# Physician Profiling and Risk Adjustment

## Second Edition

Edited by

## Norbert Goldfield, MD
Medical Director
3M Health Information Systems
Wallingford, Connecticut

## An Aspen Publication®

Aspen Publishers, Inc.
Gaithersburg, Maryland
1999

Library of Congress Cataloging-in-Publication Data

Physician profiling and risk adjustment / [edited by] Norbert Goldfield.—2nd ed.
p.   cm.
Includes bibliographical references and index.
ISBN 0-8342-1169-6 (alk. paper)
1. Manged care plans (Medical care)—Mathematical models.
2. Diagnosis related groups. 3. Risk (Insurance)—Mathematical models. 4. Patients—Classification—Mathematical models.
5. Medicine—Practice—Mathematical models. 6. Medical care—Evaluation—Mathematical models. 7. Physicians—Rating of—Mathematical models. I. Goldfield, Norbert.
[DNLM: 1. Physician's Practice Patterns—United States.
2. Managed Care Programs—United States. 3. Quality Assurance, Health Care—United States. 4. Prospective Payment System—United States. W 87 P578 1999]
RA413.P535    1999
362. 1—dc21
DNLM/DLC
for Library of Congress          98-37565
CIP

Copyright © 1999 by Aspen Publishers, Inc.
All rights reserved.

Aspen Publishers, Inc., grants permission for photocopying for limited personal or internal use. This consent does not extend to other kinds of copying, such as copying for general distribution, for advertising or promotional purposes, for creating new collective works, or for resale. For information, address Aspen Publishers, Inc., Permissions Department, 200 Orchard Ridge Drive, Suite 200, Gaithersburg, Maryland 20878.

Orders: (800) 638-8437
Customer Service: (800) 234-1660

**About Aspen Publishers** • For more than 35 years, Aspen has been a leading professional publisher in a variety of disciplines. Aspen's vast information resources are available in both print and electronic formats. We are committed to providing the highest quality information available in the most appropriate format for our customers. Visit Aspen's Internet site for more information resources, directories, articles, and a searchable version of Aspen's full catalog, including the most recent publications: **http://www.aspenpublishers.com**
**Aspen Publishers, Inc.** • The hallmark of quality in publishing
Member of the worldwide Wolters Kluwer group

Editorial Services: Lenda Hill
Library of Congress Catalog Card Number: 98-37565
ISBN: 0-8342-1169-6

*Printed in the United States of America*

1   2   3   4   5

# Dedication

This book would never have come to print without Richard Averill—intellectual collaborator and friend—who could ask for more.

# Table of Contents

Contributors . . . . . . . . . . . . . . . . . . . . . . . . . . . . . . . . . . . . . . . . . . . . .    xvii

Foreword . . . . . . . . . . . . . . . . . . . . . . . . . . . . . . . . . . . . . . . . . . . . . . . .    xxiii

Preface . . . . . . . . . . . . . . . . . . . . . . . . . . . . . . . . . . . . . . . . . . . . . . . . .    xxv

Part I—Theoretical Considerations in Physician Profiling and Risk
       Adjustment . . . . . . . . . . . . . . . . . . . . . . . . . . . . . . . . . . . .    1

Chapter 1—Trust, Obligations, and Power: Reframing the
       Relationship between Patients, Physicians, and
       Managed Care Organizations . . . . . . . . . . . . . . . . . . . . . . .    3
       *Norbert Goldfield*
       Trust . . . . . . . . . . . . . . . . . . . . . . . . . . . . . . . . . . . . . . . . . . . . .    5
       Power . . . . . . . . . . . . . . . . . . . . . . . . . . . . . . . . . . . . . . . . . . . . .    9
       Obligations . . . . . . . . . . . . . . . . . . . . . . . . . . . . . . . . . . . . . . . .    12
       Negotiating A Redefined Physician-Patient-MCO
          Relationship . . . . . . . . . . . . . . . . . . . . . . . . . . . . . . . . . . . .    14
       Recommendations For Reframing The Physician-Patient-MCO
          Relationship . . . . . . . . . . . . . . . . . . . . . . . . . . . . . . . . . . . .    16

Chapter 2—Physician Profiling—Not Whether but How . . . . . . . . . . . .    21
       *Norbert Goldfield*
       Desired Characteristics of Physician Profiles . . . . . . . . . . . . .    22
       Current Uses of Physician Profile Data . . . . . . . . . . . . . . . . . .    24
       The Need to Adjust for Severity of Illness . . . . . . . . . . . . . . .    25
       Data Elements Currently Used in Physician Profiling . . . . . . .    26
       The Future of Physician Profiling . . . . . . . . . . . . . . . . . . . . . .    31
       A Forward-Looking Strategy . . . . . . . . . . . . . . . . . . . . . . . . . .    32
       Conclusions . . . . . . . . . . . . . . . . . . . . . . . . . . . . . . . . . . . . . . .    34

**Chapter 3—Commentary on "Physician Profiling"** ...............    **39**
 *Jon Kingsdale and Harris A. Berman*

**Chapter 4—Commentary on "Physician Profiling": The Patient, The
  Organization, The Physician—Whose Profile?** .........    **43**
 *John D. Stoeckle*

**Chapter 5—Commentary on "Physician Profiling": Profiling—Necessary
  but Not Sufficient** ..............................    **45**
 *John Wasson*

**Chapter 6—Commentary on "Physician Profiling": Cautionary Notes**    **47**
 *Patrick S. Romano*
 Greater Risk of Producing Bad Information ..............    47
 Greater Harm from Releasing Bad Information ...........    51
 Suggestions for the Near Future .....................    53

**Chapter 7—Commentary on "Physician Profiling"** ...............    **57**
 *Ian H. Leverton*

**Chapter 8—Commentary on "Physician Profiling"** ...............    **63**
 *Michael L. Millenson*

**Chapter 9—Public Disclosure of Case Mix Adjusted Clinical Information:
  Practical and Theoretical Challenges** ...............    **67**
 *Norbert Goldfield*
 The Need To Emphasize Improvement Over Time versus the
   Desire To Protect the Public and Immediately Identify Poorly
   Performing Providers ...........................    69
 The Need To Provide Educational Follow-Up for All Customers
   versus the Desire To Provide an Unencumbered Free Flow of
   Information ...................................    71
 The Need To Provide Case Mix Adjusted Information Based on
   Agreed-Upon, Universally Accepted Statistical Measures That
   Are, In Turn, Explained To the Public versus the Desire To
   Avoid All Statistical Manipulations and Trust That Someone
   Will Take Care of This Issue .....................    72
 The Need To Provide Information Based on Reliable and Valid
   Methodologies versus Getting Something Out Now .....    74

The Need To Focus on Low-Income or Uninsured Individuals
   versus Focusing on Other Patients . . . . . . . . . . . . . . . . . . . .     76
The Need To Emphasize Process of Care versus Outcomes . .     76
Conclusions . . . . . . . . . . . . . . . . . . . . . . . . . . . . . . . . . . . . . .     77

**Chapter 10—Public Disclosure: A Researcher's Perspective** . . . . . . . . .     **79**
   *Lisa I. Iezzoni*
   Ensuring Quality . . . . . . . . . . . . . . . . . . . . . . . . . . . . . . . . .     80
   Understanding Strengths and Weaknesses . . . . . . . . . . . . . . .     81
   Making Choices Affecting Interpretation of Findings . . . . . . .     82
   Necessity . . . . . . . . . . . . . . . . . . . . . . . . . . . . . . . . . . . . . . .     83
   Pitfalls of Using Different Methods . . . . . . . . . . . . . . . . . . . .     84
   Conclusions . . . . . . . . . . . . . . . . . . . . . . . . . . . . . . . . . . . . . .     84

**Chapter 11—Public Disclosure: A Media Perspective** . . . . . . . . . . . . . .     **85**
   *Josh Barbanel*

**Chapter 12—Public Disclosure: A Media Perspective** . . . . . . . . . . . . . .     **87**
   *Michael L. Millenson*

**Chapter 13—Public Disclosure: A Hospital Chief Executive's Perspective**     **91**
   *Ronald Goodspeed*

**Chapter 14—Public Disclosure: A Hospital Quality Improvement Project's**
   **Perspective** . . . . . . . . . . . . . . . . . . . . . . . . . . . . . . . . . . . .     **95**
   *Vahé A. Kazandjian*
   What Is Accountability? . . . . . . . . . . . . . . . . . . . . . . . . . . . . .     96
   What Is An Outcome of Care? . . . . . . . . . . . . . . . . . . . . . . . .     97
   What Is Benchmarking? . . . . . . . . . . . . . . . . . . . . . . . . . . . . .     98
   The Usefulness of Publicly Disclosed Data . . . . . . . . . . . . . . .     99
   Immediate, Intermediate, And Ultimate Data Users . . . . . . . .    100
   The Question of Acuity Adjustment . . . . . . . . . . . . . . . . . . . .    102
   Where Will the Data Come From? . . . . . . . . . . . . . . . . . . . . .    105
   Conclusions . . . . . . . . . . . . . . . . . . . . . . . . . . . . . . . . . . . . . .    106

**Chapter 15—Public Disclosure: An Employer Response** . . . . . . . . . . . . .     **107**
   *Robert W. Hungate*

**Chapter 16—Public Disclosure: A Response from the Pennsylvania Health Care Cost Containment Council Experience** . . . . .   **111**
*Ernest J. Sessa*

**Chapter 17—Public Disclosure: A Response from "Heath Care for All"**   **117**
*Robert Restuccia*

**Chapter 18—Public Disclosure: A State Agency Response** . . . . . . . . . . .   **121**
*Tim Lynch and Randy Mutter*
Giving Consumers Power through Information . . . . . . . . . . .   122
Achieving Consensus on Methodologies . . . . . . . . . . . . . . .   123
Methodology Evaluation . . . . . . . . . . . . . . . . . . . . . . . . . . .   124
Uses And Limits Of UB-82/92 Data in Florida . . . . . . . . . .   126

**Chapter 19—Public Disclosure: A Brief Commentary** . . . . . . . . . . . . . .   **129**
*Eugene C. Nelson*
The Need to Emphasize Improvement over Time . . . . . . . . .   130
The Need To Empower the Public through Educational
    Follow-Up . . . . . . . . . . . . . . . . . . . . . . . . . . . . . . . . . . . .   130
The Need To Provide Case Mix Adjusted Information Based on
    Universal Standards and the Need To Provide Information Using
    Reliable and Valid Methods . . . . . . . . . . . . . . . . . . . . . . .   131
The Need To Focus Attention On Low-Income Populations .   131
The Need To Emphasize the Process of Care . . . . . . . . . . . .   132
Final Comment . . . . . . . . . . . . . . . . . . . . . . . . . . . . . . . . . .   132

**Chapter 20—Public Disclosure: A Researcher's Perspective** . . . . . . . . .   **135**
*Edward L. Hannan*
Data Quality . . . . . . . . . . . . . . . . . . . . . . . . . . . . . . . . . . .   135
Completeness . . . . . . . . . . . . . . . . . . . . . . . . . . . . . . . . . . .   136
Validity . . . . . . . . . . . . . . . . . . . . . . . . . . . . . . . . . . . . . . .   137
Process-Outcome Links . . . . . . . . . . . . . . . . . . . . . . . . . . .   141
Conclusions . . . . . . . . . . . . . . . . . . . . . . . . . . . . . . . . . . . .   141

**Part II—Fundamentals of Case Mix and Risk Adjustment** . . . . . . . . . .   **143**

**Chapter 21—Overview: Case Mix, Risk Adjustment, Reinsurance, and Managed Care** . . . . . . . . . . . . . . . . . . . . . . . . . . . . . . . . . . .   **145**
*Norbert Goldfield*
Conclusions . . . . . . . . . . . . . . . . . . . . . . . . . . . . . . . . . . . .   151

**Chapter 22—Understanding Your Managed Care Practice:**
         **The Critical Role of Case Mix Systems** ................    **153**
         *Norbert Goldfield*
         Historical Background of Case Mix Systems .............    155
         Ambulatory Case Mix Systems .......................    157
         Components and Challenges of an ACMS .............    157
         Ambulatory Patient Groups .........................    160
         Applying APR-DRGs To Managed Care ................    162
         Recent APG and DRG Development Trends .............    168
         Conclusions .......................................    168

**Chapter 23—DRGs and Quality Management in Hospitals** ..........    **171**
         *Robert B. Fetter*
         Definitions in Quality Assurance ......................    171
         Quality of Care in Hospitals ..........................    172
         The Process of Quality Management ....................    173
         Specifying and Using Control Charts ...................    174
         The Concept of Process Control ......................    174
         The Concept of Statistical Control .....................    175
         The Statistical Nature of Care Processes ................    176
         Control Charts for Attributes .........................    182
         Other SPC Techniques ..............................    184
         SPC and Total Quality Management ...................    186
         Total Quality Management In Hospitals ................    187
         Conclusions .......................................    187

**Part III—Risk Adjustment for Outpatient Care** ...................    **189**

**Chapter 24—Methods of Compensating Managed Care Physicians and**
         **Hospitals** ....................................    **191**
         *Norbert Goldfield, Harris Berman, Arlen Collins,*
         *Richard Cooper, Daniel Dragalin, Peter Kongstvedt,*
         *Norman Payson, David Siegel, Arthur Southam, and Ernest Weis*
         MCO Physician Reimbursement ......................    192
         Conclusions .......................................    203

**Chapter 25—Blue Shield of California Outpatient Payment Program** .    **207**
         *John F. Roughan*
         Background ........................................    208
         Procedure .........................................    209

Work Plan ....................................... 209
Results ......................................... 211
Conclusions ..................................... 212

**Chapter 26—Use of Ambulatory Patient Groups in Iowa**
**Hospitals—Revisited .............................. 215**
*James C. Vertrees and Marcia J. Stark*
General Historical Summary .......................... 215
Selection and System Criteria ........................ 216
1996 Rebasing and Recalibration ..................... 218
Key Resolution Issues and Conclusions ................ 219

**Concluding Comments ...................................... 223**
*Norbert Goldfield*
Profiling and Quality Improvement ................... 223
Profiling and Ambulatory Case Mix Systems ............ 225

**Chapter 27—The American Medical Accreditation Program: Quality,**
**Accreditation, and the AMA ....................... 229**
*William F. Jessee, Terry Hammons, and Richard Hughes*
Fragmented Credentialing, Office Review, and
Physician Profiling .............................. 230
An Integrated Solution: Physician Accreditation ......... 232
AMAP and Professional Accountability ................ 233
A Balance: Information for Improvement and
Information for Choice ........................... 233
How AMAP Accreditation Works .................... 235
From Application to Accreditation .................... 236
Developing Better Measurement for Self-Assessment and
Improvement .................................... 236
Is Professional Accreditation Equal to the Task? .......... 238

**Appendix 27–A—Principles of Physician Profiling ................ 243**

**Appendix 27–B—Principles To Guide the Collection, Release, and Use of**
**Physician-Specific Health Care Data ................. 245**

**Appendix 27–C—AMAP Standards ........................... 247**

**Chapter 28—"Best Clinical Practice": Assessment of Processes of Care and of Outcomes in the U.S. Military Health Services System** .........................     **251**
*Henry Krakauer, Monica Jia-Yeong Lin, Eric M. Schone,*
*Dae Park, Richard C. Miller, Jeffrey Greenwald,*
*R. Clifton Bailey, Barbara Rogers, Geoffrey Bernstein,*
*David E. Lilienfeld, Sidney M. Stahl, Raymond S. Crawford III,*
*and David C. Schutt*
Background ...................................     252
Methodology ..................................     253
Illustrative Results .............................     263
Discussion ....................................     274


**Chapter 29—Development of a Prospective Payment System for Hospital-based Outpatient Care** ....................     **281**
*Richard F. Averill, Norbert I. Goldfield, Laurence W. Gregg,*
*Thelma M. Grant, Boris V. Shafir, and Robert L. Mullin*
Characteristics of an Outpatient Patient Classification System     282
Overview of APGs ..............................     284
Selection of the Initial Classification Variable ...........     286
Development of Significant Procedure APGs ............     289
Development of Medical APGs .......................     291
Development of Ancillary Service APGs ...............     296
Summary of Development .........................     299
The APG Payment System .........................     305
APG Payment Simulation .........................     309
Evaluation of the 13 Alternative Formulations of an APG PPS     313
Converting Charges to Costs .......................     314
Computing APG Relative Weights ...................     315
Comparison of Alternative APG Systems ...............     317
Comparison of Version 2.0 APGs and DRGs ............     321
Hospital APG Impact Simulation ....................     322
Discussion ....................................     330
Implementation Issues ...........................     332
Conclusions ...................................     335

**Appendix 29–A—List of Version 2.0 APGs** .......................     **337**
Significant Procedure and Therapy APGs ...............     337
Ancillary Services APGs ..........................     343
Medical APGs ..................................     345

**Part IV—Case Mix Adjustment for Inpatient Care** ................ 351

**Chapter 30—Logic and Applications of the All Patient Refined DRGs: The Greater Southeast Community Hospital Experience** ..... 353
*Patricia Jones and George Strudgeon*
Greater Southeast Community Hospital ................ 353
GSCH Decision Support Function .................... 353
Information Systems Configuration for APR-DRGs ....... 355
APR-DRG Logic Overview .......................... 355
Using APR-DRGs For Managed Care ................. 364
Conclusions ....................................... 371

**Chapter 31—Physician Profiling in Seattle: A Case Study** ........... 373
*Gregg Bennett, William McKee, and Laura Kilberg*
Prerequisites for Resource Use Reduction Efforts ......... 374
Physician Profiling Components ...................... 376
Information Distribution ............................ 380
Engaging Management and Medical Staff Support ........ 381
Physician Profile Feedback and Counseling .............. 383
Results ........................................... 385
Discussion ........................................ 388
Conclusions ....................................... 389

**Chapter 32—The Evolution of Case Mix Measurement Using Diagnosis-related Groups** ......................... 391
*Richard F. Averill, John H. Muldoon, James C. Vertrees,*
*Norbert I. Goldfield, Robert L. Mullin, Elizabeth C. Fineran,*
*Mona Z. Zhang, Barbara Steinbeck, and Thelma Grant*
DRG Systems ..................................... 393
Comparison of the Structure of the DRG Systems ......... 399
Database ......................................... 401
Untrimmed $R^2$ Results ............................. 402
$R^2$ For Cost By MDC .............................. 406
Data Trimming .................................... 409
Trimmed $R^2$ Results ............................... 413
Hospital-Level Analysis for Cost ..................... 415
Payment Redistribution ............................. 420
Mortality Analysis ................................. 438
$R^2$ and C-Statistic for Mortality by MDC ............... 440
Mortality by Age and Sex ........................... 446

Hospital-Level Analysis for Mortality . . . . . . . . . . . . . . . . . .     447
Conclusions . . . . . . . . . . . . . . . . . . . . . . . . . . . . . . . . . . .     449

**Chapter 33—Using Severity-adjusted Data to Impact Clinical Pathways     455**
*Carol Fridlin*
**Concluding Comments . . . . . . . . . . . . . . . . . . . . . . . . . . . . . . . . . . . .     465**
*Patrick Romano, Richard F. Averill and Norbert Goldfield*
Point: It is Important to Judiciously Use in Provider Profiles Secondary
Diagnoses That Represent Comorbidities or, Possibly,
Complications . . . . . . . . . . . . . . . . . . . . . . . . . . . . . . . . .     465
Counterpoint: All conditions that occur after hospital admission are
potentially preventable complications . . . . . . . . . . . . . . . .     471

**Part V—Episodes of Illness** . . . . . . . . . . . . . . . . . . . . . . . . . . . . . .     477

**Chapter 34—Episodes of Illness: Introduction** . . . . . . . . . . . . . . . . . . . .     479
*Norbert Goldfield*

**Chapter 35—The Current State of Risk Adjustment Technology for**
**Capitation** . . . . . . . . . . . . . . . . . . . . . . . . . . . . . . . . . . . .     483
*Melvin J. Ingber*
Structures of Risk Adjuster Systems . . . . . . . . . . . . . . . . . . . .     485
Classifying and Evaluating Risk Adjusters . . . . . . . . . . . . . . .     485
Prospective Risk Adjusters Based on Claim or Encounter Data     488
Systems Using Inpatient Hospital Data . . . . . . . . . . . . . . . . . .     489
Full Encounter Data Models . . . . . . . . . . . . . . . . . . . . . . . . .     496
Models for Medicare . . . . . . . . . . . . . . . . . . . . . . . . . . . . . . .     499
A Model for Medicaid Expenditures for the Disabled . . . . . . .     505
Models Developed for the General Population and Medicaid .     507
Survey-Based Models . . . . . . . . . . . . . . . . . . . . . . . . . . . . . .     515
Conclusion . . . . . . . . . . . . . . . . . . . . . . . . . . . . . . . . . . . . . .     517

**Chapter 36—Prospective Risk Adjustment Classes** . . . . . . . . . . . . . . . . . .     523
*Norbert Goldfield, Richard Averill, Jon Eisenhandler,*
*John S. Hughes, John Muldoon, Barbara Steinbeck,*
*and Farah Bagadia*
Data Preparation . . . . . . . . . . . . . . . . . . . . . . . . . . . . . . . . . .     527
Assigning Risk Adjustment Classes . . . . . . . . . . . . . . . . . . . .     529
Data . . . . . . . . . . . . . . . . . . . . . . . . . . . . . . . . . . . . . . . . . . . .     535
Conclusion . . . . . . . . . . . . . . . . . . . . . . . . . . . . . . . . . . . . . .     539

**Chapter 37—The Development of a Risk-Adjusted Capitation Payment
    System: The Maryland Medicaid Model** .............. **541**
*Jonathan P. Weiner, Anthony M. Tucker, A. Michael Collins,
Hamid Fakhraei, Richard Lieberman, Chad Abrams,
Gordon R. Trapnell, and John G. Folkemer*
    The Components of the Payment System ................ 544
    The ACG-Based Health Status Adjuster ................ 549
    Database Construction ................................. 549
    Construction of RACs Based on ACGs ................ 551
    Simulating the Impact of the Risk-Adjusted Model ........ 553
    Policy Implications ..................................... 559
    Some Benefits ......................................... 560
    Some Pitfalls and Challenges ......................... 561
    Conclusions ........................................... 564

**Appendix 37–A—Distribution of Prospective Resource Use in Each
    ACG for RAC Capitation Payment Cells: AFDC and
    Other Nondisabled** ............................... **567**

**Appendix 37–B—Distribution of Prospective Resource Use in Each
    ACG for RAC Capitation Payment Cells: SSI and
    Other Disabled** ................................... **571**

**Chapter 38—Physician Profiling Using Outpatient Pharmacy Data as a
    Source for Case Mix Measurement and Risk Adjustment** **575**
*Douglas W. Roblin*
    Outpatient Pharmacy Data .......................... 576
    Data Integrity ........................................ 578
    Case Mix Measurement .............................. 584
    Case Mix Measurement and Practice Profiling for
        Improved Panel System Design and Management ....... 587
    Case Mix Measurement and Statistical Models of Health Risk    589
    Conclusions ........................................... 595

**Chapter 39—Profiling the Health Service Needs of Populations
    Using Diagnosis-based Classification Systems** .......... **599**
*John H. Muldoon, John M. Neff, and James C. Gay*
    Brief Review of Existing Population-Based Classification
        Methods ......................................... 600
    Design and Structure of NACHRI Classification of Congenital
        and Chronic Health Conditions ..................... 602

Illustration of Uses of NACHRI Classification of Congenital
and Chronic Health Conditions ..................... 607
Coding and Classification Issues ....................... 618
Public Health and Policy Applications ................. 620
Conclusions ........................................ 621

**Chapter 40—Predicting Mental Health Outpatient Services Using
Non-claims-based Characteristics** ................... **623**
*Norbert Goldfield, Richard Averill,
Herbert Fillmore, and Dennis Graziano*
Study Design ...................................... 624
Data Analysis ..................................... 630
Discussion ........................................ 640
Recommendations .................................. 641

**Chapter 41—Predicting the Cost of General Medical Outpatient and
Emergency Services Using Non-claims-based
Characteristics** ................................. **643**
*Norbert Goldfield, Richard Averill, Jon Eisenhandler,
Herbert Fillmore, and Dennis Graziano*
Abstract .......................................... 643
Methods .......................................... 645
Data Analysis ..................................... 646
Discussion ........................................ 651

**Appendix 41–A—New York State (New York Department of Health
Project Participants)** ............................ **653**

**Chapter 42—Improving the Prediction of Rehabilitation Outpatient
Services Using Patient Characteristics** ................ **655**
*Norbert Goldfield, Richard Averill, Thelma Grant,
Yvette Wang, Dennis Graziano, Herbert Fillmore,
and William Fisher*
Background ........................................ 656
Study Design ...................................... 657
Data Analysis ..................................... 661
Discussion ........................................ 667
Conclusions ....................................... 669
Recommendations .................................. 669

**Index** ................................................ **671**

# Contributors

**Chad Abrams, MA**
Program Coordinator
Health Services R & D Center
School of Public Health
Johns Hopkins University
Baltimore, MD

**Richard Averill, MS**
Research Manager
Department of Clinical Research
3M Health Information Systems
Wallingford, CT

**Farah Bagadia, MD**
Clinical Research Assistant
3M Health Information Systems
Wallingford, CT

**Josh Barbanel**
The New York Times
New York, New York

**Gregg Bennett, MHA, MBA, CPA**
President
HBS International, Inc.
Bellevue, Washington

**Harris A. Berman, MD**
Chief Executive Officer
Tufts Health Plan
Waltham, MA

**Arlen Collins, MD**
Managed Care Consultant
Amherst, MA

**A. Michael Collins, PhD**
Deputy Executive Director
Information Systems
Development and Consulting
Center for Health Program Development and
    Management
University of Maryland at Baltimore County
Baltimore, MD

**Richard Cooper, MD**
Managed Care Consultant
Franklin, TN

**Daniel Dragalin, MD**
Consultant
Blue Cross of New Jersey
Newark, NJ

**Jon Eisenhandler, PhD**
Senior Healthcare Researcher
3M Health Information Systems
Wallingford, CT

**Hamid Fakhraei, PhD**
Director of Economic Analysis
Center for Health Program Development and
   Management
University of Maryland at Baltimore County
Baltimore, MD

**Robert B. Fetter**
Roseland, VA
Carol Fidlin, RN, BS, CPHQ
St Vincent Hospitals and Health Services
Indianapolis, IN

**Elizabeth C. Fineran, CMS**
Project Manager
3M Health Information Systems
Wallingford, CT

**John G. Folkemer, MSW, MPA**
Director
Health Services Analysis and Evaluation
Maryland Department of Health & Mental
   Hygiene
Baltimore, MD

**James C. Gay, MD**
Associate Professor of Pediatrics
Vanderbilt University Medical Center
Nashville, TN

**Norbert Goldfield, MD**
Medical Director
3M Health Information Systems
Wallingford, CT

**Ronald Goodspeed, MD**
CEO
Charlton Memorial Hospital
Falls River, MA

**Thelma Grant, RRA**
Senior Product Development Analyst
3M Health Information Systems
Wallingford, CT

**Barry R. Greene, PhD**
Senior Vice President
Education and Research
Medical Group Management Association
Englewood, CO

**Laurence W. Gregg, BS**
Supervisor
3M Health Information Systems
Wallingford, CT

**Terry Hammons, MD**
American Medical Association
Assistant Vice President
Quality and Managed Care
Chicago, IL

**Edward Hannan, PhD**
Professor and Chair of the Department of
   Health Policy, Management & Behavior
SUNY-Albany School of Public Health
Rensselaer, NY

**John Hughes, MD**
Consultant
3M Health Information Systems
New Haven, CT

**Richard Hughes, MD**
Director
Clinical Reference Evaluator
American Medical Association
Chicago, IL


**Robert W. Hungate, MBA**
Principal
Physician—Patient Partnerships for Health
Wellesley, MA


**Lisa I. Iezzoni, MD, MSc**
Professor of Medicine
Harvard Medical School
Co-Director of Research
Beth Israel Hospital
Boston, MA


**Melvin J. Ingber, PhD**
Economist
Office of Strategic Planning
Health Care Financing Administration
Baltimore, MD


**William F. Jessee, MD**
Vice President
Quality and Managed Care
American Medical Association
Chicago, IL


**Patricia Jones, MHS**
Director, Decision Support Services
Greater Southeast Community Hospital
Washington, DC

**Vahé A. Kazandjian, PhD, MPH**
President
Center for Performance Sciences, Inc.
Adjunct Associate Professor
School of Hygiene and Public Health, The
    Johns Hopkins University
Baltimore, MD
Senior Scientist, The Gallup Organization
Princeton, MA
Vice President for Research
Maryland Hospital Association
Lutherville, MD


**Laura Kilberg, RN, MSPH/HSA**
Director
Quality Management
Providence Medical Center
Seattle, WA


**Jon Kingsdale, PhD**
Sr. Vice President
Planning and Development
The Tufts Health Plan
Waltham, MA


**Peter R. Kongstvedt, MD, FACP**
Partner
Ernst & Young, LLP
Washington, DC


**Henry Krakauer, MD, PhD**
Captain
USPHS
Office of the Assistant Secretary for
    Planning and Evaluation
Washington, DC

**Ian Leverton, MD**
Health Care Consultant
San Francisco, CA

**Richard Lieberman, BA**
Johns Hopkins University
Baltimore, MD

**Tim Lynch, PhD**
Tallahassee, FL

**William McKee, MD**
Medical Director
Providence Medical Center,
Seattle, WA

**Michael L. Millenson**
Visiting Scholar, Northwestern University
Center for Health Services Policy and
    Research
Evanston, IL

**John Muldoon**
Senior Fellow/Vice President
Classification Research
National Association of Children's Hospitals
    & Related Institutions
Alexandria, VA

**Robert L. Mullin, MD**
3M Health Information Systems
Wallingford, CT

**Randal C. Mutter, MPH**
Consultant
Health Information Partners, Inc.
Tallahassee, FL

**John M. Neff, MD**
Medical Director
Children's Hospital and Medical Center
Seattle, WA

**Eugene C. Nelson, DSc**
Professor
Department of Community & Family
    Medicine
Dartmouth Medical School
Hanover, NH

**Norman C. Payson, MD**
President & Chief Executive Officer
Healthsource, Inc.
Hooksett, NH

**Robert Restuccia, MPA**
Executive Director
Health Care For All
Boston, MA

**Douglas W. Roblin, PhD**
Health Economist, Special Studies
Kaiser Foundation Health Plan, Inc.
Oakland, CA

**Patrick S. Romano, MD, MPH**
Associate Professor of Medicine and
    Pediatrics
Division of General Medicine and Center for
    Health Services Research in Primary Care
University of California, Davis
Sacramento, CA

**John F. Roughan, MBA, BA**
Manager
Provider Relations
Blue Shield of California
Los Angeles, CA

**Ernest J. Sessa**
Former Executive Director
Pennsylvania Health Care Cost Containment
    Council
Harrisburg, PA

**Boris V. Shafir, BS**
Software Engineer
3M Health Information Systems
Wallingford, CT

**David Siegel, MD**
Medical Director
Health Alliance Plan, Inc.
Detroit, MI

**Arthur Southam, MD**
CEO
Care America Health Plans, Inc.
Chatsworth, CA

**Marcia J. Stark, MS**
Secretary/Treasurer
Iowa CHMIS Governing Board
Des Moines, IA

**Barbara Steinbeck, ART**
Manager
Clinical Research
3M Health Information Systems
Wallingford, CT

**John D. Stoeckle, MD**
Physician
Massachusetts General Hospital
Boston, MA

**George Strudgeon, MBA**
Administrator
Managed Care
Greater Southeast Healthcare System
Washington, DC

**Gordon Trapnell, FSA**
President
Actuarial Research Corporation
Annandale, VA

**Anthony M. Tucker, MPA**
Analyst
John Hopkins School of Public Health
Baltimore, MD

**James C. Vertrees, PhD**
President
Solon Consulting Group, Ltd.
Silver Spring, MD

**John H. Wasson, MD**
Director
Center for the Aging
Research Director
Dartmouth COOP Project
Dartmouth Medical School
Hanover, NH

**Jonathan P. Weiner, DrPH**
Professor
Deputy Director of Health Services
Research and Development Center
Johns Hopkins School of Public Health
Baltimore, MD

**Ernest Weis, MD**
CEO
Humana/Michael Reese Health Plan
Chicago, IL

**Mona Zhang, BS**
Statistician
3M Health Information Systems
Wallingford, CT

# Foreword

It was the ability to conceive of hospital outputs as a system of identifiable processes that led to the discovery of the inpatient classification system of Diagnostic Related Groups (DRGs). The analysis of these outputs in terms of product lines has completely changed the way that the economic behavior of hospitals can be analyzed and managed. That applied research began with the understanding that hospitals consisted of similar classes of treated patients. The key to the research was grouping patients by the resources they consumed.

The DRG research process was able to build on the use of the length of stay in the hospital as an effective surrogate measure of resource. The same measurement issues, of finding an effective measure to use as a surrogate for resource consumption, is the stumbling block in the derivation of classification systems in ambulatory care research. For that reason, there have been a variety of ambulatory encounter systems developed that attempt to get at resource consumption in very different ways.

Research in classifying ambulatory care visits actually began shortly after the DRG research with several of the same researchers. *Physician Profiling and Risk Adjustment* serves as an anthology of the systematic assault on these extremely important problems of conceptualization and measurement. The strategy remains one of process identification, analysis, and resource management. The solution will ultimately be folded into a continuous quality improvement system that will permit the comparison of similar classes of patients and the resources they consume.

The pressing need to solve this important problem encourages the proliferation of proprietary and premature claims of resolution. We are simply not there yet. But in the process of reaching resolution, we must carefully examine the yield of the best research efforts to date. This book allows researchers and those attempting to understand case mix issues in practice to do exactly that, and the editor is to be commended for giving us that opportunity.

**Barry R. Greene, PhD**
*Senior Vice President/Education and Research*
*Medical Group Management Association*
*Englewood, Colorado*

# Preface

Since the first edition of this book a scant two years ago, there have been tremendous advances in the field of physician profiling and risk adjustment. The stakes have gotten higher. That is, managed care plans and insurance companies are shifting more and more risk onto the physician. The advent of greater financial risk heightens the importance of profiling and risk adjustment methods of outpatient services—sections, which are considerably enhanced in this book.

The book is divided into five sections:

1. theoretical considerations in physician profiling and risk adjustment,
2. fundamentals of case mix and risk adjustment,
3. physician profiling and risk adjustment of outpatient care,
4. case mix adjustment for inpatient care, and
5. measuring episodes of illness.

## THEORETICAL CONSIDERATIONS IN PHYSICIAN PROFILING AND RISK ADJUSTMENT

Since the first edition of this book, the theoretical challenges to physician profiling and risk adjustment have become only more complex—and interesting. In part the complexities have arisen from the transfer of financial risk from payers to providers, a phenomenon which was already present at the time of the publication of the first edition but has become much more prevalent today. This shift in risk has led to changes in relationships between physicians, managed care organizations, and patients. The first chapter in this section attempts to deal with the manifold philosophical issues which emanate from this radical shift in risk from payer to provider. The second chapter in this section provides a summary of the variety of efforts underway to profile physicians. In addition to the many scientific challenges underlying physician profiling, of particular importance is the challenge of external versus internal release of physician specific information. While there has simply been an explosion in this field in the past couple of years, it is nothing in comparison to what will be available for discussion in the next edition of this book. Technological advances, summarized in this chapter, will lead physician profiling to a much more clinically and statistically sophisticated level of analysis and delivery to the customer(s). The last set of chapters in this section deals with the public disclosure of comparative information. Challenges still abound in this arena—as evidenced by the new commentaries by Nelson and Hannan.

## FUNDAMENTALS OF CASE MIX AND RISK ADJUSTMENT

This section of the book outlines the overarching challenges in developing case mix methods, statistical tools for tracking groups over time, and an overview of tools used for paying physicians and hospitals.

In the first chapter, one of the editors of this manual analyzes the many controversies in theoretical and practical aspects of case mix. Robert Fetter, one of the architects of the diagnosis related group (DRG) system, next discusses statistical applications of case mix methodologies particularly as they pertain to control charts. It is hard enough to adjust for differences between patients. This book will take you the next step and outline statistical methods for tracking over time how one group of physicians is comparing with another.

The push to compare physicians and hospitals has assumed great importance in large part due to the types of financial incentives placed on them. The dramatic push toward managed care has spawned a plethora of payment methods. The last chapter in the fundamentals section outlines the payment methods currently used.

Case mix adjustment has become more important precisely because of the varied methods used to pay practitioners and institutions. These payment methods often place the physician and/or hospital at significant financial risk. Unfortunately, the case mix adjustment tools discussed in this book are not sophisticated enough to adjust the payment made to physicians. The tools can be used to compare physician practices from a per-visit or per-episode-of-illness standpoint. Variations of capitation are used increasingly to pay hospitals. Case mix adjustment methods such as the ones discussed in this book are being used to adjust hospital capitation rates.

## PHYSICIAN PROFILING AND RISK ADJUSTMENT OF OUTPATIENT CARE

There are several new important developments in outpatient services that are highlighted in new chapters. The American Medical Association is embarking on an ambitious and exciting new accreditation program—the American Medical Accreditation Program (AMAP). Dr. Jessee and his colleagues summarize past physician accreditation efforts together with a synopsis of the AMAP program. The Health Care Financing Administration is implementing a new outpatient prospective payment system for hospital outpatient departments and ambulatory surgery centers, the details of which are summarized in the article by Averill et al. There are many new interesting independent developments in physician profiling. Some of them are summarized in the chapter on Physician Profiling in the Theoretical Considerations section. Henry Krakauer and his colleagues provide us with a summary of a new approach to physician profiling that he has developed.

## CASE MIX ADJUSTMENT FOR INPATIENT CARE

The main developments in this arena since the first edition have been with the applications of case mix adjustment, particularly in the area of economic and clinical profiling of institutions. In addition there are new developments in data collection effort. The State of California is mandating the collection of a flag identifying whether or not secondary diagnoses were present on admission. Averill, Goldfield and Romano summarize this section with a debate over ideal features in a case mix adjustment system for inpatient services. It goes without saying that the paper by Fetter, one of the pioneers in case mix adjustment, is just as valid today as in the first edition. Unfortunately, I would be willing to make a gentleman's bet and say that the vast majority of institutions, even those practicing continuous quality improvement, still could learn a great deal from Professor Fetter's application of control charts to case mix measurement.

## MEASURING EPISODES OF ILLNESS

Measuring episodes of illness is possible today largely due to technological advances in computing. Interestingly, while the demand for this type of data is ever increasing, the shift of financial risk from payers to providers highlights new challenges in the integration of disparate streams of outpatient and inpatient claims. Typically, the provider does not know the entire patient population under treatment (only those patients who have received treatment). The payer has that information. It is possible that the ownership of disparate streams of data may force providers and payers to cooperate. However, as the Oxford Health Plan experience demonstrates, having a complete and accurate file of enrolled patients or individuals (a Master Member Index) can be challenging from a computing point of view.

The articles in this section are all new and reflect the many challenges in creating an episode of illness system—for either prospective/retrospective capitation risk adjustment or for retrospective profiling.

**Norbert Goldfield**

# PART I

# Theoretical Considerations in Physician Profiling and Risk Adjustment

# Trust, Obligations, and Power: Reframing the Relationship between Patients, Physicians, and Managed Care Organizations

*Norbert Goldfield*

**ABSTRACT**

Objective: This article provides a review of the changing doctor-patient relationship in light of the advent of managed care.

Conclusions: The doctor-patient relationship is transitioning to the doctor-patient-managed care organization relationship. An analysis of trust, obligations and power can help to clarify the doctor/patient/MCO relationship. This relationship can be strengthened if:

- Financial risk assumed by providers and MCOs is limited in an effort to mitigate any incentive to inappropriately undertreat chronically ill patients
- MCOs assume responsibility for **coordination** of care, not **limitation** of care. This includes encouraging patients to manage their own care.
- Physicians are actively engaged in efforts to measure and improve upon their performance.
- Technology assessment is performed by a third party, which has no direct relationship with MCOs.

The concept of trust revolves around the physician/patient relationship rather than the institutions (i.e., managed care organizations) that surround that relationship.[1]

*A typical scenario in today's health care market place: Unlike in the past, the major insurers of care (employers, Medicare, and Medicaid) today shift the entire financial risk for medical care onto managed care organizations (MCOs). In turn, MCOs often shift the entire financial risk onto providers of care—after they have removed 15–20 % of profit. Alternatively, MCOs pay providers on a discounted fee-for-service basis and give them little or no feedback on their performance (i.e., quality of care and utilization of resources). The choice of providers by MCOs is based almost exclusively on price. Lacking information on the care they give and racing to offer the lowest price, providers of care have little opportunity to engage in quality improvement activities. MCOs frequently advertise in a variety of media. These promotions provide minimal information on the quality of care provided by the MCOs. Enrollees perceive there to be significant administrative and/or financial obstacles to getting appropriate care. While satisfaction of enrollees with medical care may be high, there is significant suspicion of the MCOs' motives. Enrollees' suspicion of MCOs has spilled over into their relationship with physicians. It goes without saying that physicians are deeply hostile to what they perceive to be MCOs' efforts to not only exert power over physician incomes but to place barriers to needed care for their patients. Both patients and physicians believe that physician obligations are not being met because of the intrusion of managed care organizations into the doctor-patient relationship.*

With the advent of managed care, consumers have witnessed a sea of change in their traditional relationship with the health care community. Most importantly, managed care organizations (MCOs) have inserted themselves into the physician-patient relationship. The traditional physician-patient relationship has in fact turned into a physician-patient-MCO relationship, resulting in a significant diminishing of *trust* and significant changes in *obligations* and *power*. These changes are not in the best interest of MCOs, providers, or patients.

This chapter presents a detailed analysis of trust, obligations, and power. Based on the analysis, it then suggests actions that can improve the relationship between consumers and the health care community in general and the relationships between MCOs, physicians, and patients in particular. All need to change the perception and reality of trust, obligations, and power if these relationships are to improve and health is to be enhanced.

Patients need to feel empowered to negotiate with health care providers for the type of care that they believe they need. If they feel empowered, they will trust not only their physicians but also the MCOs (the entities that control their access to care). The renewal of trust will depend on the willingness of physicians to commit themselves to continually studying the art and science of medicine. It will also depend on the ability of MCOs to play a positive role in the coordination of health care services and the prevention of illness. In the long term, the coordination of care can occur only if the financial risk placed on MCOs and providers of care is limited.

## TRUST

Most patients are still inclined to trust their physicians. Yet their level of trust is lower than it used to be. Indeed, not so long ago patients held physicians in higher esteem than any other group of professionals.[2]

There are many aspects of trust. A full understanding of its various aspects will help lay the ground work for a better understanding of the physician-patient-MCO relationship. Discussed in this section are the following topics:

- trust as accepted vulnerability
- trust as willingness to comply or cooperate
- trust as reliance on others

### Trust as Accepted Vulnerability

When a patient trusts his or her physician, the former is placing him- or herself in a vulnerable position. Trust as accepted vulnerability to another's possible but unexpected ill will or incompetence must be part of the relationship between patients and physicians. Ideally, it should also exist in the relationship between patients and MCOs.[3] While the traditional fee-for-service system provided opportunities for physician-patient conflict, the onset of capitation (fixed reimbursement regardless of the amount of services provided), set the stage for significant ill will between physicians and patients. Because of the tremendous publicity surrounding financial incentives, physicians have themselves fostered the perception that underservice is prevalent, thereby generating ill will between themselves and patients. The fact is that both fee-for-service and capitation provide ample opportunities for ill will. It is the contention of this chapter that the Hippocratic oath and, more importantly, the financial boundaries that are placed around either fee-for-service or capitation can strengthen accepted vulnerability. Accepted vulnerability is the key to increased trust.

## Trust as a Willingness to Comply or Cooperate Before Needing to Monitor One's Performance

Trust can also be defined as a willingness to cooperate with another person or entity before monitoring performance (perhaps without ever monitoring performance).[4] Many health care professionals, including physicians, believe that today the quality of the health care system cannot be adequately measured. In contrast, it is the author's view that quality monitoring is scientifically valid and can assist in maintaining and enhancing trust. This process can take the form of physician profiles, or "report cards." Most physician profiles developed by MCOs mostly contain clinical information that is difficult to interpret. Yet nascent efforts are underway to improve the profiles via increased communication between MCOs and physician groups. An example is the California Cooperative Health Care Reporting Initiative, which has physician groups, employers, and MCOs on its board of directors. This group is fostering the development of meaningful physician profiles. A second example is the Massachusetts Medical Society, which is actively promoting a dialogue with MCOs in the state in an effort to develop more meaningful profiles.[*]

Largely due to the challenges inherent in risk-adjusting physician panels, the profiling of physicians and MCOs is scientifically insufficient and imprecise.[5] While not every type of physician profile needs to be risk adjusted (e.g., those that focus on process measures), physician profiles of greatest interest to patients, such as satisfaction, functional health status, and mortality profiles, do need to be risk adjusted. Thus MCOs are encouraged to contract with physicians who can perform according to their current imprecise profiling tech-

---

[*]The Massachusetts Medical Society has established a company, Vital Solutions, Inc., a subsidiary of the Massachusetts Peer Review Organization, whose mission is to establish closer links between managed care organizations and physician profiling. The author is on the board of this organization.

niques and to avoid contracts with physicians who cannot. If MCOs institute limits on physician financial risk, they could "scrutinize" physician practices with greater precision and thereby inspire patient trust. Without such limits, patients will continue to impugn MCOs as organizations that have only profit-making motives.

Interestingly, the recent clamor regarding physician adherence to guidelines, the publication of risk-adjusted mortality rates, and the increase in information on patient satisfaction might appear to reflect a lack of patient trust in physicians. However, some patients do trust their physicians without concrete information pertaining to the physicians' practice patterns.[6] With the triangular relationship between the MCO, physician, and patient, such information presented appropriately can, at a minimum, validate and enhance patient trust. At its best, it can engage patients in the management of their own disease—the ultimate manifestation of patient trust in their physicians and MCOs.

## Trust as Reliance on Others

According to one ethicist, "Trust . . . is (also) letting other persons . . . take care of something the truster cares about, where such care involves some exercise of discretionary powers."[7] This definition of trust fits the relationship between patients and physicians. Patients allow physicians to exercise power because they expect physicians to fulfill their responsibility to them. Consumers can pick up the clues that indicate the limits of what is entrusted, and the limits are very closely tied to the amount of financial risk that physicians can assume. As the assumed financial risk increases, patient trust decreases. Thus, there is little possibility of trust between physicians and patients unless limits on the financial risk assumed by physicians are put into place.

While there is a human-to-human relationship between physicians and patients, this type of relationship does not exist between patients and MCOs. Can one trust an organization in the same manner one can trust another human being? People do trust longstanding institutions such as fire departments, but can patients trust a for-profit corporation that does not provide a clear indication of the relationship it expects to maintain with its patients or a clear outline of its policy of coordinating care for patients? Is it possible for patients to trust the American Association of Health Plans (AAHP), the trade group representing MCOs, when its current advertising campaign, called Putting

Patients First, is belied by the many MCOs that put their profit-loss statement first?[8] Even if an MCO is a not-for-profit organization, competition with for-profit MCOs will require it to generate significant profits (for purposes such as expansion). Although trust in organizational entities can exist, trust in today's MCOs is impossible unless significant changes in all aspects of their managerial operations and health care objectives occur. A good example of the type of change needed is the creation of staff who function as patient advocates while working with the primary care physicians to coordinate the care of chronically ill patients.

While paradoxical on the surface, an important means of enhancing trust between patients and physicians or MCOs is to allow patients substantial say in the management of their own illnesses. Yet the degree of power accepted must be up to each patient. Patients should not be "empowered" (i.e., forced) to leave the hospital less than 24 hours after a vaginal delivery or to have a radical mastectomy on an outpatient basis. Patients need to be truly empowered to make important medical decisions either by themselves or with their physicians. Taken to its logical conclusion, patients are truly empowered when they have the choice of trusting their physicians to manage all aspects of their illness.

MCOs can facilitate patient empowerment by

- providing information that could impact a joint physician-patient treatment decision and
- coordinating care once the treatment decision has been made.

This is a difficult balancing act. The perception that MCOs are not limiting care but coordinating care is needed.

It takes time to develop trust. The physician-patient relationship has developed over thousands of years and would take a long time to destroy. On the other hand, MCOs have had only 25 years to develop their relationships with patients and physicians. As a consequence, trust has not had a chance to grow. At the heart of this lack of trust are the financial incentives inherent in today's capitated contracts and perceived restrictions on access to care for enrollees.

The third side of the patient-physician-MCO relationship triangle is the relationship between physicians and MCOs. As already noted, it is difficult to have trust between these two parties without boundaries around financial incentives.

## POWER

Different aspects of power are relevant to different aspects of the patient-physician-MCO relationship. These aspects include

- power as the ability of one person to change the behavior of another
- power as the ability to prevent action by an individual by means of an implicit threat
- power as a bond that structures an ongoing relationship between two social agents
- power as influence (the most preferable form of power)

Most obviously, an individual or entity has power over another individual if the latter's behavior is partially determined by the former. The ability of MCOs to keep physicians from mentioning certain treatments represents an example of that type of power. It should be emphasized that contracts containing gag rules have diminished in frequency because of physician and consumer protests, not because of leadership on the part of MCOs.[9] Only slightly more subtle but with the same net effect is the current MCO practice, particularly common on the West Coast, of shopping around for the lowest possible capitation rate. Interestingly, power over capitation rates may change hands if integrated delivery systems develop to the point that physicians hold many of the purse strings. Power as the ability to impact behavior superficially fits the relationship between physicians and MCOs.

Power over another individual can be expressed by a lack of action by an individual in response to an implicit threat by an another individual or an entity. This form of power is more insidious and pernicious. "Indeed, is it not the supreme exercise of power to get others to have the desires you want them to have; that is to secure their compliance by controlling their thoughts and desires."[10] The ability of an MCO to alter physician practice patterns as they pertain to, for example, the utilization of services reflects the MCO's implicit power. While, in theory, physicians are in charge of their practice, they may not receive a contract renewal if their practice patterns do not conform to very specific MCO guidelines. These guidelines are occasionally developed without physician input. While this aspect of power is important, it implies specific, MCO actions that result in specific physician reactions. The fact is that the relationship between MCOs and physicians is much more complex than that.

Power can also be viewed from the perspective of the "lordship bondage" relationship.[11] In this relationship, power is conceived, not as actions which one independent agent tries to affect another independent agent, but rather as a bond that structures an ongoing relationship between two social agents.[12] Such a bond may exist today when an MCO insures or covers a substantial percentage of a physician's practice and the MCO includes rules and regulations in which the physician has little or no say. The risk of such a situation is particularly strong in staff model MCOs (where all of the patients are covered by one MCO or in which the medical group is part of the MCO). It should be emphasized that it is the senior management of a staff model MCO, particularly in the not-for-profit sector, that determines the role of physicians. There are in fact many not-for-profit MCOs that have a tradition of physician leadership and thus provide significant voice to front-line physicians. Another example of a dominating relationship exists when the entire financial risk of a capitated contract is placed on a provider, such as a physician group or a physician-hospital network alliance. Yet it is not in the MCO's interest to have a de facto lordship bondage relationship with physicians.

There is also a power relationship between physicians and patients characterized by "influence." Influence, though, is fundamentally different from the forms of power described above. That is, if a physician influences a patient, the patient may alter his or her behavior, but the change is voluntary. Ultimately, even though a patient is in a weaker "power" position when sick, the patient has self-determination. The empowerment of patients by physicians and the encouragement of patient self-determination by physicians increases physicians' influence over patients. Put differently, the historical physician-patient relationship can be described as coercive, in that implicit power is its foundation. Under a newer model, that of enhanced patient self-determination, the physician shares expertise in an appropriate manner with the patient. So, while a small number of patients prefer their physicians to exert power over them (i.e., determine their behavior), physician influence is the preferable form of power in the relationship between physicians and patients.

Unfortunately, many aspects of the current relationship between a patient covered under a capitated contract and an MCO can be described as coercive. That is, given a choice, the patient would not follow the restrictions set by the MCO, whether the restrictions are in the benefits package or part of the administrative regulations underlying the MCO's operation. In the Putting Patients First campaign, MCOs are trying to shift away from use of coercive power toward a situated power strategy. According to Thomas Wartenberg,

A situated power relationship between two social agents is thus constituted by the presence of peripheral (i.e., several) social agents in the form of a social alignment. A field of social agents can constitute an alignment in regard to a social agent if, and only if, first of all, their actions in regard to that agent are coordinated in a specific manner . . . a social alignment is thus a quasi-monopolistic structure through which individuals gain access to things that they might wish to have.[13]

If an MCO pursues a strategy of providing coordinated care (implicitly implying several different "agents"), the MCO itself represents such an "alignment of social agents." The contractual arrangements between the MCO and the patient represent the "quasi-monopolistic" structure through which patients are able to gain access to the required health services. Additional features of the concept of situated power help to describe a new power relationship between MCOs and patients. Wartenberg continues, "The situated concept of power allows us to see that there is no necessary connection between the expert knowledge possessed by the empowering agent and the structure of the power relationship itself. While the expert may be an authority about certain subject matters, this authority is indistinguishable from the authority he comes to have as a result of being situated as an empowering agent."[14] Although in the final analysis the MCO does technically have the power to be coercive in its behavior toward a patient, the MCO could better achieve its financial and organizational goals if it pursued a coordinated care or situated power strategy toward its patients.

Due to the contractual relationship inherent in the benefits agreement with enrollees, MCOs, unlike physicians, will never exert only "influence" over patients. Additionally, the putting patients first strategy fundamentally still lies within the framework of the coercive power relationship, not of the situated power relationship. As discussed in the preceding section, MCOs need to shift away from coercion toward allowing patients as much self-determination as possible. Of course, MCOs will still need to maintain a significant role in decision making, as they bear the brunt of every costly decision made. However, clearer communication between MCOs and patients can only result in better decisions—ones that are cost effective and result in better outcomes. Better communication depends on the establishment of trust between patients and MCOs and between patients and their physicians. While complete trust will never be established between MCOs and physicians, the power relationship between the two should be more defined and easier for patients to understand. Thus, while MCOs will still resort to explicit or implicit sanctions in dealing with physicians or patients, situated power should be the bond that structures the ongoing relationships between MCOs and physicians and between MCOs and patients.

## OBLIGATIONS

The changed relationship between physicians and patients is not merely a result of MCOs' entering into a separate relationship with patients; it is the result of MCOs' having their own distinct relationship with physicians. The financial arrangements between MCOs and physicians lie at the heart of this relationship, which can range from an arm's length, discounted, fee-for-service relationship to a salaried employee relationship. Each point on this continuum has distinct implications for the physician's obligations to the MCO and consequently for the physician's obligations to his or her patients.

Patients are just beginning to consider how the change in physician obligations to MCOs affects the level of trust they can or should have in their physicians. To better understand the interplay between trust and obligations, it is important to distinguish, as Baier and Scanlon do, between three types of trust: unconscious trust, conscious but unchosen trust, and conscious trust the truster has chosen to endorse and cultivate.[15] There is a *contract* between doctors and patients, a contract that has existed for so long that it has assumed an unconscious form. The danger in unconscious trust is illustrated in a statement by the philosopher David Hume: "The penalty to which a promiser subjects himself in promising is that of never being trusted again in a case of failure."[16]

Unconscious trust has characterized the physician-patient relationship until the recent and dramatic corporatization of medicine. Today, unconscious trust has shifted, for the most part, into conscious trust the truster has chosen to endorse and cultivate. This is the ideal type of trust between physician and patient in today's health care environment. That is, medicine has come to a point at which patients who are knowledgeable about their disease will likely have the best outcomes; in these circumstances patients develop conscious trust derived from the increased knowledge they have about their illness. For example, studies have documented that the outcomes of asthma care are improved if the patients actively participate in their care.[17] Such improved outcomes can only occur if two conditions are met:

1. the physicians meet their obligation to teach and involve the patients in their own care
2. the patients are interested in as well as emotionally and financially capable of learning about and managing a significant portion of their care

Philosophically, the physicians' obligation to their patients is more important than the patients' obligation to participate in their care. It is the physicians' obligation to continually assess their patients' emotional and intellectual ability to participate in managing their own care and to communicate their observations to the patients. This continual assessment and communication process represents the essence of conscious trust the truster has chosen to endorse and cultivate. Conversely, the absence of communication between physicians and patients, combined with the perverse financial incentives inherent in capitation, will lead patients to suspect appropriately that self-management is a ruse serving the financial needs of the physicians.

Physicians must not only act on their changed relationships with patients but also take into account the new payers—the MCOs. While financial risk arrangements that place too great a risk on providers are important, the change in employee status for physicians has another implication as well: they no longer answer to themselves alone but must now consider the financial and quality of care demands of their employers.

Prior to considering the physicians' dilemma of having to satisfy their new employers as well as their patients, we need to further clarify the concept of obligation. According to Peter Singer, people "ought to give until we reach the level of marginal utility—that is, the level at which, by giving more, I would cause as much suffering to myself or my dependents as I would receive by my gift."[18] This clarification is helpful in that it combines "giving" (physicians give to their patients in an effort to maintain the trust that patients place in them) and the "suffering" (physicians face the burden of reduced pecuniary compensation and have new "obligations" to MCOs).

There are two specific challenges to the obligations of physicians to their patients:

1. impartiality, or equal concern and respect, which presses physicians toward an acceptance of general obligations
2. individualism, which requires or implicitly assumes limits on the moral demands that can be made of each physician[19]

These two challenges, impartiality and individualism, are very much related to the amount of financial risk physicians should allow themselves to assume. The principle of impartiality lends weight to the belief that physicians should not assume financial risk that exceeds strict limits. The principle of individualism would allow physicians to assume as much financial risk as they desire. As Fishkin showed in "The Limits of Obligation," there is no easy resolution to the tension between impartiality and individualism if one focuses on obligation alone.[20] However, the introduction of power and trust possibly can help. As detailed in the previous section, physician power is maximized if it is transformed into "influence." With this as the basis for the physician-patient relationship, physician influence is maximized if patient decision making is enhanced. Enhanced patient decision making can occur only if trust exists between the physician and patient.

Trust can exist only if two conditions are met. First, physicians must look beyond the financial risk issue and work together with fellow physicians, MCOs, and patients to strengthen their dedication to the science of medicine. As discussed above, it is possible to produce meaningful profiles by having physicians involved in their development. Use of these improved profiles will likely result in increased trust on the part of patients and MCOs.

Second, the financial risks assumed by physicians must be clearly defined for all parties and must be limited. While the principle of individualism by itself would allow physicians to assume greater financial risks in the care of their patients, the need to use influence rather than coercion and the need to enhance trust act as barriers to the assumption of significant financial risk.

## NEGOTIATING A REDEFINED PHYSICIAN-PATIENT-MCO RELATIONSHIP

*A scenario from tomorrow's doctor-patient-managed care relationship: Patients choose MCOs on the basis of quality-of-care and cost information provided at enrollment time. The quality-of-care information includes data not only on outcomes of care but also on the ability of the MCOs to coordinate services for patients with a chronic illness. In addition, MCOs provide information from physicians that rate MCOs on a variety of parameters, including their ability to coordinate services. MCOs provide physicians with two types of information: (1) confidential information on quality and cost when sample sizes are too small or when the indicator in question is still being researched and (2) information on cost and quality issues. Such infor-mation is first provided to physicians for validation and then released to the public. MCOs take a similar approach with hospitals. While risk-based pay-ments are used for both MCOs and providers, all health care organizations and individuals have both upside and downside limits for these payments.*

The key to the reestablishment of trust between patients, physicians, and MCOs is not to protect power of any one group but to increase the power of all three groups. For this to happen, each must be aware of the potential new relationships inherent in today's health care system. These new relationships can be explored via a negotiation process. Such a process requires a basic level of trust among the three groups if the new relationships are to be maxi-mized. Essential to the process of change is readiness on the part of key con-stituents to engage in the process.[21]

The regulatory and legislative onslaught on the physician-patient-MCO relationship is evidence that the three groups have in front of them a "unique window of opportunity to reframe the basic premises that motivate the sys-tem."[22] The purpose of this chapter is to provide a philosophical and ethical background for reframing the basic motivating principles of the health care system. A new relationship based on trust, obligations, and power would have at its core an answer to a completely different question: how will MCOs keep enrollees healthy? Rather than competing only on the price of medical ser-vices, MCOs should compete on the coordination of services for individuals in need of managed care. Unfortunately, due to market constraints, MCOs today compete largely on the basis of price. It is important that consumers (employers and enrollees alike) and physicians actively work together to encourage MCOs to include coordination of services as a key variable for the evaluation of MCO performance.

In an article in the *Wall Street Journal* on the placing of financial risk onto providers, a consumer indicated that "she considers herself well informed on health care but had no idea that PacifiCare, her HMO, gives physicians incen-tives to control drug expenses. 'If costs are going to be motivating the doctors, patients' health won't be their primary concern,' she fears."[23] However, the medical director stated that "the HMO doesn't disclose the drug arrangements routinely, but would tell patients if asked."[24] This kind of information must be routinely disclosed to patients so that they can understand and provide feedback. In the same article, another HMO executive commented, "One of the main reasons for the [pharmacy] incentives is simply to get physicians to read the HMO's quarterly prescribing profiles telling how much their prescriptions cost the HMO, and how far above or below average their costs are."[25] In his view, by controlling drug costs, "the budgets and incentives help employers continue to afford prescription drug benefits."[26] There is no mention in this quote of the impact of these programs on patient health. My own first-ever physician profile provided me with the average number of prescriptions per patient per visit. This information was not adjusted for the complexity of the patients. In its current state of incompleteness, such information is ignored by physicians and thus reinforces their belief that MCOs are uninterested in improving quality.

It is difficult to develop a trusting relationship, but, once started, a trusting relationship is fairly easy to maintain. However, it is also easy to destroy trust. Both trust and mistrust tend to be self-fulfilling and contagious. Today, trust is virtually nonexistent between patients and MCOs and between physicians and MCOs, and trust between physicians and patients is under serious strain. This chapter has attempted to explore the dimensions of the trust relationships between these three groups. In addition, the obligations that all three groups have toward each other have been highlighted. A full understanding of the concept of power colors the obligations that patients, physicians, and MCOs have toward each other. Power, particularly as it pertains to the impact of financial incentives, needs to be completely defined and clearly explained to all parties. An understanding will develop as each party in the triangle realizes it is in its own interest to limit the impact of financial incentives on provider and MCO behavior. Physician and MCO power can be modulated if boundaries are placed on financial incentives. These boundaries could provide both physicians and MCOs with a renewed sense of their traditional health care obligations toward patients, which in turn could lead to maintenance of trust. Without such a renewal of commitment, the fragile bonds of trust will unravel. The ultimate consequence is that patient care—which we *all* eventually find ourselves needing—will suffer.

## RECOMMENDATIONS FOR REFRAMING THE PHYSICIAN-PATIENT-MCO RELATIONSHIP

- Physicians need to understand and act on the implications of their changed relationships with patients and evolving new relationships with MCOs.

- The financial risk assumed by providers and MCOs needs to be limited and tailored to mitigate any incentive to inappropriately undertreat chronically ill patients. Frequently, medical groups accept complete risk for services.[27] These contracts are typically not adjusted for complexity, thus providing the MCO with a disincentive to coordinate care and the physician with an incentive to select healthier patients. It is understood that other MCOs do not pay physicians using this type of incentive.
- "Very few physicians are measuring their performance."[28] Physicians should redouble their commitment to working with patients and MCOs to continuously improve the care that they provide. Such a commitment requires learning from locally built guidelines developed collaboratively by physicians and MCOs and from patient satisfaction and health status data. Information derived from valid clinical comparisons can be expressed in physician profiles. Nascent efforts in this direction are underway. These efforts need to be significantly expanded.
- Patients need to be offered the choice of increased management of their own health care. If they choose increased management, MCOs and physicians must provide them with the tools to achieve this objective. If MCOs demonstrate that they are trying to provide the best possible coordination of health care services, patients will likely cede power to them. Similarly, patients will likely cede power (or, more precisely, influence) to physicians when they are able to choose whether or not to manage their own care.
- Popular resentment against MCOs has been fueled by the perceived limitation of new technologies. In each case, technology assessment should be performed by a third party that has no direct relationship with the MCO or those who have assumed financial risk for the care of the patient. This strategy may paradoxically result in less coverage for certain expensive technologies—those that have not been proven safe or effective. While it is understood that for expensive technologies the assessment process is occasionally delegated to outside organizations, outside assessment is not typically extended to all technologies. For example, an MCO that considered two new technologies for detection of cervical cancer rejected the one with the marginally higher detection rate because the gain was so small, it wasn't worth it.[29]
- MCOs should assume responsibility for coordination of care, not limitation of care. Coordination of care is defined as the seamless integration of a network of health care and non-health-care professionals and

technologies for the purpose of improving the processes and outcomes of care. While coordination of care is most relevant for patients with significant chronic illnesses, coordinated delivery of care is useful in all types of medical care, including preventive services such as immunization. If financial risk is limited, MCOs will have an incentive to coordinate care. Moreover, it should be the obligation of MCOs to coordinate multifaceted and complex medical services, particularly for the chronically ill. As the agents who control the capitation rate, MCOs have the power to coordinate services in such a way as to increase quality and decrease costs. Today, patients perceive only the limitation of care practiced by MCOs. Patient trust would increase dramatically with a coordination-of-care approach.

---

**NOTES**

1. L. Newcomer, "Measures of Trust in Health Care," *Health Affairs* 16 (1997): 50.
2. "Kaiser/Harvard National Survey of Americans' Views on Managed Care," *Managed Care Outlook*, 14 November, 1997, 7.
3. A.C. Baier, *Moral Prejudices: Essays on Ethics* (Cambridge, MA: Harvard University Press, 1994), 99.
4. D. Gambetta, ed., *Trust: Making and Breaking Cooperative Relations* (New York: Basil Blackwell, 1988), 217.
5. A.K. Gauthier et al., "Risk Selection in the Health Care Market: A Workshop Overview," *Inquiry* 32 (1995): 14.
6. D. Lupton et al., "Caveat Emptor Blissful Ignorance? Patients and the Consumerism Ethos," *Social Science and Medicine* 33 (1991): 559–568.
7. Baier, *Moral Prejudices*, 104–105.
8. Putting Patients First, American Association for Health Plans, fall 1997, material provided by AAHP Communications Department.
9. M. Pretzer, "How HMOs Still Gag Doctors," *Medical Economics* 9 March, 1998, 42–47.
10. T. Wartenberg, *The Forms of Power: From Domination to Transformation* (Philadelphia: Temple University Press, 1990), 57.
11. Wartenburg, *The Forms of Power*, 70.
12. Wartenburg, *The Forms of Power*, 69.
13. Wartenburg, *The Forms of Power*, 107.
14. Wartenburg, *The Forms of Power*, 154.
15. T. Scanlon, "Promises and Practices," *Philosophy and Public Affairs* 19 (1990): 199–226.
16. D. Hume, *A Treatise of Human Nature*, ed. L.A. Selby-Bigge and P.H. Nidditch (Oxford: Clarendon Press, 1978), 522.

17. C.J. Homer, "Asthma Disease Management," *New England Journal of Medicine* 20 (1997): 1461–1463.
18. P. Singer, "Famine, Affluence and Morality," in *Philosophy, Politics and Society*, 5th series, ed. P. Laslett and J. Fishkin (New Haven, CT: Yale University Press, 1979), 33.
19. J.S. Fishkin, *The Limits of Obligation* (New Haven, CT: Yale University Press, 1982), chap. 19.
20. Fishkin, *The Limits of Obligation*, 59.
21. M. Leonard, *Renegotiating Health Care* (San Francisco: Jossey-Bass, 1995), 172.
22. Leonard, *Renegotiating Health Care*, 172.
23. "Dose of Austerity from HMO's Now Put Doctors on Budget for Prescriptions," *Wall Street Journal*, 22 May, 1997, 1.
24. "Dose of Austerity."
25. "Dose of Austerity."
26. "Dose of Austerity."
27. D.A. Conrad et al., "Primary Care Physician Compensation Method in Medical Groups," *JAMA* 279 (1998): 853–858.
28. Newcomer, "Measures of Trust in Health Care."
29. L. Newcomer, as quoted in "Health Care Costs Trimmed, Hold Inflation Down," *Wall Street Journal*, 30 June, 1997, 1.

# CHAPTER 2

# Physician Profiling—Not Whether but How

*Norbert Goldfield*

In an ideal world, all relevant clinical information—along with data on mortality, patient satisfaction and other important characteristics of physician practice—would be released to the public. As Michael Millenson pointedly asks in Chapter 13, "How about driving out *my* fear each time I seek treatment from my profit-driven health maintenance organization (HMO), which has just signed up a joint venture consisting of a panic-stricken community hospital and a pampered group of local physicians who could not spell *capitation* a year ago if you spotted them all the vowels? That, my friends, is fear."[1]

Yet physicians also have a legitimate concern. While public disclosure of comparative information is well established in the case of managed care organizations and hospitals, there is little experience with public release of physician-specific information. As someone who has had experience with the approximately 20 states that produce hospital-specific mortality and severity profiles, I can attest to the difference between releasing information pertaining to a hospital with thousands of employees and releasing information pertaining to one physician or a small group of physicians. Simply put, the difference is one of public relations. While large organizations such as hospitals, managed care organizations, and large medical groups either have or could have significant public relations resources to deal with negative fallout following public disclosure of comparative information, small groups of physicians could not withstand such an onslaught. Yet for physicians to burrow their heads into the sand and simply claim that currently available information is not scientifically valid is not only inadequate in today's marketplace but denies patients information that would allow them to make better choices and better manage their own care.

In light of this, the key question physicians must face is how can they best obtain information regarding their practice that will have a measurable impact on the processes and outcomes of patient care. This chapter will examine this question in light of the current state of physician profiling and future research trends. In particular, the following topics will be discussed:

- desired characteristics of physician profiles
- current uses of physician profile data
- the need for adjustment for severity of illness
- data elements used in current physician profiling (claims data, encounter data, patient questionnaires data, and medical record abstraction data)
- the future of physician profiling
- a forward-looking physician-profiling strategy

## DESIRED CHARACTERISTICS OF PHYSICIAN PROFILES

Whether used for internal or external purposes, physician profiles should share the following characteristics:

- be of interest to as many consumers of physician profiles as possible (patients, employers, managed care organizations, and of course physicians)
- help to improve the processes and/or outcomes of care.
- have a firm basis in scientific literature while recognizing that much of clinical medicine is still an art and contains many controversies
- meet certain statistical thresholds of validity and reliability
- cost the minimum amount to produce
- respect patient confidentiality (patient consent should be obtained for information from the medical record and/or when using patient-derived information)

Because of the various consumers of physician profiles, there is a need to achieve political and scientific agreement between often differing and competing interests. The process of consensus building is just as important as the final product itself. In fact, successfully integrating the needs of differing consumers will result in physician profiles that are especially likely to significantly improve both the processes and outcomes of care.

The author and several colleagues collected over 1,000 patient responses to a questionnaire on desired characteristics of physician report cards.[2] An analysis found that the patients (enrolled in three managed care organizations dispersed throughout the United States) valued information pertaining to the processes of care more than they valued information pertaining to the outcomes of care. In addition, while knowledge regarding outcomes is continuously improving, patients appear to have very high confidence in and desire to have information pertaining to processes of care (such as availability of appointment times and the friendliness of the staff).

While it is obvious that there is a need for scientific validity for any data elements within a physician profile, ensuring validity is easier said than done. Take, for example, the optimal treatment of chronic otitis media. The Agency for Health Care Policy and Research recently released a guideline on the optimal treatment of this chronic disorder.[3–5] Conversations with individuals who participated in the development of the guideline indicated that the scientific acceptability of the final guideline differed depending on whether one was a primary care practitioner or an ear, nose, and throat specialist. The optimal care of diabetics presents another example of differing points of view. Some patients tolerate a lifestyle that includes frequent examination of blood glucose level and occasional hypoglycemic episodes; others prefer to risk future complications instead of undergoing continual glucose examination. Research has demonstrated how the role of patient interaction with the physician in the decision-making process is critical.[6,7]

Differences in understanding of the best treatment (leading to different outcomes, often in the distant future) simply indicate that it is important for all consumers, including physicians, to appreciate the fact that much of medicine is still an art. Not only is medicine an art, but part of the artfulness emanates from the need to take into account patient preferences. We need to understand more about outcomes and preferences. The continuous evolution of our understanding demands that an update process be an integral feature of physician profiling.

Several factors underline the issue of the statistical performance of data elements used within physician profiles: choice of the data elements themselves, adjusting for severity of illness, and assurance of sufficient sample size. The data elements chosen for the profile need to be clinically and scientifically acceptable. According to Harry Selker, the data elements chosen need to have

- content validity

- face validity
- clinical practicality
- "consensus validity"
- demonstrated safety and effectiveness
- transportability
- an updating process[8]

Unfortunately, the "art" aspect of medicine manifests itself when different clinical perspectives emerge between different groups of medical professionals, as in the case of otitis media. In such cases, achieving a consensus becomes a major challenge. The challenge is even greater when the needs of the many consumers of physician profiles are taken into account.

The second factor, adjusting for severity of illness, is discussed in detail below. We will here discuss the third. In light of the increasing popularity of point-of-service plans, which allow enrollees greater freedom of provider choice, the need for a sufficient sample size is a real and growing concern. The only practical means of dealing with this issue is for medical professionals to work together, alone or under the auspices of an organization such as the state medical society, and collect data until the relevant statistical criteria are met.

There is at least one significant difference between physician profiles used for internal purposes (by the physician) and those used for external purposes: the threshold of statistical and clinical validity does not need to be as high when physician profiles are used for internal quality improvement activities. What is the threshold? A simple mathematical formula is not sufficient. The threshold for public release depends on the development of a community-wide approach to the need to release the information, a process for its release, and an understanding on how it will be used to improve both care and the physician-patient relationship.

## CURRENT USES OF PHYSICIAN PROFILE DATA

Physician profiles are used today for the following purposes:

- utilization management
- quality improvement
- capitation adjustment
- network determination and updating

This chapter does not deal with the latter two uses of physician profiles. Suffice it to say that currently available methodologies are not sufficient to adequately adjust capitation rates for individual physician panels—without the use of stop-loss.[9] With respect to network determination, it is unfortunate that managed care organizations still use profiling adjustments in the initial development of managed care networks. Physicians who have often never seen any data on their practice patterns can be excluded from a managed care network and not provided with the opportunity to respond by documenting different practice patterns or improving their practice patterns (if, in fact, their practice patterns need improving).

The focus here is on two other uses of physician profiling: quality improvement and utilization management. It is important to confront the issue of case mix or severity adjustment prior to analyzing past physician profiling efforts in the areas of quality improvement and utilization management.

## THE NEED TO ADJUST FOR SEVERITY OF ILLNESS

When confronted with the need to examine quality of care and utilization of services, most physicians immediately turn to the age-old excuse: my patients are sicker. Because it is repeated over and over again, this excuse needs to be explored.

Case mix adjustment for purposes of quality improvement or utilization management represents the first step and the first step only in the quality improvement process. A physician profile adjusted for case mix taken at one point in time should never be used to make final decisions regarding a physician's medical practice. This implies that, unless one can profile a physician's practice over a period of time, such information should not be released to the public. However, the seeds of a compromise are present, provided there is excellent communication between the various parties seeking physician-specific information. Initially, physician profiles should be developed with the participation of all consumers, particularly physicians. A second step involves the choice of one of several technologies, either claims-based or non-claims-based, for case mix adjustment. While it is possible to adopt the perspective that current case mix adjustment technologies represent a half-empty glass, I prefer the opposite approach if consumers insist that these technologies be open for examination and verification.

One of the most difficult questions facing a purchaser of a case mix technology is the degree to which the purchaser is comfortable with the use of potentially preventable complications as part of the severity adjustment logic. For example, with respect to myocardial infarction (MI), many secondary diagnoses present upon admission after an MI probably represent comorbidities or sequelae of the MI. Thus, if a patient develops complete atrioventricular (AV)-block on the second day of hospitalization, it is likely that this secondary diagnosis represents a comorbidity and not a complication. One could extend this analysis to a large number of other diagnoses secondary to an MI.

A purchaser needs to answer the following question as part of the case mix purchasing process: does the purchaser prefer a case mix technology that includes the potentially preventable complications in the logic? Such case mix logic gives the benefit of the doubt to the provider (hospital or physician). If these complications are not included, providers may be unfairly "rated." While my bias is to include all secondary diagnoses after admission, save for those that represent clear complications (the 9000 series of codes in ICD-9-CM), others might altogether reject such an approach. The state of California may be a leader in providing a middle ground (i.e., regarding whether a secondary diagnosis was present upon admission).[10] Such knowledge would allow the calculation of separate indices for all codes versus those codes only present upon admission.

Once this process of adjustment for case mix is completed, physician-specific profiles adjusted for case mix should be released, but only to the physician. This allows for a further process of buy-in. By this time, the physician profile could be developed with several data collection points, thus increasing its statistical power. In addition, it ensures that the profile is able to properly identify and assign patients for whom the physician has true responsibility.

The decision as to whether or not to release the profile to the public would then be based on a number of factors, principally the scientific validity of the profile itself and the level of consumer interest in the profile. Without adjustment for case mix, a physician profile has no salience, even if the profile is released for internal use only. Case mix measures will continue to improve. The many consumers for physician profiles and the decreasing cost of aggregating data elements previously too costly to combine together will lead to significant improvements in case mix measures over the coming several years.

## DATA ELEMENTS CURRENTLY USED IN PHYSICIAN PROFILING

The three main types of data elements are claims data, patient-derived information, and encounter data.

**Claims Data**

Although much maligned, claims data can be an important ingredient in a physician profile.[11] In fact, there are several advantages to the use of inpatient claims data for quality improvement and utilization management purposes:

- With the implementation of diagnosis-related groups (DRGs) there began an extended period of experience with inpatient coding.[12]
- As there are significant financial issues at stake for the hospital, a considerable effort is typically made to code as accurately as possible.[13]
- For enrollees with a chronic illness (individuals with the highest likelihood of interaction with the health care system), information pertaining to the quality of hospital care is likely to be very important.
- For at least one important indicator of quality within a hospital, mortality, the information is reliably coded and is of great importance to all consumers interested in physician profiles.
- For many physicians, there are a sufficient number of patients for examining quality and utilization issues. When that is not possible, there are statistical methods to aggregate clinically dissimilar patients into categories, adjusted for complexity.
- While using claims data for quality improvement purposes is still controversial, a considerable amount of experience in using them for this purpose has accumulated.[14–16]

The Maine Medical Assessment Project has extensively utilized inpatient claims data for the purpose of developing physician profiles.[17] These profiles are then released directly to the physicians. This project has had a significant impact on medical practice, not only because of the rigorous scientific nature of data elements used in the physician profiles but equally because of the release process. Though the physician profiles are released for internal purposes only, senior physicians have provided extensive follow-up to the physicians involved in the profile effort.

A significant controversy still exists regarding the validity of using claims data for quality improvement purposes. It is unlikely that those who dismiss the validity of claims based data for these purposes will change their minds; the same goes for those institutions and individuals that use such data. The best approach is two pronged. First, institutions and/or individuals that use claims data to improve quality need to continue to publish. More important, large organizations such as state health agencies and national centers providing input into data collection instruments such as ICD-9-CM need to include new data elements, thus increasing the validity of claims data. For example, California mandates the collection of a data element indicating whether the secondary diagnosis on a hospital claims form was present upon admission.

Over the past five years, researchers have begun to analyze claims data in other sectors of the health care system. However, once again it is important to clarify the object of using claims data. There are two types of ambulatory care claims data: visit-based data and episode-of-illness data.

With respect to visit-based claims data, profiling can provide information pertaining to utilization of services (on the condition that procedures are not a significant part of the case mix adjustment that is used to account for differences in the severity of the case).[18] So long as the objective is clearly specified, profiling can also provide information pertaining to the quality of care provided to enrollees. Thus, the following types of information obtained from visit-based claims data are useful for physician profiles for quality-monitoring purposes:

- the presence or absence of a particular procedure (such as a vaccination or mammogram), whose performance typically indicates that quality care has been provided for the particular condition
- the utilization of inappropriate site of care, such as the emergency room for an asthmatic, which, if repeated continuously, may indicate an opportunity for improvement[19]

According to a recent review of claims data used for physician report cards, "Despite their imperfections, claims data can be extremely useful probes to improve utilization, target continuing medical education, help manage complex patients, identify underserved patients, and detect misprescribing as well as fraud and abuse."[20] The author goes on to indicate that there is little training available to help physicians accurately and reliably code with ICD-9-CM and CPT-4. While training programs are important, accurate coding will emerge only when physicians have an incentive to code accurately. For example, I have seen a marked increase in physician interest in accurate coding when physicians are committed to and trusting of inpatient risk adjustment methodologies that a hospital, with input from the physicians, has decided to use for profiling purposes.

Physician profiling using episode-of-illness claims data is in a primitive state. Yet significant enhancements will shortly appear on the market, including severity-adjusted disease-specific categories that

- could be tracked over an episode of illness[21]
- begin at hospitalization and track mortality over a 90-day period of time
- identify procedure codes, which may represent a complication of care (in a recently published paper, the Center for Health Economics Research identified the performance of a CT scan shortly after discharge for an endarterectomy as a possible indicator of a complication of care)[22]

**Patient-derived Information**

Two types of information are typically drawn from enrollees: satisfaction and health status information.[23] While there is no published information on the use of patient satisfaction questionnaires to improve physician performance, there is considerable anecdotal evidence that these questionnaires can be useful. The author was involved in the development and use of a patient satisfaction questionnaire in a large staff model HMO. The results of a survey performed with this questionnaire were used to partially determine salary increases for the HMO physicians. Of greatest importance, the physicians themselves were involved in the development of the questionnaire. As for the issue of cost, it should be emphasized that patient satisfaction questionnaires do not require large numbers of enrollees to produce statistically valid information.[24]

The last few years have seen the development of a significant number of well-validated questionnaires that measure a patient's health status.[25] The Foundation for Accountability (FACCT), a competitor of the National Committee for Quality Assurance (NCQA) and the Joint Commission on Accreditation of Healthcare Organizations, emphasizes the improvement of outcomes and health status.[26–28] There appears to be little effort at the present time to add physician profiles to its portfolio of managed care organization profiles.

**Encounter Data**

Encounter data include any information drawn from the medical record and any other pieces of paper or data files completed by a provider at the time of an encounter with a patient. With respect to inpatient profiling, Medsgrps is the best-known risk adjustment system that uses information drawn from the medical record.[29] Both hospital- and physician-specific profiles have been released to the public based on this risk adjustment system. The most extensive "scorecard." emanating from Pennsylvania is its "Focus on Heart Attack."[30,31] The state of New York has released physician-specific report cards in its analysis of hospital cardiovascular surgery since 1992.[32–34] While report cards were controversial, there is ample evidence that cardiovascular surgery mortality rates did decline as a consequence of the release of this information.[35] Although many experts have argued against the use of scorecards,[36,37] in a recent review of the New York State experience with public disclosure of risk-adjusted physician profiles, the authors state, "We believe that the public release of data on mortality rates has played an important part in galvanizing physicians and hospitals to seize these opportunities to improve."[38]

Several medical specialty societies have also ventured into the field of physician profiling for specific hospital-based surgical procedures.[39,40] Unfortunately, many of these efforts are proprietary, and the developers have not opened the logic for scrutiny by independent researchers. While it is thus difficult at the present time to evaluate the reliability and validity of such efforts, it is likely that they will increase in importance. If the members of a specialty society are supportive, the resulting physician profiles, after considerable internal development, will probably be publicly released.

The Health Employer Data Information Set (HEDIS), developed under the auspices of NCQA, is the most extensive effort to draw information from encounter data.[41] Although NCQA currently uses this information just to evaluate managed care organizations, the Pacific Business Group on Health (PBGH) has begun to use the HEDIS data set to evaluate medical groups that contract with managed care organizations.[42] PBGH plans to release the evaluation information to the public. This is a significant step forward in the development of physician profiles for external release. Its importance derives from the fact that most physicians, particularly on the West Coast, are not solo practitioners or members of small medical groups. Large medical groups that contract with HMOs for the entire risk are the main providers of medical care. The American Medical Association's physician profiling program has significant potential.[43] It is currently unclear as to what, if any, impact it will have on consumer interest in physician profiles. Chapter 28 provides an update on this program.

One of the main drawbacks in all the efforts listed in this section is the cost involved in obtaining encounter information. In addition, it would appear that there has been little involvement on the part of organized medicine. It is the business community that is largely driving this process. Possibly the business community views the obtainment of NCQA-based information as an intermediate step prior to direct contracting. This is similar to what is occurring in other mature managed care markets, such as Minnesota. The net result will be the public release of physician profiles for, at least, medical groups of substantial size.

## THE FUTURE OF PHYSICIAN PROFILING

The future of physician profiling can be analyzed from two perspectives: the push for external release and the integration of disparate types of information, leading to a significant reduction in costs and simultaneous increase in validity for increasingly sophisticated physician profiles. With respect to the latter, it is likely that in the short term increasingly sophisticated yet inexpensive physician profiles will be available. We are on the threshold of lifting the electronic and organizational barriers to inexpensively linking salient elements for physician profiling. Many hospital-based systems will be able to link clinical and administrative data in the not too distant future, thus significantly increasing the power of the profiles of hospital-based services. Health care organizations are expending significant resources in an effort to link hospital and ambulatory care data. The short-term advances will include these:

- A link between the name of a pharmaceutical and severity-adjusted claims data will increase the clinical validity of, for example, examinations of the outcomes of care for diabetics. These databases are available now.
- Within a year, there will be a link with outpatient laboratory values. This will provide further clinical validity for the analysis, for example, of outcomes for diabetics. The value of a hemoglobin A1C will be an excellent outcome-dependent variable in the follow-up of diabetes.
- Within two years, there will be a link between patient health status and claim-based laboratory and pharmaceutical information.

The challenge will be implementation. Implementation is extremely difficult, and policy makers will need to pay attention to the following types of issues:

- The acceptance by individual physicians and other consumers of report cards. Acceptance includes not only participation in the development of the profiles but also an in-built quality improvement process to use the profiles effectively. This applies to all consumers of the profile, not just physicians. We still understand very little about how consumers can best use these profiles.[43]
- The protection of patient confidentiality.
- The development and implementation of new statistical and profiling techniques to enhance the validity of the physician profiles.[44,45]

In the meantime, we need to have a strategy in place for current efforts to promote valid and reliable physician profiling.

## A FORWARD-LOOKING STRATEGY

A strategy on physician profiling needs to include the following elements:

- a way of dealing with issues of patient confidentiality
- a research agenda
- internal and external release of information

### Dealing with Patient Confidentiality

Physicians and patients are understandably concerned that patient confidentiality may be violated. To my knowledge, violation has not occurred in any public release of physician-specific information. Patient confidentiality can be ensured if strict policies are rigorously adhered to. In addition, encryption methodologies are under development, which will create greater patient and physician confidence that patient confidentiality will not be put at risk by physician profiles.[46]

### A Practical Research Agenda

A forward-looking agenda for research on physician profiling would include at least the following questions:

- What profile topics are physicians and other customers interested in? As discussed earlier, we should not assume that all patients are only interested in outcomes such as mortality.
- What are the best methods for engaging physicians and other customers in the development of physician profiles?
- What new approaches, both from an informatics and a clinical perspective, can be developed to inexpensively produce reliable and valid physician profiles? Also needed is determination of which organizational arrangements will facilitate the development and implementation of physician profiles based on adequate samples.
- What educational techniques can be implemented that will enable all customers, including physicians and patients, to learn from physician profiles to improve care? All customers need to be involved; change in care cannot only emanate from change in physician practice.

A research agenda such as the one outlined above must not be used to block development and implementation of physician profiles. The following section details specific features of desired physician profiles that can be produced today.

**Internal and External Release of Information**

At a minimum, physicians need to be an integral part of the team that develops the physician profiles. For example, cardiovascular surgeons were actively involved in the development of the New York State Department of Health cardiovascular surgery project. Even so, a number of surgeons published significant criticisms of the methodology.[47]

The report format itself is an extremely important feature of physician profiles. Florida, for example, which has released hospital-specific mortality and severity-of-illness rates for several years, has established wide confidence intervals and designed a format that places great emphasis on information and deliberately underemphasizes histrionic identification of poor or excellent performers.[48]

Ideally, the report cards should be first delivered to the affected institution in an effort to solicit feedback and identify any problems with the report cards themselves. In these days, in which there is mouthing of the words "quality improvement" and a great emphasis on immediate public disclosure, it is worth summarizing the conclusions of a several-year effort at internal dissemination of physician-specific information. Physicians at the Maine Medical Assessment Foundation concluded the following:

- Physicians are willing to change their practices if they are brought into a culturally appropriate improvement program.
- Related specialties can often work together effectively on issues of common interest.
- Area- and physician-specific data are not made public so as to build a sense of confidentiality among participants.[49]

Yet the public does have a right to know. Much of the world still does not operate on the continuous quality improvement (CQI) principle of "driving out fear" by providing internal feedback only to physicians. Or as Michael Millenson states, "What a shame God never had a chance to read Deming's book before writing His."[50] One is most likely to resolve the tension and develop successful public report cards for physicians if all customers are brought to the table and are involved in a CQI manner.

## CONCLUSIONS

It is appropriate to conclude this chapter by recalling the fate of one of the earliest efforts to produce physician-specific reports. Ernest Codman, a surgeon at the Massachusetts General Hospital, proposed that de facto physician report cards be developed and publicly released.[51] For his efforts, Mass General dismissed him from the staff. The American College of Surgeons, at their annual meeting, burned his "report cards" in the hall fireplace at the Waldorf Astoria Hotel in New York City.[52,53]

Seventy-five years later we still have a long road to traverse before we fully understand what type of physician report cards are needed. This chapter has attempted to separate out threads that can then be brought back together through further research and renewed commitment to the principles of continuous quality improvement.

---

## NOTES

1. M. Millenson, "Public Disclosure: A Media Perspective," in *Physician Profiling and Risk Adjustment*, eds. N. Goldfield and P. Boland (Gaithersburg, MD: Aspen Publishers, 1996).

2. N. Goldfield et al. "Consumer Assessment of Report Card Domains," submitted for publication.

3. J.L. Paradise, "Controversies: Treatment of Acute Otitis Media," *JAMA* 279 (1998): 1784–1785.

4. A. Melhus and A. Hermansson, "Controversies: Treatment of Acute Otitis Media," *JAMA* 279 (1998): 1783–1784.

5. M.J. Harkness, "Controversies: Treatment of Acute Otitis Media," *JAMA* 279 (1998): 1783.

6. S. Kaplan and J. Ware. *The Patient's Role in Health Care and Quality Assessment in Providing Quality Care* (Ann Arbor, MI: Health Administration Press, 1995), 25–59.

7. M. Gerteis, *Through Patient Eyes* (San Francisco: Jossey-Bass, 1993).

8. H.P. Selker, "Criteria for Adoption in Practice of Medical Practice Guidelines," *American Journal of Cardiology* 71 (1993): 339–341.

9. N. Goldfield et al., "Prospective Risk Adjustment Classses," in *Physician Profiling and Risk Adjustment*, 2nd ed., ed. N. Goldfield, Chapter 36.

10. State of California, California Code of Regulation, Title 22, Division 7, Chapter 10, Article 8, Section 97225–97226.

11. R.F. Coulam and G.L. Gaumer, "Medicare's Prospective Payment System: A Critical Appraisal," *Health Care Financing Review* annual suppl. 13 (1997): 45–76.

12. Coulam and Gaumer, "Medicare's Prospective Payment System."

13. D.C. Hsia et al., "Medicare Reimbursement Accuracy under the Prospective Payment System, 1985 to 1988," *JAMA* 268 (1992): 896–899.

14. L. Iezzoni, "Severity of Illness Measures and Assessing the Quality of Hospital Care," in *Providing Quality Care*, eds. N. Goldfield and D. Nash (Ann Arbor, MI: Health Administration Press, 1995).

15. Iezzoni, "Severity of Illness Measures."

16. Iezzoni, "Severity of Illness Measures."

17. G.T. O'Connor et al., "Regional Organization for Outcomes Research," *Annals of the New York Academy of Sciences*, 31 December, 1993, 44–50.

18. R. Averill et al., "Design of a Prospective Payment Classification System for Ambulatory Care," *Health Care Financing Review* 15, no. 1 (1993): 71–100.

19. N. Goldfield, "A Quality Improvement Process for Ambulatory Prospective Payment," *Journal of Ambulatory Care Management* 16, no. 2 (1993): 50–60.

20. D.W. Shapiro et al., "Containing Costs While Improving Quality of Care: The Role of Profiling and Practice Guidelines," *Annual Review of Public Health* 14 (1993): 219–241.

21. N. Goldfield et al., "The Prospective Risk Adjustment System."

22. J.B. Mitchell et al., "Using Physician Claims to Identify Postoperative Complications of Carotid Endarterectomy," *Health Services Research* 31 (1996): 141–152.

23. Kaplan and Ware, "The Patient's Role in Health Care and Quality Assessment."

24. J. McGee et al., *Collecting Information from Health Care Consumers: A Resource Manual of Tested Questionnaires and Practical Advice* (Gaithersburg, MD: Aspen Publishers, 1996).

25. McGee et al., *Collecting Information from Health Care Consumers.*

26. J. Schroeder and S. Lamb, "Data Initiatives: HEDIS and the New England Business Coalition," *American Journal of Medical Quality* 11, no. 1 (1996): S58–S62.

27. D. Lansky, "Overview: Performance Measures—The Next Generation," *Journal on Quality Improvement* 22 (1996): 439–442.

28. D.C. Brooks, "The Joint Commission on the Accreditation of Health Care Organizations," in *Providing Quality Care*, eds. N. Goldfield and D. Nash (Ann Arbor, MI: Health Administration Press, 1995).

29. Iezzoni, "Severity of Illness Measures and Assessing the Quality of Hospital Care."

30. J.G. Jollis and P.S. Romano, "Pennsylvania's Focus on Heart Attack: Grading the Scorecard," *New England Journal of Medicine* 338 (1998): 983–987.

31. E.D. Schneider and A.M. Epstein, "Influence of Cardiac-surgery Performance Reports on Referral Practices and Access to Care: A Survey of Cardiovascular Specialists," *New England Journal of Medicine* 335 (1996): 251–256.

32. E.L. Hannan et al., "Public Release of Cardiac Surgery Outcomes Data in New York: What Do New York State Cardiologists Think of It?" *American Heart Journal* 134 (1997): 1120–1128.

33. J. Green and N. Wintfeld, "Report Cards on Cardiac Surgeons: Assessing New York State's Approach," *New England Journal of Medicine* 332 (1995): 1229–1232.

34. M.R. Chassin, "Benefits and Hazards of Reporting Medical Outcomes Publicly," *New England Journal of Medicine* 334 (1996): 394–398.

35. E.L. Hannan et al., "Assessment of Coronary Artery Bypass Surgery Performance in New York: Is There a Bias against Taking High-Risk Patients?" *Medical Care* 35, no. 1 (1997): 49–56.

36. E.J. Topol et al., "Readiness for the Scoreboard Era in Cardiovascular Medicine," *American Journal of Cardiology* 75 (1995): 1170–1173.

37. Topol et al., "Readiness for the Scoreboard Era in Cardiovascular Medicine."

38. Hannan et al., "Public Research of Cardiac Surgery Outcomes Data in New York."

39. O. Ukimura et al., "A Statistical Study of the American Urological Association Symptom Index for Benign Prostatic Hyperplasia in Participants of Mass Screening Program for Prostatic Diseases Using Transrectal Sonography," *Journal of Urology* 156 (1996): 1673–1678.

40. Schneider and Epstein, "Influence of Cardiac-surgery Performance Reports on Referral Practices and Access to Care."

41. National Committee for Quality Assurance, "Quality Compass," Washington, DC, 1998.

42. Personal communication with David Hopkins, Pacific Business Group on Health, September, 1998.

43. A.K. Rosen et al., "Developing Episodes of Care for Adult Asthma Patients: A Cautionary Tale," *American Journal of Medical Quality* 13, no. 1 (1998): 25–35.

44. K.C. Stange et al., "How Valid Are Medical Records and Patient Questionnaires for Physician Profiling and Health Services Research? A Comparison with Direct Observation of Patient Visits," *Medical Care* 36 (1998): 851–867.

45. J.L. Sardinas, Jr., and J.D. Muldoon, "Securing the Transmission and Storage of Medical Information," *Computers in Nursing* 16 (1998): 162–168.

46. M.A. Epstein et al., "Security for the Digital Information Age of Medicine: Issues, Applications, and Implementation," *Journal of Digital Imaging* 10, no. 3, suppl. 1 (1997): 122–127.

47. Topol et al., "Readiness for the Scorecard Era in Cardiovascular Medicine."

48. *1996 Guide to Hospitals in Florida* (Tallahassee: State of Florida Agency for Health Care Administration, 1996).

49. R.B. Keller et al., "Informed Inquiry into Practice Variations: The Maine Medical Assessment Foundation," *Quality Assurance in Health Care* 2, no. 1 (1990): 69–75.

50. R.B. Keller et al., "Dealing with Geographic Variations in the Use of Hospitals: The Experience of the Maine Medical Assessment Foundation Orthopaedic Study Group." *Journal of Bone and Joint Surgery [AM]* 72, no. 9 (1990): 1286–1293.

51. E.A. Codman, "The Product of a Hospital," *Archives of Pathology and Laboratory Medicine* 114 (1990): 1106–1111.

52. A. Donabedian, "Ernest A. Codman, MD, The End Result Idea and the Product of a Hospital: A Commentary," *Archives of Pathology and Laboratory Medicine* 114 (1990): 1105.

53. W.W. McLendon, "Ernest A. Codman, MD (1869–1940), The End Result Idea, and the Product of a Hospital: The Challenge of a man ahead of his time and perhaps ours," *Archives of Pathology and Laboratory Medicine* 114 (1990): 1101–1104.

CHAPTER 3

# Commentary on "Physician Profiling"

*Jon Kingsdale and Harris A. Berman*

In Norbert Goldfield's review of physician profiling, he rightly focuses on a major obstacle to its further development and broader acceptance. He repeatedly refers to the "art" of medicine, by which he means both the variability in means to a desired medical outcome and the subjective preferences of patients for different outcomes. When the optimal treatment for a given medical condition cannot be prescribed in a single, consistently applied guideline, what standard can we use to compare actual with ideal performance?

Most of the chapter focuses on this issue and related obstacles in using provider-generated data (claims and encounter data) to measure accurately the performance of physicians against professionally derived standards of care. For convenience, we can label this type of profiling as "professional" (i.e., based on provider-generated data and using physician-generated standards of care).

Goldfield's discussion of the opportunities and problems with professional profiling present a challenge to researchers and practitioners: how to utilize the tools becoming available to effectively improve health care quality and outcomes. In view of the interest of managed care organizations (MCOs) in continuously improving health care quality, they would seem to be the natural promoters of professional profiling. If properly promoted, professional profiling could improve quality, standardize practices now subject to wide variation, and document (and improve) the quality of care provided by MCOs.

However, even as the many technical problems Goldfield discusses in connection with professional profiling are addressed, the resistance of physicians to public disclosure of such comparisons may actually increase.

Given the managed care backlash currently in vogue, many MCOs will be loath to jump onto this bandwagon, for fear of further alienating their physicians. Some would wish the title of Goldfield's chapter was "*Physician Profiling — Not Whether, but Not Now!*"

Only if physicians participate in the development of the process and feel real ownership of this work will the product be accepted and not just become more fodder for the backlash against managed care. The critical challenge, then, is to excite physician leaders about the need for professional profiling and the methodologies to be used. Once they have taken ownership of the process themselves, then there will be hope for progress, both in resolving to *their* satisfaction the methodological and research issues that Goldfield raises and in the public dissemination and use of professional profiles.

There is, however, an alternative to the professional profiling on which this chapter focuses. By contrast, we might term profiles based on surveys of patients asked to rate their physicians' services or their own functionality as "consumer" profiling. Goldfield deals summarily with patient-focused questionnaires that address the intentionally subjective measure of medicine's art—what does the customer prefer and how does he or she feel or function as a result? By focusing on the many issues related to professional profiling, Goldfield seems to slight consumer profiling.

MCOs already use consumer profiling and are likely to expand such use, partly because the cost of collecting information from a sample of members is far less than that of collecting reliable encounter data. Staff and group model MCOs may be able to obtain encounter data from electronic medical records, but the vast majority of MCO members are served in IPA or network models, where such data are not readily collectible. Moreover, Goldfield rightly raises many questions about the accuracy, confidential nature, and statistical credibility of encounter data, especially for public use in assessing individual physician performance, that do not apply to consumer survey data.

A second point is that MCOs, by focusing on patients' admittedly subjective assessment of how well physicians served them and how well they feel as a result, can contribute an important perspective that professionals all too often ignore. MCOs represent the nexus between consumer and provider. They are well situated to gather data from consumers, to interpret these data back to physicians for purposes of improving physician performance, and to use such data to stimulate informed consumer demand for quality of care.

Third, returning to the issue of physician interest (or lack thereof) in professional profiling, greater use of consumer profiling may well ease the way for professional profiling. Ironically, if physicians feel threatened by the use and disclosure of consumer-generated ratings, they can hardly dismiss them as irrelevant. Rather, they may feel pressured to respond with more "credible" quality measures and therefore support the development of professional profiling as an important complement to consumer profiling. Unless forced by alternative metrics to support credible professional profiling, they will, we fear, generally prefer no profiling.

# CHAPTER 4

# Commentary on "Physician Profiling": The Patient, The Organization, The Physician— Whose Profile?

*John D. Stoeckle*

In the search for improvement in health care, the patients, the organizations, and now the physicians—what are they like and what can they do better— have all been examined. In the case of patients, a vast sociological literature has studied what prevents patients from taking preventive action, going to the doctor, taking medicines, and changing their illness-prone behaviors. These old patient themes have largely disappeared, as poor health is no longer viewed as the patient's fault. Then it was the turn of health care organizations, especially hospitals, where the systems inside supposedly did not prevent mistakes, produced less than optimal outcomes, and were inefficient and costly in providing care.

Now we are looking at the physicians and their role in determining patient outcomes. Part of this new interest is motivated by the focus on customer choice and part is motivated by the desire for information on outcomes of treatment, especially technical interventions, for the purpose of improving practice.

All good. But how certain is it that we can determine the physician's role in achieving an outcome when the main factor might be the patient, the organization, even the disease? And how can the uses of the information serve more than the market? And are physician profiles one-shot measures or longitudinal perspectives? Indeed, today it is the organization that makes the doctor, so why the physician profiles?

# CHAPTER 5

# Commentary on "Physician Profiling": Profiling—Necessary but Not Sufficient

*John Wasson*

> The nationally implemented approaches . . . currently measure quality rather than actually improve quality. To "underperformers," these measurement tools alone provide no explicit guidance to diagnose the problem and remedy the situation. Nor will this data stimulate high performers to continue improvement.[1]

Prior to the 1990s, the organization and delivery of health care primarily consisted of payment for professional services, procedures, office visits, prescriptions, supplies, and days of care in specific settings. In the 1990s, we added "payment per member months" to the list. In the 21st century we will add "payment per member month after adjustment for report card quality."

Although measurement is necessary to monitor improvement, report card quality measurement alone will not improve care. What seems to really improve outcomes for specific patients is the incorporation of a productive provider and patient interaction into daily work.[2] Better aggregate care *may result* when there is

- ongoing measurement
- monitoring of processes of care
- a process for designing and testing changes in the care

Better aggregate care and individual care is *likely to result*[3] when there is also

- a balanced assessment of processes and outcomes that matter to patients
- education of and feedback to patients and providers in real time about the quality of their interaction

- a commitment to and cooperation with these approaches at all levels of an organization[4]

**NOTES**

1. J.S. Durch et al., *Improving Health in the Community: A Role for Performance Monitoring* (Washington DC: National Academy Press, 1997).

2. M. Von Korff et al., "Collaborative Management of Chronic Illness," *Annuals of Internal Medicine* 127 (1997): 1097–1102.

3. M. Splaine et al., "Implementing a Strategy for Improving Care: Lessons from Studying Those Aged 80 and Older in a Health System," *Journal of Ambulatory Care Management* 21 (1998): 56–59.

4. R.A. Garabaldi, "Computers and the Quality of Care: A Clinician's Perspective," *New England Journal of Medicine* 338 (1998): 259–260.

CHAPTER 6

# Commentary on "Physician Profiling": Cautionary Notes

*Patrick S. Romano*

In the chapter entitled "Physician Profiling: Not Whether but How," Gold-field argues cogently that public disclosure of physician profiles, or report cards, is the wave of the future. While making this argument, he properly acknowledges the "difference between releasing information pertaining to a hospital with thousands of employees and releasing information pertaining to one physician or a small group of physicians." Unfortunately, he oversimplifies this difference by attributing it to "public relations" and the relative inability of physicians and small physician groups to withstand the effects of unfavorable publicity.

In fact, the difference between releasing information about hospitals and releasing information about physicians and physician groups is far more complex, and more intractable, than Goldfield's analysis suggests. This complexity does not preclude public disclosure of physician profiles, but it should give pause and stimulate careful consideration of alternative strategies for improving physician performance. I believe that releasing information about physician performance differs from releasing information about hospital or health plan performance for two fundamental reasons: (1) the risk of producing bad information is greater, and (2) the harm from releasing bad information is also greater.

## GREATER RISK OF PRODUCING BAD INFORMATION

There is greater risk of producing invalid or unreliable information about physician performance than about hospital or health plan performance. Identifying the sources of this increased risk is the first step toward minimizing it.

The most fundamental problem with public disclosure of physician profiles is that each physician sees relatively few patients with any specific diagnosis or procedure. Of course, this statement is more applicable to primary care physicians, who treat a wide variety of problems, than to subspecialists, who sometimes accumulate substantial experience with a limited number of conditions and procedures. With small numbers of cases, wide confidence intervals surround estimates of physician performance. In this situation, either Type I error (mislabeling a physician as a quality outlier when his or her true performance is average) or Type II error (mislabeling a physician as average when his or her true performance is better or worse than expected) rises to unacceptable levels.[1]

This problem has been explored using a technique known as Monte Carlo simulation. For example, using a conventional threshold of $p < .05$ to identify hypothetical organizations where 2 percent of patients died due to unsatisfactory care (and 9 percent died despite satisfactory care), the percentage of low-quality organizations labeled as outliers varied from 1.3 percent when each organization had 50 patients to 18.7 percent when each organization had 1,000 patients.[2] A similar analysis focusing on acute myocardial infarction (AMI) suggested that high-mortality outliers could be identified with a sensitivity exceeding 20 percent only if the minimum volume was set at 400 cases.[3] Even at that minimum volume, only about 40 percent of identified outliers actually provided poor-quality care (given the assumption that 12.5 percent of deaths at poor-quality hospitals were preventable with optimal care). In the face of such profound limitations, one might reasonably ask, "why bother releasing these data?"

This problem is compounded by difficulties in risk-adjusting physician profiles. Risk adjustment may be even more important for physician outcomes than for hospital outcomes, simply because there is more observed variability at the physician level. For example, the coefficient of variation for cesarean delivery rates, after removing the random component, was recently estimated at 0.22 (low to moderate) across hospitals and 0.45 (moderate to high) across physicians.[4] Whereas hospitals tend to admit a broad spectrum of patients with any specified condition, certain physicians, such as perinatologists, see only the highest risk patients. Not surprisingly, adjustment for age and sex captures only a small fraction of the interphysician variability in outcome rates.[5] Even the best risk-adjustment tools may fail to explain important differences in patient risk that drive referrals to specific physicians.

In the late 1990s, risk adjustment systems for ambulatory case mix adjustment remain relatively crude when compared with systems for inpatient case mix adjustment. The most commonly used system, Ambulatory Care Groups (ACGs) from Johns Hopkins University, assigns each patient to 1 of just 52 categories based on the combination of diagnoses documented on outpatient visits within a one-year period. According to its developers, this system explains 15–30 percent of the observed variation in ambulatory visits and 25–45 percent of the observed variation in log-transformed ambulatory charges during a one-year follow-up period.[6] However, in one study, ACGs accounted for only 7.5 percent of the variation in total patient expenditures during the subsequent year, after adjustment for differential unit pricing across providers.[7] This study and others[8] have shown that ACGs are far better at explaining past resource use than at predicting future resource use, perhaps because both resource use and ACG intensity are a function of the number of physician claims.

Other systems that have been used to risk-adjust ambulatory care outcomes include the Ambulatory Diagnostic Groups used to construct ACGs,[9] the Medical Outcomes Study SF-36 measure of function and perceived health status,[10,11] a list of self-reported chronic conditions,[12] and the Duke Case-Mix System (which combines the Duke Health Profile with the Duke Severity of Illness Checklist).[13] Although these systems perform about equally well in explaining future resource use, none has been validated as a predictor of morbidity, mortality, loss of function, or other clinically meaningful outcomes of ambulatory care.

Not only are risk adjustment systems based on outpatient claims data inherently weaker than comparable systems based on inpatient data, but the data are probably of poorer quality. Whereas inpatient data systems typically accommodate at least 9 diagnoses and sometimes as many as 25, outpatient data systems usually accommodate only 1 or 2. Whereas inpatient records are abstracted by medical records professionals with specialized training in ICD-9-CM coding, outpatient records are typically abstracted by clerical personnel in physicians' offices who have multiple responsibilities and variable training. Whereas hospitals have strong incentives to abstract inpatient records thoroughly to optimize diagnosis-related group (DRG) assignment, medical groups have no such incentive, because their billings are more influenced by CPT (Current Procedural Terminology) coding.

Several studies have confirmed that outpatient claims data have significant quality limitations. In a study of claims submitted to a major managed care organization, only 43 percent of patients with a medical service claim for hypertension actually had hypertension based on a mailed survey.[14] Of the same group of patients, 47 percent actually had hypertension based on medical record review. Adjusted for chance, the agreement between medical records and Medicare Part B claims in another study was adequate ($\kappa > 0.4$) for 6 diagnoses (diabetes, congestive heart failure, chronic obstructive pulmonary disease, hypertension, rheumatoid arthritis, and transient ischemic attack) but inadequate for 17 others.[15] Even the best risk-adjustment system cannot perform well if the available data do not capture patients' actual severity of illness.

A final contributor to the risk of producing bad information is that physician profiling is inherently an attempt to isolate one component of a complex, interconnected system. No physician practices in a vacuum. He or she relies on nurses to provide bedside care in hospital and home, respiratory therapists to provide respiratory care, pharmacists to dispense medications and educate patients about how to take them, physical therapists to counsel patients about activity and exercise, dietitians to provide nutrition education, and colleagues in other specialties to diagnose and treat problems outside his or her scope of practice. Most importantly, the physician's own success depends partially on whether patients communicate their questions and concerns and then adhere to his or her therapeutic recommendations. Only some of these factors are under the physician's direct or indirect control.

Determining which of several physicians is principally responsible for the patient's care is often not straightforward. A primary care physician may refer a patient to a specialist or vice versa. One primary care physician may transfer a patient to a colleague, either permanently or temporarily. Several physicians in the same call group may essentially share responsibility for a patient. For example, should AMI mortality rates be analyzed according to the emergency physician who first treated the patient, the primary care physician who admitted the patient, the cardiologist who consulted and performed a catheterization, or the physician who ultimately discharged the patient? In a study using Medicare's Cooperative Cardiovascular Project data set, cardiologists' mortality rate for AMI patients was 13.8 percent using hospital claims but only 12.4 percent using initial claims for physician services.[16]

## GREATER HARM FROM RELEASING BAD INFORMATION

Greater harm is likely to result from releasing invalid or unreliable information about physicians than from releasing similarly invalid or unreliable information about hospitals. This is partially because, as Goldfield describes, physicians and small physician groups lack the resources and skills to defend themselves when they receive an unfavorable grade in a public report. In a survey of chief executives at 374 nonfederal acute care hospitals listed in the California Hospital Outcomes Project 1996 report on risk-adjusted mortality after acute myocardial infarction,[17] 15 of the 274 respondents had been publicly labeled as high-mortality outliers. Of these 15 hospitals, 13 involved marketing or public relations professionals and 4 involved legal counsel in discussing the report and developing a coordinated response. Most submitted letters that defended the hospital's performance; these letters were published with the final report. As a result, newspaper coverage of the public release often highlighted the "spin" suggested by local hospital administrators:

> Mad River disputes hospital survey . . . Heart attack rates cast into doubt

> Health report smiles on nine of 10 Kern hospitals . . . Mitigating issues seen

> Hospital officials say report of little value

Physicians and small physician groups are less likely to be able to defend their reputations in this manner because of their limited resources and lack of familiarity with risk-adjusted performance measures. Although physicians' inability to mount a strong defense should not take them "off the hook" for potential misdeeds, it is a basic premise of our legal system that accused individuals have full access to the information that incriminates them, as well as professional assistance in interpreting and refuting such information. Whenever feasible, the same premise should be applied to proceedings that may result, not in loss of liberty, but in loss of livelihood for a physician and permanent damage to his or her reputation.

There are several other reasons why greater harm is likely to result from releasing invalid or unreliable information about physicians than from releasing similarly invalid or unreliable information about hospitals. First, consumers have much more latitude in choosing physicians than in choosing hospitals. Most consumers choose their own physician, often from a list of their health plan's approved providers, after soliciting recommendations from friends, family, coworkers, employers, or other laypersons. By contrast, hospital choice is heavily influenced by health professionals, especially physicians and paramedics, who steer patients toward specific facilities based on their own preferences and experiences. These professionals are presumably less likely to be swayed by invalid information that may mislead consumers into choosing the wrong hospital.

Perhaps because of their greater latitude in choosing physicians, consumers also seem to be more interested in information about physicians than in information about hospitals. This observation presumably reflects consumers' (and health plans') view of primary care physicians as "gatekeepers" to the health care system, guiding the choice of all other health care services. After selecting a physician, a patient tends to entrust that person with the responsibility to make various health care purchasing decisions on his or her behalf. In addition, most consumers recognize that they are far more likely to need physician services than hospital services. Information about hospital quality lacks immediacy for the great majority of consumers, who are unlikely to require inpatient care in the near future. Of course, these arguments underscore the desirability of releasing valid and reliable information about physician performance but also the undesirability of releasing invalid or unreliable information.

Finally, the characteristics of the physician marketplace are such that it is easier for a physician or medical group to benefit from a favorable report card or suffer from an unfavorable report card than a hospital or health plan. With a growing surplus of physicians, most metropolitan areas have an adequate supply of both primary care physicians and specialists. Consumers who wish to switch away from a physician, and health plans that wish to delist a physician, can easily do so. By contrast, the hospital marketplace is often a monopoly or oligopoly in which barriers to entry are high, market segmentation is common (e.g., private versus public hospitals), and consumer choice is driven largely by provider network relationships. In addition, hospitals are more heavily capitalized than physicians, more closely tied to a specific community, and better positioned to withstand a temporary loss of business. All of these factors make physicians more vulnerable than hospitals to the impact of an unfavorable but invalid report card.

These arguments relate not just to physicians but also to their patients. In other words, patients potentially suffer equally if the performance of specific physicians is publicly criticized based on invalid or unreliable information.

Patients may switch practices, seeking a more highly rated physician but ending up with one whose true performance is worse than that of their original physician. Even the patient who does not switch practices may suffer unnecessary emotional distress, anxiety, and pressure from friends and family. The physician-patient relationship may be poisoned by such misinformation; the resulting distrust may interfere with communication of important symptoms and treatment recommendations. Most seriously, physicians may systematically avoid high-risk patients because they do not believe that current risk-adjustment methods give them sufficient credit for treating these patients.[18,19] In some cases, high-risk patients would receive the greatest benefit from aggressive therapy.[20]

## SUGGESTIONS FOR THE NEAR FUTURE

Recognizing the risk of producing bad information about physician performance and the considerable harm that may result from releasing such information, I suggest a few additions to Goldfield's helpful list of "desired characteristics of physician profiles":

- Physician profiles should, as Goldfield suggests, "meet certain statistical thresholds of validity and reliability." These exact thresholds should be set by the sponsors and consumers of each profile, preferably with input from those profiled. *Physician profiles are most likely to meet these thresholds, and arouse consumers' interest, if they apply to broad groups of patients defined on the basis of demographic rather than clinical characteristics.* For example, many more women need mammograms or cervical smears in a given year than need inpatient care for stroke. Therefore, physician-specific data on mammography rates are probably much more reliable, and more useful to consumers, than physician-specific data on stroke mortality.
- *Physician profiles should feature measures with high face validity among all stakeholders in the process, including physicians and their professional societies, health plans, and consumer representatives.* Such measures might, for example, include mammography rates among women aged 50–69 years but not mammography rates among younger or older women. Such measures might include overall screening rates for colorectal cancer but not the use of individual modalities such as flexible

sigmoidoscopy. Physician profiles should steer clear of controversial areas where reasonable physicians disagree.

- *Physician profiles should feature measures that are clearly under the control of physicians rather than hospitals or hospital staff, health plans, or consumers themselves.* Mortality rates for stroke, heart attack, and other conditions requiring multiple levels of skilled inpatient care are useful measures of quality, but they reflect more on an entire system of care than on any individual component, such as physician services. Similarly, it may be invalid to compare mental health outcomes across psychiatrists if the utilization of psychiatric services is tightly regulated by managed care organizations or their contractors.

- *Physician profiles should not rely completely on ICD-9-CM coded data because of known problems with the accuracy of these data when generated in outpatient settings.* Of course, using ICD-9-CM coded data may be an excellent way to stimulate rapid improvement in their quality. The optimal strategy may involve careful use of ICD-9-CM coded claims data combined with validation sub-studies to assess their validity and explore suspected deficiencies.

- Notwithstanding Goldfield's emphasis on "the need to adjust for severity of illness," I suggest that *physician profiles prepared for public dissemination in the late 1990s should either not require risk adjustment or require only the simplest risk adjustment, such as stratification by age and gender.* More complex procedures raise legitimate concerns about the adequacy of risk adjustment and the quality of risk factor data. For this reason, process measures, which typically do not require risk adjustment, seem more attractive than outcome measures, which are meaningless without risk adjustment. Claims-based profiling systems have been developed for diabetes,[21] hypertension, congestive heart failure, and several other conditions.[22] The National Committee for Quality Assurance has developed a set of claims-based process indicators (the Health Plan Employer Data and Information Set) that focus on preventive care.[23]

As Goldfield points out, "the public does have a right to know." But what does the public have a right to know? Surely the public does not have a right to information that is inaccurate or irrelevant, such as what the physician ate for breakfast or what television shows he or she likes to watch. Surely too the public trusts persons with expertise in the field to identify valid quality indicators and analyze data about them appropriately. This trust gives us an enormous collective responsibility to proceed cautiously in releasing physician-specific profiles, for these profiles may be based on misleading data and have the potential to cause more harm than benefit.

## NOTES

1. A.R. Localio et al., "Comparing Hospital Mortality in Adult Patients with Pneumonia: A Case Study of Statistical Methods in a Managed Care Program," *Annals of Internal Medicine* 122 (1995): 125–132.
2. D.L. Zalkind and S.R. Eastaugh, "Mortality Rates as an Indicator of Hospital Quality," *Hospital and Health Services Administration* 42 (Spring 1997): 3–15.
3. T.P. Hofer and R.A. Hayward, "Identifying Poor-Quality Hospitals: Can Hospital Mortality Rates Detect Quality Problems for Medical Diagnoses?" *Medical Care* 34 (1996): 737–753.
4. E. Keeler et al. *Management and Outcomes of Childbirth Study: Secondary Data Final Report* (Santa Monica, CA: Rand Corporation, 1995).
5. S. Salem-Schatz, "The Case for Case-Mix Adjustment in Practice Profiling: When Good Apples Look Bad," *JAMA* 272 (1994): 871–874.
6. N.S. Smith and J.P. Weiner, "Applying Population-based Case Mix Adjustment to Managed Care: The Johns Hopkins Ambulatory Care Group System," *Managed Care Quarterly* 2 (Summer 1994): 21–34.
7. J.B. Fowles et al., "Taking Health Status into Account when Setting Capitation Rates: A Comparison of Risk-Adjustment Methods," *JAMA* 276 (1996): 1316–1321.
8. J.P. Weiner et al., "Development and Application of a Population-Oriented Measure of Ambulatory Care Case-Mix," *Medical Care* 29 (1991): 452–472.
9. J.B. Fowles et al., "Taking Health Status into Account when Setting Capitation Rates: A Comparison of Risk-Adjustment Methods."
10. J.B. Fowles et al., "Taking Health Status into Account when Setting Capitation Rates: A Comparison of Risk-Adjustment Methods."
11. M.C. Hornbrook and M.J. Goodman, "Assessing Relative Health Plan Risk with the Rand-36 Health Survey," *Inquiry* 32 (1995): 56–74.
12. J.B. Fowles et al., "Taking Health Status into Account when Setting Capitation Rates: A Comparison of Risk-Adjustment Methods."
13. G.R. Parkerson, Jr. et al., "Duke Case-Mix System (DUMIX) for Ambulatory Health Care," *Journal of Clinical Epidemiology* 50 (1997): 1385–1394.
14. L. Quam et al., "Using Claims Data for Epidemiologic Research: The Concordance of Claims-based Criteria with the Medical Record and Patient Survey for Identifying a Hypertensive Population," *Medical Care* 31 (1993): 498–507.
15. J.B. Fowles et al., "Agreement between Physicians' Office Records and Medicare Part B Claims Data," *Health Care Financing Review* 16 (Summer 1995): 189–199.

16.  J.G. Jollis and P.S. Romano, "Pennsylvania's *Focus on Heart Attack*: Grading the Scorecard," *New England Journal of Medicine* 338 (1998): 983–987.

17.  P.S. Romano et al. "Grading the Graders: How Hospitals in California and New York Perceive and Interpret Their Report Cards," *Medical Care* (in press).

18.  E.C. Schneider and A.M. Epstein, "Influence of Cardiac-Surgery Performance Reports on Referral Practices and Access to Care: A Survey of Cardiovascular Specialists," *New England Journal of Medicine* 335 (1996): 251–256.

19.  N.A. Omoigui et al., "Outmigration for Coronary Bypass Surgery in an Era of Public Dissemination of Clinical Outcomes," *Circulation* 93 (1996): 27–33.

20.  R.M. Califf et al., "The Evolution of Medical and Surgical Therapy for Coronary Artery Disease: A 15 Year Perspective," *JAMA* 261 (1989): 2077–2086.

21. J.P. Weiner et al., "Variation in Office-based Quality: A Claims-based Profile of Care Provided to Medicare Patients with Diabetes," *JAMA* 273 (1995): 1503–1508.

22. D.W. Garnick et al., "Focus on Quality: Profiling Physicians' Practice Patterns," *Journal of Ambulatory Care Management* 17 (1994): 44–75.

23. *HEDIS 3.0* (Washington, DC: National Committee for Quality Assurance, 1998).

# CHAPTER 7

# Commentary on "Physician Profiling"

*Ian H. Leverton*

The following does not argue with Dr. Goldfield's assertions and comments but rather is intended to be an introduction to the issues surrounding physician profiling, with particular emphasis on the cultural and emotional issues it engenders.

Physician profiling is a methodology that allows multiple aspects of a physician's professional performance to be expressed and quantified by defined sets of measurables. These measurables may be directed at quality, service (which many patients may perceive as quality of care), utilization of resources, and virtually any other aspect of health care delivery the physician is involved in. The profile (sometimes referred to as a report card) derived from these data sets may address any one of these facets of the physician's work or a mix of them.

As very few norms or standards have been identified for any of these measurables, physician profiles are essentially comparative in nature. That is, they compare the performance of physicians against each other in a defined data set (one set of measurables).

Physician profiles (defined data sets) have been designed to assure and improve quality, "weed out" the "bad apples," examine relative utilization of resources, reward "good performers," punish "bad performers," introduce the concept of 360-degree evaluation to physicians (by introducing nurses, patients, etc., into the evaluation process), provide information to health plans to allow them to better manage the infrastructure of health care delivery, and give purchasers (employers, government etc.) and patients better insight into the product they are buying.

The multitude of types of physician profiles and the different uses they can be put to create an essential need for extensive, cogent, accurate, and hence expensive data to make them credible. As many physicians are convinced that such data are not currently available, this broad spectrum of design and purpose is itself at least partially responsible for the suspicion and resentment that many physicians feel toward the whole concept of profiling.

Following are some of the hurdles, real or perceived, that stand ready to obstruct the progress, acceptance, and success of physician profiling. They are all well known, frequently spoken of, but rarely written about.

The subject of physician profiling is highly sensitive and provocative—particularly to physicians. It is, therefore, essential that the terms used in discussing this topic are clearly defined and not left open to (mis)interpretation.

For example, the word *complications* does not necessarily imply avoidability. Indeed the occurrence of an AV block following a myocardial infarction is a good example of an unavoidable sequela, comorbidity, or "complication" of myocardial infarction.

On the other hand, the identification of complicating, postinsult events that appropriate therapeutic interventions usually prevent is very important. It is equally important that physicians believe that the designers and interpreters of the data sets understand this.

The issue of "coding" of primary diagnosis and comorbidities has been further clouded by the phenomenon often referred to as "code creep."

As Medicare reimbursement to both hospitals and physicians became based on the coding of the elements of an episode of illness for a given patient, hospitals and physicians soon recognized the financial implications, both institutional and personal, of assigning different codes. Code creep manifests itself in one of two ways. The first way is to code an episode of illness higher up the scale of severity, thus usually higher up the scale of reimbursement, than is strictly warranted by the patient and the illness. The second way (sometimes referred to as "unbundling") is to purposefully add comorbidities or procedures that in fact represent no increase in complexity, severity, or intervention but simply serve to increase "codeable events" and drive up reimbursement (e.g., "hemorrhage" added to "resection of aortic aneurysm" or "left thoracotomy" added to "ligation of patent ductus arteriosus").

Code creep was particularly common before the advent of DRGs, and physicians were sometimes encouraged in this practice by hospitals and health plans. Even setting aside the more than dubious ethics involved (the practice is now viewed as Medicare fraud and a felony) the entirely erroneous severity scores that this leads to invalidates, in some eyes, any physician profile derived from their use.

My purpose in delving into clarity of definition and coding is not to stray into the technicalities of physician profiling but rather to illustrate that physician cynicism about this subject is not entirely without substance.

The above observations lead naturally to a discussion of two major issues surrounding physician profiling.

The first is complex but easily understandable: any data used must be accurate, cogent, and appropriately interpreted. At this time, many physicians simply do not believe the available data to be either accurate, cogent, or appropriately interpreted. This is "fixable," as more and more sophisticated and reliable data systems are being developed and more experience is gained in deriving important and useful information from that data.

The second is more difficult to understand and describe and therefore more difficult to resolve. It is, however, critical, especially in the context of the publication and distribution of report cards. It is a strongly held belief, deeply ingrained in the cultural norms of physicians, that it is unethical to publicly criticize a colleague. Osler said, "Let not your ear hear the sound of your voice raised in unkind criticism or ridicule or condemnation of a brother physician" and "Never let your tongue say a slighting word of a colleague."[1] This message, in subtle and sometimes direct ways, has been effectively communicated to generations of physicians. It can still be seen in the tendency to hold the mortality and morbidity "rounds" of the major disciplines in teaching institutions behind closed doors and in the absence of "strangers." It can still be seen in the willingness of physicians to criticize their peers in closed session and in their abhorrence at allowing those comments to escape the four walls. It might also be said that along with this deeply inculcated credo is an element of "There but by the grace of God go I."

It should also be noted that given the nature of medical care, the sometimes disastrous harm to human life resulting from errors, and the need to learn from errors, learning could not up to this time have taken place without a degree of secrecy (confidentiality) and the trust of one's peers.

Enveloped within the "secret" learning process (some might refer to this process today as "continuous quality improvement") is the somewhat vague but oft-mentioned concept of "the art of medicine." Most, if not all, physicians believe there is an art of medicine but are unable to define it. Being unable to define it, they are unable to communicate it to an external audience. They are fearful that an external audience will deny the existence of that art and perceive a bad outcome as the lack of scientific knowledge or expertise on the part of the physician.

In struggling to describe their art to the lay public, physicians often try to back into an understanding by talking of the "inexact" science of medicine, which may have some value but does tend to accentuate the negative (lack of knowledge, however, declining personal fault for that lack of knowledge) rather than the positive (the bringing to bear of a subtle admixture of knowledge, skill, and experience on a problem that science does not yet fully comprehend).

There are other issues related to the public dissemination of physician profiles that concern doctors. One can always argue that most of these are perceptions rather than reality, but, as always, this makes them no less powerful or pervasive.

The consumer (patient, employer, third-party payer, etc.) is not competent to appropriately interpret the profile. Thus, harm in economic and societal terms may be done to the innocent.

The real purpose (hidden agenda) of physician profiling is economic—to weed out the "expensive" provider (high utilizer) and to renumerate physicians based solely on their utilization of resources and not the quality of care they deliver. Indeed, these strategies have been used.

A less obvious but real concern of physicians who work in group and staff model HMOs is that they are inevitably targeted for profiling, or any other kind of assessment, as their environment is the most suited to data collection, economies of scale, direct comparison, and "management" pressure. Meanwhile, their colleagues in fee-for-service medicine sit in splendid isolation and sweet anonymity. In other words, scrutiny (hence force for change) is being aimed in the completely wrong direction!

The argument about using physician profiles "internally" versus "externally" seems to me to be largely fallacious, except when physician misunderstanding of the many different types and uses of profiles and previous bad experiences are factored in. As Goldfield points out, there are a plethora of different types and uses of profiles, each using different kinds of data sets and each aimed at assessing different facets of a physician's practice. It seems to me that the profile types used internally will be quite different from the types used externally. I use the plural in each case, as different reporting formats may well be used for different external and internal audiences.

Some profiles may best be suited for quality assurance and quality improvement, while others may better assist both physicians and plan administrators to better manage the delivery system. Both are internal audiences. Similarly, the employer and member are both external but will be interested in very different types of information.

There are few physicians in this country who have not been affected by the chaos of change in health care delivery over the past several years. Without exploring the justification, or lack thereof, for their emotions, we now have a nation of angry, resentful and suspicious physicians. As Goldfield pointed out in the first chapter of this book, for many of us there is a third party, the managed care organization (or "plan"), involved in what was always a sacrosanct relationship between two parties only—the physician and the patient. There is little wonder that many physicians see their own interests and, incidentally, those of their patients, as divergent from those of the plan. They see physician profiling as yet another means for the plan to interfere in the physician-patient relationship, attack their remuneration by the arbitrary measurement of utilization of resources, and withhold necessary care from the patients. The promised or implied measurement of quality they view as a thin veil to mask this ulterior motive.

Amidst all the controversies surrounding physician profiling sits the ultimate consumer—the patient. Any marketing person in any business (with the possible exception of health care) will tell you that you cannot sell what you think the consumer needs. You can only sell what the consumer wants.

Repeatedly over recent years internal surveys by one of the nation's largest HMOs have consistently shown that the vast majority of people (i.e. current or future patients) are very little impressed by, or interested in, the "scientific" data in physician profiles or report cards that purport to demonstrate the clinical expertise of doctors and differentiate them by ranking within that data set. Instead, they place great value in personal experience and reports from friends and neighbors that characterize "their" doctor as warm, personable, caring, and human.

To many of us this is a sobering thought as we consider how people can best be given information they can use to choose those physicians who do indeed deliver better care. But for the purposes of this discussion, this is just another indicator that physician profiles must be carefully tailored to the audience they are intended to impact if they are to have any value at all. Physicians may take comfort, however, from the fact that, given the above, the release of potentially damaging information that they so fear would likely have far less negative impact than they assume.

The issue of patient confidentiality, at least from the perspective of physician profiling, seems to me to be more theoretical than real. Modern data collection and reporting systems and coding methodologies can keep the identity of individuals from even the most prying eyes, and in today's society how important can this really be? To what extent this objection to profiling is a smoke screen and to what extent a genuine concern is hard to say, but in all likelihood it is directly linked to physicians' fear and resentment of possible further intrusion of third parties into the physician-patient relationship.

I am very much in agreement with the thrust of Goldfield's remarks. Physician profiling can be a valuable tool that will offer physicians the opportunity to improve the quality of the care they deliver, allow health plans to manage better and more appropriately, allow the purchasers of health care to better evaluate the products they are offered, and allow people to make better informed choices about the physicians or health plans they select.

As Goldfield points out, much work will need to be done on data, coding, and reporting systems before the benefits are fully achieved. However, I have no doubt that they will be achieved. Some would even go as far as to say that information technology will be the true engine of change in health care for the next decade.

Nevertheless, it is my contention that the "softer," less easily definable elements of culture, training, suspicion, resentment, cynicism, fear, and lack of understanding must be addressed and the issues resolved if physician profiling is to even come close to fulfilling its potential. The early and continuing involvement of physicians in all aspects of the process of development, use, and dissemination of physician-specific information will be essential to its success.

The fact that we continually have to remind ourselves that physician involvement is essential to the resolution of virtually any problem in health care is a source of constant amazement to me.

NOTE

1. "Osler, the Teacher," *Johns Hopkins Hospital Bulletin* 30 (1919):199.

CHAPTER 8

# Commentary on "Physician Profiling"

*Michael L. Millenson*

In an oft-quoted 1988 editorial, Arnold Relman, then editor of the *New England Journal of Medicine*, heralded the "dawning [of] the Era of Assessment and Accountability." Wrote Relman, "We can no longer afford to provide health care without knowing more about its successes and failures."[1]

Relman was right in his concern for improvement but wrong in his prediction that a new era was at hand. He wrote at a time when the Health Care Financing Administration was annually releasing statistics on the Medicare mortality rates of every hospital. After the 1988 presidential election, however, HCFA pressure for quality improvement measurement and management waned. The dawning of a new era turned out to be just another glimmering of moonbeams.

Ten years later, a turning point in institutionalizing assessment and accountability seems to finally have arrived. Still, the title of Norbert Goldfield's chapter, "Physician Profiling: Not Whether but How," should still be regarded with some skepticism. Goldfield is both a recognized clinical quality expert and in the front ranks of those eager to put knowledge into practice. Being willing and able to lead, however, does not by itself guarantee a large mass of followers.

Most physicians are not only less knowledgeable than Goldfield about physician accountability, but are also less committed to implementation. As a result, the "whether" of physician profiling is by no means as certain in the short run as Goldfield (and others of us) might wish. Just as importantly, the "whether" of physician profiling still has a great influence upon the "how;" that is, the audience demanding the data continues to determine what data are collected in the first place. This is true whether the audience is an internal one, such as the Joint Commission on Accreditation of Healthcare Organizations, or an external one, such as a governmental body or purchaser coalition.

The fragility of self-motivated physician profiling can be seen by taking a closer look at the Maine Medical Assessment Foundation (MMAF). The

MMAF is cited by Goldfield, as it is by other commentators, as an example of successful physician-motivated improvement for its work in bringing physicians together, showing them their practice variation data in a confidential and supportive setting, and then facilitating change. The reality, however, is that the foundation's impact has been modest, even in the small, homogeneous community in which it operates.

MMAF has not solved the "whether" problem; its programs touch only a handful of physicians treating a small number of conditions. And though the foundation claimed its work eliminated $21 million in unnecessary medical procedures in Maine over the five years ending in 1990, Maine during that time spent about $11 *billion* on health care. Even if only hospital care is counted in the mix, the foundation still managed to trim spending by less than half a percent.[2]

Change motivated by outside forces has been more substantial. In New York State, the doctors controlled neither the "whether" nor the "how" of the profiling of cardiothoracic surgeons performing coronary artery bypass graft (CABG) surgery. The effort was "voluntary" only in the sense that a warden asking a prisoner to come to lunch is putatively an invitation, not a command. The state health department, which asked the hospitals to voluntarily participate, tightly controlled the professional existence of those same hospitals. The health department's data on mortality rates of individual hospitals and surgeons, including a comparison to state norms, was eventually released directly to consumers.

Although New York State took great pains to publish its methodology in the peer-reviewed literature, its effort at profiling aroused intense hostility from the profession. Indeed, the validity of the data has been largely discredited in the public's eyes because of that hostility.

The lesson that Maine, New York, and experiences elsewhere teaches us about the "how" and "whether" of physician profiling is the same one learned by Ernest Amory Codman some 80 years ago at Massachusetts General Hospital. Goldfield is right in citing Codman as an early martyr to the cause. Codman's insights into the human behavior traits that blocked his success might also be added to Goldfield's comments.

"For whose *interest* is it to have the hospital efficient?" Codman asked pointedly. "There is a difference between interest and duty. You do your duty if the work comes to you, but you do not go out of your way to get the work unless it is for your interest."[3]

In whose interest is it for physicians to have their results compared for the purpose of improving performance? If physician profiling is not perceived as being in the best interests of the physicians whose participation is being sought, they will ignore voluntary programs (as have most physicians in Maine), be content to pay the idea lip service (as did the *New England Journal of Medicine*), or attempt to discredit the message (as in New York State) or the messenger (as with Codman himself).

Goldfield's call for "a research agenda" that addresses physician concerns is one way to attack the duty/interest dichotomy. Also helpful is Goldfield's call for participatory decision making, a continuous quality improvement focus, and sensitivity to the release of inaccurate or incomplete data. All of these elements are necessary, but they are not sufficient. To get from "whether" to "how," there must be unrelenting pressure for change.

Quality guru W. Edwards Deming understood that systemic quality improvement is a daunting task. The psychological commitment to this level of change only arises "out of the crisis," in Deming's phrase; that is, when there is no other perceived alternative.[4] It is literally a case of "quality or else."

What Relman thought was a crisis in 1988 turned out to be only a passing political storm. Today, the true crisis that is pressing the profession to consider the "how" of physician profiling is what I have called the crisis of commodification. In the days before managed care became mainstream medicine, when physicians exercised effective monopoly power, the lack of information about qualitative differences between individual physicians and hospitals was a source of economic strength. Every member of the "guild" could claim excellence and thereby command a high price. On the other hand, when physicians and hospitals have to compete for patients, what was a strength turns into a weakness. If quality is equal everywhere, then health plans or large corporations can buy medical treatment like corn, wheat, or any other commodity; that is, solely on the basis of price.[5]

The crisis of commodification argues for profiling, but the level of detail of those profiles remains an open question. Physicians typically sell their services to health plans or corporate purchasers as a group. Clinical profiles of individual doctors (save for some high-volume surgeons) may best be used by internal physician committees in selecting the members of that group and then helping the group improve its overall performance over time. On the other hand, patients will probably be interested in service report cards on individual physicians (related to timeliness of appointments and the like) and a clinical report card on the group as a whole and on the hospitals it uses.

Unfortunately the time has not yet arrived for clinical report cards on individual physicians. Indeed, apart from high-volume surgeons in a few specialties, clinical report cards on individual physicians may always be problematic.

As the threat of commodification increases, the physician community will finally turn to debating the "how" of report cards, not the "whether." At that time, Goldfield's detailed guide to operationalizing profiles will undoubtedly become a topic of lively discussion between purchasers (including health plans acting on their behalf) and providers (physicians alone or in combination with other groups). Who should collect what? How much of the data should become public? Who should pay for the effort?

As the purchasers press for clinical data, we will finally have arrived at the juncture of "quality or else." That should prove a powerful spur to the continuous quality improvement efforts in medicine that Goldfield so rightly seeks to encourage.

## NOTES

1. A.S. Relman, "Assessment and Accountability, The Third Revolution in Medical Care," *New England Journal of Medicine* 319 (1988):1220–1222.
2. Office of the Actuary, Health Care Financing Administration, personal communication, 11 December 1995.
3. E.A. Codman, "The Product of a Hospital," *Surgery, Gynecology and Obstetrics*, April 1914.
4. W. Edwards Deming, *Out of the Crisis* (Cambridge, MA: Massachusetts Institute of Technology, 1986).
5. M.L. Millenson, *Demanding Medical Excellence: Doctors and Accountability in the Information Age* (Chicago: University of Chicago, 1997).

CHAPTER 9

# Public Disclosure of Case Mix Adjusted Clinical Information: Practical and Theoretical Challenges

*Norbert Goldfield*

Clarifying objectives is critical before beginning any quality improvement project. Similarly, all customers interested in case mix should carefully and in close communication answer the question of how, not whether, to release case mix adjusted information to the public. This chapter and the following responses should collectively shed light on a complex topic about which much has been written but little illuminated.

In clarifying the objectives of disclosing case mix adjusted information to the public, it is important first to identify and characterize the various customers involved in the public disclosure process and second to describe the uses to which such data will be put by each customer. Part of the challenge in releasing information to the public is the assertion by state or federal policy makers that the patient or general public represents the only customer in the quality improvement process. In fact, the successful release of severity-adjusted information must take into account numerous other customers, including the following:

- physicians, nurses, and other hospital employees
- hospital administrators
- employers, including senior executives and benefits managers
- employees of managed care organizations
- media representatives, including print, broadcast, and cable news reporters
- government employees and their agencies, including state health data organizations and federal entities such as the Health Care Financing Administration

67

- uninsured or low-income individuals, whose health care needs must be addressed separately from those of the middle- and upper-income general population

This chapter analyzes how the interests of these different customers are indeed different. The key to successful release of severity-adjusted information to the public is identifying and building upon common interests of customers in the public disclosure process. Over time, as greater understanding develops about the strengths and limitations of different types of case mix adjusted methodologies, there will be increased dialogue and resolution of the interests described below:

- the need to emphasize improvement over time versus the desire to protect the public and immediately identify poorly performing providers
- the need to empower the public through education and information versus the desire to just give out information and hope for the best
- the need to provide case mix adjusted information based on agreed-upon, universally accepted statistical measures that are, in turn, explained to the public versus the desire to avoid all statistical manipulations and trust that an unbiased third party will take care of any problem
- the need to provide information based on clinically reliable and valid methodologies versus the desire to provide at least some information to the public
- the need to emphasize the process of care versus the desire to pay attention primarily to outcomes
- the need to focus greater attention on low-income or uninsured individuals versus the political need to satisfy the wants of middle- and upper-income individuals

Only a redoubling of customer commitment to the key principles of continuous quality improvement (CQI) will resolve the conflicts between the needs and desires. A serious commitment to CQI can succeed in providing important information (defined as information that can assist patients in making better decisions affecting their health care) to the public in a timely manner. However, this will not occur in the short term. The reason is that price cutting without sufficient regard to long-term implications is the principal driver of strategic thinking in health care today. This relentless focus on price combined with the lack of a technology to risk adjust capitation payments adequately enables managed care organizations to de facto cherry-pick their enrollees.[1] In the short term, policy makers will need to find other means of resolving differing customer needs versus wants.

## THE NEED TO EMPHASIZE IMPROVEMENT OVER TIME VERSUS THE DESIRE TO PROTECT THE PUBLIC AND IMMEDIATELY IDENTIFY POORLY PERFORMING PROVIDERS

### Case Example

A national newspaper recently published a series of articles comparing mortality statistics among hospitals. The hospital association expressed concern to this newspaper that the methodology utilized was very flawed for the purpose of the examination of mortality. The hospital association engaged an outside firm that also critiqued the methodology for adjusting for severity of illness. Among other problems the outside firm discovered was that deaths within 48 hours of admission were not considered part of the mortality rate. When confronted with this information, the reporter for this major newspaper stated, "These patients would have died anyway." Even though nationally recognized authorities called the reporter, the series was run. The hospital association criticized the series. The hospital association, however, has not responded in any other manner; for example, minimal quality initiatives were announced.

From a superficial perspective, the public disclosure of comparative health care information is antithetical to a commitment to principles of quality improvement. The general public rightfully feels (and the news media rarely does anything to disabuse it of the notion) that the provider that emerges as the "best" in whatever case mix adjusted measure is used must, ipso facto, provide the highest quality care. Other providers on the list must provide poorer care and thus should be avoided.

This is an understandable but not completely correct conclusion and, if applied to all health care controversies, would provide the death knell to any serious commitment to CQI. One of the key principles of CQI—driving out fear—must be incorporated into the organization if quality is to be improved over time. Unfortunately, cut-throat competition that focuses disproportionately on price considerations makes this impossible at the present time.

How can these important CQI principles, which emphasize open communication within an organization, be reconciled with the public's right to read in the newspaper about the "winner" in the latest case mix adjusted report card or to watch the evening news to learn how some innocent victim was virtually "killed" at a hospital characterized as having a higher than expected death rate? As depicted in Figure 9–1, newspaper editors may be inclined to sensationalize this information by broadcasting it against a backdrop of innocent victims dying at the hands of inadequately trained providers, commonly known in journalism as the human interest angle.

Nevertheless, providers must respect the public's right to know. Unfortunately, providers have traditionally stuck their heads in the sand, and many have refused to acknowledge that the public has a right to have comparative information in a timely manner. Too often, state hospital associations have been prodded into participating in such releases of information, yet when the participation occurs, it is done in a grudging manner.

Other customers for case mix adjusted information have, understandably, thought of their own organizational needs. While a number of state health agencies have tried to respond, these organizations have too often looked at the customers at the health care table and have seen only the general public or employer benefits managers as the true customers. Employees of state health agencies have not viewed it to be in their interest to identify and include the quality improvement needs of providers such as physicians and hospitals.

Historically, employers, likely the most important and influential customers today, have been interested primarily in issues pertaining to price. Recently, this has begun to change, with several employer coalitions expressing strong interest in a variety of quality-of-care measurements, such as the Health Plan Employer Data and Information Set (HEDIS).[2] Few purchasers, at this point, are using any kind of quality data to dictate purchasing decisions about providers or health plans.

# High Hospital Death Rates

**Figure 9–1** *Source:* Spotlight, Boston Globe. Monday, October 3, 1994, p. 6.

There appears to be an unresolved tension between the public's right to know and provider quality improvement. A serious commitment to educational follow-up at the time case mix adjusted information is released may provide the seeds of a compromise.

## THE NEED TO PROVIDE EDUCATIONAL FOLLOW-UP FOR ALL CUSTOMERS VERSUS THE DESIRE TO PROVIDE AN UNENCUMBERED FREE FLOW OF INFORMATION

A CQI approach that incorporates an educational component when hospital-based information is released might include the following elements:

- All parties concerned (i.e., stakeholders) should work together to develop a release plan for the case mix adjusted data.
- An agreement among the relevant parties should specify that the data in question should first be given to affected providers, including hospitals, physicians, or managed care organizations. A comment period should be incorporated.
- The information should be released to the public with a significant educational component. Providers should be involved in the development of the educational component. It is providers who are both the most knowledgeable and most biased. The educational component should emphasize that final decisions should not be made solely on the basis of case mix adjusted information. Rather, employers, the public, and other interested consumers should work with physicians, hospitals, and managed care organizations to improve the care delivered.

Put differently, a key tenet of CQI is that the "classical" health care quality assurance professional is changing from someone who directs quality improvement projects to an individual who empowers other members of the health care team to carry out projects that result in improved care. In the same vein, professionals at state health care agencies should consider empowering consumers to take charge of their own health care decisions. Merely releasing data with explanatory notes will not meet the need. A comprehensive educational component is necessary.

Opponents may argue that it will be difficult to agree upon the content of the educational component. Participants in the release of information may not even agree on the following premise underlying the release of the information itself: identifying differences in case mix adjusted comparative information represents the first step and only the first step in the quality improvement process. Case mix adjusted information, such as hospital mortality rates, cannot provide data with enough certainty to warrant immediate customer decisions about where to seek care. Still, some customers will want to take immediate action based on case mix adjusted information and, for example, eliminate certain providers.

Therefore, an educational program containing the pros and cons of these different approaches must be discussed. The question is not whether, but rather how, an educational program should be constructed.

## THE NEED TO PROVIDE CASE MIX ADJUSTED INFORMATION BASED ON AGREED-UPON, UNIVERSALLY ACCEPTED STATISTICAL MEASURES THAT ARE, IN TURN, EXPLAINED TO THE PUBLIC VERSUS THE DESIRE TO AVOID ALL STATISTICAL MANIPULATIONS AND TRUST THAT SOMEONE WILL TAKE CARE OF THIS ISSUE

### Case Example

A state health agency, working with an outside researcher, recently performed an analysis of hospital discharges using a severity adjustment case mix system. In going over the results, the outside researcher wanted to know why the addition of the severity logic did not seem to add any explanatory power to the analysis. When asked how the data were processed and prepared before they were analyzed, the researcher indicated that a "light trim" was used (claims were removed from further analysis because they were outliers in terms of costs). It is virtually certain that in performing this light trim, the outside researcher removed many of the sickest and most complex patients from the analysis.

Customers need to be reminded constantly that case mix adjusted data summarize information attached to real human beings. Too often, the debate about which severity system is "better" centers around the statistical performance of the various available systems that purport to adjust for differences in $R^2$. Is this a suitable statistic for the measurement of the validity of systems measuring differences in case mix? Should available data be trimmed before any statistics, such as $R^2$, are applied to the dataset? How much of this information should be presented to the public? How much involvement should be expected from professional associations?

The preliminary answer to all these questions is that it depends what the objectives are in collecting case mix adjusted information in the first place. If one objective is to provide the public with information to improve decision making on an individual basis, a basic primer on statistical aspects of case mix adjustment should be provided (hence the discussion of $R^2$ in this chapter). In addition, if the state health agency is trying to obtain buy-in from professional associations to which hospitals and physicians belong, an offer to discuss details on the statistical methodology should be made.

The old saying that "the devil is in the details" is nowhere more true than the statistical adjustments made before final analyses are made public. A number of statistical and nonstatistical factors must be considered by all consumers before final release of the data. Each of the following criteria should be explained in basic terms to the public:

- Which statistics should be included? $R^2$ is commonly utilized.
- What kind of trimming, if any, of variables should be performed? If trimming is used, at what point in the analysis should the statistical technique be used? Statistical techniques such as standard deviation and interquartile ranges are both utilized. Both are different and result in the trimming out of different cases.
- Should all groups within the population be treated equally in any case system?

## Case Example

United Health Care and Kaiser Permanente, two of the largest managed care organizations in the United States, recently and separately published their data on their immunization rates for different groups of enrollees. Of critical importance, the two organizations counted differently the population on which the results were based. Kaiser included a sample of enrollees who used services at least once and had been enrolled in Kaiser for at least two years. In contrast, United Health Care included all child enrollees who were members during the study time frame in question.

This case example is important because the public needs to be involved and educated about risk adjustment issues. The public's response to the following questions is essential: after what period of enrollment should a managed care organization be responsible for at least aspects of the behavior (e.g., follow through on recommended immunizations) of individual enrollees—after the first encounter, the first mailing, several visits, the first year, or simply never?

## THE NEED TO PROVIDE INFORMATION BASED ON RELIABLE AND VALID METHODOLOGIES VERSUS GETTING SOMETHING OUT NOW

The need for a clinically legitimate methodology goes to the heart of the relationship between researchers in this field; other health professionals, such as physicians and managed care administrators; and the public. Unfortunately, many health professionals have, until now, accepted the notion that as long as the case mix researcher is based at a university, the individual must be "unbiased." This is not the case. All researchers, whether or not based at a university, understandably bring their own biases to their research endeavors.

For example, many researchers answer differently the following question: for what purpose is the severity adjusted information used? The question is not necessarily indicative of bias, but disclosure of the researcher's answer puts the data and the analysis in proper perspective. For example, the intended use of the data dictates which data will be collected and for what time period, how the data will be collected, which data elements will be used, and how those elements will be defined. These are not yet universally standardized, and in a very few instances, one might not want them to be (e.g., time period).

Some researchers still say that customers can legitimately act immediately on case mix adjusted information without attempting to determine the sources of the discrepancy. Others strongly believe that case mix adjustment represents the first step and the first step only in the quality improvement process. As a consequence, this first step, while it must be clinically meaningful, must simultaneously be inexpensive (from both a time and monetary perspective) to obtain. Thus, discharge data systems should be used if possible as a beginning phase in the quality improvement process.

Customers should work together with state health agencies to improve these systems continuously. For example, together they should consider adding an extra or "Mayo" digit to the discharge abstract form that would identify whether any secondary diagnoses were present on admission. The presence of the "Mayo" digit would in turn facilitate the identification of complications of treatment.

Because of the deep biases that researchers bring to the development of case mix systems, the following steps should be undertaken in evaluating various case mix systems—with the ultimate objective of choosing one:

- Health care professionals, drawn from the many customers, must be involved in the final decision; this implies that employees within state health agencies should not be the only individuals empowered to make the final choice. Representatives of physician, hospital, and managed care groups should be involved. Employer representatives should be involved provided that they (with all other health care professionals) commit themselves to learning the basics, not the propaganda, of competing case mix adjustment systems.
- Similarly, representatives of each health care group should coordinate an educational effort to involve and educate the public on the clinical and financial aspects of competing health care systems.
- With both the public and health professionals actively involved, the state health agency can, as a last step, coordinate disparate interests to arrive at a consensus decision on a case mix system that meets clinical criteria.

## Case Example

One state health agency that has devoted considerable resources plans releasing a report card that contains the results of different case mix systems. This agency is planning to release the case mix adjusted information using the competing case mix systems without an explanation of how the systems could arrive at different results.

Does this state agency's approach constitute a process that will result in realistic education for both providers and the general public or simply an attempt to push a particular political agenda in favor of one case mix system over another? Alternatively, is this state health agency implicitly stating that it is very difficult to evaluate competing severity adjustment systems and thus is encouraging the broad public to make the decision instead?

## THE NEED TO FOCUS ON LOW-INCOME OR UNINSURED INDIVIDUALS VERSUS FOCUSING ON OTHER PATIENTS

Research has shown clearly that Medicaid patients are sicker on admission to a hospital than individuals with traditional insurance. One could argue that Medicaid patients should not be separated from the rest of the population, as the purpose of the case mix measures is to stratify on the basis of severity of illness. Or should a state health agency adopt a posture that acknowledges that low-income and uninsured individuals have the greatest difficulty in obtaining needed care and therefore publish data specifically focused on this group at risk?

Whereas uninsured and low-income individuals are at greatest risk, large employers have been the most vocal in declaring a need for risk adjusted information. Moreover, community groups representing low-income individuals have traditionally advocated for their clients without using risk adjusted information. Rather, they have concentrated on more mundane issues, such as simply obtaining access to any facility for their clients.

Advocacy groups should become familiar with case mix methodologies. In this manner, they could more effectively argue for their clients by identifying specific areas where deficiencies in care are occurring. Using these methodologics, it may even be feasible to work with employers and tie deficiencies in care for high-risk populations together with the pricing and quality-of-care needs of employers and their employees. This is occurring to a limited extent in Massachusetts, where large businesses are working with the officials in the Medicaid program to improve care for all Massachusetts residents.

## THE NEED TO EMPHASIZE PROCESS OF CARE VERSUS OUTCOMES

Severity-adjusted information primarily identifies opportunities for improvement in the process of care. Improving the process should also improve the outcomes for the population in question. However, customers for severity-adjusted information have begun to insist that severity-adjusted information be used to look at specific outcomes, notably mortality and complications. Except for specific surgical conditions, such as coronary artery bypass grafts, neither mortality nor complication rates are strong enough scientifically to merit the type of death rate comparisons that are so often presented in the print and television media. Difficulties that exist in the International Classification of Diseases,

Ninth Edition, Clinical Modification (ICD-9-CM) coding system make the use of complication rates even more challenging. In the short term, the political impetus will be to continue to identify institutions with poor outcomes. Over time, it is hoped that the various customers involved in the public disclosure process will work together to understand better the differences in case mix to improve the *process* of care.

## CONCLUSIONS

### Case Example

A state health agency recently began to release to the public case mix adjusted information based on a severity-of-illness system using discharge abstracts. While numerous customers were involved in the selection process, there was much rancor and the threat of a lawsuit. The state health agency officials committed themselves to evaluate within two years the importance of variables, such as health status and the Mayo digit, not currently collected on a claims form. This was perceived to be very important by the employer community. The first roll-out of the data was preceded by meetings with the following:

- Providers, including representatives of hospitals, physicians, and managed care organizations. Through numerous discussions, an agreement was reached whereby the state health agency would provide an annual award to the provider who was judged by an outside panel to have undertaken the best quality improvement project using the case mix adjusted data. The state health agency indicated that it would place a premium on quality improvement projects that focused on low-income or other vulnerable populations.
- Professional associations and community-based organizations (Rotary and Elks Clubs) throughout the state. The quality improvement aspect, in particular, the annual award, of the public disclosure process was emphasized.
- Media representatives. Again the quality improvement aspect of the public disclosure process was emphasized.

Approximately 1,000 individuals attended the meetings. Quarterly follow-up newsletters and yearly follow-up meetings are planned. Further enhancements of the data release are planned, and outpatient data are to be released within three to five years.

By articulating many of the controversies swirling around the presentation of case mix adjusted data to the public, this chapter demonstrates the excitement and dangers inherent in the public release of risk-adjusted information. As the previous example indicates, significant opportunity remains to improve patient care dramatically. This process has a far greater possibility of succeeding if all the customers focus on the goals of quality improvement throughout the disclosure period. Quality improvement principles insist on identification of key customers.

There should be a communications process in place between these customers, possibly led by a state health agency with input from appropriate federal groups such as the Health Care Financing Administration and Agency for Health Care Policy and Research. A well-designed communications process can foster agreement even among opposing factions over, for example, the content of an educational component to be included in any release of case mix adjusted information. This component should consider educating the public around statistical issues, not just the data themselves. Separate educational interventions may be necessary for underserved populations.

Some of the reactants to this issue emphasize what they may believe is another vision of quality improvement; the public release of case mix adjusted information allows for a free flow of ideas and, more importantly, market-based solutions to the health cost containment crisis. Such a vision places much less emphasis on cooperation between the various customers of risk-adjusted information. The main themes of this chapter—educational follow-up and open communication—do not negate such a vision. The market-based exchange of ideas within the framework of case mix adjusted information is legitimate. This chapter suggests that greater cooperation between the various customers for case mix adjusted information will, over time, result in greater satisfaction for the ultimate customer: the patient.

---

NOTES

1. E. Spragins, "Simon Says, Join Us," Newsweek, 19 June 1995, 55–57.
2. National Committee for Quality Assurance, *Health Employer Data Information Set* (Washington, DC: National Committee for Quality Assurance, 1995).

CHAPTER 10

# Public Disclosure: A Researcher's Perspective

*Lisa I. Iezzoni*

Public disclosure and dissemination of information are central to the mission of most research, particularly investigations involving health and medical care. Especially in clinical trials, publicizing findings is essential to meeting a variety of goals, including improving patients' health. Clinical trials, however, often are not performed and generally are not published until they have met certain standards of quality.

For example, before clinical research is funded by the National Institutes of Health (NIH), groups of scientific peers known as "study sections" evaluate and approve a research proposal's technical merit, including patient sampling plans, statistical power (i.e., ensuring that the number of patients is adequate to answer the research hypotheses), and analytic methods. Institutional review boards (IRBs) certify that protocols do not endanger patients. Finally, additional scientific peers judge the manuscripts prior to publication. While the peer review process is not perfect, it generally ensures that published research is of acceptable quality.

A drawback of many research studies is that they take time; answers may not be available for years. In addition, research findings may not pertain to entire populations because certain types of persons have been excluded from participating. These two factors highlight the fundamental differences between health care research and information prepared for public dissemination in the competitive health care marketplace. In the latter instance, time is often at a premium, and information must be relevant for a wide array of health care consumers.

A third major distinction between research and public data initiatives involves the data themselves. In research, data are gathered specifically to address research questions. In their evaluations of research applications, for example, NIH study sections explicitly consider whether the proposed sources of data and definitions of data elements are suitable. In contrast, public initiatives often must rely on data gathered for different purposes, such as billing or other administrative tasks. This situation frequently constrains the types of patient outcomes or clinical events that can be addressed. For instance, outcomes of greatest importance to patients, such as functional ability or quality of life, are generally unavailable in public data initiatives.

Data limitations are particularly important in devising methods for case-mix or risk adjustment. Given the variety of factors that affect patients' health risks and outcomes, even research studies are often stymied by how, exactly, to adjust for risk. This challenge is magnified manifold in public data initiatives that rely on existing data sets or that have serious practical and financial constraints on de novo data collection.

Therefore, whereas few in the research community would probably advocate withholding information from open disclosure, it is probable that most researchers would—at a minimum—urge caution in using published results comparing provider performance. Given the limitations sketched above, public data initiatives raise a variety of issues in the minds of researchers. Five of the most important issues are discussed below.

## ENSURING QUALITY

Persons or organizations publishing risk-adjusted, comparative outcome information have a fiduciary responsibility to ensure its quality. Public data initiatives are just that—initiatives presenting information intended for public consumption and discussion. Considerable effort is often expended to present results in a way that is accessible to the intended audience. For example, findings may be distilled down to a single symbol, such as an open circle for good performance, a half-filled circle for average performance, and a fully darkened circle for poor performance. Although some programs publish technical reports detailing their methods (e.g., state-sponsored hospital performance reports in California and Pennsylvania), it is unlikely that many users will read the "fine print" or caveats raised. In addition, the technical details are outside the expertise of most readers.

The fine print can, however, raise issues crucial to judging the meaning and value of the data. For example, when the Pennsylvania Health Care Cost

Containment Council first published its data on hospital performance in the late 1980s, they set the *p* value for targeting outlier providers at 0.25. That meant that 25 percent of hospitals flagged as especially good or bad by their methodology were identified as such by random chance alone, not by "true" quality of care (standard analyses set *p* values at 0.05—5 percent—or lower). Hospitals flagged by this methodology were legitimately concerned, and the state subsequently modified the methodology. However, this "technical detail" was difficult to communicate effectively to the public: newspaper stories about "bad" hospitals are far more compelling than stories about levels of statistical significance.

Given that it is unlikely that users of data will appreciate fully the way the data are produced, persons or organizations publishing this work have a responsibility to ensure that it meets certain methodological standards. This responsibility should not be seen as patronizing users of data. Instead, it derives from the general responsibility producers have toward the consumers of their products: because consumers are not manufacturing experts, they rely on producers to ensure the products' quality. For most health care products, consumers are further protected by outside regulation and oversight (e.g., the Food and Drug Administration, state and local agencies, external accreditation bodies). As yet, no such protections exist for consumers of health care data.

## UNDERSTANDING STRENGTHS AND WEAKNESSES

Users of data who make choices for others (e.g., benefits managers at companies who make choices for employees) have a responsibility to understand fully the strengths and weaknesses of the data. The first point leads directly to this second concern. Increasingly, data comparing health care providers are used by benefits managers and others for contracting or deciding who will be preferred (or allowed) providers. Persons who use these data—especially to make decisions that affect other people—must understand fully the value of the data. They must review the technical details, evaluate the caveats, and determine whether the data can be used legitimately as the foundation for their specific decisions.

This responsibility requires that these intermediary consumers of data obtain information sufficient to review all analytical choices made by the producers of the data. This need for full disclosure extends to the risk-adjustment methods used: What factors were considered in controlling for patient risk, and how were they quantified? Which data were used? How was data quality ensured? Which statistical methods were employed?

Answering these questions may be particularly challenging when a proprietary severity- or risk-measurement method is employed. Vendors of the method may legitimately claim that their business would be compromised if they were forced to reveal publicly all aspects of their approach.

However, consumers of these "information products" have rights, too. To be able to use severity software in a legitimate and responsible fashion, they need to know how it works. For risk adjustment, users especially need to know details about what clinical factors are employed and how they contribute to scoring patients. This allows users to determine whether critical risk factors for their populations of interest were included or not. For example, was prior open-heart surgery included in assessing risk for patients undergoing coronary artery bypass grafts (CABGs)? Users of severity- or risk-adjustment methods must gain access to the logic underlying the approach.

## MAKING CHOICES AFFECTING INTERPRETATION OF FINDINGS

Choices are inevitably made in risk adjustment that will affect interpretation of the findings. It is a myth that all science is completely objective. Even the most rigorous clinical trial requires decisions (e.g., about which patients to include) that could skew or subtly bias its results. In addition, there are no perfect methods, especially for risk adjustment. Given the numerous data limitations suggested above, choices in risk adjustment for comparing provider performance could become problematic and even value laden.

For example, studies have suggested that persons with low educational levels are less likely than well-educated persons to seek care early in the course of their disease. This may be a contributing reason why poorly educated persons may be sicker than better-educated ones when they finally arrive at the hospital. Therefore, educational status may be a legitimate risk factor in examining patient outcomes.

Suppose, however, that one is comparing the performance of health maintenance organizations (HMOs), which by their nature are supposed to focus on prevention and ongoing primary care. Risk adjustment using patient educational levels would mask differences across HMOs in their ability (or inability) to care effectively for poorly educated persons. In this instance, it would be more valuable to examine HMO performance within strata of patients grouped by their educational achievement—that is, to calculate outcomes for highly educated patients separately from those for patients with a grade-school-only education. Sociodemographic factors that raise similar concerns include patient race, ethnic identification, language, and income level.

Numerous other choices must be made as well, such as identifying additional clinical factors to be included in the risk adjustment, identifying the exact statistical modeling approach, and setting the $p$ value for statistical significance. In few instances is any single approach absolutely correct. Each option will have pros and cons that must be weighed in light of the data and other limitations of the particular setting. The implications of these decisions must be considered in evaluating the meaning of the results of the analyses.


## NECESSITY

In certain instances, it may not be necessary to perform risk adjustment. Risk adjustment is difficult but desirable in many settings, even if only to prove to providers that concerns about varying patient severity have been addressed. Nevertheless, in producing comparative performance data, the first question should be whether risk adjustment is absolutely essential. In certain instances, it may not be necessary to adjust for risk.

For example, important information about provider quality is suggested by the number of cases treated annually. One of the most powerful findings in New York State's initial study of mortality for CABG patients released in 1991 was how many surgeons operated on relatively few patients. Risk adjustment is not needed to support the belief that surgeons with larger volumes probably do better than those with only a handful of cases. Part of a multifaceted explanation for subsequently improved CABG mortality in New York was the withdrawal of low-volume surgeons.

Similarly, it may not be appropriate to risk adjust when looking at patient satisfaction or experience with care. Even though research has found that sicker patients are more likely to be dissatisfied with their care than healthier patients, one may not want to control for severity for reasons analogous to the education example in the section on making choices above; making sure all patients are satisfied, regardless of extent of illness, is the ultimate goal.

## PITFALLS OF USING DIFFERENT METHODS

Comparing data compiled using different methods is fraught with pitfalls. Specialized health care services increasingly cover broader markets, even cutting across states; for example, some health plans now send patients hundreds of miles to receive tertiary services such as CABG operations and transplants. In this context, it is tempting to compare providers across large geographic areas or health care systems. However, different states and different plans collect different data, and comparing data compiled using different methods can produce misleading results.

For example, many states gather only up to 5 discharge diagnoses on routine hospital discharge abstracts, while other states (e.g., California) have space for up to 25 discharge diagnoses. With more coding slots, the relevant health care personnel (e.g., physicians, medical record coders) may be more likely to list a variety of diagnoses that could more accurately reflect patient risk. Using discharge abstract data for risk adjustment, it is not fair to compare outcomes from states allowing 5 codes with those from states allowing 25 codes.

Other data distinctions may produce even more difficulties. For example, some clinical-data-based severity measures consider the extent of patient illness on admission to the hospital. By controlling only for admission severity, these methods help isolate subsequent events that could reflect poor quality of care. In contrast, most hospital discharge abstracts contain all discharge diagnoses, regardless of when they were made and when during the admission the events occurred. For example, if a cardiac arrest occurred on Day 5 due to poor quality, these discharge abstract-based methods would "control for" cardiac arrest—in effect, not holding the hospital accountable for this event. Comparing hospital death rates produced using admission data versus data encompassing the entire hospitalization would thus be misleading.

## CONCLUSIONS

These types of data issues form a core set of technical details that are often contained in the "fine print" accompanying public release of data. Other methodological decisions, such as choice of patient populations or minimal sample sizes, present similar concerns. Therefore, it is crucial for producers of comparative performance data to disclose these methodological details, and it is similarly essential for consumers of the data to understand the implications of those details.

# Public Disclosure: A Media Perspective

*Josh Barbanel*

Dr. Norbert Goldfield is absolutely right that with American medical care in enormous turmoil, the public is demanding more and more information about health care in general and local hospitals in particular. The question is not whether data will be released but by whom, how, and when.

What people want to know most of all, bluntly, is whether they are more likely to die in their neighborhood hospital—where their health plans get the best price—or at some other hospital across town. Specifically, has that magnificent local academic medical center been so damaged by competition-driven cost cutting that it no longer deserves its reputation?

Whatever its practical and statistical limitations, case mix adjustment is a technique designed to make these kinds of comparisons between hospitals more meaningful, and, so, the data will be used—not only by the medical priesthood but also by employers, insurers, and the public at large.

If the hospital industry or its regulators do not provide such information, journalists or consumer groups will provide it themselves. Some health maintenance organizations (HMOs) already do it. With the help of case mix software packages, a personal computer with a large hard disk, a state discharge dataset, and a little advice, any news organization could produce credible risk-adjusted mortality tables in a few days, trimmed or untrimmed, without the help of the Mayo Clinic (or the "Mayo" digit).

When this happens, one hopes that this hypothetical news organization would do a thoughtful job—namely, clearly describe the methodology, explain the meaning and limitations of the conclusions, examine outliers and explore alternative explanations, listen to the views of the hospitals, and avoid bad methodology.

When the local hospital association objects anyway, when a stream of politically connected chief executive officers (CEOs) bombard the publisher with protests, the crusty, cigar-smoking, statistically correct city editor will then be able to say, "What do you mean, we're unfair? We're part of the continuous quality improvement team. We're customers, just like you are."

The point is that, whereas there are many customers for hospital data, the only real customers of the health system are the patients. Everyone else is a stakeholder but not a customer. To a patient undergoing a coronary bypass, outcome is everything, but the quality improvement process his or her providers use is an incomprehensible artifact.

Dr. Goldfield brings a humane, ennobling, almost utopian perspective to the problem at hand. If only all groups could work together without fear, he says, they would be able to use the statistical power of these tools for the common good, and medical care would be better for it.

This is a huge step forward from the traditional *Father Knows Best* model, where hospitals' mistakes were examined behind closed doors and in the confidential minutes of quality assurance meetings, and less-than-competent physicians lived without fear. In that environment, the cash flow could be measured, but the medical inputs and outputs could not.

However, it may be a mistake for Dr. Goldfield to put patients and journalists, and perhaps even state regulators, on his continuous quality improvement teams. When W. Edwards Deming brought this notion to Japan, he helped Japanese industry transform itself. However, the people who bought Japanese products were not part of the quality improvement process: they were the customers who bought the best product (based on performance) at the best price.

In this respect, the hospital industry is not unlike the electronics industry. The customers want and should be able to get the best product for the money and should not be expected to worry about quality improvement or improvement methods over time.

# CHAPTER 12

# Public Disclosure:
# A Media Perspective

*Michael L. Millenson*

The idea of "report cards"—the public disclosure of provider-specific information on medical quality—simultaneously tantalizes, titillates, and terrifies physicians, hospital administrators, and executives of health plans. Norbert Goldfield is one of the few to discuss this whole area of data release with some reference to real-world problems and opportunities. His chapter "Public Disclosure of Case Mix Adjusted Clinical Information" makes a valuable contribution to the debate.

Unlike some of his confreres in the research community, Dr. Goldfield acknowledges that what is at stake involves more than a high-minded civics discussion about the public's right to know. It can be a jungle out there. Purchasers blindly pursue lower costs with deliberate ignorance about the effect their penny squeezing may have on patients. On the provider side as well, there is a shortage of candidates for sainthood. Providers, Dr. Goldfield writes, have traditionally stuck their heads in the sand, and many have refused to acknowledge that the public has a right to have comparative information in a timely manner. Too often, state hospital associations have been prodded into participating in such releases of information; when participation finally occurs, it is only in a grudging manner.

In other words, hospitals stonewall.

Unfortunately, almost all the discussion by providers about public data release has one element in common: whining. Report cards violate one of W. Edwards Deming's key principles of continuous quality improvement (CQI), providers invariably protest: you are supposed to "drive out fear." How can we expect innocent providers to join in CQI activities when they worry about being pilloried by the release of inaccurate, misleading, or confusing data to the untutored masses?

Drive out fear? How about driving out *my* fear each time I seek treatment from my profit-driven health maintenance organization (HMO), which has just signed up a joint venture consisting of a panic-stricken community hospital and a pampered group of local physicians who could not spell *capitation* a year ago if you spotted them all the vowels? That, my friends, is fear.

Of course, I *know* I can trust the HMOs to do the right thing. One New York health plan recently announced that it was listening to its customers by issuing a report card based on the measures that consumers listed as important. Forgive me if I view this as a cynical ploy. After all, is the average consumer going to ask for the case mix adjusted mortality rates for open-heart surgery or whether the physician's secretary answers the phone by the second ring?

As near as I can tell, the entire Judeo-Christian tradition violates Deming's hallowed principle. Christians believe that humans are born sinful, hardly a CQI kind of attitude. Jews, while not conceding original sin, nonetheless speak of the constant battle within each person between the Will To Do Good and the Evil Impulse. The rabbis recommend Awe/Fear of the Heavens and Fear of Sin as a way to keep people on the straight and narrow. What a shame God never had a chance to read Deming's book before writing His.

My intention is not to disparage the need for cooperation rather than vindictiveness. I completely agree with the provider community that great care must be taken in making sure that misleading indicators of quality of care are not made public in an irresponsible manner. Dr. Goldfield deals with the issues surrounding risk adjustment in a knowledgeable and sensitive way, but I am concerned about the naivete and self-centered attitude of many in the provider community.

It would be nice if these physicians and hospitals who fear for their reputations acknowledged that public data disclosure—or the threat of it—has already saved lives by motivating behavioral change that otherwise would not have occurred. The evidence is clear in New York State, where at least three hospitals have publicly acknowledged that release of data on coronary artery bypass graft surgery caused them to reexamine their processes of care and significantly improve them. If three hospitals have acknowledged this publicly, one can only wonder what the others did privately.

One of those hospitals, by the way, ignored a consultant who tried to warn earlier that there were problems. The hospital's managers finally acted in response to public pressure. Who can blame them? Taking on powerful surgeons who honestly believe that they are giving the best possible care is not a task that a hospital administrator or chief of the medical staff looks forward to doing. Sometimes, one has to be forced into self-examination. American industry, after all, only adopted CQI because of its fear about the effects of Japanese competition.

In my personal experience, some of the most eloquent physician and hospital advocates of CQI are bright, talented, and thoughtful individuals. They spend most of their time speaking to appreciative audiences, as well they should, but they do not see the underside of the medical profession. Not only "bad" physicians but many well-meaning and complacent ones honestly see no reason to change their practices.

Concerns about the downside of public disclosure of data are legitimate. I suspect that Dr. Goldfield's plan to "educate" the news media is overoptimistic, as the recent managed care "backlash" frenzy amply illustrates. Education may work in markets like Cleveland, but the press corps in Washington, New York, Chicago, and Los Angeles—places that set the national agenda—are different. I remember when the Health Care Financing Administration (HCFA) tried to precede the release of its mortality data with a day of media education. Most of the influential television types skipped the education, which is understandable. They are general assignment reporters, and their time is precious. They then attended the press conference, did not listen to the caveats presented there, and asked questions that had already been answered. In any event, the persons who need educating the most may be the editors who decide the story's tone and where it is placed.

If Dr. Goldfield thinks that he can even use the term *case mix* with the news media, he's been talking too much to the trade press and other quasi-policy-work reporters. As a group, general reporters think they are math whizzes if they can figure out that "66.66 percent" is the same as "two-thirds."

There is no easy solution to the difficult balancing act Dr. Goldfield describes. To my mind, the situation we have today offers a number of advantages. Call it the "good cop/bad cop" strategy. The bad cop is the mean media threatening public humiliation, or it is the ogre of government-run health care, or it is those purchasers with the glint of cost-cutting blood lust in their eyes. Because of these threats, medical providers are flocking to seminars on outcomes measurement and quality improvement—in other words, the courses run by the good cops.

Fortunately for providers, the threats of the bad cops have so far proven empty. Reform of Medicare has not meant new requirements for data release by providers, and when the news media publish data on quality, it is mostly ignored, which is not surprising: consumers do not yet understand the data. Besides, consumers often ignore far more well established sources of information. Every year, auto makers sell millions of cars that receive negative reviews in *Consumer Reports* magazine.

As long as providers stay scared, though, the bad cops will be doing their job. My advice to providers: drive out your fear long enough to effectively drive out mine. Then both of us will be happy.

CHAPTER 13

# Public Disclosure: A Hospital Chief Executive's Perspective

*Ronald Goodspeed*

The potential benefit from disclosure of risk-adjusted clinical performance data is certainly more likely to be realized if accomplished with well-planned educational follow-up and open communication. The enormity of the task is well described and illustrated in Chapter 9. Using the framework of continuous quality improvement is appropriate and increases the chances of some benefit to all parties from the disclosure. Naturally, customer identification is the crucial first step; however, the more interesting questions are these: Who are the real customers? Who are the sellers? What is each seller's intent?

The first case example described a newspaper appearing to attempt to protect the public by printing the data. Though plausible, it is more likely just one more way to sell newspapers. The reporter has visions of a Pulitzer Prize. The hospital association clearly recognized the futility of attempting to straighten out the mess and wisely did not feed the media fires with more fuel to sell newspapers. This opinion may be described as cynical or perhaps just realistic.

Other providers or sellers of the adjusted data have other agendas that also contribute to making the release of clinical information a political process. The state agencies need to justify their budgets and existence. Researchers developing the risk adjustment methods or analyzing the data need further funding, promotion, and tenure. Purveyors of risk adjustment methods want to promote and sell their products. These are not dishonorable intents, but it is important to recognize them as part of a political process and make every attempt to change and limit the impact of the political process.

Knowledge, completely provided to all involved parties, has the best chance of removing the political forces in the process of disclosing clinical information. Any process that is being politicized experiences the presentation of highly selected information by parties with a particular agenda or self-interest. Education is, therefore, the most hopeful solution because it prepares the recipient of information to interpret it in a less biased manner. However, due to the complexity of case mix adjustment methodologies, educational efforts are difficult and must be well designed.

Educating the parties involved about individual statistical techniques, such as analysis of variance or logistic regression, should not be a focus. The case mix adjustment method itself is much more important. Purely clinical adjustments of case mix categories are more readily understood by recipients of education than the nuances of the statistics being used in the analysis of the data.

There are multiple case mix adjustment methods but few that were designed to produce a level playing field for the comparison of medical care outcomes. Most methods were developed to enhance the financial case mix adjustment system known as diagnosis-related groups (DRGs). Hence, most were developed to predict resource utilization better—which is the main purpose for which DRGs are used in other nations—but these case mix adjusters are now being promulgated as methods to predict clinical outcome. All too often, the "severity" that is being measured is the severity of financial resource utilization. Comparing observed outcomes with expected outcomes requires solid methods to develop expected—that is, predicted—outcomes.

With some case mix adjustment products, education about the method is more difficult to accomplish because of the seller's desire to protect "proprietary" information. This phenomenon underscores the need for open disclosure of more than just the outcomes data. Even with open disclosure of how a given method adjusts for case mix, there are limits to the results. As Dr. Goldfield's analysis implies, there are no case mix adjustments for demographic factors that may have significant impact, such as socioeconomic status, type of health insurance coverage, or presence/lack of coverage.

Currently, case mix adjusted clinical data being released are mostly institution specific and usually hospital specific, yet more and more care today is provided outside the hospital. A physician's outpatient practice controls the prevention of illness or hospitalization, prehospital preparation, the decision to admit, and posthospital care. With the release of these data, the hospital is being held solely accountable, although at times only part of the process has occurred in the hospital.

For example, many obstetrical admissions are of 12 to 24 hours' duration, and two patients (mother and child) are discharged into the hands of their family, an attending physician, and possibly a home health agency. Where is the public disclosure of outcomes of the physician's practice and the home health agency's care for these cases? Is the clinical information being measured meaningful, or is it just measuring the most readily available data?

Quality improvement is intuitively a good thing. In the health care marketplace, however, the first five priority issues for purchasers (i.e., third party payers and employers) are (1) price, (2) price, (3) price, (4) price, and (5) price.

Experience confirms this opinion. Recently, during a long and arduous negotiation between a local hospital and a third-party payer, the hospital was asked to provide data demonstrating the quality of care provided to be superior to that of competitors. After presenting two hours' worth of data that established superior structure, process, and outcome, the hospital was told that the data did not matter, the discount was the issue.

Who is the real customer in this process of disclosing case mix adjusted clinical information? Who is the seller? Dr. Goldfield lists many potential customers, yet, all too often, it appears that the sellers are serving only themselves and their own purposes. The sellers are their own best customers.

Neither reporters, news media, researchers, nor state agencies protect the public if they are not willing to engage in a process similar to Dr. Goldfield's final case example. The example of educational follow-up and open communication between collaborative parties seems too good to be true. May this ideal and productive state of affairs soon arrive or be created.

# CHAPTER 14

# Public Disclosure: A Hospital Quality Improvement Project's Perspective

*Vahé A. Kazandjian*

No matter which arena of health care performance assessment is explored, a few terms are encountered in a repetitive and overwhelming way: *outcomes research, benchmarking,* and *accountability.* Although none of these terms means the same thing to its different users, public policy is often based on the interaction of these terms, under the seemingly trustworthy objectivity of health services research.

Chief among recent policy reforms is the issue of accountability. The spirit of accountability is proposed to encompass the duty and obligation institutions producing social services have toward society in demonstrating goodness of the product. How will it be assessed that the product or service was good? Perhaps by comparing the producer to other producers of the same service and by assigning a decreasing order of "goodness"[1] to the various producers of the service. Such an activity is often referred to as *benchmarking.* Finally, what can be more trustworthy than establishing a relationship between "what is done for what, for whom" and "what was the outcome"? Such an activity is classified as *outcomes research.*

The purpose of this commentary is threefold:

1. to challenge the beliefs and expectations associated with concepts of outcomes research and its evaluation
2. to discuss the usefulness of publicly disclosed performance information
3. to fulfill the accountability mandate by defining three types of audiences: immediate, intermediate, and ultimate

## WHAT IS ACCOUNTABILITY?

According to *Webster's Ninth New Collegiate Dictionary, accountable is* synonymous with *answerable.*[2] It seems logical to assume that in order to obtain an answer, a question should first be asked. From that point of departure, it should be agreed, therefore, that there is a set of questions that a group has asked the health care providers regarding the goodness of the services or the care.

Who are these groups? Are they the purchasers of care, looking at health care as yet another service they buy for their employees? Are they payers, looking to justify premiums and provider charges to their purchaser customers? Are they the recipients of the care, who look at health care as a fundamental and deserved social service? Are they the researchers eager to break new ground in the understanding of the relationship between care, medicine, and healing? Are they powerful representatives of a subgroup of patients with disabilities, with special needs, or of a special age segment? Are they professional colleagues requesting an "internal dialogue on performance" before answering for their performance to the less clinically versed members of society?

If there are so many groups, is it possible to find a unique mode or method of accountability? Will a purchaser of care be satisfied with raw data on hospital mortality while a clinician refuses to discuss the matter unless the data are case mix adjusted? Will a high mammography rate indicate a highly accountable health plan? Will a high cesarean-section rate denote a resource-wasteful hospital where obstetricians practice as they please or a public hospital that takes in high-risk mothers with little or no prenatal care?

What is the question health care professionals are trying to answer? What standard are they trying to meet? Is it to demonstrate that health care was delivered as needed or most cost-effectively? Most cost-efficiently? That the care resulted in expected and best results? That the recipients of care were pleased and comfortable with the clinical and humane treatment? That physicians, nurses, administrators, physical therapists, and colleagues were fulfilled as professionals practicing the noble art of healing?

No matter who the audience is, there is a pressing conclusion to reach about accountability: it may not be possible to be accountable to all groups through a single mode or method of accountability. If so, it seems quite acceptable that more than one approach will be necessary to fulfill the larger social accountability mandate to quantify and publicly report on health care quality and efficiency of resources used. Therefore, the various projects available to all kinds of providers—hospitals, health plans, subacute and long-term care facilities, physician practices, ambulatory care settings, physician networks, hospital networks, and academic centers—are necessary and contribute to a better understanding of the questions.

The field may be at the stage of understanding the questions. However, the unsuspecting reader of an article on the local hospital's mortality rate rankings or report cards on individual health plans may believe that these examples represent definitive proof of goodness of service and care.

The question "What is accountability?" is not answered yet. If accountability is all of the above, and if one is answerable to only one audience, that will constitute partial accountability—and anything partial is open to criticism and challenge.

## WHAT IS AN OUTCOME OF CARE?

An outcome of care is different from an outcome in manufacturing. For example, an outcome of hip replacement is not that there were two types of postoperative infections but that the patient was able to walk, climb stairs, and perhaps play golf three or six months after the surgery. In this example, the postoperative infections constitute an immediate "output" of the care, whereas the restoration or improvement of patient's functional health status constitute the outcome of the care. In industry, the completion of a pair of boots may be the outcome of the manufacturing instead of how the wearer of these boots fared on hiking trips.

Why is this distinction important? Because outputs of care deal with efficiency and effectiveness of the production of that service, whereas the improvement in patients' physical and functional health is a gauge of the appropriateness of that service. It should be no surprise, therefore, that primary emphasis should be placed on demonstrating the effectiveness of the care and not the efficiency of the production. After all, it is possible to produce unnecessary and potentially harmful services in a very efficient and environmentally safe way. Does that mean that the services provided were of good quality?

What, therefore, is real outcomes research? It is research wherein patients are followed after discharge or after the receipt of care, and their evaluations of the care as well as functional health status are quantified and included in the analysis. This is the simplest way of saying that there may not be any outcomes research without a systematic focus on the community—and that makes a lot of sense if it is the community or society asking us to be answerable to its inquiry into the goodness of the service or care received.

Is outcomes research as defined above commonly encountered? No. Most research projects focus on "output" analysis, which is an important but incomplete dimension of outcomes research. The reasons are understandable, although they may not be justifiable: there is pressure by payers to describe and report on performance, community-based research takes too long, there are no databases conducive to following the patients within a continuum-of-care framework, and high variation in the output rates of selected aspects of care is strong and sufficient proof of "something being wrong."

Any project that does not address the issue of outcomes will not respond to any social accountability mandate. Output-based and output-limited research is conducive to poor policy making and societal frustration. It is the project that attempts outcomes research by including patients' evaluation of care and their changing functional and emotional health status that will come closer to fulfilling its accountability to a community or society at large.

## WHAT IS BENCHMARKING?

*Benchmarking is* one of the newest words added to the health services research lexicon. Sometimes it is tempting to say that benchmarking is just scribbling on public seating. What it really means is comparing one organization or person to a better performer (or the best) and learning why the poorer performer is not as good.

The relationship that benchmarking has to accountability and outcomes research is an important one. When it can be demonstrated through outcomes research that one provider (hospital, health plan, or individual) is better than another, society then will have a rational basis for selecting providers. Furthermore, the better provider will have performed a more desirable set of activities—ones that resulted in the better outcomes. Thus, knowing the processes or activities of care, any performer could use the comparison to improve on certain aspects of practice and become a voluntary participant in the performance improvement cycle.

Unfortunately, benchmarking is used differently in health care. It is used to describe any comparative analysis of *output rates*. For example, a hospital that has a 10-percent bacteremia nosocomial infection rate would search for a hospital with a less-than-10-percent rate to establish its benchmark. However, there are no warranties that a lower infection rate will also have a higher proportion of appropriateness—the corollary of which is that a higher rate may reflect more appropriateness of the processes of care than a lower rate. After all, the two most potent ways to achieve an artifactually lower nosocomial infection rate are not to have patients or not to report all infections. Clearly, true benchmarking is performed only on the activities encompassing the care and not the resulting outputs or even outcomes. This terminological misuse sometimes provides an unwarranted credibility to an otherwise simple and limited initiative of contrasting provider performance output rates.

The repercussions that such activities have on public accountability are serious: if a higher rate is deemed less desirable than a reference output rate—which is often insufficiently adjusted for disease acuity and patients' functional health status—then those with higher rates will end up being rated unfavorably on the roster of social accountability.

## THE USEFULNESS OF PUBLICLY DISCLOSED DATA

The fact that some concepts of performance assessment and evaluation are not always applied correctly does not diminish the usefulness of public data disclosure. The disclosure of information about the effectiveness and efficiency of curative, preventive, or palliative care is a rational evolution for the medical profession. The public, however it is defined, should participate in the evaluation of certain aspects of the health system's performance. The challenge is this: which aspects of performance can be popularized—to become amenable to general scrutiny—and how?

Perhaps the inability to identify unequivocally these aspects of performance is at the basis of the controversy about report cards, indicators of quality, and public disclosure debates. Should the public know about the rate at which a health plan provided prevention services to the community it serves? Should the local television stations display and debate the flowcharts where care management at some hospital is described for all or selected modalities of case management? Should the public evaluate the extent of adverse outcomes based on the extent to which an institution applies and requires adherence to protocols of case management?

Crucial to the above argument is the ability of the health care professionals to identify the few target aspects of performance that are true reflections of performance goodness. The "all or nothing at all" argument is not valid for accountability; "the few, the valid" pointers of performance should be the goal.

What are the next steps? Once the debate about the usefulness of public disclosure is brought to an end, the logistics of that disclosure need to be organized. To do that, the audiences of such disclosure should be identified.

## IMMEDIATE, INTERMEDIATE, AND ULTIMATE DATA USERS

This commentary proposes that there are three leading audiences expecting to receive information on health care's performance: (1) providers of care, (2) researchers, and (3) all others. The information type, intensity, and specificity needed by each of the three audiences are different.

### Providers of Care

Providers of care constitute the immediate audience for performance data. That quality assurance and quality improvement professionals, clinicians, management, and trustees should be involved in the review of their own performance data is so obviously reasonable that it is sometimes overlooked. The joint attention paid by the providers of care internally should be based on objective indices or pointers of performance. These indicators can be constructed internally or be part of a larger project in which the hospital participates. An external program has the added usefulness of providing comparative information about the performance of peers. Many of the presently available indicators (e.g., mortality, cesarean sections, readmissions, waiting time, nosocomial infections) fall into this category.

The providers of care should first be knowledgeable about these indicators' profiles because, through time and pattern analysis, they will be able to identify aspects of their own performance amenable to further review. That means making the transition from output indicators to process indicators. This transition is not only crucial for improving performance but also for understanding all the activities that are performed well or even in an exemplary manner. It is the basis of benchmarking.

## Researchers

Providers of care should not be expected to demonstrate the statistical validity of any relationship between process and output. That is, although a certain disease management strategy was followed and the output was predicted and desirable, it does not unequivocally establish the effectiveness of that treatment or the accuracy of the provider's decision making. Other factors and their possible contribution to explaining the relationship between what was done and what happened must be considered.

More important, it is the researchers who will present the options for outcomes research. The outcomes-based design will longitudinally establish a linkage between the processes of care and the changes in the functional, emotional, and behavioral status of the patients. By aggregating the experiences of these groups of patients, a community profile will be built, wherein the effect of the health care provider on the health of the community is established. That is the ultimate test of performance goodness. Consequently, researchers constitute the intermediate audience, with a potential for some overlap with the ultimate audience (i.e., all others).

## All Others

In this category are payers, community representatives, and all actual and potential users of health care services. The distinction between this group and the previous two is not only in the type of information they could receive but also the timing of the release of this information. It may be most constructive to release the data to "all others" once the providers of care have a good understanding of their performance profiles and have established a baseline strategy to quantify and evaluate the activities of care. In addition, information to all others should be released with the understanding that researchers are designing the necessary accountability framework—that which will establish the relationship between the performance of a hospital or health plan and changes in the population's health status.

Necessary time should be allowed for the first two audiences to establish the inquisitive and evaluative data capabilities. Sometimes, it can take a number of years to reach the maturity needed to interpret data through ongoing evaluation and monitoring of trends.

## THE QUESTION OF ACUITY ADJUSTMENT

The proverbial plaint "my patients are different" has accelerated the discussion about the usefulness of patient acuity adjustment when comparing provider performance profiles. The concept is certainly not new; the basic requirement of epidemiological analysis is identifying "populations at risk" and comparing *only* those with equivalent risk. The idea of acuity[3] adjustment based on clinical and sociodemographic patient characteristics falls in the same conceptual framework.

One noteworthy difference is the time frame within which the observations are made. In epidemiological designs, the study populations are followed for a predetermined period of time, and patterns of differences in the outcomes of their exposures are established. For example, if a group is exposed to magnetic fields resulting from high-voltage electric lines, the prevalence of certain cancers is identified over time. Further, a causal or confounding relationship between exposure and symptoms or change in health status is investigated. Thus, the study of that correlation includes population cohorts that are adjusted for risk, signs and symptoms, or voluntary or involuntary exposures to potential carcinogens.

The question of acuity adjustment could be addressed differently by each of the three audiences identified above, based on the purpose of each audience. Acuity adjustment *at the patient level may not be as important* if the output rates of one institution are compared to its own rates over time or to those of peer institutions. The determination of peer institutions is important to this distinction. Here, a peer institution is characterized through its overall aspects, such as *resources* (e.g., number of beds, special care units by type, teaching status, types of services, location); *utilization* (e.g., number of discharges, proportion of admissions from emergency department, ambulatory surgery by type and volume); and *goals and mission* (e.g., tax status, ownership, membership in a multihospital system or a regional hospital network). The purpose of comparing output rates is to establish a baseline and provide performance reference points to providers of care (the immediate audience) to guide them in focusing on activities of care. The baseline can be established through a rank-order observational study. That is, the ranking of a hospital's rate is analyzed over time vis-à-vis the position or rank of its peers. It is very reasonable to expect that when peer institutions are compared, patient-level acuity adjustment will have marginal effect on the rank ordering compared with non-acuity-adjusted ranking.

The immediate audience would use the performance data for internal analysis and not for public disclosure. In this type of data, the goal is to have *relative* reference points; the magnitude of the rate is not important. That Hospital A's unadjusted cesarean-section rate was 18 percent whereas Hospital B's was 22 percent has practically no usefulness for questions about quality of care because the difference only indicates that the two hospitals are performing abdominal deliveries at a different rate. Instead, a number of pertinent questions may be asked to understand these rates better, such as these:

* Is the difference in these two rates a reflection of the complications of labor?
* Is the difference between the rates influenced by patient demographics?
* Is the difference between the rates a result of provider propensity for abdominal delivery or of provider inability to interpret fetal monitor readings correctly?

The rates alone cannot tell the reason since rates only describe and cannot explain; people explain. Without explanation, "gold standard" rates for good practice cannot be identified. What this means is that it makes little difference to the professionals what the cesarean-section rate is so long as such deliveries are attempted for the right reasons.

It is, however, very useful to know about the difference in cesarean-section rates between Hospitals A and B, especially if these rates have a temporal pattern and trend. Thus, a consistently different rate from peer institutions, or noteworthy fluctuations over time, may be sufficient to trigger an internal analysis of the processes of care. That is the first crucial step toward amelioration of performance, which can be achieved without individual-patient-level acuity adjustment.

Acuity adjustment is crucial for researchers in their search for explanations of the observed performance profiles. This intermediate audience faces, however, a systematic challenge: often the results of health services research do not arrive in time for clinicians and administrators to alter course, philosophy, or strategy. The rapid metamorphosis of the U.S. health care system is especially vulnerable to this time lag. This issue is most acutely felt when the use of new technologies is evaluated within the context of provider philosophy or practice style of care. The emergence of new technologies or the confounding effects of patient preferences may render the research findings only partially or marginally useful. However, for its intended purposes, researchers would see benefits in the more specific acuity-adjustment methods.

Finally, acuity adjustment may be marginally important to the general public if the sequence of public release of data has progressed from provider-targeted data to researcher-specific data to information made public for general, societal consumption. The reason for the marginal benefits of acuity adjustment in publicly disclosed data (ultimate audience) is that if performance data, such as outputs, were trended over time by the providers in search of self-evaluation and amelioration, special attention already would have focused on processes of care. When processes of care are studied, providers of care will have a more satisfactory answer to their communities regarding the appropriateness of care. If the care provided was not appropriate, and no effort was made to ameliorate the care, the community will have solid grounds for dissatisfaction.

Policy decisions will then be made to audit, evaluate, and monitor the services from specific institutions by external organizations. Perhaps "quality superboards" will then be formed to coordinate the effort. However, accountability may still not have been reached. In this sequence of events, the researchers will play an additional crucial role: determining the effect of care on the health status of patients. Eventually, patients' health statuses will add up to the community's health status.

There are at least two caveats capable of jeopardizing the validity of an acuity-adjusted comparison: (1) the acuities adjusted for may themselves be complications of the care, and (2) the same variables may not be valid for acuity adjustment across all conditions or patient complaints. Although both limitations are conceptual in nature, their influence on the applicability of acuity-adjustment methods is substantial. The two caveats are discussed next, but first a clarification of their underlying concepts may be appropriate.

If the adjustment method is generic (e.g., adjustment for patient demographics, secondary diagnoses, gender), the clinical validity of the adjustment may be questionable. Indeed, is it possible to fathom that a single adjustment algorithm could apply to and satisfy the constellation of diseases alleviated by the medical professionals? Is it more reasonable to think that the acceptability of the acuity-adjustment algorithm is a function of its flexibility to encompass and cover characteristics relevant to each disease, symptom, or complaint? If true, then a viable, specific, and sensitive acuity-adjustment methodology should be tailored to each patient or, at least, group of patients. An effort-benefit analysis may cautiously discourage the routine adoption of an individual-patient-level acuity-adjustment methodology.

In the case of the first caveat—that risks adjusted for may themselves be complications of the care—there is one thing to remember. If an adjustment system cannot discriminate between physiological and anatomical changes resulting from the care itself and those due to patients' medical history, acuity adjustment may serve a perverse incentive: poorer performance may be accepted by falsely attributing the observed results to patients' "severity."

The second caveat—that the same variables may not be valid for acuity adjustment across all conditions or patient complaints—is affected by the biological reality of patients as well as their preferences for care. Indeed, the identification and treatment of different health conditions depend on an understanding of the different patient characteristics clinically and specifically associated with those very conditions. A "canned" acuity-adjustment algorithm may not be sensitive to such requirements. However, to prove itself, an algorithm needs a timely and responsive health information system.

## WHERE WILL THE DATA COME FROM?

The above discussion will remain academic and unapplicable unless the most basic types of data are routinely collected and reliably catalogued. The best algorithm is useless if it cannot run on necessary data, and necessary data are few and far between.

Consider two issues: (1) the availability of clinical, demographic, preference-reflective data to describe the elements of the hospital experience and (2) the presence or lack of posthospitalization data about functional health status and quality of patient life. In most situations, such a database will require new data collection, added cost, and increased opportunity for adding unreliability to the health services data sources. In addition, any new effort, especially when associated with new cost, is looked upon with a jaundiced eye: will it provide added value or will it just "make us feel good that we're doing something"?

There are burgeoning initiatives across the United States to inspire confidence in the usefulness of data on patient preference and community health status. It is not yet known how the knowledge about these aspects of care would alter providers' philosophies or patients' expectations. That should rank high among the goals of "health outcomes" research.

## CONCLUSIONS

There may be a necessary sequence to the release of data to different audiences. The sequence starts with the providers of care, follows a parallel path with data released to researchers, and culminates in public disclosure of performance profiles built on the findings of the previous two sequences.

The question of acuity adjustment was also discussed. It is argued that if data are trended over time *and* if the comparison of the rates is among peers treating a comparable patient mix, additional adjusting for patient acuity of illness may provide only marginal benefit. It is suggested that trended data will identify patterns of performance with enough specificity to guide further inquiry into processes of care. Acuity adjustment is crucial, however, if interhospital comparisons are made with no stratification by type of hospitals. Interestingly, that may be the main shortfall of the data release and comparison logic, not the extent to which the data are adjusted for patient acuity levels.

There remains one more intriguing problem to be solved: what value do patients' choices have in explaining practice patterns and provider performance? How can these choices or patient compliance be taken into account so that provider evaluations reflect only those things within providers' control?

Most of the voluminous research about various procedures' utilization trends has focused on provider proclivity to prescribe or perform. However, it is interesting to note that the frequency of some procedures is substantially more affected by patient preference than is others, and there is as yet no systematic collection of patient preference data. Therefore, until data analysis systematically and rationally combines data on patient preference, compliance, and change in functional health status with practice patterns and availability of resources, the health care field cannot be fully answerable to society for the "goodness" of care.

---

NOTES

1. "Goodness" is defined as a synthesis of clinical efficacy, caring, and affordability.

2. *Webster's Ninth New Collegiate Dictionary*, s.v. "accountable."

3. "Acuity" is used instead of the traditional "risk," since this commentary considers these terms separate and noninterchangeable. Acuity is the severity of a patient's disease, thus a clinical concept. Risk is an epidemiological concept whereby a group's extent of exposure is evaluated vis-à-vis the chance for developing a disease.

# CHAPTER 15

# Public Disclosure: An Employer Response

*Robert W. Hungate*

The role of the employer as major purchaser is explicit in evolving a competitive health care market. Employers seek to empower employees as effective consumers of health care. These two steps in the value chain of health care benefits have had clear ways to view costs.

Benefit, in effect, quality, has been far less quantifiable. Quality has been largely subjective, set by the vignette of other patient experiences, general image, and often a vague sense that the more money spent, the better the quality. Public data release is sought to correct the existing market deficiency.

Employers know that employees trust the cost decisions that benefit managers make only if the benefit, or quality, to the individual gets better and/or the cost to the individual also decreases. These benefit tensions play out at three market levels—plan, place, and procedure—each of which requires effective risk adjustment for patient health status.

The issues Dr. Goldfield raises in Chapter 9 for the public disclosure of case mix adjusted clinical information are real and very significant. They apply to risk adjustment of employers' payments to plans and to appropriate patient expectations of results or outcomes. Patient expectations become the final determinant of quality.

In his discussion of the interrelationships among the press, continuous quality improvement (CQI), and public disclosure of provider-specific data, Dr. Goldfield raises the issue of driving out fear of the continuous improvement process on the part of those providing health care. What about patients' fear?

Most people I know do not regard days spent in the hospital with the same kind of pleasant anticipation as a vacation, a good night's sleep, or a decent meal. How they feel about health care is more akin to how they feel about taxes: "I'd like as little as necessary, but I sure want the best when I need it because the best will mean that I get to do more of the other things I really prefer." This almost negative interpretation of benefit is, perhaps, the ultimate underpinning driving disclosure, hence the need for effective, correct risk adjustment.

Unmet patient expectations will always be understood as bad quality. If an individual's true risk of mortality for, say, coronary bypass surgery is 20 percent due to comorbidities, then setting expectations based on institutional performance at 4-percent mortality will not lead to valid decisions. If, within the institution, there is a variance among surgeons of 2-percent to 8-percent mortality, it must be established whether that is a result of patient risk or other factors. Whichever set of facts exists is very material to the patient and to presentation of a valid basis for decisions.

Institutions that wish to lead in CQI must also lead in accountability. In effect, institutions and health plans that wish to enjoy the label *high quality* must now publish or perish. However, we have no hope of establishing high-quality measurement systems unless valid risk adjusting for each patient is used to set procedure expectations for both patient and physician. Results for those procedures are summarized as place accountability and summarized further in health plans' descriptions of their plan quality. Quality means meeting expectations, and expectations are for results.

If a provider's process control measurement systems exist without explicit objectives, what assurance is there that what patients seek—their expectations and objectives—are the same as the provider's goals? Perhaps the institutional or individual provider is no longer driven by patient needs but only by an employer's or health plan's demand for low cost. In that case, patients' blind faith in the good intentions of caring providers is no longer enough.

Patients are a clear part of the process control in health care. The positive results of trust, hope, and the placebo effect are part of this process control; so is patient compliance with drug or other treatment regimens. Patients' trepidations cannot always be removed but can be reduced by accurate information that describes current capability, past outcomes for a procedure, and the direction of change (the intended improvement). To be useful, this information must meet all its customers' needs, be they employers, plans, or patients. Employers must know that they get value for money spent, plans must be assured that they are appropriately compensated and that their providers perform well, and patients need objective information on which to base their judgments of plans and providers.

Dr. Goldfield refers to a seemingly unresolved tension between the public's right to know and provider quality improvement. He suggests that educational follow-up accompany a data release as a method of compromise. In the end, no compromise in the free flow of correct information will be possible. All parties in this equation have an essential need for accurate information. Although this need can only be met partially at the present time, denying it only delays achieving demonstrable high quality of care.

There is a continued reluctance to release less-than-perfect information, but if patients must live with imperfect information, will they be denied an opportunity to understand their own real risks from a medical procedure? The truth at the moment is that patients have to live with imperfect information about medical procedures all the time, and other stakeholders (plans, purchasers, practitioners, even policy makers) expect patients to make do with the scientific information currently available, perfect or not. To choose which physician or hospital to use is in no way more important or more requiring of perfect information than to choose whether to have a lumpectomy or a mastectomy. If patients can make do with less-than-perfect information about the latter, they presumably can make do with less-than-perfect data on the former; the lack of perfection does not necessarily invalidate the process of informed consent or the ability to choose.

However, both practitioner and patient must have realistic expectations regarding both risks and desired outcomes. Understating risk or overstating results both set the stage for unmet expectations, that is, bad quality. Unless detailed individual, risk-adjusted cases are used to set procedure expectations, the result is an uncontrolled system that will not learn what it needs to learn from the information system that supports it. Accountability, then, means that patient expectations are based on the same statistical, risk-adjusted outcome measures that an institution and its clinicians use to assess their own performance.

It is over 10 years since the initial release of Health Care Financing Administration (HCFA) hospital mortality data, which were much criticized for their questionable validity. At the same time, there is virtually no visible initiative on the part of institutions to become qualitatively accountable on a basis that supports their own quality improvement initiatives. To say it can be done without public accountability for outcomes is to ignore patients' critical role in those end results. Regrettably, HCFA has since discontinued the release of this data, stating its susceptibility to error rather than improving its risk adjustment system.

Dr. Goldfield's example of the state agency and its case mix adjustment, as well as the related questions he raises, brings home the point that, unless all patients are included in the sample, all patients cannot trust the data! Unless professionals agree to the validity of the data, they will not be committed to improvement. In the case example on immunization rates and responsibility, some adjustments to the system could be suggested to reduce the measurement differences. For example, if all enrollees were always included in the data sample, and charge-backs to a patient's prior health plan were used for appropriate but undelivered preventive care, the incentives for continuous improvement would have been more appropriate to the goal and more effective.

Specific criticisms of the inadequacy of economic risk adjusting, the lack of a Mayo digit, emphasis on process measurement because outcome measures are inadequate for differentiation—all these are valid observations. However, to suggest that customers talk to health departments to get recordkeeping systems changed or cooperate in the education needed to understand deficiencies in the data misplaces the responsibility for action. Patients—the correctly identified true customer—and payers may be misled by bad measures, but they are not responsible for fixing them. Those who provide the product, the caregivers, are responsible for congruence between their own performance measures and those of their customers.

The U.S. auto industry paid the price of such incongruence: it lost buyers. Health care's purchasing is driven differently, largely by intermediary purchasers rather than the direct beneficiaries, meaning patients. To reorient health care providers to their real customers now requires a change from simple trust by patients to trust based on accurate, valid, risk-adjusted outcomes information. Inspection can be done externally, as it now largely is, but improvement can only come from internal effort.

Perhaps building physician-hospital organizations, coupled with capitated payments for all providers, will realign structures and incentives so that progress on risk adjustment will proceed more rapidly. The difficulties that Dr. Goldfield articulately outlines are real, but the question remains: why is there not more urgency on providers' part to fix them?

CHAPTER **16**

# Public Disclosure: A Response from the Pennsylvania Health Care Cost Containment Council Experience

*Ernest J. Sessa*

One must approach the issue of public disclosure of data about the quality of medical treatment and surgical outcomes with a certain amount of sympathetic appreciation. Everyone has said or done things that can be looked back upon with regret, everyone makes mistakes, and everyone has a bad day now and then. However, rarely are those mistakes played out on the front page of a local or even a national newspaper, let alone reported on the 6 o'clock news. Such an event certainly triggers embarrassment, fear, anger, and perhaps blame. For better or for worse, it also changes behavior.

The Pennsylvania Health Care Cost Containment Council, an independent state agency, was created in 1986 and given the mission of restraining health care costs by stimulating market-based reforms. As health care costs rose dramatically, and the ranks of uninsured persons swelled, group purchasers of health benefits as well as individual patients grew increasingly determined to try to identify which physicians and hospitals provided the best care at the best price. Their attempts to gain the cooperation of the medical community were largely futile, and, in the end, they turned to state government to create an agency that would require providers to submit selected data and would require such data to be made public.

The council was charged with collecting, analyzing, and publicly releasing information that purchasers and consumers could use to help identify the most efficient and effective providers of care. The strategy was this: as those providers benefited from positive publicity and gained more patients, the remaining health care providers would be forced to respond by restraining or lowering their costs and improving the quality of their patient outcomes.

When the council first began to publish hospital performance data, there was a great outcry from the medical community. One would have imagined that the world was about to end. Six years later, life goes on. Hospitals have not gone out of business. Reputations have not been destroyed. What has happened is that over time a relatively cooperative relationship has developed—a process strengthened by the spotlight of public attention and awareness of hospital and physician performance. More important, a number of hospitals are responding in positive and constructive ways; costs are being lowered, and more emphasis than ever is being placed on quality improvement. In what is not an isolated example, a hospital in Pennsylvania—one that each year faced newspaper headlines labeling it the highest-priced medical provider in the county—recently announced that it has made dramatic cost reductions, that it now has the lowest prices in the area, and that these claims will be substantiated by future public data releases. Would this have occurred without the aspect of public reporting now in full swing in our state? With all due respect to the medical community, the answer is no.

During the last four years, the council has published 36 regional *Hospital Effectiveness Reports,* which cover 175 of the commonwealth's largest hospitals and report data on between 50 and 60 diagnosis-related group (DRG) categories. These reports provide the public with comparative information on the number of patients treated at each hospital, the average charges, the average length of stay, and risk-adjusted mortality and morbidity statistics. The council also has produced four annual *Consumer Guides to Coronary Artery Bypass Surgery,* which provide risk-adjusted patient mortality figures for hospitals and cardiac surgeons as well as the average amount charged by hospitals for coronary artery bypass graft (CABG) procedures. Also, the council has published nine regional *Small Area Analysis Reports,* three years of aggregated financial data about every Pennsylvania hospital, and a report on major organ transplants. In addition, the council has an active special reports department that has produced customized data analysis for hundreds of businesses, insurers, researchers, hospitals, and government organizations.

This constitutes an enormous amount of public data. It is only fair to ask: what has the effect of all this information been on the public, on providers, and on the people paying the bills? The impact has been significant, and it confirms that the strategy set in motion by the state legislature eight years ago was a sound one. Consider the following evidence:

- Accutrex, Inc., which employs 100 people in Washington, Pennsylvania, has used the council's reports to cut its health care bill by 13 percent. The savings allowed the company to expand its health coverage to include prescription drugs and routine checkups. Accutrex is part of a business alliance in southwestern Pennsylvania that has saved its members more than $1 million recently using the council's reports.
- Hershey Foods Corp. has used the council's data to select 10 central Pennsylvania hospitals and 200 physicians for its new managed care plan—one that was developed to emphasize outcome measurements and cost efficiency. The company's strategy of shifting the majority of its workers into managed care appears to be working. Hershey's health care costs for the last few years have been virtually flat across the board.
- The Northeast Pennsylvania Regional Health Care Coalition, a group of businesses and employees that represents some 5,000 people, has used the council's data to prepare for direct negotiations with physicians and hospitals.
- Pennsylvania Power and Light, Binney and Smith, General Electric Co., Rohm and Haas, and ALCOA are among a growing number of companies that have used the council's data to affect the skyrocketing cost of health care.
- Managed care plans such as HealthAmerica have used the council data to construct more efficient and effective provider networks. Pennsylvania Blue Shield, with six million subscribers, has used council data as well as its own to find physicians who can deliver quality care while keeping down costs. The HMO of Northeast Pennsylvania (a Blue Cross affiliate) has used our data to determine who it would contract with as exclusive service providers for its subscribers in the Wilkes-Barre–Scranton market.
- One of the topics that has received a great deal of recent attention involves measuring the performance of health plans, not just providers. We have demonstrated that the council can do just that. The Welfare Fund of the Laborers' District Council of Western Pennsylvania used our data to decide among various managed care alternatives. The data showed that an efficient provider network would yield better clinical results and lower costs for the fund's 7,500 members. With the assistance of consulting firm A. Foster Higgins, Inc., and extensive data from the council, the fund was able to select the preferred provider network offered by the local Aetna Health Plan. This new plan increased benefits

for the fund's members, reduced out-of-pocket expenses, and reassured members about the quality of care being delivered.

- Finally, thousands of individual consumers have requested copies of these reports each year, and our office staff regularly field phone calls from people who are facing treatment or surgery and are anxiously seeking information to help them find the best physician or hospital.

How have hospitals reacted? Positively, from a consumer standpoint. Here are several examples of actions taken by hospitals following data releases:

- In October 1993, Berwick (Pennsylvania) Hospital Center said the council's reports were largely responsible for its decision to order a complete review of the hospital's charge structure. Berwick's chief executive officer announced changes that would make Berwick more competitive.
- In January 1992, St. Vincent's Health Center in Erie lowered its prices for cardiac procedures by $5 million annually, following disclosure of council data showing that a nearby hospital was less expensive for the same procedure.
- Following the publication of the first *Consumer Guide to Bypass Surgery* in November 1992, Mercy Hospital in Pittsburgh promoted its cost and quality bypass surgery results on billboards, purchased ads in publications like the *Wall Street Journal,* and sent packets of promotional material to referring cardiologists, businesses, and health maintenance organizations (HMOs) throughout Southwestern Pennsylvania.
- Pocono Medical Center in Stroudsburg, Lehigh Valley Hospital, St. Joseph's Hospital in Lancaster, and Bradford Regional Medical Center (all in Pennsylvania) are among a growing number of hospitals that have acted to reduce their prices in the light of public reporting.

Since its inception, the council has worked diligently to avoid many of the concerns raised by Dr. Goldfield in Chapter 9. Many are legitimate, and exploring how the council established and sustained a cooperative working relationship with Pennsylvania's medical community might be instructive.

Although the council has many audiences, its primary mission is to provide the purchasers of health care services (i.e., businesses, organized labor, state government, insurers, and consumers) with a mechanism to cut swiftly rising health care costs. These costs were undermining the local economy, wreaking havoc on the financial health of Pennsylvania companies, and threatening salary and benefits negotiations between management and labor. While the council endeavors to be as helpful to hospitals as possible, its primary mission is not to take over the job of hospital quality improvement. The data simply point to the results of hospital care. If those results are not adequate, it is the job of the hospitals in question to respond and fix the problem.

The council has always sought the feedback of the medical community. Our agency engages in an ongoing dialogue with physicians and hospitals about a wide range of topics. The advice of our Technical Advisory Group, an independent, ad-hoc committee of experts in the fields of outcomes measurements, quality improvement, and health policy, has been extremely helpful. The council works closely with MediQual Systems, the designer of the primary outcomes measurement system that we use.

The council uses a state-of-the-art, clinically based outcomes measurement system (formerly known as MedisGroups, now called Atlas MQ) to rate providers. We have supplemented that system for our specialty reports and consumer guides.

The outcome data are also severity or risk adjusted. In other words, physicians and hospitals are in a sense given extra credit for treating high-risk patients and thus are not penalized for it. It is important to point out that an advantage cannot be achieved by turning away high-risk cases; that only reduces the *expected* numbers of mortalities and morbidities.

The council has not sought to overstate what can be concluded from the data. The information is basically a means of providing people with the ability to ask intelligent questions. The reader is always cautioned not to use our data as a sole source of information. Additionally, the agency takes pains to deal with the media in a professional way that does not attempt to sensationalize the results of the data.

The issues of education and measurement of the process of care as opposed to outcomes are valid ones. However, to pursue an educational program such as Dr. Goldfield suggests, while laudable, would take a great amount of time and resources. The same is true of measuring care processes, which would require the collection and analysis of numerous variables—an enormous undertaking.

Every idea for expanding the breadth and depth of the quality reporting system has to be weighed against the demand for timely and more comprehensive data as well as the cost of collecting the data. Moreover, is it or should it be the responsibility of an outside agency to examine the process of care in a hospital to determine where things could be improved? No—again, that is the hospital's responsibility.

Dr. Goldfield began Chapter 9 by stating that the focus should not be on whether data should be made available to the public but how. That is a question that those of us in the public reporting business wrestle with as honestly and as competently as we can.

The process of publicly disclosing provider-specific patient outcomes cannot be easy for physicians and hospitals. While none of the measuring systems that exist today are perfect, the message from the purchasing, consumer, and public policy communities is that they are unwilling to wait for some vague future time when "perfect" data that the medical community is comfortable with are available. Purchasers want timely data quickly and in as manageable a form as possible.

It is our challenge to ensure that the data and the way they are reported are fair and, at the same time, credible. By being accountable to its purchaser constituency and remaining sensitive to the legitimate concerns of medical providers, the commonwealth of Pennsylvania has been successful in doing just that: providing fair and credible data in a timely fashion.

CHAPTER 17

# Public Disclosure: A Response from "Health Care for All"

*Robert Restuccia*

In Chapter 9, Norbert Goldfield asserts that uninsured and low-income people should be viewed as a customer group for case mix adjusted data distinct from the middle- and upper-class population. He challenges organizations representing the poor and the uninsured to expand their focus beyond access to care to address quality-of-care issues. In viewing the poor and uninsured as a separate group, Dr. Goldfield is acknowledging that these people are at particular risk for poor quality of care and that the strategies to improve their health may be very different from the strategies for typical middle-income Americans.

The health care system is much less likely to respond to the needs of the poor and uninsured than to the needs of middle-income Americans with employment-based coverage. The great majority of the poor and near-poor have no insurance or have Medicaid coverage. They have a limited choice of providers and plans. They are much more likely to experience poor health and to be disabled than the rest of the population.

The problem is not just one of access to care. There is a documented relationship between lack of insurance coverage and poor quality. For example, the Medical Practice Study after reviewing 31,000 medical records in New York concluded that "the uninsured are systematically at risk for poor quality."[1] While Medicaid recipients fare better than the uninsured in terms of quality, there are still significant differences between the care and treatment of people on Medicaid and the privately insured.[2]

However, the problem of quality care for the poor and uninsured does not relate just to problems with the health care provided. The health of

117

low-income people is more likely to be affected by unemployment, poor housing, poor nutrition, inadequate education, violence, and other socioeconomic factors. These problems have a profound impact on the health of the poor but are usually outside the control of health care providers. Also, low-income populations are more likely to face cultural barriers than middle-class populations. They are more likely to be non-English speaking and less familiar with the American health care system.

The most effective interventions to improve the health of people living in poverty may not be related to direct health care services. Health care systems that work well for middle-class populations may not be appropriate for the low-income populations. The care that an organization provides to patients in a white middle-class suburb may not meet the needs of people in a multicultural, inner-city neighborhood. A health organization skilled in the care of a diverse population and able to integrate other (e.g., social) services into a comprehensive care plan may provide better care for that population.

Some consumer organizations that have worked on quality-of-care issues have focused on making case mix adjusted information available in a form that would be useful for people choosing health plans and providers. Report cards based on case mix adjusted data are proliferating throughout the country. These data are risk adjusted so that differences in outcomes can be attributed to the quality of care provided, not to the characteristics of the consumers. Dr. Goldfield describes the significant problems of adjusting for comparative purposes across institutions. It is questionable how helpful this approach is to consumers in picking a health plan or provider. It is certainly of little use to uninsured and Medicaid recipients, who are very limited in their choice of providers.

Also, in the process of risk adjusting data, much relevant information is lost for low-income patients. Because socioeconomic status is typically part of the risk adjustment formula, differences in the treatment of low-income patients are masked. For low-income consumers, a different approach would be more relevant in improving the quality of care. Rather than ignore the differences between socioeconomic groups, case mix data could be stratified so that differences between groups can be identified and different approaches evaluated.

Consumer groups could have an important role to play in using this case mix data to improve the quality of care for low-income constituencies. Dramatic changes in health care for the poor provide an important opportunity for consumer organizations to expand their focus to quality-of-care issues.

In a managed care system in particular, issues of access and quality are increasingly intertwined. Over 16 million Medicaid recipients are now covered under Medicaid-managed care programs. Some Medicaid officials are open to consumer input regarding the development of case mix adjustment methods. If included in such discussions, the unique perspective of consumer organizations representing the poor and uninsured could make a significant impact on the process to improve the quality of care.

However, the involvement of these groups will be very different from that of providers, health plans, or employers. Consumer and community groups bring an important perspective but often do not have the technical capacity or resources to work on these issues. If the poor and uninsured are going to be an audience for this information, resources and methods need to be developed to allow them to be effective participants.

Dr. Goldfield notes that it is impossible for health care organizations to achieve the continuous quality improvement goal of "driving out fear" because case mix adjusted data could be used against these organizations in the current cut-throat competitive environment. However, this information also could be used similarly against the special populations that consumer organizations are trying to help. For example, case mix adjusted data may show higher rates of preventable illnesses and the need for additional resources for drug treatment or pregnancy prevention. This information could be used to blame rather than to help people in poverty—a rather well-known phenomenon in politics. Moreover, the insurance industry could use this case mix information to avoid groups and redline communities with higher than average needs.

This suggestion is not as preposterous as it sounds. In the current political climate, few policy makers and much of the public at large are not sympathetic to the needs of low-income people. Welfare reform has resulted in millions of people losing entitlement to public benefits. Moreover, the insurance industry is already accused of using health data, risk factors, and other information to screen out potential high-risk applicants; what reason is there to think that it would discontinue this practice with poor patients when more highly refined, risk-adjusted data become available?

There are important opportunities and risks to improving health care quality. Case mix adjusted data can be a way of helping us to understand how to use resources more effectively and improve the quality of care. Risk adjustment is also likely to expose fundamental inequities in the health system. In the end, a commitment to high-quality health care means that society will need to address the differing needs of all its members.

---

**NOTES**

1. H. Burstin, et al., "Socioeconomic Status and Risk for Substandard Medical Care," *JAMA* 268 (1992): 2383–2387.
2. Office of Technology Assessment, *Does Health Insurance Make a Difference?* background paper (Washington, DC: Office of Technology Assessment, September 1992), 22.

# CHAPTER 18

# Public Disclosure: A State Agency Response

*Tim Lynch and Randy Mutter*

Dr. Goldfield consistently taps into a number of current concerns about health care information and its uses in Chapter 9. However, attempting to resolve any of the key issues raised is a bit like trying to drink from a fire hose: one does so very carefully.

Dr. Goldfield cites the unenviable choice public health care policy managers so often have to face: "the need to provide case mix adjusted data based on universally accepted, statistically valid measures that are explained to the public versus the desire to avoid all statistical manipulations and trust that an unbiased third party will take care of any problem."

This statement rests on a set of fairly heroic assumptions—one of them being that anyone in this field can achieve close to universal consensus on anything when deeply vested interests are at play. These often prove almost impossible to bring together in the complex real-world settings, given the diverse and powerful vested interests involved, the legitimate complexities of the analysis at hand, and the inherent limits of the data.

Further, his statement reflects several underlying assumptions:

- Anything can be universally agreed upon by all potentially affected parties.
- The statistical procedures and data available are sufficiently robust to achieve the desired ends.
- Statistically based case mix measures can be developed for all of the complex tasks at hand desired by all interest groups.
- These efforts and conclusions can be adequately explained to the public.

Finally, his statement also suggests that, alternatively, public health managers might choose to do nothing for now, waiting instead for someone else to resolve the problems. Clearly, neither of these polar alternatives are an option; rather, as in so many areas of a real-world application, a middle ground is the only rational path to pursue.

Floridians understand these concerns as well as anyone else in the nation. We have been struggling with these issues directly for well over a decade, and resolving complex health data and analysis issues has been a major undertaking. This task became even more sensitive as the mission and focus of our agency's analysis evolved into a driving force of health care reform in Florida.

Health data analyses are being increasingly used to foster competition, assess resource use and procedure charge/cost, and judge the quality of services rendered by providers across the state. These assessments highlight the most and least successful providers. The public release of these data ultimately should result in changing the behavior of the most wasteful, least effective providers while rewarding the most successful ones.

A second, increasingly important step in this process is to delineate the limits of one's capabilities and fully address only those issues within the reach of one's resource capabilities. Analysts must qualify their research conclusions where need outstrips capabilities. They face multiple sets of needs from different users of health care data research. There is an always present demand to extrapolate results and extend available tools and research methods well beyond their limits in order to answer pressing issues the methods and data were not intended to address. Researchers must be vigilant in guarding against this kind of abuse.

## GIVING CONSUMERS POWER THROUGH INFORMATION

Part of the mission of the Florida Agency for Health Care Administration (AHCA) is to collect health care data and analyze it into usable knowledge that gives consumers the ability to make informed and efficient purchasing decisions. It is assumed that this information will also be used within the health care industry to help create truly competitive markets within the state where none has previously existed. The data also should help physicians, hospitals, health maintenance organizations (HMOs), and insurers to evaluate and ally themselves correctly with other providers in new relationships.

The Florida Health Care and Insurance Reform Act of 1993 allowed small businesses to organize into community health purchasing alliances (CHPAs), which means pooling for the purpose of buying health coverage, and allowed suppliers to organize into accountable health partnerships (AHPs) (i.e., integrated groups of health care providers and insurers.) The act also required the agency to measure "both the efficient utilization of medical resources and the effectiveness of medical care" and mandated the creation and use of practice parameters and standardized outcomes reports to help the CHPAs evaluate the AHPs. Lastly, the agency was required to issue annual reports, starting in December 1994.

## ACHIEVING CONSENSUS ON METHODOLOGIES

From 1992 through 1994, AHCA convened more than 20 specialized, legally mandated, and other data committee meetings and workshops throughout the state. The committees were composed of representatives of all segments of the Florida health care industry, including consultants, university and government researchers, and consumers. All hospitals were invited to the meetings, as were members of the press. These meetings were held to establish what Dr. Goldfield refers to as the need to provide universally accepted, risk-adjusted statistical information based on universally accepted standards.

Such meetings helped to develop consumer and industry consensus on the kind of data and analysis needed to ensure the success of Florida's managed competition information model. The meetings brought together all of the involved interest groups in an open forum and combined the best data, minds, tools, and research capabilities available to us. The agency issued a series of reports that summarized the conclusions of these initiatives.

The mandates of the health reform act were carried out with explicit recognition of several important guiding principles and caveats:

- Government's role must be to act as a single, consistent, reliable, and unbiased source of comparative health care information.
- Purchaser and provider demand dictates that development of information from existing data sources is essential before any new data collection initiatives are warranted.
- All affected parties must be included in the deliberation of how these issues are addressed and resolved.

- The quality and limitations of the data and analytical methods must be sufficiently examined, understood, and qualified in any analysis:
  - Evidence of wide variability in both process and outcome measures do exist and point to opportunities for quality improvements.
  - Comparing and analyzing these variations across providers will, itself, lead to improved performance (the Hawthorn or sentinel effect).
  - The resolution and quality of the data must match the uses to which the information is put, and producers of the information must not overstate its purpose or capability.
  - Wide variability in the depth and quality of data within the UHDDS/UB-92 datasets exists.
- Using these data for performance assessment will stimulate improvement of the data.
- Market accountability is a natural extension of a longstanding commitment by providers to total quality management (TQM) and continuous quality improvement (CQI) initiatives.
- Extensive provider, consumer, and media education is essential for successful dissemination and use of these data.

The Patient Outcome Workgroup concluded that insufficient information exists, in a centralized and standardized form, with which a CHPA or consumer can evaluate acute-care hospitals. There is also a scarcity of data to foster comparisons of outcomes for ambulatory surgery centers and nursing homes.

Even within the health care industry, there is no common benchmark for comparison among peers. Thus, it is difficult for CHPAs and AHPs to identify the sources of variation between providers. Additionally, representatives from hospitals, ambulatory surgery centers, and nursing homes are expected to employ the database for their own use in internal improvement, including mapping their current positions within the emerging managed competition marketplace.

## METHODOLOGY EVALUATION

The work group, after completing a systematic evaluation of commercially available severity adjustment systems and an assessment of UB-92–based versus clinical abstracting systems, reached several conclusions:[1]

- The agency will be the single data repository for data collection and will severity adjust all hospital data.
- Every reasonable attempt must be made to ensure that agency data are complete and accurate.
- The agency should develop a method of trimming outliers.
- Outcome measures should be expanded to include evaluation of the entire episode of illness and focus on the continuum of care.
- Adjusting patient severity of illness results in enhanced outcome comparisons among providers and among AHPs.
- However, no single severity-of-illness adjustment method is consistently more accurate or reliable in explaining the variance in outcomes than any other method currently available.
- Hospitals, therefore, should not be forced to acquire a specific vendor system.
- A clinical abstracting system is very much more expensive than a UB-82/92 system.
- A UB-82/92 system should, therefore, be used to complete the required severity adjustment, with the agency considering the all-patient-refined diagnosis-related groups (APR-DRG) system as one of the preferred systems.
- Practice guidelines will help guide positive change but will require special study or ad hoc analysis to supplement existing UB-82/92 data collection.

The outcomes work group, with the guidance of the State Center for Health Statistics, completed a variety of data analyses consistent with combined committee recommendations. The analyses led to the development of an initial comprehensive acute-care hospital report card. These resource use and quality profile progress reports were produced in draft form in January 1994. The reports evaluated each of Florida's 213 acute-care hospitals and reported their average charges, average length of stay, mortality rates—all of which were adjusted for age, sex, payer mix, case mix, case illness severity (APR-DRG), and regional price variation. Readmission rates were also evaluated.

The release of these progress reports generated considerable interest within the industry and resulted in a wide number of valuable recommendations for refining and improving our methodology. Suggestions included reevaluating pediatric and other specialty hospitals with unique missions, grouping hospitals

**Table 19–1** Use of UB-82/92 Patient Administrative Data for TQM/CQI Profiling Assessments of Florida Acute-Care Hospitals

| Purpose | UB-82/92 utility | Additional data needed | Cost of additional data |
|---|---|---|---|
| Hospital performance profiles (report cards) | Medium/high | None | N/A |
| Variation in physician practice | | | |
| Medical complexity—low | | | |
| Cesarean delivery | Medium/high | Some | Low |
| Pneumonia | Medium | Moderate | Moderate |
| Medical complexity—moderate | | | |
| Low back pain | Low/moderate | Moderate | Moderate |
| Medical complexity—high | | | |
| (Coronary artery bypass graft) | Poor | Extensive | Medium/high |
| Other medical procedures | | | |
| (Rehabilitation, mental health, outpatient, long-term care, other) | Low | Moderate/high | Moderate/high |

*Source:* Reprinted from Florida Agency for Health Care Administration.

by discharges rather than bed size, developing an outlier methodology, and developing measures of statistical significance confidence bounds.

AHCA contracted with University of Florida researchers to undertake the necessary technical refinements, under the guidance of the State Center for Health Statistics. Researchers have reestimated these performance profiles, and another version was available in mid-1995. This effort was one of the first comprehensive evaluations of its kind developed anywhere in the United States and will serve as a model for other states for the foreseeable future.

## USES AND LIMITS OF UB-82/92 DATA IN FLORIDA

AHCA staff have evaluated the uses and limits of state administrative inpatient acute-care hospital data for a variety of purposes. Table 19–1 provides examples of the analyses' conclusions, the use of administrative data, and the limits of the data. It also provides a relative estimate of costs associated with any additional data collection efforts necessary to fully achieve intended purposes, where appropriate. Table 19–1 attempts to profile some of the limits of the existing data and analysis capabilities described earlier.

Existing UB-82/92 data sources are more than adequate to complete comprehensive hospital report card profiles of the sort undertaken in Florida. This includes evaluation and comparison of 24 separate, clinically coherent service lines (neonatology, vascular surgery, orthopedics, etc.) within each Florida hospital. No additional data are needed; however, extensive statistical manipulation and quality assessment efforts are essential to ensure high-quality, meaningful comparisons.

The use of UB-82/92 data to profile physician practice becomes more selective. Certain practices, such as evaluation of cesarean-section deliveries, can be completed with only minimal additional data collection. Other more complex invasive medical procedures, such as coronary artery bypass grafts, warrant extensive additional data collection and analysis well beyond the UB-82/92 data currently collected. Achieving consensus on the required data and analysis methods for complex procedures of this sort is far more selective and must be managed on a case-by-case basis, with the experts in each field guiding data collection and analysis.

Finally, UB-82/92 data often do not adequately capture sufficient information for a wide number of procedures or conditions and omit treatment in settings outside the acute-care hospital. These include mental and behavioral health care facilities, both residential and outpatient; long-term care units; rehabilitation care; and a wide variety of other outpatient settings. Far more analysis and detailed data gathering will be required to develop sufficient data for properly evaluating these categories of care into a meaningful TQM/CQI profiling process.

CHAPTER **19**

# Public Disclosure: A Brief Commentary

*Eugene C. Nelson*

The aim of this commentary is to discuss some of the issues raised by Dr. Goldfield in his chapter "Public Disclosure of Case Mix Adjusted Clinical Information: Practical and Theoretical Challenges." Dr. Goldfield first points out that many different types of people in diverse sectors—health care, industry, government, media, and consumers—stand to benefit, or suffer, from public release of clinical information. He then observes that these different types of beneficiaries, or "data customers," in fact have different uses for the information based on their diverse needs. The central message of the chapter is that "public release of case mix adjusted clinical information must be done in a manner that meets the diverse needs of multiple customers. These needs will not be met, unless key principles of continuous quality improvement (CQI) are understood and acted upon."

Although I agree with this assertion, I detect a red flag fluttering in the midst of the central message. To some people, continuous quality improvement and total quality management are fads that have already faded. Management fads come and go quickly in North America; if it is hot today it will be cold tomorrow. The tragedy is that principles worthy of endurance may be lost as the tide of a management fad crests and then recedes. Therefore, it is probably smarter to emphasize the key principles on which continuous quality improvement is based than to worry about the name *CQI*. Modern improvement principles are alive and well in many of the world's best-managed organizations. These principles must be followed if public release of clinical information is to actually fulfill its promise. In short, the "customer needs" and "key principles" of modern improvement should be placed in the foreground and the worldwide quality and value improvement movement placed in the background.

Goldfield's chapter addresses six different needs for data. Each of these is discussed below.

## THE NEED TO EMPHASIZE IMPROVEMENT OVER TIME

The public does need protection from truly dangerous care, yet this protection must be based on an accurate diagnosis of causes (processes) and effects (outcomes). For this to be possible, there must be a safe learning environment, which in turn requires the active cooperation of the professional health community. Thus, a "sorting and shooting" approach will only drive fear into the providers of healthcare and preclude a serious attempt to unravel the tangled web of causation.

What is needed is the creation of an environment that emphasizes learning, allows steady improvement of outcomes, *and* fosters the use of statistical methods. Statistical methods make it possible to determine if an upward trend is really up, if a downward trend is really down, or if a provider is really operating in an inferior or superior performance zone. Therefore, another key improvement principle—in addition to the principle to drive out fear—must be invoked: make an effort to understand variation and to separate common cause variation from special cause variation. This requires the use of statistical process analysis techniques that are not commonly used in healthcare.

## THE NEED TO EMPOWER THE PUBLIC THROUGH EDUCATIONAL FOLLOW-UP

We are drowning in data and parched for useful information. Education for all stakeholders before, during, and after data release (and not just in follow-up) is essential to move from raw data to interpretable, useful, and actionable information. Education must emphasize an understanding of (1) statistical process analysis methods to give stakeholders criteria for interpreting fluctuations in outcomes over time and to avoid tampering, (2) the necessity for building outcomes analysis on clinically homogeneous subgroups to provide apples-to-apples comparisons, and (3) underlying systems of causation to avoid the simplistic assumption that "this alone" caused "that."

## THE NEED TO PROVIDE CASE MIX ADJUSTED INFORMATION BASED ON UNIVERSAL STANDARDS AND THE NEED TO PROVIDE INFORMATION USING RELIABLE AND VALID METHODS

The aim of case mix adjustment is to provide fair, apples-to-apples comparisons. The key here is to look at actual differences in outcomes among clinically homogeneous populations in order to determine if some groups of patients fare better or worse over time because of the treatment that they received (as opposed to their underlying biological condition). Consequently, to provide apples-to-apples comparisons, either statistical adjustment for measurable case mix differences is needed (this usually requires a multivariate regression approach) *or* stratification (sorting cases into clinically homogeneous subgroups) is required.

Trimming out patients from the analysis (i.e., excluding some cases) should only be done based on biological considerations (for the purpose of creating clinically homogeneous subgroups), so that the results of the analysis can be accurately interpreted. It is a canon of science that the data collection and analysis methods must be reliable and valid, while it is a law of working in the real world that these methods be affordable and efficient (otherwise they will not be widely used). Hence, *current* discharge data systems, which were developed primarily for billing purposes, are not sufficiently standardized or refined to generate reliable and valid data for analysis of clinical outcomes. These discharge data systems will require substantial upgrading if they are going to be able to produce reliable and valid data needed for clinical outcomes analysis.

Another issue that is sometimes buried in discussions of case mix adjustment is this: adjustment for what? The case mix adjustment system can be geared to explain variation in death and complications, functional outcomes, or costs of care. Different variables will be used to adjust for different outcomes. Thus, there must be agreement about the purpose of the case mix adjustment process, and different combinations and weightings of "adjusters" will be needed for different outcomes.

## THE NEED TO FOCUS ATTENTION ON LOW-INCOME POPULATIONS

Separate analysis of case mix adjusted outcomes for vulnerable populations would be very helpful. Published literature has shown that the elderly with chronic problems and impoverished minorities do tend to have poorer outcomes than other groups. Moreover, stratified analyses of vulnerable populations may reflect subtle, unmeasured case mix differences associated with nonbiological factors and will dramatize the true discrepancies in outcomes between the advantaged and the disadvantaged. Consequently, placing a bright analytic spotlight on these groups will provide more knowledge about key outcomes for vulnerable populations, who receive care largely through tax-supported dollars.

## THE NEED TO EMPHASIZE THE PROCESS OF CARE

It is precisely because outcomes matter most that there must be a special focus on processes of care. The processes of care, interacting with the patient and the sociocultural and physical environment, produce the outcomes, and if we wish to improve the outcomes, we must first understand the actual system of causation. Unless we get better at detecting what actually causes what, we can do little more than admire superior results and lament poor outcomes.

## FINAL COMMENT

Dr. Goldfield has provided a wonderful overview of public disclosure by highlighting the different (and sometimes conflicting) needs of different customers of case mix adjusted clinical information. He has shown how some key principles of modern improvement must be used if we are to reap the benefits of knowing more about variations in outcomes of care between different providers, practicing in different locations, and changes in trends over time. Yet it seems to this observer that there are two more needs that must be met for the power of case mix adjusted results to be unleashed.

### The Need to Foster Active, Cooperative, Action-Learning Networks

Outcomes will only improve if the delivery system improves. Improvement of this system will require detailed, professional knowledge about what works and what does not work and application of that knowledge in a systematic way. Cooperative networks of health professionals with a shared interest in attaining the optimal outcomes for the patients that they care for—when coupled with data feedback, reflection on results, interdisciplinary learning, and measured improvement trials—can accelerate interest in better results and can rapidly generate much improved outcomes at sharply reduced cost. The Northern New England Cardiovascular Group, the Dartmouth Primary Care Cooperative Information Project, the Vermont-Oxford Perinatal Network, and the Institute for Healthcare Improvement's Breakthrough Initiatives, to mention just a few examples, have shown how professional networking for learning and measuring and taking action can lead to substantially enhanced outcomes.

## The Need To Expand the Publication of Case Mix Adjusted Clinical Results To Include Measures of Value

The challenge that we face is to maximize biological outcomes, functional status, health risk status, and patient satisfaction with care while minimizing the short- and long-term direct and indirect costs of care. In other words, the public wants, and the providers need, to generate best *value* results today and improved value tomorrow. Healthcare value is a function of health outcomes (i.e., appropriateness of care, biological outcomes, functional status, risk status, and patient satisfaction) in relationship to health care–related costs (i.e., the direct medical care costs and the indirect social costs of receiving care and suffering from illness). Just as intelligent decisions about where to seek care cannot be made only on the basis of cost information, they cannot be made only on the basis of traditional clinical outcomes, even when they are appropriately case mix adjusted. What is needed is a parsimonious, balanced set of health outcome measures (including satisfaction) and costs for discrete patient populations followed over a relevant time frame.

Let us hope that the ideas expressed in Chapter 9, as well as the concepts discussed in the other contributions, will help push the technical knowledge base and health policy field closer to realizing the benefits that can flow from the measurement and communication of important information on the value of clinical care.

CHAPTER 20

# Public Disclosure: A Researcher's Perspective

*Edward L. Hannan*

I would like to comment briefly on some of the most important issues that arise in trying to ensure that publicly released outcomes data are as representative as possible of the relative quality of care that they are purportedly measuring and also to discuss briefly the process-outcome link. The examples pertain primarily to acute care outcomes reporting, but most of them are also applicable to the reporting of managed care outcomes.

In considering the release of risk-adjusted outcomes data, the accuracy, completeness, and validity of the data are of primary concern. The following discussion contains definitions of these criteria as well as recommended initiatives that can be taken to ensure that they are adequately addressed.

## DATA QUALITY

By the term *data quality*, I mean to refer to whether the data elements being used are accurately reported. To some extent, data quality depends on the original purpose of the data system being utilized for risk adjustment and public dissemination. For example, most administrative databases were created primarily for reimbursement purposes, and the patient's DRG is generally the determinant of the reimbursement level. Also, the DRG usually varies only according to the presence of an additional "complication," which actually means a complication or a comorbidity. Once a secondary diagnosis that places the patient into a higher paying DRG has been coded, there is no payment incentive for coding additional secondary diagnoses. Thus, there is frequently a large variation among hospitals in the number of secondary diagnoses that are coded. This can have an impact on the risk adjustment process, since the hospitals that code the most secondary diagnoses will benefit the most from risk adjustment.

For clinical databases that have been developed for the purpose of public dissemination or are eventually used for that purpose, the incentive is to code as many diagnoses or comorbidities as possible, because the sicker patients look, the better a hospital's risk-adjusted outcomes will be. Consequently, there is a need to audit the medical records that are the source of the data used for publicly reported risk-adjusted outcomes, and the audits must be extensive in order to avoid inattentiveness to data definitions and gaming of the system.

This means examining medical records to confirm the accuracy of what has been reported. The process is expensive and time consuming, but if public releases have the potential of ruining a provider's reputation, there is no other acceptable alternative. Sampling schemes can be developed to identify the cases and the hospitals most likely to have reporting problems, but there is no substitute for auditing a considerable number of records. This has been the policy of New York's Cardiac Surgery Reporting System since its inception. Nearly every year, the Department of Health has found the need to ask at least one hospital to recode all or part of its data, and the errors generally involve overcoding of risk factors. In contrast, undercoding of risk factors was found in the year prior to public release.

## COMPLETENESS

Completeness of data is also an important consideration. A hospital's mortality rate, and consequently its risk-adjusted mortality rate, can be drastically different if a few patients who died are not reported in the system (particularly for low-mortality procedures or DRGs). For administrative data that are linked to payment, this may not be as important, because hospitals would not receive reimbursement for cases that are not reported. However, some administrative databases are not linked to payment for all patients, and most clinical databases are not linked to payment. When databases that are not linked to reimbursement are used for risk adjustment, it is important that they be matched with another database known to be complete because it has the proper incentives for completeness. Even databases that are used for reimbursement do not necessarily contain all cases, and it is desirable to have another source for cross-checking.

## VALIDITY

### Multiple Measures of Quality

Ideally, validity is a measure of how accurately the risk-adjusted outcomes reflect relative quality of care. Unfortunately, there is no gold standard for quality of care. It should encompass patient satisfaction, appropriateness (the correct intervention being undertaken), effectiveness (the best possible outcomes having occurred, both in the long and in the short term), and arguably even efficiency (no more resources consumed than are necessary to achieve the best possible outcomes).

Because of data and resource limitations, most publicly disseminated acute care outcomes reports are limited to mortality and occasionally length of stay. However, it is important that all constituents of the provider-profiling effort commit themselves to obtaining and disseminating information on the other measures mentioned above. Rather than considering this concern to be a component of validity, a case could be made that it deserves its own moniker, perhaps the term *comprehensiveness*.

### Assessing Validity for a Specific Outcome

With respect to assessing the validity of a given measure such as mortality or length of stay, it is important to ensure that all (or as many as possible) measures of patient severity are available for use in the risk adjustment process. One way this can be done is by perusing the existing literature regarding important risk factors for patients with the procedure, diagnosis, or DRG of interest. If the literature identifies key risk factors that are not available in the database being used, this is a potential danger. This process should also include the examination of variables that represent socioeconomic status, because it has been demonstrated that Medicaid and uninsured patients' limited access to health care over an extended period of time can have an adverse effect on their ability to survive acute episodes of care.

Also, if statistical models presented in the literature yield much better predictions of adverse events than the model being used (based on measures such as $R^2$ for length of stay models and the $C$ statistic for mortality models), this is a warning sign that risk is not adequately being adjusted.

## Threats to Validity of Administrative Data

There are numerous studies that conclude that administrative or claims data are inadequate when used to adjust for severity for different groups of patients. In general, there are several problems associated with the use of administrative data for risk adjustment. First, they are usually not audited to ensure sufficient data quality (California represents an exception to this statement, although I am not knowledgeable enough about its system to opine whether its audits are comprehensive enough).

Second, administrative databases frequently do not contain important risk factors that are not diagnoses per se. For example, for coronary artery bypass graft patients, ejection fraction (the percentage of blood in the left ventricle that is expelled when it contracts) is not contained in administrative databases. Also, the stenosis (degree of blockage) in the carotid artery is not contained in administrative databases, but it is an important determinant of mortality, as is perioperative stroke among carotid endarterectomy patients.

Third, users (e.g., analysts) cannot generally determine whether the secondary diagnoses reported in administrative databases are comorbidities (present at admission to the hospital and therefore a necessary element of the risk-adjustment process) or complications of care (which should not be used to adjust for patient severity because they are reflective of the quality of inpatient care). Regions that use administrative data generally use risk adjustment software, such as Dr. Goldfield's APR-DRGs, to perform the risk adjustments. Most of these packages assign each patient to one or a limited number of severity groups based on the specific combination of diagnoses the patient has. When regions use administrative data and do not use one of these packages, they generally develop a statistical model using individual risk factors (e.g., this is what is done in California).

Regardless of whether a software package is used for administrative data or a statistical model is developed de novo, the analyst or software developer is confronted with a difficult problem: each secondary diagnosis must be classified as a complication or a comorbidity, because comorbidities but not complications are legitimate to use in a risk adjustment process.

For some diagnoses, there should be no doubt about their genesis. A chronic illness such as hypertension, diabetes, or asthma is clearly a comorbidity. Also, diagnoses in the International Classification of Diseases, Ninth Edition, Clinical Modification (ICD-9-CM) 996–999 range are clearly complications of care, because the description of these diagnoses is "Complications of Surgical and Medical Care, Not Elsewhere Classified." These diagnoses include problems such as "infection and inflammatory reaction due to in-dwelling urinary catheter," "postoperative shock," and "accidental puncture or laceration during a procedure."

Unfortunately, there are a multitude of other diagnoses that are not clearly complications or comorbidities. Sometimes, the nature of the patient admission will provide a clue. A patient admitted to a hospital for elective surgery who has a secondary diagnosis of pneumonia can be assumed to have contracted the pneumonia during the hospital admission (i.e., pneumonia is a complication in this case) because elective surgery would not be performed on a patient with pneumonia. On the other hand, a secondary diagnosis of pneumonia for a medical patient with a principal diagnosis having another pneumonia code can be assumed to be a comorbidity.

There are other situations that are not as straightforward but for which the preponderance of evidence is in favor of one alternative. Anemia or infection for a surgical patient would appear to be more likely a result of the surgery than a problem the patient had at admission to the hospital. It should be noted that, in theory, these problems could be coded as complications of care in the ICD-9-CM 996–999 range. For example, septicemia in elective surgery patients is frequently coded as ICD-9-CM code 038.9 (which indicates that the patient had septicemia prior to admission) rather than as 998.59 (which denotes post operative septicemia). Although it is possible that some elective surgery patients have pre-operative septicemia, one would expect that the vast majority of surgical patients with septicemia would have acquired it during the course of the hospital stay.

There are also patient types (procedures, DRGs) for which a particular secondary diagnosis could legitimately be either a complication or a comorbidity. One example is a myocardial infarction for coronary artery bypass surgery patients. Another is stroke for carotid endarterectomy patients. Clinical databases can distinguish between complications and comorbidities by having different sections of the form or data entry package devoted to each one. However, almost no administrative database has the so-called Mayo digit that notes for each secondary diagnosis whether it was present at admission. An exception is New York's Statewide Planning and Research Cooperative System (SPARCS), which has contained these fields since 1991, and California's administrative database. Nevertheless, an inspection of the coding of these fields in SPARCS does not inspire confidence in their accuracy (e.g., hypertension is sometimes coded as a complication and wound infection following surgery is sometimes coded as a comorbidity).

Thus, in many situations there is no way to confirm whether a secondary diagnosis is a complication or comorbidity without inspecting the patient's medical record. This option is usually too expensive and time consuming to be a viable alternative. Hence, what is done in practice by analysts who develop statistical risk adjustment models from scratch without using software packages is to either use the diagnosis as a comorbidity for all patients with the diagnosis (i.e., use it in the risk adjustment process if it is statistically significant) or assume it is a complication (i.e., never use it in the risk adjustment process). Presumably this is also the strategy used by the severity software packages, although it is impossible to know for sure because of the proprietary nature of their business.

If a secondary diagnosis is used in the risk adjustment process irrespective of whether it is a complication or comorbidity, the model will work better (i.e., have a higher $R^2$ for continuous outcome measures like length of stay and a higher $C$ statistic for binary outcome measures like mortality or live discharge), because complications are more strongly related to other adverse outcomes such as mortality or length of stay than comorbidities are. Thus, if a severity package errs in including secondary diagnoses that are primarily complications, it will benefit by looking better than packages that are more conservative about using secondary diagnoses, despite the fact it is flawed. Also, when this package is used for risk adjustment, hospitals with relatively more complications will benefit unfairly and hospitals with fewer will be disadvantaged.

My colleagues and I have published articles in *Medical Care* and *Health Services Research* that demonstrate that an administrative database (in one case SPARCS and in another case MEDPAR, the Medicare database) performs nearly as well as clinical data when predicting mortality for coronary artery bypass graft patients. However, when the clinical database is used to eliminate the inappropriate use of complications to predict mortality in the administrative database, the clinical database predicts mortality substantially better than the administrative database.

The only way to ensure that complications and comorbidities are accurately distinguished from one another is to add binary codes for secondary diagnoses that denote whether they were present at admission and to accompany this action with an audit process that confirms the accuracy of the codes.

## PROCESS-OUTCOME LINKS

I agree that it is important that efforts be made to relate significant differences in risk-adjusted outcomes among groups (hospitals, surgeons, regions, etc.) to differences in processes of care used by these groups. Without this critical step, quality improvement is doomed to be minimal.

I believe that health care providers must be responsible for improving the quality of care that they provide, because they are the ones who are in the best position to do so. However, I also believe that employer organizations, government, and the public should attempt to convince providers that altering processes of care will actually lead to better outcomes. This can be done by striving to make sure that process measures are part of the data system used for case mix adjustment whenever possible (note: this is not the case for most administrative data systems). The other effective mechanism is to advocate for public release of the data. Several New York cardiac surgeons and administrators have admitted off the record that they would never have examined their processes of care if the coronary artery bypass graft data had not been released to the public. I think the reason for this was not that they believed that the risk-adjusted data were reflective of quality of care, but that they needed to review the data since their names and their hospital's name were going to be in the newspaper. In many cases, the public releases have led to scrutiny that would not otherwise have occurred. Providing hospitals with as much process data as possible (particularly comparative process data in conjunction with risk-adjusted outcomes data) will serve to make hospitals' and surgeons' quality improvement efforts more effective.

## CONCLUSIONS

We are still in the infancy of the development of medical care scorecards and the dissemination of these scorecards to the public. There is much room for improvement with respect to the statistical methods that are used, the format for reporting provider assessments, the documentation of methods and data restrictions in public reports, and the careful statement of caveats associated with public releases. For lack of space, none of these important concerns has been discussed here. However, as important as they are, none is more important than the adequacy of the database being used to generate the provider assessments. The foregoing discussion has addressed several qualities that the database should possess. Most databases currently used for provider assessments lack at least one of these qualities, and it is essential that the "customers" of public releases (as Dr. Goldfield calls them) strive to develop new databases or alter current ones with these concerns in mind.

# PART II

# Fundamentals of Case Mix and Risk Adjustment

CHAPTER 21

# Overview: Case Mix, Risk Adjustment, Reinsurance, and Managed Care

*Norbert Goldfield*

The editor of this book poses a set of questions that policy makers, researchers, and practitioners must face as health reform, whether market or government driven, continues its torrid pace:

- Should a risk assessment methodology used to adjust capitation rates or to profile physicians and hospitals be based on differences in a patient's diagnosis (or diagnoses), health status, prior use of health services, or a combination of all three?
- What are the challenges in using the same risk adjustment for many purposes?
- Are claims-based data sufficient for the first step in the continuous quality improvement (CQI) process?
- What challenges do currently available case mix measures face in their use for risk adjustment for the purpose of adjusting capitation rates? Does reinsurance mitigate any of these issues?

On which factors should risk assessment methodology be based? The purpose of developing a risk assessment method for adjusting capitation rates is to predict future medical expenditures. Medical expenditures can be fairly predictable (e.g., maternity visits prior to a delivery) or random (e.g., gunshot

*Source*: Adapted from N. Goldfield, Foreword, *Managed Care Quarterly*, Vol. 2, No. 3, pp. iv–viii, Aspen Publishers, Inc., © 1994.

wound, automobile accident, or earthquake injuries). However, there is a broad range of predictability between these two extremes.

Thus, the treatment for heart disease (even if one knows detailed clinical information such as the patient's functional status) can vary dramatically and can differ by tens of thousands of dollars. Among other reasons, clinical differences and past treatment history must be taken into account in developing risk assessments for prediction of future medical expenditures. A managed care organization might prefer to utilize a risk assessment that limits itself to the current health status/diagnoses of an individual (e.g., ACGs or the RAND SF-36 questionnaire, a patient-completed form measuring health status). Although the use of past health services may be a more accurate reflection of future expenditures for an individual, a managed care plan might argue that including prior procedures would bias the capitation risk adjustment in favor of performing future procedures. This argument can be rebutted by the following example. Knowing whether a diabetic had a below-knee amputation is a critical piece of information regarding not only the current health status of this patient but also what the likelihood is of future treatment (such as another amputation) for this type of diabetic. Currently, no single risk assessment methodology is robust enough for capitation adjustment on a nationwide basis.

What are the problems inherent in using the same risk adjustment method for many purposes? There is considerable debate about which variables should be included when using a case mix measure for even one purpose, such as quality of care. The following exchange in the letters to the editor section in the *Journal of the American Medical Association*, discussing a study of mortality rates following coronary artery bypass grafts, illustrates this debate. Nontechnical readers may be put off by the clinical terms mentioned, but there is no need to worry about the specific words: you will still get the point. This exchange provides a glimpse of the range of opinions on which data should be included in a risk adjustment model for (in this case) quality management.

One of the letter writers criticizing the risk adjustment model wrote,

> The data elements may depend greatly on [individual] physician judgment, and the data elements may be a consequence of care rather than a risk factor. For example, the use of internal mammary artery bypass grafts, delays between cardiac catheterization and surgery, the performance of carotid endarterectomies during the same stay, and admitting patients through the emergency department . . .

may depend as much on clinical judgment and hospital practice as patient risk. . . . The diagnosis of congestive heart failure or the performance of certain abdominal surgeries may be a consequence of bypass surgery rather than a risk factor prior to surgery.

Therefore, certain types of complications may increase the apparent patient risk and therefore reward the hospitals whose patients have these complications. . . . If equations largely dependent on clinical judgment become standards for evaluating quality of care, physicians may change their practice to improve their risk-adjusted outcomes.[1]

The developers of the model, Luft and Romano, responded thus:

Hartz et al. note that some data elements . . . may actually be consequences of care rather than risk factors. Other variables . . . may reflect physician practice patterns. . . . Our model might have had less predictive power if such variables had been excluded. We fully agree with these comments. The investigator must make reasoned judgments about which variables are likely to represent underlying patient characteristics and which variables are more likely to represent the quality of care. The latter variables should not be used as predictors in a risk adjustment model. . . . Others may disagree with our judgments, but our approach gave hospitals the benefit of the doubt.[2(p.2298)]

In an era in which there is a great deal of talk about the necessity of continuous quality improvement (CQI), the tendency is still to find the bad apple. With all the pressures to disclose comparative information, it is important to give providers the benefit of the doubt where warranted while at the same time continuing to investigate opportunities for improvement using reliable and valid case mix measures.

Although this book includes case studies of a variety of methods well suited for both utilization management and quality-of-care purposes, the above debate shows why it is important to use these measures with care. Unfortunately, many managed care organizations do not appreciate the limitations of these methodologies and may use these case mix measures in deciding who should and should not be included in a provider network.

When comparing physicians with each other, or one hospital with another, the use of claims-based data versus data obtained from the medical record represents an important issue. As will be discussed in detail in the next chapter, the issue represents a flash point of debate. The editor believes that while case mix measures must be continuously improved, they only represent the first step in the quality improvement process. As such, the information derived must be easy and inexpensive to obtain, which restricts the information-gathering process to either claims-based data or to infrequently collected information from the medical record or other sources. At the same time, developers of case mix methodologies have the obligation to improve continuously the type of information collected. For example, when the state of California recently mandated the use of a claims-based method for comparison of hospitals, the state also mandated that hospitals determine whether the secondary diagnoses listed on the discharge form were present on admission. This relatively simple data collection step will enable hospitals and consumers to assess better whether secondary diagnoses represent complications or comorbidities.

What are the caveats for using case mix measures to adjust capitation rates? Does reinsurance or the establishment of risk corridors for capitation rates mitigate any of these issues? A national expert recently summarized the problems facing risk adjusters for capitation payment: implementing a risk adjustment system based only on age and gender is equivalent to implementing a per-case hospital payment system, such as the Medicare Prospective Payment System, without an adequate case mix measure.

If the Clinton Administration had proposed a reform of Medicare hospital payment to adjust rates only for age and gender, it would have been obvious that some type of case mix classification system was necessary. If the administration had been told that it would take several years until a DRG-type case mix system could be developed, Congress would have told the administration to come back after a viable case mix measure was developed. Unfortunately, the administration is making just this type of argument for risk adjusters.[3]

It is true that the list of risk adjusters from Exhibit 21–1 includes a large number of variables beyond age and sex. However, the reason for hesitancy by experts is that, whereas DRGs represent a per-case payment, capitation constitutes the entire payment for a group of patient expenditures for a whole year, paid on a per-person, per-month basis. Each month, the practitioner/institution will have to provide all the care required for that member for a flat fee. If the estimate of expected care on which the payment is based is too low, the provider risks underpayment; if too high, the plan pays for services not

**Exhibit 21–1** Variables Used in Creating Risk Adjustment Models

Demographic factors
Diagnostic information
Patient-derived health status
Claims-derived health status
Prior use of all services
Prior use of nonelective hospitalization
Prior use of procedure performed

*Source*: Reprinted from *Managed Care Quarterly*, Vol. 2, No. 3, p. iv, Aspen Publishers, Inc., © 1994.

rendered. That is the risk both parties assume with capitation—and the reason a realistic projection is desirable.

However, it is little known that the value of the multiple correlation coefficient, or $R^2$, of less than 0.15 for the total payment of DRGs provided to a hospital is 0.9, much higher than the current 0.5, which in turn is better than any risk adjustment methodology available today.[4] This means that even if one were to accept 0.5 (50 percent of the variation in medical expenditures is explained by the risk assessment method), that means that half is left unexplained.

Promising a primary care physician that 15 percent of the payment for his entire panel of patients covered by the HMO has been adjusted simply means that 85 percent is still unexplained. This allows for a large margin of error, particularly if the information is used to make final determinations on which physicians should be selected for inclusion in a managed care network. Rather, this information should be used in a quality improvement manner to feed back information to physicians and work with them to effect changes in practice patterns.

Put another way, how much faith should a managed care plan have in a risk adjustment model used for adjusting capitation rates—even one as good as ACGs or Health Chex (Rochester, New York)—when, according to the Risk Adjustment Work Group of the American Academy of Actuaries (AAA), 4 percent of claimants in a typical insurance plan generate as much as 50 percent of the claim costs?[5]

Is it not conceivable that within this framework, managed care plans will figure out ways to improve their chances of picking out the good risks? Again, according to the AAA, "In such an environment, there would be a tremendous incentive for insurers to take advantage of any gaps in the regulatory structure and attempt to create new ways to avoid the worst health risks in order to assure survival, gain profitability, or simply minimize the risk of insolvency."[6(p.9)]

The cherry-picking problem is compounded when one is trying to assess the risk for the individual who decides to switch plans after a year. The risk adjustment for the entire health plan may be a problem if, for example, most of the sick individuals all opt for a specific plan. Whatever $R^2$ is present for any of the currently available risk adjusters, the reality is that "risk adjusters currently being proposed would not be accurate enough to protect carriers from the adverse selection that can result within a purchasing cooperative where individuals are allowed to choose any plan they want," according to the AAA work group's report.[7(p.5)]

The challenge facing the adjustment of capitation rates for clinicians treating certain types of patients is even greater. In many managed care plans, a patient typically can decide to choose the plan offering the widest array of services at the best price and often has a choice of physician from a wide panel. While this is the theory, the reality is that all practitioners participating in managed care arrangements know a variety of ways to avoid chronically ill or difficult-to-manage patients and to target populations that have lower illness burdens.

There are two interim solutions to adjust the results obtained with currently available risk assessment methods: (1) reinsurance and (2) risk corridors for different types of capitation payments. New York State implemented a risk pool for 15 specific diseases in 1993. Under a nationwide approach, health plans would share the costs of treating patients who incur expenses above a certain level. Unfortunately, the reinsurance approach does not provide any respite for low-income, community-based clinics. The fairest approach to solving the capitation risk adjustment problem is to establish different capitation rates and, just as importantly, the use of risk corridors. Capitation rates should be different for healthy middle-class groups than for low-income groups with a large number of acquired immune deficiency syndrome (AIDS) patients. Just as importantly, the upside profit potential and downside loss potential should be limited by the imposition of actuarially determined reimbursement corridors.

In the short term, differing capitation rates with risk corridors will not be acceptable in a political climate that emphasizes the wonders of the free market. In the long term, it is likely that the relatively small number of health plans that remain after the initial free market push will demand such an approach for their own economic survival.

## CONCLUSIONS

Case mix measures are used to compare hospitals, managed care plans, and physicians with each other. Case mix measures are also utilized to adjust payment rates for these same groups. Case mix measures represent the fundamental building blocks that measure clinical differences in groups of patients. It is important to be careful how these measures are used, as quality of care delivered to patients is at stake. Risk adjustment methodologies are excellent for physician profiling if one adopts them as the first step in the quality improvement process. Differences in hospital or primary care practice profiles, adjusted for the case mix measures, often reveal quality improvement opportunities.

This first step is the easy part. The hard part comes in working together with the health care team to determine the sources for these differences. After identifying and implementing solutions, the quality improvement process just continues. As befits true commitment to quality improvement, risk assessment methodologies will only improve. In turn, this will provide the health care team with a greater ability to deal with "treasures" uncovered by applying case mix measures.

---

NOTES

1. Letters to the editor, A.J. Hartz, E.M. Kuh, and E.L. Kayser letter to editor on "Coronary Artery Bypass Graft Mortality: Patient Risk or Physician Practice," *JAMA* 270 (1993): 2298.

2. H. Luft and P. Roman, reply to Hartz, Kuh, and Kayser letter, *JAMA* 270 (1993): 2298.

3. Testimony by Gerard F. Andersen, Ph.D., Director of the Center for Hospital Finance and Management, Johns Hopkins University School of Public Health, before the Subcommittee on Health Committee on Ways and Means, U.S. House of Representatives, Hearings on Risk Selection and Health Plan Adjustment Issues in Health Care Reform, 9 November 1993.

4. Information provided by Jim Vertrees, Solon Inc.

5. Testimony by the Risk Adjustment Work Group, American Academy of Actuaries before the Subcommittee on Health Committee on Ways and Means, U.S. House of Representatives, Hearings on Risk Selection and Health Plan Adjustment Issues in Health Care Reform, 9 November 1993.
6. Testimony by the Risk Adjustment Work Group.
7. Testimony by the Risk Adjustment Work Group.

CHAPTER 22

# Understanding Your Managed Care Practice: The Critical Role of Case Mix Systems

*Norbert Goldfield*

Without being directly used for physician payment, case mix systems have had a significant effect on physician practice patterns.[1] Case mix systems have been used, with dramatic results, for the payment of hospitals. This effect has grown from the original legislative intent as a hospital payment system for inpatient care to one that is used for contracting and severity-adjusted physician profiling by health maintenance organizations (HMOs) and other managed care organizations (MCOs; for a discussion of severity, see Exhibit 22–1) and identification of areas to be targeted for quality improvement for both hospitals and MCOs. Over the past decade, this increased use of case mix adjusters has been aided by significant refinements of diagnosis-related group (DRG) case mix systems and the development of case mix systems for ambulatory care.

The use of inpatient case mix systems for payment has had a significant effect on other aspects of the health care system. Of great significance, the use of DRGs for Medicare payment encouraged an already strong trend toward the use of outpatient services.[2] This rapid growth of outpatient services prompted a managerial and regulatory demand for outpatient case mix systems such as ambulatory patient groups (APGs).[3]

Health professionals and institutions can derive significant benefits from ambulatory and inpatient case mix adjustment systems. These sys-

*Source*: Adapted from *Managed Care Quarterly*, Vol. 2, No. 3, pp. 12–20, Aspen Publishers, Inc., 1994.

**Exhibit 22–1** The Meanings of Severity

If possible, *severity* is even more misunderstood than the term *quality improvement*. In discussing severity it is important to first define several terms that are often used interchangeably. It is critical that the applied research community clearly distinguish between these terms.

*Severity of illness* refers to the relative levels of loss of function. At a minimum, this function can be measured in physiologic terms and the ability to perform activities of daily living. *Treatment difficulty* refers to the patient management problems that a particular illness presents to the health care provider. Such management problems are associated with illnesses without a clear pattern of symptoms, illnesses requiring sophisticated and technically difficult procedures, and illnesses requiring close monitoring and supervision. *Need for intervention* relates to the severity of illness that lack of immediate or continuing care would produce. *Resource intensity* or *severity of service* refers to the relative volume and types of diagnostic, therapeutic, and bed services used in the management of a particular illness.

*Source*: Reprinted from *Managed Care Quarterly*, Vol. 2, No. 3, p. 17, Aspen Publishers, Inc., © 1994.

tems are useful for quality improvement in that classification systems such as DRGs and APGs can be used to break down health care services into basic building blocks. Each component is unique because each contains diagnoses and/or procedures that are similar from both a clinical and resource consumption point of view. Thus, the components can be used to improve understanding of resource consumption and aspects of quality for inpatient and outpatient activities.

As these basic building blocks consist of a variety of services packaged together, they can also be used to provide an incentive for appropriate resource use, although this is not exactly how the Medicare program uses DRGs. However, institutions are using quality improvement techniques to understand how to improve resource use, thereby maximizing reimbursement per DRG. In either case, institutions are looking to quality improvement in an effort to enhance quality and lower costs.

It should be emphasized that case mix systems are useless without the significant interest, capability, and support of medical leaders. DRGs and APGs are merely tools; they do not provide answers by themselves. They do not constitute action. In turn, medical leaders need support from both front-line practicing physicians and senior nonphysician administrators from the institution. Case mix tools are very important but are only one of many weapons in the medical director's armamentarium. They can be most effectively used within a context of overall institutional commitment to quality improvement. In fact, once a commitment to quality improvement exists, follow-through will be difficult without the use of case mix tools.

## HISTORICAL BACKGROUND OF CASE MIX SYSTEMS

The current commitment to quality improvement can be traced back to the late Eugene Codman, a surgeon at the Massachusetts General Hospital in Boston. Whereas much of his work has been seen as a precursor to outcomes studies, his work can also be seen as an antecedent of DRGs and APGs. In his path-breaking article, appropriately entitled "The Product of a Hospital," Dr. Codman wrote, "It would be supposed that in the annual reports of hospitals, some account of their products would be found. To a certain extent this is true, but often, much of the material in an annual report is but a mere account of money subscribed and the proportionate amounts which are spent on the different departments."[4]

When Dr. Codman presented his data examining outcomes of care to his colleagues at the annual conference of the American College of Surgeons meeting at the Waldorf Astoria, they responded by burning his report in the fireplace of the meeting hall. Case mix research remained at this unappreciated level until the late 1960s, when Robert Fetter and other researchers at Yale University began to adopt a fresh look at this issue. "In 1967, a group of physicians at our local university hospital asked for help with a problem regarding utilization review. At the time, two years after the start of the Medicare program, all hospitals were required to operate a program of UR [utilization review] and quality assurance as a condition of Medicare participation. The physicians asked whether industrial methods of cost and quality control could be adapted and applied to the hospital industry."[5]

Sixteen years later, DRGs were implemented by the Health Care Financing Administration (HCFA) for inpatient hospital care reimbursement under

Medicare's Prospective Payment System (PPS). It must be emphasized that the DRGs' developers did not initially envision their use for payment. In responding to the request by physicians at Yale–New Haven Hospital, Fetter and his colleagues tried to develop a system that would be useful for managerial purposes. In creating this management tool, the developers were guided by several considerations. Their goals included having

- class definitions based on information routinely collected on hospital abstracts
- a manageable number of classes
- similar patterns of resource intensity within a given class
- clinically similar types of patients in a given class[6]

This organizational approach resulted in the DRGs implemented in the early 1980s. There are four critical parts to understanding the structure of DRGs:

1. organ system
2. distinction between surgical and medical procedure
3. categorization of procedures and categorization of medical problems
4. other indicators that differentiate processes of care

Age, comorbidities, and complications constitute indicators that modify the DRG assignment. Physician panels were involved in examining each ICD-9-CM code (International Classification of Diseases, Ninth Edition, Clinical Modification) to identify codes that constituted comorbidities and complications according to the following algorithm: a substantial complication or comorbidity was defined as a condition that, in combination with a specific principal diagnosis, would cause an increase in length of stay by at least one day in at least 75 percent of the patients.[7] This effort to identify complications and/or comorbidities resulted in a list of approximately 1,000 ICD-9-CM codes. Virtually this same list of codes is still used by HCFA.

Medicare PPS has been successful in controlling the growth in Medicare inpatient expenditures, which in 1990 were annually $18 billion less than during the early 1980s.[8] As a result, it was natural that the federal government would look for an outpatient equivalent, given the staggering rise in Medicare outpatient expenditures.

## AMBULATORY CASE MIX SYSTEMS

The cost of ambulatory care services has exploded over the past 10 years. The reasons for this dramatic increase are many and include clinical, regulatory, and competitive factors. Analysts point to the implementation of Medicare DRGs in 1983 as a key factor contributing to the rise in demand for ambulatory services.[9] Other key factors include the introduction of new, rapidly changing medical technology and the spread of managed care. Regulators and employers who demanded better control of inpatient costs in the 1980s have now shifted their attention to ambulatory care, which has increased in both quantity and cost. This increase has prompted payers, clinicians, and health services researchers to try to understand better the content of the ambulatory care encounter.

It is particularly important that the conceptual issues pertaining to ambulatory case mix systems (ACMS) be discussed to fully understand how to measure resource consumption and quality of care for managed care services. Accurate understanding of resource consumption and clinical coherence are two keys to developing a valid ambulatory care classification system for payment and quality improvement purposes. Whether one uses an ACMS for either visits or episodes, for quality management or payment, it is imperative that the different classes statistically reflect differences in current resource consumption, prediction of future resource consumption, or clinical status of patient groups. However, the complexity of ambulatory care services increases the challenge of making an ACMS clinically cogent. This must be accomplished; otherwise, health professionals who use the ACMS will not perceive it as clinically cogent.

## COMPONENTS AND CHALLENGES OF AN ACMS

There can be up to three parts to an ACMS: (1) the classification system; (2) the "bundling" algorithm of the classes that serves to describe the entire ambulatory encounter; and (3) if the ACMS is to be used for reimbursement, a payment computation. Some ACM systems consist only of a classification component. In these systems, each member of a class consumes similar resources. Each class purports to describe similar ambulatory encounters, from either a resource consumption or clinical cogency perspective. Ambulatory visit groups and diagnosis clusters are examples of this type of ACMS.

Other ACMSs combine or bundle different classes that together describe an ambulatory episode or visit. The bundling logic depends on clinical and non-clinical factors such as cost and frequency of performance of a test. Thus, a plain radiology film might represent a service that could be bundled into primary care services provided during an encounter. APGs are examples of this type of ACMS. Ambulatory care groups (ACGs) represent a combination of a larger number of groups, ambulatory diagnosis groups (ADGs).

If the system is to be used for payment, a third component of the ACMS must be developed. That is, the resources consumed in each class, or combination of classes, must be translated into a dollar amount. APGs are an example of a system specifically developed to be used for payment.

There are two main obstacles to creating an ACMS: (1) the complexity of ambulatory encounters and (2) problems inherent in current coding systems. Ambulatory encounters are complex for both clinical and organizational reasons. Ambulatory care represents services that are frequently provided for poorly understood clinical conditions.[10] A large percentage of ambulatory care visits have as their principal diagnosis a sign, symptom, or finding for which, at the completion of the visit, the clinician has not decided on a firm diagnosis.[11]

The poorly understood nature of many conditions seen in outpatient encounters is exacerbated by a poor understanding of patient motivations for seeking medical care.[12] Not only do patients often complain of symptoms for which medical science has not developed effective treatment (e.g., back pain), but there also is often a difference of opinion between physician and patient as to whether the condition was fully and satisfactorily treated. Thus, the inadequate medical understanding of back pain, for example, presents significant difficulties in creating a clinically cogent class of similarly costing visits for back pain, which is one of the most frequent reasons for ambulatory encounters.

There are two aspects to the administrative complexity of ambulatory care. From a geographic perspective, patient and physician alike are typically confronted with myriad possible institutions or care settings from which needed services may be obtained. Many of these are widely scattered across a service area. In addition, unlike the inpatient setting where physicians and nurses typically coordinate all aspects of patient care, there is usually no such coordination in the ambulatory care arena unless the patient specifically has been assigned a case manager by his or her health plan, a not uncommon occurrence with high-risk or high-cost cases in managed care or workers' compensation but a less common phenomenon for routine care. Even if the patient is enrolled in an HMO that aims to provide managed care, there often is little true coordination of care among physician offices, laboratories, and radiology facilities, which, in health plans that are not based on group practices or staff clinics, may be located miles apart.

The diffuse nature of ambulatory care merely adds to the difficulty of packaging ambulatory encounters into one category. In contrast to outpatient services, there is little difficulty in defining beginning and end points for inpatient care. When a patient remains overnight in the hospital, his or her entire daily existence occurs within those four walls, making the content of inpatient care far easier to measure.

Another major difficulty in developing an ACMS is the appropriate definition of a new ambulatory care patient. This critical issue is one that bridges clinical and organizational concerns. Several of the visit-based systems use new patient versus old patient as a classifying variable. This variable is used based on the assumption that a new patient consumes a different quantity of resources than an old patient.

However, the validity of this distinction becomes suspect when one attempts to define *new*. A patient can be new to the primary care practitioner, to the practitioner seeing the patient on that occasion, to the institution, or to the health plan but not to the practitioner. Newness may represent a structural element of the physician-patient encounter that, similar to many other structural measures of quality, intuitively appears to be a reasonable predictor of resource consumption but on further examination cannot be clearly specified with a high degree of reliability.

The inadequacy of current coding systems further complicates the already difficult task of developing an ACMS. Two coding systems are in common use in the United States today, ICD-9-CM and the Current Procedures and Terminology, Fourth Edition (CPT-4). CPT-4 is procedure oriented and is primarily used in physician offices. ICD-9-CM is primarily intended and organized for inpatient care. They are not parallel coding systems.

As if this were not enough, ambulatory encounters are poorly understood and difficult to classify for several other reasons, including the following:

- deficiencies in clinical knowledge
- varied patient responses to the same poorly understood clinical condition
- different settings, even within the same institution or health plan, from which the patient can choose to obtain ambulatory services

- facility-specific variables such as queuing

The next sections describe two case mix systems in common use today: APGs and all-patient-refined DRGs (APR-DRGs).

## AMBULATORY PATIENT GROUPS

APGs were developed under a HCFA contract as an ACMS that could be used for ambulatory care prospective payment. The Department of Health and Human Services has published in the *Federal Register* the proposed implementation of outpatient prospective payment system using a derivative of Ambulatory Patient groups—ambulatory patient categories (APCs).[13] While this discussion will use the term APGs, the APCs the Health Care Financing Administration is considering share many characteristics with APGs. APGs are a patient classification scheme designed to explain the amount and type of resources used in an ambulatory care visit. Cases in a given APG have similar patient clinical characteristics, similar resource uses, and similar costs. The process of formulating the APGs was highly iterative—statistical data derived from large claims-based data sources were compared with clinical judgment. The end result is a clinically consistent group of patient classes that are homogeneous in resource use.

There are 145 procedure APGs, 80 medical APGs, and 72 ancillary service APGs, for a total of 297. APGs as currently constructed describe the complete range of services provided in the outpatient setting. They can form the basic building blocks of a visit-based outpatient PPS and/or provide a flexible structure that allows managed care organizations to use APGs for contracting and physician-profiling purposes.

APGs contain several significant departures from DRGs:

- The initial classification variable for APGs is whether or not a significant procedure was performed. A significant procedure is scheduled normally, represents the main reason for the visit, and dominates the time and resources expended during the visit. A medical visit occurs if a provider was seen, but a significant procedure was not performed. Examples of *significant procedure APGs* include carpal tunnel repair and stress tests. Examples of *medical APGs* include hypertension, headache, and hematological malignancy.

- There can be only one DRG per hospital stay, but there can be more than one APG per ambulatory visit.
- DRGs use ICD-9-CM for classification; APGs use both ICD-9-CM and CPT-4 codes.

## Payment for Ambulatory Services Using APGs

In constructing APGs, the developers decided that a visit-based PPS for ambulatory care had to have three components: (1) a patient classification scheme (APGs themselves), (2) a significant procedure consolidation and ancillary packaging process, and (3) payment computation and discounting. When a patient has multiple significant procedures, some of the significant procedures may require minimal additional time or resources. Significant procedure consolidation refers to collapsing multiple related significant-procedure APGs into a single APG to determine payment. For example, if both a simple repair and complex repair (two separate APGs) are coded on a patient bill, only the complex skin incision will be used in the APG payment computation.

A patient with a significant procedure or a medical visit may have ancillary services performed as part of the visit. Ancillary packaging refers to including certain ancillary services into the APG payment rate for a significant procedure or medical visit. A uniform list of ancillary APGs that are always packaged into a significant procedure or medical visit was developed. Examples of packaged APGs are plain films and electrocardiograms. Packaging is a critical part of the APG system. Without it, there would be no economic incentive to use appropriately services such as complete blood counts and plain films. These services may appear to be inconsequential. However, such small ticket items constitute almost 60 percent of all claims submitted to Medicare for outpatient services.

## Monitoring Quality of Care

Whereas APGs were developed for Medicare outpatient services payment, they can assist continuous quality improvement (CQI) efforts. For example, an institution attempting to document the results of a CQI intervention in the area of vaccination can effectively use APGs because they combine a large number of vaccine-related CPT-4 codes into one of three groups, based on resource cost of the three groups—thus profiling vaccination rates more effectively than using more than 50 CPT-4 codes, which is the usual approach.

APGs can also identify potential areas of inappropriate use of services or resources. For example, using control charts, one might track the use of ancillaries for elective procedures such as upper gastrointestinal endoscopies, herniorrhaphies, and cataract removals. These results could be profiled by physician, ambulatory care setting, or other organizational variables. Of course, aberrant results provided by APGs should not be used as definitive measures of inappropriate utilization. Instead, the results could be tracked over time using a control chart, if a large database is available. If results show consistent inappropriate utilization, a CQI team could then attempt to determine the sources of or reasons for the aberrant statistics.

Lastly, APGs give decision makers, particularly those in managed care organizations, an accurate picture of the types of patients served by their primary care practitioners. This information can be used to assign them reasonably sized patient loads that can, in turn, result in increased practitioner and patient satisfaction.

## APPLYING APR-DRGs TO MANAGED CARE

APR-DRGs can help physicians in managed care organizations target areas for quality improvement. Most managed care plans contract with hospitals on the basis of either simplistic combinations of DRGs, per diems, or capitation. This approach assumes that it is the hospital and its full-time personnel that have the responsibility for understanding the factors leading to increased resource consumption and poor quality. Managed care physicians increasingly will be asked by hospital managers to involve themselves in hospital operations and to understand how they can contribute to quality improvement that benefits their patients.

Using claims-based case mix systems will improve managed care physicians' ability to identify the best contracting opportunities and to work with their administrative colleagues in explaining variations in resource consumption and quality of care. Many hospitals and managed care companies are currently using severity-adjusted DRGs. Over the past year, interest in severity-adjustment tools has risen dramatically, particularly with the arrival of claims-based analytic tools such as APR-DRGs, which are much less labor-intensive than medical-records-based tools such as MedisGroups (created by Medi-Qual, Inc.) and the computerized severity index (CSI).

Before discussing current DRG variants used throughout the world, it is important to specify a lexicon of the confusing DRG terminology (see Exhibit 22–2). When the DRG definitions were originally developed in the 1970s, DRGs were intended to describe all types of patients seen in the acute-care hospital. Unfortunately, conventional analyses by DRG can provide an insufficient and incomplete comparison of cost, length of stay, and mortality data.

When the efficiency of providers showing higher costs or length of stay is questioned, the typical response is, "My patients are sicker." A more refined classification system, then, is needed to identify the patients with different resource needs and outcomes. Beginning in 1985, considerable effort was extended to refine DRGs to account for complexity without having to resort to examining the medical record; these refinements described all use information derived from the claims form. The result is that DRGs have become a universal language that hospitals, managed care organizations, and insurers now use in discussing the product of the hospital.

## Refining DRGs for Severity of Illness

Researchers have refined DRG technologies in an effort to defuse the never-ceasing tension among the many purposes for measuring case mix. For managed care organizations, this tension is between understanding differences in resource consumption in contrast to an enhanced comprehension of the differences in extent of illnesses in patients.

While it is often the case that understanding resource consumption and understanding the extent of illness are one and the same, this is not always so. Many managed care administrators are most interested in a severity-adjusted case mix system that provides an improved statistical explanation of the variance in resource consumption within a DRG category. In contrast, managed care physicians can best understand the reasons for treatment pattern differences if and only if they believe that these differences have taken into account the extent or severity of the illness of the patients.

In deciding whether to concentrate primarily on intensity of resource consumption or on severity of illness, it is important to question who is most likely to benefit from an improved explanation of variance in resource consumption: the physicians, managed care organizations, or other members of the health care team. Both the medical and administrative leadership need to

**Exhibit 22–2** DRG Terminology

---

**HCFA DRGs:** These DRGs are used by HCFA for hospital reimbursement on a prospective basis for Medicare (over 65) patients. They are updated annually. A contract for their enhancement is provided to researchers at 3M/Health Information Systems, with final decisions resting with researchers and policy makers within HCFA.

**AP-DRGs:** All-patient DRGs are used by New York State for prospective payment for all non-Medicare inpatient services provided in the state. They have been specifically developed to account for cost variance for all ages and types of patients. Thus, the National Association of Children's Hospitals and Related Institutions (NACHRI) provides input in the formation of these DRGs as they apply to pediatric populations. They are updated annually with input provided by researchers at 3M/Health Information Systems and researchers/policy makers working at the New York State Department of Health.

**Yale Refined DRGs:** In the mid-1980s, the researchers developing the original DRGs subdivided the HCFA DRGs into subclasses (three for medical and four for surgical) based on differences in resource consumption resulting from the presence of specific comorbidities and complications.

**APR-DRGs:** All-patient-refined DRGs are used by hospitals and governmental organizations to examine issues of complexity or severity within a DRG. They are applicable to all ages and types of patients. They have not been used for payment or budgeting purposes, as many of the APR-DRG categories are too small for the purpose of setting a payment weight. Four classes are created for both medical and surgical DRGs. Classes represent distinct differences between patients in both resource consumption and severity of illness.

*Source*: Reprinted from *Managed Care Quarterly*, Vol. 2, No. 3, p. 17, Aspen Publishers, Inc., 1994.

---

decide which dependent variable (i.e., costs, length of stay, mortality, or complications) needs to be better explained.

The intended audience for DRG refinements, such as the APR-DRGs, is both the administrative and medical leadership in the managed care setting. That is to say, the APR-DRGs attempt to explain, using claims information, the variance in severity of illness and intensity of service for patients enrolled in a managed care plan. The APR-DRGs attempt to bridge these two diverse audiences by providing insight into cost differences between illness categories that have been adjusted for severity. While variance in cost may represent a variance in severity of illness in 80 percent of the cases, there are notable exceptions. An example can help clarify the severity of illness debate.

There is likely to be no disagreement that a patient with a decubitus ulcer consumes more resources than a similar patient without one. However, is that same patient more severely ill simply by virtue of the fact that the patient has a decubitus ulcer? This is a difficult question to answer, one that needs clinical research for a definitive response. Many clinicians would indicate that a pneumonia patient with a decubitus ulcer is not much more severely ill than one without. On the other hand, most clinicians would similarly agree that a diabetic patient with a decubitus ulcer is indeed more severely ill than one without such an ulcer.

The many issues undergirding this example demonstrate why there is confusion within both the academic research community and the market over what, exactly, the competing severity of illness systems really measure: severity of illness, intensity of service, or both.

To compound the severity determination problem, many clinicians and marketers of proprietary severity products encourage belief in the following hypothesis: increased severity of illness during a hospital stay, as measured by their system, correlates with increased problems in quality of care delivered to the patient. Little research has been performed to investigate this assertion.

A recent study examined whether two frequently used severity-of-illness systems, CSI and MedisGroups, are able to identify quality-of-care problems.[14] Worsening severity of illness for hospitalized patients was correlated with physician assessments of quality problems. They found inconsistent correlation between increased severity and problems in quality of care as measured by examination of the medical record.

## The APR-DRG Logic

The APR-DRGs are used by hundreds of hospitals and are used by 20 organizations in 20 states for public comparative purposes. The logic of the APR-DRGs is provided in an effort to enable readers to ask challenging questions of vendors as they decide between the many competing systems present in the market.

APR-DRGs determine class assignments by examining several aspects of a patient's stay in the hospital, according to these guidelines:

- Each of the APR-DRGs is divided into four possible subclasses—minor, moderate, major, and extreme—to which a case may be assigned. The more classes a severity system contains, the better the statistical performance. While there may be better statistical performance, the number of cases in each class will be less and less, thus diminishing the value in having more classes.
- There are two scores for each patient: one for severity of illness and one for risk of mortality. It is important for the user to identify institutional objectives and see whether these objectives are met with the score(s) provided by the severity-of-illness measure under review.
- APR-DRGs are based on the all-payer DRGs (AP-DRGs), not HCFA DRGs. Thus, the base APR-DRGs are more relevant for the entire population, whereas the HCFA DRGs are most relevant for Medicare. For example, there are virtually no HCFA neonatal DRGs, an area of critical importance for managed care plans and physicians trying to manage these very expensive patients.
- Class assignment is adjusted if the secondary diagnosis is typically part of the principal diagnosis. Urinary retention, usually a Class 2 type comorbidity, becomes Class 1 if the principal diagnosis is prostatic hypertrophy or if a transurethral resection of the prostate is performed.
- Class assignment is also adjusted in the reverse direction. An uncomplicated diabetic patient having a vaginal delivery is placed into a higher class by virtue of the diabetes itself.
- Age per se constitutes a modifier. For example, pediatric patients with bone infections are placed into a higher class than adults with similar comorbidities. Bone infections in pediatric patients are frequently more severe due to the active growth plate in their bones.
- The principal diagnosis itself may modify class assignment. Thus, for example, a patient with diabetic hyperosmolar coma as a principal diagnosis is certainly different from a straightforward diabetic patient, regardless of whatever other secondary diagnoses the two patients may have. A patient with an anterior wall myocardial infarction has a higher risk of mortality than a patient with an inferior wall myocardial infarction.

- The performance of a non-operating-room invasive procedure, such as the implantation of a temporary pacemaker, can also at times serve to adjust the class assignment of a patient's comorbidities. For example, it is difficult, if not impossible, to assess the clinical significance for a patient who has complete heart block as a secondary diagnosis. It is certainly more than a Class 1 secondary diagnosis; however, there is a range in the severity of illness of patients who have complete heart block. Some patients walk around with this condition while others need immediate and intensive medical intervention. Thus, the class assignment of a patient with complete heart block is modified if a temporary pacemaker is implanted during the hospitalization.
- The most significant theoretical advance in the APR-DRGs is that the interaction of secondary diagnoses is taken into account. This has represented a significant conundrum for researchers in the field. A thorough examination is particularly important for more severely ill patients. For example, traditional DRG refinements have not been able to adequately explain the severity of illness of patients in intensive care units. An examination of patients with multiple comorbid diagnoses represents a significant advance in the DRG refinement technology. All physicians appreciate that many patients who are admitted have multiple comorbidities. Thus, a patient with diabetes out of control may have a pulmonary problem on top of congestive heart failure. Surely this patient is distinct from a diabetic patient who has a decubitus ulcer and cellulitis. Not only are these patients clinically distinct, but, more important, it is necessary to know whether each of these two patients' multiple comorbidities interact.

Managed care plans have many hospitals under contract and need to compare and contrast performance on a number of clinical variables over time. There is also an increased trend toward capitation of hospital services. Not surprisingly, hospitals also use severity systems such as APR-DRGs for contracting purposes when negotiating with managed care plans. Hospital systems use APR-DRGs to adjust capitation rates paid them by managed care plans.

Once a severity adjustment tool is adopted by an institution, a managed care physician might use the following strategy. If top leadership supports quality improvement and believes in the value of severity-adjusted case mix data, then comparisons among classes of patients should be made over a period of time. These data should then be plotted on a graph using a control chart methodology to identify whether a difference in cost, for example, represents a true difference or a random event.

If differences remain, a comparison of groups of patients in similar classes will, at minimum, reveal whether these classes of patients contain differences in costs. If so, it would not be unreasonable to ask why such a difference exists. If the methodology defining the severity-of-illness classes is valid, two possibilities exist: (1) either the cost differentials between the two groups of patients in the same class represent differences in practice style that occasionally lead to unnecessary utilization of services, or (2) problems in quality resulted in the increased utilization of services to rectify the quality-of-care problems.

If the administrative leadership is either unsupportive or unclear about the benefits of case mix systems, it is up to the managed care physician to work with the medical director and create a critical mass of understanding and support for the case mix system among the other physicians. Clinical coherence and claims-based inpatient case mix systems represent an important advance in efforts to understand better the sources of variation in resource consumption and quality of care.

## RECENT APG AND DRG DEVELOPMENT TRENDS

Several development efforts involving DRGs and APGs are currently underway. These development efforts represent a microcosm of similar refinement efforts in many case mix systems. Continued refinement of APR-DRGs proceeds with a particular emphasis on (1) understanding specific aspects of interactions between comorbidities and primary/secondary diagnoses (current research will likely improve the capacity of these case mix systems to measure variance of cost, length of stay, or other variables) and (2) determining the differences between mortality and charges in constructing a severity system.

With ongoing refinement of APGs and APR-DRGs, the development of ways of measuring episodes of illness represents the next challenge. There are several approaches to the measurement of episodes of illness, and these are summarized in a new section of this book.

## CONCLUSIONS

Given the increasing role of managed care and the need to understand cost and quality issues, case mix systems will have significantly wider applications in the future. This is particularly true on the managed care side, whether the provider is paid on a capitated (per patient, per month) or discounted fee-for-service basis. Physicians working in managed care organizations will want to use case mix systems that accurately describe the basic building blocks of inpatient and outpatient services.

This discussion demonstrates that case mix systems have a wide variety of uses, not just for payment but also for understanding treatment outcomes (analyses of morbidity and mortality) and process measures of quality. The key to the use of any case mix system is how the system was developed. Can it be used for risk adjustment of managed care plans or for adjusting the severity of illness for patients of either physicians or hospitals?

An effective quality improvement program must include adequate institutional support for the continuous quality improvement (CQI) process. Critical to improvement is a thorough institutional commitment to understanding the information provided by tools that describe both processes and outcomes of care. Case mix adjustment methods represent a critical part of that toolbox. This chapter outlines the questions the user should consider asking as the evaluation of a case mix system proceeds.

---

## NOTES

1. L. Russell, *Medicare's New Hospital Payment System* (Washington, DC: The Brookings Institution, 1989).
2. S. Leader and M. Moon, Medicare Trends in Ambulatory Surgery, *Health Affairs* (Spring 1989).
3. R. Averill et al., *Design and Development of a Prospective Payment System for Ambulatory Care*, final report (Rockville, MD: Health Care Financing Administration, December 1990).
4. E.A. Codman, "The Product of a Hospital," *Surgery, Gynecology and Obstetrics* 18 (1914): 196.
5. R.B. Fetter et al., *DRGs: Their Design and Development* (Ann Arbor, MI: Health Administration Press, 1991), 4.
6. Fetter et al., *DRGs*.
7. Fetter et al., *DRGs*.
8. W. Schwartz and D. Mendelson, "Hospital Cost Containment in the 1980s: Hard Lessons Learned and Prospects for the 1990s," *New England Journal of Medicine* 234, no. 15 (1991): 1037–1042.
9. K. Davis et al., *Health Care Cost Containment* (Baltimore, MD: Johns Hopkins University Press, 1990).

10. E.C. Nelson and D.M. Berwick, "The Measurement of Health Status in Clinical Practice," *Medical Care* 27, no. 3 (1989): 577–590.

11. A.J. Barsky, "Hidden Reasons Some Patients Visit Doctors," *Annals of Internal Medicine* 94 (1981): 492.

12. J. Burnum, "The Worried Sick," *Annals of Internal Medicine* 88 (1978): 572.

13. 14 *Federal Register*, September 9, 1998.

14. L.I. Iezzoni et al., "Predicting In-Hospital Mortality," *Medical Care* 30, no. 4 (1992): 347–359.

CHAPTER 23

# DRGs and Quality Management in Hospitals

*Robert B. Fetter*

Most of you are aware that the original motivation for the development of diagnosis-related groups (DRGs) was to make them a basis for identifying cases for utilization review (UR) and quality assurance (QA) programs in hospitals.[1] The initial applications, however, were for hospital payment and financing systems, and this continues to be the major area of applications.

It was thought by many that the original DRGs introduced in 1981 were insufficiently precise for use by UR and QA programs. Specifically, the problem of variable severity of illness within these DRGs was seen as a major hindrance. Recently, however, with improvements in the accuracy and completeness of the medical record abstract and the development by 3M of the all-patient-refined DRGs (APR-DRGs), it now seems that the time is right to begin serious application of DRGs in hospital QA and quality management programs.

This does not mean simply grafting DRG-centered applications onto existing QA programs. It is time to rethink and redesign such programs by taking advantage of knowledge and experience from industrial quality assurance programs. This requires a change of approach from one of investigating possible cases of poor quality (i.e., targeting "bad apples" and cost outliers) to a program of total quality management (TQM) aimed at continual improvement of care processes in hospitals (constantly improving the average level of care).

## DEFINITIONS IN QUALITY ASSURANCE

To establish a basis for this discussion, a few definitions are necessary:

- *Inspection* is the act of comparing actual results with predetermined norms or standards so as to identify defective output.
- *Quality control* is the systematic recording of actual results in order to draw inferences concerning the stability of the process employed in producing those results.
- *Quality assurance* is the result of a program of investigation into causes of instability in processes and the correction of identified causes resulting in process stability and improvement.
- *Quality conformance* refers to a system of inspection, control, and investigation based on agreed standards that produces output in conformance with those standards.
- *Total quality management* is concerned with the involvement of all of the participants in any process in a designed program that includes as necessary all of the elements defined above and that leads to consistent and provable results in accordance with agreed standards of output.

## QUALITY OF CARE IN HOSPITALS

There are, unfortunately, differing views as to both definitions of and approaches to quality of care in hospitals. The American Medical Association espouses a definition vaguely linked to outcomes, calling high-quality care that which consistently contributes to improvement or maintenance of the quality and/or duration of life. Unfortunately, reaching this laudable goal is not subjected to measurement and control by any systematic approach. It is left to those involved to devise their own methods.

The Joint Commission on the Accreditation of Healthcare Organizations judges hospitals to be of better or poorer quality based on the degree of adherence to generally recognized standards of good practice and achievement of anticipated outcomes. A hospital with good procedural manuals, high-quality records systems, good credentialing procedures, and the like, is rated highly based on these structural features. In industry, the usually accepted definition of quality always includes the phrase "ensuring conformance of output to agreed upon standards."

What is needed is a system of quality management similar in scope and approach to the best of those found in industrial settings, a system based on the principles first advocated in the 1920s by Walter Shewhart at Bell Telephone Laboratories and put into practice at Western Electric.[2] These methods recently have been widely adopted by and improved by applications in Japanese industries and are gradually finding their way back to U.S. industry.[3]

## THE PROCESS OF QUALITY MANAGEMENT

There are a number of basic premises on which modern quality management rests.[4] First, inspection as a means of quality improvement is ineffective and inefficient. Simply locating and discarding poor-quality output does not get at the basic problem of how and why it was produced in the first place. Second, management, not the worker, is primarily responsible for quality of output. It is up to management to create and maintain the conditions of work and appropriate facilities and to lead the efforts toward process improvement. Third, the participation of all parties in any given process is fundamental to understanding both the present state of that process and identifying the means by which it may be improved. Fourth, the statistics descriptive of each process must be recorded in a reliable, informative manner so that process stability can be established and maintained. Fifth, the cause and effect of process instability should be identified in advance by those who understand the process, and measurements must be made to identify quickly and accurately instances of instability.

How can these principles be brought to bear on quality management in hospitals? To begin with, a number of conditions must be met. First, there must be an organizational structure that identifies as much as possible the common processes of illness and treatment. This argues for clinical organization along body system lines. Thus, one would have separate units devoted to cardiology, musculoskeletal problems, gynecology, urology, ophthalmology, and the like. It is important that these departments each identify specific personnel in both clinical and administrative areas. Personnel may belong to more than one unit, but each unit should be defined in terms of a specific roster of individuals.

Second, the distinctive processes that are employed by each unit should be identified. Here, DRGs can help by providing an initial framework by which each unit can define more fully the processes in which it engages as it treats patients. Each of these processes should identify normal expectations of resource use. These expectations may be expressed in precise terms (presurgical laboratory and x-ray procedures) or in statistical terms (probability distribution of normal surgical theater times).

Third, the results of any process should be identified in measurable terms. The probability of death, postoperative infection, complications, treatment errors, expected length of stay, expected intensive care unit time, and expected cost should all be established in advance. Those who participate in the process should all participate in specifying such results. The possible causes of process aberration and the effects expected should be made the subject of a process manual. Thereby, when something goes wrong—that is, when process instability is detected—the team is ready to proceed, in most cases, with a predetermined response.

Finally, statistical process control (SPC) charts must be established to record systematically the results of the care processes used.[5] In this way, information is available on the current state of each process, and problems can be detected virtually as soon as they occur.

## SPECIFYING AND USING CONTROL CHARTS

In order to improve any process, it is necessary first to define in measurable terms the specifications against which outputs are evaluated. When output does not meet specifications—meaning it is of low quality—resources are wasted. In the hospital, such waste occurs whenever poor outcomes result, extra costs are required to remedy a poorly performed procedure, or results obtained are of limited value. Examples of quality waste include postoperative wound infections, performance of unnecessary procedures, and overutilization of ancillary services.

Whereas traditional hospital quality assurance has long rested on medical care evaluation studies and UR, the best quality assurance programs in industry are concerned with continuous process improvement through measurement and understanding of the processes by which output is produced. As noted earlier, the basic ideas were originated by Shewhart to improve quality in the production of telephones.[6]

## THE CONCEPT OF PROCESS CONTROL

A process consists of a set of inputs (labor, materials, equipment, management), a conversion process, and a set of outputs characterized by some measurements of these outputs. In any process, variation in the outputs will occur. Variation in output is a function of variation in inputs, in the conversion process, and/or in the measurements of output. The problem of control is to ensure that the outputs are stable and thus predictable over time. Whether or not they conform to a specified set of requirements is a different question from that of whether or not the process is stable. A stable process may be one that produces output in conformance with management's requirements, that exceeds specifications, or that falls short of requirements.

A process is *in control* when output variation remains within predetermined limits from a statistical point of view. SPC consists of a set of powerful techniques to ensure the continued stability of any process and to detect the presence of sources of instability.

In a hospital, for example, postoperative infection rates may be observed as occurring at the rate of 15 percent for a particular kind of case and may be stable over time. Whether or not 15 percent is a reasonable and appropriate rate is a second question to be asked. Measures may be undertaken to improve the processes of care and to reduce the rate to, for example, 10 percent, again with measurements indicating a stable process.

## THE CONCEPT OF STATISTICAL CONTROL

If the variation between and within the input factors of a process is stable, then the variation in output will be stable. This is referred to as a *stable system of chance causes*. That is, the variation is a function of known cause factors and is predictable in statistical terms.

For example, the variation in the cost of treating a particular kind of case may be discovered by an analysis of past performance. Through application of statistical control techniques, the expected value and limits of variation of this cost may be determined. With these expectations, when some change occurs in the underlying system of chance causes, a signal would be generated that the process has gone "out of control." Those responsible for the process would be alerted to attempt to discover an assignable cause for the unexpected variation that was observed. In this way, the process may be brought back into control through removing the assignable cause that introduced instability into the system.

Shewhart postulated three principles for SPC:[7]

1.  All chance systems are not alike in the sense that they enable us to predict the future in terms of the past. That is, one may be willing to gamble on the outcome of a coin-tossing game but not on the outcome of a particular horse race.

2. Constant systems of chance causes do exist in nature. The ability to produce mortality tables is certainly evidence of the existence of such systems.
3. Assignable causes of variation may be discovered and eliminated.

## THE STATISTICAL NATURE OF CARE PROCESSES

Figure 23–1 shows a typical example of the statistical nature of health care processes. This records the cost of hospital care during a one-year period for treating 631 patients who received coronary artery bypass grafts (CABGs). For the most part, the process exhibits considerable stability, but a small percentage of the results are definitely aberrant. The basic logic of SPC rests on

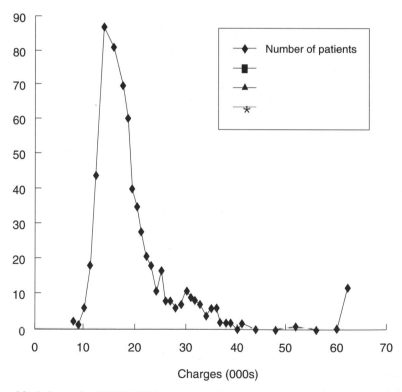

**Figure 23–1** Costs for DRG 107 Coronary Artery Bypass Graft

the *central limit theorem* of statistics.[8] This theorem states that if a distribution of individual items (e.g., measurements) are from a stable underlying process, then any statistic computed from samples of these individual items (such as the mean or variance) will have a normal distribution. This guarantees that we can know in advance the characteristics of these distributions of small-sample statistics even if we have no knowledge of the shape of the underlying distribution of individual items.

If the Figure 23–1 data were organized sequentially by date of patient discharge and grouped into small samples, say, of 4 patients each, then the process statistics could be estimated for each such sample.

This would result in 157 values (631/4) estimating the mean and variation of the process. The central limit theorem guarantees that if the process is the result of a stable system of chance causes, these process statistics will have a normal distribution. Since the characteristics of the normal distribution are well known, there is an expected prediction of the mean and variation. If this prediction is not satisfied for any sample, then one can infer that the process was not "in control" at the point that the sample in question was drawn.

Table 23–1 shows the first 100 values of the data from Figure 23–1 organized into 25 subgroups of 4 values each, expressed as thousands of dollars. Two statistics, mean (arithmetic average) and standard deviation, are calculated for each sample and shown as XBAR and SDEV. Standard deviation is a measure of the variance in a process and is computed by taking the square root of the sum of the squared deviations from the mean. Using the square root transforms the measure into the same units as the mean, rather than the squared value of such measurements. The terms XBAR and SDEV are simply conventions usually used in SPC to identify the mean and standard deviation, respectively.

Based on the hypothesis that the process is in control, the limits (+/–3 SDEV for the sample means and deviations) are shown also. Figures 23–2 and 23–3 plot these results and show one "out-of-control" point at Subgroup 19 for XBAR, with a value above the upper control limit. The sample shows one value of 53,000, which is the value to be investigated. If one or more assignable causes could be found, this sample could be eliminated, and the control limits reset for further use. In Figure 23–3, there is one out-of-control point for SDEV on Subgroup 3. This indicates a source of instability that is unexpected, and the values of 39 and 37 would need to be investigated to try to find assignable causes.

**Table 23–1** Control Chart for Charges—DRG 107

| Subgroup | C1 | C2 | C3 | C4 | XBAR | SDEV |
|---|---|---|---|---|---|---|
| 1 | 13 | 22 | 14 | 24 | 18.25 | 4.81534 |
| 2 | 11 | 15 | 20 | 15 | 15.25 | 3.191786 |
| 3 | 39 | 37 | 14 | 12 | 25.5 | 12.53994 |
| 4 | 11 | 17 | 20 | 26 | 18.5 | 5.408329 |
| 5 | 29 | 18 | 16 | 16 | 19.75 | 5.402546 |
| 6 | 17 | 16 | 16 | 16 | 16.25 | 0.433013 |
| 7 | 37 | 15 | 18 | 14 | 21 | 9.354143 |
| 8 | 23 | 14 | 21 | 31 | 22.25 | 6.057021 |
| 9 | 16 | 16 | 21 | 15 | 17 | 2.345208 |
| 10 | 16 | 16 | 13 | 14 | 14.75 | 1.299038 |
| 11 | 16 | 27 | 17 | 15 | 18.75 | 4.81534 |
| 12 | 39 | 19 | 15 | 11 | 21 | 10.77033 |
| 13 | 18 | 15 | 18 | 18 | 17.25 | 1.299038 |
| 14 | 18 | 29 | 15 | 26 | 22 | 5.700877 |
| 15 | 33 | 15 | 31 | 14 | 23.25 | 8.785642 |
| 16 | 13 | 20 | 14 | 14 | 15.25 | 2.772634 |
| 17 | 13 | 16 | 14 | 17 | 15 | 1.581139 |
| 18 | 33 | 15 | 11 | 19 | 19.5 | 8.291562 |
| 19 | 22 | 22 | 15 | 53 | 28 | 4.71394 |
| 20 | 20 | 18 | 13 | 13 | 16 | 3.082207 |
| 21 | 14 | 14 | 16 | 27 | 17.75 | 5.402546 |
| 22 | 17 | 31 | 31 | 13 | 23 | 8.124038 |
| 23 | 22 | 13 | 15 | 15 | 16.25 | 3.418699 |
| 24 | 15 | 15 | 23 | 18 | 17.75 | 3.269174 |
| 25 | 15 | 13 | 24 | 19 | 17.75 | 4.205651 |
|  |  |  |  | Mean | 19.08 | 5.483107 |

*Note*: Upper control limit for XBAR is 26.28, lower control limit for XBAR is 11.88, upper control limit for SDEV is  11.29, and lower control limit for SDEV is 0.0.

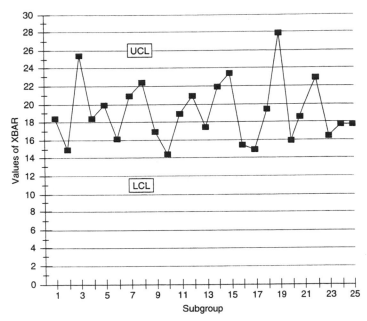

**Figure 23–2** Control Chart for XBAR, DRG 107—Charges

---

Thus, the cases treated in this sample exhibit unexpected values based on the statistics of the entire set of samples. The costs of care are outside the expected range for these cases, and some cause of variation needs to be investigated.

As a further simple example of SPC, in Table 23–2 are shown the length of stay (LOS) for patients who were treated for cataracts by lens extraction, organized consecutively by discharge date and into subgroups of 4 patients each. For each such subgroup, the mean, range (R), and standard deviation are calculated. The overall statistics indicate a grand mean of 3.96 days and an average standard deviation of 1.16 days.

With respect to the means, if the process were stable, one would expect only 3 in 1,000 such estimates to be beyond 3.96 plus 3 SDEV. The standard deviation can be estimated as 1.16 divided by the square root of 4, the sample size. This gives 5.70 as the upper limit. Results are plotted in Figure 23–4 for XBAR and Figure 23–5 for SDEV. As sample 10 is beyond this limit, we infer that at that point something unexpected happened—an assignable cause

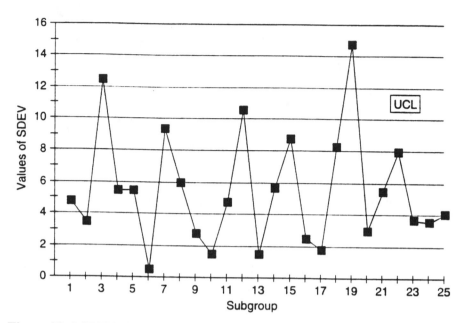

**Figure 23–3** SDEV Chart, DRG 107—Charges

occurred. That is, the process of care that resulted in this set of LOS values for sample 10 was in some way significantly different. It is important to discover the cause of the unexpected result and, if possible, remove the cause from the system. Both the range and standard deviation estimates are also out of limits for this sample. Subgroup 17 also shows the mean out of limits, but for this group the variance is inside the limits.

Assuming that the cause for the out-of-control indications is found, these samples could be eliminated from the set of observations, the statistics recalculated, and the limits reset for future operation. If this sample can be eliminated in this way, control limits for future observations will be tighter and more sensitive to abnormalities in the process of care.

An interesting pattern is observed for Subgroups 19 through 25, which all fall below the value of XBAR. Four values in a row on either side of the central line are also an indication that the process is unstable. In this case, one could infer that the level of the process has changed, and a new series started after Subgroup 18. In fact, in this case, an intervention did occur at that point in time and was the cause for the change in system behavior. The process is

**Table 23–2** Control Chart for LOS—DRG 39

| Subgroup | LOS1 | LOS2 | LOS3 | LOS4 | XBAR | SDEV |
|---|---|---|---|---|---|---|
| 1 | 4 | 4 | 6 | 3 | 4.25 | 1.258306 |
| 2 | 4 | 4 | 1 | 4 | 3.25 | 1.5 |
| 3 | 3 | 3 | 4 | 8 | 4.5 | 2.380476 |
| 4 | 6 | 4 | 3 | 4 | 4.25 | 1.258306 |
| 5 | 4 | 4 | 4 | 2 | 3.5 | 1 |
| 6 | 5 | 4 | 5 | 4 | 4.5 | 0.57735 |
| 7 | 3 | 4 | 3 | 5 | 3.75 | 0.957427 |
| 8 | 4 | 2 | 4 | 4 | 3.5 | 1 |
| 9 | 4 | 4 | 5 | 4 | 4.25 | 0.5 |
| 10 | 3 | 7 | 4 | 11 | 6.25 | 3.593976 |
| 11 | 6 | 5 | 3 | 4 | 4.5 | 1.290994 |
| 12 | 2 | 4 | 4 | 3 | 3.25 | 0.957427 |
| 13 | 5 | 5 | 4 | 4 | 4.5 | 0.57735 |
| 14 | 3 | 7 | 6 | 5 | 5.25 | 1.707825 |
| 15 | 4 | 3 | 4 | 3 | 3.5 | 0.57735 |
| 16 | 4 | 4 | 4 | 2 | 3.5 | 1 |
| 17 | 8 | 6 | 7 | 4 | 6.25 | 1.707825 |
| 18 | 4 | 5 | 5 | 4 | 4.5 | 0.57735 |
| 19 | 3 | 4 | 3 | 3 | 3.25 | 0.5 |
| 20 | 2 | 3 | 5 | 4 | 3.5 | 1.290994 |
| 21 | 3 | 3 | 1 | 3 | 2.5 | 1 |
| 22 | 2 | 5 | 5 | 3 | 3.75 | 1.5 |
| 23 | 3 | 2 | 3 | 4 | 3 | 0.816497 |
| 24 | 4 | 3 | 4 | 3 | 3.5 | 0.57735 |
| 25 | 3 | 1 | 2 | 3 | 2.25 | 0.957427 |
| | | | | Mean | 3.96 | 1.162569 |

*Note:* Upper control limit for XBAR is 5.70, lower control limit for XBAR is 2.22, upper control limit for SDEV is 2.39, and lower control limit for SDEV is 0.0.

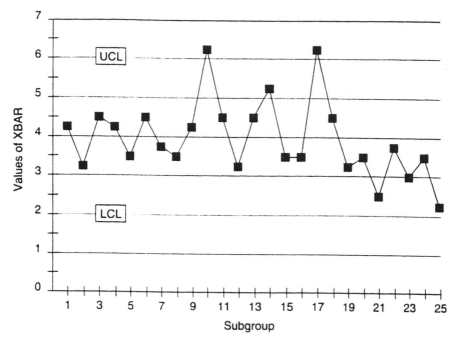

**Figure 23–4** XBAR Chart, DRG 39—LOS

now "in control" but at a different level for both the mean and variance. Using SPC in this way, it is possible to monitor any process that can be characterized by numerical measurements of its output.

This example illustrates a change in the process that was deliberately introduced, resulting in a reduction in average LOS. The level of the process has responded appropriately, as indicated by the sample statistics. In this case, "out of control" indicates a favorable event, and the process statistics are reset to allow future monitoring at this new level of expectations.

## CONTROL CHARTS FOR ATTRIBUTES

In many cases, variables of interest are not subject to measurement as in the case of cost or LOS. Analysts may be interested in the rate of occurrence of phenomena such as postoperative infection, decubitus, or an unscheduled return to the operating room as indicators of process quality. In such cases, the appropriate statistic for the control chart is the proportionate occurrence of the

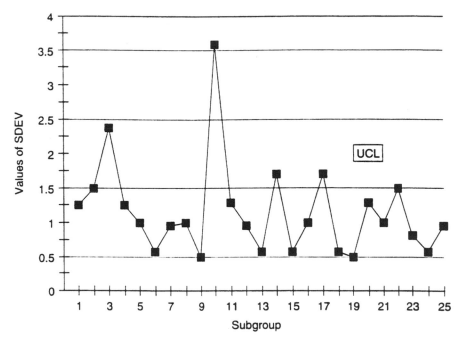

**Figure 23–5** SDEV Chart, DRG 39—LOS

event of interest. Such charts can be used with constant or varying sample sizes.

In addition, in instances in which differing rates are expected within the same set of observations, a standardized chart can be employed. Thus, if one were monitoring physicians with respect to the incidence of postoperative infection, different rates might be expected dependent on the type of case treated.

Table 23–3 shows data for each of four surgeons treating patients in four DRGs for which different rates of infection are considered normal. The expected rates can be set based on experience, judgment, or a combination of both. In each case, the sample consists of 50 patients broken down by DRG.

For each DRG and for each sample size, a critical number is calculated based on the central limit theorem—a number indicative of an unexpected event. In this case, the definition given to the out-of-limits event is as in the control chart for LOS—that is, 1 sample in 300 might normally be expected to exceed this limit.

As shown in the table, there are two out-of-control samples. This clearly illustrates the advantages of organizing data into small subgroups and focusing on individual actors in the process. For DRG 1, the occurrence of 1 in 25 is not an unusual event, as is the result of 1 in 27 for DRG 4, but the sample of 8 for Surgeon 2 and of 6 for Surgeon 3 pinpoints the problem quite precisely.

For attributes, a table can be constructed in advance, giving out-of-control values for any expected rate and for any sample size. Table 23–4 is an excerpt from such a table showing critical values based on expected rate and sample size. Whereas the first part of Table 23–4 gives these values based on expectations of 1 in 300, the second part gives the same values based on expectations of 1 in 20. Often, the 1-in-20 values are used as warning limits, whereas the 1-in-300 values are considered definite indications of assignable causes.

## OTHER SPC TECHNIQUES

Although control charts for variables and for attributes are the main tools of SPC, additional types of charts can prove useful. If one examines accident rates such as falls, the appropriate statistic is Poisson rather than the binomial illustrated above. The Poisson is a distribution originally devised to reflect the behavior of accident statistics for which the probabilities are very small. If a situation can be described in this way, the Poisson is a very useful distribution, because its values depend only on the mean of the process, whereas standard deviation is always the square root of the mean. Thus, Poisson is much easier to use than the binomial, which depends on both mean and variance. However, the binomial can be used in a wider range of situations than the Poisson.

Also, the Poisson is used when the statistic recorded is the number of defects per unit. For example, it can be useful to identify a number of vari-

**Table 23–3** Infection Rates by DRG

| DRG | IR | S1 | | S2 | | S3 | | S4 | | TC | TI |
|-----|-----|----|----|----|----|----|----|----|----|----|----|
| 1 | .01 | 5 | 0 | 8 | 1 | 6 | 0 | 6 | 0 | 25 | 1 |
| 2 | .15 | 20 | 2 | 15 | 3 | 19 | 3 | 25 | 2 | 79 | 10 |
| 3 | .04 | 15 | 1 | 20 | 2 | 19 | 0 | 15 | 2 | 69 | 5 |
| 4 | .00 | 10 | 0 | 7 | 0 | 6 | 1 | 4 | 0 | 27 | 1 |

**Table 23–4** Critical Values for Attributes

| | | | | | Sample size | | | | |
|---|---|---|---|---|---|---|---|---|---|
| | P | 5 | 10 | 15 | 20 | 25 | 30 | 35 | 40 |
| | .01 | 1 | 1 | 1 | 2 | 2 | 2 | 2 | 2 |
| | .02 | 1 | 2 | 2 | 2 | 3 | 3 | 3 | 3 |
| | .03 | 1 | 2 | 2 | 3 | 3 | 4 | 4 | 4 |
| .003 | .04 | 2 | 2 | 3 | 3 | 4 | 4 | 5 | 5 |
| | .05 | 2 | 3 | 3 | 4 | 5 | 5 | 6 | 6 |
| | .10 | 3 | 4 | 5 | 6 | 7 | 8 | 9 | 10 |
| | .15 | 3 | 5 | 6 | 8 | 9 | 10 | 12 | 13 |
| | .25 | 4 | 7 | 9 | 11 | 13 | 15 | 16 | 18 |
| | .01 | 1 | 1 | 1 | 1 | 1 | 1 | 2 | 2 |
| | .02 | 1 | 1 | 1 | 2 | 2 | 2 | 2 | 3 |
| | .03 | 1 | 1 | 2 | 2 | 2 | 3 | 3 | 3 |
| .050 | .04 | 1 | 2 | 2 | 3 | 3 | 3 | 4 | 4 |
| | .05 | 1 | 2 | 2 | 3 | 3 | 4 | 4 | 5 |
| | .10 | 2 | 3 | 4 | 5 | 5 | 6 | 7 | 8 |
| | .15 | 2 | 4 | 5 | 6 | 7 | 8 | 9 | 11 |
| | .25 | 3 | 5 | 7 | 9 | 11 | 12 | 14 | 15 |

ables representing unexpected and undesirable events for each case treated in a hospital. These different kinds of events could be weighted and an overall measure of the quality of care developed in terms of errors and/or abnormalities in the care process, on a per-case basis. This kind of measure was originally developed to monitor the quality of assembled products such as radios, telephones, and television sets. It allows the melding of a great deal of disparate data into a single measure indicative of case quality in an institution.

The control charts for variables illustrated earlier are quite effective at signaling the presence of an assignable cause of variation that is suddenly introduced into a process. However, there are situations in which a process changes slowly over time in response, for example, to an ongoing training program. In these cases, the control chart may be slow to signal a change. For such circumstances, the cumulative sum chart (CUSUM) has been developed.[9] This technique rests on the statistics of cumulative changes over time and can guarantee detection of change in such cases in a timely manner.

There are additional techniques available to accommodate a wide variety of circumstances that may be encountered in practice. These techniques are described and illustrated in many modern textbooks available today, some of which are included in the reference list at the end of this chapter.

## SPC AND TOTAL QUALITY MANAGEMENT

Process control is a useful technique in and of itself, but it should always be viewed as only one component of a quality assurance program that is comprehensive and that aims at continual improvement of processes within an institution. In a hospital, each different kind of case that is treated represents a different process and needs to be the object of a quality improvement effort. The team responsible for treating each such case should meet regularly to review SPC monitoring results and to suggest ways to improve the care of patients. These teams—sometimes called *quality circles*—should identify the variables that must be monitored and should try to anticipate assignable causes of variation that may occur. These anticipations also must include responses to change so that little time is lost in correcting a process.

There are many variables that are candidates for SPC. However, each case will require specification of those variables most useful for quality control. The following variables are typical of those that might be included:

- length of stay (LOS)
- preoperative LOS
- cost of care (by type of cost)
- surgical time
- severity level
- hospital-acquired (nosocomial) infection
- complications of anesthesia
- transfusion error
- medication error
- death
- unscheduled return to operating room
- unplanned removal/repair of normal organ
- patient satisfaction

Other variables may be specified depending on the type of case being considered.

If one is to understand both absolutely and relatively the quality of care being delivered by each health care institution, it is essential that these techniques be much more widely applied. This requires both education for and understanding by providers seriously interested in quality-of-care improvement in their respective care settings.

## TOTAL QUALITY MANAGEMENT IN HOSPITALS

The explicit involvement of management at all levels in quality improvement activities is crucial to systematic and systemwide process improvement. Hospital executives and managers cannot remain aloof from the problems of clinical process improvement. Clinicians cannot blame others for supply or equipment failures. All members of a process team are involved and responsible for the success of that process. This *quality circle* philosophy has made enterprises that practice it highly effective and successful.[10]

## CONCLUSIONS

It will be argued by some that they have no time to do all this extra work, but poor quality is costly. Blaming someone else for system failures is easy. Being truly effective in the use of time and talents requires recognition of the interdependencies that exist in one's activities. Making the process of caring for each patient *optimally effective* will produce maximum efficiency in the use of all the resources devoted to that process. Physicians, nurses, technicians, maintenance personnel, administrators, and everyone else involved will be more effective if the system in which they operate is subject to these principles of continual improvement.

---

NOTES

1. R.B. Fetter, ed., *DRGs: Their Design and Development* (Ann Arbor, MI: Health Administration Press, 1991).

2. W.A. Shewhart, *Statistical Methods from the Viewpoint of Quality Control* (Washington, DC: U.S. Department of Agriculture Graduate School, 1939).

3. W.E. Deming, *Out of the Crisis* (Cambridge, MA: Massachusetts Institute for Technology, 1986).

4. J.M. Juran, *Juran on Planning for Quality* (New York, NY: The Free Press/Macmillan, 1988).

5. R.B. Fetter, *The Quality Control System* (Homewood, IL: Richard D. Irwin, 1967).

6. Shewhart, *Statistical Methods.*

7. Shewhart, *Statistical Methods.*

8. Fetter, ed., *DRGs.*

9. Fetter, ed., *DRGs.*

10. M. Walton, *The Deming Management Method* (New York, NY: Dodd, Mead & Company, 1986).

# PART III

# Physician Profiling and Risk Adjustment of Outpatient Care

CHAPTER 24

# Methods of Compensating Managed Care Physicians and Hospitals

*Norbert Goldfield, Harris Berman, Arlene Collins,*
*Richard Cooper, Daniel Dragalin, Peter Kongstvedt,*
*Norman Payson, David Siegel, Arthur Southam, and Ernest Weis*

Physicians are the Hippocratic guarantors of the high-quality care every patient hopes to receive as well as the decision makers on many aspects of the rising costs of health care services. While Hippocrates does not enter into a hospital's credo, these institutions also must balance the need to provide high-quality care with the demand to control the cost of care. A managed care organization's (MCO's) choice of reimbursement mechanisms used to compensate physicians and hospitals need to reflect these two, intertwined, aspects of physician activity.[1]

As a prelude to reading about the many systems used to adjust payment rates it is necessary to understand the range of payment systems currently used in managed care. It is precisely the wide variety of payment strategies in use which prompts consumers to demand that comparisons between managed care physicians and hospitals adjust for differences between patients. This review details and assesses the types of financial arrangements offered by MCOs contracting with physicians and hospitals. Information was synthe-

*Source*: Adapted from N. Goldfield, H. Berman, A. Collins, R. Cooper, D. Dragalin, P. Kongstvedt, N. Payson, D. Siegel, A. Southam, E. Weis, "Methods of Compensating Physicians Contracting with Managed Care Organizations," *Journal of Ambulatory Care Management*, Vol. 15, No. 4, pp. 81–92, Aspen Publishers, Inc., © 1992.

sized from a combination of literature review and the authors' assessment of these reimbursement mechanisms on the basis of their individual experiences.

These are the basic types of financial incentives that MCOs utilize today:

- managed fee-for-service
- capitation
- case mix based payment such as ambulatory patient groups (APGs) and diagnosis-related groups (DRGs)
- risk pools, withholds, and bonuses
- stop-loss or risk-limiting protection

All MCOs utilize at least capitation or managed fee-for-service. The third payment category represents either an intermediate phase between fee-for-service and capitation or a year-end capitation adjustment. The fourth and fifth incentives are typically utilized to complement compensation.

## MCO PHYSICIAN REIMBURSEMENT

### Managed Fee-for-Service

*Fee-for-service* is defined as payment for a specific medical service. Managed fee-for-service is typically based on a discount off the usual and customary charge (UCR) or a fee schedule developed by the MCO based on claims data. The payment may or may not include all ancillary services and tests such as supplies and laboratory tests. Interestingly, the renewed emphasis on primary care practitioners has pushed some MCOs to return to forms of fee-for-service payment for primary care physicians and place specialists under capitation.

*Global fees* involve a single fee for all services related to a medical procedure or episode of care. This approach is particularly common for obstetrics, as when a single fee is paid for all prenatal visits, the delivery, and all ancillary tests. The Health Care Financing Administration, on a demonstration project basis, uses global fees for the payment of both physicians and hospitals for coronary artery bypass graft procedures and aftercare. Many MCOs contract with tertiary care institutions for all aspects of transplantation care. This type of contract allows MCOs to compare outcomes of care for procedures with high visibility for enrollees.

Global fees that include specific outcomes involve a global fee, for example, for arthroscopic knee surgery, including any reoperations for the first two years after the initial operation. Another example would be a global fee for any operation on breast masses, including operations ranging from lumpectomies to radical mastectomies.

*Target expenditures* represent a pool of money allocated for physician expenditures (primary care physicians, or PCPs, and specialists). If the sum is exceeded, payment adjustments are made to achieve financial targets. Ideally, the manager of the pool is an already existing organization such as a group practice.

While there is a voluminous literature pertaining to the impact of traditional fee-for-service and discounted fee-for-service compensation on physician practice patterns, there is limited information pertaining to the managed fee-for-service variants described above.[2] In the experience of most of the authors of this review, managed fee-for-service arrangements can be effective in controlling health care costs. However, several authors of this review believe that capitation, to be discussed below, represents the most effective means of influencing health care costs and providing decision-making autonomy to the physician. The more difficult, as yet unanswered, question is the comparative advantages and disadvantages of managed or performance-based fee-for-service arrangements as compared to capitation.

## PCP Capitation

Capitation represents a flat-rate payment, typically on a per-member per-month basis (pmpm), paid to a practitioner or hospital for providing specified services to enrolled members as frequently as is necessary. Capitation is intended to cover services which the PCP ordinarily provides in the office or hospital; capitation of PCP services rarely involves solely physician care and usually includes certain basic tests or procedures which have low cost and are performed in the office setting. Services typically covered under capitation include all visits to the PCP, selected laboratory tests such as hematocrits and urinalyses, and selected office procedures such as electrocardiograms and spirometries.

The number and type of tests and procedures which are capitated vary. Notably, the capitation will vary depending on whether or not immunizations and laboratory tests are included. Immunizations are often excluded because their cost has risen in recent years due to product liability concerns. If immunizations are included, MCOs either make a separate payment or include it as part of the capitation payment.

Unlike traditional fee-for-service, capitation means that the physician or hospital takes on a form of risk. There are two types of risks that a PCP can assume: service risk and financial risk. Service risk refers to the risk a physician assumes for providing as many needed services as specified under the contract in return for a fixed payment. In economic terms, a physician's time can also be viewed as a marginal cost whereas an x-ray constitutes a direct cost. The PCP is at total service risk for what is included in the pmpm capitation. This service risk pertains to the services the PCP would routinely provide to the patient in the office. Under this arrangement, the typical one for primary care capitation, the PCP bears service risk but no direct financial risk in that the PCP is guaranteed the agreed-upon pmpm payment. However, a physician can be placed at financial risk for a variety of risk funds described below.

The service risk assumed by a PCP in a monthly capitation agreement implies that there typically is no after-the-fact capitation adjustment. If such an adjustment were adopted, it would provide the physician with a supplementary payment for an "insufficient" capitation in light of actual practice expenses. This can occur if the physician has a particularly sick "panel" or group (e.g., acquired immunodeficiency syndrome [AIDS]) of patients. The "my patients are sicker" argument represents the biggest physician criticism of the calculation of capitation payments. The factors that determine the capitation rate for a group of patients assigned to the physician may include age, level of benefit, plan copayment, sex, severity, and provider specialty.

Capitation is rapidly gaining acceptance as a preferred form of payment to hospitals, particularly on the West Coast. The adequacy of the capitation payment is more complex for hospitals, as these institutions assume both a service and financial risk when they accept capitation as the form of payment.

Almost all MCOs in the United States rely solely on patient age and sex data to calculate the capitation rate, despite the fact that age and sex account for less than 20 percent of the variation in costs among individual patients.[3] Two types of refinements may be desirable: adjustments to health status for the purposes of improving the accuracy of capitation payments and retroactive adjustments to PCP payments already made. Based on International Classification of Diseases, Ninth Edition, Clinical Modification (ICD-9-CM) diagnoses, researchers have developed a methodology, ambulatory care groups (ACGs), which better adjusts capitation rates than use of age and sex.[4] The recently developed outpatient DRG (APGs) system could also be used for this purpose.[5] ACGs, APGs, and other systems useful for risk adjustment are described in this book.

MCOs defend their current reliance on age and sex in calculating the capitation rate by pointing to the law of large numbers and the fact that capitation only includes primary care visits and minor tests or procedures. There can be significant underpayment or overpayment to physicians who are placed on capitation when their patient enrollment is too low. With respect to other factors that may impact the capitation rate, the relationship between the benefit plan copayment and the capitation rate typically represents an actuarial calculation. Unfortunately, there is little empirical research documenting the use of a severity adjustment for capitation payments for physicians. There is significant experience in the use of severity adjustments for modifying capitation rates in hospitals. While the enrollee group is typically not small for a hospital, there is tremendous variability in costs for these enrollees. Without the use of severity adjustment or financial backstops to minimize loss, hospitals can easily slide into financial distress.

There are several different forms of capitation:

- *Fee-for-service with group capitation:* Individual physicians in a group practice are paid on a fee-for-service basis while the entire group is paid a fixed capitation. The group is typically capitated only for outpatient costs.
- *Individual hospital/physician group capitation or physician-hospital organization (PHO):* In this situation, both the hospital and the group are paid on a pmpm basis. This mechanism just shifts the risk from the payer to a provider intermediary. This in turn forces the provider to devise a payment mechanism. Case mix adjusted fee-for-service payments such as APGs for physicians and all-patient-refined DRGs (APR-DRGs) for hospitals are becoming increasingly popular.
- *Group capitation with individual physician capitation:* Both individual physicians and the entire group are capitated.
- *Individual physician capitation with fee-for-service guarantees:* Physicians are guaranteed that the total amount paid under capitation will at least equal a payment amount that would have been received under fee-for-service.
- *Individual physician capitation:* The physician is paid on a pmpm basis.

- *Individual hospital capitation:* The use of capitation for hospital payment is relatively new, and no studies have been published.
- *Individual physician capitation only:* The use of capitation for those patients who come to the physician during a defined period of time, typically a quarter. This method has been extensively used in other countries, notably Israel, and is making an appearance in the United States.

No empirical studies unequivocally demonstrate the impact of capitation on quality and efficiency. Of greater importance for the contemporary policy debate, no studies compare the relative advantages of the different forms of capitation described above. Several case studies have been published that examine the impact of capitation on physician practice patterns.[6-8] Several econometric studies have concluded that financial incentives do influence the behavior of physicians toward patients.[9-11] The chapters in this book provide some of the first studies that use severity adjustment for both inpatient and outpatient capitation payments.

There are two distinct schools of thought on the impact of capitation on physician behavior. Most experts believe that capitation encourages physicians and hospitals to examine their own practice patterns and thereby control costs. The authors of this review believe that capitation, more importantly, assists in influencing PCPs' willingness to manage the care of their patients. This perspective is grounded in the belief that physicians and hospitals are impacted by both financial and nonfinancial incentives. Advocates of capitation believe that this financial incentive is particularly important for those physicians and hospitals who already provide cost-effective, high-quality health care—these are the physicians who need to be most rewarded and are typically underpaid in the classical fee-for-service system.

Capitation can have a moderating impact on physician costs on a long-term basis if PCPs are paid adequate capitation rates and a small number of physician-specific quality and cost data profiles are regularly fed back to providers. While capitation provides the principal quality and cost incentive, the authors of this review believe that providers need to see their quality and cost profiles on a regular, comparative basis in order to act on the incentive.

## Group versus Individual Physician Capitation

Group capitation is becoming more important as PHOs represent an increasingly important provider-controlled payment intermediary. Often a medical group will be capitated for services to an enrolled population. In this situation, the group practice can pay individual PCPs in the group using a variety of methods, including salary or discounted fee-for-service. Alternatively, the group practice may elect to reimburse its physicians using capitation. There is no empirical literature on group capitation as it compares with capitation of individual physicians. Capitation of a group may provide more actuarially precise reimbursement than could be provided to an individual physician in independent practice. A large number of MCOs, such as CareAmerica, contract only with medical group practices on a capitated basis. On the other hand, individual physician capitation may provide for more direct feedback and communication between the MCO and a specific physician. US HealthCare capitates primary care physicians on an individual basis.

If an MCO chooses to capitate a group practice, the latter must be able to obtain information on the types and cost of services it is providing. Ideally this information should be physician specific, though this is often difficult to obtain. Capitation of medical groups has become increasingly prevalent as medical group practices have gained financial and marketing sophistication. When this increased management ability is present, MCOs often delegate utilization review and quality assurance (UR and QA) to the prepaid medical groups, transforming UR and QA from an intrusive, confrontational process between the MCO and the group to a collegial, collaborative one administered by the group medical practice.[12]

## Withhold

"Withholding" of a percentage of a PCP's capitation or discounted fee-for-service payment is a frequently utilized MCO tool. The withhold, typically 5 percent to 15 percent of the capitation payment, is returned to the PCP depending on the financial health of the MCO. While typically the withhold is a separate sum of money independent of the funds described above, some MCOs make the return of the withhold dependent on risk pool performance. There are no published studies on the impact of the withhold on physician behavior. A significant problem with any discussion of the withhold is that, historically, some MCOs have not returned the withhold, creating a perception among providers that the withhold is simply a discount from the capitation or fee-for-service payment. Withholds were particularly popular during the 1980s, a time of relative financial distress for many MCOs. With the financial robustness of most MCOs, withholds have fallen into disuse for the reimbursement of physicians. Withholds have not historically been much used with hospitals.

## Bonus

A "bonus" payment represents a monetary reward for meeting performance standards. A bonus or supplementary payment can have a significant impact, particularly if it can be provided at the discretion of the MCO manager; that is, one does not need to provide a bonus only once a year. Over the past few years, bonus type payments are becoming more common. The most common type is one that is applied in a step-wise fashion in response to physicians' meeting quality or utilization standards. Bonuses are generally not applied to hospitals.

## Risk-based Payment

Risk pools or other funds are sums of money set aside by an MCO for distribution to a physician or group practice. Risk pools specifically oriented toward cost containment have become less common as MCOs have become more actuarially familiar with the development and maintenance of capitation payments that do not place the MCO at undue risk. Furthermore, the rapid rise in capitation for specialists has removed much of the impetus for risk pool use for primary care practitioners. Risk pools are generally not applied to hospitals.

A risk fund, typically, constitutes a portion of an MCO's direct medical expenses or percentage of profit that the MCO contracts to pay a provider if specific performance goals are met. These funds, which may be given to the individual physician or group practice, are typically over and above the capitation. While a physician can assume financial risk, in the form of a risk fund, for the capitation payment, risk funds are typically established for other direct medical expenses, such as those attributable to the hospital. The actuarial calculation of a hospital risk pool, for example, begins with a detailed knowledge of the MCO's total hospital expenses and those of the individual physician or group. The MCO, and often the physician, then decides what risk the physician or group can reasonably assume for these hospital expenses. This can be actuarially difficult to calculate. The amount of risk assumed by the physician may be related to factors such as a sufficiently large panel and understanding how to manage risk through cost and utilization control.

There are two ways of distributing risk pool funds: budgeted distributions and traditional risk pools. The main difference between the two involves the MCO's commitment to distribute all the funds in the pool irrespective of individual physician performance on the pool. The term *budgeted distribution* means that a specified amount of money is set aside for a group of physicians at the beginning of the fiscal period; this money will be distributed even if several physicians perform poorly in all the dimensions defined below. In a budgeted distribution, if several physicians do not achieve performance goals, a larger amount is left over for distribution to the other physicians in that group.

An MCO may utilize several types of risk pools or budgeted distributions:

- institutional (hospital)
- emergency room
- consultative services
- quality assurance

Institutional or hospital referral pools are often further split out by specific populations, notably obstetrics and mental health. If these differentiations by specific populations are not separated out, the pool may be completely inaccurate.

Emergency department (ED) pools may be important as a tool to encourage availability of PCPs in their office and refer only to those patients of the ED who are truly in need of emergency services.

Consultative pools allot an actuarially determined pmpm payment for all referrals to specialists. It is important to track these referrals, particularly if the MCO is attempting to utilize the PCP as a true gatekeeper of patient care. This pool often represents an important influence on PCP behavior.

Quality assurance funds are becoming popular with MCOs. In part this is due to adverse publicity resulting from lawsuits filed against MCOs, charging that the incentives inherent in the capitation structure encourage underservice.[13] Payments to physicians based on the quality of care fall into two categories:

1. payment independent of performance on other risk pools
2. payment tied to other risk pool performance

When QA fund distributions are made (it appears that these occur in less than half of the MCOs), they may be tied to performance on the physician's other risk pools. Therefore, if the PCP performs poorly on hospital, ancillary, and specialist funds, for example, no payment is made, irrespective of the physician's performance on the QA standards.

MCOs use several types of tools to measure a PCP's performance on the quality assurance pool, including chart audits, examination of offices to ascertain proper functioning of equipment and office cleanliness, and patient satisfaction information. Patient-derived information includes surveys and other items, such as the length of time it takes to obtain an appointment.[14]

The majority of MCOs use the risk pool concept. However, this approach may not be beneficial to either the MCOs or the PCPs or hospitals under contract if the pools are not actuarially accurate. This inaccuracy can be due to factors such as

- inadequate demographic or cost information
- lack of physician control over services (such as in many aspects of hospitalization)
- adverse selection resulting in a large number of outliers, which will not be captured by actuarial calculations and could result in significant losses to the PCPs or hospitals under contract

One mechanism to prevent certain high-cost services from adversely impacting the risk pool is to eliminate specific services from the risk pool arrangement. Examples would be the exclusion of cardiac surgery or organ transplant costs from the provider's risk pool. In general, high-cost services that occur with low and unpredictable frequency and for which the cost of care is not significantly affected by the provider's choice among acceptable clinical approaches should be excluded from risk pools.

## Stop-loss

*Stop-loss, risk-limiting* protection, or *reinsurance* are terms used to describe financial arrangements whereby the MCO provides financial protection to a capitated provider or protects the reasonableness of a risk pool arrangement against the effects of extraordinarily costly cases. Different levels of stop-loss provide varying degrees of protection to the provider (typically a group practice, though it can be an individual physician) assuming financial risk-sharing with the MCO. For example, stop-loss insurance is purchased so that one hospitalization or sick patient does not significantly deplete a group practice's hospital or outpatient (e.g., ancillary and referral) risk fund. No empirical data on stop-loss document its impact on practice behavior.

As with all forms of insurance, the decision to buy and the selection of the appropriate deductible depends on the possibility of costs which substantially exceed the expected range of costs, the probability of such occurrences, the impact of the potential loss on the provider, the risk aversion preference of the provider, and to a lesser extent the cost of coverage. A provider's desire to cover catastrophic loss may indicate that stop-loss coverage should be established at a low dollar level. In contrast, a medical group may want to assume increased risk, generating increased profit, and thus establish the stop-loss coverage at a relatively high dollar level. The extent of risk most medical groups assume is typically dependent on two factors: the number of enrollees for which the medical group is assuming risk and whether the services placed at risk are under direct management supervision by the group.

As referrals outside the medical group are under the control of the medical group, most providers are willing to place themselves at risk for specialty referrals. In contrast, medical groups have less influence over hospital services and therefore are often less willing to assume significant risk for these services unless they have a very large enrollee base. Typical stop-loss policies range from $1,000 to $9,000 for outpatient referral services and $10,000 to $100,000 for hospital services on a claims per member per year basis. Medical groups tend to assume hospital risk at the lower end of the range for hospital services, while MCOs with substantial enrollment assume a larger stop-loss risk for hospital services.

Both the group practice and the MCO should mutually agree on the level of catastrophic loss above which stop-loss coverage would apply. A large number of admissions costing $30,000 with the stop-loss set at $50,000 could lead to serious financial difficulties for the providers. Unfortunately, the ramifications of inadequate or absent stop-loss are not sufficiently explained to most providers before they sign their contract. This is at least in part due to the fact that many MCOs do not understand themselves the potential financial implications of inadequate stop-loss coverage.

## Specialist Capitation

While MCOs typically utilize capitation only for PCPs, increasingly MCOs are beginning to capitate specialists. This action would effectively remove portions of the PCPs' specialist risk fund pool or budgeted distribution. Capitation of specialists is used for two particular groups of physicians: those specialists whose utilization is hard to actuarially predict (e.g., mental health) or those specialists whose care can be very expensive either due to large volume of services provided (e.g., radiology) or particular procedures utilized (e.g., ophthalmology). MCOs are applying the same philosophy to capitation of specialty health maintenance organizations (HMOs); that is, there is an increasing tendency to capitate specialty services which have historically had difficult-to-predict resource consumption (for example, mental health and oncology services).

### Ancillary Service Capitation

Capitating ancillary services, such as laboratory and pharmacy, enables the MCO to know its expenses in advance. It also is important for reasons of physician feedback. Pharmacy and laboratory will be explained as models, though the authors appreciate the significant differences in capitating different ancillary services. Capitation of laboratory services is made possible by the low marginal cost of incremental laboratory tests. From a financial perspective, laboratory companies are often interested in capitating this service because it provides a marketing entree to physicians covered under the contract. On the other hand, capitation of pharmacy services is made possible by discretionary dispensing behavior (e.g., generic versus brand name) and ability to obtain bulk discounts, both of which can be influenced by pharmacists. No published research studies examine the impact of capitation of ancillary services on physician behavior.

From a purely financial perspective, if an MCO capitates pharmacy services, it knows in advance the cost of an important portion of an MCO's expense. In addition, the MCO typically receives management information system (MIS) reports from the vendor documenting physician practice patterns for pharmacy utilization. If pharmacy and laboratory information can be provided on a concurrent or retrospective basis, the data can serve as an excellent sentinel marker for the physician's overall utilization and quality of care. It should be emphasized that in the long term, the MCO will wish to work closely with its physicians and the vendor to assure well-managed and, therefore, stable rates of ancillary usage. Otherwise, physicians will have no incentive to carefully examine their prescribing patterns.

It may appear surprising that laboratory services could be capitated. However, such a figure can be actuarially calculated, and there are large laboratory companies that are eager to assume this risk. Only a few lab tests are excluded from this type of capitation contract. Laboratory capitation has become a very common feature of managed care.

## CONCLUSIONS

Figure 24–1 summarizes the variants of the four types of financial incentives discussed in this review. Capitation and managed fee-for-service are represented on the same line because they constitute the MCO's principal physician payment. Risk-based payments are supplementary payments over and above capitation. Medical groups, in particular, typically retain stop-loss protection to ensure that a small number of patients requiring very costly care do not deplete risk funds. Each line depicts increased financial or service risk assumed by the physician.

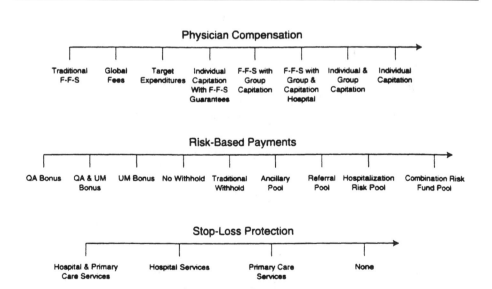

**Figure 24–1** Financial Incentives for Physicians in Managed Care Organizations (MCOs). *Source*: Reprinted from *Journal of Ambulatory Care Management*, Vol. 15, No. 4, p. 90, Aspen Publishers, Inc., © 1992.

While there are many unknowns pertaining to financial incentives, these incentives represent an important feature of today's health care landscape. However, considerable empirical work needs to be undertaken if both physicians and MCOs are to maximize the benefits obtainable from financial incentives. There is a significant need for research which examines the impact of differing capitation arrangements, managed fee-for-service, risk pools, and bonus or withhold on cost and quality. Information based on further studies will complement the information summarized in this review. The authors see the following specific questions as meriting research:

- What are the effects of financial versus nonfinancial incentives on physician or hospital behavior?
- What forms of performance-based fee-for-service systems have an impact on utilization?
- Do alternative capitation arrangements differentially impact quality of care and cost of services? How do these results differ from managed fee-for-service?
- Does capitation differentially impact quality of care for various socioeconomic groups?
- Is the impact of capitation across the board or are laboratory services, for example, impacted to a greater extent than patient visits?
- What other variables could be utilized to enhance the accuracy of capitation rate calculation?
- Is there a minimum number of prepaid enrollees a physician must have before the PCP is compensated via capitation in lieu of discounted fee-for-service?
- What, if any, are the advantages of group versus individual capitation?
- Does capitating hospitals impact physician behavior in the same manner as hospital prospective payment?
- What is the interaction between a group practice's risk-taking behavior and the level of stop-loss coverage obtained for the physicians through the plan?

Broader ethical and professional questions also need to be asked. While there have been a number of excellent articles pertaining to the ethical conflicts in general aspects of capitation, these lines of inquiry need to be directed to the particular types of financial incentives currently in existence and discussed here. A different line of inquiry opened up by capitation is its impact on physician autonomy. It is important to understand from a theoretical perspective whether capitation allows physicians to practice with a greater degree of freedom than other current reimbursement mechanisms. As one can argue both sides of this coin, theoretical and empirical analyses of this critical issue are needed.

The use of increased financial and service risk to influence behavior will increase, particularly if physicians and hospitals continue to receive cost and quality information on their practice. The authors also believe that these incentives will, over time, be structured more as rewards, as opposed to the current systems which tend to emphasize risks. "Risks" implies a financial penalty for failing to practice in a specified manner; a reward system, on the other hand, offers additional compensation for meeting practice standards.

---

### NOTES

1. G. Povar and J. Moreno, "Hippocrates and the Health Maintenance Organization," *Annals of Internal Medicine* 109 (1988): 419–424.

2. E.M. Livingstone, "Will Endoscopic Global Fees Destroy Gastroenterology as a Specialty?" *Journal of Clinical Endocrinology and Metabolism* 13 (1991): 358–361.

3. K.G. Manton et al., "Controlling Risk in Capitation Payment: Multivariate Definitions of Risk Groups," *Medical Care* 27 (1989): 259–272.

4. J.P. Weiner et al., "Development and Application of a Population Oriented Measure of Ambulatory Care Case Mix," *Medical Care* 29 (1991): 452–472.

5. R. Averill et al., *Design and Evaluation of a Prospective Payment System for Ambulatory Care* (Wallingford, CT: 3M Health Information Systems, 1990).

6. T.X. Carey et al., "Prepaid versus Traditional Medicaid Plans: Lack of Effect on Pregnancy," *Health Services Research* 90 (1991): 165–181.

7. R.E. Hurley et al., "Gatekeeping Effects on Patterns of Physician Use," *Journal of Family Practice* 32 (1991): 167–174.

8. S.M. Retchin and B. Brown, "Elderly Patients with Congestive Heart Failure under Prepaid Care," *American Journal of Medicine* 90 (1991): 236–242.

9. A.L. Hillman, "Financial Incentives for Physicians in HMOs. Is there a Conflict of Interest?" *New England Journal of Medicine* 317 (1987): 1743–1748.

10. A.L. Hillman et al., "How Do Financial Incentives Affect Physician's Clinical Decisions and the Financial Performance of Health Maintenance Organizations?" *New England Journal of Medicine* 321 (1989): 86–92.

11. W.P. Welch, *Giving Physicians Incentives To Contain Costs under Medicare: Lessons from Medicaid* (Washington, DC: The Urban Institute, 1989).

12. M. Moser, "The Growth of Multispecialty Medical Groups," *Journal of Care Management* 14 (1991): 13.

13. "Symposium: The Dark Side of Health Care Cost Containment," *Seton Hall Legislature Journal* 14 (1990).
14. N. Goldfield, "Measurement and Management of Quality in Managed Care Organizations: Alive and Improving," *Quality Review Bulletin*, 17, no. 11 (1991).
15. Povar and Moreno, "Hippocrates and the Health Maintenance Organization."

CHAPTER **25**

# Blue Shield of California Outpatient Payment Program

*John F. Roughan*

Outpatient medical care has been one of the fastest-growing sectors of health care costs. Many of the causes are familiar: technology changes, an ever-increasing supply of physicians, practice pattern changes in both surgery and anesthesia, and an increasingly greater use of utilization review in inpatient settings.

The rising trend for outpatient charges has been alarming. Between 1988 and 1990, average charges for these services for Blue Shield subscribers increased 15 percent to 17 percent on an annual basis. Existing Blue Shield payment approaches, based on a percentage discount on charges, provided little opportunity to implement utilization management or cost controls. Given this situation, new payment strategies needed to be adopted. The organization moved to develop and implement a prospective payment system that could be used for contracting with hospitals and free-standing facilities.

The main objectives of the outpatient payment program were to

- move to negotiated case rates versus percentage of charges, thereby improving payment predictability (a major objective of the project was to contain Blue Shield's reimbursement of outpatient services by developing case rates that would be negotiated periodically;

*Source:* Adapted from J.F. Roughan, "Blue Shield of California Outpatient Payment Program," *Managed Care Quarterly*, Vol. 2, No. 3, pp. 70–73, Aspen Publishers, Inc., © 1994.

payments based on charges did not allow for predictable actuarial estimates of benefit costs)

- develop a methodology that could be used for all outpatient services
- provide reasonable correlation between costs and reimbursements
- ensure outpatient payment that was less than or equal to inpatient diagnosis-related group (DRG) case rates for the same procedure (with an increasing number of inpatient procedures being performed in an outpatient setting, there was a need to control reimbursement regardless of the place of service)
- develop a reasonable rate differential between hospitals and free-standing facilities
- eliminate facility payments for minor surgical procedures
- include all significant ancillary costs (i.e., lab, radiology) in the case rate
- give Blue Shield a competitive advantage over other private payers in the California marketplace who had not attempted to more effectively manage outpatient services

## BACKGROUND

Several issues confronted Blue Shield during the search for a new payment system. Among them were developing a payment method for classifying surgical procedures as well as ground rules for visits that involve multiple procedures, developing rates that would take into account cost differences between hospitals and free-standing facilities as well as differences between inpatient and outpatient rates, and obtaining comparative outpatient data.

In 1990, Blue Shield of California, along with other Blue Cross and Blue Shield plans, participated in an ambulatory surgery study coordinated through the Center for Health Policy Studies on behalf of the Health Care Financing Administration (HCFA). Blue Shield thereby became aware of HCFA's efforts regarding development of ambulatory patient groups (APGs). APGs are an outpatient classification system originally developed for Medicare under the leadership of Health Systems International. They were designed to categorize outpatient visits with similar clinical characteristics as well as similar resource uses and costs. APGs could then be used to create a payment system that reimburses outpatient facilities (hospital and ambulatory centers) a fixed amount for each distinct APG.

APGs are determined by Current Procedural Terminology, Fourth Edition (CPT-4) codes assigned to services provided during an outpatient visit. A special definitions manual was available that defined all APGs by broad procedural categories and, for each APG, all of the related CPT codes used. In general, all CPTs for a given APG require a similar resource usage during the provision of the outpatient service.

## PROCEDURE

In September 1991, Blue Shield decided to move forward with the development of an outpatient prospective payment system based on the APG classification system. The approach was appealing because it not only provided for prospective payment, but it also enabled a measurement of case mix. A decision was made initially to limit the program to outpatient surgeries and later to expand the program to radiology and other services. As a percentage of total outpatient business, surgery accounted for 55 percent, whereas radiology and laboratory services totaled 27 percent.

Blue Shield decided to implement the payment system in a pilot program with a selected group of its network hospitals and free-standing outpatient centers. The project was undertaken to gain concrete experience in negotiating prospective payment contracts with providers as well as to develop and test appropriate claims and operational systems.

The development process required the use of outpatient surgery claims data and pricing information from both hospitals and free-standing facilities. Blue Shield used its existing claims data and analyses as a starting point and worked with the California Ambulatory Surgical Association to supplement the data. The Blue Shield database included three years of data (1988–1990) and involved over 300,000 claims.

The foundation of the new payment system is the CPT-4 coding system. There are approximately 8,000 procedure codes under the CPT-4 system. Each of the 2,000 surgery-related codes has been assigned to an APG. The APG classifications used by this system are taken directly from the 3M Classification Version 1.0, which was being developed for use by Medicare.

## WORK PLAN

Blue Shield's APG program encompasses 119 surgical APGs for hospitals and 111 surgical APGs for free-standing surgery centers. The following is a summary of the work plan used to develop the payment system:

- Review existing Blue Shield outpatient claims analyses.
- Use Blue Shield data to create a current payment baseline.
- Create payment profiles within APG classifications from baseline claims data.
- Investigate large dollar variances resulting from such factors as the type of hospital (tertiary, rural) and the geographical location of the provider.
- Organize and summarize pricing information from hospitals and free-standing facilities.
- Based on results of pricing analyses, develop a pricing strategy to be used in contracting while recognizing large variations in charge practices between providers.

Decisions needed to be made regarding the details of the program. The following work flow and program requirements were established:

- *Provider submits claim with CPT code detail.* The outpatient facility must report all procedures performed during the visit by coding the appropriate CPT codes on the claim form. Without these codes, no APG can be assigned to the claim (claims with missing CPT codes would be returned to the provider).
- *APGs are assigned to CPT codes.* This assignment was controlled by the APG definition manual (note that many claims will have more than one APG).
- *Claim is classified as to type of service.* If any of the APGs on the claim are surgical, the claim is paid according to the APG methodology. If no surgical procedure is involved, then the claim is paid on a percentage of charges as specified in the provider contract.
- *Multiple procedure claims are reduced to a single APG.* Some claims will involve multiple surgical procedures that are performed during a single outpatient visit. Whereas 15 percent of the cases have multiple APGs, only the most expensive APG will be assigned to the visit (the extra cost of performing the multiple procedures has been factored into the payment system).

  Any nonsurgical APGs involved in the surgical procedure would not be reflected in the payment calculation; again, the extra cost of these services has been factored into the system. Also, all CPT-4 procedures classified as minor procedures (procedures more appropriately performed in a physician's office) have been assigned an APG weight of zero.

As an example of an APG assignment, consider the following claim:

| CPT-4 Code Procedure | Provider-Charge ($) | APG Group Number | APG Weight |
|---|---|---|---|
| 43239 (Upper gastrointesti-nal endoscopy) | $350.00 | 162 | 0.38253 |
| 45380 (Colonoscopy) | 600.00 | 164 | 0.40544 |
| 81005 (Urinalysis) | 8.00 | 431 | 0.00999 |

This claim contains two surgical APGs (162 and 164) and one nonsurgical APG (431). Because the surgical procedure is primary, the nonsurgical APG would have no bearing on reimbursement. Because APG 164 has the highest weight value (0.40544), it would become the determining APG for the claim.

• *Reimbursement is calculated using APG weights.* Charge-based weights were developed for each APG by using historical Blue Shield outpatient claims data. APG weights are calculated by dividing these average charges by the overall outpatient average charge. Relativity between the APGs resulted from these calculations. Separate sets of weights were calculated for hospital and free-standing surgery centers to reflect differences in their costs of operation.

Each provider's claims are analyzed to determine historical APG mix and reimbursement patterns. This information is then used to negotiate provider rates to be used in the APG reimbursement calculation. A theoretical unit value of one (multiplier) is finalized with the provider. The multiplier (e.g., $1,050) is then applied against the APG weights to create an overall schedule unique to the provider.

## RESULTS

The negotiation of APG contracts with hospitals has proven to be more involved than contracts with free-standing surgery centers. Several factors have accounted for this situation. All of the free-standing centers that were approached use global case rates for their standard billings. These centers also use CPT-4 codes for billing purposes. Because their sole business is surgical services, the centers have a reasonable understanding of their costs on a per-case basis. Given these factors, the centers readily agreed to the APG concept, and the negotiations regarding the provider multiplier were concluded with minimal problems.

In comparison, most hospitals have itemized billings for outpatient surgeries rather than case rates. As a result, Blue Shield has had to assist hospitals in calculating expected reimbursement under the APG payment methodology. Also, whereas hospitals use CPT-4 codes for their Medicare and Medicaid billings, many facilities use ICD-9 codes for billings to commercial payers. Because outpatient bills must contain CPT-4 codes for the APG program, Blue Shield has had to work with hospitals so they can comply with this requirement.

Blue Shield has achieved many of the objectives initially established for the APG program. For example:

- APGs have greatly improved payment predictability. Once the initial provider multiplier is established, face-to-face negotiations determine the rate of increase. These negotiations have resulted in a relatively narrow range of annual increases.
- There is now a 15-percent to 20-percent price difference between hospitals and free-standing surgery centers.
- While accounting for less than 2 percent of total claims, facility payments have been eliminated for minor procedures.
- All significant ancillary costs (i.e., lab, radiology) are included in the case rate; contract negotiations have not resulted in provider-specific modifications or exceptions to the basic payment methodology.
- APGs have provided Blue Shield with a competitive advantage in the marketplace. This is especially true for large employers (500+ employees) that have seen double-digit increases in outpatient costs and are seeking a vehicle to control these expenses.
- APGs provide a reasonable correlation between costs and payments. Several providers have used the relativity of the weights to reprice their services.

## CONCLUSIONS

Currently, 30 percent of Blue Shield's provider network is on the APG program. The organization is currently expanding the program with its remaining preferred providers. A challenge will be to assess the impact of health care reform efforts on provider reimbursement and payer/provider relationships.

In the future, Blue Shield plans to expand the APG program to include non-surgical outpatient services. Because nearly 45 percent of outpatient services involve nonsurgical services, predictability of payment is a business necessity. As outcome analysis becomes a more important element in the evaluation of the quality of health care, methodologies such as APGs will become critical evaluation tools.

CHAPTER 26

# Use of Ambulatory Patient Groups in Iowa Hospitals— Revisited

*James C. Vertrees and Marcia J. Stark*

This chapter describes the initial implementation and decision-making process for Iowa's APG system in 1994 and subsequent rebasing and recalibration efforts in 1996. To fully understand the theory and requirements of the APG prospective payment system as designed for Iowa, see the October 1994 issue of *Journal of Ambulatory Care* and other related sources. This chapter summarizes the full extent of the policy options involved in Iowa's system when initially implemented, examines the rationale for those decisions, and then compares the initial Version 1.0 implementation policy decisions with the analysis and changes adopted subsequent to Version 2.0 implementation (based on more extensive and complete data interpretation) in 1996.

## GENERAL HISTORICAL SUMMARY

In 1992, the Iowa General Assembly had instructed Iowa Medicaid to develop and implement a new outpatient reimbursement system that would encourage efficient use of health care dollars and maintain the standards of quality inherent in the Iowa program. Subsequent to that directive, the Iowa Department of Human Services (Iowa Medicaid) released a request for proposal (RFP) for technical assistance with the development and implementation of a new outpatient system. After the selection of the ambulatory patient group (APG) system in 1993, the state implemented the Version 1.0 system (with modifications) in 1994 and then subsequently rebased and recalibrated the entire system in 1996 to implement the modified Version 2.0 system. The initial decision process and implementation issues are described along with the various changes that were initiated by the rebasing and recalibration.

## SELECTION AND SYSTEM CRITERIA

The selection of a new outpatient reimbursement system and methodology for Iowa was based on several criteria. First, the system would be required to comprehensively reimburse all services (without professional fee components) that were provided in a hospital-based ambulatory setting. Second, to encourage support from the provider community, the basic system design was required to utilize to the greatest extent possible the existing Iowa Universal Bill 92 (UB-92) coding conventions and claim completion methods in place. Last, the new outpatient data and reimbursement system needed to support Iowa's requirements of classifying services into clinically meaningful groups, allow for reasonable resource comparison between different areas, and prevent future gaming or upcoding problems within the system.

Iowa Medicaid contracted with Solon Consulting (now 3M-Health Information Systems [3M-HIS]) to design and develop a system. Although a number of systems were evaluated, the decision was made to use APGs. The APG system allowed for total service inclusion, utilized the commonly collected data elements, grouped services in meaningful and distinct ways, and allowed the state to retain individual program policies that it deemed necessary to ensure that the basic requirements of the Iowa Medicaid program were met.[1]

In 1994, the Iowa Medicaid program became the first payer to fully implement an outpatient reimbursement system based on Version 1.0 APGs. Until that time, the development of APGs had been mainly connected to the 3M demonstration project done in conjunction with the Health Care Financing Administration (HCFA) for use in Medicare. Most of the previous development work had centered around data and policy needed to support the Medicare program. Based upon the primary design developed for HCFA, Iowa Medicaid's policies and requirements were evaluated to determine the optimum requirements for the APG program for Medicaid.[2]

As the previous outpatient reimbursement methodology used in Iowa had been retrospective cost based, the system lacked both any real incentives to support efficient service delivery or significant review of how claim-coding conventions impacted reimbursement. This situation, coupled with the lack of Current Procedural Terminology (CPT) coding (on previously paid claims to set APG weights), became the biggest obstacle to overcome in the development of the APG system in Iowa. As Iowa had identified a need to compute APG weights specific to its program, without needed CPT-4 claim coding, mapping accommodations using International Classification of Diseases, Ninth Edition (ICD-9) and UB-92 hospital revenue codes were developed to support weight-setting activities. Using ICD-9– and UB-92–based revenue codes, the appropriate CPT code and APG assignment were imputed, allowing grouping to occur. Analysis of the APG assignments showed expected statistical distribution relating to the APG assignments. Cost analysis, however, showed a somewhat larger than expected per case variance, encouraging the state and providers to programmatically support the use of an "outlier" provision.[3]

Similar deviance appeared with services that included multiple timed units per visit (such as occupational, physical, or speech therapies) and proved difficult to assign in a consistent unit. Surveys of various Iowa hospitals providing those therapy services had no "standard" time unit, and costs varied widely. In the initial Iowa Version 1.0 implementation, the standard therapy time unit was defined as 15 minutes; however, the mapping of the actual claims showed significant disparity, thereby affecting relative weights.

Based on the need for mapping and utilizing an "untried" system, the Iowa Legislature also mandated that hospitals would not be placed in financial jeopardy by using a system that could potentially reimburse below reasonable levels. Iowa Medicaid was instructed to utilize a risk corridor for two years to verify that the level of payments (based upon APGs) were within 5 percent plus or minus the level of payments reimbursed using the previous cost-based system, and DHS was instructed to maintain global budget neutrality for the outpatient budget lines.[4] Similarly, Medicaid was required to rebase and recalibrate the system after its first two years of operations, with the understanding that the actual "grouped" Iowa data (from the first two years) would be superior to the initial "mapped" data, resulting in better accuracy.

As a departure from the Version 1.0 design, Iowa used the original Version 1.0 grouper, but implemented the packaging and consolidation logic set that was to be part of the Version 2.0 grouper (the Version 2.0 grouper was incomplete during the initial implementation). Since there were no inherent logic differences with the packaging or consolidation information, the logic worked equally well with Version 1.0. Some hospitals expressed concerns over the packaging of ancillary services (such as magnetic resonance imaging (MRI), certain chemotherapies, computed tomography (CT) scans, and other higher cost services) and consolidation of significant procedures, especially bilateral procedures. Although the higher cost ancillary services normally did not package and the issue became moot, the bilateral procedures would consolidate into the same APG and would consistently underpay these procedures.[5] Similar concerns surfaced regarding procedures that were terminated or modified and would not directly fit into the APG coding and reimbursement format. It was decided to give these cases special consideration when they occurred to determine the size and scope of this issue and make appropriate reimbursement determinations.

On a quarterly basis, Medicaid was required to demonstrate that the reimbursements were within the respective risk corridor and make adjustments as needed. As a result of those calculations, it was apparent that the system was trending payments toward the higher side, requiring funds to be returned to the state from many hospitals during the cost settlement process. The three-year cost settlement support of the APG risk corridor was demanding but did allow the state to better monitor the APG system and to make adjustments on an ongoing basis.

## 1996 REBASING AND RECALIBRATION

After the first two years of operation, the rebasing and recalibration occurred, using data from these two years. During analysis of those data, several key data and design issues were noted, leading to state policy changes. As previously indicated, the mapped claims that identified expected outlier amounts seemed to be relatively high in comparison with the experience for Medicare. After review of Iowa's second data set, it appeared that the initial mapping did not correctly interpret the data and had miscategorized some of these claims. The level of outlier claims, which were expected to be at a 1- to 2-percent level, was at nearly 10 percent, using the initial tolerance levels for outlier determination. Based on these findings, the dollar tolerance levels for outliers was raised, resulting in more normal outlier rates.

Similarly, the timed units for therapies also seemed to be skewed. Analysis of those services indicated that providers were incorrectly coding many of the therapy units and costs. The most common errors were found to be these:

- not listing or incorrectly listing the appropriate number of units of service
- using charges that were incompatible with the units listed
- incorrectly or inconsistently batching service data when submitting claims

During the 1996 training sessions, additional information was distributed to hospitals to correct these errors.

Additional analysis uncovered several other common data entry and claim completion errors that caused reimbursement errors. Most of these anomalies were discussed and corrective action was presented as part of the 1996 APG training session held in Fall 1996. As an example, state policy directives indicated that payment could be made for the assessment of a patient regardless of the outcome of the visit. It appeared that many hospitals did not code the assigned HCPCS assessment code and hence did not receive reimbursement for that service if it was provided. Other similar claim completion issues resulted in underpayment for the use of observation beds hours.

Key concerns included the larger than expected expenditures. Because of the rebasing and recalibration, more accurate data aggregation was possible (using claims that had been already grouped during payment), resulting in more accurate APG weights and APG assignments. Some recalibrated APG weights changed significantly, average costs per unit decreased (as a result of better data aggregation and cost-finding steps), and errors in unit reporting were corrected when identified. Additionally, the use of the Version 2.0 grouper enhanced the assignment of APGs, making the groups more consistent with current service provision and treatment protocols.

## KEY RESOLUTION ISSUES AND CONCLUSIONS

Both HCFA and the state of Iowa have continued to study the project to ascertain needed information for future implementations with other state Medicaid programs or Medicare. With regard to internal state concerns, most of these have been successfully resolved by the state agency. Many of the initial concerns voiced by hospitals either did not materialize or were handled.[6] HCFA's review showed most areas were positive, although the difficulty of initial implementation was noted.

With nearly four years of operation completed, the state seems to be well positioned to foster continued use and growth of the system. The multiple years of experience in operation and implementation will be helpful not only for continued use in Iowa but also to other payers wishing to use the system. The major issues in the state seem to reflect the rapidly changing environment of the ambulatory service sector and the updating necessary to support the changes occurring. Procedures considered to be inpatient procedures a short time before may now be considered to be ambulatory in nature. The volatility of these changes will require more frequent grouper updates as well as the design of individual options that are primarily dependent upon local characteristics of service provision. Similarly, the changes in electronic claim submission have resulted in further shortening of the time available to support the grouper and payment module changes.[7] It was noted that Iowa's enhanced electronic data interchange (EDI) claim submission has resulted in many APG claims being submitted on Thursday afternoon and adjudicated at the close of business the next day. Thus, hospitals that initiate ICD-9 or CPT-4 yearly coding changes may receive errors because of the lack of time for updating the groupers and APG system. More modular approaches to updating the grouper may alleviate this type of error.

Iowa's use of the classification portion of APGs continues to grow. As many portions of the state are now covered by managed care organizations (MCOs), the APG system will provide Iowa with a method to assess the differences in the MCO delivery system as well as the ability to compare the managed care blocks to the remaining fee-for-service sector. As all of the hospital providers have the ability to code the needed conventions, the state is considering requiring the use of that coding so that it can be imported into the MCO encounter data system. Given HCFA's requirements (under the Balanced Budget Act of 1997) that Medicaid agencies must assess the quality of care provided by the contracted plans, the use of the APG system to extract the data is timely and appropriate. While Iowa has been enjoying several years of declining medical expenditures, the most recent trend has been toward increasing costs and services. The comparative data available in the APG system will likely prove invaluable for identifying and controlling the increases appearing in the Medicaid program.

---

NOTES

1. Most Medicaid programs have numerous local coding dictates as well as many nonroutine clinical services, distinct service limitations, or unique medical necessity issues germane only to individual state Medical programs or individual beneficiaries. The design of the APG system allowed Iowa the flexibility to include and maintain the distinct program contents.

2. Vertrees et al., "Developing an Outpatient Prospective Payment System Based on APGs for the Iowa Medicaid Program," *Journal of Ambulatory Care, October 1994,* pp. 82–96. This article discusses the reasons for using cost versus charge data, unit-of-service data, and utilization data and other system-based decisions.

3. It had been the general consensus during the development of the APG system that most cases requiring an outlier status would ultimately switch venues (either by being admitted or by requiring another O/P visit) and negate the need for an outlier policy provision. Iowa still maintains an outlier provision in the program.

4. This risk corridor was intended to be used until the system was rebased using actual Iowa data in 1996. However, for SFY 1997, the Association of Iowa Hospitals and Health Systems successfully lobbied for the continuation of the risk corridor as well as the expansion of the levels to 10 percent plus or minus. As the rebasing normalized the payments even further, the risk corridor became less of a concern to hospitals in total. The intent of the legislatively mandated expansion (from 5 to 10 percent plus or minus) was not totally clear to the state. Regardless, the risk corridor was due to sunset at the end of SFY 1997 (June 30, 1998) and was not readopted.

5. Additional attention has been given to the recording and payment of bilateral procedures in the subsequent release of APGs.

6. Hospitals initially expressed worries about staffing increases demanded by claims coding, reimbursement levels, trying out a "new" system, unknown system issues, and other similar concerns. Most of these concerns tended to diminish when the system had been underway for a period of time. Similarly, the reimbursement levels remained adequate and claim-processing statistics for clean claims remained on a par with other claim types after the initial implementation period. Many of the larger hospitals, as well as the IH&HS, also employed an outside vendor to perform training activities adjunct to the claims completion training done by the state.

7. The state had also changed MMIS contractors during this time period. The APG system in its entirety was transferred from one mainframe to another without significant complications. The majority of work involved changing edit specifications (as opposed to reprogramming large portions of the MMIS). The ability of the APG system to transfer from mainframe to mainframe is crucial to its acceptance in the payer marketplace.

# Concluding Comments

*Norbert Goldfield*

## PROFILING AND QUALITY IMPROVEMENT

A large number of methods are available for risk adjusting outpatient care. My concluding comments will focus on

- the overarching standards one should utilize before considering a risk adjustment system
- the specific criteria one should employ before deciding on a risk adjustment methodology
- a listing of available methods

Before discussing the advantages and disadvantages of currently available tools in the field, it is important to step back and discuss the different uses of these tools and the appropriate time for their introduction. Two articles published in 1994 in the *New England Journal of Medicine* brought the issue of using ambulatory case mix measures into sharp relief.[1,2] In an editorial responding to an article that demonstrated sharp differences in utilization patterns between Oregon and Florida, the editor of the journal, Dr. Kassirer, advocated stringent criteria for the use in practice of these ambulatory case mix measures. Most controversially, Dr. Kassirer stated that the criteria for the use of these should be the same as those used by the Food and Drug Administration (FDA) for the evaluation of new medications. He specifically recommended that physicians work together to reject the use of health policy tools that do not pass a set of criteria equivalent to the FDA's safe and effective test.

223

Dr. Kassirer's pronouncement reveals two profound misunderstandings regarding the differences between the timing of approval of the use of advances in medical research and advances in practical health services research and the ability (or possibly even the need) of health policy tools to achieve the same statistical properties as those required by the FDA. Whereas the FDA process has one purpose and one purpose only (the safety and efficacy of a proposed new medicine), practical health services research is subject to the problem and challenge that the same tool is used for multiple purposes. From a quality improvement perspective, Dr. Kassirer would have better served the health system, and the medical profession in particular, if he had insisted that developers and users work together to identify the manifold uses of these health policy tools. With this understanding in hand, users, such as medical professionals, should in turn work with other members of the health care team, such as insurers or managed care organizations, to encourage insurers not to use these tools for purposes that may cause irreparable harm to the medical profession.

Dr. Kassirer and others could appropriately object that demanding the specification of when a tool can cause irreparable harm merely skirts the issue. How does one identify such a situation? A careful examination and understanding of the quality improvement process holds the key to such an understanding. In fact, the quality improvement process (plan-do-check-act) in a positive way demands that different members of the health care team utilize health policy tools useful for a quality improvement project and make suggestions for improvements in these tools. Thus as long as the health care team, whether at a local or national level, continues to work together toward continuous improvement, it is legitimate and mandatory to utilize ambulatory case mix tools.

The process of physician profiling within a quality improvement context can be contrasted with a process that too often is used in today's rapidly changing market and that does result in irreparable harm to the medical profession. Physician profiling based on quality improvement shares the following characteristics:

- individual feedback
- peer comparison
- face-to-face communication
- continuous program
- an understanding of the costs of overutilized services

Compare this approach with the manner in which these profiling tools are often utilized today. Tools such as Health Chex and ambulatory care groups are often used in the initial development of a managed care network. In these situations, physicians who have often never seen any data on their practice patterns are excluded from a managed care organization and not provided with the opportunity either to respond to the charges or to improve their practice patterns (if, in fact, their practice patterns need improving). Such a use of an ambulatory case mix tool can only result in direct harm and demoralization of the medical profession, a complete disregard for the quality improvement process, and, more fundamentally, a misdirection of efforts at improving our health care system.

Thus Dr. Kassirer's blanket demand that all health policy tools operate under the same evaluation process as that of the FDA not only reveals a misunderstanding of the changes affecting the health care system but, more important, also neglects the critical significance of integrating quality improvement principles into health care reform.

## PROFILING AND AMBULATORY CASE MIX SYSTEMS

It needs to be emphasized that we are at a preliminary stage in the development of tools to measure differences in the case mix of ambulatory services. This is not for lack of trying but rather because dependent variables likely to be important, such as health status, are not collected on a routine basis and because independent variables, such as charges, may have little relationship to the true cost of services. Although there is much to be learned, it is important to use what is available and, from a quality improvement perspective, to continue to assess new and improved available tools. For example, unpublished work in progress indicates that costs and charges are closely related from a proportional perspective. In addition, other current research reveals that health status appears to be quite helpful in explaining variations in resource consumption, particularly in areas of health care that have been traditionally difficult to measure, such as rehabilitation and mental health services.

The key issue in determining the adequacy of the case mix system is the use to which it will be put. Profiling of ambulatory services can be used for purposes of

• quality improvement, including outcomes management

- utilization management (e.g., efficiency of physician practice)
- capitation adjustment
- technology assessment
- network determination and updating

Ambulatory Patient Groups (APGs) can be used to manage the underutilization or overutilization of specific discrete services (e.g., herniorrhaphy or diabetes), and Ambulatory Care Groups, Diagnostic Episode Clusters, and Health Chex all use different methodologies to assess whether there may be overutilization or underutilization of services cutting across both procedures and diagnoses.

Customers are always asking consultants, which is best? A good consultant will answer: It depends on what you want to use the system for. The questions listed in Exhibit 1 should be considered when examining an ambulatory case mix system.

**Exhibit 1** Questions To Consider When Choosing an Ambulatory Case Mix System

---

**CLINICAL**

Are the base units expressed in clinical terms easily understood and supported by health care professionals?

Are the base units driven by International Classification of Diseases, Ninth Edition, Clinical Modification (ICD-9-CM), Current Procedural Terminology, Fourth Edition (CPT-4), or both?

Does a mapper exist to trace codes utilizing the code system currently in use in your system?

If you are looking at episodes, is the unit of analysis the total episode of care (inpatient and outpatient) or are outpatient services only considered?

Can case examples of the use of the system be provided?

**STATISTICAL**

What is the predictive capability of the case mix adjustment?

How are outliers treated? (It should be pointed out that the more outliers removed, the more the statistics will improve, at the expense of explaining the entire ambulatory care contact.)

*continues*

**Exhibit 1** Continued

Is it an ICD-9 code-driven system?

Is the unit of analysis the total episode of care (i.e., all outpatient and inpatient care and prescription drugs are linked)?

Does it have a large number of diagnostic groupings (i.e., medical conditions)?

Is a valid method for assigning an ICD-9 code to encounters with missing and nonspecific ICD-9 codes available?

Does it place all available encounter and claims data for each patient into at least one episode of care?

Is an episode duration defined by the maximum number of days between contact with a physician (i.e., window period)?

For multiple concurrent episodes, is an encounter placed into only one episode (e.g., one lab is placed into one and only one episode)?

Do episodes have an adjustment for comorbidities, severity of illness, and patient age?

Is the predictive ability of the episode adjustments very high?

Can outlier episodes be excluded from analysis?

To reduce fragmentation of episodes, are two years of encounter data required?

Can pattern-of-treatment results for treating specific medical conditions easily be compared across networks and physicians?

Is the system flexible enough to be used for the following software products?
- Global pattern-of-treatment profiling
- Prescription drug performance/risk
- Clinical guideline development
- Outcomes research
- Physician compensation
- Physician group composition
- High-cost patient risk management
- Medical capitation performance/risk
- Workers' compensation performance/risk
- Chronic disease management
- Health Plan Employer Data and Information Set (HEDIS) 2.0/3.0 reporting

Changing physician behavior is most successful when physicians receive individualized feedback that compares their practice patterns with those of a peer group in the same specialty and in the same patient and catchment area. Moreover, the physician feedback needs to address single clinical actions that a respected clinical leader can present in a face-to-face meeting. The diagnostic cluster approach was designed to provide clinical leaders with the information necessary to develop physician feedback on single clinical actions.[3]

## NOTES

1. J.P. Kassirer, "The Use and Abuse of Practice Profiles," *New England Journal of Medicine* 330 (1994): 634–636.

2. H.G. Welch et al., "Physician Profiling: An Analysis of Inpatient Practice Patterns in Florida and Oregon," *New England Journal of Medicine* 330, no. 9 (1994): 607–612.

3. D. Cave and E. Geehr, "Analyzing Patterns of Treatment Data To Provide Feedback to Physicians," *Medical Interface*, July, 1994, 125.

CHAPTER 27

# The American Medical Accreditation Program: Quality, Accreditation, and the AMA

*William F. Jessee, Terry Hammons, and Richard Hughes*

On May 7, 1847, Nathan Davis, a young physician from Binghamton, New York, along with some 80 like-minded colleagues, met in Philadelphia to form the American Medical Association (AMA). As one of its first actions, the young association set standards for ethical behavior and medical education and established a standing committee on medical practice.[1] Ever since, the AMA has had as its guiding principle to "promote the art and science of medicine and the betterment of public health." Setting professional standards and providing physicians with the information and means to meet or exceed those standards are critical elements in continuously improving the quality of care and service and bettering public health.

In 1997, the AMA launched a major new effort to advance the quality of medical care. The new American Medical Accreditation Program[SM] (AMAP) is an ambitious effort by the AMA, in partnership with state, county, and national medical specialty societies, to set standards that can serve as a national benchmark of quality for individual physicians.[2] AMAP collects and verifies information on a physician's credentials, performance, and commitment to quality and provides this information to hospitals and health plans for their use in credentialing. And AMAP will provide to each physician key information on both processes and outcomes of care as a foundation for self-assessment and improvement.

AMAP does not seek to duplicate or replace the myriad attempts to generate "profiles" and "report cards" for physicians, but it does offer a comprehensive and balanced approach to using information for choosing physicians and for fostering physician self-assessment and improvement. AMAP provides information on physician accreditation status that patients can use to help them choose their physicians. This summary measure complements other physician-specific information that is available to the public, including that available through AMA Physician Select on the Internet. (Physician Select can be accessed through the "Doctor Finder" feature on the AMA website at www.ama-assn.org/aps/amahg.htm. Physician Select provides basic information on a physician's training and other credentials, and for many physicians it provides additional personalized practice information, such as office hours, admitting privileges held, practice philosophy, and professional achievements.)

To health plans and hospitals that the physician designates, AMAP provides a standardized portfolio of information on the physician's credentials, personal qualifications, office practice, and participation in self-assessment and improvement. Through standardization of specific quality measures used by physicians and the health care organizations through which they provide care, AMAP will enable more consistent measurement of patient care and outcomes by physicians, health plans, and other health care organizations—enabling better coordinated and more effective efforts to improve care across organizational and geographic boundaries.

Physicians receive a summary of the information provided to hospitals and health plans they designate and will in the future receive detailed comparative analyses of care processes and clinical outcomes for their patients. Only physicians will receive these detailed, comparative data on their own practices and outcomes; AMAP will not use these data to generate detailed clinical report cards for public use.

AMAP is committed to this balanced approach to information for choice and information for improvement—providing accurate, useful summary measures of quality to physicians, health care organizations, and the public while providing more extensive information to physicians, coupled with support and tools for using the data to improve care. The decision to provide detailed comparative clinical measurements only to physicians reflects a belief that by invigorating and informing the professional commitment to quality, AMAP can make its greatest contribution to better care for the public.

## FRAGMENTED CREDENTIALING, OFFICE REVIEW, AND PHYSICIAN PROFILING

The process through which health plans, hospitals, and other organizations assemble and verify physicians' credentials has grown into a huge task that is replete with redundancy. Similarly, a growing variety of attempts to measure isolated aspects of physicians' care and outcomes has added an additional layer of inconsistent, costly, and largely ineffective profiling to the effort to evaluate and select physicians. AMAP provides a means to reduce cost and improve the effectiveness of credentialing, office review, and measurement and feedback while providing information that patients can use to identify physicians who have met nationally recognized standards of quality.

In managed care, information about a physician's education, training, and credentials is collected and verified by each health plan in order to meet its own regulatory or accreditation requirements. For similar purposes, hospitals, ambulatory surgery centers, physician networks, and others go through the same data collection, verification, and review process as the first step in evaluating the qualifications for every physician that applies for membership. A 1996 study by the Colorado Physicians Insurance Company (COPIC) estimated the annual cost for these duplicative credentialing efforts at $43 million in Colorado alone,[3] and it seems safe to assume that nationally these credentialing activities add at least several hundred million dollars annually to the administrative costs of health plans and health care organizations. The value of such activities has not been shown to justify the costs incurred.

In addition, every health plan that seeks accreditation, from either the National Committee for Quality Assurance (NCQA) or the Joint Commission on Accreditation of Healthcare Organizations (Joint Commission), must conduct a biennial on-site review of the office of every primary care physician and high volume specialist.[4,5] Since the average physician now participates in more than 11 plans,[6] these reviews add unnecessary expense through massive duplication of effort.

Finally, each health plan (and each hospital as well) attempts to profile physicians on the basis of clinical performance, outcomes, cost, or other measures. But each includes only its own patients, usually a small proportion of a physician's total practice, and variability in the specific definitions of the measures leads to different measurements—and interpretations—from different sources. As a consequence, physicians may receive widely divergent feedback on their performance. For example, one plan may ask a physician for action to lower his rate of cesarean deliveries at the same time that another plan draws the same physician's attention to his "lower than expected" rate for such deliveries.[7] Each plan may have had good intentions, but each has access to information on only a small and unrepresentative sample of the physician's total patient population. It is not surprising that many physicians react negatively to such data and that most regard them as irrelevant.

Yet most physicians probably would find credible feedback on their performance to be of interest and potentially valuable to them. Physicians are by nature both altruistic and competitive. By training, they learn to become skeptical and conservative. But for feedback on clinical performance, patient satisfaction, clinical outcomes, or cost to be effective in influencing physicians' decisions, it must be credible, relevant, and comprehensive.[8-10] The current fragmented analysis of data by payer, rather than by physician, generally fails that test.

## AN INTEGRATED SOLUTION: PHYSICIAN ACCREDITATION

AMAP addresses these problems by substituting a single physician-driven, national program for the current fragmented, duplicative, and wasteful system. Physicians who apply for and achieve AMAP accreditation biennially complete one application, have their credentials verified one time, undergo a single practice operations review, and will receive periodic performance profiles across all their patients. Participating health plans, hospitals, networks, and others can then be provided with the information they require at a fraction of the cost of collecting and verifying it themselves. Physicians save time, money, and hassle. Health plans, hospitals, networks, and others can drastically reduce administrative overhead that adds no value to their operations. Purchasers and consumers gain from a nationally standardized process that provides recognition for physicians who meet AMAP's national standards for physician quality.

Through physician accreditation, AMAP will provide mechanisms and measures to assess and improve the quality of patient care and service. The measures that physicians will use to evaluate the care they provide will capture key aspects of the process and outcomes of care. Key measures for care of specific clinical conditions are being developed and selected in collaboration with national medical specialty societies, who are the profession's leaders in quality measurement and physician performance assessment. Measures will be tested in collaboration with medical societies to ensure that the data generated on physicians' practices are useful to physicians in evaluating what they do and in their efforts to improve. Finally, AMAP measures will be defined to be consistent with measures required (by the Joint Commission and NCQA) for accreditation of hospitals and health plans so that physicians and provider organizations will be spared the cost and waste of multiple inconsistent attempts to collect such data and so that each physician can more easily interpret the data from his or her own practice in light of the measurements provided by a hospital or health plan. This integrated approach will also increase the effectiveness of measurement and feedback by these provider organizations.

## AMAP AND PROFESSIONAL ACCOUNTABILITY

AMAP is an ambitious undertaking. It represents much more than an effort to eliminate waste, duplication, and hassle for physicians, health plans, and other health care organizations, and it is not just a rationalization of the measurement and feedback of data on quality. AMAP reasserts the historic role of the medical profession and the AMA in setting standards to help advance the art and science of medicine. By invigorating and informing physicians' commitment to high quality care for their patients, AMAP has the potential not just to rationalize credentialing and measurement of quality but to be a vehicle for pervasive improvement of patient care and outcomes.

AMAP sets quality standards and will provide physicians with the information and support to meet or exceed those standards. For the first time, physicians will gain access to standardized measurements that provide information about the most important aspects of care and outcomes for their patients, analyses that show physicians how their care—and their outcomes—compare with their peers. Using programs for self-assessment and improvement from specialty societies, local medical societies, and other professionally driven organizations, physicians will receive support to evaluate their practices and improve their outcomes.

## A BALANCE: INFORMATION FOR IMPROVEMENT AND INFORMATION FOR CHOICE

As we move further into the information age, individual patients increasingly use comparative data to examine a physician's credentials. Many physician report cards and physician profiles are intended to provide the public with information they can use to choose physicians. These are well-intentioned beginnings, but like in the story of the blind men and the elephant, a host of unmeasured or idiosyncratic variables and other problems limit their usefulness. In an unknown number of instances, these profiles are potentially misleading because the data are not representative of the physician's usual practices and performance.

While recognizing the importance of and the public's need for information to choose their personal physicians (and to choose hospitals and health plans), AMAP emphasizes the physicians' need for better information for self-assessment and improvement. To balance these needs, AMAP will make a physician's accreditation status publicly available, but only the physician will receive the detailed comparative data from measurements of quality and patient outcomes. Hospitals and health plans to which the physician applies will receive the entire portfolio of credentials, personal qualifications, and the results of office review. As the profession learns how to make quality of care more consistent across regions and states, the accreditation status earned by physicians will become increasingly credible and valuable to patients and purchasers.

This balanced approach to information—summary information for patients and the public, a portfolio of information for health care organizations with which physicians work, and detailed clinical data on care processes and outcomes to physicians to support self assessment and improvement—reflects the strength of AMAPS's belief in the power of the profession's accountability for quality of care. The greatest potential for continuous improvement of patient care and outcomes lies in the profession's commitment to excellence and physicians' commitment to self-assessment and improvement. AMAP will provide information for improvement—information to fuel the engine of professional accountability.

The public deserves valid information they can use to select their physicians. AMAP accreditation status will be useful for that purpose, and the AMA also provides additional information to the public through Physician Select. But it is still early in our collective understanding of how best to provide information on the quality of physicians, hospitals, and plans for use by patients and consumers.[11,12] We do not know how to use detailed comparative clinical data for this purpose. There is not only the risk of misinterpretation and misuse of such data but also the potential to induce defensive resistance by physicians to the measurements that are needed for improvement.[13,14] As we learn how to provide more useful information to patients that they can use in selecting physicians (and to do so without inviting misinterpretation and misuse of incomplete data), AMAP and the AMA will make more information available to the public. The AMA's "Principles of Physician Profiling" and "Principles To Guide the Collection, Release, and Use of Physician-Specific Health Care Data" give useful guidance for developing good information for use in evaluating and choosing physicians (see Appendixes 27–A and 27–B).

## HOW AMAP ACCREDITATION WORKS

AMAP sets standards in five areas: credentials, personal qualifications, environment of care, clinical performance, and patient care results. Physicians must satisfy all of the 12 required standards and score at least 11 of 22 possible points from 10 supplemental standards in order to achieve AMAP accreditation (see Appendix 27–C). The standards were developed through a structured process of review and consensus development that included medical societies, managed care plans, hospitals, consumers, patient groups, employers, purchasers, and various other stakeholders. They were given final approval by a 22-member governing body that included representation from consumers, patient groups, employers, managed care organizations, hospitals, health care accreditors, and government as well as physicians. The standards address the multiple aspects of quality physician care and are the same throughout the nation. The standards cover education and training, continuous professional self-improvement, ethical behavior, participation in peer review, and operation of a safe, patient-friendly office.

A set of standardized clinical performance measures, derived primarily from work done by medical specialty societies and health plan accreditation groups, will in the future give physicians a source of credible information on how they compare with their colleagues. Among the variables to be measured will be key processes of care, selected clinical outcomes, patient satisfaction, and health status. The unique value of AMAP will be in providing consistent feedback from data on *all* the patients in a physician's practice, not just those covered by a particular health insurance product, and in the consistency of the measurements used to generate the individual physician's results and the aggregated measurements by hospitals and health plans. Physician participation in a quality measurement system—whether it is one offered by the physician's specialty society, by a health system, or by other compatible systems—will eventually become a requirement for accreditation.

Funding for AMAP comes primarily from charges to health plans and hospitals that use it as a source of information about the credentials and performance of affiliated physicians. AMAP also charges physicians an application fee of $50 for AMA members and $125 for nonmembers every two years. By collecting and verifying the data once and providing them to multiple users, AMAP greatly reduces the cost to each hospital, health plan, or other user and reduces hassle and overhead costs to the physician while remaining economically viable. The fee charged to users of the information is significantly less than the amount each user organization would have to spend to collect and verify the information. Similarly, use of a carefully selected and representative set of clinical performance and patient care result measures will greatly reduce the collection time and associated administrative costs for physicians and health plans.

AMAP began operating in New Jersey late in 1997 and in the District of Columbia, Montana, and Idaho in early 1998. We anticipate that another 6 to 12 states will have the program available by the end of 1998 and that it will be offered to physicians in the balance of the country over the next three years. The AMA is developing partnerships with specialty societies, state medical societies, physician networks, and others engaged in measurement and feedback of clinical performance and patient care results, and testing of some standardized performance measures is planned to begin in 1998. Analysis of the data and feedback of clinical performance and outcomes measures to physicians should be an operating part of the program by 2001.

## FROM APPLICATION TO ACCREDITATION

The process and standards used to accredit physicians are the same in every state (see Figure 27–1). Once accredited, a physician applies for reaccreditation every two years, and the information in his or her portfolio is updated and verified.

## DEVELOPING BETTER MEASUREMENT FOR SELF-ASSESSMENT AND IMPROVEMENT

AMAP, in partnership with state and national medical specialty societies, intends to "manage the evolution" of measurement systems that physicians can use to measure, evaluate, and improve the care they provide. The intent is

| | |
|---|---|
| PHYSICIAN OR CLIENT REQUESTS APPLICATION | Physician may be asked to apply by hospital, health plan, PHO, network, etc. |
| ↓ | |
| AMAP PRE-POPULATED APPLICATION SENT | Some of the required information is already in the AMA Masterfile and is already verified with primary sources |
| ↓ | |
| PHYSICIAN RETURNS APPLICATION | Application contains all the information required by Joint Commission-accredited hospital, NCQA-accredited plan, etc. |
| ↓ | |
| CREDENTIALS VERIFIED BY CVO CONTRACTOR | CVO is under contract to AMAP or to state partner; CVO verifies information and forwards it to AMAP |
| ↓ | |
| PERSONAL QUALIFICATIONS VERIFIED BY AMAP | These include participation in peer review, commitment to ethical behavior, participation in continuing medical education (CME), and self-assessment |
| ↓ | |
| OFFICE SITE REVIEW BY ENVIRONMENT OF CARE (EOC) CONTRACTOR | EOC review body is under contract to AMAP or to state partner and uses AMAP-designed software; physician gets immediate summary of review; results are forwarded to AMAP |
| ↓ | |
| ACCREDITATION DATA COMPARED TO STANDARDS | This generates a yes-no accreditation decision based on objective comparison of data elements to written standards |
| ↓ | |
| ACCREDITATION STATUS AND PORTFOLIO OF DATA TO PHYSICIAN | Physician receives full information about accreditation status, how it was determined, and all data elements—no black boxes |
| ↓ | |
| ACCREDITATION STATUS AND PORTFOLIO OF INFORMATION TO HOSPITALS, PLANS, ETC., AS SPECIFIED BY PHYSICIAN | This information is provided to entities that have contracted with AMAP, if also designated by the physician |

Courtesy of American Medical Association.

**Figure 27–1** AMAP Accreditation Process

not for AMAP to develop entirely new measurement systems but rather for AMAP, in partnership with specialty societies, to identify from existing sources or if necessary to develop a small, coherent set or cluster of key measures of process and outcomes for each of a number of clinical conditions and demographic groups: diabetes, low back pain, otitis media, pregnancy and childbirth, infants, healthy women of child-bearing age, and so forth. This might result in a set of six measures for diabetes, eight measures for management of low back pain, and seven for major depressive disorder. Each such "core set" of clinical performance measures could be incorporated into all the clinical performance measurement systems in which physicians participate. The core measures for a condition will be reliable, valid, and important clinically for assessing the quality of care and patient outcomes for patients with that condition and for use by physicians to improve patient care.

The identification and development of measures will occur in collaboration with NCQA, the Joint Commission, and other bodies that have an interest in better systems of measurement so that the physician-level measurements that are of greatest interest to AMAP are consistent with the more aggregated measurements that are of greater interest to hospitals, health plans, and other organizations. The intent is that measures identified as members of a core set will be widely adopted for use not only in physician-level clinical performance measurement systems but also—in aggregated form—for organizational assessment and improvement so that measurements for the physician's use and for the plan's use can be done just once for a particular patient. This would reduce the cost and hassle for physicians and for their patients, and it would result in measurements and analyses used by plans that would be consistent with measurements used by physicians in those plans.

AMAP anticipates that most measures will come from existing physician-level systems, particularly those that have been and are being developed by medical specialty societies. Other measures will include those that are being identified or developed by NCQA for use in aggregated health plan measures or by the Joint Commission for use in aggregated hospital- or facility-level measures.

## IS PROFESSIONAL ACCREDITATION EQUAL TO THE TASK?

The design of AMAP reflects an assumption that the medical profession is accountable for the quality of care that physicians provide their patients and the public and a belief that by setting professional standards and informing the profession's commitment to meet or exceed those standards the quality of patient care will be most effectively improved. There is a growing body of literature describing effective approaches to improving health care and the promising results of that work.[15-21] But many people believe that market mechanisms—consumers choosing health plans, patients choosing hospitals and physicians—provide the more effective path to quality. AMAP's balanced approach to information for choice and for improvement has the potential to harness both forces for improvement.

Some have questioned whether the AMA, as a membership organization, should set quality standards for physicians.[22] Clearly, any such effort should not supplant and does not diminish the importance of existing medical licensure requirements or specialty board certification. It is the role of state medical licensure boards to set minimum standards for licensure to practice medicine and to act to protect the public from physicians whose clinical performance does not meet criteria of minimal acceptability. Specialty boards are, and should be, arbiters of the qualifications necessary to profess oneself to the public as a specialist in an area of medicine. But the advent of managed care has placed new pressures on the trust once enjoyed between patients and physicians. Consumers and purchasers increasingly are seeking more information about physicians. They want to know not only about education, training, and specialty board certification but whether physicians are clinically current, behave ethically, participate in peer review, and operate safe practices. They want to know whether a physician's patients are satisfied and how patient treatment patterns and results compare to those of others treating similar patients. Accreditation responds to these needs and complements certification and licensure.

It is appropriate that the medical profession undertake the responsibility for accreditation. Setting standards for the profession must be seen as one of the principal obligations of any professional association. These associations establish standards, evaluate members of the profession against those standards, and help the profession to meet or exceed those standards. To do less would be to abrogate responsibility for meeting the obligations of the trust that society has placed in the profession.

If standards addressing these issues are not set by physicians and their professional associations, then they will, by default, be set by other groups. The American Diabetes Association has already staked out its claim as the standards setter for diabetes care.[23] In Massachusetts, the Board of Registration in

Medicine has responded to public demands for information about physicians by developing an Internet-accessible database of physician profiles that includes detailed professional liability claims experience,[24] lending credibility, in the public's eye, to such experience as a quality measure. And the President's Advisory Commission on Consumer Protection and Quality in the Health Care Industry has recommended that physicians should be included, with health plans, in a proposed new federal initiative to shape the definition and disclosure of data on standard measures of performance.[25]

If the AMA does not assume a leadership role in setting standards for physicians, then who shall? AMAP, while initiated by the AMA, relies heavily on state medical societies and their county components as local partners in implementation. National medical specialty societies are also a part of the program, developing clinical self-assessment programs, specialty-specific site review criteria, and relevant condition–specific measures of clinical performance and patient care results. For the program to succeed, it must unite the various components of organized medicine in a cohesive effort to continuously advance the quality of our profession.

Will any of this make a difference? Is there any evidence that accreditation improves quality—in medicine, education, or any other field? Supporting anecdotes are manifold, but controlled studies are absent. Some things, however, have sufficient face validity that they are widely accepted not only as elements of professional behavior but as fundamental elements of public policy. For example, we know of no controlled study that shows that persons who satisfactorily complete a four-year education in medicine and are able to pass the National Board or U.S. Medical Licensure exams provide better medical care than persons who do not. But such standards seem appropriate on their face and are widely accepted as necessary prerequisites to the practice of medicine in the United States.

If the standards set by physicians and used by AMAP have face validity, they should be useful in advancing the cause of quality medical care. The standards are fully available for examination, and they will be examined for evidence that they are too stringent or not stringent enough. Pilot testing has shown that even well-trained board-certified physicians are challenged by the office review criteria but find them fair and relevant to patient care quality.[26] In the end, the AMAP standards must stand on their own merits, and they will be repeatedly examined and tested as they are used by physicians, hospitals, health plans, and the public. Where appropriate, the standards will evolve.

AMAP accreditation will not ensure that every patient treated by an accredited physician receives quality care, but it should increase the likelihood of good care. AMAP will also have value in restoring patient confidence and in reasserting physician leadership in setting standards for the practice of medicine.

**NOTES**

1. American Medical Association, *Caring for the Country: A History and Celebration of the First 150 Years of the American Medical Association* (Chicago: American Medical Association, 1997), 13–15.

2. P.J. Seward, "Restoring the Ethical Balance in Health Care," *Health Affairs* 16 (1997): 195–197.

3. Colorado Physicians Insurance Company, "Initial Physician Credentialing Costs for the Colorado Marketplace," (unpublished report, 1996).

4. National Committee for Quality Assurance, *Standards for Accreditation* (Washington: National Committee for Quality Assurance, 1997), 45.

5. Joint Commission on Accreditation of Healthcare Organizations, *Accreditation Manual for Health Care Networks* (Oakbrook Terrace, IL: Joint Commission on Accreditation of Healthcare Organizations, 1996), 100.

6. M.L. Gonzales, ed., *Physician Marketplace Statistics 1996: Profiles for Detailed Specialties, Selected States and Practice Arrangements* (Chicago: American Medical Association, 1997), 134.

7. J.D. Nelson, personal communication, 1996.

8. J.M. Eisenberg, *Doctors' Decisions and the Cost of Medical Care* (Ann Arbor, MI: Health Administration Press, 1986), 91–119.

9. N.A. Nadler, *Feedback and Organizational Development: Using Data Based Methods* (Reading, MA: Addison-Wesley, 1997).

10. W.F. Jessee, "Approaches To Improving the Quality of Health Care: Organizational Change," *Quality Review Bulletin* 7, no. 7 (1981): 13–18.

11. J.H. Hibbard and J.J. Jewett, "Will Quality Report Cards Help Consumers?" *Health Affairs* 16, (1997): 218–228.

12. P.D. Cleary and S. Edgman-Levitan, "Health Care Quality: Incorporating Consumer Perspectives," *JAMA* 278 (1997): 1608–1612.

13. J.P. Kassirer, "The Quality of Care and the Quality of Measuring It," *New England Journal of Medicine* 329 (1993): 1263–1264.

14. A. Epstein, "Performance Reports on Quality: Prototypes, Problems, and Prospects," *New England Journal of Medicine* 333 (1995): 57–61.

15. E.C. Nelson et al., "Improving Health Care: Part 1: The Clinical Value Compass," *Joint Commission Journal on Quality Improvement* 22 (1996): 243–258.

16. E.C. Nelson et al., "Improving Health Care: Part 2: A Clinical Improvement Worksheet and Users' Manual," *Joint Commission Journal on Quality Improvement* 22 (1996): 531–548.

17. J.J. Mohr et al., "Improving Health Care: Part 3: Clinical Benchmarking for Best Patient Care," *Joint Commission Journal on Quality Improvement* 22 (1996): 599–616.

18. P.B. Batalden et al., "Improving Health Care: Part 4: Concepts for Improving Any Clinical Process," *Joint Commission Journal on Quality Improvement* 22 (1996): 651–659.

19. M.R. Chassin, "Quality of Health Care: Part 3: Improving the Quality of Care," *New England Journal of Medicine* 335 (1996): 1060–1063.

20. D.M. Berwick and T.W. Nolan, "Physicians as Leaders in Improving Health Care: A New Series in *Annals of Internal Medicine*," *Annals of Internal Medicine* 128 (1998): 289–292.

21. D.M. Berwick, "Developing and Testing Changes in Delivery of Care," *Annals of Internal Medicine* 128 (1998): 651–656.

22. J.L. Kassirer, "The New Surrogates for Board Certification: What Should the Standards Be?" *New England Journal of Medicine* 337 (1997): 43–44.

23. American Diabetes Association, "New Program Recognizes Physicians Who Provide Quality Diabetes Care," *Clinical Diabetes* 15, no. 3 (1997): 134.

24. Commonwealth of Massachusetts, Board of Registration in Medicine, 1997. See http://www.docboard.org.

25. T.R. Reardon, personal communication, 1997.

26. American Medical Association, "Environment of Care Advisory Committee Briefing: May 1997 Field Tests" (unpublished report, 1997).

## A P P E N D I X   2 7 – A

# Principles of Physician Profiling

The AMA believes that managed care organizations, third party payers, government entities, and others that develop physician profiles should adhere to the following principles.

- The active involvement of physician organizations and practicing physicians in all aspects of physician profiling shall be essential.
- The methods for collecting and analyzing data and developing physician profiles shall be disclosed to relevant physician organizations and physicians under review.
- Valid data collection and profiling methodologies, including establishment of a statistically significant sample size, shall be developed.
- The limitations of the data sources used to develop physician profiles shall be clearly identified and acknowledged.
- Physician profiles shall be based on valid, accurate and objective data and used primarily for educational purposes.
- To the greatest extent possible, physician profiling initiatives shall use standards-based norms derived from widely accepted, physician-developed practice parameters.
- Comparisons among physician profiles shall adjust the patient case-mix, control for physician specialty, and distinguish between the ordering or referring physician and the physician providing the service or procedure.
- The quality and accuracy of physician profiles, data sources, and methodologies shall be evaluated regularly.
- Physician profiling data and any other information that has been compiled related to physician performance shall be shared with physician under review.
- Effective safeguards to protect against the unauthorized use or disclosure of physician profiles shall be developed.
- Any disclosure or release of physician profiles shall follow strict conformance to the AMA's "Principles To Guide the Collection, Release, and Use of Physician-Specific Health Care Data."

Courtesy of American Medical Association.

A P P E N D I X  **27 – B**

# Principles To Guide the Collection, Release, and Use of Physician-Specific Health Care Data

The AMA believes that managed care organizations, third party payers, government entities, and others that collect, analyze, release, and use or intend to use physician-specific health care data should adhere to the following principles.

- The methods for collecting and analyzing physician-specific health care data shall be disclosed to physicians under review and the public.
- Physician-specific health care data shall be valid, accurate, objective, and used primarily for the education of both consumers and physicians.
- Data elements used in the collection of physician-specific health care data, including severity adjustment factors, shall be determined by advisory committees which include actively practicing, and where relevant, specialty-specific physicians from the region where the data are being collected.
- Statistically valid data collection, analysis, and reporting methodologies, including establishment of a statically-significant minimum number of cases, shall be developed and appropriately implemented prior to the release of physician-specific health care data.
- Effective safeguards to protect against the dissemination of inconsistent, incomplete, invalid, inaccurate, or subjective physician-specific health care data shall be established.
- Physicians under review and relevant physician organizations shall be provided with an adequate opportunity to review and respond to proposed physician-specific health care data interpretations and disclosures prior to their publication or release.
- Reliable administrative, technical, and physical safeguards to prevent the unauthorized use or disclosure of physician-specific health care data shall be developed.

- Such safeguards shall treat all underlying physician-specific health care data and all analyses, proceedings, records, and minutes from quality review activities on physician-specific health care data as confidential and provide that none of these documents shall be subject to discovery or admitted into evidence in any judicial or administrative proceeding.
- The quality and accuracy of the physician-specific health care data shall be evaluated by conducting periodic medical record audits.

Courtesy of American Medical Association.

APPENDIX 27–C

# AMAP Standards

To be AMAP accredited, a physician must fully meet all required (**R**) standards and achieve a score of at least eleven (11) of twenty-two (22) points on the supplemental (**S**) standards. All references to periods of time refer to the date from which a physician's application is received by AMAP.

**Credentials**

| | | |
|---|---|---|
| *** | **1R** | Graduation from an accredited allopathic or osteopathic medical school *or* a foreign medical school recognized by the World Health Organization as determined by the Educational Commission on Foreign Medical Graduates |
| *** | **2R** | Current, active, unrestricted medical or osteopathic license in the U.S. state, district, or territory of practice (exception: physicians employed by the federal government may have a current active medical or osteopathic license in *any* U.S. state, district, or territory) |
| *** | **3R** | Current, unrestricted DEA registration (schedules II–V) *or* no history of revocation of DEA registration (schedules II–V) within the past five years |
| *** | **4R** | No disciplinary action (final judgments) within the past five years against any medical or osteopathic license; or by any U.S. state, district, or territory; or by any federal agency, including Medicare and Medicaid |
| *** | **5R** | No record of felony or fraud conviction since graduation from medical school |
| 4 points | **6S** | Completion of a residency training program approved by the Accreditation Council for Graduate Medical Education, the American Osteopathic Association, the Royal College of Physicians and Surgeons of Canada, or the College of Family Physicians of Canada |
| 3 points | **7S** | Initial certification (*or* permanent certification) by an American Board of Medical Specialties recognized board *or* completion of residency within the past four years |
| 3 points | **8S** | Current recertification by an American Board of Medical Specialties recognized board[1] |

| [1 point] | 9S | Professional liability claims experience at or below the 50th percentile for the past five years (based on final judgments and/or paid claims, risk-adjusted for frequency and severity with respect to specialty, years in practice, and jurisdiction of practice)[2] |
|---|---|---|
| 1 point | 10S | No record of disciplinary action in the National Practitioner Data Bank (NPDB) within the past five years |

### Personal Qualifications

*Ethics*

| *** | 11R | Agree in writing to abide by the AMA *Principles of Medical Ethics* |
|---|---|---|
| *** | 12R | Have no report of any adjudicated violation of AMA *Principles of Medical Ethics* or any adjudicated ethical violation reported by any medical society or medical or osteopathic licensing board |
| 1 point | 13S | Membership in a medical professional association that has a published code of ethics or an equivalent, and whose members subscribe to that code and agree to submit themselves to the ethical review process of that organization |

### Continuing Medical Education

| *** | 14R | Completion of 100 hours of CME (within two years) of which 40 hours are in ACCME Category 1 |
|---|---|---|
| | | *or* |
| | | Current AMA Physician's Recognition Award (PRA) |
| | | *or* |
| | | Completion of current CME requirements of any specialty society or other organization with which the AMA PRA award has a reciprocity arrangement[3] |
| *** | 15R | Compliance with any state requirements for CME |
| 1 point | 16S | At least 50 hours of Category 1 CME credit within the past two years in the primary specialty of practice |
| 1 point | 17S | AMA PRA has been earned *with commendation for self-directed learning* |

*Peer Review[4]*

| *** | 18R | Member of an organization that conducts peer review of its members, including any one of the following |
|---|---|---|

- the organized medical staff of a hospital accredited by Joint Commission, or the American Osteopathic Association, or certified to participate in the Medicare program
- a group practice, health care organization, physician network, or health plan accredited by an AMAP-recognized accreditation organization that requires a peer review process

### *Self-assessment[5]*

| | | |
|---|---|---|
| *** | 19R | Completion of one or more AMAP-approved self-assessment programs within 24 months; any combination of self-assessment programs used to meet this requirement must total at least 5 hours of Category 1 CME credit and must include both |
| [1 point] | | • clinical performance *and* |
| [1 point] | | • medical practice operations |

**Environment of Care**

| | | |
|---|---|---|
| | 20R | Satisfactory completion of an office site review in accordance with AMAP criteria with a score of at least 70%[6] |
| | | *or* |
| | | At least 75% of the physician's practice is in an office, clinic, group practice, or hospital that is currently accredited by an AMAP-recognized accreditation organization[6] |
| 2 points | 21S | Satisfactory completion of an office site review in accordance with AMAP criteria with a score of at least 80% |
| | | *or* |
| 4 points | | Satisfactory completion of an office site review in accordance with AMAP criteria with a score of at least 90% |
| | | *or* |
| 2 points | | At least 75% of the physician's practice is in an office, clinic, group practice, or hospital that is currently accredited *with commendation* by an AMAP-recognized accreditation organization |

### *Clinical Performance and Patient Care Results[7]*

| | | |
|---|---|---|
| 2 points | 22S | Current participation in an ongoing process that evaluates the clinical performance and/or patient care results of the applicant and of other physicians (continuous quality improvement) |

[1]Credit for 8S will be granted only if recertification has been completed prior to the date of expiration of the initial certification or any subsequent recertification.

*** Indicates required standard.

[2]Data relevant to this standard will initially be monitored to ascertain its pertinence. The standard will not become effective before January 1, 1999, and no points will be awarded prior to the effective date.

[3]Programs with which the AMAP has a reciprocity arrangement are identified in *Instructions for Completing the AMAP Accreditation Application.*

[4]For purposes of these standards, the term *peer review* refers to review of the clinical performance and/or patient care results of an individual physician by other physicians with similar levels of training and qualifications.

[5]This requirement is effective for AMAP applications submitted on or after January 1, 2000. Applications received before that date may receive two supplemental points toward accreditation for completion of an approved *clinical performance* self-assessment.

[6]This requirement may be waived in cases where a physician does not maintain an office nor treat patients in a facility where the *AMAP Environment of Care Survey Criteria* would be applicable.

[7]Pilot testing is ongoing to evaluate and select specific clinical performance and patient care results measures for inclusion in AMAP. Until such time, medical records will be reviewed during the environment of care site review for the following items in recognition of their use by other accreditation organizations. These items, however, which are subject to interpretation, will warrant no points in AMAP accreditation.

- Laboratory and other studies are ordered, as appropriate.
- Working diagnoses are consistent with findings.
- Treatment plans are consistent with diagnoses.
- Review for under- and over-utilization of consultants.
- Evidence that preventative screening and services are offered in accordance with the (organization's) practice guidelines.
- No evidence that the patient is placed at inappropriate risk by a diagnostic or therapeutic procedure.

Courtesy of American Medical Association.

CHAPTER 28

# "Best Clinical Practice": Assessment of Processes of Care and of Outcomes in the U.S. Military Health Services System

*Henry Krakauer, Monica Jia-Yeong Lin, Eric M. Schone,*
*Dae Park, Richard C. Miller, Jeffrey Greenwald,*
*R. Clifton Bailey, Barbara Rogers, Geoffrey Bernstein,*
*David E. Lilienfeld, Sidney M. Stahl,*
*Raymond S. Crawford III, and David C. Schutt*

The National Quality Management Program of the Military Health Services System of the United States has undertaken a series of projects whose objective is the active, ongoing monitoring and improvement of the effectiveness and efficiency of the care provided to a broad population that encompasses troops on active duty, retirees, and dependents. The analytic activities consist of (1) identification by clinical panels of conditions and procedures of interest; (2) collection of data from electronic repositories and from charts to characterize the patients, how they are managed, the clinical outcomes they experience, the resource costs their care entails, and, from questionnaires, their functional status and level of

The views expressed herein are the opinions of the authors and do not necessarily represent the official positions of the federal agencies with which they are associated.

*Source:* Reprinted with permission from H. Krakauer et al., Best Clinical Practice: Assessment of Processes of Care and of Outcomes in the US Military Health Services System, *Journal of Evaluation in Clinical Practice*, Vol. 4, No. 1, pp. 11–29, © 1998, Blackwell Science Ltd.

satisfaction; and (3) generation of "report cards" that inform organizational units down to the level of the hospital of the characteristics of their patients, their practices, and the risk-adjusted outcomes they achieve. The patterns of care employed by the hospitals that obtain the best risk-adjusted outcomes and resource utilization ("best clinical practice") are identified and made known. In addition, a systematic process of developing outcomes-based practice guidelines has been devised. Its intent is to serve as a decision-support tool to clinicians. Initial estimates have been obtained of the probable consequences of the application of this tool to operative interventions in childbirth. Use of the tool would result in a higher occurrence of elective cesarean sections (C-sections), a reduced rate of emergency cesarean sections, and much lower use of forceps, with an overall improvement in outcomes and lower resource costs.

This program is currently in the early phases of implementation. The two principal requirements for the immediate future are (1) education of the clinical and administrative communities in the use of the data and the decision-support tools and (2) evaluation of the consequences of the use of the data by the clinical and administrative communities.

## BACKGROUND

The Military Health Services System of the United States is a substantial provider and purchaser of health care services for about 8.3 million persons, including uniformed personnel, retirees, and their dependents. The services include about 1 million hospitalizations and 50 million outpatient visits, and they cost about $15 billion yearly. Approximately 75 percent of the care is provided directly in military hospitals and clinics, and the remainder is purchased from civilian facilities. Oversight of the quality of care is the responsibility of the National Quality Management Program (NQMP) of the Department of Defense.[1] Its component activities include the formulation of policy pertaining to the verification of the credentials of physicians and of their practice privileges, accreditation of hospitals and other facilities, utilization management, and, the subject of this chapter, the ongoing assessment of practices and outcomes for the purpose of improving the quality of medical care.

At present, attention is focused on conditions and problems identified by clinical and administrative staff as being worthy of special attention because the services are provided in high volume, entail high clinical and medicolegal risk and cost, or bear substantially on the ability of persons on active duty to perform their work. The mechanism for the evaluation of the practices associated with these conditions and procedures is termed "special studies"; it principally involves the collection of data through the abstraction of charts but encompasses the use of administrative data and surveys of facilities and patients. The studies initiated in the past three years have addressed maternity care, with a special focus on cesarean section; cholecystectomy;[2] hysterectomy; ankle injuries; pediatric head trauma; pediatric asthma; and clinical preventive services. Ischemic heart disease, diabetes, and mental health and substance abuse are currently under evaluation. Because of its prominence, maternity care is undergoing continuing review.

The objective of the analyses is to identify from current clinical experience the patient care strategies that constitute most effective and efficient practice—"best clinical practice." With a few exceptions, such as the evaluation of "clinical preventive services," which was a descriptive assessment of processes of care, the studies address outcomes of care, including costs.

The focus of attention is the care provided by the military facilities, but, with the progressive integration under a new program, TRICARE, of services purchased in the civilian sector into the overall care of defined populations for which the regional medical commander is responsible, the medical practices of contracting civilian facilities are also coming under review.[3]

## METHODOLOGY

A deliberate attempt is made to structure the analyses to reflect the approaches and thought processes of clinicians. The projects begin, therefore, with a specification of (1) what data about the patient and his or her condition clinicians feel are useful and necessary for the management of the patient, (2) the significant diagnostic and therapeutic interventions that were undertaken during the episode of care, (3) the patient's responses to the interventions, and (4) the patient's condition at the conclusion of the episode. The analyses then attempt to establish the linkages between the characteristics of the patients, the interventions, and the results or outcomes achieved.

### Case Sampling

The sampling strategies follow from the objectives of studies. In certain instances—for example, in the analyses of cholecystectomy and hysterectomy—all hospitalizations within a year for the relevant procedures were identified and abstracted. In the case of the maternity care projects, such an approach would have been impractical because it would have required the abstraction of about 70,000 charts. Because the characterization of the practice patterns of individual military hospitals was deemed important and because the volume of deliveries varies greatly among the military hospitals, a strategy was devised to yield a minimum of 100 (or all deliveries if there were fewer than 100) and a maximum of 200 cases per hospital. These cases were selected by random sampling of the admissions for delivery of each hospital. (Consequently, in the analyses, each case was weighted by the inverse of its sampling probability, i.e., by the number of cases it represents.)

## Data Acquisition

The first step consists of the specification of a "data dictionary" by a panel of clinicians. Although diagnoses are collected, the great majority of the items used to describe the condition of the patient are "basic biological facts," signs (e.g., edema), symptoms (e.g., nausea), and findings (e.g., hematocrit). Interventions are characterized at a similar level of detail (e.g., the type and volume of blood products used for transfusion). The resulting dictionaries are quite voluminous, containing generally several thousand items.

The second step consists of insertion of the data dictionaries into a software program that guides and structures the process of chart abstraction. The software is installed on laptop computers issued to the chart abstractors.

Chart abstraction is carried out by trained medical record specialists, in most instances at the hospital or clinic that provided the care. In some instances, copies of charts are sent to a central location for abstraction. The resulting files are transmitted to the statistical center.

The data are assembled, reviewed, and "cleaned" at the statistical center and converted to files suitable for analysis.

In addition to chart abstraction, questionnaires are also used to acquire data. The two principal applications of questionnaires are the collection of information from facilities on their physical resources, their staff, and their policies and the collection of information from patients on their functional status and their satisfaction with the care received.

## Scoring of Outcomes

Although four classes of outcomes are evaluated—morbidity, functional status, patient satisfaction, and resource utilization—the utility of functional status and patient satisfaction is limited by the incompleteness of the response to the questionnaires sent to patients. Measures of morbidity and resource utilization are obtained directly from the chart abstracts.

## *Morbidity*

The assessment of morbidity, following the clinical model, entails the identification in the abstracted data of all the adverse occurrences experienced by the patient. The list is presented to a panel of clinicians and patients, and each occurrence is assigned a weight that reflects its severity in the opinion of the panel. The criteria of severity are (1) the likelihood of causing a fatal outcome, (2) the likelihood of causing prolonged or permanent physiologic or functional impairment, and (3) the likelihood of causing a prolonged and difficult process of recovery. The scale of severity is chosen for convenience and usually lies in the range of 0–12 or 0–20. A score of 1 signifies a minor and transient problem, and the highest score is for death. Although the scale is hierarchical rather than truly proportional, scores are aggregated. The process of aggregation proceeds in steps (Figure 28–1). First, scores for individual occurrences are combined to form a score for a pathophysiologic cluster. Then, pathophysiologic clusters are combined into intermediate outcomes. Finally, overall aggregate outcome scores are formed. The rules of aggregation are as follows: (1) scores are added if they reflect independent occurrences or processes, (2) the largest of a group of scores is taken if the scored occurrences or processes are manifestations of a common underlying injury or disturbance, and (3) scores are incremented by an intermediate amount if the severity of a finding is increased by the presence of another finding.

## *Resource Utilization*

The objective of this component of the analyses is to ascertain how much effort or work was required to manage a case rather than to assign actual dollar costs, something that is in fact not feasible in the health care system of the Department of Defense. Its conceptual basis lies in two tools devised for the Health Care Financing Administration (HCFA) of the U.S. Department of Health and Human Services, the Resource Based Relative Value Scale (RBRVS)[4] and the diagnosis-related group (DRG) weight.[5] The former assigns a specific value, the relative value unit (RVU), to each diagnostic and therapeutic service provided by physicians as defined the American Medical Association's Current Procedural Terminology (CPT) codes, and the latter is

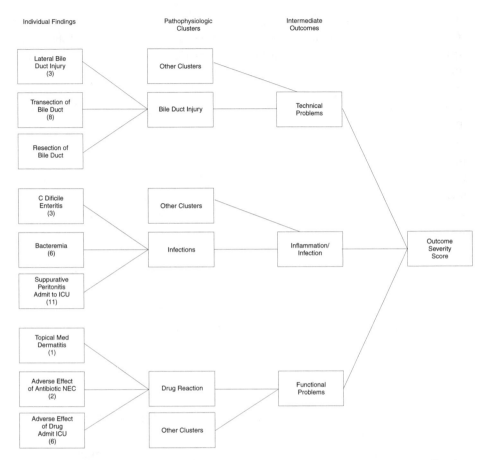

**Figure 28–1** Illustrative Scheme for the Development of Outcome Scores Following Cholecystectomy from Discrete Postprocedure Clinical Findings

an analogous measure of the utilization of resources by a facility entailed by an admission.

The RVU is an estimate of the quantity of the work, based on the time, difficulty, required training, practice expense, and so on, entailed in the provision of a service. Because the ultimate purpose of the RBRVS is to establish prices for services provided by physicians, a conversion factor, approximately $33 per RVU in 1993, is defined.

Similarly, the DRG weight reflects an average intensity of care provided by a hospital to manage a patient admitted for the particular DRG condition or procedure. Because an average length of stay is also associated with each DRG, a weight per day of care can be computed for each DRG. The two major contributors to departures from an average intensity of service are variations in length of stay (LOS) and use of intensive care units. The first can be accounted for simply by obtaining the product of the actual LOS of the particular patient and the weight per day for the DRG for which the patient was admitted. The conversion factor for the DRG weight per day in maternity admissions is about $1,240, and therefore one DRG weight per day is equivalent to 37 RVUs. Similarly, a charge per ICU day can be calculated from the data maintained by HCFA, and ICU utilization resource costs can then be added to the DRG weight adjusted for the LOS. The sum, converted to the scale of the RVUs, then represents the total utilization of resources by the facility for the care of the patient.

The overall utilization of resources is the sum of the facility "costs" and of the diagnostic and therapeutic services, whether provided in the hospital or on an outpatient basis. For example, in the case of the maternity care project, data were available to cover the care for the pregnancy from the first prenatal visit to discharge from the hospital following delivery (Figure 28–2).

### Patient Satisfaction and Functional Status

Summary measures reported on the patient questionnaires on hierarchical scales are used directly. The analysis of these data and their integration with the data on morbidity and on resource costs is more problematic because of the incompleteness of the responses from the patients.

## Statistical Analysis

The statistical analysis of the data has two objectives: the preparation of a report card on the components of the Military Health Services System and the development of decision support tools to assist decision makers (clinicians as well as administrators) in the use of the results to improve the effectiveness and efficiency of care.

### Preparation of the Report Card

The report card consists of (1) a descriptive component that simply characterizes the populations of patients, their intermediate and aggregate clinical morbidity scores, the details of the care they received, and the resource utilization entailed by their care; and (2) an analytic component in which the observed outcomes are compared to the outcomes expected for the case mix

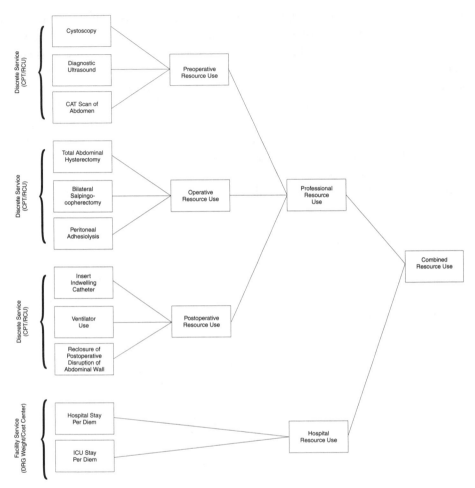

**Figure 28–2** Illustrative Scheme for the Development of Aggregate Resource Costs of Hospitalization for Hysterectomy from Individual Services

represented by the populations. The analytic component employs the construction of predictive models by means of multiple regression to provide the patient-specific parameters to be used for risk adjustment in the estimation of the influence of (1) interventions and facility characteristics and (2) organizational units (services, regions, and hospitals) on outcomes and resource costs.

## *Development of Decision Support Tools*

The identification of best clinical practices can be approached by two means. One makes use of the report card to locate organizational components whose clinical outcomes and resources utilization are substantially and statistically significantly better than expected and to specify their policies and practices and compare them with those of other components. The intent is to initiate a dialog among the components, informed by the data on practices and outcomes, that, it is hoped, will result in improvements.[6] The second focuses on patients who are candidates for a type of intervention (e.g., operative delivery), and attempts to develop outcomes-based practice guidelines that identify which patients, given the experience of similar patients in the very near past, are likely to have superior outcomes if provided with the intervention. This approach requires the construction of models predictive of the occurrence of the intervention as well as of the outcomes.

## Development of Predictive Models

The general process of building the predictive model consists of the following steps:

1. selection of patient characteristics observed sufficiently frequently to support a reasonably stable assessment of their association with the outcome (the threshold was about 30 occurrences)
2. selection from those only of the variables that had a reasonably statistically significant association ($p < 0.1$) with the outcome in bivariate analysis
3. correlation analysis to identify and eliminate instances of strong collinearity (correlation coefficient greater than about 0.4)
4. stepwise regression to select the variables to populate the final predictive model

The measure of resource utilization fits a log-normal distribution quite satisfactorily. Consequently, the modeling employed linear regression on the logarithms of the resource costs.

The distributional properties of the clinical outcomes are more highly varied and can be complex (Table 28–1). In the case of the most recent maternity project, the assigned scores had a bimodal pattern. A general approach to the assessment of hierarchically ranked outcomes was, therefore, devised. In the first step, the scores are formed into a reasonable number of groups. The

**Table 28–1** Outcome Scores. (a) Hysterectomy and cholecystectomy; (b) maternity care

(a)

| Grouped Score | Hysterectomy Number of Cases | Percent | Cholecystectomy Number of Cases | Percent |
|---|---|---|---|---|
| 0 | 4972 | 77.03 | 8807 | 88.99 |
| 1 | 1173 | 18.17 | 697 | 7.04 |
| 2 | 208 | 3.22 | 265 | 2.68 |
| 3 | 86 | 1.33 | 102 | 1.03 |
| 4 | 16 | 0.25 | 26 | 0.26 |
| Total | 6455 | 100.00 | 9897 | 100.00 |

(b)

| Total Score | Maternity Care Number of Cases | Percent |
|---|---|---|
| 0 | 2640 | 33.40 |
| 1 | 743 | 9.40 |
| 2 | 781 | 9.88 |
| 3 | 1147 | 14.51 |
| 4 | 792 | 10.02 |
| 5 | 466 | 5.90 |
| 6 | 362 | 4.58 |
| 7 | 362 | 4.58 |
| 8 | 193 | 2.44 |
| 9 | 118 | 1.49 |
| 10 | 94 | 1.19 |
| 11 | 59 | 0.75 |
| 12 | 57 | 0.72 |
| 13 | 22 | 0.28 |
| 14 | 29 | 0.37 |
| 15 | 15 | 0.19 |
| 16 | 7 | 0.09 |
| 17 | 3 | 0.04 |
| 18 | 1 | 0.01 |
| 19 | 6 | 0.08 |
| 20 | 1 | 0.01 |
| >20 | 6 | 0.08 |
| Total | 7904 | 100.00 |

*Source:* Reprinted with permission from H. Krakauer et al., Best Clinical Practice: Assessment of Processes of Care and of Outcomes in the U.S. Military Health Services System, *Journal of Evaluation in Clinical Practice*, Vol. 4, No. 1, pp 11–29, © 1998, Blackwell Science Ltd.

result for cholecystectomy and hysterectomy is illustrated in Table 28–1. For maternity care, the scores were regrouped into six intervals, and the resulting six-valued ordinal outcome variable was subjected to ordered logistic regression. The prediction produced by this process is the set of probabilities that the outcome score of a given patient falls into each of the score intervals. A predicted outcome score for each patient was then obtained by summing the products of these probabilities and the population average value of the score associated with each interval. In models that only contain patient characteristics, the predicted outcome score is a measure of "severity of illness" and can be used as the risk adjustor in subsequent analyses.

Because the regression coefficients in the ordered logistic regression do not directly report the magnitude of the effect of a given predictor variable on the outcome, a further application of the predicted weighted outcome score was devised. Regressions were carried out in which all patients were assigned, for example, first one value of a binary (0,1) variable and then the complementary value. All other variables had the true values applicable to the patients. The difference in the population-average predicted weighted scores obtained from the two regressions represents the direction and magnitude of the effect of that variable on the outcome score. The meaning of this quantity is analogous to that of the regression coefficient in linear regression: it is the increment in the dependent variable associated with a unit change in an independent variable, all other independent variables being held constant. (The validity of this approach was evaluated in a circumstance in which the outcome scores were in fact approximately normally distributed. The estimators of the effect of covariates based on ordered logistic regression on grouped scores, obtained in the manner just described, were very similar to the coefficients of the covariates obtained by linear regression over the full span of their values. A full technical exposition of the use of ordered logistic regression and its subsidiary techniques will be presented elsewhere.)

## Application of Predictive Models

The purpose of the models that contained only patient characteristics as predictors or covariates was to obtain a predicted outcome score that could be used as a risk adjustor in the estimation of the influence of interventions, facility characteristics, and policies on outcomes. Such predicted scores were calculated by means of separate models for each outcome (clinical, resource cost, satisfaction, functional status) of interest.

**Formulation of Outcomes-based Practice Guidelines**

As the patient's condition evolves, clinicians must choose among alternative courses of action. Their decisions, at best, are based on estimates of which course is likely to most benefit the patient. Practice guidelines are statements by panels of experts intended to specify this optimal course to practicing clinicians. The approach adopted in the present analyses attempts to identify the characteristics of patients that result in better outcomes when one or the other of the available alternatives is used. This was accomplished in two steps.

First, models were built to predict the occurrence of an intervention. The models represent the collective judgment of the clinical community as to which patient characteristics indicate or contraindicate the performance of the procedure. They reflect not assertions but the observed strength of the association of the patient characteristics with the actual performance of the procedure. The analytic techniques employed simple logistic regression when only two alternatives were under consideration (e.g., the scheduling of a C-section at the time of admission) and multinomial logistic regression when multiple alternatives entered into the decision (e.g., emergency C-section and forceps delivery during labor). Simultaneously, models were built to predict the outcomes based on patient characteristics known at the time the decision about the intervention is to be made. Thus, in the development of the practice guideline on elective C-section, data on the patient known up to the time of admission are used, but in the case of emergency C-section precipitated by the adverse progress of labor, data accumulated during the course of labor are also incorporated into the model.

Second, a decision threshold for the use of the intervention was obtained by comparing the probability of the intervention with the outcomes achieved. Although the predictive power of the models of the use of C-sections was substantial with a proportion of concordant pairs of patients (i.e., pairs of patients who did and did not receive the intervention), the patient who did receive the intervention had the higher predicted probability of the intervention (equivalent to the area under the receiver operating characteristics [ROC] curve),[7] 0.90 for scheduled C-sections and 0.95 for unscheduled C-sections—significant proportions of patients with relatively low predicted probabilities of the intervention did receive it, and vice versa. Therefore, a relationship between the predicted probability and the risk-adjusted outcome (the difference between the observed and the predicted outcome) could be explored for patients who did and who did not receive the intervention over the range of predicted probabilities. In the case of C-section and forceps delivery, for women who received the intervention, the risk-adjusted outcome improved with increasing predicted probability, whereas for women who did not receive the intervention, the risk-adjusted outcome deteriorated with increasing probability. The point of intersection of these trends represents the decision threshold, the predicted probability of the intervention at which the risk-adjusted outcome is equal whether the intervention is or is not used. At higher probabilities, the outcome is better with the intervention, and at lower predicted probabilities it is better without. As an approximation, the trends in the relationships between the risk-adjusted outcomes and the predicted probabilities of the intervention were fitted by linear regression.

The practice guideline consists of determining whether, for a given patient, the decision threshold probability is or is not exceeded. A listing of the statistically and biologically significant characteristics and of their regression coefficients was generated. For a given patient, the sum of the regression coefficients of the characteristics that were present was calculated and compared to the value that corresponds to the decision threshold probability. The strength of the guidance provided in this manner is clearly related to the magnitude of the difference between the sum applicable to the patient and the decision threshold sum.

## ILLUSTRATIVE RESULTS

### The Report Cards

The report cards contain a descriptive component and an evaluative component, which report the frequency with which the interventions that had statistically significant associations with either outcomes or with resource use were carried out in each region and throughout the Department of Defense (Table 28–2). To provide insight into the potential impacts on the performance of each major geographic jurisdictional unit or region, the report cards also contain the estimated impacts of the interventions, adjusted for patient risk, on outcome scores ("Change in score") on an absolute scale and on resource costs ("Change in RCU") on a proportional scale, along with an estimate of the statistical significance of the association ("P value"). Thus, epidural anesthesia is associated with a worsening of the outcome by 0.39 points and a 5

**Table 28–2** Effect of Processes of Care on Combined Outcome and Resource Use

| Process of Care | Change in Score | p value | Change in RCU | p value | Frequencies of Processes of Care | | | | | | | | | | |
| --- | --- | --- | --- | --- | --- | --- | --- | --- | --- | --- | --- | --- | --- | --- |
| | | | | | DoD | Region 7 | Region 8 | Region 9 | Region 10 | Region 11 | Region 12 | Caribbean | Tricare Euroope | Tricare Pacific |
| **Pre-delivery Processes** | | | | | | | | | | | | | | |
| BPP monitored during admission | 1.73 | 0.00 | 0.58 | 0.00 | 0.5% | 0.2% | 0.4% | 0.0% | 4.3% | 0.6% | 1.0% | 0.0% | 0.0% | 0.8% |
| Number of BPPs obtained during admission | 1.05 | 0.00 | 0.15 | 0.00 | 0.0 | 0.0 | 0.0 | 0.0 | 0.2 | 0.0 | 0.0 | 0.0 | 0.0 | 0.0 |
| NST performed during admission | 0.28 | 0.00 | 0.15 | 0.00 | 11.8% | 9.3% | 9.1% | 9.4% | 16.4% | 5.2% | 51.3% | 10.8% | 6.7% | 5.4% |
| Number of NSTs performed during admission | 0.22 | 0.00 | 0.11 | 0.00 | 0.2 | 0.1 | 0.1 | 0.1 | 0.4 | 0.1 | 0.9 | 0.1 | 0.1 | 0.1 |
| CST performed during admission | 0.52 | 0.06 | 0.08 | 0.06 | 1.1% | 1.0% | 0.9% | 4.2% | 0.6% | 1.0% | 0.0% | 0.0% | 1.2% | 1.0% |
| Number of CSTs performed after admission | 0.04 | 0.85 | 0.05 | 0.09 | 0.0 | 0.0 | 0.0 | 0.0 | 0.0 | 0.0 | 0.0 | 0.0 | 0.0 | 0.0 |
| Ultrasound examination performed during admission | 0.80 | 0.00 | 0.29 | 0.00 | 5.9% | 7.6% | 3.7% | 4.2% | 17.6% | 5.9% | 16.6% | 1.5% | 4.2% | 3.6% |

| | | | | | | | | | | | | | | |
|---|---|---|---|---|---|---|---|---|---|---|---|---|---|---|
| Number of ultrasound exams performed during admission | 0.71 | 0.00 | 0.20 | 0.00 | 0.1 | 0.1 | 0.0 | 0.1 | 0.3 | 0.1 | 0.2 | 0.0 | 0.0 | 0.0 |
| Monitoring by auscultation | 0.16 | 0.68 | −0.04 | 0.53 | 0.6% | 0.2% | 2.1% | 1.6% | 0.7% | 1.2% | 0.0% | 0.0% | 0.1% | 0.0% |
| Internal fetal monitoring | 0.36 | 0.00 | 0.04 | 0.00 | 57.6% | 62.0% | 50.7% | 54.6% | 61.4% | 58.2% | 54.8% | 56.9% | 45.1% | 47.0% |
| External fetal monitoring | −0.12 | 0.13 | −0.07 | 0.00 | 84.1% | 84.8% | 87.0% | 87.0% | 23.1% | 94.5% | 93.0% | 93.8% | 72.6% | 71.2% |
| Epidural anesthesia | 0.39 | 0.00 | 0.05 | 0.00 | 37.9% | 43.3% | 19.1% | 37.1% | 45.9% | 47.6% | 58.8% | 0.0% | 15.8% | 28.2% |
| General anesthesia | 2.27 | 0.00 | 0.47 | 0.00 | 1.7% | 2.2% | 1.1% | 2.4% | 0.9% | 1.0% | 0.5% | 1.5% | 1.8% | 2.2% |
| Intrathecal anesthesia | 0.19 | 0.05 | 0.02 | 0.12 | 9.9% | 1.7% | 7.9% | 15.0% | 13.6% | 37.7% | 2.0% | 20.0% | 30.5% | 7.0% |
| Subarachnoid anesthesia | −0.22 | 0.21 | 0.23 | 0.00 | 2.6% | 1.0% | 5.3% | 1.4% | 2.9% | 4.8% | 0.0% | 0.0% | 5.0% | 1.3% |
| Any spinal anesthesia | 0.01 | 0.92 | 0.13 | 0.00 | 18.8% | 8.7% | 21.8% | 26.3% | 18.1% | 46.0% | 8.0% | 36.9% | 39.1% | 15.1% |
| Narcotic analgesia | 0.51 | 0.00 | 0.14 | 0.00 | 53.3% | 58.1% | 58.3% | 64.4% | 52.3% | 72.5% | 55.3% | 70.8% | 51.2% | 56.2% |
| Artificial rupture of membranes | 0.01 | 0.81 | −0.02 | 0.02 | 51.9% | 51.7% | 52.0% | 47.5% | 51.4% | 58.7% | 51.8% | 44.6% | 51.2% | 48.6% |
| Medical augmentation of labor | 0.38 | 0.00 | 0.09 | 0.00 | 40.3% | 41.5% | 34.5% | 41.6% | 61.0% | 38.5% | 47.7% | 7.7% | 38.4% | 33.7% |
| Surgical augmentation | 0.01 | 0.85 | −0.02 | 0.02 | 51.9% | 51.7% | 52.0% | 47.5% | 51.4% | 58.7% | 51.8% | 44.6% | 51.2% | 48.7% |
| Amnioinfusion | 0.56 | 0.00 | 0.10 | 0.00 | 7.8% | 9.1% | 7.3% | 7.6% | 6.1% | 11.4% | 21.1% | 4.6% | 5.1% | 4.2% |

continues

**Table 28-2** Continued

| Process of Care | Change in Score | p value | Change in RCU | p value | DoD | Region 7 | Region 8 | Region 9 | Region 10 | Region 11 | Region 12 | Region Caribbean | Tricare Europe | Tricare Pacific |
|---|---|---|---|---|---|---|---|---|---|---|---|---|---|---|
| | | | | | | | | | *Frequencies of Processes of Care* | | | | | |
| Fetal scalp stimulation | 0.64 | 0.00 | 0.08 | 0.00 | 8.0% | 10.2% | 5.7% | 12.0% | 5.4% | 7.6% | 7.5% | 0.0% | 4.1% | 6.2% |
| Intrauterine pressure catheter placement | 0.43 | 0.00 | 0.09 | 0.00 | 37.7% | 46.6% | 35.0% | 32.9% | 29.9% | 46.5% | 38.7% | 40.0% | 25.6% | 21.0% |
| **Delivery Processes** | | | | | | | | | | | | | | |
| Delivery by obstetrician | 0.34 | 0.00 | 0.07 | 0.00 | 51.4% | 41.1% | 66.3% | 51.3% | 30.0% | 26.8% | 26.6% | 60.0% | 77.0% | 66.8% |
| Delivery by family practitioner | −0.10 | 0.24 | −0.08 | 0.00 | 11.0% | 0.8% | 10.7% | 16.8% | 15.4% | 7.7% | 0.5% | 0.0% | 14.3% | 12.1% |
| Delivery by midwife | −0.24 | 0.01 | −0.12 | 0.00 | 11.1% | 13.9% | 14.5% | 18.8% | 0.0% | 1.9% | 4.0% | 38.5% | 3.3% | 12.0% |
| Delivery by nurse | −0.54 | 0.00 | 0.07 | 0.00 | 4.9% | 0.3% | 0.5% | 2.5% | 0.9% | 0.3% | 0.0% | 0.0% | 0.7% | 3.0% |
| Delivery by resident | −0.02 | 0.71 | 0.02 | 0.04 | 23.7% | 32.5% | 6.1% | 8.4% | 28.6% | 72.3% | 88.9% | 0.0% | 0.1% | 0.2% |
| Delivery by other physician | −0.33 | 0.25 | −0.02 | 0.64 | 0.8% | 0.9% | 0.5% | 0.8% | 0.6% | 1.0% | 0.5% | 0.0% | 0.2% | 0.0% |
| Spinal anesthesia | −0.06 | 0.57 | 0.21 | 0.00 | 6.9% | 6.1% | 9.3% | 10.7% | 3.1% | 5.1% | 6.0% | 16.9% | 4.8% | 7.4% |
| Local anesthesia | −0.13 | 0.03 | −0.09 | 0.00 | 33.9% | 32.2% | 34.4% | 25.3% | 19.6% | 25.6% | 25.1% | 43.1% | 37.2% | 42.0% |
| Vaginal delivery | −0.34 | 0.00 | −0.40 | 0.00 | 83.9% | 81.9% | 85.1% | 81.3% | 84.0% | 85.0% | 80.4% | 78.5% | 86.8% | 83.1% |
| Vaginal breech delivery | 1.77 | 0.00 | −0.05 | 0.59 | 0.3% | 0.4% | 0.0% | 0.1% | 0.0% | 0.2% | 1.0% | 0.0% | 0.1% | 0.1% |

| | | | | | | | | | | | | | |
|---|---|---|---|---|---|---|---|---|---|---|---|---|---|
| Forceps delivery, successful or failed | 1.63 | 0.00 | 0.02 | 0.20 | 5.9% | 8.7% | 4.7% | 4.9% | 8.6% | 10.3% | 4.0% | 0.0% | 4.5% | 3.8% |
| Vacuum forceps delivery, successful or failed | 0.98 | 0.00 | −0.01 | 0.58 | 8.0% | 7.2% | 10.3% | 7.0% | 4.3% | 8.7% | 7.0% | 10.8% | 12.8% | 8.6% |
| VBAC | 0.19 | 0.19 | −0.19 | 0.00 | 3.6% | 5.7% | 2.8% | 2.8% | 0.7% | 5.0% | 6.5% | 0.0% | 5.7% | 3.2% |
| Scheduled/elective C-section | −0.37 | 0.00 | 0.22 | 0.00 | 5.4% | 6.1% | 6.0% | 8.0% | 7.1% | 3.8% | 9.5% | 9.2% | 4.3% | 4.6% |
| Unscheduled/non-elective C-section | 0.70 | 0.00 | 0.42 | 0.00 | 11.4% | 13.1% | 9.6% | 11.6% | 10.6% | 12.7% | 10.6% | 9.2% | 9.9% | 12.1% |

*Note:* The "Change in Score" represents an absolute increase or decrease, but "Change in RCU (Resource Cost Unit)" represents a proportional change. The column labeled "DoD" refers to the experience in the hospitals of the Department of Defense overall and includes purchased care in civilian hospitals. The "Regions" are major administrative units assigned responsibility for the care of a defined population. Typically, they contain several hospitals. BPP: biophysical profile; NST: non-stress test; CST: contraction stimulation test; VBAC: vaginal birth after Caesarean section.

*Source:* Reprinted with permission from H. Krakauer et al., Best Clinical Practice: Assessment of Processes of Care and of Outcomes in the U.S. Military Health Services System, *Journal of Evaluation in Clinical Practice*, Vol. 4, No. 1, pp 11–29, © 1998, Blackwell Science Ltd.

percent increase in resource use. (Note that, to produce these tables, the interventions were assessed one at a time rather than in a multiple regression model containing the listed set. The effects are only adjusted for the condition of the patient at the time of admission. Consequently, the effects shown also contain the effects of other processes entrained by the one whose effects are given. For example, a delivery performed by a nurse-midwife could not have been an unscheduled C-section necessitated by a deterioration of the condition of the patient or her baby during labor.)

Similar data are provided in the reports on maternity care for interventions carried out during prenatal care prior to admission. Separate reports on practices are prepared for individual hospitals. In addition, data on the characteristics of the patients are also provided in similar form (frequencies of findings and the strength of their associations with outcomes). Facility characteristics (e.g., the number of deliveries, the obstetrical level, the ratio of house staff to attending physicians) and policies (e.g., pertaining to same-day surgery or to reuse of laparoscopic instruments in cholecystectomy) are also echoed back to the relevant organizational units. Such data inform local, regional, and national decision makers and place the patient populations, the practices, and their settings in proper perspective.

Measures of risk-adjusted performance of organizational units in terms of clinical outcomes and resource costs (Table 28–3). The risk adjustment takes the form of a comparison of the observed outcome scores and resource costs to those that are predicted by means of the models for the patients cared for by the listed military hospitals of one TRICARE region. Although no measures of the statistical significance of the difference between the observed and the predicted results are shown, they are available, and one of their uses is illustrated in Figure 28–3. This presents the results obtained by the five hospitals whose outcome scores and resource use were statistically significantly superior to those expected and that had the best results. The column in Figure 28–3 labeled "Best Clinical Practice" provides a calibration with respect to what is achievable. The civilian hospitals with which the region contracted for the provision of maternity care because the capacity of the military hospitals was insufficient use a distinctly lower amount of resources but also had distinctly poorer clinical outcomes. The latter effect was further isolated to two large community hospitals. Whether this observation reflects a substantive problem with the quality of care or an anomaly in the collection and reporting of data is not yet clear. Because this report is the first attempt to evaluate the care pro-

**Table 28–3** Actual and Expected Outcome Scores and Cost

|  | *Best Clinical Practice* | *DoD* | *Region 11 (Military)* | *Region 11 (Civilian)* | *MTF 125* | *MTF 126* | *MTF 127* |
|---|---|---|---|---|---|---|---|
| Sample Size | 901 | 7,393 | 398 | 511 | 200 | 100 | 98 |
| Total Number of Births FY95 | 6,135 | 53,861 | 3,208 | 972 | 2,070 | 625 | 513 |
| **Combined maternal and neonatal score** | | | | | | | |
| Expected | 2.88 | 2.91 | 3.18 | 2.80 | 3.32 | 3.11 | 2.68 |
| Actual | 2.14 | 2.91 | 2.87 | 3.21 | 3.15 | 2.68 | 1.98 |
| **Maternal score** | | | | | | | |
| Expected | 1.12 | 1.15 | 1.36 | 1.06 | 1.53 | 1.11 | 1.01 |
| Actual | 0.99 | 1.15 | 1.43 | 0.96 | 1.72 | 1.15 | 0.64 |
| **Neonatal score** | | | | | | | |
| Expected | 1.75 | 1.75 | 1.86 | 1.66 | 1.88 | 1.96 | 1.67 |
| Actual | 1.16 | 1.75 | 1.44 | 2.24 | 1.43 | 1.53 | 1.34 |
| **Combined maternal and neonatal cost** | | | | | | | |
| Expected | 227.35 | 230.57 | 243.30 | 226.60 | 254.91 | 232.60 | 212.94 |
| Actual | 188.43 | 230.57 | 228.89 | 179.31 | 249.40 | 218.13 | 171.68 |
| **Maternal cost** | | | | | | | |
| Expected | 177.34 | 181.04 | 188.93 | 177.39 | 198.34 | 179.65 | 165.14 |
| Actual | 151.23 | 181.04 | 178.95 | 136.84 | 191.00 | 175.67 | 140.68 |
| **Neonatal costs** | | | | | | | |
| Expected | 41.72 | 42.29 | 44.68 | 41.73 | 47.47 | 41.75 | 38.01 |
| Actual | 32.28 | 42.29 | 41.71 | 32.13 | 46.08 | 40.00 | 29.35 |

Note: The abbreviation MTF stands for Military Treatment Facility or, in the present study, military hospital.

*Source*: Reprinted with permission from H. Krakauer et al., Best Clinical Practice: Assessment of Processes of Care and of Outcomes in the U.S. Military Health Services System, *Journal of Evaluation in Clinical Practice*, Vol. 4, No. 1, pp 11–29, © 1998, Blackwell Science Ltd.

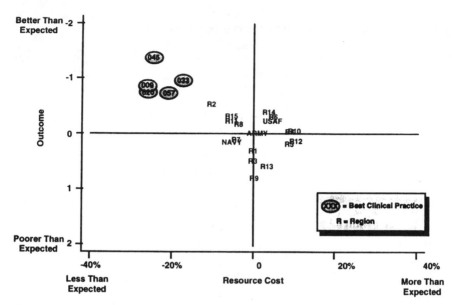

**Figure 28–3** Illustrative "Clinical Practice Profile" for Maternity Care. The vertical axis gives the increment in outcome severity associated with delivery within the organizational unit specified (TRICARE regions R1–R14, the military services, and the hospitals exhibiting best clinical practice), and the horizontal axis gives the percent increment in resource cost over that expected for the case mix of the organizational unit.

vided directly by military facilities and by their civilian contractors, anomalies in the data are a clear possibility.

The coordinates of the data points are increments in the clinical outcome scores (vertical axis) and proportional increments in resource costs (horizontal axis) of the patients of the services, the regions, and the five military hospitals identified as having the best clinical practices. An organizational unit that falls on the zero lines for outcomes or costs has outcomes or costs exactly what would be expected for its patient population. The services and regions represent rather large aggregations. As a result, their departures from the expected results tend to be quite small. On the other hand, the data for the best clinical practice hospitals indicate the magnitude of possible deviations. As a practical matter, these hospitals can serve as role models for the others. Their outcomes scores are 1 point below the expected 2.8, and their resource utilization is more than 20 percent (approximately $1,500) less than the predicted 230 RVUs (approximately $7,600).

## Outcomes-based Practice Guidelines

Figure 28–4 consists of a simplified decision tree that identifies the principal logical decision points in the management of an admission for delivery. A distinctive characteristic of the data obtained in the present studies is that the terminal node utilities (the difference between the observed and expected outcome scores for individual patients or groups of patients) are available as continuous functions of the level of indication (predicted probability) of the procedure as calculated for individual patients by means of checklists such as that in Table 28–4, the checklist for scheduled C-section. If the sum of the weights associated with the findings exceeds the threshold weight, the analyses suggest that scheduling a C-section is advisable, as the outcome is likely to be better with it than without. The degree to which the patient's sum of weights exceeds the threshold score is a measure of the strength of the indication.

Decision thresholds were obtained for scheduled (elective) and unscheduled (emergency) C-sections and for forceps delivery. Although sought, none could be found for epidural analgesia, nor for medical or surgical induction or augmentation of labor. These interventions are associated, on average, with poorer risk-adjusted outcomes. The present analyses, therefore, failed to identify clinical circumstances in which these interventions are superior to their alternatives. In the case of epidural analgesia, whose justification is not clinical but comfort related, evidence could also not be obtained that its use resulted in a higher level of patient satisfaction than its alternatives.

Two important points stand out. First, "best clinical practice" is *not* projected to be achieved by the reduction in the rate of C-sections (Table 28–5). Indeed, if the decision rules were followed, the overall rate would increase from 17 to 22 percent of deliveries. Second, application of the decision rules would reverse the proportion of scheduled to unscheduled C-sections. In 1995, the latter were two-thirds of all C-sections performed in Department of Defense facilities but would fall to 28 percent of the total. In addition, the use of forceps delivery would nearly disappear because the data suggest that there are very few circumstances in which forceps produce a superior outcome than that achievable with the alternatives.

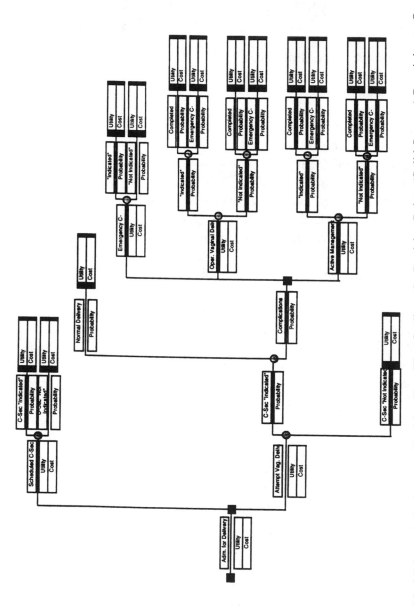

**Figure 28–4** Schematic Pathway or Decision Tree That Outlines the Decision Points (Solid Squares) Pertaining to Operative Interventions In Delivery. The branches that emanate from the circles represent possible patient characteristics that may be present and events that may follow the decisions. The terminal nodes permit the specification and weighting of the final outcomes.

**Table 28–4** Indications for Scheduled Caesarean Section. Threshold Probability of Scheduled Cesarean (C-) section = 0.31 Decision Threshold Score = 1.11

| Risk Factor | Value | Checklist score |
|---|---|---|
| Previous pregnancy, vaginal delivery | −1.49 | _____ |
| Cervical abnormality | −1.37 | _____ |
| Patient age <18 | −1.16 | _____ |
| Mother, Hispanic | −0.70 | _____ |
| Mother, White | −0.49 | _____ |
| Premature labor: antepartum | −0.43 | _____ |
| Education-undocumented, both parents | 0.22 | _____ |
| Moderate edema: on admission | 0.29 | _____ |
| Preeclampsia-mild/moderate: before/during pregnancy | 0.38 | _____ |
| Hypertension, gestational or chronic or HELP: before/during pregnancy, or present on admission | 0.39 | _____ |
| Previous pregnancy, fetal distress | 0.48 | _____ |
| Premature rupture of membranes | 0.58 | _____ |
| Oligohydramnios: at admission | 0.62 | _____ |
| Placenta previa/low-lying: antepartum and/or present | 0.63 | _____ |
| Previous pregnancy, cord, placental, or amniotic fluid | 0.67 | _____ |
| Proteinuria: last prenatal visit | 0.71 | _____ |
| Uterine leiomyomata: before/during pregnancy | 0.71 | _____ |
| Nonstress test result abnormal: before admission | 0.79 | _____ |
| Patient age >35 | 0.83 | _____ |
| High birth weight: antepartum or post admission | 0.91 | _____ |
| Chorioamnionitis: diagnosed antepartum | 1.10 | _____ |
| Malpresentation: antepartum and/or present on admission | 1.16 | _____ |
| Previous pregnancy, Caesarean section | 1.83 | _____ |
| Placental abruption: diagnosed antepartum | 2.63 | _____ |
| Malpresentation at first vaginal exam | 3.24 | _____ |
| Active herpes: at admission | 3.28 | _____ |
| Contracted or abnormal pelvis on admission | 4.51 | _____ |
| **Total** | | _____ |

Decision Threshold Score=1.11

*Source*: Reprinted with permission from H. Krakauer et al., Best Clinical Practice: Assessment of Processes of Care and of Outcomes in the U.S. Military Health Services System, *Journal of Evaluation in Clinical Practice*, Vol. 4, No. 1, pp 11–29, © 1998, Blackwell Science Ltd.

**Table 28–5** Projected Consequences of Implementation of Decision Rules. (a) Changes in Frequencies of Procedures; (b) Changes in Outcomes and Resource Use

| (a) Procedure | Frequencies (percent of deliveries) | |
| --- | --- | --- |
| | Current | Projected |
| Total operative deliveries | 29.3 | 22.2 |
| All C-sections | 16.8 | 21.5 |
|   Scheduled C-sections | 5.5 | 15.4 |
|   Unscheduled C-sections | 11.3 | 6.1 |
| Operative vaginal deliveries | 12.5 | 0.7 |

| (b) Outcomes | |
| --- | --- |
| Overall change in score per patient | −0.26 |
| Overall change in resource cost per patient | $264.00 |
| Change in score per patient for patients affected by the decision rules | −0.99 |
| Change in resource costs per patient for patients affected by the decision rules | $1,009.00 |

*Source*: Reprinted with permission from H. Krakauer et al., Best Clinical Practice: Assessment of Processes of Care and of Outcomes in the U.S. Military Health Services System, *Journal of Evaluation in Clinical Practice*, Vol. 4, No. 1, pp 11–29, © 1998, Blackwell Science Ltd.

Application of the decision rules is projected to result in improved outcomes because of the reductions in unscheduled C-sections and in attempted forceps deliveries, both associated with poorer outcomes when adjusted for the condition of the mother at the time of admission (Table 28–2). In addition, despite the increase in the C-section rates, a reduction in resource costs is also projected, principally because of the reduction in the much more costly unscheduled C-sections (Table 28–5).

## DISCUSSION

The methodological approaches to the evaluation of clinical practices in the Military Health Services System described herein were devised to meet specific needs. This system is simultaneously undergoing regionalization and is attempting to integrate the care delivered directly by military facilities with services purchased from the civilian sector. The devolution of responsibility to regional commanders for the management of both components carries with it the requirement that they be sufficiently informed of the absolute and relative effectiveness and efficiency of their facilities and services. In addition, severe budgetary limitations are creating demands for constraining the activities of medical practitioners.[8] The pressures on the Military Health Services System are, of course, not unique. However, the command environment permits somewhat distinct responses. These include the ability to focus quickly and clearly on specific problems and to marshal resources to quickly address them.

The form of the responses is conventional: report cards[9,10] and practice guidelines.[11] In addition, the structure of the analytic process attempts to mimic the clinical thought process. It is the combination of format and orientation that gives the present approaches their distinct character.

First, clinical outcomes are characterized broadly, encompassing all facets of the biological experience of the patient. This necessitates a scoring algorithm rather than a focus on one event or a very narrow set of events, as often occurs in conventional clinical studies. Scoring is, in fact, fairly commonly used in medicine whenever multiple dimensions of the patient's condition must be evaluated (e.g., in assessing functional status by means of the SF36, a standardized questionnaire developed to support research on outcomes).[12]

Second, the operational requirement of an ongoing process of monitoring and assessment dictates reliance on observational rather than experimental approaches (clinical trials). The need for speedy results also requires that retrospective methods based on existing data obtainable from electronic systems and from charts be used. The challenge has been to construct efficient tools for the systematic abstraction of data from charts, and various solutions have been devised (e.g., MedisGroups[13] and the UCDSS).[14] The tools used for the present project are distinguished by the richness of clinical detail that they make available for analysis (because they focus on specific medical conditions) and the intent to have a consistent design for the data dictionaries (reflecting the commonalities of medicine).

Third, a consistent analytic methodology applicable to the great majority of medical conditions is highly desirable. Because the outcome scores assigned to patients are hierarchical but do not predictably follow any convenient distribution, analytic techniques based on ordered logistic regression combined with the generation of the estimators of effect analogous to regression coefficients to provide intelligible estimates of the impact of individual predictors on the outcome scores had to be devised.

The most substantive innovation developed in this project is the formulation of clinical decision rules, which are outcomes-based practice guidelines.[15] They specifically address the need of clinicians to marshal and bring to bear the collective experience of their peers on the specific patients for whom a course of action must be selected. The results of a conventional clinical trial indicate the utility of this approach, but only for the specific types of patients and under the specific conditions of the trial. The results of a regression analysis of observational data, as in Tables 28–3 and 28–4, report only the average effect of an intervention on the entire population of the study. They do not answer the question of whether a particular intervention is more advisable under one set of circumstances than under another. But the selective use of the elements of the medical armamentarium is the essence of medical practice.

The decision rules are direct responses to this need. They address, first, the question of what patient characteristics have been observed to drive the decision to perform the intervention, and, second, the question of what arrays of these characteristics have been observed to be associated with superior outcomes if the intervention is performed.

The hallmark of medical decision-making at present is its variability, and the objective of practice guidelines is to reduce this variability. However, the conventional approach to the formulation of practice guidelines relies on collective judgments expressed through committees. This approach is subject to three limitations: (1) the diversity of medical opinion results in frequent failure to agree on the appropriateness of an intervention under specific circumstances;[16] (2) the simplicity and rigidity of guidelines frequently limits their applicability to only a subset of patients for whom a decision is required;[17] and (3) the adoption of practice guidelines developed by consensus has been, at best, erratic.[18]

Our studies contain substantial numbers of patients with documented arrays of characteristics, many of whom were subjected to a given intervention and many of whom were not. Thus, the current environment provides ample opportunity to assess the relative merits of interventions in patients with comparable levels of indication. The decision rules explicitly array the level of indication for an intervention (as revealed by current practice in the Military Health Services System) against the outcomes achieved in patients who did or did not receive that intervention, and they thereby suggest the probably superior course of action at any level of indication. They also permit the accumulation of indications as a patient's condition evolves, allowing sufficient indications to appear to cause the threshold to be exceeded (assuming the condition does not resolve prior to that point).

The use of quantitative empirical data to assist in clinical decision-making is well established. For example, a tool has been available for some time to determine when a patient complaining of chest pain is sufficiently likely to have a myocardial infarction and thus should be admitted to an intensive care unit.[19]

The limitations of the approach adopted in the present project are, on the one hand, inherent in the use of observational data and, on the other hand, due to the relative novelty of the techniques dictated by the operational requirements.

The limitations associated with observational data follow from (1) incompleteness of the information contained in the charts; (2) incompleteness in the specification of the data to be abstracted to capture the condition of the patient, its evolution, and the manner in which the patient was managed; and (3) inaccuracies in the abstraction of information. Uncertainty about the completeness of the chart is a given, but it impairs confidence in the results of analysis, and also undermines the ability of the clinical team to care for the patient. The specification of the data items to be collected (the data dictionaries) was guided by the need to obtain that information deemed by clinicians to be required for the management of the patient. An important advantage results from the biological redundancy of much of the information collected by clinicians: many signs, symptoms, and findings reflect on the same underlying problem, and if one is not available, another nearly equivalent one will do (e.g., blood urea nitrogen [BUN] and serum creatinine as measures of the impairment of renal function, and ejection fraction, edema, respiratory symptoms, and chest radiographic findings as indicators of heart pump failure). Techniques to ensure the accuracy of chart abstraction, including training, reabstraction, and edit checks, have been used in various phases of the projects.

The most critical component of the present approach, the one on which the validity and usefulness of the analyses hinge, is the scoring of the outcomes. It is the one component that depends on clinical judgment. Because the scores are assigned to elementary events, it is hoped that variability in scoring will be minimized. The initial (learning) phases are always the most difficult. For example, a clear shift in scoring philosophy was evident between the panels that scored outcomes in the first maternity care project in the program (births that occurred in 1993) and the second project (births that occurred in 1995), although the same key clinicians served on both panels. The second panel rather consistently assigned somewhat lower scores (lower by about 1 point) to the same findings, especially to the less severe ones. One consequence was that, whereas the scores produced by the first panel accorded with a normal distribution, the shift at the low end of the scoring range in the second panel resulted in a bimodal distribution. However, the clinicians are becoming more comfortable with the scoring process as they gain experience.

Three significant technical matters have not yet been addressed. The first is the construction of an integrated measure of performance from the multiple dimensions of outcome (clinical, resource use, functional status, satisfaction). To this point, because of the limited return of patient questionnaires, the focus had been on only two dimensions. They can be conveniently presented on a graph such as Figure 28–3 to provide the reader with a qualitative insight into the consistency of performance or into the trade-offs that occur. Thus, overall in maternity care better risk-adjusted outcomes tend to be associated with lower risk-adjusted resource use. But, focusing on C-sections, those hospitals that have higher than expected C-section rates have better outcomes but also higher resource use. However, if more than 2 dimensions of outcome need to be considered and if quantitative estimates of the trade-offs are desired, then multivariate techniques will have to be brought to bear.[20] These are now being explored.

Second, the analyses to date have focused on specific events or episodes (e.g., an admission). However, disease runs a course over time, punctuated by acute events and interventions, and patients move among levels of health. The full assessment of the effectiveness and efficiency of patient care strategies requires, therefore, that the evolution of each patient's condition be considered. This problem will acquire prominence in the analysis of the management of ischemic heart disease. Various approaches are available. Modeling of time-to-event that yields projections of the evolving probability of an event such as death over time can be carried out quite effectively.[21] Concatenation of events can be carried out using Markov processes, path analysis, or conditional probability techniques.[22] These approaches are also now being explored.

Third, and most importantly, a more effective, more reliable, and less costly and cumbersome method for obtaining the needed detailed clinical data than abstraction of paper charts is needed. The proper solution to this problem lies in the implementation of the electronic patient record system.[23] The true justification of this system is that it is needed for patient care, especially when multiple sites are involved in that care, as in the case of the military. The availability of data for analysis is but a useful byproduct. The Department of

Defense is indeed committed to speedy implementation of the electronic patient record system.

The Military Health Services System requires ongoing and rapidly responsive monitoring and assessment of its practices for the purpose of continually improving its effectiveness and efficiency in caring for the population for which it is responsible. The approaches devised and described herein represent a response based on the resources available to it. Their objective is to provide decision makers at all levels not only with up-to-date information about the populations cared for and about prevalent patterns of practice but also with indications of what changes in practice might be beneficial. The data that emerge from these analyses are best used to focus attention and as starting points for more detailed reconsiderations and reevaluations by clinicians and commanders.

The Military Health Services System is a large, complex managed care organization with the distinctive mission of maintaining the readiness of the troops on active duty while also caring for dependents and retirees. Because of its command structure, it offers a unique opportunity for the development and evaluation of techniques for the monitoring and management of medical practice. As experience is gained with the tools described herein, their applicability to and usefulness for a broad range of managed care organizations and medical care as a whole should become clarified.

---

NOTES

1. Department of Defense Directive 6025.13, National Quality Management Program in the Military Health Services System, 20 July, 1995.
2. D.C. Wherry et al., "An External Audit of Laparoscopic Cholecystectomy in the Steady State Performed in Medical Treatment Facilities of the Department of Defense," *Annals of Surgery* 224 (1996): 145–154.
3. S.C. Johnson, "Tricare: The Military's Version of Managed Care," *Medical Interface* 9 (1996): 86–89.
4. "Physician Fee Schedule Update for Calendar Year 1996 and Physician Volume Performance Standard Rates of Increase for Federal Fiscal Year 1996–HCFA: Final Notice," *Federal Register*, 8 December 1995, 63358–63366.
5. "Changes to the Hospital Inpatient Prospective Payment Systems and Fiscal Year 1995 Rates; Correction—HCFA: Final Rule; Correction," *Federal Register*, 3 December 1994, 64153–64156.
6. G.T. O'Connor et al., "A Regional Intervention to Improve the Hospital Mortality Associated with Coronary Artery Bypass Graft Surgery. The Northern New England Cardiovascular Disease Study Group," *JAMA* 275 (1996): 841–846.

7. J.A. Hanley and B.A. McNeil, "The Meaning and Use of the Area under the Receiver Operating Characteristic (ROC) Curve," *Radiology* 143 (1982): 29–36.

8. Johnson, "Tricare."

9. "Report Card Pilot Project Technical Report," National Committee for Quality Assurance, Washington, DC, 1995.

10. D.M. Nadzam et al., "Data-driven Performance Improvement in Health Care: The Joint Commission's Indicator Measurement System (IMSystem)," *Joint Commission Journal of Quality Improvement* 19 (1993): 492–500.

11. M.J. Field and K.N. Lohr, *Clinical Practice Guidelines: Directions for a New Program* (Washington DC: National Academy Press, 1990).

12. J. Ware et al., *SF-36 Health Survey: Manual and Interpretation Guide* (The Health Institute, New England Medical Center, 1993).

13. R.C. Bradbury et al., "Interhospital Variations in Admission Severity-adjusted Hospital Mortality and Morbidity," *Health Services Research* 26 (1991): 407–424.

14. A.J. Hartz et al., "Severity of Illness Measures Derived from the Uniform Clinical Data Set System (UCDSS)," *Medical Care* 32 (1994): 801–901.

15. F.J. Crosson, "Why Outcomes Measurement Must Be the Basis for the Development of Clinical Guidelines," *Managed Care Quarterly* 3 (1995): 6–11.

16. R.E. Park et al., "Physician Ratings of Appropriate Indications for Three Procedures: Theoretical Indications vs. Indications Used in Practice," *American Journal of Public Health* 79 (1989): 445–447.

17. E.F. Ellerbeck et al., "Quality of Care for Medicare Patients with Acute Myocardial Infarction. A Four-State Pilot Study from the Cooperative Cardiovascular Project," *JAMA* 273 (1995): 1509–1514.

18. D.A. Brand et al., "Cardiologists' Practices Compared with Practice Guidelines: Use of Beta-blockade after Acute Myocardial Infarction," *Journal of the American College of Cardiology* 26 (1995): 1432–1436.

19. R.A. McNutt and H.P. Selker, "How Did the Acute Ischemic Heart Disease Predictive Instrument Reduce Coronary Care Unit Admissions?" *Medical Decision Making* 8 (1988): 90–94.

20. T.W. Anderson, *An Introduction to Mutivariate Statistical Analysis* (New York: Wiley, 1984), chap. 12.

21. H. Krakauer and I. Jacoby, "Predicting the Course of Disease," *Inquiry* 30 (1991): 115–127.

22. J.K. Lindsey, *Models for Repeated Measurements* (Oxford: Oxford University Press, 1993).

23. R.S. Dick and E.B. Steen, eds., *The Computer-based Patient Record* (Washington, DC: National Academy Press, 1991).

CHAPTER 29

# Development of a Prospective Payment System for Hospital-based Outpatient Care

*Richard F. Averill, Norbert I. Goldfield, Laurence W. Gregg, Thelma M. Grant, Boris V. Shafir, and Robert L. Mullin*

The OMNIBUS Budget Reconciliation Act (OBRA) of 1990 required the U.S. Health Care Financing Administration (HCFA) to design and evaluate a prospective payment system (PPS) for the facility cost of outpatient care. OBRA called for the evaluation of a PPS for all hospital outpatient services (e.g., same-day surgery units, emergency departments, outpatient clinics, etc.). The facility cost refers to the hospital cost for providing care (e.g., room charges, medical and surgical supplies, etc.) and excludes the physician's professional service.

During the period 1988–1990, HCFA funded the development of Version 1.0 of the Ambulatory Patient Groups (APGs).[1] The APGs are a patient classification system that was designed to be used as the basis of an outpatient PPS. Version 1.0 of the APGs was released in the spring of 1991. During the period 1991–1994, a number of payers, including state Medicaid agencies and Blue Cross and Blue Shield plans, began using APGs for outpatient payment.[2] Individual providers also began using APGs for internal management. The availability of improved data, the expanding use of APGs, and the potential use of APGs as the basis of a Medicare outpatient PPS resulted in HCFA funding the development of Version 2.0 of the APGs. One of the objectives of the development of Version 2.0 was to simplify the APG system so that it could be more easily implemented as the basis of a Medicare outpatient PPS.

Courtesy of 3M Health Information Systems, Wallingford, Connecticut.

The research project to develop Version 2.0 of the APGs was initiated in 1992. The development of Version 2.0 of the APGs was performed by 3M Health Information Systems in close cooperation with HCFA. Version 2.0 of the APGs was completed and released in August 1995.[3]

In March 1995, HCFA submitted a report to the U.S. Congress recommending that the APGs or an APG-like patient classification system be used as the basis of a Medicare outpatient PPS. In August 1997, the U.S. Congress passed the Balanced Budget Act of 1997, which included the requirement that a Medicare outpatient PPS be implemented beginning in January 1999.

This chapter discusses the development of the APG patient classification system and its use in an outpatient PPS. Financial simulations of an APG-based PPS are presented and various policy alternatives are evaluated.

## CHARACTERISTICS OF AN OUTPATIENT PATIENT CLASSIFICATION SYSTEM

Fundamental to the design of any PPS for ambulatory care is the selection of the basic unit of payment. The Medicare inpatient PPS uses the hospital admission as the basic unit of payment. The basic unit for ambulatory care is the visit, which represents a contact between the patient and a health care professional. The visit could be for a procedure, a medical evaluation, or an ancillary service such as a chest x-ray. For each type of visit, a prospective price could be established that includes all routine services (e.g., blood tests, chest x-rays, etc.). If the cost of the routine services rendered during a visit were included in the payment for the visit, hospitals would have the financial incentive to control the amount of services rendered.

An ambulatory patient classification system serves the same function as the diagnosis related groups (DRGs) in the Medicare inpatient PPS: the patient classification system provides the basic product definition for the ambulatory setting and will have important secondary effects. For example, DRGs have brought about fundamental changes in management, communications, cost accounting, and planning within hospitals. These changes have resulted in improved efficiency in the delivery of inpatient care. The benefits to hospital management that resulted from the adoption of DRGs would also be expected to occur in the ambulatory setting. Thus, the selection of an appropriate patient classification system is critical to the success of an outpatient PPS. An ambulatory patient classification system should have the following characteristics.

## Comprehensiveness

The patient classification system must be able to describe every type of patient seen in an ambulatory setting. This includes medical patients, patients undergoing a procedure, and patients who receive ancillary services only.

## Administrative Simplicity

The patient classification system should be administratively straightforward to implement. The number of patient classes should be kept to a reasonable number. A patient classification system containing relatively few patient classes (e.g., fewer than the number of DRGs) will be more easily understood by providers and will ease the administrative burden on both facilities and payers. In addition, the data used to define the patient classes should be compatible with existing billing, data collection, coding, storage, and processing practices. Such compatibility will decrease implementation costs, data errors, and other administrative problems.

## Homogeneous Resource Use

The amount and type of resources (e.g., operating room time, medical surgical supplies, etc.) used to treat patients in each patient class should be homogeneous. If resources used vary widely within a patient class, it would be difficult to develop equitable payment rates. If a facility treated a disproportionate share of either the expensive or inexpensive cases within a patient class, then the aggregate payments to that facility might not be appropriate. Further, the facility might be encouraged to treat only the less costly patients within the patient class, causing a potential access problem for the complex cases. Thus, a homogeneous pattern of resource use is a critical characteristic of any patient classification system used in a PPS.

## Clinical Meaningfulness

The definition of each patient class should be clinically meaningful. For example, a patient class involving a procedure should, in general, contain only procedures on the same body system that are of the same degree of extensiveness and utilize the same method (e.g., surgical, endoscopic, percutaneous, etc.). The underlying assumption in a PPS is that hospitals will respond to the financial incentives in the system and become more efficient. Clinical meaningfulness is critical, because in order to respond effectively hospitals must communicate the incentives to their medical staffs. A clinically meaningful patient classification system will be more readily accepted by providers and will be more useful as a communication and management tool.

## Minimal Upcoding and Code Fragmentation

In the patient classification system, there should be minimal opportunities for providers to assign a patient to a higher paying class through upcoding. A patient classification system with many classes that are based on subtle distinctions is susceptible to upcoding. In general, the patient classes should be as broad and inclusive as possible without sacrificing resource homogeneity or clinical meaningfulness. In addition, there should be minimal opportunities for increasing payment by separately reporting the constituent parts of a procedure.

## Flexibility

In a visit-based payment system, there is a wide array of options in terms of which ancillary services should be included in the visit payment. The extent to which ancillary services are included in the visit payment is a policy decision. The patient classification system must be flexible enough to accommodate a full range of options for incorporating ancillary services into the visit payment. In addition, the patient classification system should be structured to allow changes in technology and practice patterns to be easily incorporated. This system should provide a flexible framework that can adapt to such change without requiring a major restructuring of the classification system.

Because of the fundamental role that the patient classification system plays in a PPS, it is essential that the patient classification system possess substantially all of the above characteristics.

## OVERVIEW OF APGs

APGs are designed to explain the amount and type of resources used in an ambulatory visit. Ambulatory resources include pharmaceuticals, supplies, ancillary tests, type of equipment needed, type of room needed, treatment time and so on. Patients in each APG have similar clinical characteristics, resource use, and costs. Similar resource use means that the resources used are relatively constant across all patients within each APG. However, some variation in resource use will remain among the patients in each APG. In other words, the definition of the APG is not so specific that every patient included in the same APG is identical, but rather the level of variation in patient resource use is known and predictable. Thus, although the precise resource use of a particular patient cannot be predicted by knowing the APG of the patient, the average pattern of resource use of a group of patients in an APG can be accurately predicted.

Patients in each APG also have similar clinical characteristics. Similar clinical characteristics mean that the patient characteristics included in the definition of the APG should relate to a common organ system or etiology and that a specific medical specialty should typically provide care to the patients in the APG. In addition, all available patient characteristics that consistently affect resource use should be included in the definition of the APGs. For example, patients with diabetes may or may not have ketoacidosis. Although these patients are the same from organ system, etiology, and medical specialist perspectives, the APGs will assign patients with and without ketoacidosis to different patient classes, because the presence of ketoacidosis consistently increases the resource use of diabetic patients. On the other hand, sets of unrelated surgical procedures should not be used to define an APG because there is no medical reason for expecting that the resource use would be similar.

The definition of similar clinical characteristics is, of course, dependent on the goal of the classification system. For APGs, the definition of clinical similarity relates to the medical rationale for differences in resource use. If, on the other hand, the classification goal was related to patient prognosis, then the definition of patient characteristics that were clinically similar might be different. The requirement that APGs be clinically homogeneous caused more patient classes to be formed than is necessary for explaining resource use alone. For example, patients with a dilation and curettage or a simple hemorrhoid procedure are quite similar in terms of most measures of resource use. However, different organ systems and different medical specialties are involved. Thus, the requirement that APGs have similar clinical characteristics precludes the possibility of these types of patients being in the same APG.

APGs were developed to encompass the full range of ambulatory settings, including same-day surgery units, hospital emergency rooms, and outpatient clinics. APGs, however, do not address phone contacts, home visits, nursing home services, or inpatient services. Data from several sources, including hospital outpatient departments and ambulatory surgical centers, were used in developing the APGs. However, better cost data from nonhospital sites are needed in order to determine if there are any problems with applying APGs to nonhospital sites.

Although the anticipated initial application of APGs focuses on Medicare patients, APGs were developed to represent ambulatory patients across the entire patient population. For example, APGs relating to pregnancy were developed even though pregnancy is not often encountered in the Medicare population.

APGs were developed to differentiate facility costs and not professional costs. However, professional costs relate primarily to professional time and therefore directly relate to facility time. Professional time can serve as a proxy for the amount of time a patient used the resources of the facility. During the development of APGs, facility costs such as supplies and equipment as well as professional time were taken into consideration.

The data elements used to define APGs were limited to the information routinely collected on the Medicare claim form and consisted of the diagnoses coded in International Classification of Diagnoses 9th Revision Clinical Modifications (ICD-9-CM) and procedures coded in Current Procedural Terminology Fourth Edition (CPT-4). The patient characteristics used in the definition of the APGs were restricted to those readily available in order to ensure that the APGs could be readily implemented.

## SELECTION OF THE INITIAL CLASSIFICATION VARIABLE

The first step in developing a patient classification system is to choose the initial classification variable. In the DRGs, the principal diagnosis is used to classify patients into a set of mutually exclusive major diagnostic categories (MDCs). Within each MDC, procedure, age, and complications and comorbidities are used to complete the DRG classification system. APGs use procedure instead of diagnosis as the initial classification variable. The decision to do so was based on the following considerations:

- When a significant procedure is performed in an ambulatory setting, it is normally the reason for the visit. The procedure will normally be scheduled in advance and will consume the vast majority of resources associated with the visit.

- With procedure as the initial classification variable, each procedure will be assigned to only one APG. With principal diagnosis as the initial classification variable, the same procedure could be assigned to many different APGs depending on the principal diagnosis. Having each procedure in only one APG also reduces the number of APGs and simplifies the establishment of prospective prices.

Once the decision to use procedure as the initial classification variable was made, it was then necessary to partition all procedures into a set of mutually exclusive and exhaustive procedure groups. The first step in the process was to identify all procedures that could be done only on an inpatient basis. An inpatient procedure was defined as a procedure that requires at least 24 hours of postoperative recovery time or monitoring before a patient can be safely discharged. Some procedures, such as craniotomies, are clearly inpatient procedures. However, there are other procedures, such as the treatment of an open fracture, that are normally done on an inpatient basis but can sometimes be done on an ambulatory basis. Further, patients with the same CPT-4 procedure code can have a great deal of variation in the complexity of the procedure performed. For example, the treatment of an open humeral fracture can vary considerably in complexity.

Only the simplest cases of procedures normally done on an inpatient basis are done on an ambulatory basis. Thus, an open humeral fracture treated on an ambulatory basis will have minimal bone displacement and tissue damage. Such procedures are included in the APG procedure classification. When grouping procedures together to form homogeneous subclasses, it is important to recognize that variations of severity exist within a CPT-4 code and that only the simplest cases of complex procedures are treated in an ambulatory setting.

The procedures that could be performed on an ambulatory basis were then assigned to one of the following two classes:

1. *Significant procedure.* This is a procedure that is normally scheduled, constitutes the reason for the visit, and dominates the time and resources expended during the visit (e.g., the excision of a skin lesion). Significant procedures range in scope from debridement of nails to pacemaker replacements as well as significant tests, such as a stress test.
2. *Ancillary services.* The term *ancillary services* is used to refer to both ancillary tests and ancillary procedures. An ancillary test is one that is

ordered by the primary physician to assist in patient diagnosis or treatment. Radiology, laboratory, and pathology constitute ancillary tests. An ancillary procedure is a procedure that increases but does not dominate the time and resources expended during a visit. Examples of ancillary procedures include immunizations and the insertion of an intrauterine device (IUD).

Only patients with a significant procedure were assigned to significant procedure APGs. All medical services provided to the patient were assumed to be an integral part of the procedure. Patients who received medical treatment but who had no significant procedures performed were assigned to medical APGs. Examples of medical treatments that do not involve a significant procedure include treatment for poisoning, neonatal care, and well care.

Figure 29–1 illustrates the APG partition based on services rendered or procedures performed. Patients who undergo a significant procedure are assigned to a significant procedure APG. For example, a patient who had a simple skin excision performed to remove a skin lesion would be placed in a significant procedure APG based on the CPT-4 code that describes the precise procedure. Patients receiving medical treatment that does not involve a significant procedure were assigned to medical APGs. A patient who visited a physician to have a skin lesion evaluated and had no significant procedures performed would be assigned to a medical APG based on the ICD-9-CM diagnosis code.

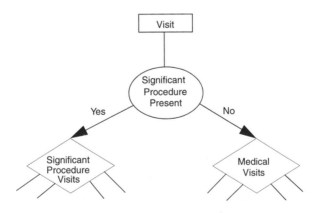

**Figure 29–1** Initial APG Partition Based on the Presence of a Significant Procedure. Courtesy of 3M Health Information Systems, Wallingford, Connecticut.

A patient who neither received medical treatment nor underwent a significant procedure but had an ancillary service performed would be assigned to only an ancillary service APG.

## DEVELOPMENT OF SIGNIFICANT PROCEDURE APGs

Significant ambulatory procedures are subdivided into groups of CPT-4 codes based on the body system associated with the procedure:

- integumentary system
- musculoskeletal system
- respiratory system
- cardiovascular system
- hematologic, lymphatic, and endocrine
- digestive system
- urinary system
- male genital system
- female genital system
- nervous system
- eye and ocular adnexa
- facial, ear, nose, mouth and throat
- therapeutic and other significant radiological procedures
- physical medicine and rehabilitation
- mental illness and substance abuse therapies

Body systems were formed as the first step toward ensuring that the procedures in each APG were clinically similar. The significant procedures in each body system generally correspond to a single organ system and are associated with a particular medical specialty. The body systems used in the procedure APGs are similar to the MDCs for the DRGs. However, there are some significant differences. For example, the body system for skin and subcutaneous tissue includes muscle, whereas muscle is in the musculoskeletal MDC. Muscle was included in the skin and subcutaneous tissue body system because most procedures involving the fascia (connective tissue) are clinically similar to dermal procedures and have similar patterns of resource use. If fascia or muscle procedures were included within the bone and joint body system, then it would have been necessary to form separate APGs for muscle procedures.

Thus, the inclusion of muscle in the skin and subcutaneous tissue body system reduced the overall number of APGs. Further, there are MDCs for etiologies such as infectious diseases for which there are no corresponding body system in the significant procedure APGs.

Some body systems had few procedures performed on an ambulatory basis. For example, except for biopsies or excisions of the thyroid, there are no endocrine procedures performed on an ambulatory basis. Thyroid procedures were included with lymph node biopsies and excisions because they are clinically quite similar.

Once each significant procedure was assigned to a body system, the procedures in each body system were subdivided into clinically similar classes. The classification variables considered in the formation of the procedure classes are shown in Table 29–1. In general, method was used as the primary classification variable. Different methods such as surgery, endoscopy, manipulation, dilation, catheterization, laser, and needle often require different types of rooms, equipment, and supplies as well as different amounts of time. For example, procedures in the respiratory body system were initially divided by method into endoscopic, needle or catheter, and noninvasive test subgroups. On the other hand, most male reproductive procedures are surgical; therefore, the male reproductive body system was initially subdivided based on site and not method. Surgical procedures were usually subdivided based on type (i.e., incision, excision, or repair). The time required to perform a procedure depends on the type of procedure, with repairs generally taking the most time. Thus, surgical skin procedures were divided into separate incision, excision, and repair groups. Endoscopic procedures were often divided into separate classes depending on purpose (i.e., diagnostic or therapeutic). Therapeutic endoscopic procedures generally require more time. The extent of a procedure was often taken into consideration. Thus, skin excisions of 2 cm and 20 cm are assigned to different APGs.

Another aspect of extent is the complexity of the procedure. Complexity basically refers to the amount of time normally required to perform a procedure. For example, the excision of a pressure ulcer will generally require more time than the excision of a skin lesion. Thus, the excision of the pressure ulcer was viewed as more complex and therefore assigned to a different APG. Anatomical site (e.g., face, hand, etc.) within a body system was used in order to ensure clinical similarity (e.g., procedures of the external ear versus the internal ear) and was also used to implicitly reflect complexity (e.g., treatment of a

**Table 29–1** Classification Variables Considered in the Development of the Significant Procedure APGs

| Variable | Example |
|---|---|
| Site | Face, hand, etc. |
| Extent | Excision size: 2 cm versus 20 cm |
| Purpose | Diagnostic or therapeutic |
| Type | Incision, excision or repair |
| Method | Surgical, endoscopic, etc. |
| Device | Insertion or removal |
| Medical specialty | Urology, gynecology, etc. |
| Complexity | Time needed to perform procedure |

Courtesy of 3M Health Information Systems, Wallingford, Connecticut.

closed fracture of a finger is usually less complex than treatment of a closed fracture of other sites).

If a procedure involved the insertion of a device (e.g., neurostimulator), then a separate APG was formed in order to recognize the cost of the device. Medical specialty was never explicitly used in the significant procedure APG formation, but procedures normally done by different medical specialties were usually put in different APGs.

## DEVELOPMENT OF MEDICAL APGs

Medical APGs describe patients who receive medical treatment but do not have a significant procedure performed during the visit. The fact that a patient had a specific significant procedure performed provides a great deal of precise information regarding the amount and type of resources typically used during the visit. Patients without a significant procedure (i.e., medical patients) can use a wide range of resources depending on their condition at the time of the visit. Medical patients can be described using the diagnoses of the patient coded in ICD-9-CM, which allows specific diseases (e.g., pneumonia) as well as signs, symptoms, and findings (SSFs) (e.g., chest pain, melena, elevated sedimentation rate, etc.) to be coded. The term "diagnosis" will be used to refer generically to SSFs and diseases. The standard Medicare claims form and the ICD-9-CM ambulatory coding guidelines require that the diagnosis that was the primary reason for the visit be indicated. Further, any additional diagnoses that are present may be listed on the claim as secondary diagnoses. The primary variable used to form the medical APGs is the diagnosis coded as the reason for the visit. The reason for the visit is the primary determinant of the resources used (e.g., time, tests ordered, etc.) during the visit. Thus, the medical APGs are based on the type of patient being treated.

The treatment of a medical patient is often highly influenced by the SSFs present at the time of the visit. In general, the coding of a disease simply indicates that the disease was present but gives no indication of how extensive or severe the disease was at the time of the visit. The coding of SSFs in addition to the underlying disease provides some indication of the extensiveness of the disease. The use of SSFs in the definition of the medical APGs was difficult because of the following limitations in the ICD-9-CM codes for SSFs:

- Many of the ICD-9-CM codes for SSFs are not precise. For example, abdominal rigidity (code 7894) has no precise clinical definition.
- There are a large number of SSF codes that refer to abnormal laboratory results that are imprecise. For example, a diagnosis of hypokalemia does not convey useful information because the range of potassium levels associated with hypokalemia can vary significantly in terms of clinical significance.

In addition to the imprecision of many of the SSF codes, the use of SSFs as a primary variable in the medical APGs could create opportunities for upcoding. If the APGs for SSFs had a high payment weight, then there would be a financial motivation to code the SSFs instead of the underlying disease. The fact that the ICD-9-CM coding rules allow only nonroutine SSFs to be coded also limited the applicability of SSFs in the definition of the medical APGs. As a result of the problems associated with SSFs, the SSFs used in the definition of the medical APGs were restricted to SSFs

- that had relatively precise clinical meaning
- that were significant enough not to be a routine part of most diseases
- that were significant enough to tend to dominate the resources used during the visit (ensuring that upcoding is not an issue because assignment to the SSF APG is appropriate irrespective of the underlying disease)

A single major SSF APG for medical patients was formed. Examples of SSFs included in the major SSF APG are meningismus and gangrene. In addition to the SSF codes, there were also ICD-9-CM codes included in the major SSF APG that specify both the underlying disease and the SSF (e.g., diabetic ketoacidosis). A patient is assigned to the major SSF APG whether the major SSF is coded as the reason for the visit or as a secondary diagnosis. The major SSF APG identifies the medical patients with extensive diseases who are usually treated in emergency rooms and who require significant amounts of resources. Patients who have nonmajor SSFs coded as the reason for the visit are assigned to the medical APG that is usually associated with the SSF (e.g., cough is assigned to the upper respiratory infection APG).

After patients who had a major SSF were assigned to a separate APG, the medical APGs were formed on the basis of the ICD-9-CM diagnosis code that was the reason for the visit. Thus, all possible ICD-9-CM diagnoses were divided into a set of mutually exclusive and clinically similar classes. The classification variables considered in the formation of the medical classes are shown in Table 29–2.

The initial variable used to form the medical APGs was the etiology of the diagnosis that was the reason for the visit:

* well care and administrative
* trauma
* infections
* pregnancy

---

**Table 29–2** Classification Variables Considered in the Development of the Medical APGs

| Variable | Example |
| --- | --- |
| Etiology | Trauma, malignancy, etc. |
| Body system | Respiratory, digestive, etc. |
| Type of disease | Acute or chronic |
| Medical specialty | Ophthalmology, gynecology, etc. |
| Patient age | Pediatric, adult, etc. |
| Patient type | New or old |
| Complexity | Time needed to treat the patient |

Courtesy of 3M Health Information Systems, Wallingford, Connecticut.

- malignancy
- poisoning
- neonate
- other

As a first step in the formulation of the medical APGs, each ICD-9-CM diagnosis code was assigned to one of the etiology subgroups. Malignancies and trauma were assigned to separate subgroups because they had unique resources associated with the care provided (e.g., frequent radiology and laboratory services). The body system group encompasses a broad spectrum of diseases from acute diseases such as pneumonia to chronic diseases such as hypertension. The "other" group was then divided into subgroups based on the specific body system of the diagnosis that was the reason for the visit:

- malignancy
- poisoning
- trauma
- neonate
- pregnancy
- infectious diseases
- nervous system diseases
- eye diseases
- ear, nose, mouth and throat diseases
- respiratory system diseases
- cardiovascular system diseases
- digestive system diseases
- major signs, symptoms, and findings
- musculoskeletal diseases
- skin and breast diseases
- endocrine, nutritional, and metabolic diseases
- kidney and urinary tract diseases
- male genital system diseases
- female genital system diseases
- immunologic and hematologic diseases

The initial subdivision of the medical APGs is shown in Figure 29–2. Once all the subclasses based on the etiology and the body system were formed,

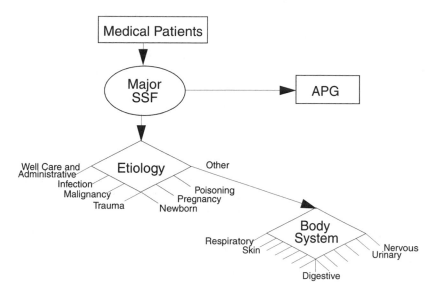

**Figure 29–2** Initial Medical APG Logic. Courtesy of 3M Health Information Systems, Wallingford, Connecticut.

---

then the other classification variables in Table 29–2 were used to further subdivide each etiology and body system.

Whether a diagnosis was acute or chronic was not explicitly used in the formation of the medical APGs. There are medical APGs that contain only diagnoses that are acute or chronic, but a medical APG was never formed for the explicit purpose of identifying acute or chronic diseases. Medical specialty was never explicitly used in the medical APG formation, but diseases normally treated by different medical specialties were usually put in different APGs. Age was not used in the definition of medical APGs.

Whether a patient was a new patient or an old patient was considered as a possible variable in the formation of the medical APGs. However, the new patient–old patient distinction was not used for the following reasons:

- There is difficulty in establishing a precise definition of a new patient. New can refer to either the physician or the facility. Thus, a patient may be considered new only the first time the patient is treated as an outpatient at the hospital. Alternatively, the patient may be considered new for each visit in which the patient is treated by a different physician. From a resource use perspective, the presence of new diagnoses or problems is often just as important as whether the patient is new to the facility or physician. The only definition of new that is not prone to upcoding is new to the facility.

- The impact on resources of whether a patient is a new patient varies by setting. For emergency room and same-day surgery units, the fact that the patient is new has little impact on resource use. For an outpatient clinic, a new patient often utilizes more resources.
- To the extent that there are follow-up visits for a patient, they typically occur at the same facility as the initial visit. These lower cost visits balance out the often more costly initial visit.
- The designation of whether a patient is a new or old patient is not present on the Medicare Universal Bill 92 (UB-92) claim form. Thus, a change in reporting requirements would have been necessary.

Patient complexity basically refers to the amount of time and tests normally required to treat a patient. In a visit-based payment system, visit time is an important determinant of facility fixed cost because it directly affects both the number of visits that can be provided and the amount of overhead costs that are allocated to each visit. In forming the medical APGs, visit time was considered an important factor in the determination of resource use and the associated facility cost. Thus, separate medical APGs were formed to recognize differences in visit time. For example, a visit for a skin malignancy normally takes considerably less time than a visit for a hematologic malignancy.

The final issue that was considered in the formation of the medical APGs was the amount and type of ancillary services that are typically provided to a patient. Because the cost of some ancillary services would be included in the base visit payment, patients with different profiles of ancillary service use needed to be in different APGs.

## DEVELOPMENT OF ANCILLARY SERVICE APGs

Ancillary services refer to ancillary tests (i.e., laboratory, radiology, and pathology) and ancillary procedures (e.g., immunization, anesthesia, insertion of an IUD, etc.). Ancillary APGs were formed for each type of ancillary service.

## Laboratory

The laboratory department in which the laboratory test is typically performed was used as the primary variable in the formation of the laboratory APGs. Thus, tests performed by the different laboratory departments (e.g., hematology, microbiology, toxicology, etc.) were assigned to different APGs. The testing method (e.g., radioimmunoassay) was used to a limited extent when the method represented a substantially different type of test with relatively clear indication for usage. However, in general, different methods of performing the same test were placed in the same APG. A laboratory technician will typically employ different methods depending on the precision of result that is needed. However, different methods are also employed depending on the training of the laboratory professional. For example, although there is a clear difference between a fluorimetric and a chromatographic method in the determination of the calcium level, there frequently are not precise indications when to do one versus the other. As a consequence, the different methods for performing the same test were usually assigned to the same APG. The same type of laboratory test (e.g., chemistry) was sometimes differentiated by the source of specimen (e.g., blood versus urine) in order to account for the labor cost of collecting and transporting the specimen. Finally, the same type of laboratory test was usually differentiated based on the complexity of the test. Tests that required more time, technicians with greater skill levels, or expensive equipment were assigned to different APGs. For example, multichannel chemistry tests were assigned to a separate APG from other chemistry tests because of the cost of the equipment used to perform a multichannel chemistry test. Laboratory tests that require no equipment and are typically performed during a visit (e.g., blood or urine dipstick tests) were assigned to a single APG as a result of their very low level of complexity. During the development of the laboratory APGs, physicians who either headed or worked in hospital laboratory departments and technicians who perform the tests were consulted. In addition, the laboratory relative value units (RVUs) developed by the College of American Pathologists were utilized.

## Radiology

The type of equipment (magnetic resonance imaging [MRI], computed tomography [CT], plain film, etc.) was the primary classification variable for the radiology APGs because the cost of the radiology equipment varies considerably across the different types of radiological procedures. Nuclear medicine was separated into diagnostic and therapeutic groups. Five of the radiological APGs were considered significant procedures. These radiological APGs were interventional and met the definition of a significant procedure.

## Pathology

Pathology was divided into two APGs based on the complexity of the pathology test. Pathology tests requiring more time or greater skill levels were assigned to the complex pathology APG. In addition, Pap smears were assigned to a separate APG.

## Anesthesia APG

All of anesthesiology was assigned to a single APG. The APG payment system includes the cost of anesthesia in the payment for a significant procedure. The CPT-4 codes do not differentiate between general and local anesthesia, and it was therefore not possible to create separate general and local anesthesia APGs. However, the procedures in each significant procedure APG typically have the same type of anesthesia administered. Thus, the absence of a differentiation on the type of anesthesia did not present a problem.

## Ancillary Tests and Procedures

Other ancillary tests include electrocardiograms, other minor cardiac and vascular tests, and pulmonary function tests. Ancillary procedures are procedures that do not dominate the time and resources expended during a visit but do increase the time and resources expended during a visit. Thus, ancillary procedures can be performed as part of a medical visit and do increase the cost of the medical visit. Ancillary procedures include immunizations, introduction of needles and catheters, biofeedback, infusion therapy, tube changes, minor reproductive procedures, and minor ophthalmological procedures. Immunizations were divided into three APGs based primarily on the cost of the vaccine (e.g., rabies vaccination is considered a complex immunization).

## Chemotherapy

There are two significant procedure APGs for chemotherapy that are based on the route of administration of the chemotherapy (i.e., intravenous push versus continuous infusion). These two significant procedure APGs reflect the difference in supplies and the labor cost of monitoring the administration of the chemotherapy drug. There is a second major cost component associated with chemotherapy and that is the cost of the chemotherapy drug. Chemotherapy drug costs can vary considerably, and therefore five additional chemotherapy APGs were formed to reflect the costs of chemotherapy drugs. Thus, the payment for a chemotherapy visit is composed of two APGs, one for the route of administration and one for the chemotherapy drug.

## SUMMARY OF DEVELOPMENT

The process of formulating the APGs was highly iterative, involving statistical results from historical data combined with clinical judgment. A preliminary classification was developed based solely on clinical judgment. The preliminary classification was then evaluated using several databases, including both Medicare and non-Medicare patients and contact time between provider and patient as well as charge data. The databases used in the development of Version 1.0 of the APGs were as follows:

- 1987 Part B Medicare annual data consisting of summary charges by CPT-4 code
- 1987 Medicare outpatient sample consisting of a 5-percent outpatient sample containing 232,827 procedure claims
- 1988 Medicare outpatient data for all Medicare hospital outpatients with a date of service from the last two weeks of October 1988, totalling 1.6 million outpatient claims
- 1988 New York State data containing approximately 400,000 claims from New York hospitals and community health centers, including contact time between provider and patient
- 1985 National Ambulatory Care Survey data derived from 72,000 visits drawn from 2,789 office-based physicians that included contact time between provider and patient
- U.S. Army Ambulatory Care data derived from 516,006 visits to army hospitals and clinics that included contact time between provider and patient
- relative value scales, including relative values for physicians[4] and the Resource Based Relative Value Scale (RBRVS)[5]

The database used in the development of Version 2.0 of the APGs was the HCFA Common Working File (CWF). The CWF is a comprehensive file of all services rendered to Medicare beneficiaries. An extract from the CWF of all visits to hospital outpatient departments during the first three months of 1992 was obtained. The 1992 data from the CWF contained 14,883,101 claims. All claims for the same patient, for the same provider, on the same day were collapsed together into a single claim. The collapsing of claims reduced the CWF database from 14,883,101 claims to 14,513,354 claims. The 14,513,354 claims were then evaluated for ambiguities in the identification of claims as a single visit and edited for the presence of errors. After eliminating claims with errors and claims with unreasonable charges or cost values, there were 11,412,738 claims in the CWF database.

The preliminary APG patient classes formed, based on clinical judgment, were evaluated using reports that displayed aggregate frequency and charge statistics as well as available RVU scales. For each CPT-4 code within an APG, the report for significant procedure and ancillary service APGs displayed the count, mean charge, and standard deviation of charges from each database as well as the available RVU scales. Using this report, the CPT-4 codes that comprise each APG were evaluated across all databases and RVU scales simultaneously. The evaluation looked for consistency of average charges across the CPT-4 codes within an APG across all the databases as well as for consistency across the available RVU scales. For each ICD-9-CM diagnosis code, the report for the medical APGs displayed the summary statistics for charges and visit time. The evaluation of the medical APGs looked for consistency of average charges and visit time across the ICD-9-CM codes within an APG across all the databases. As the APGs were being formed, the definitions were circulated to clinical consultants for comments on clinical appropriateness. Nearly 100 professionals throughout the country commented and consulted on the construction of the APGs. This process of defining APGs and reviewing them both clinically and with the data was repeated numerous times. The overall objective of the process was to have clinically similar groups of patients with similar resource use but to achieve these objectives with as few APGs as possible.

During the formation of DRGs, charge data were, in general, found to reflect the relative needs of patients. The number of bed days and ancillary services consumed by inpatients depended on their needs. However, hospital ambulatory charges are also highly influenced by physician charges. A great deal of effort has been expended in the development of RVUs, such as the

RBRVS developed for physician payment. RVU systems have been widely used for many years. Ambulatory charges for a procedure do not necessarily reflect the actual needs or complexity of an individual patient but are often based on the established RVU for the procedure. As a consequence, statistical results from charge data often simply reflect the established RVU scales. Although charge data were used extensively in the APG development, it was necessary for the clinical team to make judgments on whether observed hospital charge differences across different procedures reflected real differences in the resources required to perform the procedure or any bias in the established RVU scales.

For example, there are different CPT-4 codes for excisions of benign and malignant skin lesions. RVU and charge data implied that excisions of malignant skin lesions of the same site and size used significantly more resources than benign skin lesions. However, the histology of the lesion is often not known at the time of the procedure but is established when a pathology report is returned. Further, the excision of a malignant and benign skin lesion of the same site and size is fundamentally the same procedure, except that a wider margin is excised for lesions that are suspected to be malignant. Thus, the significant procedure APGs do not differentiate between malignant and benign skin excisions. In addition, procedure APGs avoid assigning procedures to different APGs based on subtle or easily gameable distinctions in the CPT-4 codes. For example, deep and superficial muscle biopsies are in the same APG because the distinction between deep and superficial lacks a precise definition in the CPT-4 system.

The development of the APGs required a balance between the number of APGs, clinical consistency, and homogeneity in charges and visit time. Clinical consistency was required in order for any procedures or diagnoses to be grouped into an APG. However, in general, APGs were not formed solely on clinical grounds. Verification of consistent differences in charges or visit time was required in order to form an APG. In general, infrequent APGs were not formed unless there was strong clinical justification and a large charge difference. For example, pacemaker replacements are infrequent on an outpatient basis, but pacemaker replacements do represent a clinically distinct group of patients with a very high cost. Thus, a pacemaker replacement APG was formed. The end result of the process of forming the APGs is a clinically consistent group of patient classes that are homogeneous in terms of resource use.

The development of Version 2.0 of the APGs involved a complete reevaluation of the Version 1.0 APG definitions. The decision to make any APG

Version 2.0 modifications was based on a combination of clinical judgment and the results from the review of the CWF data. Decisions on specific Version 2.0 modifications were made in the following manner:

- Project medical staff, in conjunction with HCFA staff, made an initial assessment of the clinical meaningfulness of any potential APG modification. Potential APG modifications that are clinically unreasonable often occur when reviewing statistical data on the average charges or cost of individual CPT-4 procedure or ICD-9-CM diagnosis codes. An individual code with a relatively low frequency of occurrence can sometimes appear to be in the wrong APG based on historical data. Statistical results that had no clinical rationale were not used as the basis of APG modifications. In general, potential APG modifications that were clinically unreasonable were not given further consideration. However, if the procedure or diagnosis in question occurred with a high frequency, additional confirmation was obtained from experts in the specialty area.

- If, in the judgment of the project medical staff and HCFA staff, there was any possible clinical merit to a potential APG modification, then the modification was reviewed with either the internal clinical consultants or outside experts in the specialty area of the modification. A wide cross section of outside experts were consulted during the development of Version 2.0 of the APGs. The purpose of the review was to provide additional clinical confirmation for APG modifications. While this was not a formal consensus panel process, every attempt was made to have all APG modifications clinically confirmed by outside experts.

- Any supporting data for the APG modifications was also reviewed. The supporting data that was evaluated included the historical cost or charges, the relative values if available, the amount and type of packaged ancillaries, the overall frequency of occurrences, and the frequency of treatment in the emergency room. The coding implications of any APG modification were also taken into consideration.

- All APG modifications were developed in close collaboration with HCFA staff. Frequent meetings and briefings were held with members of the research, operations, coding, and policy staffs at HCFA. Operational and policy implications of any APG modifications were discussed and evaluated with HCFA staff. The final decision on all APG modifications represents a consensus between the project staff and HCFA staff.

Version 2.0 of the APGs has 282 APGs plus 8 error APGs, whereas Version 1.0 of the APGs had 298 APGs plus one error APG. Table 29–3 contains the number of APGs by the different APG types. While the total number of APGs is relatively similar, the vast majority of APGs had some significant modifications. Appendix 29–A contains a complete list of the Version 2.0 APGs.

Figure 29–3 provides an overview of the APG Version 2.0 assignment logic. Patients with any significant procedures or therapies are assigned to one or more significant procedure APGs. If there are no significant procedures present and there is a medical visit indicator, the patient is assigned to a medical APG. If there is neither a significant procedure nor a medical visit indicator present, but there are ancillary tests or procedures present, then the patient is only assigned one or more ancillary APGs. If there is no significant procedure, medical visit indicator, or ancillary services present, the claim is considered an error.

The APGs describe the complete range of services provided in the outpatient setting. The APGs can form the basic building blocks for the development of a

**Table 29–3** Number of APGs by APG type

| APG type | Version 1.0 | Version 2.0 |
|---|---|---|
| Significant procedure | 145 | 126 |
| Radiological significant procedure | 0 | 5 |
| Mental health and substance abuse significant procedure | 0 | 8 |
| Medical | 80 | 83 |
| Laboratory | 23 | 20 |
| Ancillary radiology | 20 | 11 |
| Pathology | 2 | 3 |
| Anesthesia | 1 | 1 |
| Ancillary tests and procedures | 15 | 18 |
| Chemotherapy | 3 | 5 |
| Incidental | 8 | 2 |
| Admitted or died | 1 | 0 |
| Error | 1 | 8 |
| Total | 299 | 290 |

Courtesy of 3M Health Information Systems, Wallingford, Connecticut.

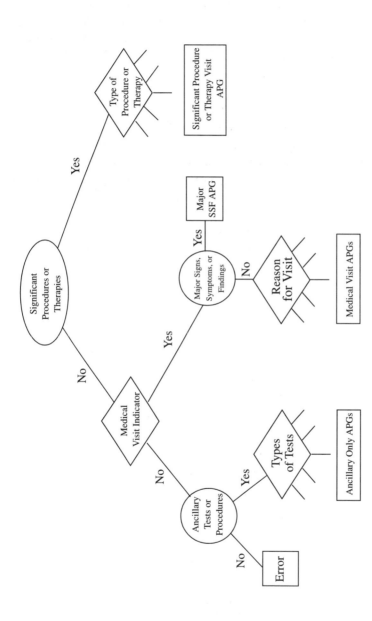

**Figure 29–3** Overview of APG Assignment Logic. Courtesy of 3M Health Information Systems, Wallingford, Connecticut.

visit-based outpatient prospective system and can provide a flexible structure for configuring a payment system to meet specific policy objectives.

## THE APG PAYMENT SYSTEM

In the APG payment system, a patient is described by a list of APGs that correspond to each service provided to the patient. The assignment of multiple APGs to a patient is in contrast with the DRG system, which always assigns an inpatient to a single DRG. If a patient has multiple procedures, then the DRGs use a procedure hierarchy to select the most appropriate DRG. The DRG payment includes the cost of all ancillary services provided to the patient. In the outpatient setting, the diversity of sites of service (i.e., same-day surgery units, emergency rooms, and outpatient clinics), the wide variation in the reasons patients require outpatient care (e.g., well care to critical trauma care), and the high percentage of cost associated with ancillary services (i.e., the cost of ancillary services can often exceed the cost of the base visit) necessitate a patient classification scheme that can closely reflect the services rendered to the patient. The APGs address the diversity within the outpatient setting by assigning patients to multiple APGs when needed. For example, if a patient had two procedures performed plus a chest x-ray and a blood test, then there would be four APGs assigned to the patient (i.e., one APG for each procedure plus the APGs for the chest x-ray and the blood test). In a PPS, each APG would have a standard payment rate, and the payment for a patient could be computed by summing the payment rates across all the APGs assigned to the patient. However, in order to provide incentives for efficiency and to minimize opportunities for upcoding of APGs, not all the APGs assigned to a patient are used in the computation of the payment. The APG system uses two techniques for grouping different services provided into a single payment unit: ancillary packaging and multiple significant procedure and ancillary discounting.

### Ancillary Packaging

A patient with a significant procedure or a medical visit may have ancillary services performed as part of the visit. Ancillary packaging refers to the inclusion of certain ancillary services into the APG payment rate for a significant procedure or medical visit. For example, a chest x-ray is packaged into the payment for a pneumonia visit. The packaging of ancillaries does not imply that there would be no payment associated with the packaged ancillary. The cost of the packaged ancillaries would be included in the payment amount for the significant procedure or medical APG. For example, if a packaged ancillary cost $20 and is performed for 50 percent of the patients in a medical APG, then $10 (i.e., 50 percent of $20) would be included in the payment rate for the medical APG.

Under Medicare's DRG-based PPS for hospital inpatient care, all ancillary services provided to a patient are packaged into the payment for the DRG to which the patient is assigned. Because of the nature of outpatient care, it is not clear that all services provided or ordered during a visit can be packaged into one payment rate. Medicare's current payment system for ambulatory care involves separate payments for ancillary services provided in conjunction with a visit. Ancillary packaging will allow the Medicare program to make a single payment for a well-defined package of ambulatory services, thereby creating a consistent definition of services across providers. Packaging will give providers the incentive to improve their efficiency by avoiding unnecessary ancillaries and by substituting less expensive but equally effective ancillary services for more costly options.

There are also some potential problems in the packaging of ancillaries. Packaging places providers at financial risk. If expensive ancillaries that are not usually performed for a particular type of visit are included in the packaged payment, then the financial risk may be excessive. For example, if a $500 test that occurs on average only once per hundred visits was packaged, then the packaged payment for each visit would include only $5 for this test. Therefore, only relatively inexpensive, frequently performed ancillaries are packaged.

There are basically two alternative approaches to packaging: partial packaging and all-inclusive packaging. Under partial packaging, ancillary services that are inexpensive or frequently provided are packaged into the payment for the significant procedure or medical visit. However, other ancillary services, particularly those that are expensive or infrequently performed (such as MRIs), are paid as separate ancillary APGs. Partial packaging limits the providers' risk. Under all-inclusive packaging, all services (including expensive ancillaries) that are provided during a visit are packaged into the visit payment. The partial packaging option is the most appropriate option because it does not impose a high level of risk for providers.

Because partial packaging was utilized in the APG payment system, the subset of ancillary services that would be packaged into a procedure or medical visit needed to be determined. There are two approaches to selecting the ancillaries to be packaged: clinical and uniform.

A clinical packaging approach selects the ancillaries to be packaged on an APG-specific basis. The ancillaries to be packaged are selected primarily on clinical grounds. Thus, only ancillaries that are clinically expected to be a routine part of the specific procedure or medical visit are packaged. The clinical approach has the benefit that the resulting package for a visit is clinically meaningful.

The alternative to clinical packaging is to develop a uniform list of ancillaries that are always packaged into every significant procedure or medical visit. There are several advantages associated with a uniform packaging of ancillaries. A uniform packaging is administratively simple. Once the uniform list of ancillaries is developed, both the Medicare fiscal intermediaries and providers will know that every ancillary on the list is always packaged. Thus, the tracking of the ancillaries that are packaged is straightforward. Further, a uniform list of packaged ancillaries is simple for hospitals to explain to their medical staff, and thus the incentive to efficiently utilize the packaged ancillaries can be effectively communicated.

A uniform list of ancillaries is also less prone to manipulation by providers. With a clinical packaging of ancillaries, procedure or medical visits have different levels of ancillaries packaged across the different APGs. Thus, there is an incentive to code the patient into the significant procedure or medical APG with the fewest packaged ancillaries. This presents a particular problem for medical visits in which multiple diagnoses are present. For medical visits with multiple diagnoses, the ancillary tests may be performed for the secondary diagnoses. Under a clinical packaging, low-cost nonroutine tests are not packaged into the visit payment. This provides a financial incentive for providers to perform such nonroutine tests. A uniform packaging includes a wider array of ancillaries in the packaging for each APG, and thus there is less opportunity for additional payments from nonroutine ancillaries.

A uniform packaging of ancillaries was selected for use in the APG payment model. An attempt to develop a clinical packaging of ancillaries proved difficult. The administrative simplicity, the relative freedom from manipulation, and the wider scope of uniform packaging of ancillaries led to its adoption. In general, the ancillaries in the uniform packaging included ancillaries that are performed for a wide range of different types of visits and were relatively low cost compared with the average cost of the procedure and medical APGs. Only relatively low cost ancillaries were included in the uniform packaging, because if high-cost ancillaries were packaged into the visit payment, the patients who required such ancillaries would cause a substantial financial loss for the hospital. The list of ancillaries included in the uniform packaging is a policy decision. The cost of medical surgical supplies and drugs and all other facility-related costs are included in the payment for a significant procedure or medical visit. The only exception is the cost of chemotherapy medication, because it is frequently very costly.

## Discounting

When multiple significant procedures are performed or when the same ancillary service is performed multiple times, a discounting of the APG payment rates can be applied. Discounting refers to a reduction in the standard payment rate for an APG. Discounting recognizes that the marginal cost of providing a second procedure to a patient during a single visit is less than the cost of providing the procedure by itself. For example, discounting could compensate for the reduced cost per procedure of doing multiple significant procedures at the same time. When multiple significant procedures are performed, in general the patient preparation, use of the operating room, and recovery time are shared between the procedures. Thus, the cost of doing multiple procedures at the same time is less than the cost of doing the procedures at different times.

Discounting can also be used to provide a financial incentive not to repeat the same ancillary service multiple times. Because the performance of multiple ancillaries in the same APG may be clinically necessary and appropriate, there is no consolidation of ancillaries within the same APG. Thus, each non-packaged ancillary in the same APG will result in an additional payment. However, in order to provide some financial incentive not to repeat ancillary tests, multiple ancillaries in the same APG could be discounted. The level of any discounting is a policy decision and would be determined during system implementation.

The components of an APG payment system are shown in Figure 29–4. In this example, although there are four APGs assigned to the claim, only three of the APGs are used to compute the final payment amount. The bunion procedure (APG 32) and the hand and foot tenotomy (APG 34) are significant

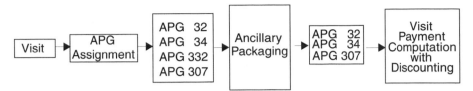

**Figure 29–4** APG Payment System. Courtesy of 3M Health Information Systems, Wallingford, Connecticut.

---

procedures and would have separate APG payments. The payment amount for the second significant procedure would be discounted. The simple surgical pathology (APG 332) is packaged, but the CAT scan (APG 307) is not. A visit-based APG PPS with uniform ancillary packaging and multiple APG discounting would have many advantages over the current outpatient payment method, such as the following:

- Many similar units of service are aggregated, greatly reducing the number of units of service.
- The need to establish separate payment rates for minor differences in the unit of service is eliminated.
- The opportunity for unbundling the units of service is greatly reduced.
- There is a financial incentive to use packaged ancillary services efficiently.
- Multiple procedures during a visit are reasonably compensated but not excessively rewarded.
- Payment of medical visits is based on the type of patient treated and not on the level of effort reported by the physician.

The structure of the APG payment model provides considerable flexibility. By modifying the level of ancillary packaging and discounting, the incentives in the system can be altered in order to achieve specific policy objectives.

## APG PAYMENT SIMULATION

In order to evaluate the APG payment model, a payment simulation using the historical Medicare CWF data was performed.[6] The objective of the APG payment simulation was to evaluate the alternative formulations of the APG payment model. The design of an APG-based outpatient PPS has five essential components, described below.

## Basis of Payment Weights

The APG payment weights can be computed based on either the charges or cost reported by hospitals. Since the markup from cost to charges can vary considerably across hospital outpatient departments, there can be substantial differences in the payment weights computed from charges versus those computed from cost.

## Ancillary Packaging

A patient with a significant procedure or a medical visit may have ancillary services performed as part of the visit. Ancillary packaging refers to the inclusion of certain ancillary services into the APG payment rate for a significant procedure or medical visit. The extent of ancillary packaging is a policy decision and can vary from none to the full packaging of all low-cost, routine ancillary tests and procedures.

## Outlier Policy

Outliers are atypical cases that have costs much higher than the APG payment amount. Additional payments can be provided to outlier cases. The extent of outlier payments can vary from none to a significant percentage of cases.

## Discounting

When multiple significant procedures are performed or when the same ancillary service is performed multiple times, a discounting of the APG payment rates can be applied.

## Window of Time for Ancillary Packaging

Packaged ancillary services delivered on the day of a significant procedure or medical visit will always be included in the APG payment. The window of time for including packaged ancillaries in the APG payment can be expanded beyond the day of the visit.

The above components of an APG system can be configured to produce different formulations of an APG PPS. Thirteen different formulations of an APG PPS were selected for evaluation. These are summarized in Table 29–4.

Three alternative lists of packaged ancillaries were examined in the APG impact simulations. The three alternative packaging lists are summarized in Table 29–5. The cost of medical surgical supplies and drugs, except for chemotherapy, are always packaged and included in the APG relative weights. The cost of all incidental services (i.e., APG 421) are also always packaged and included in the APG relative weights. The limited packaging option only packages the anesthesia services. The simple packaging option adds simple ancillary tests to the lists of packaged ancillaries. The full packaging option adds some additional ancillary services, plus some minor medical services, to the list of packaged ancillaries.

**Table 29–4** Components of Alternative APG Systems

| APG System | Basis of relative weights | Ancillary packaging | Outliers | Ancillary discounting | Window of time |
|---|---|---|---|---|---|
| 1 | Cost | Limited | 1% | No | Same day |
| 2 | Charge | Limited | 1% | No | Same day |
| 3 | Cost | Full | 1% | No | Same day |
| 4 | Charge | Full | 1% | No | Same day |
| 5 | Cost | Simple | 1% | No | Same day |
| 6 | Cost | Limited | None | No | Same day |
| 7 | Cost | Full | None | No | Same day |
| 8 | Cost | Full | 3% | No | Same day |
| 9 | Cost | Limited | 3% | No | Same day |
| 10 | Cost | Limited | 1% | Yes | Same day |
| 11 | Cost | Full | 1% | Yes | Same day |
| 12 | Cost | Full | 1% | No | Three days |
| 13 | Cost | Full | 1% | No | Seven days |

Courtesy of 3M Health Information Systems, Wallingford, Connecticut.

**Table 29–5** Alternative APG Packaging Options

| Full | Simple | Limited | | APG |
|---|---|---|---|---|
| X | X | | 310 | Plain Film |
| X | X | X | 321 | Anesthesia |
| X | X | | 332 | Simple Pathology |
| X | X | | 343 | Simple Immunology Tests |
| X | X | | 345 | Simple Microbiological Tests |
| X | X | | 347 | Simple Endocrinology Tests |
| X | X | | 349 | Simple Chemistry Tests |
| X | X | | 350 | Basic Chemistry Tests |
| X | X | | 351 | Multichannel Chemistry Tests |
| X | X | | 356 | Simple Clotting Tests |
| X | X | | 358 | Simple Hematology Tests |
| X | X | | 359 | Urinalysis |
| X | X | | 360 | Blood and Urine Dipstick Tests |
| X | | | 371 | Simple Pulmonary Function Tests |
| X | X | | 373 | Cardiogram |
| X | X | | 383 | Intro of Needle and Catheter |
| X | | | 384 | Dressings and Other Minor Proc |
| X | | | 385 | Other Misc Ancillary Proc |
| X | | | 386 | Biofeedback and Other Training |
| X | | | 411 | Psychotropic Med Management |

Courtesy of 3M Health Information Systems, Wallingford, Connecticut.

Outlier payments essentially represent a stop-loss provision that protects providers from extreme losses on any individual patient. Cost outlier values were established for each significant procedure and medical APG. If the cost of the patient exceeds the cost outlier value, then the total payment for the patient was computed as the standard APG payment amount plus 100 percent of the difference between the actual cost and the cost outlier value. The cost outlier value was established based on a specified number of standard deviations above the mean for each APG. The precise number of standard deviations above the mean was established such that a specified percentage of total payments would be associated with outlier payments. Thus, the number of standard deviations varied depending on the exact percentage of total payments associated with outlier payments. Since there are some administrative costs associated with outlier payments, the cost outlier value was constrained to be, at a minimum, $1,700 for significant procedure APGs and $350 for medical APGs. Thus, for patients whose cost exceeds the cost outlier value, the total payment would be:

Total payment = APG payment + (actual cost – outlier value)

Outlier payments are only associated with significant procedure and medical claims; there are no outlier payments associated with ancillary-only claims. Three outlier alternatives were evaluated: no outliers, 1 percent of total payments associated with outlier payments and 3 percent of total payments associated with outlier payments. The inpatient DRG system currently has 5.1 percent of total payments associated with outlier payments. A 5.1 percent of total payments associated with outlier payments was not evaluated, since it would produce a large volume of claims with outlier payments.

If there are multiple significant procedures, the significant procedure with the highest relative weight is paid at 100 percent and each additional significant procedure is discounted by 50 percent. The 50-percent multiple significant procedure discounting was included in all APG systems that were evaluated. In addition, a 20-percent discounting of multiple ancillaries in the same APG was evaluated.

Packaged ancillary services delivered on the day of a significant procedure or medical visit are always included in the APG payment. The impact of expanding the window of time for including packaged ancillaries in the APG payment was evaluated. A three-day and seven-day window of time around the visit was evaluated.

## EVALUATION OF THE 13 ALTERNATIVE FORMULATIONS OF AN APG PPS

For each of the 13 formulations of an APG PPS, the APG payment amount for each patient was computed and compared to historical patient cost (referred to as an APG simulation). The APG payment levels for each of the APG simulations were set such that the aggregate APG payment, including any outlier payments, was equal to the aggregate cost across all patients. Thus, each APG simulation was performed on a budget-neutral basis. The

APG simulation adjusted each hospital's APG payments for variations in wage rates using the 1993 Medicare inpatient PPS wage rate adjustment factors. In applying the wage rate adjustment factors, it was assumed that each hospital had 71.4 percent of its cost associated with labor. This is the same percentage used in the inpatient PPS.

Medicare payment for hospital outpatient services is based on a complex and confusing collection of payment methods. The current Medicare system pays hospital outpatient services under a number of different methods, including fee schedules, blended payment methods, and cost-based payments. It was beyond the scope of this project to compute actual historical Medicare outpatient payments and compare actual payments to APG-based payments. Thus, the results of the 13 APG simulations do not reflect the actual payment impact on hospitals, because the actual payments to hospitals based on the current complex and confusing system were not calculated. In addition, APG payment rates were not calculated based on the current level of Medicare program expenditures, which are less than hospital costs, but instead were calculated based on what total program expenditures would be under a pure cost-based system. Thus, for purpose of comparing the 13 different APG simulations, hospital payments under each formulation of an APG PPS were computed with the constraint that, in the aggregate, Medicare total expenditures under any of the APG simulations were equal to total hospital costs. The most basic of the 13 formulations of an APG PPS was selected as the reference APG simulation, and the relative APG payment impact was computed by comparing cost-based APG payments under each of the other APG simulations to the reference APG simulation. The relative APG payment impact was computed for different categories of hospitals and was used to evaluate each component of the APG system (e.g., the extent of outlier payments) in terms of its relative payment impact across the different categories of hospitals.

## CONVERTING CHARGES TO COSTS

Based on the provider number, each claim was linked to a file provided by HCFA that contained departmental cost-to-charge ratios for each hospital. The charges on a claim were converted to cost by using the departmental cost-to-charge ratios. If there were no cost-to-charge ratios available for a hospital, the claims from that hospital were eliminated from the analysis. If a cost-to-charge ratio for the hospital was missing for only a subset of departments in a hospital, then the overall hospital cost-to-charge ratio was used for those departments. In general, the cost-to-charge ratios for ancillary departments tended to be lower than for other hospital departments. For example, the average cost-to-charge ratios for diagnostic radiology, laboratory, and electrocardiology were 0.66, 0.54, and 0.39, respectively. In comparison, the average cost-to-charge ratios for clinics, emergency room, and operating room were 1.30, 1.06, and 0.77, respectively.

## COMPUTING APG RELATIVE WEIGHTS

Relative weights for each APG were computed. Relative weights can be computed based on either historical charges or cost. APG simulations were performed using relative weights computed from both charges and cost in order to determine if the basis of the relative weights resulted in a substantial impact in relative APG payment. The APG relative weights for significant procedure or medical APGs include the costs associated with any ancillaries that are packaged into these APGs.

Using charges and the three different packaging options, three sets of charge-based APG relative weights were computed. In addition, using costs and the three different packaging options, three sets of cost-based APG relative weights were computed. The relative weights were computed based on the average cost or charge in each APG. The relative weights for significant procedure APGs were computed using only claims that had a single significant procedure because it was not possible to allocate accurately the costs (e.g., pharmaceuticals, medical-surgical supplies, etc.) across multiple significant procedure APGs.

In order to obtain an accurate estimate of the average cost or charge, it was necessary to eliminate the extreme charge or cost values from the computation of the average. In the computation of the inpatient DRG relative weights, claims with charges that were more than three standard deviations above the mean of the log of charges were eliminated. The same method of eliminating extreme charge or cost values was used in computing the six sets of APG relative weights. The percentage of claims trimmed from the computation of the relative weights was only a fraction of 1 percent.

The relative weights computed from charges and costs were essentially the same. The Pearson correlation coefficient between charge-based and cost-based relative weights, with limited, simple, and full packaging, was

0.990, 0.991, and 0.992, respectively. However, due to the lower cost-to-charge ratio for ancillary departments, the relative weights for ancillary APGs tend to be proportionately lower for cost-based weights than for charge-based weights.

Table 29–6 contains the overall percentages of the relative weights derived from packaged ancillaries for the six sets of relative weights. In general, the percentage of the relative weight from packaged ancillaries tends to be lower for cost-based relative weights than for charge-based relative weights. This reflects the relatively low cost-to-charge ratios associated with the ancillary departments. The medical APGs have a much higher percentage of the APG relative weight from packaged ancillaries than the significant procedure APGs. For the cost-based relative weights with full packaging, the relative weight with the highest percentage of the APG relative weight from packaged ancillaries is the medical APG for chest pain with cardiac enzymes to rule out myocardial infarction (APG 573), at 46.2 percent. The high percentage of packaged ancillaries associated with this APG is the result of the packaging of the extensive laboratory tests that are performed for this type of patient. In general, the percentage of the relative weight from packaged ancillaries tends to be 3 to 4 times higher for medical APGs than for significant procedure APGs. The high percentage of the relative weights from packaged ancillaries

**Table 29–6** Percentage of APG Relative Weights Derived from Packaged Ancillaries

| | | Charge-based relative weights | | | Cost-based relative weights | | |
|---|---|---|---|---|---|---|---|
| | Count | Full pack-age | Simple pack-age | Limited pack-age | Full pack-age | Simple pack-age | Limited pack-age |
| Significant procedure claims | 1,567,263 | 11.90 | 11.64 | 3.62 | 9.24 | 9.00 | 2.51 |
| Medical claims | 2,186,728 | 45.38 | 45.20 | 0.94 | 31.34 | 31.18 | 0.52 |
| Significant procedure and medical claims combined | 3,753,991 | 20.00 | 19.76 | 3.20 | 15.44 | 15.22 | 2.07 |

Courtesy of 3M Health Information Systems, Wallingford, Connecticut.

for medical patients is primarily the result of the relatively low payment for a medical claim. The APG with the lowest percent of the APG relative weight from packaged ancillaries is the significant procedure APG for laser eye procedures (APG 213), at 0.22 percent.

## COMPARISON OF ALTERNATIVE APG SYSTEMS

The 13 APG simulations were compared by computing an overall $R^2$, which provides a measure of the amount of variance in historical cost explained by the APG payment system. Positive values that approach 1.0 for $R^2$ would indicate that the relative value of the total APG payment closely approximates the relative value of the historical cost. Table 29–7 contains the $R^2$ for all 13 APG simulations. Based on the results in this table, the impact of each of the alternative formulations of an APG PPS was evaluated.

### Cost-based and Charge-based Relative Weights

From Table 29–7, APG Systems 1 and 2 compare the effects of using relative weights based on charges and costs with the limited packaging option, while APG Systems 3 and 4 make the same comparison with the full packaging option. All four APG systems have 1 percent of payments associated with outliers, no ancillary, and a same-day window. The $R^2$ values for APG System 1 and APG System 2 are virtually identical, and the $R^2$ values for APG System 3 and APG System 4 are also virtually identical. Thus, the cost of individual patients can be predicted equally well (i.e., obtain the same $R^2$) using relative weights computed from charges or relative weights computed from costs.

### Alternative Ancillary Packaging Lists

APG Systems 1, 3 and 5 use limited, full, and simple packaging, respectively, with cost-based relative weights, 1 percent of payments associated with outliers, no ancillary discounting, and a same-day window of service. The simple packaging and the full packaging have virtually identical $R^2$ results. The $R^2$ for significant procedure claims is 2.2 percent lower with full packaging (0.668 versus 0.683). For medical claims, the $R^2$ is 21.1 percent lower with full packaging than it is with limited packaging (0.588 versus 0.745).

**Table 29–7** $R^2$ for Alternative APG Systems

| APG systems | Sig proc | Medical | Medical plus sig proc | Anc only | Total | Basis wghts | Anc pkg | Out | Anc disc | Window of time |
|---|---|---|---|---|---|---|---|---|---|---|
| 1 | 0.683 | 0.745 | 0.686 | 0.746 | 0.773 | Cost | Lim | 1% | No | Same day |
| 2 | 0.688 | 0.744 | 0.690 | 0.739 | 0.774 | Chg | Lim | 1% | No | Same day |
| 3 | 0.668 | 0.588 | 0.660 | 0.746 | 0.757 | Cost | Full | 1% | No | Same day |
| 4 | 0.669 | 0.589 | 0.661 | 0.739 | 0.756 | Chg | Full | 1% | No | Same day |
| 5 | 0.668 | 0.590 | 0.660 | 0.746 | 0.757 | Cost | Sim | 1% | No | Same day |
| 6 | 0.620 | 0.439 | 0.605 | 0.746 | 0.721 | Cost | Lim | None | No | Same day |
| 7 | 0.601 | 0.264 | 0.575 | 0.746 | 0.701 | Cost | Full | None | No | Same day |
| 8 | 0.734 | 0.726 | 0.733 | 0.746 | 0.804 | Cost | Full | 3% | No | Same day |
| 9 | 0.760 | 0.804 | 0.762 | 0.746 | 0.823 | Cost | Lim | 3% | No | Same day |
| 10 | 0.682 | 0.744 | 0.684 | 0.746 | 0.772 | Cost | Lim | 1% | Yes | Same day |
| 11 | 0.668 | 0.587 | 0.660 | 0.746 | 0.756 | Cost | Full | 1% | Yes | Same day |
| 12 | 0.665 | 0.592 | 0.657 | 0.747 | 0.755 | Cost | Full | 1% | No | 3 days |
| 13 | 0.664 | 0.596 | 0.656 | 0.747 | 0.754 | Cost | Full | 1% | No | 7 days |

Courtesy of 3M Health Information Systems, Wallingford, Connecticut.

The lower $R^2$ for medical claims with the full packaging option reflects the combined effect of the variability in the use of ancillaries for medical visits coupled with ancillaries being a large percentage of the cost of a medical visit.

## Outliers

APG Systems 6, 1, and 9 use 0 percent, 1 percent, and 3 percent of payments associated with outliers, respectively, with the limited packaging option, cost-based relative weights, no ancillary discounting and a same-day window of time. For significant procedure APGs, the 3-percent outlier option has the highest $R^2$, while the 1-percent outlier option is 10.1 percent lower (0.760 versus 0.683) and the no outlier option is 18.4 percent lower (0.760 versus 0.620). For medical APGs, the 3-percent outlier option has the highest $R^2$, while the 1-percent outlier option is 7.3 percent lower (0.804 versus 0.745) and the no outlier option is 45.4 percent lower (0.804 versus 0.439). Thus, there is a small reduction in $R^2$ if outlier payments are reduced from 3 percent to 1 percent but a large reduction in $R^2$ for medical claims if outlier payments are eliminated entirely.

APG Systems 7, 3, and 8 use 0 percent, 1 percent, and 3 percent of payments associated with outliers, respectively, with the full packaging option, cost-based relative weights, no ancillary discounting, and a same-day window of service. For significant procedure APGs, the 3-percent outlier option has the highest $R^2$, while the 1-percent outlier option is 9.0 percent lower (0.734 versus 0.668) and the no outlier option 18.1 percent lower (0.734 versus 0.601). For medical APGs, the 3-percent outlier option has the highest $R^2$, while the 1-percent outlier option is 19.0 percent lower (0.726 versus 0.588) and the no outlier option is 63.6 percent lower (0.726 versus 0.264). Thus, with full packaging, there is a modest reduction in $R^2$ by reducing the outlier payments from 3 percent to 1 percent and a large reduction in $R^2$ for medical claims if outlier payments are eliminated entirely.

While the 3-percent outlier option has the highest $R^2$, it also results in significantly more claims having outlier payments. APG Systems 1 and 3, which use the 1-percent outlier option, have 1.277 percent and 1.241 percent of claims with outlier payments, respectively. APG Systems 8 and 9, which use the 3-percent outlier option, have considerably more claims with outlier payments, 4.571 percent and 3.588 percent, respectively.

## Ancillary Discounting

APG System 10 adds ancillary discounting to APG System 1. APG Systems 1 and 10 have limited packaging, with cost-based relative weights, 1 percent of payments associated with outliers, and a same-day window of service. APG System 11 adds ancillary discounting to APG System 3. APG Systems 3 and 11 have full packaging, with cost-based relative weights, 1 percent of payments associated with outlier, and a same-day window of service. The $R^2$ for APG Systems 1 and 10 and the $R^2$ for APG Systems 3 and 11 are virtually identical. Thus, there is virtually no reduction in $R^2$ from ancillary discounting.

## Window of Time

In order to simulate windows of time of three days and seven days for APG Systems 12 and 13, respectively, it was necessary to collapse some of the ancillary-only claims into a significant procedure or medical claim. Thus, if there was an ancillary-only claim for a patient two days following a medical visit, the ancillary-only claim was deleted and the ancillary services provided were incorporated into the medical visit claim. In addition, the expanded window of time created some ambiguous situations, which necessitated the exclusion of some additional claims. For example, if the same ancillary-only claim occurred two days after a medical visit and two days prior to a significant procedure visit, then it would be open to question whether the ancillary-only claim should be associated with the medical visit or the significant procedure visit. In this example, all three claims would be excluded from the analysis because of the ambiguity. There was only a small percentage of significant procedure or medical claims eliminated due to ambiguities, and 3.02 percent and 6.65 percent of the ancillary-only claims were collapsed or eliminated due to ambiguities for the three-day and seven-day windows of time, respectively.

As a result of the expanded window of time, a larger proportion of the cost of a significant procedure or medical visit was associated with packaged ancillaries. For the full packaging option, the percentages of the APG cost associated with packaged ancillaries were 15.94, 15.83, and 16.32 for the one-day, three-day, and seven-day windows of time, respectively. Thus, there was only a very small increase in the percentage of APG cost from packaged ancillaries as the window of time was expanded.

APG Systems 3, 12, and 13 use same-day, three-day, and seven-day windows of time, respectively, with cost-based weights, full ancillary packaging, 1-percent outliers, 50-percent multiple significant procedure discounting, and no ancillary discounting. The $R^2$ for all three APG systems is virtually the same. Thus, there is no substantial impact on $R^2$ as a result of expanding the window of time of ancillary packaging.

## COMPARISON OF VERSION 2.0 APGs AND DRGs

Medicare inpatient data was used to compute the $R^2$ for the DRGs. In the payment model used for the DRG analysis, the payment for each patient was computed as the average standardized charge for the DRG to which the patient was assigned.

The APG simulation that most closely approximates the untrimmed DRGs is APG System 7, which uses cost-based weights with full packaging, no outliers, significant procedure discounting, no repeat ancillary discounting, and a same-day window of time. Table 29–8 compares the $R^2$ for APGs and DRGs.

The $R^2$ for untrimmed (i.e., without outliers for APGs) procedure and medical claims combined is higher for APGs than for DRGs (0.575 for APGs versus 0.394 for DRGs). For procedure claims, the APGs have a higher $R^2$ than the DRGs (0.601 for APGs versus 0.425 for DRGs). For medical claims, the DRGs have a slightly higher $R^2$ than the APGs for untrimmed claims (0.264 for APGs versus 0.267 for DRGs). The higher $R^2$ for the APGs means that the APGs predict historical outpatient costs better than the DRGs predict historical standardized inpatient charges.

**Table 29–8** $R^2$ for DRGs and APGs

|  | Untrimmed DRGs | APG System 7 |
|---|---|---|
| Procedure discharges/visits | 0.425 | 0.601 |
| Medical discharges/visits | 0.267 | 0.264 |
| Combined procedure/medical discharges visits | 0.394 | 0.575 |

Courtesy of 3M Health Information Systems, Wallingford, Connecticut.

## HOSPITAL APG IMPACT SIMULATION

Hospital characteristics were identified by linking the provider number on each claim to the FY1993 PPS Payment Impact File. Hospitals were categorized into 67 categories. The categories were not mutually exclusive, and the same hospital could appear in multiple categories. The hospital categories replicated the hospital categories used by HCFA to display the inpatient PPS impact results. All information necessary to create the hospital categories was available in the FY1993 PPS Payment Impact File except hospital ownership. Hospital ownership was obtained using a separate file provided by HCFA.

The hospital categorization was done in two different ways, one based on geographic location and the other on payment categories. In the geographic location section, the metropolitan statistical area (MSA), the region of the country, and the urban/rural status are based on the *actual* location of the hospital. Since these hospital location characteristics affect the inpatient PPS payment levels, the Executive Office of Management and Budget reclassifies the urban/rural designation as well as the MSA and geographic region. In the payment categories section the MSA, the region of the country, and the urban/rural status were based on the *reclassified* location of the hospital used in the inpatient PPS.

The FY1993 PPS Payment Impact File contained 5,491 hospitals. Only hospitals covered by the inpatient PPS were included in the PPS Payment Impact File. The analysis database included 5,118 (92.3 percent) of the PPS hospitals. In addition, the analysis database contained data from 356 hospitals that were not covered by the inpatient PPS (e.g., psychiatric hospitals). The non-PPS hospitals had very few claims per hospital in the analysis database. For PPS hospitals there was an average of 2,222 claims per hospital in the analysis database, but for non-PPS hospitals there was only an average of 60.2 claims per hospital. There were also 16 hospitals that were PPS hospitals that were not in the FY1993 PPS Payment Impact File. Since the data were from 1992, these are probably hospitals that closed or merged with other hospitals in 1993. In total, there were 5,490 hospitals in the analysis database.

Tables 29–9 and 29–10 contain for each hospital category the impact of each of the 13 APG systems. APG System 6 represents the most basic version of an APG system. APG System 6 uses cost-based relative weights, limited packaging, no outliers, no ancillary discounting, and a same-day window of time. The impact of an APG system was measured by taking the aggregate APG payment to hospitals in the hospital category under the APG system,

**Table 29–9** Impact by Hospital Category by Geographic Location across APG Systems

| Hospital categories | APG system | | | | | | | | | | | | |
|---|---|---|---|---|---|---|---|---|---|---|---|---|---|
| | 1 | 2 | 3 | 4 | 5 | 6 | 7 | 8 | 9 | 10 | 11 | 12 | 13 |
| Location | | | | | | | | | | | | | |
| Urban hospitals | 0.00 | -0.25 | -0.07 | -0.34 | -0.05 | 0.00 | -0.08 | 0.01 | 0.12 | -0.01 | -0.07 | -0.16 | -0.68 |
| Large urban areas | 0.13 | -0.68 | 0.19 | -0.62 | 0.23 | 0.00 | 0.04 | 0.55 | 0.56 | 0.11 | 0.18 | 0.11 | -0.42 |
| Other urban areas | -0.13 | 0.23 | -0.35 | -0.03 | -0.36 | 0.00 | -0.21 | -0.59 | -0.38 | -0.13 | -0.36 | -0.47 | -0.97 |
| Rural areas | -0.07 | 1.11 | 0.17 | 1.42 | 0.10 | 0.00 | 0.26 | -0.17 | -0.51 | -0.03 | 0.20 | -0.20 | -0.82 |
| Bed size (urban) | | | | | | | | | | | | | |
| 0–99 beds | 0.55 | 0.87 | 0.43 | 0.71 | 0.41 | 0.00 | -0.13 | 1.27 | 1.38 | 0.60 | 0.47 | 0.12 | -0.41 |
| 100–199 beds | 0.05 | 0.36 | -0.31 | -0.07 | -0.29 | 0.00 | -0.39 | 0.27 | 0.74 | 0.03 | -0.31 | -0.44 | -1.03 |
| 200–299 beds | 0.06 | 0.76 | -0.58 | -0.02 | -0.55 | 0.00 | -0.65 | -0.52 | 0.15 | 0.05 | -0.59 | -0.68 | -1.11 |
| 300–499 Beds | -0.17 | -0.36 | -0.34 | -0.57 | -0.33 | 0.00 | -0.18 | -0.63 | -0.47 | -0.18 | -0.35 | -0.34 | -0.79 |
| 500 or more beds | -0.06 | -3.02 | 1.42 | -1.23 | 1.43 | 0.00 | 1.51 | 1.25 | -0.18 | -0.07 | 1.40 | 1.28 | 0.56 |
| Bed size (rural) | | | | | | | | | | | | | |
| 0–49 beds | 0.50 | 0.87 | 2.77 | 3.65 | 2.59 | 0.00 | 2.38 | 2.85 | 0.14 | 0.51 | 2.81 | 2.31 | 1.75 |
| 50–99 beds | 0.03 | 1.29 | 0.34 | 1.72 | 0.25 | 0.00 | 0.34 | 0.21 | -0.27 | 0.05 | 0.38 | -0.17 | -0.91 |
| 100–149 beds | -0.25 | 1.43 | -0.66 | 0.95 | -0.72 | 0.00 | -0.38 | -1.12 | -0.78 | -0.20 | -0.64 | -1.00 | -1.65 |
| 150–199 beds | -0.30 | 0.88 | -0.50 | 0.65 | -0.53 | 0.00 | -0.19 | -1.30 | -1.09 | -0.25 | -0.48 | -0.65 | -1.18 |
| 200 or more beds | -0.33 | 0.86 | -0.97 | 0.10 | -0.96 | 0.00 | -0.64 | -1.48 | -0.73 | -0.28 | -0.95 | -1.24 | -1.71 |
| Urban by census div. | | | | | | | | | | | | | |
| New England | -0.59 | -2.36 | 0.25 | -1.44 | 0.29 | 0.00 | 0.83 | -0.24 | -0.87 | -0.59 | 0.25 | -0.30 | -1.50 |
| Middle Atlantic | -0.23 | -0.01 | 0.36 | 0.66 | 0.37 | 0.00 | 0.60 | 0.63 | 0.36 | -0.18 | 0.37 | -0.12 | -1.83 |
| South Atlantic | 0.18 | 0.21 | -0.76 | -0.90 | -0.75 | 0.00 | -0.98 | -0.47 | 0.38 | 0.15 | -0.77 | -0.72 | -0.83 |

*continues*

**Table 29–9** continued

# 324 PHYSICIAN PROFILING AND RISK ADJUSTMENT

**Table 29–9** continued

| Hospital categories | 1 | 2 | 3 | 4 | 5 | 6 | 7 | 8 | 9 | 10 | 11 | 12 | 13 |
|---|---|---|---|---|---|---|---|---|---|---|---|---|---|
| East North Central | -0.28 | 0.16 | -0.57 | -0.22 | -0.56 | 0.00 | -0.30 | -0.81 | -0.40 | -0.31 | -0.57 | -0.78 | -1.50 |
| East South Central | 0.24 | 0.38 | -0.57 | -0.55 | -0.59 | 0.00 | -0.83 | -0.67 | 0.08 | 0.22 | -0.60 | -0.63 | -0.81 |
| West North Central | 0.22 | -0.18 | 0.10 | -0.30 | 0.17 | 0.00 | -0.12 | -0.08 | -0.04 | 0.18 | 0.08 | 0.13 | 0.04 |
| West South Central | 0.68 | 0.36 | -0.41 | -0.88 | -0.48 | 0.00 | -1.16 | 0.57 | 1.64 | 0.58 | -0.43 | -0.12 | 0.12 |
| Mountain | 0.38 | -2.35 | 1.81 | -0.58 | 1.73 | 0.00 | 1.46 | 2.13 | 0.39 | 0.37 | 1.79 | 1.91 | 1.56 |
| Pacific | 0.10 | -0.43 | 0.51 | 0.03 | 0.60 | 0.00 | 0.46 | 0.49 | -0.06 | 0.15 | 0.50 | 0.71 | 0.39 |
| Puerto Rico | -0.93 | -4.28 | 2.07 | -0.14 | 2.16 | 0.00 | 3.03 | 0.34 | -2.51 | -0.87 | 2.14 | 2.46 | 1.33 |
| Rural by census div. | | | | | | | | | | | | | |
| New England | -0.51 | 1.57 | 0.02 | 2.11 | 0.02 | 0.00 | 0.56 | -0.44 | -0.91 | -0.37 | 0.08 | -0.41 | -1.15 |
| Middle Atlantic | -0.70 | 1.03 | 0.16 | 1.98 | 0.09 | 0.00 | 0.89 | -1.32 | -2.11 | -0.63 | 0.15 | -0.87 | -2.86 |
| South Atlantic | 0.15 | 1.06 | -1.00 | -0.23 | -0.97 | 0.00 | -1.18 | -0.91 | -0.03 | 0.14 | -0.97 | -1.19 | -1.51 |
| East North Central | -0.21 | 2.26 | -0.82 | 1.53 | -0.88 | 0.00 | -0.59 | -1.30 | -0.69 | -0.21 | -0.79 | -1.37 | -2.33 |
| East South Central | -0.27 | 0.80 | 0.00 | 1.23 | -0.08 | 0.00 | 0.31 | -0.76 | -1.10 | -0.25 | 0.02 | -0.36 | -0.76 |
| West North Central | 0.18 | 0.67 | 1.43 | 2.19 | 1.36 | 0.00 | 1.34 | 1.23 | -0.15 | 0.27 | 1.46 | 1.02 | 0.45 |
| West South Central | 0.26 | 0.17 | 0.97 | 1.12 | 0.76 | 0.00 | 0.72 | 1.30 | 0.49 | 0.24 | 0.99 | 0.76 | 0.52 |
| Mountain | 0.07 | 1.12 | 1.82 | 3.22 | 1.66 | 0.00 | 1.84 | 1.48 | -0.44 | 0.15 | 1.86 | 1.65 | 1.61 |
| Pacific | -0.16 | 0.76 | 1.10 | 2.25 | 1.00 | 0.00 | 1.31 | 0.63 | -0.85 | -0.07 | 1.14 | 1.13 | 0.90 |
| Puerto Rico | -0.96 | 1.41 | 2.35 | 5.64 | 2.52 | 0.00 | 3.39 | 0.51 | -2.86 | -0.73 | 2.44 | 0.16 | -5.43 |

APG system

Courtesy of 3M Health Information Systems, Wallingford, Connecticut.

**Table 29–10** Impact by Hospital Category and by Payment Category across APG Systems

| Hospital Category | APG Systems | | | | | | | | | | | | |
|---|---|---|---|---|---|---|---|---|---|---|---|---|---|
| | 1 | 2 | 3 | 4 | 5 | 6 | 7 | 8 | 9 | 10 | 11 | 12 | 13 |
| Payment location | | | | | | | | | | | | | |
| Urban hospitals | 0.00 | -0.18 | -0.10 | -0.31 | -0.09 | 0.00 | -0.11 | -0.03 | 0.10 | -0.01 | -0.11 | -0.21 | -0.74 |
| Large urban areas | 0.07 | -0.55 | 0.08 | -0.55 | 0.12 | 0.00 | -0.01 | 0.38 | 0.42 | 0.05 | 0.08 | -0.01 | -0.55 |
| Other urban areas | -0.09 | 0.29 | -0.33 | 0.00 | -0.35 | 0.00 | -0.23 | -0.55 | -0.32 | -0.09 | -0.34 | -0.47 | -0.98 |
| Rural areas | -0.06 | 1.00 | 0.36 | 1.53 | 0.28 | 0.00 | 0.45 | 0.00 | -0.52 | -0.01 | 0.39 | -0.01 | -0.57 |
| Teaching status | | | | | | | | | | | | | |
| Non-teaching | 0.05 | 1.28 | -0.55 | 0.56 | -0.55 | 0.00 | -0.61 | -0.48 | 0.04 | 0.05 | -0.54 | -0.72 | -1.14 |
| Resident-to-bed ratio < 25 | -0.12 | 0.06 | -0.18 | -0.04 | -0.18 | 0.00 | -0.05 | -0.30 | -0.14 | -0.11 | -0.17 | -0.24 | -0.80 |
| Resident-to-bed ratio ≥25 | -0.05 | -6.95 | 3.33 | -2.84 | 3.37 | 0.00 | 3.42 | 3.27 | 0.05 | -0.08 | 3.31 | 3.02 | 1.91 |
| Disprop share hospitals | | | | | | | | | | | | | |
| Non-DSHs | -0.05 | 0.97 | -0.36 | 0.58 | -0.36 | 0.00 | -0.32 | -0.34 | -0.01 | -0.03 | -0.35 | -0.55 | -1.08 |
| Urban DSHs | | | | | | | | | | | | | |
| 100 beds or more | 0.06 | -1.59 | 0.56 | -0.96 | 0.57 | 0.00 | 0.51 | 0.56 | 0.03 | 0.03 | 0.55 | 0.48 | -0.08 |
| Fewer than 100 beds | 0.25 | 0.29 | 0.08 | 0.17 | 0.08 | 0.00 | -0.16 | -0.15 | -0.53 | 0.24 | 0.12 | 0.07 | -0.05 |
| Rural DSHs | | | | | | | | | | | | | |
| Sole community (SCHs) | 0.08 | -0.08 | 0.02 | 0.01 | -0.12 | 0.00 | -0.04 | 0.29 | 0.09 | 0.02 | 0.05 | -0.13 | -0.29 |
| Rural referral centers (RRCs) | -0.23 | -0.96 | -0.33 | -1.00 | -0.25 | 0.00 | -0.08 | -0.65 | -0.56 | -0.19 | -0.32 | -0.51 | -0.96 |
| Other rural DSH hosp | | | | | | | | | | | | | |
| 100 beds or more | -0.37 | 0.27 | -0.68 | -0.05 | -0.77 | 0.00 | -0.30 | -1.17 | -0.75 | -0.30 | -0.64 | -1.06 | -1.45 |
| Fewer than 100 beds | -0.06 | 0.10 | 1.25 | 1.83 | 1.12 | 0.00 | 1.33 | 0.73 | -0.95 | -0.08 | 1.28 | 1.04 | 0.85 |

*continues*

**Table 29–10** Continued

| Hospital Category | APG systems | | | | | | | | | | | | |
|---|---|---|---|---|---|---|---|---|---|---|---|---|---|
| | 1 | 2 | 3 | 4 | 5 | 6 | 7 | 8 | 9 | 10 | 11 | 12 | 13 |
| Urban teaching hospitals and DSHs | | | | | | | | | | | | | |
| Both teaching and DSH | 0.09 | −3.26 | 1.62 | −1.38 | 1.62 | 0.00 | 1.57 | 1.45 | −0.11 | 0.05 | 1.61 | 1.49 | 0.71 |
| Teaching and no DSH | −0.28 | −0.14 | −0.23 | −0.13 | −0.22 | 0.00 | 0.05 | −0.20 | 0.04 | −0.25 | −0.22 | −0.35 | −0.98 |
| No teaching and DSH | 0.03 | 0.86 | −0.97 | −0.32 | −0.95 | 0.00 | −1.03 | −0.73 | 0.22 | −0.01 | −0.99 | −0.98 | −1.22 |
| No teaching and no DSH | 0.10 | 1.54 | −0.85 | 0.38 | −0.83 | 0.00 | −0.98 | −0.65 | 0.23 | 0.10 | −0.85 | −0.98 | −1.41 |
| Rural hospital types | | | | | | | | | | | | | |
| Nonspecial status hospitals | 0.00 | 1.09 | 0.60 | 1.86 | 0.52 | 0.00 | 0.64 | 0.31 | −0.43 | 0.03 | 0.63 | 0.09 | −0.58 |
| RRC | −0.43 | 0.83 | −0.67 | 0.53 | −0.70 | 0.00 | −0.24 | −1.39 | −1.06 | −0.36 | −0.65 | −0.90 | −1.37 |
| SCH | 0.12 | 1.29 | 0.77 | 2.12 | 0.66 | 0.00 | 0.71 | 0.74 | −0.16 | 0.16 | 0.81 | 0.47 | −0.03 |
| SCHs and RRCs | −0.01 | 0.46 | −0.10 | 0.34 | −0.11 | 0.00 | −0.08 | −0.95 | −0.95 | 0.06 | −0.08 | −0.13 | −0.33 |
| Medicare dependent small rural hospital | 0.39 | 0.94 | 1.93 | 2.84 | 1.80 | 0.00 | 1.60 | 2.05 | 0.24 | 0.40 | 1.96 | 1.36 | 0.53 |
| Type of ownership | | | | | | | | | | | | | |
| Voluntary | −0.16 | 0.35 | −0.27 | 0.18 | −0.27 | 0.00 | −0.12 | −0.36 | −0.19 | −0.14 | −0.27 | −0.45 | −1.07 |
| Proprietary | 0.40 | 0.82 | −0.75 | −0.49 | −0.71 | 0.00 | −1.21 | −0.14 | 0.82 | 0.32 | −0.77 | −0.69 | −0.74 |
| Government | 0.43 | −2.23 | 1.84 | −0.46 | 1.82 | 0.00 | 1.45 | 1.82 | 0.32 | 0.41 | 1.84 | 1.67 | 1.20 |

*Note:* DSH = disproportionate share hospital

Courtesy of 3M Health Information Systems, Wallingford, Connecticut.

subtracting the aggregate APG payments to hospitals in the hospital category under APG System 6, and dividing the difference by the aggregate APG payments to hospitals in the hospital category under APG System 6. The result is the percentage difference between hospital payments under the APG system being evaluated and hospital payments under APG System 6. An impact of +2.0 would indicate that the hospitals in the hospital category would receive 2 percent more in aggregate payments under the APG system being evaluated than the hospitals would have under the basic APG system (APG System 6). The relative APG payment impact measures how the aggregate payments to hospitals in each hospital category would change as the basic APG system (APG System 6) is expanded (e.g., more extensive ancillary packaging, the addition of outlier payments, etc.). Thus, the relative APG payment impact provides a means of evaluating each component of the APG system in terms of its effect on aggregate APG-based payments to different categories of hospitals. It does *not* provide a measure of the change in actual payments that hospitals would receive under an APG payment system.The discussion of the relative APG payment impact is based on Tables 29–6 and 29–7. APG System 1 adds 1-percent outlier payments to the basic APG system (APG System 6), and APG System 9 adds 3-percent outlier payments. There was relatively little APG payment impact across categories of hospitals as a result of adding outlier payments to the APG system. In general, the APG payment impact with outlier payments added was within 1 percent of the basic APG system.

The discussion of the relative APG payment impact is based on Tables 29–9 and 29–10. APG System 1 adds 1-percent outlier payments to the basic APG system (APG System 6), and APG System 9 adds 3-percent outlier payments. There was relatively little APG payment impact across categories of hospitals as a result of adding outlier payments to the APG system. In general, the APG payment impact with outlier payments added was within 1 percent of the basic APG system.

APG System 7 adds full packaging to the basic APG system. The addition of full packaging does tend to have a substantial APG payment impact across categories of hospitals. As a result of the addition of full packaging to the basic APG system, teaching hospitals with a resident-to-bed ratio greater than 0.25 have a 3.42-percent increase relative to the basic APG system. Urban hospitals over 500 beds, urban disproportionate share teaching hospitals, rural Medicare-dependent hospitals, small rural hospitals, and government hospitals experienced an increase between 1 and 2 percent as a result of adding full packaging to the basic APG system. There were no hospital categories that experienced a substantial decrease, except for proprietary hospitals, which experienced a 1.21-percent decrease.

APG Systems 3 and 8 add 1-percent and 3-percent outlier payments to the full packaging option in APG System 7, respectively. The addition of outliers to the full packaging option of APG System 7 does not substantially change the results, except that with full packaging and 3-percent outliers, rural hospitals over 100 beds do experience a substantial decrease.

The addition of ancillary discounting (APG System 11) or the addition of an expanded window of service (APG Systems 12 and 13) to the full packaging APG system with 1-percent outliers (APG System 3) does not substantially change the results across categories of hospitals.

APG Systems 2 and 4 use charge-based relative weights whereas all other APG systems use cost-based relative weights. The change to charge-based relative weights has a substantial APG payment impact across hospital categories. APG Systems 3 and 4 are the same except that APG System 3 uses cost-based relative weights and APG System 4 uses charge-based relative weights. For example, for teaching hospitals with a resident-to-bed ratio greater than 0.25, APG System 3 would result in an increase relative to the basic APG system of 3.33 percent, while APG System 4 would result in a decrease of 2.84 percent. The cause of this relative APG payment impact is the low cost-to-charge ratios for ancillary departments. Hospitals that have the majority of their outpatient services as ancillary services would experience a decrease using cost-based relative weights, since cost-based ancillary APG relative weights are proportionately lower. Conversely, hospitals that have the majority of their services as direct patient care services (e.g., emergency room visits) would have an increase using cost-based relative weights, since cost-based significant procedure and medical APG relative weights are proportionately higher. To illustrate this impact, hospitals were categorized based on the percentage of patients who only received ancillary services (i.e., no significant procedure or medical visit). APG System 3 and APG System 4 are the same, except that APG System 3 uses cost-based relative weights and APG System 4 uses charge-based relative weights. The difference in APG payment under APG System 3 and APG System 4 was computed and divided by the APG payment under APG System 4. The result is the percentage difference in APG payment due to cost-based relative weights as opposed to charge-based relative weights. Table 29–11 shows the results across hospitals categorized by the percentage of ancillary-only claims.

In Table 29–11, the 269 hospitals having less than 5 percent of their claims with only ancillaries had an increase equal to 6.921 percent by using cost-based relative weights instead of charge-based relative weights. Conversely, the 72 hospitals having 95 percent or more of their claims with only ancillaries had a decrease equal to 10.948 percent by using cost-based relative weights instead of charge-based relative weights.

**Table 29–11** Percentage Difference in Impact between APG System 3 and APG System 4 by Percentage of Ancillary-only Hospital Claims

| Percentage ancillary only | Count hosp | Percentage diff APG impact |
|:---:|:---:|:---:|
| 0–5 | 269 | 6.921 |
| 5–10 | 50 | 11.776 |
| 10–15 | 62 | 14.121 |
| 15–20 | 47 | 9.556 |
| 20–25 | 65 | 8.580 |
| 25–30 | 82 | 6.679 |
| 30–35 | 119 | 3.845 |
| 35–40 | 130 | 2.008 |
| 40–45 | 184 | 1.807 |
| 45–50 | 268 | 1.384 |
| 50–55 | 361 | 0.569 |
| 55–60 | 398 | 0.033 |
| 60–65 | 467 | −0.426 |
| 65–70 | 574 | −1.146 |
| 70–75 | 592 | −1.759 |
| 75–80 | 666 | −2.775 |
| 80–85 | 578 | −4.043 |
| 85–90 | 340 | −5.609 |
| 90–95 | 166 | −7.439 |
| 95–100 | 72 | −10.948 |

Courtesy of 3M Health Information Systems, Wallingford, Connecticut.

In summary, the alternative formulations of APG systems did not result in substantial differences in impact across different categories of hospitals. The only components of the APG system that caused any substantial variations in impact across different categories of hospitals were the selection of charge versus cost-based relative weights and the extent of ancillary packaging.

## DISCUSSION

The statistical performance of the APGs, in terms of $R^2$ was evaluated for 13 different APG systems. The statistical results provide a measure of the extent to which simulated APG payments for a patient correspond to the historical cost for the patient. In general, the statistical performance of the APGs is better than the statistical performance of the inpatient DRGs. The evaluation of the 13 different APG systems resulted in the following conclusions:

- There is virtually no difference in $R^2$ results for APG relative weights derived from charges or cost.
- The extent of ancillary packaging does affect the $R^2$ of the APGs. The $R^2$ results for the simple packaging and full packaging are virtually identical. In comparison to limited packaging, full packaging has minimal impact on $R^2$ for significant procedure claims but causes a modest decrease in $R^2$ for medical claims.
- The APG outlier policy has a significant impact on the $R^2$ of the APGs. Failure to have any outlier policy causes a large reduction in $R^2$, especially for medical claims. An outlier policy of having 1 percent of total APG payments associated with outliers results in a large improvement in $R^2$. A 3-percent outlier policy further improves $R^2$ but results in a substantial increase in the number of claims with outlier payments.
- The addition of a 20-percent discount for repeated ancillaries within the same APG has no substantial impact on $R^2$.
- Expanding the ancillary packaging of window of service for significant procedure and medical claims beyond the same day has no substantial impact on $R^2$.
- Across the 13 APG systems, the only factors that have a substantial payment impact by category of hospital are the extent of ancillary packaging and the basis of the relative weights.

Based on the above results, the recommended APG system is as follows:

- Although the charge- and cost-based APG relative weights were highly correlated and there was virtually no difference in $R^2$ between the charge- and cost-based APG relative weights, the use of cost-based relative weights is preferable. Since the cost-to-charge ratio for ancillary departments tends to be lower than for other departments, the charge-based APG relative weights for ancillary services tend to be higher than the cost-based APG relative weights. This would result in proportionately higher APG payments for ancillary services with charge-based relative weights than with cost-based relative weights. In particular, it would result in an increase for hospitals that deliver ancillaries as their primary outpatient service. As a result of this bias, cost-based relative weights are recommended. This bias is the source of the impact differences across hospital categories that would result from using charge-based relative weights.

- Ancillary packaging provides the financial incentives for hospital outpatient departments to utilize ancillary services efficiently. In order to provide such incentives, the full ancillary packaging option is preferable. There was a moderate decrease in $R^2$ for medical claims associated with the full packaging option, and there was some impact across hospital categories as a result of full ancillary packaging.

- Failure to have an outlier policy would result in a significant decrease in $R^2$ of the APGs. An outlier policy in which 1 percent of total payments are associated with outliers is preferable.

- While the discounting of repeated ancillary services did not affect $R^2$, the discounting of high-volume, low-cost ancillary services in the same APG would add complexity to the system, with relatively few benefits. Thus, discounting of repeated ancillary services is not recommended.

- While it would be desirable to have a wide window of time for ancillary packaging, in order to avoid the incentive to have ancillaries provided on a different day, the current UB-92 does not identify the provider who ordered the ancillary service. Thus, the packaging of ancillaries ordered by a provider and delivered on a different day would impose a significant administrative burden, because there is no automated way to identify such ancillaries within the Medicare billing system. It is recommended that the initial implementation of the APGs should have a same-day window of time for ancillary packaging. If a wider window of time for ancillary packaging is desired, identification of the provider who ordered the ancillary must be added to the claim.

In summary, the recommended APG system is APG System 3, which consists of cost-based relative weights, full ancillary packaging, a 1-percent outlier policy, 50-percent discounting of each additional significant procedure, no repeat ancillary discounting, and a same-day window of time for ancillary packaging. The statistical performance of this APG system exceeded the statistical performance of the current inpatient DRGs. Relative to the basic APG system, APG System 3 does impact relative APG payment in some categories of hospitals. The magnitude of the APG payment impact in any hospital category is always less than 4 percent. The APG payment impact in some hospital categories due to APG System 3 is largely the result of the full ancillary packaging.

## IMPLEMENTATION ISSUES

The APG system provides the framework for a hospital-based outpatient prospective payment system. However, there are a series of additional issues that must be addressed as part of the implementation of an APG-based prospective payment system:

### Volume of Visits

In any visit-based system, hospitals can increase revenue by increasing the number of visits. Under the existing Medicare outpatient payment system, an increase in visits will increase hospital revenue but not necessarily hospital profits. A change to an APG-based PPS may create greater incentives to increase visits for certain services. Thus, some means of monitoring and controlling the number of visits should be implemented.

### Upcoding and Fragmentation of Procedure Codes

Although the aggregation of codes into the APGs minimizes the opportunities for upcoding, hospital coding practices will need to be monitored. Procedure code fragmentation occurs when a single procedure is reported using multiple procedure codes. Currently, the Outpatient Code Editor is applied by Medicare to outpatient claims. The Outpatient Code Editor should be expanded in scope to address issues such as procedure code fragmentation.

## Identification of Visits

Since APGs are a visit-based payment system, it is essential that visits can be unambiguously identified from the claim form. Batch bills, in which the dates of service span more than one day, present difficulties for the identification of individual visits. Clear rules for the reporting of the dates of service, the units field on the revenue trailers, and the submission of batch bills need to be established. These rules should be designed so as to result in the identification of each individual visit and the services rendered during that visit.

## Shift of Ancillaries to Nonhospital Settings as a Result of Ancillary Packaging

If the implementation of an APG-based PPS includes the full packaging of ancillary services, hospitals will have a financial incentive not to provide the ancillary services directly but to send the patient to a nonhospital setting for the ancillary tests. The nonhospital facility could then bill Medicare separately for the ancillary tests. Thus, ancillaries ordered by hospital outpatient departments but delivered by nonhospital settings must be able to be identified within the claims-processing system. In order to expand the window of services for ancillary packaging and to include within the ancillary packaging all ancillaries ordered by the hospital outpatient department, the claim-processing system must identify the provider that ordered an ancillary service.

## Payment of Ancillaries Ordered Outside the Hospital

A large volume of the services provided by the ancillary department of hospitals are ordered by private physicians or other non-hospital-based providers. If hospitals are paid on an APG basis for ancillaries ordered outside the hospital, and nonhospital facilities are paid on a different basis, then there will be a payment differential for the same ancillary depending on whether the ancillary service is delivered by a hospital or a nonhospital facility. If hospital ancillary departments are paid less than nonhospital facilities, then hospitals will be at a competitive disadvantage. A negative price differential could cause a shift of ancillary services out of the hospital.

## Applicability

An outpatient PPS need not be limited to hospital outpatient departments but could also include entities that provide similar services. For example, ambulatory surgery centers and free-standing radiology centers that provide services similar to hospital outpatient departments could also be included in an outpatient PPS.

## Consistency with Inpatient Payment Levels

The increase in hospital-based ambulatory surgery was, in part, the result of the financial incentives in the Medicare payment system. Since inpatient surgery was paid at the fixed DRG rate and hospital-based ambulatory surgery was essentially paid at cost, there was a financial incentive to shift patients to the ambulatory setting, where there were no cost controls. If ambulatory surgery is paid at a fixed price, then, depending on the payment rate for surgery performed on an inpatient basis, there may be a financial incentive to perform surgery on an inpatient basis. The inpatient and outpatient payment rates for the same surgical procedure need to be established to provide the proper financial incentives.

## Computation of Prospective APG Payment Rates

Historical charges or costs can be used to compute an initial set of APG relative weights. If the historical charges or costs for some procedures are artificially high, then the APG relative weights would be disproportionately high. Consideration needs to be given to reevaluating some of the APG relative weights based on actual resource use instead of historical costs.

## Hospital-Specific Payment Adjustments

The inpatient PPS adjusts the DRG payment levels for hospitals based on hospital-specific factors such as disproportionate share and teaching status. The APG simulations included adjustments for labor costs and outliers. An evaluation needs to be performed to determine whether additional adjustments are necessary in an APG-based outpatient PPS.

## APG Update Process

The APGs will need to be reviewed and updated on an annual basis to reflect changes in technology and practice patterns as well as the annual changes in the procedure and diagnosis codes.

## CONCLUSIONS

A visit-based APG prospective payment system can provide an effective system for the payment of the facility component of hospital-based outpatient care. The APGs form a manageable, clinically meaningful set of patient classes that relate the attributes of patients to the resource demands and associated costs experienced by a hospital outpatient department. The components of the APG payment system can be configured to achieve specific policy objectives and to provide financial incentives for hospitals to provide efficient care. Based on the $R^2$ results and relative APG payment impact across the alternative formulations of the components of an APG system, an APG system with cost-based weights, full ancillary packaging, 1 percent of payments derived from outlier payments, 50-percent multiple significant procedure discounting, no repeat ancillary discounting, and a same-day window of time is recommended. Remaining implementation issues can be readily resolved, and an APG-based outpatient PPS can be implemented within a short time frame. The current Medicare payment system for outpatient services is a complex and confusing collection of payment methods, many of which are based on the cost in the hospital department providing the service. In an era of health care cost containment, a cost-based payment system for hospital outpatient care is an anachronism that provides no incentives for the efficient delivery of care and, therefore, must be replaced. An APG-based outpatient prospective payment system can be a practical and effective basis for the reform of the Medicare cost-based outpatient payment system.

---

**NOTES**

1. R. Averill et al., "Design of a Prospective Payment Patient Classification System for Ambulatory Care," *Health Care Financing Review* 15, no. 1 (1993): 71–100.
2. J. Vertrees et al., "Developing an Outpatient Prospective Payment System Based on APGs for the Iowa Medicaid Program," *Journal of Ambulatory Care Management* 17, no. 4 (1994): 82–96.

3. N. Goldfield et al., "The Clinical Development of an Ambulatory Classification System: Version 2.0 Ambulatory Patient Groups," *Journal of Ambulatory Care Management* 20, no. 3 (1997): 49–56.

4. Relative Value Studies, Inc., *Relative Values for Physicians* (New York: McGraw-Hill, 1984).

5. W.C Hsiao et al., "Estimating Physician' Work for a Resource-Based Relative Value Scale," *New England Journal of Medicine* 319 (1988): 835–841.

6. R. Averill et al., "Evaluation of a Prospective Payment System for Hospital-based Outpatient Care," *Journal of Ambulatory Care Management* 20, no. 3 (1997): 31–48.

# APPENDIX 29-A

# List of Version 2.0 APGs

## SIGNIFICANT PROCEDURE AND THERAPY APGS

### APC 1 Integumentary System

| | |
|---|---|
| 001 | PHOTOCHEMOTHERAPY |
| 002 | SUPERFICIAL NEEDLE BIOPSY AND ASPIRATION |
| 003 | COMPLEX INCISION AND DRAINAGE |
| 004 | SIMPLE INCISION AND DRAINAGE |
| 005 | NAIL PROCEDURES |
| 006 | SIMPLE DEBRIDEMENT AND DESTRUCTION |
| 007 | COMPLEX EXCISION, BIOPSY AND DEBRIDEMENT |
| 008 | SIMPLE EXCISION AND BIOPSY |
| 009 | COMPLEX SKIN REPAIRS INCL INTEGUMENT GRAFTS, TRANSFER & REARRANGE |
| 010 | SIMPLE SKIN REPAIR |
| 011 | SIMPLE INCISION AND EXCISION OF BREAST |
| 012 | BREAST RECONSTRUCTION AND MASTECTOMY |

### APC 2 Musculoskeletal System

| | |
|---|---|
| 021 | COMPLEX MUSCULOSKELETAL PROCEDURES EXCLUDING HAND AND FOOT |
| 022 | SIMPLE MUSCULOSKELETAL PROCEDURES EXCLUDING HAND AND FOOT |
| 023 | COMPLEX HAND AND FOOT MUSCULOSKELETAL PROCEDURES |
| 024 | SIMPLE HAND AND FOOT MUSCULOSKELETAL PROCEDURES |
| 025 | ARTHROSCOPY |

Courtesy of 3M Health Information Systems, Wallingford, Connecticut.

026    REPLACEMENT OF CAST
027    SPLINT, STRAPPING AND CAST REMOVAL
028    CLOSED TREATMENT FX & DISLOCATION OF FINGER, TOE & TRUNK
029    CLOSED TREATMENT FX & DISLOCATION EXC FINGER, TOE & TRUNK
030    OPEN OR PERCUTANEOUS TREATMENT OF FRACTURES
031    BONE OR JOINT MANIPULATION UNDER ANESTHESIA
032    BUNION PROCEDURES
033    ARTHROPLASTY
034    HAND AND FOOT TENOTOMY
035    ARTHROCENTESIS AND LIGAMENT OR TENDON INJECTION

## APC 3 Respiratory System

051    PULMONARY TESTS
052    NEEDLE AND CATHETER BIOPSY, ASPIRATION, LAVAGE AND INTUBATION
053    COMPLEX ENDOSCOPY OF THE UPPER AIRWAY
054    SIMPLE ENDOSCOPY OF THE UPPER AIRWAY
055    ENDOSCOPY OF THE LOWER AIRWAY
057    RESPIRATORY THERAPY

## APC 4 Cardiovascular System

071    EXERCISE TOLERANCE TESTS
072    ECHOCARDIOGRAPHY
073    PHONOCARDIOGRAM
074    CARDIAC ELECTROPHYSIOLOGIC TESTS
075    PLACEMENT OF TRANSVENOUS CATHETERS
076    DIAGNOSTIC CARDIAC CATHETERIZATION
077    ANGIOPLASTY AND TRANSCATHETER PROCEDURES
078    PACEMAKER INSERTION AND REPLACEMENT

079     REMOVAL AND REVISION OF PACEMAKER AND VASCU-
        LAR DEVICE
080     MINOR VASCULAR REPAIR AND FISTULA CONSTRUCTION
081     SECONDARY VARICOSE VEINS AND VASCULAR INJEC-
        TION
082     VASCULAR LIGATION
083     RESUSCITATION AND CARDIOVERSION
084     CARDIAC REHABILITATION

**APC 5 Hematologic, Lymphatic and Endocrine**

091     CHEMOTHERAPY BY EXTENDED INFUSION
092     CHEMOTHERAPY EXCEPT BY EXTENDED INFUSION
093     PHLEBOTOMY
094     BLOOD AND BLOOD PRODUCT EXCHANGE
095     DEEP LYMPH STRUCTURE AND THYROID PROCEDURES
096     ALLERGY TESTS
097     TRANSFUSION

**APC 6 Digestive System**

111     ALIMENTARY TESTS AND SIMPLE TUBE PLACEMENT
112     ESOPHAGEAL DILATION WITHOUT ENDOSCOPY
113     ANOSCOPY WITH BIOPSY AND DIAGNOSTIC PROCTOSIG-
        MOIDOSCOPY
114     PROCTOSIGMOIDOSCOPY WITH EXCISION OR BIOPSY
115     DIAGNOSTIC UPPER GI ENDOSCOPY OR INTUBATION
116     THERAPEUTIC UPPER GI ENDOSCOPY OR INTUBATION
117     LOWER GASTROINTESTINAL ENDOSCOPY
118     ERCP AND MISCELLANEOUS GI ENDOSCOPY PROCE-
        DURES
119     HERNIA AND HYDROCELE PROCEDURES
120     COMPLEX ANAL AND RECTAL PROCEDURES
121     SIMPLE ANAL AND RECTAL PROCEDURES

122    MISCELLANEOUS ABDOMINAL PROCEDURES
123    COMPLEX LAPAROSCOPIC PROCEDURES
124    SIMPLE LAPAROSCOPIC PROCEDURES

## APC 7 Urinary System

131    RENAL EXTRACORPOREAL SHOCK WAVE LITHOTRIPSY
132    SIMPLE URINARY STUDIES AND PROCEDURES
133    URINARY CATHETERIZATION AND DILATATION
134    COMPLEX CYSTOURETHROSCOPY AND LITHOLAPAXY
135    MODERATE CYSTOURETHROSCOPY
136    SIMPLE CYSTOURETHROSCOPY
137    COMPLEX URETHRAL PROCEDURES
138    SIMPLE URETHRAL PROCEDURES
139    HEMODIALYSIS
140    PERITONEAL DIALYSIS

## APC 8 Male Genital System

151    TESTICULAR AND EPIDIDYMAL PROCEDURES
152    INSERTION OF PENILE PROSTHESIS
153    COMPLEX PENILE PROCEDURES
154    SIMPLE PENILE PROCEDURES
155    PROSTATE NEEDLE AND PUNCH BIOPSY

## APC 9 Female Genital System

171    ARTIFICIAL FERTILIZATION
172    PROCEDURES FOR PREGNANCY AND NEONATAL CARE
173    TREATMENT OF SPONTANEOUS ABORTION
174    THERAPEUTIC ABORTION
175    VAGINAL DELIVERY
176    COMPLEX FEMALE REPRODUCTIVE PROCEDURES

177    SIMPLE FEMALE REPRODUCTIVE PROCEDURES
178    DILATION AND CURETTAGE
179    HYSTEROSCOPY
180    COLPOSCOPY

## APC 10 Nervous System

191    EXTENDED EEG STUDIES
192    ELECTROENCEPHALOGRAM
193    ELECTROCONVULSIVE THERAPY
194    NERVE AND MUSCLE TESTS
195    NERVOUS SYSTEM INJECTIONS, STIMULATIONS OR CRA-
       NIAL TAP
196    REVISION AND REMOVAL OF NEUROLOGICAL DEVICE
197    NEUROSTIMULATOR AND VENTRICULAR SHUNT IMPLAN-
       TATION
198    NERVE REPAIR AND DESTRUCTION
199    SPINAL TAP

## APC 11 Eye and Ocular Adnexa

211    MINOR OPHTHALMOLOGICAL TESTS AND PROCEDURES
212    FITTING OF CONTACT LENSES
213    LASER EYE PROCEDURES
214    CATARACT PROCEDURES
215    COMPLEX ANTERIOR SEGMENT EYE PROCEDURES
216    MODERATE ANTERIOR SEGMENT EYE PROCEDURES
217    SIMPLE ANTERIOR SEGMENT EYE PROCEDURES
218    COMPLEX POSTERIOR SEGMENT EYE PROCEDURES
219    SIMPLE POSTERIOR SEGMENT EYE PROCEDURES
220    STRABISMUS AND MUSCLE EYE PROCEDURES
221    COMPLEX REPAIR AND PLASTIC PROCEDURES OF EYE
222    SIMPLE REPAIR AND PLASTIC PROCEDURES OF EYE
223    VITRECTOMY

**APC 12 Facial, Ear, Nose, Mouth and Throat**

231      COCHLEAR DEVICE IMPLANTATION
232      OTORHINOLARYNGOLOGIC FUNCTION TESTS
233      NASAL CAUTERIZATION AND PACKING
234      COMPLEX FACIAL AND ENT PROCEDURES
235      SIMPLE FACIAL AND ENT PROCEDURES
236      TONSIL AND ADENOID PROCEDURES
237      SIMPLE AUDIOMETRY

**APC 13 Therapeutic and Other Significant Radiological Procedures**

251      THERAPEUTIC NUCLEAR MEDICINE
252      RADIATION THERAPY AND HYPERTHERMIA
253      VASCULAR RADIOLOGY EXCEPT FOR VENOGRAPHY OF EXTREMITY
254      MYELOGRAPHY
255      MISCELLANEOUS RADIOLOGICAL PROCEDURES WITH CONTRAST

**APC 14 Physical Medicine and Rehabilitation**

271      OCCUPATIONAL THERAPY
272      PHYSICAL THERAPY
273      SPEECH THERAPY

**APC 15 Mental Illness and Substance Abuse Therapies**

281      NEUROPSYCHOLOGICAL TESTING
282      FULL DAY PARTIAL HOSPITALIZATION FOR SUBSTANCE ABUSE
283      FULL DAY PARTIAL HOSPITALIZATION FOR MENTAL ILLNESS
284      HALF DAY PARTIAL HOSPITALIZATION FOR SUBSTANCE ABUSE

285    HALF DAY PARTIAL HOSPITALIZATION FOR MENTAL ILL-
       NESS
286    COUNSELLING OR INDIVIDUAL BRIEF PSYCHOTHERAPY
287    INDIVIDUAL COMPREHENSIVE PSYCHOTHERAPY
288    FAMILY PSYCHOTHERAPY
289    GROUP PSYCHOTHERAPY


**ANCILLARY SERVICES APGs**


**APC 16 Radiology**

301    COMPLEX DIAGNOSTIC NUCLEAR MEDICINE
302    INTERMEDIATE DIAGNOSTIC NUCLEAR MEDICINE
303    SIMPLE DIAGNOSTIC NUCLEAR MEDICINE
304    OBSTETRICAL ULTRASOUND
305    DIAGNOSTIC ULTRASOUND EXCEPT OBSTETRICAL
306    MAGNETIC RESONANCE IMAGING
307    COMPUTERIZED AXIAL TOMOGRAPHY
308    MAMMOGRAPHY
309    DIGESTIVE RADIOLOGY
310    PLAIN FILM
311    THERAPEUTIC RADIATION TREATMENT PREPARATION


**APC 17 Anesthesia**

321    ANESTHESIA


**APC 18 Pathology**

331    COMPLEX PATHOLOGY
332    SIMPLE PATHOLOGY
333    PAP SMEARS

## APC 19 Laboratory

341    BLOOD AND TISSUE TYPING
342    COMPLEX IMMUNOLOGY TESTS
343    SIMPLE IMMUNOLOGY TESTS
344    COMPLEX MICROBIOLOGY TESTS
345    SIMPLE MICROBIOLOGY TESTS
346    COMPLEX ENDOCRINOLOGY TESTS
347    SIMPLE ENDOCRINOLOGY TESTS
348    COMPLEX CHEMISTRY TESTS
349    SIMPLE CHEMISTRY TESTS
350    BASIC CHEMISTRY TESTS
351    MULTICHANNEL CHEMISTRY TESTS
352    ORGAN OR DISEASE ORIENTED PANELS
353    TOXICOLOGY TESTS
354    THERAPEUTIC DRUG MONITORING
355    COMPLEX CLOTTING TESTS
356    SIMPLE CLOTTING TESTS
357    COMPLEX HEMATOLOGY TESTS
358    SIMPLE HEMATOLOGY TESTS
359    URINALYSIS
360    BLOOD AND URINE DIPSTICK TESTS

## APC 20 Other Ancillary Tests and Procedures

371    SIMPLE PULMONARY FUNCTION TESTS
372    INFUSION THERAPY EXCEPT CHEMOTHERAPY
373    CARDIOGRAM
374    COMPLEX IMMUNIZATION
375    MODERATE IMMUNIZATION
376    SIMPLE IMMUNIZATION AND ALLERGY IMMUNOTHER-
       APY
377    MINOR REPRODUCTIVE PROCEDURES
378    MINOR CARDIAC AND VASCULAR TESTS

379      MINOR OPHTHALMOLOGICAL INJECTION, SCRAPING AND TESTS
380      PACEMAKER ANALYSIS
381      TUBE CHANGE
382      PROVISION OF VISION AIDS
383      INTRODUCTION OF NEEDLE AND CATHETER
384      DRESSINGS AND OTHER MINOR PROCEDURES
385      OTHER MISCELLANEOUS ANCILLARY PROCEDURES
386      BIOFEEDBACK AND OTHER TRAINING

## APC 21 Chemotherapy Drugs

391      CLASS ONE CHEMOTHERAPY DRUGS
392      CLASS TWO CHEMOTHERAPY DRUGS
393      CLASS THREE CHEMOTHERAPY DRUGS
394      CLASS FOUR CHEMOTHERAPY DRUGS
395      CLASS FIVE CHEMOTHERAPY DRUGS

## APC 22 Ancillary Mental Illness and Substance Abuse Services

411      PSYCHOTROPIC MEDICATION MANAGEMENT
412      ACTIVITY THERAPY

## APC 23 Incidental Procedures and Services

421      INCIDENTAL TO MEDICAL, SIGNIFICANT PROCEDURE OR THERAPY VISIT
422      MEDICAL VISIT INDICATOR

## MEDICAL APGS

## APC 24 Malignancy

431      HEMATOLOGICAL MALIGNANCY
432      PROSTATIC MALIGNANCY

433     LUNG MALIGNANCY
434     BREAST MALIGNANCIES
435     GI MALIGNANCIES
436     SKIN MALIGNANCY
437     OTHER MALIGNANCIES

## APC 25 Poisoning

451     POISONING

## APC 26 Trauma

461     HEAD AND SPINE INJURY
462     MINOR SKIN AND SOFT TISSUE INJURIES EXCEPT BURNS
463     SKIN AND SOFT TISSUE INJURIES EXCEPT BURNS
464     FRACTURE, DISLOCATION AND SPRAIN
465     BURNS
466     OTHER INJURIES

## APC 27 Neonate

481     NEONATE AND CONGENITAL ANOMALY

## APC 28 Pregnancy

491     ROUTINE PRENATAL CARE
492     MATERNAL ANTEPARTUM COMPLICATION
493     ROUTINE POSTPARTUM CARE
494     MATERNAL POSTPARTUM COMPLICATION

## APC 29 Infectious Diseases

501     COMPLEX INFECTIOUS DISEASE
502     MISCELLANEOUS INFECTIOUS DISEASES
503     INFECTIOUS DISEASES OF GENITAL ORGANS

## APC 30 Nervous System Diseases

511     TIA, CVA AND OTHER CEREBROVASCULAR EVENTS
512     HEADACHE
513     EPILEPSY
514     NONTRAUMATIC LOSS OF CONSCIOUSNESS
515     OTHER DISEASES OF THE NERVOUS SYSTEM

## APC 31 Eye Diseases

531     CATARACTS
532     REFRACTION DISORDER
533     CONJUNCTIVITIS AND OTHER SIMPLE EXTERNAL EYE INFLAMMATION
534     EYE DISEASES EXCEPT CATARACT, REFRACTION DISORDER & CONJUNCTIVITIS

## APC 32 Ear, Nose, Mouth and Throat Diseases

541     DENTAL DISEASE
542     INFLUENZA, URI AND ENT INFECTIONS
543     HEARING LOSS
544     OTHER COMPLEX EAR, NOSE, THROAT AND MOUTH DISEASES
545     OTHER SIMPLE EAR, NOSE, THROAT AND MOUTH DISEASES

## APC 33 Respiratory System Diseases

561     EMPHYSEMA, CHRONIC BRONCHITIS, AND ASTHMA
562     PNEUMONIA
563     COMPLEX RESPIRATORY DIS EXC EMPHYSEMA, CHR BRONCHITIS & ASTHMA
564     SIMPLE RESPIRATORY DIS EXC EMPHYSEMA, CHR BRONCHITIS & ASTHMA

**APC 34 Cardiovascular System Diseases**

571     CONGESTIVE HEART FAILURE AND ISCHEMIC HEART DISEASE
572     HYPERTENSION
573     CHEST PAIN W CARDIAC ENZYMES TO RULE OUT MYO-CARDIAL INFARCT
574     CHEST PAIN WO CARDIAC ENZYMES TO RULE OUT MYO-CARDIAL INFARCT
575     SIMPLE CARDIOVASCULAR DIS EXC CHF, ISCHEMIC HEART DIS & HYPERTN
576     COMPLEX CARDIOVASCULAR DIS EXC CHF, ISCHEMIC HEART DIS & HYPERTN

**APC 35 Digestive System Diseases**

591     NONINFECTIOUS GASTROENTERITIS
592     ULCERS, GASTRITIS AND ESOPHAGITIS
593     HEPATOBILIARY DISEASE
594     HERNIA
595     HEMORRHOIDS AND OTHER ANAL-RECTAL DISEASES
596     OTHER COMPLEX GASTROINTESTINAL DISEASES
597     OTHER SIMPLE GASTROINTESTINAL DISEASES

**APC 36 Major Signs, Symptoms and Findings**

611     MAJOR SIGNS, SYMPTOMS AND FINDINGS

**APC 37 Musculoskeletal Diseases**

621     BACK DISORDERS
622     COMPLEX MUSCULOSKELETAL DISEASES EXCEPT BACK DISORDERS
623     SIMPLE MUSCULOSKELETAL DISEASES EXCEPT BACK DISORDERS

## APC 38 Skin and Breast Diseases

| | |
|---|---|
| 631 | DISEASE OF NAILS |
| 632 | CHRONIC SKIN ULCER |
| 633 | CELLULITIS, IMPETIGO AND LYMPHANGITIS |
| 634 | BREAST DISEASES |
| 635 | SKIN DISEASES |

## APC 39 Endocrine, Nutritional and Metabolic Diseases

| | |
|---|---|
| 651 | DIABETES |
| 652 | COMPLEX ENDOCRINE, NUTRIT & METABOLIC DIS EXC DIABETES & OBESITY |
| 653 | SIMPLE ENDOCRINE, NUTRITIONAL & METABOLIC DISEASE EXC DIABETES |
| 654 | FLUID AND ELECTROLYTE DISORDERS |

## APC 40 Kidney and Urinary Tract Diseases

| | |
|---|---|
| 661 | URINARY TRACT INFECTION |
| 662 | RENAL FAILURE |
| 663 | COMPLEX URINARY DIS EXC URINARY TRACT INFECTN & RENAL FAILURE |
| 664 | SIMPLE URINARY DIS EXC URINARY TRACT INFECTN & RENAL FAILURE |

## APC 41 Male Genital System Diseases

| | |
|---|---|
| 671 | BENIGN PROSTATIC HYPERTROPHY |
| 672 | MALE REPRODUCTIVE DISEASES EXCEPT BENIGN PROSTATIC HYPERTROPHY |

## APC 42 Female Genital System Diseases

| | |
|---|---|
| 681 | GYNECOLOGIC DISEASES |

## APC 43 Immunologic and Hematologic Diseases

| | |
|---|---|
| 691 | HIV INFECTION |
| 692 | ANEMIA |
| 693 | OTHER COMPLEX IMMUNOLOGIC AND HEMATOLOGIC DISEASE |
| 694 | OTHER SIMPLE IMMUNOLOGIC AND HEMATOLOGIC DISEASE |

## APC 44 Well Care, Administrative

| | |
|---|---|
| 701 | ADULT MEDICAL EXAMINATION |
| 702 | WELL CHILD CARE |
| 703 | CONTRACEPTION AND PROCREATIVE MANAGEMENT |
| 704 | AFTERCARE |
| 705 | NONSPECIFIC SIGNS & SYMPTOMS & OTH CONTACTS W HEALTH SVCS |

## APC 45 Unknown Cause of Mortality

| | |
|---|---|
| 721 | UNKNOWN CAUSE OF MORTALITY |

## APC 46 Error

| | |
|---|---|
| 992 | INVALID PROCEDURE CODE |
| 993 | INPATIENT PROCEDURE |
| 994 | AUTOPSY SERVICES |
| 995 | NONCOVERED CARE SETTINGS AND SERVICES |
| 996 | INVALID RVDX CODE |
| 997 | ECODE CANNOT BE USED AS RVDX |
| 998 | UNACCEPTABLE RVDX, REQUIRES PROCEDURE |
| 999 | UNGROUPABLE |

# PART IV

# Case Mix Adjustment for Inpatient Care

CHAPTER 30

# Logic and Applications of the All Patient Refined DRGs: The Greater Southeast Community Hospital Experience

*Patricia Jones and George Strudgeon*

## GREATER SOUTHEAST COMMUNITY HOSPITAL

Greater Southeast Healthcare System is located on the border of Southeast Washington, D.C., and Prince George's County, Maryland. The System's major entity is Greater Southeast Community Hospital (GSCH), a 494-licensed-bed facility (424 acute beds, 26 subacute beds, 44 bassinets) that treats approximately 14,000 acute inpatients per year. The inpatient population represents a complex case mix with high severity and major social disposition problems. Nearly a quarter of the area's residents live below the poverty line, and about half have not graduated from high school. The population has the highest rates of infant mortality, cancer, and coronary disease in the local area. Approximately one out of every three inpatients is admitted through the emergency department with no private physician on the hospital's medical staff. While overall admissions have declined sine 1988, the more complex and severely ill subsets of the population have increased; these subsets include acquired immunodeficiency syndrome (AIDS), dialysis, and geriatric patients. Since the mid-1980s, Greater Southeast's administration has recognized accurate measurement of case mix complexity as a major priority.

## GSCH DECISION SUPPORT FUNCTION

Since 1987, the hospital has operated a case mix decision support function that consists of merged clinical, demographic, and financial data.

GSCH uses HBOC's TRENDSTAR decision support modules, which run on a DEC Micro-VAX minicomputer (refer to Figure 30–1). Specifically, a computer program compiles data routinely collected by the hospital's transaction systems (registration, medical records, patient accounts, and operating room) and merges them into a single record for each inpatient stay or outpatient visit. The financial components of decision support include fully integrated cost-accounting, budget, and reimbursement modules, thereby creating the capability to generate profit/loss statements by International Classification of

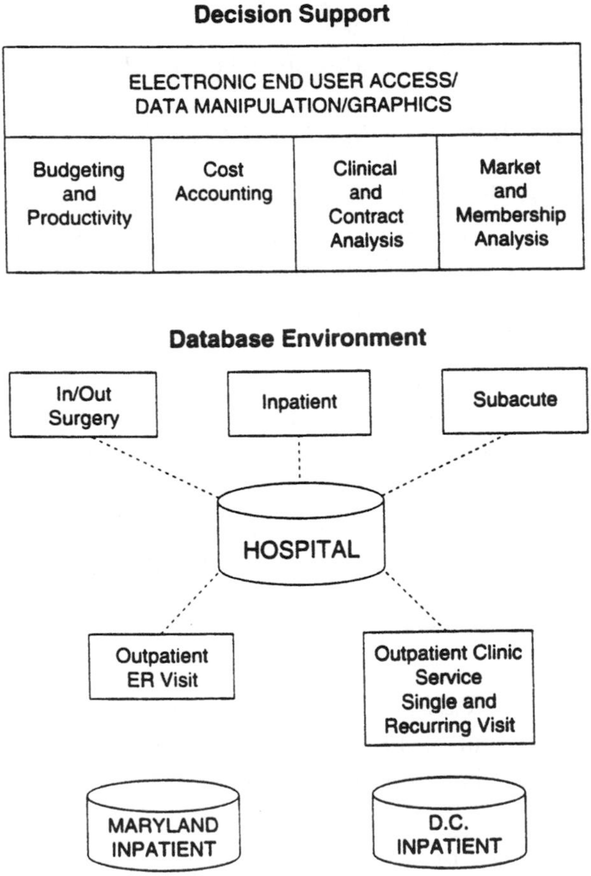

**Decision Support**

| ELECTRONIC END USER ACCESS/ DATA MANIPULATION/GRAPHICS | | | |
|---|---|---|---|
| Budgeting and Productivity | Cost Accounting | Clinical and Contract Analysis | Market and Membership Analysis |

**Database Environment**

**Figure 30–1** Greater Southeast Healthcare System Decision Support Configuration and Database Environment

Disease (ICD) codes, diagnosis-related groups (DRGs), product lines, and so forth. The data serve as the foundation for clinical assessment, reimbursement analysis, budgeting, and strategic planning.

Physicians had mandated early on that analysis of their practice patterns would be contingent on appropriate risk adjustment. The hospital had used an internally developed adjustment in the first two years, which was replaced by one major severity system that required manual abstracting and data entry of clinical elements. In 1991, the hospital turned to all patient refined DRGs (APR-DRGs; vendor, 3M-Health Information Systems [3M/HIS]) as the basis for refined case mix classification and risk adjustment.

## INFORMATION SYSTEMS CONFIGURATION FOR APR-DRGs

Because the decision support system had the most comprehensive inpatient dataset, along with powerful flexible reporting capability, GSCH made the decision to incorporate directly APR-DRG data into the case mix databases. The hospital's information system configuration consists of integrated UNIX-based applications that run on Hewlett Packard (HP) minicomputers. As a result GSCH uses a personal computer (PC) approach for APR-DRG grouping. In order to assign APR-DRG values, input data are captured directly from TRENDSTAR and formatted into an input file. The file is downloaded onto a PC, where the APR-DRG grouper resides. The grouper processes the data and returns the APR-DRG values, which are then placed into a file. In turn, this file is used to update a case mix database.

Two other features of the grouper are important to note. One is logical mapper software, which provides the capability to "map" outdated, invalid ICD codes to their current values, thereby providing automated capability to group historic data. Second, the grouper provides a complete audit trail of specific components of logic. GSCH stores all of this output in each patient record in order to validate grouper assignment. APR-DRG severity logic is also available in a comprehensive reference manual.

## APR-DRG LOGIC OVERVIEW

The most current version of APR-DRGs was released in May 1995. (*Note:* Prior versions are 10.0, 1993, and 7.0, 1991.) The APR-DRG value, severity subclass, and risk of mortality subclass comprise the three core data elements provided by the grouper for each inpatient (refer to Figure 30–2). It is notable that separate adjustments have been created to measure differences in resource utilization (severity subclass) versus mortality (risk of mortality subclass). Severity of illness and risk of mortality relate to distinct patient attributes. Severity of illness relates to the extent of physiologic decompensation or organ system loss of function experienced by the patient, while risk of mortality relates to the likelihood of dying. Citing one example, a patient with acute cholecystitis as the only secondary diagnosis is considered a major severity of illness but a minor risk of mortality. The severity of illness is major because there is significant organ system loss of function associated with acute cholecystitis. On the other hand, it is unlikely that acute cholecystitis alone will result in mortality; therefore, the mortality subclass for this patient is minor. A sample patient classification using Version 12.0 logic is illustrated in Exhibit 30–1.

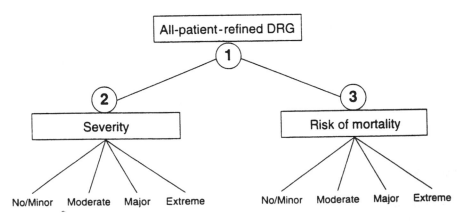

Figure 30–2 APR-DRG Descriptors

**Exhibit 30–1** Version 12 All Patient Refined DRGs Case Study

| | |
|---|---|
| Age: | 69 |
| Disposition: | 1, Home, self-care |
| Acute LOS: | 24 |
| APR-MDC: | 18, Generalized infectious disease |
| APR-DRG: | 416, Septicemia |
| Severity: | 4, Extreme |
| Risk of mortality: | 3, Major |

| ICD-9-CM | Diagnosis | Severity | Risk of Mortality |
|---|---|---|---|
| 0389.9 | Septicemia | — | — |
| 263.8 | Protein-Calorie Malnutrit | 4 | 2 |
| 537.0 | Acquired Pyloric Stenosis | 4 | 1 |
| 402.91 | Hypertens Heart Disease w/Congestive Heart Failure | 3 | 3 |
| 276.8 | Hypokalemia | 3 | 1 |
| 285.9 | Anemia | 1 | 1 |
| 535.10 | Atrophic Gastritis | 1 | 1 |
| 531.98 | Stomach Ulcer | 1 | 1 |
| 438 | Late Effect, Cerebrovascular Disease | 1 | 2 |
| 342.91 | Unspecified Hemiplegia/Paresis | 2 | 2 |

| ICD-9-CM | Procedure |
|---|---|
| 99.15 | Parenteral Nutrition |
| 45.16 | EGD w/Closed Biopsy |

## Base APR-DRGs

APR-DRGs provide the benefit of refined case mix classification for all patients seen in an acute care setting. First, it is important to distinguish how APR-DRGs differ from the two other prominent case mix classification systems used for inpatients: Medicare DRGs and the "all patient" or New York DRGs (AP-DRGs). Medicare DRG and AP-DRG classification systems have a breakout of select case-mix groupings based on age, significant comorbidities or complications (CCs), and discharge disposition. These are eliminated in almost all of the APR-DRGs, rolling back the logic to the base APR-DRGs (refer to Figure 30–3). As discussed in the previous section, the base DRGs are then classified further into four uniform severity subclasses and four risk of mortality subclasses. There are 382 base APR-DRGs.

The refinements achieved in the development of AP-DRGs serve as the first major component of case mix classification for the APR-DRGs. Additional modifications were made to a subset of the AP-DRGs, and some new base DRGs were also created that are unique to the APR classification system. Regarding the latter, additional improvements in classification of the newborn/neonate population were created based on the research of the National Association for Children and Health Related Institutions (NACHRI). New DRGs have been developed based on significant differences in resource utilization (e.g., a new DRG for fusion of scoliosis) or mortality (e.g., separate DRGs for hemorrhagic vs. ischemic stroke).

## APR Severity Logic and GSCH Validation Process

Again, it is important to compare APR severity logic with that of the Medicare and AP-DRG classification systems. AP-DRGs use CCs and major CCs

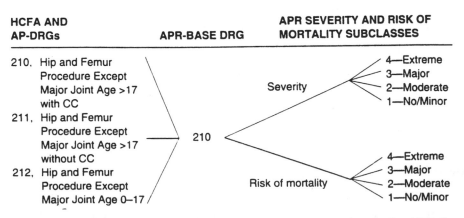

**Figure 30–3** Comparison of HCFA and AP-DRGs with All Patient Refined DRGs

(a subset of CCs that have an even greater effect on resource consumption; e.g., stomach ulcer with perforation and acute myocardial infarction). Medicare DRGs use a CC adjustment, and in 1994 the Health Care Financing Administration (HCFA) published a proposal for a major CC adjustment tailored to its own research. This results in a nonuniform severity adjustment: some DRGs have no CC adjustment, some have CCs, and some have major CCs. Also, neither system addresses the issue of adjusting severity for patients who present with multiple significant secondary diagnoses. Both deficiencies are eliminated in the APR-DRG severity logic.

Regarding the use of severity data at GSCH, it is imperative that physicians have a working knowledge of risk adjustment if they are going to accept and use these data to modify clinical practice. As a result, the physician group responsible for evaluating risk classification systems identified having complete access to the logic as one of their key requirements.

A summarized description of APR-DRG severity logic is provided in the following paragraphs. This overview parallels the general information that was provided to physicians in order to begin the validation process.

The APR severity subclass measures the total burden of illness for an inpatient stay as related to the resource demands and associated costs experienced by the hospital. This measure is based on complete evaluation of all secondary diagnoses, which are defined as any diagnosis present on admission (comorbidity) or developing after admission (complication) that affected treatment received and/or length of stay. The latter is an important point to remember, because one of the questions most frequently asked by GSCH physicians was whether or not the severity adjustment took into account those conditions that developed after the patient was admitted. The physicians did not want a severity adjustment that was based solely on the patient's condition at the time of admission; instead, they wanted a measure of maximal severity that was based on the total stay. The APR-DRG severity logic satisfies this requirement.

In order to obtain the overall severity subclass, each secondary diagnosis is assigned to one of four complexity levels: no/minor, moderate, major, or extreme. These values are subject to change for select diagnoses based on other variables (principal diagnosis; age, in particular 0–17 years; select non-operating-room procedures, such as temporary pacemaker). In general, secondary diagnoses that are defined as CCs are classified to the moderate, major, or extreme complexity levels, whereas non-CCs are classified as no/minor. It is important to note that the 3M-HIS physician research group significantly improved CC classification in the APR-DRGs. Specific examples of diagnoses that are classified as non-CCs in the HCFA and AP-DRG system but are recognized as CCs in the APR-DRGs include aseptic necrosis of the femur (ICD-9-CM, Code 733.42, moderate), bacterial enteritis (ICD-9-CM, Code 008.49, major) and salmonella meningitis (ICD-9-CM Code 003.21, extreme).

During the evaluation of the general logic, another question frequently asked by physicians focused on the impact of multiple, significant CCs. In their judgment, patients with multiple CCs typically require a longer and more complex treatment course. The APR-DRG severity logic adjusts for interactive effects between select secondary diagnoses (e.g., a patient who has congestive heart failure and diabetic ketoacidosis) by increasing the final overall severity subclass assignment for the patient.

After reviewing this general conceptual framework, the group conducted its own independent evaluation of the logic. Each member was provided with a list of the hospital's top-volume secondary diagnoses in the adult medical-surgical population and was asked to rate their complexity. As a second major exercise, members reviewed actual patient records and rated the final severity subclass as well.

The third part of the validation process focused on answering the question, "Does the APR severity adjustment explain differences in resource utilization?" The Director of Decision Support Services conducted extensive analysis of the hospital's top-volume adult medical-surgical APR-DRGs. Specifically, the objective was to measure severity mix and to then determine the impact of severity on length of stay, ancillary cost, and hospital financial performance. Figure 30–4 provides a series of severity-adjusted profiles for one of GSCH's significant volume APR-DRGs. In another study, physicians conducted record review on no/minor severity cases with high resource utilization to determine if the logic accurately identified overutilization problems.

The physicians' initial response to the APR-DRG logic was one of skepticism, focusing mainly on the concern that medical records coding might not accurately measure the severity of their patient population; however, having gone through the validation exercises, they found a very high rate of agreement between their own clinical judgment and the actual logic.

The findings of the third exercise showed excellent explanatory power of the APR severity adjustment for resource utilization in the adult medical-surgical population. The results of the record review showed accurate identification of cases with overutilization, but some cases were identified as having incorrect severity subclass assignment because of medical records coding; for

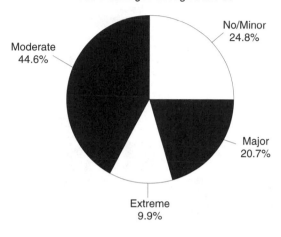

APR-DRG 127, CONGESTIVE HEART FAILURE SEVERITY MIX

1995 Discharges through June 30

No/Minor
24.8%

Moderate
44.6%

Major
20.7%

Extreme
9.9%

N = 343
AMAs and transfers to other acute hospitals were excluded.

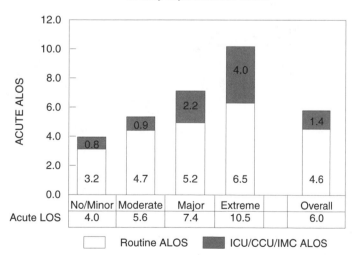

APR-DRG 127
Severity-adjusted Acute ALOS

| | No/Minor | Moderate | Major | Extreme | | Overall |
|---|---|---|---|---|---|---|
| ICU/CCU/IMC ALOS | 0.8 | 0.9 | 2.2 | 4.0 | | 1.4 |
| Routine ALOS | 3.2 | 4.7 | 5.2 | 6.5 | | 4.6 |
| Acute LOS | 4.0 | 5.6 | 7.4 | 10.5 | | 6.0 |

☐ Routine ALOS    ■ ICU/CCU/IMC ALOS

**Figure 30–4** Impact of APR-DRGs on Resource Utilization and Financial Performance                                                                    *continues*

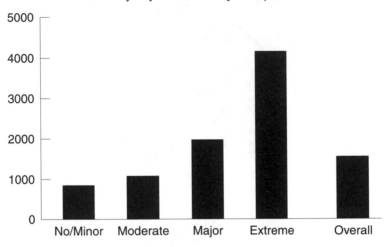

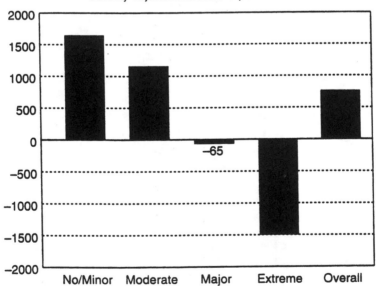

**Figure 30–4** continued

example, not coding the etiology of cardiomyopathy in a congestive heart failure patient resulted in assignment of subclass 1 instead of the correct value of 2. The clinician group approved the use of APR-DRGs for clinical assessment and physician profiling. In order to improve accuracy and consistency in coding, the hospital also purchased 3M's encoder software. GSCH physicians have continued their dialogue with the 3M-HIS medical director regarding components of the logic that merit further analysis based on their clinical judgment.

## Mortality Risk Adjustment and GSCH Validation Process

At the time of this writing, GSCH physicians are validating the risk of mortality subclass that became available with the 12.0 logic. The approach used to compute the final risk of mortality subclass value is similar to the severity logic. Each secondary diagnosis is assigned to one of four levels: no/minor, moderate, major, extreme. These values are then subject to adjustments based on different variables (age, principal diagnosis, non-operating-room procedures, etc.). The final subclass assignment is further subject to modification based on certain variables; for example, interactive effects between secondary diagnoses. 3M has identified important differences when using death as the dependent variable (risk of mortality subclass) versus total charges (severity subclass). In general, except for malignancies and certain extreme acute diseases such as intracranial hemorrhage, the risk of mortality level will be lower than the severity level.

The validation process that is underway parallels what had been done with severity. Major emphasis is placed on case-level analysis where physicians evaluate a patient's risk of mortality and then compare this with the APR logic. Another focus is aggregate mortality rate analysis by APR-DRG (refer to Figure 30–5 for a sample analysis). The preliminary findings show good explanatory power to support mortality outcomes assessment; however, additional data are needed to ensure accurate analysis. Ideally, a separate risk of mortality score should be calculated based upon comorbidity only (secondary diagnoses present on admission) and then compared with the final score, which is based upon *all* secondary diagnoses (i.e., comorbidities and complications). Additional adjustment should be made for patients with Do Not Resuscitate (DNR) orders.

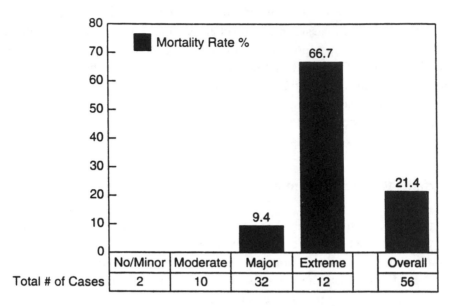

**Figure 30–5** APR-DRGs Version 12.0 Risk of Mortality Correlated with Mortality Rates, APR-DRG 416, Septicemia, Adult Patients. Six Month Sample, 10/1/94–3/31/95; AMAS and Transfers to Other Hospitals Excluded.

## USING APR-DRGs FOR MANAGED CARE

GSCH participates in many health maintenance organization (HMO) and preferred provider organization (PPO) arrangements. Most of the managed care payment rates are given as per diems or per-case amounts; however, in preparation for capitated contracts, the hospital is developing a physician-hospital organization (PHO). Specific applications of APR-DRGs for managed care are covered in the following sections.

### A Case Study in Managed Care Contracting

A managed care company with significant volume approached the hospital requesting a reduction in rates. Specifically, the company had targeted this reduction to an amount that they perceived was the rate being offered by GSCH to other managed care companies. GSCH perceived that patients belonging to this particular plan were more resource intensive than the patients of other plans and thus commenced a major project to quantify this perception and bring the issue to the negotiating table.

Quantification of differences in the relative costliness of a specific hospital's patient mix is computed using case mix indices. To date, the available indices are the Medicare DRGs and those of several state Medicaid programs that use AP-DRGs; however, these indices do not completely and uniformly adjust for differences in resource intensity attributable to severity of illness.

GSCH's initial analysis resulted in a profile of the managed care population under negotiation that showed significant differences in base APR-DRGs and severity subclasses; however, in the absence of a weighting factor, no quantitative conclusions could be reached. GSCH contacted the 3M-HIS research and development (R&D) staff to investigate how APR-DRGs could be used to support managed care contract negotiations. The R&D staff referred GSCH to the use of APR-DRG normative data. These norms were developed using the APR-DRG grouping methodology *and* Universal Bill 82 (UB-82) data, which contains statistics for length of stay, mortality, total charges, and charges by revenue center. The norms represent a geographically disperse sample of over 375 hospitals with approximately 3,850,000 discharges. The sample contains data from teaching and nonteaching hospitals, both urban and rural locations, and both Medicare and non-Medicare patients. Charge data are adjusted for regional wage differences. Exhibit 30–2 provides a listing of available elements from the normative data set.

In order to quantify the perception of difference, relative weights had to be calculated. The mechanics of calculating weights is open to negotiation. The data provided by 3M/HIS does not contain a weight; as discussed previously, the case count, length of stay, and charges are provided for each occurrence in the file. Therefore, weights can be developed through a mutually agreed-upon algorithm. Potentially, other data from either the hospital or the managed care plan could be merged with the data to calculate specific reimbursement weights. In this instance, it was agreed to use the 3M/HIS data exclusively. The weights for extreme low-volume case types were not identified as an issue as they would be in a federal- or state-mandated reimbursement method.

Table 30–1 illustrates how the normative charge data for APR-DRGs can be converted into relative weights that are sensitive to case mix (i.e., mix of base APR-DRGs) *and* severity. Table 30–2 computes an index for a single APR-DRG. Computation of the weighted average of all relative weights for specific APR-DRGs *and* severity levels results in an APR-DRG/severity index. The

**Exhibit 30–2** APR-DRG Normative Data Set

---

For specific severity subclasses within APR-DRGs, the following data are provided:

**TOTAL PATIENTS**

- Count
- ALOS
- Deaths
- Average Total Charges per Case*
- Low Trim Point
- High Trim Point

**INLIERS**

- Count
- ALOS
- Average Total Charges per Case*
- Average Charges per Case by UB Revenue Code, ex., Pharmacy, Lab & Lab Path, O.R., ICU/CCU, etc.

**LOW TRIM OUTLIERS**

**HIGH TRIM OUTLIERS**

- Count
- ALOS
- Average Total Charges per Case

*Can be used to calculate relative weights.

---

index was calculated for the specific managed care plan under negotiation as well as the aggregated index of all other plans.

The analytical result was a finding that the managed care plan's weighted average APR-DRG/severity index was 1.048, whereas the average for the other plans was .88. This difference translated into a 19.1 percent difference in resource intensity, which was acknowledged by the company as significant.

**Table 30–1** Converting APR-DRG Charge Data into Relative Weights

| APR-DRG 127, CHF | Inlier avg. total charges ($) | Inlier avg. total charges across all APR-DRGs ($) | APR-DRG relative weight |
|---|---|---|---|
| No/minor severity | 5,846 | 8,759 | 0.6674 |
| Moderate severity | 7,500 | 8,759 | 0.8562 |
| Major severity | 10,658 | 8,759 | 1.2167 |
| Extreme severity | 18,084 | 8,759 | 2.0645 |

The negotiations concluded with new rates that reflected the historical case intensity of the plan's patient population. Inasmuch as the calculations have a credible base and can be reproduced and audited, it was further agreed that the sum of annual payments would be subject to a settlement adjusting for actual case mix results.

GSCH plans to extend the use of this adjustment methodology to capitation calculations for its PHO. There are two opportunities for use. The first is to index the capitation received from a managed care plan as a method of reducing the risk assumed. As a managed care plan enters into capitation arrangements with integrated providers, the marketing incentives for the plan change; that is, the plan could market to higher risk patients than it would otherwise be inclined to market to. Formula-based adjustments should be the subject of negotiations between the two parties, thereby retaining proper alignment of responsibility for actions taken.

**Table 30–2** Using APR-DRG Relative Weights To Compute a DRG/Severity Index for APR-DRG 127, Congestive Heart Failure

| | Cases | % of total | Relative weight |
|---|---|---|---|
| No/minor severity | 86 | 18 | 0.6674 |
| Moderate severity | 232 | 47 | 0.8562 |
| Major severity | 112 | 23 | 1.2167 |
| Extreme severity | 59 | 12 | 2.0645 |
| Total APR-DRG 127 | 489 | 100 | 1.0514 |

Second, the adjustment methodology can be used to distribute risk pools within the PHO. Clearly, a PHO with more than one hospital in its equity organization could use case mix based formulas to distribute dollars. In addition, such formulas could be used in the algorithms for distributing profits and losses between hospital and physician pools. For instance, actual versus budgeted patient days per thousand population is commonly used in the formula. An index specific to length of stay could be applied to normalize the actual versus budgeted calculation.

This study is presented as demonstrating one method of building objective equity into a traditional managed care contract and potentially building protection from risk into a capitation contract.

## Physician Profiling for the PHO

In the D.C. area, Blue Cross/Blue Shield of the National Capital Area already has implemented physician profiling as the basis for selecting physicians to participate in their Select Preferred Provider Plan. Their computer-based system "Pro/File" is a powerful relational database that screens physicians in terms of various measures of resource consumption for an episode of care. Examples of the latter include the frequency with which physicians order diagnostic tests and refer patients, their average charge per episode (physician office *and* hospital), how they code and charge for visits, and how often their patients change physicians. Ronald M. Klar, a physician-consultant who developed the software, said in an interview, "Our research reveals that physicians differ markedly in their styles and patterns of practice, the consequences of which impact both the cost and quality of their patients' care. Physician evaluation and selection based on their performance has the promise of decreasing reliance on micromanagement or benefit cutbacks and the prospect for greater overall savings and acceptance."[1]

Over the last seven years, Greater Southeast has provided to physicians highly accurate and reliable data that measures resource utilization. The data set is fully adjusted for relevant characteristics of the patient population in order to ensure that practices treating more complex, sicker, and/or older patients will be fairly compared with their peers.

The PHO Steering Committee, composed of 10 physicians, supported the concept of focusing on patterns of care. After detailed review of available data and analytic methodology, they approved the creation of a profiling mechanism to select primary care physicians (PCPs). In addition, the committee uses a separate evaluation of utilization and quality issues that are identified by the hospital's Health Care Review Department.

APR-DRG data serve as the foundation for this profiling mechanism. Specific components are summarized as follows:

- All cases that qualify for analysis are classified into their respective APR-DRGs.
- Using the normative data described in the previous section (refer again to Table 30–1), outliers are defined using APR-DRG–specific high trim points (severity 4 only) and are excluded from analysis.
- Using the normative data, internal utilization statistics are adjusted for APR-DRG mix *and* severity. APR-DRG–specific relative weights are tabulated into an APR-DRG/severity index.

The practice pattern of a solo practitioner or an interdependent group is analyzed during a defined time period. Decision rules were established to ensure fair and accurate assessment; for example, excluding major service transfers (e.g., transfer of a surgical case to PCP) and excluding cases that did not receive the full course of treatment (e.g., transfer to another hospital). A sufficient number of observations must be included to ensure that differences are not due to chance; therefore, low-volume practices are evaluated on a case-by-case basis. APR-DRG/severity-adjusted average length of stay (ALOS), APR-DRG/severity-adjusted routine ancillary cost per case, and Medicare PPS case mix adjusted ALOS variance (as compared with the national case mix adjusted average) were selected as the basis for evaluating resource utilization. For these three statistics, the practice receives separate percentile rankings (low percentile equates with efficient performance) that are also accumulated into a final overall ranking. The percentage of excluded outliers is noted. If a practice has a high percentage of outliers, these cases are reviewed by the Health Care Review Department. Another set of statistics that are noted but not currently used in the evaluation focus on use of consultants (average # per case; % cases managed without consults; % cases with three or more consults). A sample profile for two practices is reviewed in Table 30–3. Based on the findings of this analysis, significantly different utilization patterns have been identified.

The Steering Committee believes that physicians who demonstrate a consistent pattern of efficient performance—the "best demonstrated practice"—

**Table 30–3** PCP Practice and Utilization Profiles

*PCP practice profile*

| Practice | # of cases | DRG/sev index | % major/ extreme severity | Average age | % cases age 75+ |
|---|---|---|---|---|---|
| #32 | 33 | 1.3898 | 70 | 79 | 70 |
| #5 | 56 | 1.1666 | 39 | 67 | 38 |

*PCP utilization profile*

| Prac- tice | Adj acute ALOS | %* | Adj anc cost $ | % | PPS LOS var | % | % LOS outlier excl | % |
|---|---|---|---|---|---|---|---|---|
| #32 | 4.45 | 7 | 660 | 17 | 1.92 | 7 | 0 | 1 |
| #5 | 8.37 | 97 | 1,010 | 86 | (3.64) | 97 | 3.6 | 82 |

*Percentile ranking.

will become the leaders in developing practice guidelines. The statistics of these physicians also could be used as internal benchmarks. In addition, physicians in this group would have the potential to be excluded from case-level utilization management, the only requirement being to continue to demonstrate efficient performance based on biannual profiling.

For practices that did not have utilization statistics comparable with the best demonstrated practice but that were not significantly different, these physicians have been invited to join the PHO; however, there will be greater scrutiny of their cases through concurrent utilization management and counseling.

A low number of practices differed significantly from their peers in all key parameters of utilization (defined as equal to or beyond the 75th percentile). In addition, there was consensus with these findings based upon the independent evaluation of the Health Care Review Department. These practices were not initially invited into the PHO; however, the performance of all practices is reevaluated annually.

Regarding selection of specialists, the steering committee is using PCP recommendations generated through a detailed survey process. These physicians also will be profiled for efficient resource utilization.

### Other Applications for Managed Care: Outcomes Assessment

Outcomes assessment at GSCH is based on three major components: (1) external comparative data of relevant peer hospitals; (2) uniform case mix classification, severity, and mortality risk adjustment across internal and external databases; and (3) use of statistical quality control techniques for data analysis. Specifically, GSCH uses external data purchased from D.C. and Maryland, which are programmed in the TRENDSTAR decision support system. This programming includes uniform case mix and risk adjustment using APR-DRGs. Statistical analysis is conducted using another software package, JUSE-QCAS (Japanese Union of Statistical Engineers–Quality Control Assisted Software). A sample study plan for mortality outcomes assessment using APR-DRGs is presented in Exhibit 30–3.

## CONCLUSIONS

The APR-DRGs are an integral component of GSCH's decision support function. The severity data have consistently been shown to be a powerful adjustment for explaining differences in resource utilization, and the mortality risk adjustment promises to offer similar explanatory power for mortality outcomes assessment. Having the opportunity to critically evaluate all components of the logic has proven to be a key factor in the medical staff's acceptance of these data to profile practice patterns.

---

**Exhibit 30–3** Sample Mortality Assessment, APR-DRG 1, Craniotomy for Intracranial Hemorrhage

- Compute an "expected mortality," i.e., the mortality rate that would have occurred if GSCH's specific proportion of risk subclasses within APR-DRG 1 had been treated by a relevant peer group of hospitals.
- Benchmark clinical practice for those hospitals with the lowest mortality rates in subclass 4 for APR-DRG 1.

The value of automated severity data relates not only to its low cost to hospitals (i.e., no additional full-time equivalents) but also in having the ability to group historic data easily for trend analysis. Hospitals could also assign APR values in real time through a properly configured concurrent medical record abstracting function. The benefit-to-cost ratio of these data is significant.

---

**NOTE**

1. J.K. Iglehart, "The New England Journal of Medicine: Excerpts on Physician Profiling," *New England Journal of Medicine* 327, no. 10 (1992): 742–747.

# CHAPTER 31

# Physician Profiling in Seattle: A Case Study

*Gregg Bennett, William McKee, and Laura Kilberg*

In response to anticipated changes in major reimbursement systems, many managed care and hospital administrators are interested in pursuing approaches to sharing physician-specific information with their medical staffs. Many of these executives believe that information sharing can be a useful tool to improve length of stay (LOS) and ancillary resource use. These improvements would lead to better financial performance and higher quality care under per-case and per-capita payment systems.

Generally, health care managers have been reluctant to share information with their medical staffs for a variety of rational and irrational reasons. There have been conflicting financial incentives and signals, especially for hospitals, regarding whether improvements in resource use are desired. Certainly, for Medicare inpatient services, which have been paid for a decade on a diagnosis-related group (DRG) basis, there are strong financial incentives for hospitals to maximize resource use. However, in most hospital settings, a larger portion of inpatient care is paid on a per-diem or percentage-of-charges basis, providing a different set of financial incentives.

Providence Medical Center (PMC) in Seattle reduced its LOS from 5.3 days to 4.8 days in one year (from 1991 to 1992) as a direct result of

*Source*: Adapted from F. Bennett, W. McKee, and L. Kilberg, "Case Study in Physician Profiling," *Managed Care Quarterly*, Vol. 2, No. 4, pp. 60–70, Aspen Publishers, Inc., © 1994.

information sharing with its medical staff. This produced a reduction in inpatient days of more than 7,700, or about 10 percent, in just one year.

PMC is a 400-bed teaching hospital with a full range of tertiary services, including a major cardiovascular program. It is one of five significant tertiary medical centers in the downtown Seattle area. Historically, the hospital has had high levels of uncompensated care and shares medical staff with its largest competitor (Swedish Hospital Medical Center). Although hospital costs at PMC have been relatively low compared with peer-group hospitals, charges have been high because of the uncompensated care load and significant discounts provided to high-volume payers.

In 1989, the hospital attempted to distribute comparative data to its medical staff for educational purposes. Unfortunately, the data were perceived to be incomplete and misleading. There were no severity adjustments, no outlier concepts, and no local benchmarks for comparison purposes. Summary scoring concepts were absent, and no relative ranking was provided to summarize the observations. As is typical of most hospital information systems designed primarily to produce claims and track dollars, the hospital's information systems were no help in developing credible data for clinicians, either retrospectively or concurrently. This failed effort at data sharing with physicians was a significant barrier to physician acceptance of the later effort.

About half of state governments collect final bill images (Universal Bill 82 [UB-82]) from short-term, acute-care general hospitals and make these data public. Washington State is one of them, accumulating approximately 550,000 final bills on an annual basis. This data set provided the opportunity to develop local benchmarks and allowed researchers to make comparisons of hospitals and physicians in a statistically significant manner. The challenge to PMC was how best to develop credible comparative data and distribute them to physicians with minimal internal disruption.

## PREREQUISITES FOR RESOURCE USE REDUCTION EFFORTS

It seems obvious that physicians admit and discharge patients, order tests, and are otherwise responsible for the resource use decisions made for the benefit of an individual patient. Physicians indisputably hold the key to better inpatient cost efficiencies. Missing from resource improvement processes in hospitals have been three essential ingredients. These missing ingredients, graphically shown in Figure 31–1, are as follows:

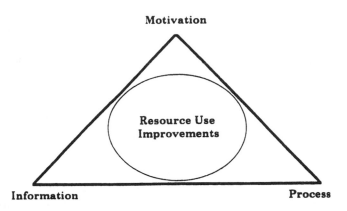

**Figure 31–1** Ingredients Missing from Inpatient Resource Use Improvement Processes. *Source:* Reprinted from *Managed Care Quarterly*, Vol. 2, No. 4, p. 61, Aspen Publishers, Inc., © 1994.

- *Motivation*: In many settings, there are limited motivating factors for hospital managers and practitioners to work toward reducing resource use. Historically, high-resource-use providers have been financially rewarded for inefficient practices. From a hospital standpoint, improved resource use may result in lower payment. From a clinician's standpoint, practice standardization requires time and effort, loss of intellectual independence, and potentially lower payment. Still, in many areas of the nation, neither hospitals nor practitioners are motivated to improve resource use.
- *Information:* Without data, well-informed decisions cannot be made. In most inpatient settings, very poor information is available or distributed at the physician level. Physicians have historically viewed hospital data sharing of physician-specific practice patterns as punitive. Essential tools, such as credible severity adjustments, outlier identification processes, and local benchmarks, have not been available. With little or no comparative data provided to clinicians about their practices, it is understandable that there is wide variation in inpatient practice for essentially the same conditions.
- *Process:* Even when practitioners are motivated and have data, without a structured process, there may be no improvement. The quality

improvement process therefore needs to focus on education rather than isolation, but hospital management processes tend to be top-down in orientation and tend to isolate rather than educate. Hospital managers will accommodate motivated physicians, whether or not that activity is in the organizational plan for the year. Data sharing with physicians can lead to physicians driving resource use improvement efforts. This runs counter to some administrators' need to control management process through budgeted operations plans.

These three essential ingredients came together at PMC to accomplish the rapid reduction in patient days. The reduction was far greater than other local hospitals experienced during the same time period. With subsequent implementation of DRG-based payment and the development of selective physician networks by most of the local payers (in 1993), the hospital was strategically well positioned.

## PHYSICIAN PROFILING COMPONENTS

In order to develop individual physician profiles and share physician-specific information, there are a number of prerequisites. Eight were considered, including severity adjustments, outlier removal, variance calculations, and physician scoring.

### Severity Adjustments

When physicians were queried early in the project, it was clear that a severity-adjustment system was essential to minimize the inevitable "my patients are sicker" argument. The physicians were not particularly concerned with which severity-adjustment system to use but wanted to make sure that a clinically meaningful tool was implemented. For the purpose of this project, 3M all patient refined DRGs (APR-DRGs) were used to assign patients to DRGs and to severity adjust those DRGs. There were 1,450 APR-DRGs, consisting of a DRG and up to four severity levels based on the interactions among the principal and secondary diagnosis.

### Outlier Removal

Because the focus of attention was on transmitting information to physicians, it was necessary to develop and implement a system for identifying and removing patients with very high charges and LOS compared to other patients in the same APR-DRG. Because one or two patients with unusually high resource use might invalidate the analysis at the individual physician level, this was viewed as a very important component of the analysis. In the aggregate, 8 percent of all cases were removed using interquartile variation concepts. In practice, the percentage of patients identified as outliers had very little impact on an individual physician profile. High-resource-use physicians were consistently high regardless of how the outlier cutoffs were defined.

### Regional Benchmarks

After outliers were removed, inliers were used to develop regional benchmarks. For the purpose of this project, two regional benchmarks were developed for each APR-DRG. The first was for LOS, and the second was for average charges.

### Variance Calculations

For each patient in the regional discharge data set, two variances were calculated, one for LOS and one for charges. For example, the average LOS for a low-severity routine vaginal delivery (APR-DRG 372.1) was 1.72 for all 40,000 inlier cases for 1992. If a patient had an LOS of two days, the LOS variance was +0.28 days (2 − 1.72). Variances were defined as the difference between expected and observed values, based on the average for inlier patients within the region as determined by the patient's APR-DRG.

### Service Line Identification

APR-DRGs were grouped into specialty service lines, closely approximating the hospital medical staff structure. For example, there were 40 APR-DRGs that composed the obstetrics service line, including vaginal deliveries and cesarean sections at all severity levels. These service lines served as the universe for discussing observations with medical staff departments. Most APR-DRGs fit reasonably well within a service line. Back surgeries were the largest area of overlap between two hospital departments (orthopedic surgery and neurosurgery).

## Variance Roll-ups by Physician

Variances were summarized and calculated for individual physicians in the aggregate within their service lines of practice. Values were calculated per admission and per case mix adjusted and severity-adjusted admission. One fault with previous data-sharing efforts by the hospital was the distribution of data at the DRG level without severity adjustments. The initial focus for this effort with individual physicians was at the aggregate level. The aggregate level, with many cases averaged together, was a more compelling statistic to obtain physician interest and attention.

## Specialty Peer-Group Comparisons

Physicians were compared to other physicians, both within PMC and across the state within their specialty areas or service lines. In the development of specialty peer groups, discharge volume thresholds were used as the sole inclusion criteria. As an example, physicians with high volumes of obstetrical cases (greater than 25 during the year) were included in the obstetrics peer group. Thus, obstetricians as well as specific family practitioners and general practitioners were all assigned to the obstetrics peer group. This also allowed physicians to be included in multiple peer groups; in fact, it was not uncommon for an individual physician to be included in four or more peer groups. This was most common with high-volume internists, who might be included in cardiology, pulmonology, gastroenterology, oncology, and other medicine peer groups.

## Physician Scoring

A mechanism was needed to convey quickly to individual physicians their resource use ranking compared with their peers across the state. By comparing LOS and charges on a case mix adjusted and severity-adjusted basis for high-volume physicians within a service line across the state, percentile rankings were assigned to each physician.

For example, the 1992 Washington State Cardiology Peer Group consisted of 390 physicians each of whom was identified as the attending physician for more than 25 cardiology-DRG patients. These 390 physicians were rank ordered by their LOS and charge experiences on a case mix adjusted and severity-adjusted basis (with outliers removed), and a percentile ranking was assigned. A percentile ranking of 25 percent indicated that a physician was at the 25th percentile of resource use compared to statewide peers in cardiology. Twenty-five percent of peer physicians had lower resource-use profiles. An example of physician scores for a group of cardiologists is shown in Table 31–1.

According to a physician focus group established to help in developing a presentation format, there were four comparison groups against whom an individual physician desired to be benchmarked:

- peer group physicians at the hospital(s) where they practice
- peer group physicians who practice in the local competitive area
- peer group physicians who practice in the geographic region
- all peer group physicians in the state

**Table 31–1** Cardiologists' PIRS*

| Physician | PIRS | Admits | Case mix | Charge index | Per day index |
|-----------|------|--------|----------|--------------|---------------|
| Phys A | 1% | 28 | 0.97 | 0.89 | 0.71 |
| Phys B | 4% | 100 | 1.17 | 0.93 | 0.99 |
| Phys C | 7% | 39 | 0.95 | 0.96 | 0.74 |
| Phys D | 9% | 87 | 1.01 | 1.06 | 1.00 |
| Phys E | 20% | 38 | 1.20 | 1.15 | 1.01 |
| Phys F | 23% | 26 | 0.97 | 0.99 | 0.93 |
| Phys G | 58% | 83 | 0.97 | 1.16 | 1.09 |
| Phys H | 77% | 62 | 1.04 | 1.12 | 1.10 |
| Phys I | 85% | 50 | 0.79 | 1.29 | 1.25 |
| Phys J | 89% | 36 | 0.94 | 1.15 | 1.21 |
| Phys K | 90% | 93 | 0.98 | 1.25 | 1.12 |
| Phys L | 95% | 32 | 0.87 | 1.18 | 1.31 |
| Phys M | 97% | 27 | 0.75 | 1.24 | 1.25 |
| Phys N | 98% | 50 | 0.96 | 1.23 | 1.07 |

*PIRS (Physician Inpatient Resource Scores) represent percentile ranking within peer group across the state. High scores suggest higher resource use. In addition, index = actual/expected (case mix and severity adjusted).

*Source*: Reprinted from *Managed Care Quarterly*, Vol. 2, No. 4, p. 64, Aspen Publishers, Inc., © 1994.

Percentile rankings provided a convenient and easily conveyed mechanism to communicate these comparisons.

## INFORMATION DISTRIBUTION

With comparative data, it was a challenge deciding how best to communicate the information to individual physicians. A structured process was developed in advance of implementation.

Where possible, summary information was presented visually and in color. Specialty summaries by physician, without individual physician labels, were especially effective. The emphasis of these presentations was on the range of observations between the low- and high-resource-use physicians. Specifically avoided were discussions or inferences of "good" or "bad" practitioners or resource use, because the data did not include quality indicators.

Several goals were identified, including improved quality, lower cost, better strategic positioning in the market, and increased physician participation in clinical pathway development. Because of relatively high LOS at PMC compared with other hospitals across the state, the immediate focus was to reduce LOS significantly. All other downtown Seattle area hospitals also had high LOS compared to statewide benchmarks. It was reiterated at this stage that it was in the short- and long-term interest of the hospital and its physicians to reduce resource use and that there was no fault to be ascribed for the current situation. LOS reduction was easily conveyed, was easily measured, and was very clear in its message.

In anticipation of hospital staff and physician requests for more data, specific staff members were identified as project support personnel. The project team thought the best internal location for both the project and supporting personnel was within the office of the medical director and the quality management department. The department committed a half-time person to the information dissemination effort.

Members of the project team shared anecdotes on how destructive cross-physician data sharing could be in a hospital. It was strongly believed that physician-specific data were to be made available only to individual physicians and department leaders. Physician-specific data were specifically not made available to physician colleagues. Curiously, one medical department (psychiatry) unanimously voted to share information among its staff—and did so.

## ENGAGING MANAGEMENT AND MEDICAL STAFF SUPPORT

Senior managers were very supportive of this project. There were many times throughout the study when physicians had means to discredit the effort, particularly those who had high resource use profiles; however, management support was unwavering.

To develop a critical understanding of the methods used to analyze resource use, inservice education was provided to all senior and department managers in the hospital. They were expected to help identify specific areas for improvement. By the time information was shared with physicians, management and medical staff shared a common language with which to communicate on resource use issues. There was also an understanding of common concepts and vocabulary; for example, patient day variances for DRG 209/ Severity Level 1 had a specific meaning.

Early in the project, an overview presentation was made to the entire medical staff at one of the scheduled quarterly meetings. A complete review of the overall methodology and an assessment of how the hospital compared with other hospitals in the area were presented from an unbiased third-party perspective. A particularly effective technique was to present data for competing hospitals as an example during the methodology discussion. Physicians were interested in these comparative data and were not preoccupied with rationalizing potential high-resource-use in their own specialty areas.

For each of the medical staff departments, a tailored presentation was developed that summarized department activity by DRG and by physician compared with regional benchmarks. These tailored presentations included

- concepts and methodology
- hospital overview by service line
- department summary by APR-DRG
- competing hospital benchmarks by APR-DRG
- anonymous resource use variation by physician

Receptive departments were scheduled first. Receptivity was predicted by the support of key department members and the high- or low-resource-use profiles of the department leaders. Almost all of the presentations were productive, were unemotional, and lasted approximately an hour and a half. Physicians were able to identify a number of reasons why the department appeared better or worse than other departments in other area hospitals.

It was important to convey to practitioners that there should be no quality implications from this profiling effort. However, they were also reminded that in the absence of reasonable quality measures, payers would have difficulty justifying higher payments to providers claiming higher quality without substantiation.

Distinctly different receptivity and levels of interest of different medical staff departments were observed. At the risk of generalizing beyond the known cases, surgeons, for example, tended to want to know conclusions and implications. For such departments, the overall methodology was abbreviated, and more effort was put into showing ranges of resource use across physicians within the same APR-DRG.

In contrast, medical specialties wanted to feel comfortable about the methodology, especially severity adjustments, before they would acknowledge conclusions or implications. For these departments, many more slides were included in the presentation that statistically supported the APR-DRG grouping methodology, with specific examples as to how severity levels were determined for specific patients. Medical specialties were more likely to fall back to the "my last patient" line of argument. They would try to relate the overall methodology to their last complex patients to see whether it made sense.

Oncologists and cardiologists, on the other hand, were preoccupied—sometimes to a fault—with statistical significance. As such, those presentations had many more statistically oriented slides, and there was much less time to discuss ranges in physician resource use.

One of the major goals of these meetings was to make certain there was an appreciation for the range of resource use observations across hospitals at the individual physician level. It was typical to show a 30-percent to 40-percent variance in LOS and resource use on a case mix adjusted and severity-adjusted basis, even within the same APR-DRG. The presenters described how the data were generally publicly available and posed the question: how did practitioners think insurers use these data? This line of questioning proved very effective in overcoming methodological objections, because this type of data was, in most cases, the only source of comprehensive profiling information relating to specialists that is available to the major payers.

Physicians were often surprised at the variance and at a loss to explain why there should be such a wide range. Generally, physicians at the low and high end of the resource use scales were quickly identified on the blinded charts by the physicians in attendance. Peers tended to know how individual peers practiced on the resource use scale.

An example of a particularly effective visual display is shown in Figure 31–2. Each physician is designated by a separate "bubble," with the size of the bubble representing the relative number of discharges. The charge and LOS indices are benchmarked at the regional average on a case mix adjusted and severity-adjusted basis. An LOS index of 1.1 would indicate LOSs were 10 percent more than expected after taking into consideration the case mix and severity of the underlying patients (excluding outliers). As expected, there were strong relationships between LOS and charge indexes.

## PHYSICIAN PROFILE FEEDBACK AND COUNSELING

At the end of the department meetings, each physician received a detailed 30- to 40-page physician profile comparing his or her practice (adjusted for case mix and severity) with that of peers. This profile included detailed patient listings, color charts, and a series of reports that summarized total practitioner activity and activity with outliers removed. This profile was

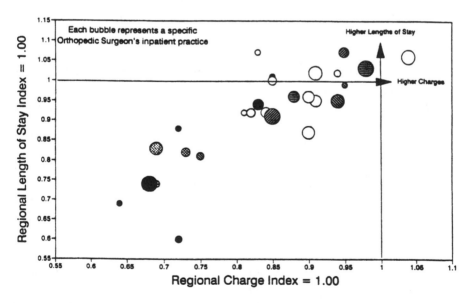

**Figure 31–2** Orthopedic Surgeons' LOS Index versus Charge Index. *Source:* Reprinted from *Managed Care Quarterly*, Vol. 2, No. 4, p. 65, Aspen Publishers, Inc., © 1994.

designed by a work group of generalists and specialists and was constructed to be interpreted and understood by clinicians within a 15-minute sitting, without the need for an education session. These individual, hard-copy physician profiles were an effective communication tool. The basic sections of the distributed profile included the following elements:

- *Transmittal.* This section described the data source and general methodologies and asked physicians to identify any errors they could find in the underlying data.
- *Executive summary.* This was a factual narrative summary of the overall profile and included sections for discharges, case mix/severity adjustments, inliers, patient day variances, charge variances, peer comparisons, and percentile rankings for the individual physician's specialty. Also included were summary color-chart comparisons of the individual physician's practice compared with that of peers within the hospital, peers in the area, peers in the region, and peers across the state. Separate charts were provided for charges and patient days.
- *Peer comparisons.* This section provided tables of percentile rankings of physicians in the area, with the individual physician highlighted. This gave physicians an opportunity to see how they compared with their local peers outside the hospital.
- *Discharge listing and summary.* To provide comfort to skeptical clinicians and demonstrate that the patients being summarized and attributed to a specific physician were authentic, a detailed patient listing was provided.
- *Variance analysis.* This section was summarized by service line and by APR-DRG. If there were high or low rankings, the physician could easily see which areas seemed to be the proximate cause.
- *Appendixes.* These included much more detail on methodology, severity adjustment methodology, and peer-group rankings for the entire region.

Armed with these profiles, the physicians had a number of questions and requests for more detailed data to support their profiles. These questions were addressed by the quality management department on a real-time basis, using microcomputer technology. Most physician requests were efforts to rationalize high resource use; however, in almost all cases, the additional requests were unable to further explain high-resource-use profiles.

Abbreviated feedback was provided on a semiannual basis to individual physicians. Detailed profiles continue to be provided annually. When data systems and data availability improve, it is expected that physician feedback will be provided quarterly, about two months after the end of each quarter.

## RESULTS

As shown in Figure 31–3, the case mix indices of each service line were very similar from 1991 to 1992. These case mix indices were developed using statewide average charges for each APR-DRG. There were separate case weights for each of the 1,450 APR-DRGs. The average of the case weights for all patients within a service line was the case mix index for the service line. The observation of minimal changes in case mix by department was confirmed with key medical staff.

Although the case mix indices of each of the service lines essentially remained unchanged, there were sharp reductions in LOS. This is shown in Figure 31–4. In orthopedics, for example, there was a 1.3-day decrease in LOS. This was attributed to a number of factors, but perhaps the most impor-

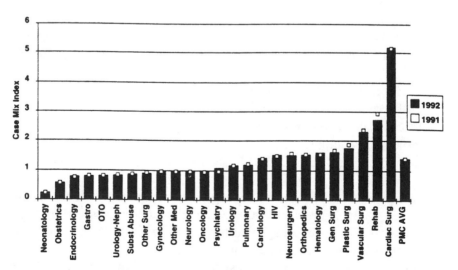

**Figure 31–3** Case Mix Index, 1991 and 1992. *Source:* Reprinted from *Managed Care Quarterly*, Vol. 2, No. 4, p. 66, Aspen Publishers, Inc., © 1994.

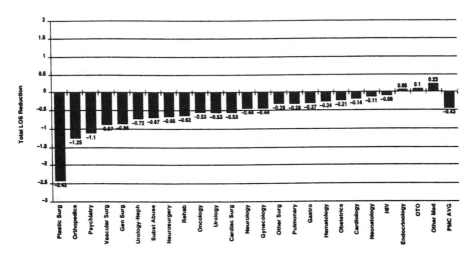

**Figure 31–4** 1992 LOS Reduction: 1992 versus 1991. *Source:* Reprinted from *Managed Care Quarterly*, Vol. 2, No. 4, p. 68, Aspen Publishers, Inc., © 1994.

tant was that physicians were motivated to work with the hospital to discharge patients faster and to communicate more fully with their patients about discharge timing expectations. The hospital's LOS dropped from 7 days for DRG 209 (total joint replacement, hips and knees) to 5 days in less than a year.

With orthopedic surgeons' active assistance, a number of differences in physician care routines for these cases were documented. These included:

- 13 different physical therapy orders
- 8 different prophylactic antibiotics
- different social work referrals and discharge planning
- variation in equipment use
- variation in occupational and physical therapy use

With support from the quality management department, which identified and worked to develop more standardized treatment protocols, a clinical pathway was developed. The hospital estimates it saved $500,000 alone from these improvements over the one-year period.

The overall patient-day savings by service line are shown in Table 31–2 and Figure 31–5. Overall, there was a reduction of about 7,700 patient days from 1991 to 1992 after volume and case mix adjustments.

**Table 31–2** 1992 Patient Day "Savings"

| Service line | 1991 LOS | 1992 LOS | Variance | 1992 admits | Patient day savings |
|---|---|---|---|---|---|
| Cardiovascular | 9.3 | 8.8 | −0.5 | 2,055 | −1,089 |
| Cardiology | 3.3 | 3.2 | −0.1 | 1,058 | −148 |
| Endocrinology | 4.8 | 4.9 | 0.1 | 218 | 13 |
| Gastroenterology | 4.3 | 4.0 | −0.3 | 716 | −193 |
| General surgery | 6.6 | 5.7 | −0.9 | 1,094 | −941 |
| Gynecology | 3.9 | 3.5 | −0.4 | 364 | −160 |
| Hematology | 7.7 | 7.5 | −0.2 | 96 | −23 |
| Human immunovirus | 7.2 | 7.1 | −0.1 | 158 | −13 |
| Neonatology | 2.2 | 2.1 | −0.1 | 1,426 | −157 |
| Neurology | 5.7 | 5.3 | −0.4 | 499 | −220 |
| Neurosurgery | 5.1 | 4.4 | −0.7 | 594 | −386 |
| Obstetrics | 2.6 | 2.4 | −0.2 | 1,608 | −338 |
| Oncology | 5.1 | 4.6 | −0.5 | 423 | −224 |
| Orthopedics | 5.7 | 4.4 | −1.3 | 1,371 | −1,714 |
| Other medicine | 5.3 | 5.5 | 0.2 | 347 | 80 |
| Other surgery | 5.2 | 4.9 | −0.3 | 170 | −49 |
| Otolaryngology | 1.5 | 1.6 | 0.1 | 290 | 29 |
| Plastic surgery | 10.2 | 7.8 | −2.4 | 69 | −167 |
| Psychiatry | 11.5 | 10.4 | −1.1 | 889 | −978 |
| Pulmonary medicine | 5.8 | 5.5 | −0.3 | 726 | −203 |
| Rehabilitation | 13.7 | 13.1 | −0.6 | 296 | −184 |
| Substance abuse | 6.0 | 5.3 | −0.7 | 32 | −21 |
| Urology | 4.4 | 3.9 | −0.5 | 313 | −166 |
| Urology-nephrology | 5.0 | 4.3 | −0.7 | 169 | −122 |
| Vascular surgery | 6.4 | 5.5 | −0.9 | 408 | −355 |
| Total | 5.3 | 4.8 | −0.5 | 15,389 | −7,729 |

*Source:* 1991 and 1992 PIRAMED Hospital Profile.

*Source:* Reprinted from *Managed Care Quarterly,* Vol. 2, No. 4, p. 69, Aspen Publishers, Inc., © 1994.

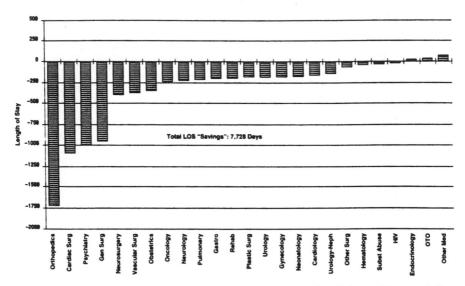

**Figure 31–5** 1992 Patient Day "Savings." *Source:* Reprinted from *Managed Care Quarterly*, Vol. 2, No. 4, p. 68, Aspen Publishers, Inc., © 1994.

## DISCUSSION

Hospital management views this project as a resounding success. The hospital continues to reduce LOS and resource use at a rate higher than its local competitors.

In retrospect, there were a number of additional key factors that contributed to the success of the project. Without question, the sharing of comparison information on a physician-specific basis was the proximate cause of much of the LOS reduction. The strongest motivation and interest for improvement by physicians was from the high end of the resource use scale. These physicians became genuinely interested in their profiles and actively sought additional data.

Confidential data sharing minimized the potential for medical staff disruption. If physicians wanted to share information with each other, they were free to do so; however, data dissemination policies were and continue to be rigidly enforced.

Physicians who were unable to change their high-resource-use practice profiles received a confidential request to meet with the medical director. There were nine physicians who received such a notice, all of whom met with the medical director. In almost all cases, these meetings were productive and led to subsequent behavioral changes.

Because purchasers of care have access to similar data, physicians were encouraged to know what other parties might know and conclude about their practices. Purchasers typically have little or no data beyond those that are available to them from claims. Part of the success of this project was probably due to the demonstration that purchasers could undertake the same type of analysis, would most likely create the same type of information, and could reasonably draw similar conclusions as to the low- and high-cost physicians.

An important perspective for the project team was joint hospital-physician responsibility for resource use issues. Physicians were very skilled at identifying institutional delays in discharging patients. Where possible, the hospital quickly made changes to remove these barriers. Perhaps hospital managers' commitment to this effort was best demonstrated by how fast barriers were overcome, once identified.

## CONCLUSIONS

Although some physician groups showed more interest in and denoted more effort to reducing resource use than others, virtually all areas of the hospital showed significant patient-day reductions, even areas that showed very little apparent interest during the project. This suggests evidence of an emerging culture within the organization that better positions both physicians and the hospital for the at-risk payment environment.

CHAPTER 32

# The Evolution of Case Mix Measurement Using Diagnosis-related Groups

*Richard F. Averill, John H. Muldoon, James C. Vertrees,*
*Norbert I. Goldfield, Robert L. Mullin, Elizabeth C. Fineran,*
*Mona Z. Zhang, Barbara Steinbeck, and Thelma Grant*

The diagnosis-related groups (DRGs) constitute a patient classification scheme originally developed as a means of relating the type of patients a hospital treats (i.e., its case mix) to the costs incurred by the hospital. The design and development of the DRGs began in the late 1960s at Yale University.[1] The initial motivation for developing the DRGs was to create an effective framework for monitoring the utilization of services in a hospital setting. The first large-scale application of the DRGs was in the late 1970s in the state of New Jersey. The New Jersey State Department of Health used DRGs as the basis of a prospective payment system (PPS) in which hospitals were paid a fixed DRG-specific amount for each patient treated. In 1983 Congress enacted a DRG-based PPS for all Medicare patients. Subsequent to the enactment of the Medicare PPS, a number of states and large payers implemented DRG-based hospital PPSs for non-Medicare patients. In addition, DRGs have been used as the basis of global budget allocation and payment in several countries in Western and Eastern Europe as well as Australia.

The evolution of the DRGs and their use as the basic unit of payment in Medicare's hospital reimbursement system represent a recognition of the fundamental role that a hospital's case mix plays in determining its costs. Although the concept of case mix may appear straightforward, clinicians, administrators, and regulators have attached different meanings to it. *Case*

---

Courtesy of 3M Health Information Systems, Wallingford, Connecticut.

391

*mix* has been used to refer to an interrelated but distinct set of patient attributes that include severity of illness, risk of dying, prognosis, treatment difficulty, need for intervention, and resource intensity. When clinicians use *case mix*, they typically are referring to one or more aspects of clinical complexity. For clinicians, *complex case mix* refers to greater severity of illness, greater risk of mortality, greater treatment difficulty, poorer prognoses and/or a greater need for intervention. Thus, from a clinical perspective, *case mix* refers to the condition of the patients treated and the treatment difficulty associated with providing care. On the other hand, administrators and regulators usually use the concept of case mix to indicate that the patients treated require more resources, which results in a higher cost of providing care. Thus, from an administrative or regulatory perspective, *case mix* refers to the resource intensity demands that patients place on an institution. While the two interpretations of *case mix* are often closely related, they can be very different for certain kinds of patients. For example, while terminal cancer patients are severely ill and have a poor prognosis, they require few hospital resources beyond basic nursing care.

The original purpose of the DRGs was to relate the case mix of a hospital to the resource demands and associated costs experienced by the hospital. Thus, DRGs focused exclusively on resource intensity. Therefore, a hospital with a complex case mix from a DRG perspective treated patients who required more hospital resources but who did not necessarily have a greater severity of illness, a greater risk of dying, greater treatment difficulty, poorer prognoses, or a greater need for intervention. As the health care industry has evolved, there has been increased demand for a patient classification system that can be used for applications beyond resource use, cost, and payment. In particular, a patient classification system is needed to

- compare hospitals across a wide range of resource and outcome measures
- evaluate differences in inpatient mortality rates
- implement and support critical pathways
- facilitate continuous quality improvement projects
- support internal management and planning systems
- manage capitated payment arrangements

For a DRG system to meet these needs, the objective of the DRG system had to be expanded in scope. In fact, five distinct DRG systems have been developed. This chapter describes and contrasts the five DRG systems and evaluates the performance of each system using a 1993 national sample of patient data that includes 675 general acute care hospitals and a 20-percent sample of patients from 40 free-standing acute children's hospitals.

## DRG SYSTEMS

DRG technology has experienced an evolutionary development process in which the later generations of DRG systems have incorporated the improvements made by earlier generations. The five DRG systems that have been developed are

- Medicare DRGs
- Refined DRGs (RDRGs)
- All Patient DRGs (AP-DRGs)
- Severity DRGs (SDRGs)
- All Patient Refined DRGs (APR-DRGs)

Each of these DRG systems was created to address specific limitations in the original DRGs.

### Medicare DRGs

The initial DRG definitions developed at Yale were intended to describe all the types of patients seen in an acute care hospital. Thus, the DRGs encompassed both the elderly patient population and the newborn, pediatric, and adult populations. However, with the implementation of the Medicare prospective payment system in October 1983, the responsibility for the maintenance and modification of the DRG definitions became the responsibility of the Health Care Financing Administration (HCFA). HCFA updates the Medicare DRGs on an annual basis. The focus of all DRG modifications instituted by HCFA subsequent to 1983 has been on problems relating primarily to the elderly population. Version 12.0 of the Medicare DRGs, effective October 1, 1995, has 492 DRGs and was used in this analysis.[2]

### Refined DRGs

During the mid-1980s the Health Care Financing Administration funded a project at Yale University to revise the use of complications and comorbidities

(CCs) in the Medicare DRGs.[3] In the Medicare DRGs a secondary diagnosis is considered a CC if it causes a significant increase in hospital resource use. For certain types of patients, a different Medicare DRG is assigned depending on whether or not a CC is present. The Yale project mapped all secondary diagnoses that were considered a CC in the Medicare DRGs into 136 secondary diagnosis groups each of which was assigned a CC complexity level. For surgical patients, each secondary diagnosis group was assigned to one of four CC complexity levels (non-CC, moderate CC, major CC, and catastrophic CC). For medical patients, each secondary diagnosis group was assigned to one of three CC complexity levels (non-CC, moderate or major CC, and catastrophic CC). All age splits and CC splits in the Medicare DRGs were eliminated and replaced by the four subgroups for surgical patients or the three subgroups for medical patients. The Yale project did not reevaluate the categorization of secondary diagnosis as a CC versus a non-CC. Only the diagnoses on the standard Medicare CC list were used to create the moderate, major, and catastrophic subgroups. The DRG system developed by the Yale project is referred to as Refined DRGs (RDRGs).

In the RDRGs, all secondary diagnoses in a secondary diagnosis group are assigned the same level, and a patient is assigned to the subgroup corresponding to the highest level secondary diagnosis. Thus, a surgical patient with two moderate CCs and one major CC is assigned to the major CC subgroup. The number of secondary diagnoses has no effect on the subgroup assigned to the patient (i.e., multiple secondary diagnoses at one level do not cause a patient to be assigned to a higher subgroup). Thus, although a surgical patient may have four moderate CCs present, the patient is still assigned to the moderate CC subgroup.

In general, the categorization of the secondary diagnosis groups as moderate, major, or catastrophic was independent of the DRG to which the patient was assigned. However, in a limited number of cases the standard level for a secondary diagnosis group was modified for a specific major diagnosis category (MDC) or RDRG.

For medical patients in each MDC, a separate DRG was created for early deaths primarily as a means of identifying patients admitted for terminal care. Early death DRGs were not created for surgical patients, since patients admitted for terminal care would normally not have surgery performed. Early deaths were defined as patients who died within two days of admission. Thus, length of stay as well as death was used to assign the RDRG.

There is no central source for RDRGs, and several vendors produce versions of RDRGs. The RDRGs used in this analysis incorporated all changes in Medicare DRGs through Version 10.0. There are a total of 1,170 RDRGs in Version 10.0 of the RDRGs. There are virtually no differences between Version 10.0 and 12.0 of the Medicare DRGs, and therefore the use of RDRGs updated only through Version 10.0 of the Medicare DRGs has no implications for the study results.

The version of RDRGs used for this analysis was produced by Information Strategies of McGraw Hill, Inc. It is different from the original Yale RDRGs in three ways. First, it retained pediatric age splits for 10 of the 43 Medicare DRGs that have pediatric age spits. Second, instead of attempting to implement complexity subclasses for mental health and substance abuse DRGs, it used pediatric and adult age subgroups for the 3 mental health DRGs with significant case volume. Third, it introduced some further refinements to the complexity subclasses based upon data analysis performed subsequent to the completion of the Yale RDRG study project. Thus, this version of RDRGs follows the original Yale RDRG model, with some updates that its developers felt were improvements along with technical updates to incorporate annual changes to the Medicare DRGs.

## All Patient DRGs

In 1987, the state of New York passed legislation instituting a DRG-based prospective payment system for all non-Medicare patients. The legislation included a requirement that the New York State Department of Health (NYDH) evaluate the applicability of the Medicare DRGs to a non-Medicare population. In particular, the legislation required that the DRGs be evaluated with respect to neonates and patients with human immunodeficiency virus (HIV) infections. The evaluation concluded that the Medicare DRGs were not adequate for a non-Medicare population. NYDH entered into an agreement with 3M Health Information Systems (3M HIS) to research and develop all necessary DRG modifications. The DRG definitions developed by NYDH and 3M HIS are referred to as the All Patient DRGs (AP-DRGs).

During the mid-1980s extensive research had been performed independently by the National Association of Children's Hospitals and Related Institutions (NACHRI) on alternative approaches to improving the DRG categories for neonates and other pediatric patients.[4] The system developed by

NACHRI was called the Pediatric Modified Diagnosis-Related Groups (PM-DRGs). The PM-DRGs created many additional DRGs specifically for neonatal and pediatric patients. As part of the New York DRG evaluation effort, NYDH and 3M HIS examined the NACHRI neonatal definitions and adopted a modified version of them. For example, the neonatal PM-DRG modifications introduced birth weight as a classification variable. In the AP-DRGs, six birth weight categories are used as the primary variable in formulating the neonatal AP-DRGs.

In addition to the changes for the neonatal AP-DRGs, MDC 24 was created for HIV infection patients. Assignment to MDC 24 is based on a principal diagnosis of an HIV infection or a principal diagnosis of an HIV-related complication combined with a secondary diagnosis of an HIV infection (e.g. principal diagnosis of pneumocystosis and a secondary diagnosis of an HIV infection). The initial release of the AP-DRGs in January 1988 included the addition of MDC 24 and the restructuring of the neonatal MDC.

Subsequent updates have made additional enhancements to the AP-DRGs. For example, as demonstrated by the RDRGs, some CCs have a greater impact on hospital resource use than other CCs. The AP-DRGs designate a subset of the CCs as major CCs. These major CCs are similar to the catastrophic CCs in the RDRGs. In order to avoid significantly increasing the number of DRGs, major CC AP-DRGs for surgical patients within an MDC and major CC AP-DRGs for medical patients within an MDC were formed for some MDCs. In total, 60 major CC AP-DRGs were created. As part of the development of the major CC AP-DRGs, a limited reevaluation of the CC list was performed.

The AP-DRGs introduced many other changes to the Medicare DRGs. Some of these primarily affect pediatric patients while others affect patients of all ages. The pediatric modifications include some of the recommendations originally developed by NACHRI as well as other significant modifications. MDC 25 was added for patients with multiple trauma. In addition, significant modifications have been made for transplants, long-term mechanical ventilation patients, cystic fibrosis, nutritional disorders, high-risk obstetric care, acute leukemia, hemophilia, and sickle cell anemia.

Some of the DRG modifications originally developed in the AP-DRGs have subsequently been adopted in the Medicare DRGs. For example, in Version 8.0 of the Medicare DRGs, an HIV infection MDC was added. However, the Medicare HIV infection MDC consists of three DRGs and does not discriminate among HIV infection patients at the level of detail contained in the AP-DRGs.

The AP-DRGs have been updated in January of every year since 1988. Version 12.0 of the AP-DRGs was effective January 1, 1995, and was used in this analysis.[5] There are a total of 641 AP-DRGs in Version 12.0 of the AP-DRGs.

## Severity DRGs

In 1993, HCFA initiated a reevaluation of the use of complications and comorbidities within the Medicare DRGs.[6] The DRG system developed by this reevaluation is referred to as the severity DRGs (SDRGs) (sometimes also referred to as severity refined DRGs [SR-DRGs]). The reevaluation excluded the DRGs associated with pregnancy, newborns, and pediatric patients. The major CC list from the AP-DRGs was used to identify an initial list of major CCs. Using Medicare data, the categorization of each secondary diagnosis as a non-CC, nonmajor CC, or major CC was reevaluated. The end result was that 111 diagnoses that were non-CCs in the Medicare DRGs were made a CC, 220 diagnoses that were a CC were made a non-CC, and 395 CCs were considered a major CC. This evaluation differed from the RDRGs in that both non-CCs and CCs were evaluated and the evaluation was performed independently for each individual diagnosis as opposed to aggregate secondary diagnosis groups.

All CC splits in the Medicare DRGs were eliminated, plus an additional 24 Medicare DRGs were merged together. The resulting base DRGs were then subdivided into three, two, or no subgroups based on an analysis of Medicare data. The result was 84 DRGs with no subgroups, 124 with two subgroups, and 85 with three subgroups. This plus the 63 DRGs not evaluated resulted in a total of 652 SDRGs.

In SDRGs, a patient is assigned to a subgroup corresponding to the highest level secondary diagnosis. Like RDRGs, multiple secondary diagnoses at one level do not cause a patient to be assigned to a higher subgroup. The categorization of a diagnosis as non-CC, nonmajor CC, or major CC is uniform across the SDRGs, and there are no modifications for specific SDRGs. HCFA published the SDRGs in 1994 but did not establish an implementation date. The SDRGs have not been updated by HCFA since the original 1994 release.

## All Patient Refined DRGs

The All Patient Refined DRGs (APR-DRGs) further refine the basic AP-DRG structure by adding four subgroups. In contrast to the SDRGs and RDRGs, the initial version of the APR-DRGs used the AP-DRGs instead of the Medicare DRGs as the base DRGs. The only exception was the neonatal MDC, for which an entirely new set of base DRGs was developed. In subsequent updates of the APR-DRGs the base AP-DRGs have been substantially modified. All age, CC, and major CC distinctions in the AP-DRGs were eliminated and replaced by two sets of four subgroups. One set of subgroups addresses patient differences relating to severity of illness, and the second set addresses risk of mortality. In APR-DRGs, severity of illness is defined as the extent of organ system loss of function or physiologic decompensation, while risk of mortality is the likelihood of dying. Since severity of illness and risk of mortality are distinct patient attributes, separate subgroups are assigned to a patient for severity of illness and risk of mortality. Thus, in the APR-DRG system, a patient is assigned three distinct descriptors:

- the base APR-DRG (e.g., APR-DRG 127—Congestive Heart Failure)
- the severity-of-illness subgroup
- the risk-of-mortality subgroup

The four severity-of-illness subgroups and the four risk-of-mortality subgroups represent minor, moderate, major, or extreme severity of illness or risk of mortality. The assignment of a patient to one of these four subgroups takes into consideration not only the specific secondary diagnoses but also the interaction between the secondary diagnoses, age, the principal diagnosis, and the presence of certain non-OR procedures. The assignment of a patient to a subgroup for each APR-DRG is performed separately for severity of illness and risk of mortality.

The creation of the four levels created the opportunity for a complete reevaluation of the diagnoses categorized as a complication or comorbidity. With the expansion to four subclasses, many non-CC diagnoses could be assigned to at least the moderate level, whereas previously there was not sufficient justification to include them with the heterogeneous set of diagnoses categorized as a CC. As a result of this reevaluation, there were 1,693 diagnoses considered non-CCs in the AP-DRGs and Medicare DRGs that were assigned to the moderate, major, or extreme level in the APR-DRGs. Conversely, 418 secondary diagnoses that are considered CCs were moved to the non-CC (minor) level in the APR-DRGs.

In the APR-DRGs, the assessment of the severity of illness or risk of mortality of a patient is specific to the APR-DRG to which a patient is assigned. In other words, the determination of the severity of illness and risk of mortality is disease specific. The significance attributed to a secondary diagnosis is dependent on the underlying problem. Thus, in APR-DRGs the severity-of-illness or risk-of-mortality level of a secondary diagnosis is assigned separately for each base APR-DRG.

The most important component of determining the final patient subgroup is the recognition of the impact of interactions among secondary diagnoses. In APR-DRGs, high severity of illness or risk of mortality is primarily determined by the interaction of multiple diseases. Patients with multiple diseases involving multiple organ systems constitute the patients who have a more extensive disease process, who are difficult to treat, and who have poor outcomes. In APR-DRGs specific combinations of secondary diagnoses interact, causing the severity-of-illness or risk-of-mortality subgroup to be increased.

The combination of the base APR-DRG and the final patient severity-of-illness and risk-of-mortality subgroups constitutes the complete APR-DRG description of the patient. For applications such as evaluating resource use or establishing patient care guidelines, the APR-DRG in conjunction with the severity-of-illness subgroup is used. For evaluating patient mortality, the APR-DRG in conjunction with the risk-of-mortality subgroup is used.

The subdivision of the 382 base APR-DRGs into the four severity subgroups, combined with the two error APR-DRGs (i.e., 469, 470), results in a total of 1,530 APR-DRGs. The APR-DRGs were a joint development of 3M HIS and NACHRI. The APR-DRGs encompass all the DRG modifications developed for the original PM-DRGs plus all subsequent NACHRI research. APR-DRGs are updated every two years. Version 12.0 of the APR-DRGs was released in September 1995 and was used in this analysis.[7]

## COMPARISON OF THE STRUCTURE OF THE DRG SYSTEMS

Table 32–1 compares the major features of the alternative DRG systems. The five DRG systems differ substantially both with respect to the base DRGs and the subgroups within each base DRG. Base DRG categories can be formed for each DRG system by merging together all CC and age splits. The base DRG categories cannot be formed for AP-DRGs because the major complication and comorbidity groups in the AP-DRGs were created by combining together patients from multiple base DRGs. Thus, in AP-DRGs it was not possible to unambiguously separate out the base DRGs from the secondary diagnosis subgroups. The number of base DRG categories is not substantially different across the DRG systems. The Medicare DRGs, SDRGs, and RDRGs

**Table 32–1** Comparison of the Structure of the DRG Systems

| | Medicare DRGs Version 12.0 | SDRGs | RDRGs Version 10.0 | AP-DRGs Version 12.0 | APR-DRGs Version 12.0 |
|---|---|---|---|---|---|
| Number of base DRG categories | 338 | 316 | 367 | NA | 384 |
| Number of DRGs | 492 | 652 | 1,170 | 641 | 1,530 |
| Multiple trauma MDC | Limited | Limited | Limited | Complete | Complete |
| HIV infection MDC | Limited | Limited | Limited | Complete | Complete |
| Newborn birthweight used | No | No | Limited | Complete | Complete |
| NACHRI pediatric changes | No | No | No | Limited | Complete |
| Major (extreme) CCs | No | Yes | Yes | Yes | Yes |
| Death used in definition | Yes | Yes | Yes | Yes | No |
| LOS used in definition | No | No | Yes | Newborn only | No |
| CC list reevaluated | No | Substantial | No | Limited | Complete |
| Multiple CCs recognized | No | No | No | No | Yes |
| Number of CC subgroups | 2 | 3 | 3 med, 4 surg | 3 | 4 |
| CC subgroup structure | Variable | Variable | Relatively uniform | Variable | Uniform |
| Risk-of-mortality subgroup | No | No | No | No | Yes |
| Base DRGs used | — | Medicare | Medicare | Medicare | AP-DRGs except neonates |

Courtesy of 3M Health Information Systems, Wallingford, Connecticut.

are focused primarily on the Medicare population while the AP-DRGs and APR-DRGs contain extensive modifications for the pediatric and adult populations. The categorization of a secondary diagnosis as a CC or non-CC was originally developed in 1980, when the ICD-9-CM version of the DRGs was created. The Medicare DRGs and RDRGs have not reevaluated the CC list, while to varying degrees the AP-DRGs, SDRGs, and APR-DRGs have reevaluated the CC list. The APR-DRGs are the only DRG system that incorporates the impact of multiple CCs. The number of CC subgroups within a DRG varies by DRG for the Medicare DRGs, SDRGs, and AP-DRGs. The CC subgroup structure for the RDRGs is relatively uniform since, with the exception of a few DRGs, such as the early death DRGs, which have no subgroups, there are always three subgroups for the medical DRGs and four subgroups for the surgical DRGs. The CC subgroup structure in the APR-DRGs is uniform across the DRGs, with all DRGs having four subgroups. A uniform CC subgroup structure facilitates the communication of comparative results to medical staffs. Death is used as a variable for assigning the DRG in all DRG systems except APR-DRGs. The use of death in the definition of the DRG makes the DRG system meaningless for mortality analysis. APR-DRGs are the only DRG system with a separate risk-of-mortality component.

## DATABASE

The database for the study was a calendar year 1993 hospital medical record abstract discharge data set that included 675 acute general hospitals and 40 free-standing acute children's hospitals.[8] The national hospital sample data set used for this study included all the patients from the 675 general hospitals and a 20-percent random sample of patients from the 40 children's hospitals.

The 675 general hospitals were generally representative of acute general hospitals throughout the United States with respect to bed size, teaching status, and urban/rural status, though there was a slight underrepresentation of rural hospitals. The 675 general hospitals included a generally representative number of hospitals from the four Census Bureau regions of the country, with the exception of the Northeast, which was underrepresented. It should be noted that this sample did not include any psychiatric hospitals or rehabilitation hospitals, though some hospitals did have psychiatric units or rehabilitation units. The 40 free-standing children's hospitals included nearly all hospitals identifying themselves as free-standing acute children's hospitals in 1993 (40 of 45).

The charge data was adjusted for area wage differences by applying the HCFA area wage index to the "labor" portion of the charges. HCFA assumes that 71 percent of charges are associated with labor. The wage index–adjusted charge data was converted to an estimate of cost using a hospitalwide ratio of costs to charges (RCCs) from Medicare cost report files. This was done using the Medicare cost report values for allowable operating and capital costs but excluding graduate medical education costs. For children's hospitals, since Medicare cost report data do not routinely exist, similar numbers were obtained from the children's hospitals.

A series of edits were applied to remove from the data patient discharge records that contained incomplete or inaccurate information. The edits eliminate patients with incalculable, invalid, or unreasonable age, length of stay, or charge values. For example, patients with length of stays greater than two years and patients with zero total charges were eliminated from the data. In addition, patients who were transferred to another acute care hospital were eliminated. These patients were eliminated since they represent an incomplete hospital stay. The original database contained 4,987,773 patients. The data quality edits eliminated 404,934 patients, primarily as the result of missing charge information. The exclusion of the transfer patients eliminated an additional 97,745 patients. To ensure a correct proportional representation of children's hospitals, only 20 percent of the patients in the children's hospitals were retained, which reduced the final number of patients in the analysis database to 4,203,646. The analysis also excluded the error DRGs 469 and 470 (in the SDRGs the error DRGs are 651 and 652). The number of patients in the error DRGs differed slightly across the five DRG systems.

## UNTRIMMED $R^2$ RESULTS

The most common statistical measure used to compare patient classification systems is reduction of variance ($R^2$), which measures the proportion of variation that is explained by a DRG system. $R^2$ provides a summary measure of the extent to which a DRG system is able to predict the value of a resource use or outcome variable based on the characteristics of individual patients. For a categorical variable such as DRG, $R^2$ is computed as

$$\frac{\sum_i (y_i - A)^2 - \sum_i (y_i - A_g)^2}{\sum_i (y_i - A)^2}$$

where $y_i$ is the value of the variable (i.e., cost or LOS) for the *ith* patient, $A$ is the average value of the variable in the database, and $A_g$ is the average value of the variable in DRG $g$. The square of the difference between the actual value $(y_i)$ and the predicted value ($A$ or $A_g$) is a measure of the variation in the data. The term

$$\sum_i (y_i - A)^2$$

is the amount of variation before subdividing the data into DRGs, and the term

$$\sum_i (y_i - A_g)^2$$

is the amount of variation after subdividing the data into DRGs. The difference between these two terms is the reduction in variation resulting from the subdivision of the data into DRGs. $R^2$ is the ratio of the reduction in variation to the amount of variation before subdividing into DRGs. $R^2$ ranges between 0 and 1 and measures the fraction of variation explained by the DRGs. Thus, an $R^2$ of 0.415 would mean that subdividing the data into DRGs reduces the amount of variation in the data by 41.5 percent.

For each of the five DRG systems, an $R^2$ for cost and LOS was computed based on untrimmed data. The $R^2$ was computed separately for medical patients, surgical patients, and medical and surgical patients combined. Table 32–2 summarizes the $R^2$ results.

Using cost for all patients, the percentage increases in $R^2$ relative to the Medicare DRGs are 8.1, 13.5, 15.0, and 30.3 percent for SDRGs, RDRGs, AP-DRGs, and APR-DRGs, respectively. The percentage increases in $R^2$ for cost are most dramatic for medical patients, at 10.6, 40.4, 50.7, and 68.9 percent for SDRGs, RDRGs, AP-DRGs, and APR-DRGs, respectively. The APR-DRGs always perform better in terms of $R^2$ than the other DRG systems. For cost, the $R^2$ for surgical and medical patients combined is sometimes higher than for either the surgical or medical patients separately. Since the cost for surgical patients tends to be much higher than for medical patients,

**Table 32–2** Untrimmed $R^2$ for Cost and Length of Stay

| Variable | Patients | Medicare DRGs | SDRGs | RDRGs | AP-DRGs | APR-DRGs |
|---|---|---|---|---|---|---|
| LOS | All | 0.3126 | 0.3439 | 0.3702 | 0.3692 | 0.4213 |
| LOS | Surgical | 0.3254 | 0.3751 | 0.3757 | 0.3665 | 0.4507 |
| LOS | Medical | 0.2878 | 0.3046 | 0.3535 | 0.3583 | 0.3820 |
| Cost | All | 0.4076 | 0.4407 | 0.4627 | 0.4689 | 0.5309 |
| Cost | Surgical | 0.4111 | 0.4506 | 0.4560 | 0.4503 | 0.5218 |
| Cost | Medical | 0.2485 | 0.2748 | 0.3488 | 0.3744 | 0.4196 |

Courtesy of 3M Health Information Systems, Wallingford, Connecticut.

the variation before subdividing into DRGs for surgical and medical patients combined is high. Since the DRGs assign surgical and medical patients to separate groups, the reduction in variation ($R^2$) for surgical and medical patients combined can be higher than either the reduction in variation for medical patients or surgical patients separately.

Any classification system that subdivides data into mutually exclusive groups of patients will exhibit a higher $R^2$ as the number of groups increases. An $R^2$ of 1.0 is achieved if the number of groups equals the number of patients. Since there is a substantial difference in the number of groups in the various DRG systems, it is possible that some of the $R^2$ differences are due to the difference in the number of groups and not due to differences in the performance of the DRG system. The $R^2$ that would be achieved by randomly splitting N observations into K groups is given by the formula.[9]

$$\frac{K-1}{N-1}$$

Since there were 4,203,646 patients in the analysis database, the expected $R^2$ values from randomly splitting the data into subgroups are 0.00012, 0.00016, 0.00028, 0.00015, and 0.00036 for the Medicare DRGs, SDRGs, RDRGs, AP-DRGs, and APR-DRGs, respectively. Thus, the $R^2$ associated with the number of groups within each DRG system is negligible, and virtually none of the $R^2$ difference across the DRG systems is due to the difference in the number of groups in the different DRG systems.

As a means of comparing the DRG systems, the DRG structure can be viewed as consisting of four distinct components.

- MDCs
- MDCs with medical/surgical distinction
- base DRG categories based on principal diagnosis, procedure, and discharge status
- subgroups within DRGs based primarily on secondary diagnoses and age

The MDCs with medical and surgical patients separated into distinct groups have virtually the same definition for all five systems. The base DRG categories are very similar across the DRG systems, with the exception of the AP-DRGs and the APR-DRGs, which contain substantial modifications to the base DRG categories. The most substantial difference in the five systems is in the definition of the subgroups within each base DRG category. The subgroups within each base DRG category are primarily based on secondary diagnoses and age and essentially provide a measure of the relative severity of patients within each DRG category. The separation of the DRG structure into four components provides a means of identifying the source of $R^2$ differences across the different DRG systems. Table 32–3 contains the $R^2$ for cost across all patients for the five DRG systems for each component of the DRG structure.

**Table 32–3** Untrimmed $R^2$ for Cost for All Patients for Each Component of the DRG Structure

| | MDC | MDC plus medical, surgical | Base DRG categories | Complete system |
|---|---|---|---|---|
| Medicare DRGs | 0.1134 | 0.1852 | 0.3969 | 0.4076 |
| SDRGs | 0.1125 | 0.1844 | 0.3960 | 0.4407 |
| RDRGs | 0.1100 | 0.1823 | 0.4024 | 0.4627 |
| AP-DRGs | 0.1090 | 0.1916 | NA | 0.4689 |
| APR-DRGs | 0.1078 | 0.1987 | 0.4381 | 0.5309 |

Courtesy of 3M Health Information Systems, Wallingford, Connecticut.

As expected, the $R^2$ values for the MDCs and the MDCs with the medical/surgical distinction are very similar across the five DRG systems (approximately 0.11 and 0.19, respectively). At the base DRG category level, the $R^2$ is approximately 0.40 for all the DRG systems, with the exception of APR-DRGs, which has an $R^2$ that is about 10 percent higher than the other DRG systems. The percentage increase in $R^2$ from the addition of the subgroups to the base DRG categories differs substantially across the DRG systems, ranging from 2.69 percent for the Medicare DRGs to 21.18 percent for the APR-DRGs. Thus, it is the secondary diagnosis subgroups that account for most of the difference in $R^2$ across the DRG systems

## $R^2$ FOR COST BY MDC

The untrimmed $R^2$ within each MDC for cost and the percentage difference in $R^2$ relative to the Medicare DRGs are contained in Table 32–4. The $R^2$ varies not only across the DRG systems but also across the MDCs. There is a systematic variation in $R^2$ across the MDCs, reflecting the fact that cost is more predictable in some MDCs, such as the circulatory system, and less predictable in other MDCs, such as mental health. This systematic variation across MDCs reflects both the extent to which there is a relatively standard treatment for the diseases in the MDC and the need for information not currently collected, such as mental health status.

The $R^2$ results across the individual MDCs are consistent with overall $R^2$ results. The APR-DRGs have the highest $R^2$ for all MDCs, except alcohol and drugs. The magnitude of the difference in $R^2$ is quite substantial for many MDCs. For example, the percentage increases in $R^2$ relative to the Medicare DRGs for MDC 24 HIV infections are 71.38, 146.62, 284.00, and 361.23 percent for SDRGs, RDRGs, AP-DRGs, and APR-DRGs, respectively. By weighting the percentage difference in $R^2$ relative to the Medicare DRGs for each MDC by the number of patients in each MDC, a weighted percentage increase in $R^2$ can be computed. Table 32–5 contains the weighted percentage difference in $R^2$ relative to the Medicare DRGs. The weighted percentage difference in $R^2$ relative to the Medicare DRGs provides a composite measure of the magnitude of the difference in $R^2$ across MDCs. The weighted percentage difference in $R^2$ relative to the HCFA DRGs is quite substantial. For APR-DRGs, the weighted percentage differences in $R^2$ are 63.27, 126.31, and 70.62 percent for medical patients, surgical patients, and all patients combined,

**Table 32–4** Untrimmed $R^2$ for Cost across All Patients by MDC

| MDC | MDC Description | Medicare | SDRG | | RDRG | | AP-DRG | | APR-DRG | |
|---|---|---|---|---|---|---|---|---|---|---|
| | | $R^2$ | $R^2$ | % Diff | $R^2$ | % Diff | $R^2$ | % Diff | $R^2$ | % Diff |
| 1 | Nervous | 0.1853 | 0.2830 | 52.73 | 0.3006 | 62.22 | 0.2849 | 53.75 | 0.3761 | 102.97 |
| 2 | Eye | 0.0722 | 0.0748 | 3.60 | 0.1519 | 110.39 | 0.1303 | 80.47 | 0.2278 | 215.51 |
| 3 | Ear, nose, mouth and throat | 0.1190 | 0.1518 | 27.56 | 0.1826 | 53.45 | 0.1998 | 67.90 | 0.2977 | 150.17 |
| 4 | Respiratory | 0.2533 | 0.2905 | 14.69 | 0.3142 | 24.04 | 0.2921 | 15.32 | 0.3635 | 43.51 |
| 5 | Circulatory | 0.4734 | 0.5315 | 12.27 | 0.5353 | 13.08 | 0.5353 | 13.08 | 0.5710 | 20.62 |
| 6 | Digestive | 0.2829 | 0.3535 | 24.96 | 0.3689 | 30.40 | 0.3621 | 28.00 | 0.4370 | 54.47 |
| 7 | Hepatobiliary and pancreas | 0.1903 | 0.2815 | 47.92 | 0.2846 | 49.55 | 0.2627 | 38.05 | 0.3359 | 76.51 |
| 8 | Musculoskeletal and connective tissue | 0.2841 | 0.3425 | 20.56 | 0.3588 | 26.29 | 0.3564 | 25.45 | 0.4319 | 52.02 |
| 9 | Skin, subcutaneous tissue and breast | 0.1729 | 0.2137 | 23.60 | 0.2225 | 28.69 | 0.2091 | 20.94 | 0.2821 | 63.16 |
| 10 | Endocrine, nutritional and metabolic | 0.1295 | 0.1938 | 49.65 | 0.2171 | 67.64 | 0.2088 | 61.24 | 0.3184 | 145.87 |
| 11 | Kidney and urinary | 0.3730 | 0.4315 | 15.68 | 0.4391 | 17.72 | 0.3982 | 6.76 | 0.5025 | 34.72 |
| 12 | Male reproductive | 0.2757 | 0.2865 | 3.92 | 0.3578 | 29.78 | 0.3103 | 12.55 | 0.3964 | 43.78 |
| 13 | Female reproductive | 0.1645 | 0.2403 | 46.08 | 0.2884 | 75.32 | 0.1928 | 17.20 | 0.3424 | 108.15 |
| 14 | Pregnancy, childbirth and the puerperium | 0.2306 | 0.2150 | -6.76 | 0.2715 | 17.74 | 0.2496 | 8.24 | 0.3110 | 34.72 |

*continues*

**Table 32–4** continued

| MDC | MDC Description | Medicare R² | SDRG R² | SDRG % Diff | RDRG R² | RDRG % Diff | AP-DRG R² | AP-DRG % Diff | APR-DRG R² | APR-DRG % Diff |
|---|---|---|---|---|---|---|---|---|---|---|
| 15 | Newborns | 0.2917 | 0.2894 | −0.79 | 0.4234 | 45.15 | 0.5070 | 73.81 | 0.6274 | 115.08 |
| 16 | Blood and immunological | 0.0574 | 0.1065 | 85.54 | 0.1591 | 177.18 | 0.1368 | 138.33 | 0.2228 | 288.15 |
| 17 | Myeloproliferative and poorly diff neop | 0.1810 | 0.2635 | 45.58 | 0.3157 | 74.42 | 0.2884 | 59.34 | 0.3543 | 95.75 |
| 18 | Infectious and parasitic | 0.1577 | 0.2376 | 50.67 | 0.2624 | 66.39 | 0.2308 | 46.35 | 0.3108 | 97.08 |
| 19 | Mental | 0.0417 | 0.0506 | 21.34 | 0.0511 | 22.54 | 0.0427 | 2.40 | 0.1176 | 182.01 |
| 20 | Alcohol and drug | 0.1593 | 0.1741 | 9.29 | 0.1158 | −27.31 | 0.0617 | −61.27 | 0.1549 | −2.76 |
| 21 | Injuries, poisonings and toxic effects | 0.1134 | 0.1993 | 75.75 | 0.1959 | 72.75 | 0.2063 | 81.92 | 0.3026 | 166.84 |
| 22 | Burns | 0.3375 | 0.3618 | 7.20 | 0.4209 | 24.71 | 0.3376 | 0.03 | 0.4627 | 37.10 |
| 23 | Factors influencing health status | 0.1266 | 0.1602 | 26.54 | 0.1979 | 56.32 | 0.1210 | −4.42 | 0.2414 | 90.68 |
| 24 | Human immunodeficiency virus infections | 0.0650 | 0.1114 | 71.38 | 0.1603 | 146.62 | 0.2496 | 284.00 | 0.2998 | 361.23 |
| 25 | Multiple significant trauma | 0.1096 | 0.1096 | −0.09 | 0.2032 | 85.23 | 0.2109 | 92.25 | 0.2385 | 117.41 |
| 26 | Other (pre-MDC) | 0.4070 | 0.4151 | 1.99 | 0.4162 | 2.26 | 0.4243 | 4.25 | 0.4721 | 16.49 |

Courtesy of 3M Health Information Systems, Wallingford, Connecticut.

**Table 32–5** Untrimmed Weighted Percentage Difference in $R^2$ for Cost across MDCs Relative to the Medicare DRGs

|  | SDRGs | RDRGs | AP-DRGs | APR-DRGs |
|---|---|---|---|---|
| All | 18.78 | 34.26 | 30.45 | 70.62 |
| Surgical | 38.36 | 67.10 | 56.78 | 126.31 |
| Medical | 49.91 | 86.93 | 73.59 | 163.27 |

Courtesy of 3M Health Information Systems, Wallingford, Connecticut.

respectively. The weighted percentage difference in $R^2$ across the MDCs is a better measure of the relative performance of the DRG systems than the overall $R^2$, since it removes the contribution of the MDCs and medical/surgical distinction, which is comparable across all the DRG systems. The weighted percentage increase in $R^2$ is lower for all patients combined than for medical and surgical patients separately, because the medical/surgical distinction increases the $R^2$ of Medicare DRGs, lowering the percentage increase in $R^2$ of the other DRG systems relative to the Medicare DRGs.

## DATA TRIMMING

The $R^2$ results have been presented using untrimmed data. Data trimming excludes from the analysis patients who have extreme values of the variable being analyzed (e.g., LOS or cost). The extent and method of data trimming can have a substantial impact on $R^2$ and can lead to biased results. There are numerous methods for data trimming. The more common methods for establishing high and low trim points include using

- a specified number of standard deviations above and below the mean
- a specified number of interquartile ranges above the 75th percentile and below the 25th percentile
- a specified multiple of the geometric mean for the high trim points and a fraction of the geometric mean for the low trim points

- a specified percentage of the patients with the highest values of the variable being analyzed and with the lowest values of the variable being analyzed

The first three methods of trimming would result in a different number of patients being trimmed in each of the DRG systems. The patients being trimmed are the patients who deviate the most from the value predicted by the classification system. Thus, if the $R^2$ of two classification systems is being compared and one of the classification systems has more patients trimmed, the $R^2$ results will be biased in favor of the classification system with the most patients trimmed. As an example of the magnitude of the difference in the number of patients trimmed and amount of cost trimmed across the different DRG systems, a high trim point equal to nine times the geometric mean of cost was used. The resulting percentages of patients and cost trimmed are contained in Table 32–6.

As shown in Table 32–6, across the DRG systems the number of patients trimmed varied by more than 60 percent and the amount of cost trimmed varied by nearly 80 percent. In this example, the increase in $R^2$ due to trimming would be greater for the Medicare DRGs than for the other DRG systems, especially the APR-DRGs. The computation of the untrimmed $R^2$ was based on an identical patient population across the DRG systems. Ideally, any comparison of the $R^2$ for trimmed data across DRG systems would also be based on an identical patient population for each system. Unfortunately, there is no trimming method that would result in an identical patient population across

**Table 32–6** Percentage of Patients and Cost Trimmed Using a High Trim of Nine Times the Geometric Mean

| DRG system | Percentage of patients trimmed | Percentage of cost trimmed |
|---|---|---|
| Medicare DRGs | 2.39 | 13.45 |
| SDRGs | 2.06 | 11.33 |
| RDRGs | 1.95 | 10.42 |
| AP-DRGs | 1.94 | 10.36 |
| APR-DRGs | 1.47 | 7.57 |

Courtesy of 3M Health Information Systems, Wallingford, Connecticut.

the DRG systems that would not be biased toward one of the systems. For example, a trimmed patient population defined by excluding patients who were trimmed in *any one* of the DRG systems or, alternatively, a trimmed patient population defined based on only those patients who were trimmed in *all* the DRG systems would create distortions within each system by not trimming patients who should be trimmed or unnecessarily excluding patients. Thus, there is no method of trimming that would produce an identical trimmed patient population across all DRG systems without creating distortions in the $R^2$ results.

Since it is common for trimmed $R^2$ results to be reported for a DRG system, the data were trimmed by excluding within each DRG the 1 percent of patients with the highest values of the variable being analyzed and .5 percent of patients with the lowest values. Thus, a total of 1.5 percent of the patients from each DRG were trimmed. The trimming was done independently for each DRG system. Thus, although approximately the same number of patients were trimmed from each DRG system, the patients who were trimmed differed across the DRG systems. Patients who are trimmed are referred to as outliers, and patients who are not trimmed are referred to as inliers.

The patients identified as outliers differed substantially across the DRG systems. For example, the percentages of high outliers for Medicare DRGs, SDRGs, RDRGs, and AP-DRGs that are inliers in APR-DRGs are 54.50, 50.49, 51.90, and 50.44, respectively. Thus, approximately half of the high outliers in each of these DRG systems are inliers for APR-DRGs. In order to illustrate the differences in the extent to which patients are identified as outliers across the DRG systems, Table 32–7 contains the high outlier patients in each DRG system that are inliers in the APR-DRG system and shows the distribution of these patients by the APR-DRG severity-of-illness subclasses.

Table 32–7 shows that the majority of these patients are severity-of-illness level 3 and 4 in APR-DRGs. Of the high outliers in each system that are inliers in APR-DRGs, 77.32, 71.87, 61.02, and 63.40 percent are severity level 3 and 4 in the APR-DRGs for the Medicare DRGs, SDRGs, RDRGs, and AP-DRGs, respectively. Thus, each of the other DRG systems tends to exclude as high outliers a disproportionate number of the high-level severity-of-illness patients that are inliers in APR-DRGs.

There is greater consistency across the DRG systems in the patients who are identified as low outliers. The percentages of low outliers for Medicare DRGs, SDRGs, RDRGs, and AP-DRGs that are inliers in APR-DRGs are 24.29, 23.98, 26.99, and 23.36 percent, respectively. Thus, approximately a

**Table 32–7** Distribution of High Outliers in Each DRG System That Are Inliers for APR-DRGs

| DRG system | APR-DRG severity subgroup | | | |
|---|---|---|---|---|
| | 1 (%) | 2 (%) | 3 (%) | 4 (%) |
| Medicare DRGs | 8.09 | 14.59 | 24.83 | 52.49 |
| SDRGs | 8.48 | 19.64 | 35.55 | 36.32 |
| RDRGs | 9.46 | 29.52 | 29.33 | 31.69 |
| AP-DRGs | 8.12 | 28.48 | 37.08 | 26.32 |

Courtesy of 3M Health Information Systems, Wallingford, Connecticut.

quarter of the low outliers in each system are inliers for APR-DRGs. Table 32–8 contains the low outlier patients in each DRG system that are inliers in APR-DRGs and shows the distribution of these patients by the APR-DRG severity-of-illness subclasses.

Table 32–8 shows that the majority of these are severity-of-illness level 1 in APR-DRGs. Thus, each of the other DRG systems tends to exclude as low outliers a substantial number of severity-of-illness level 1 patients that are inliers in APR-DRGs.

Not only are the patients defined as outliers different, but the costs of the outlier patients are also substantially different. To illustrate the difference in

**Table 32–8** Distribution of Low Outliers in Each DRG System That Are Inliers for APR-DRGs

| DRG system | APR-DRG subgroup | | | |
|---|---|---|---|---|
| | 1 (%) | 2 (%) | 3 (%) | 4 (%) |
| Medicare DRGs | 76.24 | 21.86 | 1.72 | 0.18 |
| SDRGs | 67.56 | 27.04 | 4.98 | 0.42 |
| RDRGs | 53.31 | 38.36 | 7.57 | 0.76 |
| AP-DRGs | 63.83 | 30.23 | 5.61 | 0.32 |

Courtesy of 3M Health Information Systems, Wallingford, Connecticut.

cost, the difference between the average inlier cost and average outlier cost for each DRG weighted by the number of patients in each DRG was computed for each DRG system. The differences are $32,395, $28,077, $27,332, $26,742, and $22,097 for the Medicare DRGs, SDRGs, RDRGs, AP-DRGs, and APR-DRGs, respectively. Thus, there is a substantial variation in the difference between average inlier and average outlier cost across the DRG systems. For example, the weighted difference between average inlier and outlier cost is 46.6 percent higher for Medicare DRGs than for APR-DRGs. In essence, more of the unexplained variability is being excluded by trimming in the DRG systems with a greater difference between inlier and outlier average cost. The more the outliers differ from the average of the DRG to which the outlier is assigned, the greater will be the improvement in $R^2$. In other words, the poorer the classification system, the greater the improvement in $R^2$ from trimming. A system that classifies patients into highly homogeneous groups, such as the APR-DRGs, would experience relatively little increase in $R^2$ as a result of data trimming.

## TRIMMED $R^2$ RESULTS

Table 32–9 contains the $R^2$ results using trimmed data. In general, the $R^2$ results for trimmed data are higher than for untrimmed data, and the difference in $R^2$ across the DRG systems is smaller. For cost for all patients, the percentage increases in $R^2$ relative to the Medicare DRGs are 3.5, 8.3, 8.7, and 16.7 percent for the SDRGs, RDRGs, AP-DRGs, and APR-DRGs, respectively.

**Table 32–9** Trimmed $R^2$ for Cost and Length of Stay

| Variable | Patients | HCFA DRG | SDRG | RDRG | AP-DRG | APR-DRG |
|---|---|---|---|---|---|---|
| LOS | All | 0.3797 | 0.4070 | 0.4385 | 0.4358 | 0.4787 |
| LOS | Surgical | 0.3935 | 0.4363 | 0.4370 | 0.4289 | 0.5033 |
| LOS | Medical | 0.3523 | 0.3667 | 0.4259 | 0.4273 | 0.4419 |
| Cost | All | 0.5151 | 0.5331 | 0.5577 | 0.5600 | 0.6009 |
| Cost | Surgical | 0.5132 | 0.5342 | 0.5396 | 0.5372 | 0.5883 |
| Cost | Medical | 0.3432 | 0.3646 | 0.4583 | 0.4709 | 0.4981 |

Courtesy of 3M Health Information Systems, Wallingford, Connecticut.

These are roughly half of the percentage increases in $R^2$ relative to the Medicare DRGs observed for untrimmed data.

As expected, the trimming caused a disproportionate increase in $R^2$ for the DRG systems that had lower $R^2$ values for untrimmed data. For example, for cost across all patients, trimming resulted in a 26.4-percent increase in $R^2$ for HCFA DRGs (40.76 versus 51.51) and a 13.2-percent increase in $R^2$ for APR-DRGs (53.09 versus 60.09). As discussed previously, the reason for the greater increases in $R^2$ due to trimming for the DRG systems with lower untrimmed $R^2$ results is that the trimming excludes more of the unexplained variability in the DRG systems with lower untrimmed $R^2$ values. Table 32–10 contains the increase in $R^2$ due to trimming and the difference between the average inlier cost and average outlier cost for each DRG weighted by the number of patients in each DRG.

As expected, there is a direct relationship between the magnitude of the increase in $R^2$ and the weighted difference between the average inlier and outlier cost. Thus, even though the number of patients trimmed was approximately the same across the DRG systems, the difference in the population of patients defined as outliers and the difference in the average cost of the outliers had a substantial impact on the trimmed $R^2$ results. The trimmed $R^2$ measures both the performance of the classification system and the characteristics of the patients trimmed. The net impact of the trimming is that the $R^2$ results are artificially compressed across the DRG systems.

---

**Table 34–10** Relationship between $R^2$ Increase due to Trimming and Difference between Inlier and Outlier Cost

| DRG system | Increase in $R^2$ due to trimming | Weighted difference in average inlier and outlier cost |
|---|---|---|
| Medicare DRGs | 26.37% | $32,395 |
| SDRGs | 20.97% | $28,077 |
| RDRGs | 20.53% | $27,332 |
| AP-DRGs | 19.43% | $26,742 |
| APR-DRGs | 13.19% | $22,097 |

Courtesy of 3M Health Information Systems, Wallingford, Connecticut.

**Table 32–11** Trimmed $R^2$ for Cost for All Patients for Each Component of the DRG Structure

|  | MDC | MDC plus medical and surgical | Base DRG categories | Complete system |
|---|---|---|---|---|
| Medicare DRGs | 0.1422 | 0.2329 | 0.5024 | 0.5151 |
| SDRGs | 0.1361 | 0.2243 | 0.4811 | 0.5331 |
| RDRGs | 0.1314 | 0.2195 | 0.4862 | 0.5577 |
| AP-DRGs | 0.1288 | 0.2273 | NA | 0.5600 |
| APR-DRGs | 0.1203 | 0.2239 | 0.4968 | 0.6009 |

Courtesy of 3M Health Information Systems, Wallingford, Connecticut.

Table 32–11 contains the trimmed $R^2$ for cost for all patients for each component of the DRG structure. Across all DRG systems the trimmed $R^2$ is higher than the untrimmed $R^2$ for each component of the DRG systems. At the MDC level, the trimmed $R^2$ differs across DRG systems even though the definition of the MDCs is very similar across DRG systems. The reason for the difference in $R^2$ is that the patients who are trimmed are different for each DRG system.

Table 32–12 contains the trimmed $R^2$ by MDC. The trimmed $R^2$ for each MDC is higher than the untrimmed $R^2$, and the difference in $R^2$ across the DRG systems is smaller for trimmed data than for untrimmed data. Table 32–13 contains the trimmed weighted percentage difference in $R^2$ for cost across MDCs relative to the Medicare DRGs. While the trimmed $R^2$ results are lower than the untrimmed results (see Table 32–5), there are still substantial differences across DRG systems in the trimmed weighted percentage difference in $R^2$ for cost across MDCs relative to Medicare DRGs.

## HOSPITAL-LEVEL ANALYSIS FOR COST

The analysis has focused on the ability of the DRG systems to predict cost at the individual patient level. The DRGs can also be used to predict cost at the hospital level. In the preceding patient-level analysis, the average cost of the DRG to which the patient is assigned was used to predict each individual

**Table 32–12** Trimmed $R^2$ for Cost across All Patients by MDC

| MDC | MDC description | Medicare $R^2$ | SDRG $R^2$ | SDRG % Diff | RDRG $R^2$ | RDRG % Diff | AP-DRG $R^2$ | AP-DRG % Diff | APR-DRG $R^2$ | APR-DRG % Diff |
|---|---|---|---|---|---|---|---|---|---|---|
| 1 | Nervous | 0.2903 | 0.3877 | 33.55 | 0.3880 | 33.65 | 0.3898 | 34.27 | 0.4512 | 55.43 |
| 2 | Eye | 0.1197 | 0.1272 | 6.27 | 0.1923 | 60.65 | 0.1629 | 36.09 | 0.2696 | 125.23 |
| 3 | Ear, nose, mouth and throat | 0.2659 | 0.2914 | 9.59 | 0.2994 | 12.60 | 0.3411 | 28.28 | 0.4302 | 61.79 |
| 4 | Respiratory | 0.3625 | 0.3967 | 9.43 | 0.4243 | 17.05 | 0.3925 | 8.28 | 0.4562 | 25.85 |
| 5 | Circulatory | 0.6007 | 0.6336 | 5.48 | 0.6318 | 5.18 | 0.6265 | 4.29 | 0.6490 | 8.04 |
| 6 | Digestive | 0.4025 | 0.4577 | 13.71 | 0.4710 | 17.02 | 0.4588 | 13.99 | 0.5290 | 31.43 |
| 7 | Hepatobiliary and pancreas | 0.2859 | 0.3690 | 29.07 | 0.3695 | 29.24 | 0.3522 | 23.19 | 0.4243 | 48.41 |
| 8 | Musculoskeletal and connective tissue | 0.4069 | 0.4380 | 7.64 | 0.4403 | 8.21 | 0.4666 | 14.67 | 0.5089 | 25.07 |
| 9 | Skin, subcutaneous tissue and breast | 0.2729 | 0.3109 | 13.92 | 0.3021 | 10.70 | 0.3044 | 11.54 | 0.3634 | 33.16 |
| 10 | Endocrine, nutritional and metabolic | 0.2218 | 0.2826 | 27.41 | 0.2742 | 23.62 | 0.2992 | 34.90 | 0.3988 | 79.80 |
| 11 | Kidney and urinary | 0.5030 | 0.5287 | 5.11 | 0.5326 | 5.88 | 0.5081 | 1.01 | 0.5797 | 15.25 |
| 12 | Male reproductive | 0.4347 | 0.4310 | -0.85 | 0.4347 | 0.00 | 0.4277 | -1.61 | 0.4435 | 2.02 |
| 13 | Female reproductive | 0.2520 | 0.3221 | 27.82 | 0.3460 | 37.30 | 0.2624 | 4.13 | 0.3881 | 54.01 |
| 14 | Pregnancy, childbirth and the puerperium | 0.3881 | 0.3809 | -1.86 | 0.3948 | 1.73 | 0.3983 | 2.63 | 0.4262 | 9.82 |

| | | | | | | | | | |
|---|---|---|---|---|---|---|---|---|---|
| 15 | Newborns | 0.3569 | 0.3557 | −0.34 | 0.5516 | 54.55 | 0.5726 | 60.44 | 0.6549 | 83.50 |
| 16 | Blood and immunological | 0.1218 | 0.1809 | 48.52 | 0.2415 | 98.28 | 0.2157 | 77.09 | 0.2844 | 133.50 |
| 17 | Myeloproliferative and poorly diff neop | 0.2461 | 0.3420 | 38.97 | 0.3644 | 48.07 | 0.3587 | 45.75 | 0.4106 | 66.84 |
| 18 | Infectious and parasitic | 0.2343 | 0.3200 | 36.58 | 0.3436 | 46.65 | 0.3056 | 30.43 | 0.3834 | 63.64 |
| 19 | Mental | 0.0598 | 0.0733 | 22.58 | 0.0770 | 28.76 | 0.0617 | 3.18 | 0.1613 | 169.73 |
| 20 | Alcohol and drug | 0.2530 | 0.2421 | −4.31 | 0.2155 | −14.82 | 0.0868 | −65.69 | 0.1792 | −29.17 |
| 21 | Injuries, poisonings and toxic effects | 0.2114 | 0.3096 | 46.45 | 0.2942 | 39.17 | 0.3118 | 47.49 | 0.3770 | 78.33 |
| 22 | Burns | 0.3845 | 0.3988 | 3.72 | 0.4523 | 17.63 | 0.3845 | 0.00 | 0.4924 | 28.06 |
| 23 | Factors influencing health status | 0.1748 | 0.2054 | 17.51 | 0.2407 | 37.70 | 0.1696 | −2.97 | 0.2909 | 66.42 |
| 24 | Human immunodeficiency virus infections | 0.1014 | 0.1605 | 58.28 | 0.2079 | 105.03 | 0.3178 | 213.41 | 0.3603 | 255.33 |
| 25 | Multiple significant trauma | 0.1519 | 0.1518 | −0.07 | 0.2459 | 61.88 | 0.2599 | 71.10 | 0.2865 | 88.61 |
| 26 | Other (pre-MDC) | 0.4788 | 0.4799 | 0.23 | 0.4935 | 3.07 | 0.5005 | 4.53 | 0.5405 | 12.89 |

Courtesy of 3M Health Information Systems, Wallingford, Connecticut.

**Table 32–13** Trimmed Weighted Percentage Difference across MDCs in $R^2$ for Cost Relative to Medicare DRGs

|  | SDRGs | RDRGs | AP-DRGs | APR-DRGs |
|---|---|---|---|---|
| All | 11.19 | 20.67 | 18.54 | 41.15 |
| Surgical | 24.15 | 39.15 | 38.24 | 74.22 |
| Medical | 36.66 | 63.80 | 50.69 | 107.61 |

Courtesy of 3M Health Information Systems, Wallingford, Connecticut.

patient's actual cost. In the hospital-level analysis, a case mix index based on each DRG system was computed and used to predict the actual total cost (i.e., budget) of the hospital. It is possible that one DRG system might be superior in predicting cost at the patient level but *not* be superior in predicting cost at the hospital. This would occur if the kinds of patients for which the DRG system was yielding a superior cost prediction were randomly distributed across hospitals. Conversely, if the kinds of patients for which the DRG system was yielding a superior cost prediction are concentrated in certain types of hospitals, there would be superior cost prediction at the hospital level.

Using untrimmed data, a regression was performed with total hospital cost as the dependent variable and the case mix index of the hospital as the only independent variable. In addition, a multiple regression was performed using the following hospital characteristics:

- case mix index
- percent Medicaid
- percent Medicare
- teaching hospital
- children's hospital
- urban hospital
- bed size less than 100
- bed size between 100 and 199
- bed size between 200 and 299
- bed size between 300 and 449
- bed size 450 and greater

With the exception of the case mix index, percent Medicaid, and percent Medicare, which are continuous variables, all variables were dummy variables (i.e., 0 or 1) that indicated whether or not the characteristic applied to the hospital (e.g., was or was not an urban hospital). Only hospitals that were major teaching hospitals (a ratio of interns and residents to beds greater than 0.25) were considered teaching hospitals. Table 32–14 contains the $R^2$ results for cost at the hospital level for each DRG system for the case mix index alone and for the case mix index combined with the hospital characteristics listed above. Ideally, the kinds of patients a hospital treats (i.e., its case mix) would predict its cost, and the addition of hospital characteristics would not increase the $R^2$ at the hospital level. If the addition of hospital characteristics increases $R^2$, then this increase may be caused by one or more of the following:

- The patient classification system may not adequately describe certain types of patients who tend to be treated in hospitals with specific characteristics.
- Patient attributes not directly related to patients' medical problems (e.g., income status) may increase the cost of care for hospitals treating a disproportionate number of these patients.
- Hospital characteristics such as size may affect the cost of care independent of the case mix of the hospital (e.g., economies and diseconomies of scale).

**Table 32–14** Untrimmed $R^2$ for Cost at Hospital Level across DRG Systems

|  | Medicare DRGs | SDRGs | RDRGs | AP-DRGs | APR-DRGs |
|---|---|---|---|---|---|
| $R^2$ Case mix index only | 0.5292 | 0.5358 | 0.5646 | 0.6065 | 0.6410 |
| $R^2$ case mix index plus hospital characteristics | 0.6326 | 0.6465 | 0.6512 | 0.6549 | 0.6719 |
| Percentage increase in $R^2$ from hospital characteristics | 19.56 | 20.66 | 15.34 | 7.98 | 4.82 |

Courtesy of 3M Health Information Systems, Wallingford, Connecticut.

The hospital level $R^2$ for the case mix index is between 20 and 30 percent higher than the patient level $R^2$ for cost contained in Table 32–2. Relative to the Medicare DRGs, the hospital level $R^2$ for the case mix index is 1.27, 6.71, 14.63, and 21.15 percent higher for SDRGs, RDRGs, AP-DRGs, and APR-DRGs, respectively.

The addition of the hospital characteristics increased the $R^2$ for all the DRG systems. The percentage increases in $R^2$ due to the addition of the hospital characteristics were 19.56, 20.66, 15.34, 7.98, and 4.82 for the Medicare DRGs, SDRGs, RDRGs, AP-DRGs, and APR-DRG, respectively. Thus, the addition of the characteristics of the hospital does increase $R^2$, but for AP-DRGs and APR-DRGs the magnitude of the increase is relatively small. This means that AP-DRGs and especially APR-DRGs explain most of the difference in cost that is observed across different types of hospitals. In a payment context, AP-DRGs and APR-DRGs greatly reduce the need for payment adjustments based on hospital characteristics, such as a teaching status adjustment.

## PAYMENT REDISTRIBUTION

Historically, the primary use of DRGs has been as a payment mechanism. In payment applications, DRGs are the basic unit of payment and provide the basis for allocating aggregate payments to individual hospitals. The five DRG systems result in a different allocation of aggregate payments to individual hospitals. Thus, there is a redistribution of payments across hospitals associated with use of the alternative DRG systems. The extent to which the payment redistribution impacts certain groups of patients or hospitals is an important factor in the evaluation of alternative DRG systems. It is important not only for payment applications but also for hospital profiling by state data commissions, planning and budgeting by hospital systems, and utilization review and pricing by individual hospitals.

In order to measure the payment redistribution impact, hospital payments under each DRG system were simulated and compared to hospital cost. DRG payment systems can be complex, involving adjustments for factors such as teaching status and separate payments for outliers. The payment redistribution analysis simulated a basic DRG payment system in which payment for a patient is equal to the average cost in the DRG to which the patient is assigned without any adjustment factors or separate payments for outliers.

A basic DRG payment model was used because the purpose of the analysis was to evaluate the performance of the DRG classification systems themselves and not the additional payment adjustment polices, which are typically a part of a prospective payment system. Secondarily, the use of a basic DRG payment model provides some insight as to where payment system adjustments may be most needed and whether such adjustments are less important for the more refined DRG systems.

The payment redistribution impact was measured by the ratio of payment to actual cost (RPAC), which is computed as

$$RPAC_s = \frac{\sum\limits_g n_{g,s} A_g}{\sum\limits_{i \in s} y_i}$$

where $s$ is the subset of patients being evaluated (e.g., patients aged 80 or greater), $y_i$ is the actual cost of the $i$th patient, $n_{g,s}$ is the number of patients in DRG $g$, subset $s$, and $A_g$ is the average cost in DRG $g$ in the entire database. The numerator of RPAC is equivalent to the total amount a hospital would be paid if the payment it received for each patient was equal to the average cost in the DRG assigned to the patient. The computation of the RPAC is budget neutral, since across all patients the value of RPAC will be 1.00.

RPAC is useful because it provides two comparative measures. First, RPAC provides a measure of the extent to which hospital payments correspond to actual hospital cost. Values of RPAC near 1.00 mean that hospital payments closely correspond to hospital costs. Thus, DRG systems that have RPAC values close to 1.00 provide payments that are close to historical hospital cost. Second, the relative value of RPAC provides a measure of the redistribution impact of the different DRG systems. For example, suppose for a certain subset of hospitals the RPAC value for one DRG system was 1.20 and for another DRG system it was 1.10. Under the first DRG system, the subset of hospitals would be paid 20 percent more than cost and under the second DRG system they would be paid 10 percent more than cost. Relative to the first DRG system, payments to the subset of hospitals under the second DRG system would be 8.3 percent less ((1.1–1.2)/1.2). The primary focus of the payment redistribution analysis is to identify whether certain DRG systems produce RPAC values closer to 1.00 than other DRG systems. It is the direction and magnitude of the difference in RPAC that is critical, not whether a value of 1.00 is produced.

The degree to which hospital DRG-based payments correspond to hospital costs and the payment redistribution impact of alternative DRG systems are critical issues. If certain hospitals dominate the care rendered to patients for which DRG payments are significantly less than cost, then these hospitals will financially be disadvantaged. This is especially important in a highly managed care context where health plans are actively directing inpatient admissions to selected hospitals that may appear more price competitive. Ultimately, there may be financial pressure not to offer selected services. The result will be that groups of patients might find it difficult to access needed hospital services.

The RPAC was calculated for different subsets of patients and hospitals for each of the five DRG systems. Payment redistribution was measured by computing the percent difference in RPAC relative to the Medicare DRGs. A percent difference of +20 percent means that the subset of patients or hospitals are paid 20 percent more under the specified DRG system than under the Medicare DRGs. For brevity of presentation, the tables show the RPAC for each DRG system but only show the percentage difference of APR-DRGs relative to Medicare DRGs. In most instances, the largest percentage difference occurs with the APR-DRGs.

Patients transferred to acute hospitals were removed from the analysis database. This is because they do not have a complete hospitalization. Thus, the analysis of payment redistribution is not complicated by the issue of how to handle transfer patients.

Payment redistribution results are presented for the following subsets of patients and hospitals:

- age
- admission source
- discharge destination
- primary payer
- hospital service line and age
- hospital type and age

RPACs were also generated for other combinations of variables, including admission source and age, discharge destination and age, and primary payer and age. For brevity, these tables are not included, but the most salient patterns are incorporated into the presentation of findings.

## Age Range

Table 32–15 contains RPACs for five different patient age ranges. The pediatric age range also includes a separate breakout for children with chronic diseases and children without chronic diseases. Chronic is defined as a disease expected to last 12 months or longer for at least 75 percent of the patients. The definition of chronic was based on Version 3.0 of the NACHRI classification of congenital and chronic conditions, which included physical conditions but not mental health conditions.

There are substantial differences in RPAC by patient age. For five of the six age ranges, the RPAC is closer to 1.00 for the more refined DRG systems, in particular, the APR-DRGs. For neonates, the RPAC increases from approximately 0.900 for Medicare DRGs, SDRGs, and RDRGs up to approximately 1.00 for AP-DRGs and APR-DRGs. In the Medicare DRGs, SDRGs, and RDRGs, neonates are defined by the presence of certain newborn and perinatal diagnoses codes, which results in certain very expensive neonates being assigned to nonneonatal DRGs. In contrast, the AP-DRGs and APR-DRGs define neonates by age (0–28 days at admission) and therefore more appropriately classify the neonatal patients.

The RPACs show that hospitals are substantially underpaid for children who have chronic diseases and substantially overpaid for children who do not have chronic diseases. The RPACs for Medicare DRGs are 0.824 for chronically ill children and 1.105 for nonchronically ill children. The RPACs move somewhat closer to 1.00 with the SDRGs, RDRGs, and AP-DRGs, but only by 2 to 3 percent. With APR-DRGs, the RPAC for chronically ill children increases 9.0 percent to 0.898, and the RPAC for nonchronically ill children decreases 6.2 percent to 1.036. Thus, with the APR-DRGs, the underpayment for chronically ill children is substantially decreased, but a significant gap remains. This means that hospitals that specialize in the care of chronically ill children will be underpaid by all DRG systems but will get paid substantially closer to cost with APR-DRGs.

The RPAC for adult patients aged 18–64 is a little above 1.00 for Medicare DRGs, SDRGs, RDRGs, and AP-DRGs but decreases 3.8 percent to 0.990 for APR-DRGs. This reflects a lower distribution of severity-of-illness subclasses

**Table 32–15** Comparison of RPACs for DRG Systems by Patient Age Group

| Patient age groups | Total cases | Total costs (000s) | Medicare DRGs | SDRGs | RDRGs | AP-DRGs | APR-DRGs | % Diff |
|---|---|---|---|---|---|---|---|---|
| Neonates | 492,558 | 1,066,290 | 0.899 | 0.893 | 0.914 | 0.994 | 1.000 | +11.2% |
| Patients age 1 mo–17 years | | | | | | | | |
| With chronic DX | 115,608 | 888,040 | 0.824 | 0.816 | 0.853 | 0.849 | 0.898 | +9.0% |
| Without chronic DX | 195,871 | 673,475 | 1.105 | 1.076 | 1.124 | 1.067 | 1.036 | −6.2% |
| Subtotal | 311,479 | 1,561,515 | 0.945 | 0.928 | 0.970 | 0.943 | 0.957 | +1.3% |
| Patients 18–64 years | 1,953,661 | 10,813,169 | 1.029 | 1.019 | 1.014 | 1.019 | 0.990 | −3.8% |
| Patients 65–79 years | 956,908 | 8,002,197 | 0.982 | 0.988 | 0.987 | 0.976 | 0.996 | +1.4% |
| Patients 80+ years | 472,641 | 3,386,990 | 1.009 | 1.034 | 1.028 | 1.025 | 1.063 | +5.4% |

Courtesy of 3M Health Information Systems, Wallingford, Connecticut.

in the APR-DRGs for adults. The RPAC for elderly patients aged 65–79 increases from 0.982 for Medicare DRGs to 0.996 for APR-DRGs (1.4 percent), reflecting a slightly higher distribution of higher severity-of-illness subclasses in the APR-DRGs for elderly patients.

Elderly patients aged 80 and older show a different pattern, with RPACs having values above 1.00 and the values increasing with the more refined DRG systems. The RPAC increases from 1.009 for Medicare DRGs to 1.063 for APR-DRGs (5.4 percent). It is likely that this increase reflects two factors. First, a higher proportion of this age population will have organ failure diagnoses, placing them in high severity-of-illness subclasses. Second, it is likely that a higher proportion of this age population will receive treatment aimed more at comfort than cure, including "do not resuscitate" orders.

Overall, the more refined DRG systems decrease payment for adults and pediatric patients without chronic illnesses and increase payments for neonates, children with chronic diseases, and elderly patients. In the more refined DRG systems, the RPACs are closer to 1.0 for all age ranges except elderly patients aged 80 and older.

## Admission Source

Table 32–16 contains RPACs by patient admission source. The patterns are very striking. With the more refined DRG systems, the RPACs are much closer to 1.00 for patients who are transferred in from another acute hospital but are further from 1.0 for patients transferred in from a skilled nursing facility (SNF).

The RPACs for patients transferred in from another acute hospital start at 0.849 for Medicare DRGs and increase to 0.874 and 0.876 for SDRGs and RDRGs, to 0.899 for AP-DRGs, and to 0.930 for APR-DRGs. It is likely that these are very sick patients. It is also likely that the patients transferred from another acute hospital are concentrated in certain types of hospitals, and thus it is very important that this be reflected in the DRG system. For example, the RPAC for neonates who are transferred from another acute hospital increases 73.0 percent, from 0.548 for Medicare DRGs to 0.948 for APR-DRGs.

The RPACs for patients who are transferred in from a skilled nursing facility (SNF) start at 0.997 for Medicare DRGs and increase to 1.025 for RDRGs, to 1.053 and 1.058 for SDRGs and AP-DRGs, and to 1.113 for APR-DRGs. The majority of these patients are elderly, and it is likely that the higher

**Table 32–16** Comparison of RPACs for DRG Systems by Patient Admission Source

| Patient admission source | Total cases | Total costs (000s) | Medicare DRGs | SDRGs | RDRGs | AP-DRGs | APR-DRGs | % Diff |
|---|---|---|---|---|---|---|---|---|
| Other/unknown | 4,034,699 | 23,101,242 | 1.010 | 1.008 | 1.008 | 1.006 | 1.003 | -0.7% |
| Acute hospital | 119,186 | 1,485,889 | 0.849 | 0.874 | 0.876 | 0.899 | 0.930 | +9.5% |
| SNF | 33,362 | 243,031 | 0.997 | 1.053 | 1.025 | 1.058 | 1.113 | +11.6% |

Courtesy of 3M Health Information Systems, Wallingford, Connecticut.

RPACs, especially for APR-DRGs, reflect the fact that many of these patients have organ failure and other severe complicating or comorbid conditions but do not always receive aggressive cure-oriented treatment, especially when "do not resuscitate" orders are given.

## Discharge Destination

Table 32–17 contains RPACs by patient discharge destination. Again there are some rather striking patterns, with the RPACs closer to 1.00 for the more refined DRG classification systems, especially the APR-DRGs. The RPAC for patients discharged to home decreases 4.7 percent, from 1.085 for Medicare DRGs to 1.034 for APR-DRGs. The RPAC for patients who left against medical advice decreases 5.4 percent, from 1.313 to 1.242. This suggests the APR-DRG system is classifying many of these patients in lower severity subclasses. The RPAC is still very high, however. This is not surprising given that these patients, by their choice, do not receive the full treatment that would normally be provided.

The RPACs for patients discharged to a home health service, SNF, intermediate care facility (ICF), or another institution (e.g., rehabilitation facility) show a similar pattern. The RPACs are in the range of 0.796 to 0.890 for Medicare DRGs, increase 3 to 5 percent for SDRGs, RDRGs, and AP-DRGs, and increase 7 to 10 percent for APR-DRGs, resulting in RPACs in the range of 0.855 to 0.957 for APR-DRGs. It is likely that patients with ongoing treatment needs, whether in the home setting or a facility, have a higher severity-of-illness and that the higher RPACs for the more refined DRG systems, especially the APR-DRGs, are appropriate.

The most striking discharge destination pattern is for patients who die. The RPACs increase from 0.745 for Medicare DRGs to 0.800 for RDRGs, to 0.852 and 0.860 for SDRGs and AP-DRGs, and to 0.992 for APR-DRGs. This primarily reflects the experience of the elderly (65+ years), who account for three-quarters of the inpatient hospital deaths. The RPACs for patients who die are very variable through the different age ranges. For example, the RPACs for chronically ill children, which begin at a very low 0.385 with Medicare DRGs, increase to 0.433, 0.455, and 0.487 for SDRGs, RDRGs, and AP-DRGs, respectively, and to 0.589 for APR-DRGs. It is important to realize that the cost of patients who die is extremely variable. There are patients who die within the first or second day of admission, those who die after many

Table 32–17 Comparison of RPACs for DRG Systems by Patient Discharge Destination

| Patient discharge destination | Total cases | Total costs (000s) | Medicare DRGs | SDRGs | RDRGs | AP-DRGs | APR-DRGs | % Diff |
|---|---|---|---|---|---|---|---|---|
| Home | 3,475,196 | 16,797,798 | 1.085 | 1.062 | 1.066 | 1.064 | 1.034 | –4.7% |
| Left against medical advice | 28,888 | 101,002 | 1.313 | 1.300 | 1.290 | 1.283 | 1.242 | –5.4% |
| Home health service | 241,555 | 2,544,250 | 0.860 | 0.882 | 0.894 | 0.879 | 0.919 | +6.9% |
| Other institution | 92,643 | 1,074,774 | 0.796 | 0.825 | 0.836 | 0.818 | 0.855 | +7.4% |
| SNF | 201,238 | 2,189,539 | 0.821 | 0.869 | 0.865 | 0.856 | 0.907 | +10.5% |
| ICF | 33,802 | 283,399 | 0.890 | 0.923 | 0.918 | 0.914 | 0.957 | +7.5% |
| Died | 113,128 | 1,833,529 | 0.745 | 0.852 | 0.800 | 0.860 | 0.992 | +33.2% |
| Unknown | 797 | 5,871 | 0.969 | 1.060 | 1.038 | 1.059 | 1.162 | +20.0% |

Courtesy of 3M Health Information Systems, Wallingford, Connecticut.

weeks of intensive treatment, and terminally ill patients who receive only comfort-oriented treatment.

Overall, the more refined DRG systems decrease payment for patients discharged home and patients who left against medical advice and increase payment for all other discharge destinations.

## Primary Payer

Table 32–18 contains RPACs by primary payer. There are two patterns. First, the RPACs are closer to 1.00 for the more refined DRG systems, especially the APR-DRGs, for all primary payers except Other government, for which the RPACs are slightly further from 1.00. Second, the RPACs for Medicare, Medicaid, and Title V (maternal and child health) increase 2 to 3 percent from values that are less than 1.00. For other primary payers (except Other government), the RPACs decrease 2 to 6 percent from values that are greater than 1.00. In other words, the Medicare DRGs tend to underpay Medicare, Medicaid, and Title V patients and overpay most other payers. The more refined DRG systems, especially the APR-DRGs, provide more accurate payment levels for different primary payers.

For Medicare patients the RPAC increases 2.8 percent, from 0.983 for Medicare DRGs to 1.011 for APR-DRGs. The largest increases in RPAC for Medicare patients are for chronically ill children, presumably many of whom are ESRD patients, followed by patients aged 18–64, presumably many of whom are SSI disabled, and then by patients aged 80 and over, and patients aged 65–79. RPACs for chronically ill children and 18- to 64-year-old Medicare patients are very low for Medicare DRGs and increase closer to but not up to 1.00 for the more refined DRG systems.

For Medicaid patients, the RPACs increase from 0.921 for Medicare DRGs to 0.941 for the APR-DRGs. The largest increases in RPACs are for neonatal patients and chronically ill children, both of whom have very low RPACs for Medicare DRGs and low RPACs even for the more refined DRG systems.

The decrease in RPAC for patients with nongovernment payers was largest with the APR-DRGs. Of all the primary payers, the decrease in RPAC was largest for workers' compensation patients (6.6 percent), followed by Blue Cross, commercial insurance, "no charge" patients (3.6 percent), and self-pay patients (2.5 percent).

**Table 32–18** Comparison of RPACs for DRG Systems by Primary Payer

| Patient third-party payer | Total cases | Total costs (000s) | Medicare DRGs | SDRGs | RDRGs | AP-DRGs | APR-DRGs | % Diff |
|---|---|---|---|---|---|---|---|---|
| Medicare | 1,457,912 | 11,610,304 | 0.983 | 0.996 | 0.993 | 0.984 | 1.011 | +2.8% |
| Medicaid | 705,439 | 3,075,711 | 0.921 | 0.918 | 0.940 | 0.948 | 0.941 | +2.2% |
| Title V | 648 | 6,434 | 0.734 | 0.720 | 0.748 | 0.821 | 0.839 | +14.3% |
| Other government | 55,300 | 324,592 | 0.996 | 0.988 | 0.989 | 0.998 | 0.975 | −2.1% |
| Workers' compensation | 31,697 | 205,526 | 1.036 | 1.008 | 1.010 | 1.023 | 0.968 | −6.6% |
| Blue Cross/insur/other/ no charge | 1,722,248 | 8,558,782 | 1.046 | 1.033 | 1.028 | 1.035 | 1.008 | −3.6% |
| Self-pay | 214,003 | 1,048,813 | 1.033 | 1.026 | 1.027 | 1.036 | 1.007 | −2.5% |

Courtesy of 3M Health Information Systems, Wallingford, Connecticut.

## Hospital Service Line and Age

Table 32–19 contains RPACs by service line and patient age group. For this analysis, five service lines were defined. Table 32–19 also contains the results for each age group within each service line for which there was appreciable patient volume.

The methodology for defining service lines was the following hierarchical assignment logic:

- *Normal newborn.* Patients classified as normal newborn in any of the five DRG systems.
- *Mental health/drug and alcohol abuse.* Patients classified in the mental health and drug and alcohol abuse DRGs in any of the five DRG systems.
- *Obstetrical.* Patients classified in an obstetric DRG in any of the five DRG systems.
- *Surgical.* Patients classified in a surgical DRG in any of the five DRG systems.
- *Medical.* All patients not classified into one of the prior four service lines.

For normal newborns, the RPACs decrease 17.5 percent, from 1.231 for Medicare DRGs to 1.016 for APR-DRGs. In Medicare DRGs and SDRGs, many neonates who are really normal newborns are considered to have significant problems, and as a result the RPAC is as high as 1.231. While these newborns are relatively inexpensive and dollar differences per case are small, total case volume is very large, resulting in a significant financial impact. Approximately one-fourth of the newborns classified by the APR-DRGs as normal newborns are classified by Medicare DRGs and SDRGs as having significant problems.

Across all age ranges, the RPACs for mental health and drug and alcohol patients are substantially different from 1.00. Costs are generally underpaid for pediatric and elderly patients and overpaid for adult patients. There is one DRG system, the RDRGs, which uses age 0–17 years instead of secondary diagnoses to define mental health subclasses, and this largely removes the underpayment for children, except for those who also have physical chronic diseases. There appear to be distinctive mental health and drug and alcohol abuse problems that present at different ages, and the more refined DRG systems have RPACs closer to 1.0, but the extent of the improvement is limited given the available diagnostic information.

Table 32–19 Comparison of RPACs for DRG Systems by Hospital Service Line and Patient Age

| | Total cases | Total costs (000s) | Medicare DRGs | SDRGs | RDRGs | AP-DRGs | APR-DRGs | % Diff |
|---|---|---|---|---|---|---|---|---|
| Normal newborn | | | | | | | | |
| Normal newborn | 427,131 | 264,942 | 1.231 | 1.221 | 1.028 | 0.988 | 1.016 | −17.5% |
| Mental health/drug and alcohol abuse (MDCs 19 and 20) | | | | | | | | |
| 1 mo–17 yrs w/ chronic DX | 1,722 | 13,338 | 0.641 | 0.638 | 0.770 | 0.640 | 0.669 | +4.4% |
| 1 mo–17 yrs w/o chronic DX | 13,351 | 78,444 | 0.789 | 0.785 | 0.986 | 0.780 | 0.727 | −7.9% |
| 18–64 yrs | 124,633 | 497,177 | 1.110 | 1.103 | 1.066 | 1.102 | 1.073 | −3.3% |
| 65–79 yrs | 19,512 | 122,177 | 0.794 | 0.786 | 0.761 | 0.788 | 0.882 | +11.1% |
| 80+ yrs | 9,643 | 57,813 | 0.868 | 0.865 | 0.842 | 0.862 | 0.961 | +10.7% |
| Subtotal | 168,861 | 768,949 | 1.000 | 0.994 | 0.987 | 0.993 | 0.992 | −0.8% |
| Obstetrics (MDC 14) | | | | | | | | |
| 1 mo–17 yrs w/ chronic DX | 679 | 1,954 | 0.729 | 0.724 | 0.804 | 0.722 | 0.841 | +15.4% |
| 1 mo–17 yrs w/o chronic DX | 23,902 | 47,965 | 0.981 | 0.975 | 0.978 | 0.974 | 0.979 | −0.2% |
| 18–64 yrs | 384,210 | 750,279 | 1.015 | 1.008 | 1.008 | 1.008 | 1.004 | −1.1% |
| Subtotal | 408,791 | 800,198 | 1.013 | 1.006 | 1.005 | 1.006 | 1.002 | −1.1% |

| | | | | | | | |
|---|---|---|---|---|---|---|---|
| **Surgical** | | | | | | | |
| Neonates | 3,880 | 209,068 | 0.319 | 0.316 | 0.403 | 0.869 | 1.004 | +214.7% |
| 1 mo–17 yrs w/ chronic DX | 30,473 | 450,259 | 0.850 | 0.829 | 0.856 | 0.855 | 0.899 | +5.8% |
| 1 mo–17 yrs w/o chronic DX | 39,400 | 239,053 | 1.142 | 1.068 | 1.089 | 1.109 | 1.037 | −9.2% |
| 18–64 yrs | 691,629 | 6,004,421 | 1.037 | 1.025 | 1.021 | 1.025 | 0.997 | −3.9% |
| 65–79 yrs | 338,344 | 4,505,992 | 0.990 | 1.003 | 0.996 | 0.983 | 1.004 | +1.4% |
| 80+ yrs | 110,956 | 1,405,391 | 0.997 | 1.040 | 1.038 | 1.109 | 1.063 | +6.6% |
| Subtotal | 1,214,682 | 12,814,184 | 1.000 | 1.000 | 1.000 | 1.002 | 1.004 | +0.4% |
| **Medical** | | | | | | | |
| Neonates | 61,452 | 591,673 | 0.956 | 0.950 | 1.044 | 1.041 | 0.991 | +3.7% |
| 1 mo–17 yrs w/ chronic DX | 82,734 | 422,489 | 0.802 | 0.808 | 0.853 | 0.851 | 0.904 | +12.7% |
| 1 mo–17 yrs w/o chronic DX | 119,207 | 307,994 | 1.176 | 1.172 | 1.209 | 1.121 | 1.122 | −4.6% |
| 18–64 yrs | 753,189 | 3,561,291 | 1.006 | 1.000 | 0.997 | 1.000 | 0.963 | −4.3% |
| 65–79 yrs | 599,050 | 3,374,022 | 0.977 | 0.977 | 0.982 | 0.973 | 0.988 | +1.1% |
| 80+ yrs | 352,039 | 1,923,781 | 1.022 | 1.034 | 1.026 | 1.033 | 1.067 | +4.4% |
| Subtotal | 1,967,671 | 10,181,250 | 0.993 | 0.993 | 1.000 | 0.997 | 0.996 | +0.3% |

Courtesy of 3M Health Information Systems, Wallingford, Connecticut.

For adult obstetrical patients, the RPACs decrease 0.9 percent, from 1.015 for Medicare DRGs to 1.004 for APR-DRGs. For pediatric obstetrical patients without chronic conditions, the RPACs remain essentially the same, with a value of 0.981 for Medicare DRGs and 0.979 for APR-DRGs. For pediatric obstetrical patients with chronic conditions, the RPACs increase 15.4 percent, from 0.729 for Medicare DRGs to 0.841 for APR-DRGs. In general, adult obstetric patients have RPACs slightly above 1.00 and pediatric obstetrical patients have RPACs below 1.00.

Although overall surgical patients have RPACs very close to 1.00 for all DRG systems, there is substantial variation by patient age. The difference is most dramatic for neonatal surgical patients, with an increase in RPAC of 214.7 percent, from 0.319 for Medicare DRGs to 1.004 for APR-DRGs. From the standpoint of financial risk, this is very important, since only a very small number of hospitals offer neonatal surgical services. The RPACs for surgical patients increase for the more refined DRG systems for pediatric patients with chronic conditions and patients over 64 and decrease for pediatric patients without chronic conditions and patients age 18–64.

Overall, medical patients have RPACs very close to 1.00 for all DRG systems, but there is substantial variation by patient age. The RPACs for medical patients increase for the more refined DRG systems for neonates, pediatric patients with chronic conditions, and patients over 64 and decrease for pediatric patients without chronic conditions and patients aged 18–64.

## Hospital Type and Age

Table 32–20 contains RPACs by hospital type and patient age. Hospital type is defined as follows:

- *Children's hospital (n = 40).* Based on 20-percent random sample of patients from children's hospitals.
- *Major teaching hospital (n = 28).* Hospitals with a ratio of interns and residents to beds equal to or greater than 0.25.
- *Other urban hospital (n = 413).* Excludes children's and major teaching hospitals.
- *Other rural hospital (n = 234).* Excludes children's and major teaching hospitals.

**Table 32–20** Comparison of RPACs for DRG Systems by Hospital Type and Patient Age

| Hospital type | Total cases | Total costs (000s) | Medicare DRGs | SDRGs | RDRGs | AP-DRGs | APR-DRGs | % Diff |
|---|---|---|---|---|---|---|---|---|
| Children's hospitals | | | | | | | | |
| Neonates | 5,751 | 148,548 | 0.440 | 0.440 | 0.485 | 0.769 | 0.910 | +106.8% |
| 1mo–17 yrs w/ chronic DX | 36,266 | 368,130 | 0.715 | 0.706 | 0.728 | 0.739 | 0.790 | +10.5% |
| 1mo–17 yrs w/o chronic DX | 27,627 | 121,587 | 0.923 | 0.893 | 0.903 | 0.888 | 0.866 | −6.2% |
| 18+ yrs | 389 | 3,100 | 0.771 | 0.707 | 0.669 | 0.763 | 0.672 | −12.3% |
| Subtotal | 70,033 | 641,365 | 0.691 | 0.680 | 0.705 | 0.774 | 0.832 | +20.4% |
| Major teaching hospitals | | | | | | | | |
| Neonates | 61,906 | 291,737 | 0.623 | 0.611 | 0.785 | 0.871 | 0.892 | +43.2% |
| 1mo–17 yrs w/ chronic DX | 27,203 | 249,267 | 0.819 | 0.814 | 0.850 | 0.853 | 0.920 | +12.3% |
| 1mo–17 yrs w/o chronic DX | 27,121 | 133,424 | 0.914 | 0.887 | 0.910 | 0.890 | 0.885 | −3.2% |
| 18–64 yrs | 282,160 | 2,286,074 | 0.888 | 0.882 | 0.884 | 0.889 | 0.879 | −1.0% |
| 65–79 yrs | 73,533 | 853,848 | 0.862 | 0.878 | 0.874 | 0.868 | 0.894 | +3.7% |
| 80+ yrs | 23,275 | 227,647 | 0.840 | 0.872 | 0.862 | 0.865 | 0.904 | +7.6% |
| Subtotal | 495,198 | 4,041,997 | 0.857 | 0.857 | 0.872 | 0.880 | 0.887 | +3.5% |

*continues*

**Table 32–20** Continued

| Hospital type | Total cases | Total costs (000s) | Medicare DRGs | SDRGs | RDRGs | AP-DRGs | APR-DRGs | % Diff |
|---|---|---|---|---|---|---|---|---|
| Other urban hospitals | | | | | | | | |
| Neonates | 368,327 | 583,296 | 1.119 | 1.113 | 1.064 | 1.099 | 1.068 | -4.6% |
| 1mo–17 yrs w/ chronic DX | 45,574 | 252,123 | 0.953 | 0.945 | 1.002 | 0.974 | 1.002 | +5.1% |
| 1mo–17 yrs w/o chronic DX | 113,686 | 350,938 | 1.195 | 1.165 | 1.235 | 1.155 | 1.112 | -6.9% |
| 18–64 yrs | 1,450,127 | 7,648,775 | 1.055 | 1.045 | 1.040 | 1.044 | 1.012 | -4.1% |
| 65–79 yrs | 754,834 | 6,360,267 | 0.984 | 0.991 | 0.990 | 0.977 | 0.999 | +1.5% |
| 80+ yrs | 375,489 | 2,728,092 | 1.007 | 1.032 | 1.028 | 1.023 | 1.066 | +5.9% |
| Subtotal | 3,108,037 | 17,923,490 | 1.026 | 1.027 | 1.024 | 1.020 | 1.019 | -0.7% |
| Other rural hospitals | | | | | | | | |
| Neonates | 56,574 | 42,710 | 1.388 | 1.386 | 1.231 | 1.195 | 1.122 | -19.2% |
| 1mo–17 yrs w/ chronic DX | 6,565 | 18,520 | 1.286 | 1.271 | 1.360 | 1.290 | 1.309 | +1.8% |
| 1mo–17 yrs w/o chronic DX | 27,437 | 67,527 | 1.340 | 1.318 | 1.366 | 1.278 | 1.245 | -7.1% |
| 18–64 yrs | 220,995 | 875,330 | 1.165 | 1.149 | 1.131 | 1.146 | 1.084 | -7.0% |
| 65–79 yrs | 128,535 | 788,039 | 1.094 | 1.086 | 1.082 | 1.078 | 1.074 | -1.8% |
| 80+ yrs | 73,873 | 431,184 | 1.112 | 1.128 | 1.112 | 1.122 | 1.130 | +1.6% |
| Subtotals | 513,979 | 2,223,310 | 1.140 | 1.133 | 1.121 | 1.123 | 1.097 | -3.8% |

Courtesy of 3M Health Information Systems, Wallingford, Connecticut.

The refined DRG systems, and especially the APR-DRGs, produce RPACs that are much closer to 1.00 for all four hospital types. The percentage change is greatest for those hospital types for which the RPAC for Medicare DRGs is furthest from 1.00.

For children's hospitals, the RPACs increase 20.4 percent, from 0.691 for Medicare DRGs to 0.832 for APR-DRGs. The percentage increase is 106.8 for neonates, nearly all of whom are transfers in or readmissions, and 10.5 for pediatric patients with chronic conditions. The percentage decrease is 6.2 for pediatric patients without chronic conditions.

For major teaching hospitals, the RPACs increase 3.5 percent, from 0.857 for Medicare DRGs to 0.887 for APR-DRGs. The percentage increases in RPAC are 43.2 for neonates, 12.3 for pediatric patients with chronic conditions, 3.7 for patients aged 65–79, and 7.6 for elderly patients 80 years and older. The percentage decreases in RPAC are 3.2 percent for pediatric patients without chronic conditions and 1.0 percent for adults aged 18–64. The RPAC results for pediatric patients are fairly similar for major teaching hospitals and children's hospitals.

For other urban hospitals, the RPACs decrease 0.7 percent, from 1.026 with Medicare DRGs to 1.019 with APR-DRGs. The percentage decreases are 4.6 for neonates, 6.9 for pediatric patients without chronic conditions, and 4.1 for adults age 18–64. The RPACs increase 5.1 percent for neonates, 1.5 percent for patients aged 65–79, and 5.9 percent for elderly patients 80 years and older.

For other rural hospitals, the RPACs decrease 3.8 percent, from 1.140 for Medicare DRGs to 1.097 with APR-DRGs. The percentage increases in RPAC are 1.8 for pediatric patients with chronic conditions and 1.6 for elderly patients 80 years and older. The percentage decreases in RPAC are 19.2 for neonates, 7.1 for pediatric patients without chronic conditions, 7.0 for patients aged 18–64, and 1.8 for patients aged 65–79.

Overall, the more refined DRG systems, especially the APR-DRGs, generate RPACs that are substantially closer to 1.00 for most age ranges and hospital types, in particular, for children's hospitals and major teaching hospitals. Thus, the more refined DRG systems redistribute payment so that the extent of under- and overpayment is significantly reduced. This greatly reduces the need for payment adjustments, such as teaching adjustments, which are common in most DRG payment systems. It also provides classifications that are far more reliable for a variety of purposes, including hospital profiling, planning and budgeting, utilization review, and pricing.

## MORTALITY ANALYSIS

The purpose of the mortality analyses is to compare the ability of the various DRG systems to predict inpatient mortality. The DRGs, especially the APR-DRGs, are increasingly being used for this purpose. Numerous states are now publishing hospital risk-adjusted mortality rates in order to permit consumers to compare hospital outcomes. The Medicare DRG, SDRG, RDRG, and AP-DRG systems were developed for predicting resource use and were not intended for mortality prediction. In these systems, mortality is one of the variables used to define the DRGs (i.e., patients are assigned to different DRGs depending on whether they lived or died). This is not appropriate for a mortality prediction model, since it would be circular logic to use mortality to predict mortality. Therefore, for the mortality analyses, the data were regrouped to eliminate all mortality distinctions (i.e., patients were grouped into the DRG to which they would have been assigned if the patient had not died). Since APR-DRGs do not use mortality as a grouping variable, regrouping was not necessary for APR-DRGs.

The APR-DRGs have a separate set of severity subclasses that group patients based on the risk of mortality. These APR-DRG risk-of-mortality subclasses were used for the mortality analyses instead of the APR-DRG severity-of-illness subclasses, which were used for the analyses of cost and length of stay.

Mortality in the hospital is used in this analysis. Mortality in the hospital is commonly available in hospital administrative records, but if the patient dies the day following discharge from the hospital, this would not be reflected in the hospital's records. Ideally, mortality subsequent to discharge would have been merged with the data, but this information was not available.

The literature that assesses the ability of various models to predict mortality relies on two basic statistics, $R^2$ and the area under the receiver operating characteristics (ROC) curve. In order to be consistent with this literature, the same two statistics were used for evaluating the ability of the different DRG systems to predict inpatient mortality. The $R^2$ for mortality is computed by assigning each patient a value of 0 or 1 indicating whether the patient was discharged alive or dead, respectively. The predicted mortality for the patient is equal to the average value of the zero/one variable in the DRG to which the patient is assigned. The average value of the zero/one variable is equivalent to the fraction of patients who died in the DRG. Based on the zero/one variable, the $R^2$ for mortality is computed in the same manner as the $R^2$ for cost or length of stay.

The area under the ROC curve is commonly used to evaluate alternative methods for predicting a zero/one outcome. The area under the ROC curve is typically used for evaluating the efficacy of a method that predicts that a given patient will or will not experience the event of interest. The basis of the ROC curve is sensitivity and specificity. In this context, sensitivity is the probability that someone classified as dead actually died, while specificity is the probability that someone classified as alive actually did not die. Sensitivity and specificity are computed as follows:

$$\text{Sensitivity} = \Sigma n_i p_i \, I(p_i \geq P)/\Sigma n_i p_i$$

$$\text{Specificity} = \Sigma n_i \, (1 - p_i) \, I(p_i < P)/\Sigma n_i (1 - p_i)$$

where $n_i$ is the number of patients in DRG $i$, $p_i$ is the fraction of patients who died in DRG $i$, and $I(p_i)$ is an indicator that takes the value 1.0 if, in a particular DRG, the proportion of dead is at least $P$ for sensitivity and less than $P$ for specificity. The computation of the sensitivity and specificity assumes that all patients in a DRG died if $p_i \geq P$ and conversely that all patients in a DRG lived if $p_i < P$.

The ROC curve plots sensitivity against one minus specificity as the value of $P$ varies. The area under the ROC curve is referred to as the c-statistic. The c-statistic measures how well a DRG system discriminates between patients who lived and those who died. A c-statistic value of 0.5 indicates no ability to discriminate, while a value of 1.0 indicates perfect discrimination.

In order to understand the interpretation of the c-statistic, assume that patients are separated into two groups comprising those who died and those who did not. If a patient is drawn from each group at random, then each of these patients will have an associated DRG and each DRG will have an associated mortality rate (i.e., fraction of patients who die). The c-statistic is the probability that the mortality rate in the DRG assigned to the patient who died is higher than the mortality rate in the DRG assigned to the patient who lived. This probability would be expected to be high (i.e., near 1.0) for all DRG systems, since the deaths tend to be concentrated in relatively few DRGs. Thus, the c-statistic should be relatively high for each DRG system and as a result is unlikely to provide much differentiation across the DRG systems.

**Table 32–21** $R^2$ and C-statistic for Mortality

| Statistic | Patients | Medicare DRGs | SDRGs | RDRGs | AP-DRGs | APR-DRGs |
|---|---|---|---|---|---|---|
| $R^2$ | All | .1076 | .1662 | .1532 | .1507 | .2638 |
| $R^2$ | Surgical | .0773 | .1467 | .1247 | .1258 | .2431 |
| $R^2$ | Medical | .1149 | .1707 | .1601 | .1567 | .2676 |
| c | All | .8926 | .9230 | .9189 | .9252 | .9481 |
| c | Surgical | .8810 | .9315 | .9238 | .9275 | .9570 |
| c | Medical | .8935 | .9186 | .9157 | .9228 | .9439 |

Courtesy of 3M Health Information Systems, Wallingford, Connecticut.

Table 32–21 contains the $R^2$ and c-statistic for mortality. Across all patients, the percentage increases in $R^2$ relative to the Medicare DRGs are 54.5, 42.4, 40.1, and 145.2 for SDRGs, RDRGs, AP-DRGs, and APR-DRGs, respectively. As expected, the c-statistic was high for all DRG systems. Across all patients, the percentage increases in the c-statistic relative to the Medicare DRGs are 3.4, 2.9, 3.7, and 6.2 for SDRGs, RDRGs, AP-DRGs, and APR-DRGs, respectively.

Table 32–22 contains the $R^2$ and c-statistic for mortality for each DRG system for each component of the DRG structure. The $R^2$ and c-statistic for mortality at the MDC and DRG category level are virtually the same across the DRG systems. The percentage increases in $R^2$ from the addition of the subgroups to the DRG categories range from 9.02 percent for the Medicare DRGs to 141.35 percent for the APR-DRGs. The percentage increases in the c-statistic from the addition of the subgroups to the DRG categories range from 1.40 percent for the Medicare DRGs to 7.15 percent for the APR-DRGs. Thus, it is the secondary diagnosis subgroups that account for virtually all of the difference in $R^2$ and the c-statistic across the DRG systems.

## $R^2$ AND C-STATISTIC FOR MORTALITY BY MDC

The $R^2$ within each MDC for mortality and the percentage difference in $R^2$ relative to the Medicare DRGs are contained in Table 32–23. The c-statistic within each MDC for mortality and the percentage difference in the c-statistic relative to the Medicare DRGs are contained in Table 32–24.

**Table 32–22** $R^2$ and C-statistic for Mortality for Each Component of the DRG Structure

| Statistic | DRG system | MDC | MDC plus medical, surgical | DRG categories | Complete system |
|---|---|---|---|---|---|
| $R^2$ | Medicare DRGs | 0.0248 | 0.0263 | 0.0987 | 0.1076 |
| $R^2$ | SDRGs | 0.0249 | 0.0264 | 0.1024 | 0.1662 |
| $R^2$ | RDRGs | 0.0247 | 0.0262 | 0.1019 | 0.1532 |
| $R^2$ | AP-DRGs | 0.0247 | 0.0264 | NA | 0.1507 |
| $R^2$ | APR-DRGs | 0.0247 | 0.0266 | 0.1093 | 0.2638 |
| c | Medicare DRGs | 0.7635 | 0.7720 | 0.8803 | 0.8926 |
| c | SDRGs | 0.7639 | 0.7723 | 0.8834 | 0.9230 |
| c | RDRGs | 0.7635 | 0.7720 | 0.8843 | 0.9189 |
| c | AP-DRGs | 0.7629 | 0.7723 | NA | 0.9252 |
| c | APR-DRGs | 0.7632 | 0.7732 | 0.8848 | 0.9481 |

Courtesy of 3M Health Information Systems, Wallingford, Connecticut.

The magnitude of the difference in $R^2$ for mortality across the DRG systems can be very large for some MDCs. Since $R^2$ for mortality for the Medicare DRGs is very low for some MDCs, the difference in $R^2$ can be several thousand percent. Since the c-statistic is relatively high for all DRG systems, the magnitude of the difference in the c-statistic across the DRG systems tends to be in the 5- to 20-percent range for most MDCs. For example, the percentage increase in the c-statistic for the APR-DRGs relative to the Medicare DRGs ranges from 2.75 percent for newborns to 40.25 percent for HIV infections, with 18 of the MDCs in the 5- to 20-percent range. An increase in the c-statistic of 5–20 percent does represent a substantial improvement. In general, the c-statistic tends to be very high in MDCs where death is relatively rare (e.g., for APR-DRGs, the c-statistic is 0.9892 for the eye MDC) and lower in MDCs in which death is more frequent (e.g., for APR-DRGs, the c-statistic is 0.7725 for the HIV MDC).

A composite measure of the magnitude of the difference in $R^2$ and c-statistic across the MDCs can be obtained by computing the weighted percentage difference in $R^2$ and c-statistic across MDCs. Table 32–25 contains the weighted percentage difference in $R^2$ and c-statistic relative to the Medicare DRGs. This

**Table 32–23** $R^2$ for Mortality by MDC

| MDC | MDC Description | Medicare $R^2$ | SDRG $R^2$ | SDRG % Diff | RDRG $R^2$ | RDRG % Diff | AP-DRG $R^2$ | AP-DRG % Diff | APR-DRG $R^2$ | APR-DRG % Diff |
|---|---|---|---|---|---|---|---|---|---|---|
| 1 | Nervous | 0.0631 | 0.1430 | 126.62 | 0.1267 | 100.79 | 0.1343 | 112.83 | 0.2513 | 298.25 |
| 2 | Eye | 0.0035 | 0.0016 | 54.28 | 0.0375 | 971.42 | 0.0232 | 562.85 | 0.1558 | 4351.42 |
| 3 | Ear, nose, mouth and throat | 0.0773 | 0.1245 | 61.06 | 0.1408 | 82.14 | 0.0732 | −5.30 | 0.2354 | 204.52 |
| 4 | Respiratory | 0.1173 | 0.1364 | 16.28 | 0.1447 | 23.35 | 0.1417 | 20.80 | 0.2195 | 87.12 |
| 5 | Circulatory | 0.0978 | 0.1923 | 96.62 | 0.1473 | 50.61 | 0.1351 | 38.13 | 0.2855 | 191.92 |
| 6 | Digestive | 0.0464 | 0.1174 | 153.01 | 0.1079 | 132.54 | 0.1005 | 116.59 | 0.2197 | 373.49 |
| 7 | Hepatobiliary and pancreas | 0.1028 | 0.1704 | 65.75 | 0.1644 | 59.92 | 0.1371 | 33.36 | 0.2894 | 181.51 |
| 8 | Musculoskeletal and connective tissue | 0.0249 | 0.0938 | 276.70 | 0.0837 | 236.14 | 0.0702 | 181.92 | 0.2136 | 757.83 |
| 9 | Skin, subcutaneous tissue and breast | 0.0705 | 0.0998 | 41.56 | 0.1001 | 41.98 | 0.0914 | 29.64 | 0.2128 | 201.84 |
| 10 | Endocrine, nutritional and metabolic | 0.0267 | 0.0831 | 211.23 | 0.0718 | 168.91 | 0.0695 | 160.29 | 0.1723 | 545.31 |
| 11 | Kidney and urinary | 0.0585 | 0.1101 | 88.20 | 0.0966 | 65.12 | 0.1019 | 74.18 | 0.1831 | 212.99 |
| 12 | Male reproductive | 0.0851 | 0.1189 | 39.71 | 0.1154 | 35.60 | 0.0942 | 10.69 | 0.1853 | 117.74 |
| 13 | Female reproductive | 0.1087 | 0.1506 | 38.54 | 0.1561 | 43.60 | 0.1100 | 1.19 | 0.2318 | 113.24 |

| | | | | | | | | | |
|---|---|---|---|---|---|---|---|---|---|
| 14 | Pregnancy, child-birth and the puerperium | 0.0006 | 0.0005 | −16.66 | 0.0136 | 2166.66 | 0.0006 | 0.00 | 0.0717 | 11850.00 |
| 15 | Newborns | 0.0834 | 0.0830 | −0.47 | 0.2956 | 254.43 | 0.3036 | 264.02 | 0.4155 | 398.20 |
| 16 | Blood and immu-nological | 0.0062 | 0.0590 | 851.61 | 0.0664 | 970.96 | 0.0469 | 656.45 | 0.1806 | 2812.90 |
| 17 | Myeloproliferative and poorly diff neop | 0.1400 | 0.2005 | 43.21 | 0.1533 | 9.50 | 0.1875 | 33.92 | 0.2588 | 84.85 |
| 18 | Infectious and par-asitic | 0.0657 | 0.1379 | 109.89 | 0.1079 | 64.23 | 0.1311 | 99.54 | 0.2374 | 261.33 |
| 19 | Mental | 0.0056 | 0.0157 | 180.35 | 0.0057 | 1.78 | 0.0051 | −8.92 | 0.1533 | 2637.50 |
| 20 | Alcohol and drug | 0.0051 | 0.0360 | 605.88 | 0.0009 | −82.35 | 0.0044 | −13.72 | 0.2015 | 3850.98 |
| 21 | Injuries, poisonings and toxic effects | 0.0253 | 0.1044 | 312.64 | 0.0902 | 256.52 | 0.0574 | 126.87 | 0.2057 | 713.04 |
| 22 | Burns | 0.2346 | 0.2413 | 2.85 | 0.3263 | 39.08 | 0.2308 | −1.61 | 0.4269 | 81.96 |
| 23 | Factors influencing health status | 0.0089 | 0.0119 | 33.70 | 0.0331 | 271.91 | 0.0093 | 4.49 | 0.0923 | 937.07 |
| 24 | Human immunode-ficiency virus infections | 0.0053 | 0.0535 | 909.43 | 0.0530 | 900.00 | 0.0836 | 1477.35 | 0.1535 | 2796.22 |
| 25 | Multiple significant trauma | 0.0281 | 0.0283 | 0.71 | 0.0496 | 76.51 | 0.0713 | 153.73 | 0.1951 | 594.30 |
| 26 | Other (pre-MDC) | 0.1310 | 0.1651 | 26.03 | 0.1271 | −2.97 | 0.1285 | −1.90 | 0.2329 | 77.87 |

Courtesy of 3M Health Information Systems, Wallingford, Connecticut.

**Table 32–24** C-statistic for Mortality by MDC

| MDC | MDC Description | Medicare C | SDRG C | SDRG % Diff | RDRG C | RDRG % Diff | AP-DRG C | AP-DRG % Diff | APR-DRG C | APR-DRG % Diff |
|---|---|---|---|---|---|---|---|---|---|---|
| 1 | Nervous | 0.7758 | 0.8490 | 9.43 | 0.8377 | 7.97 | 0.8532 | 9.97 | 0.8989 | 15.86 |
| 2 | Eye | 0.7843 | 0.7484 | -4.57 | 0.9620 | 22.65 | 0.9532 | 21.53 | 0.9892 | 26.12 |
| 3 | Ear, nose, mouth and throat | 0.9263 | 0.9523 | 2.80 | 0.9668 | 4.37 | 0.9501 | 2.56 | 0.9814 | 5.94 |
| 4 | Respiratory | 0.8279 | 0.8464 | 2.23 | 0.8534 | 3.08 | 0.8593 | 3.79 | 0.8895 | 7.44 |
| 5 | Circulatory | 0.8154 | 0.8817 | 8.13 | 0.8595 | 5.40 | 0.8792 | 7.82 | 0.9146 | 12.16 |
| 6 | Digestive | 0.8130 | 0.8859 | 8.96 | 0.8688 | 6.86 | 0.8895 | 9.40 | 0.9261 | 13.91 |
| 7 | Hepatobiliary and pancreas | 0.8622 | 0.9085 | 5.36 | 0.9046 | 4.91 | 0.9005 | 4.44 | 0.9406 | 9.08 |
| 8 | Musculoskeletal and connective tissue | 0.8353 | 0.9130 | 9.30 | 0.9199 | 10.12 | 0.9188 | 9.99 | 0.9592 | 14.83 |
| 9 | Skin, subcutaneous tissue and breast | 0.8630 | 0.8904 | 3.17 | 0.9072 | 5.12 | 0.9192 | 6.51 | 0.9509 | 10.18 |
| 10 | Endocrine, nutritional and metabolic | 0.7532 | 0.8398 | 11.49 | 0.8090 | 7.40 | 0.8412 | 11.68 | 0.8832 | 17.25 |
| 11 | Kidney and urinary | 0.8256 | 0.8780 | 6.34 | 0.8602 | 4.19 | 0.8763 | 6.14 | 0.9151 | 10.84 |
| 12 | Male reproductive | 0.8682 | 0.8961 | 3.21 | 0.9508 | 9.51 | 0.9462 | 8.98 | 0.9681 | 11.50 |
| 13 | Female reproductive | 0.9527 | 0.9687 | 1.67 | 0.9840 | 3.28 | 0.9763 | 2.47 | 0.9886 | 3.76 |

| | | | | | | | | | | |
|---|---|---|---|---|---|---|---|---|---|---|
| 14 | Pregnancy, childbirth and the puerperium | 0.8015 | 0.7649 | -4.56 | 0.8599 | 7.28 | 0.8096 | 1.01 | 0.8602 | 7.32 |
| 15 | Newborns | 0.9468 | 0.9454 | -0.14 | 0.9651 | 1.93 | 0.9688 | 2.32 | 0.9729 | 2.75 |
| 16 | Blood and immunological | 0.6427 | 0.7845 | 22.06 | 0.8023 | 24.83 | 0.7988 | 24.28 | 0.8901 | 38.49 |
| 17 | Myeloprofroliferative and poorly diff neop | 0.8729 | 0.8956 | 2.60 | 0.8957 | 2.61 | 0.9069 | 3.89 | 0.9256 | 6.03 |
| 18 | Infectious and parasitic | 0.7438 | 0.8294 | 11.50 | 0.8025 | 7.89 | 0.8242 | 10.80 | 0.8773 | 17.94 |
| 19 | Mental | 0.7805 | 0.7928 | 1.57 | 0.7889 | 1.07 | 0.7748 | -0.73 | 0.9561 | 22.49 |
| 20 | Alcohol and drug | 0.8584 | 0.8583 | -0.01 | 0.6667 | -22.33 | 0.8531 | -0.61 | 0.9555 | 11.31 |
| 21 | Injuries, poisonings and toxic effects | 0.7859 | 0.8851 | 12.62 | 0.8658 | 10.16 | 0.8824 | 12.27 | 0.9308 | 18.43 |
| 22 | Burns | 0.8272 | 0.8768 | 5.99 | 0.9603 | 16.09 | 0.8259 | -0.15 | 0.9685 | 17.08 |
| 23 | Factors influencing health status | 0.6970 | 0.7123 | 2.19 | 0.7834 | 12.39 | 0.6985 | 0.21 | 0.8479 | 21.64 |
| 24 | Human immunodeficiency virus infections | 0.5508 | 0.6549 | 18.89 | 0.6805 | 23.54 | 0.6998 | 27.05 | 0.7725 | 40.25 |
| 25 | Multiple significant trauma | 0.6243 | 0.6234 | -0.14 | 0.6846 | 9.65 | 0.7251 | 16.14 | 0.8035 | 28.70 |
| 26 | Other (pre-MDC) | 0.7791 | 0.8360 | 7.30 | 0.7745 | -0.59 | 0.7763 | -0.35 | 0.8752 | 12.33 |

Courtesy of 3M Health Information Systems, Wallingford, Connecticut.

**Table 32–25** Weighted Percentage Difference in $R^2$ and C-statistic across MDCs Relative to Medicare DRGs

| Statistic | Patients | SDRGs | RDRGs | AP-DRGs | APR-DRGs |
|-----------|----------|-------|-------|---------|----------|
| $R^2$ | All | 98.30 | 391.14 | 94.95 | 1974.03 |
| $R^2$ | Surgical | 302.36 | 968.27 | 311.12 | 3945.78 |
| $R^2$ | Medical | 83.07 | 189.33 | 96.90 | 922.67 |
| c | All | 4.48 | 5.61 | 5.87 | 11.07 |
| c | Surgical | 7.79 | 12.49 | 11.16 | 18.03 |
| c | Medical | 4.29 | 4.69 | 5.20 | 10.30 |

Courtesy of 3M Health Information Systems, Wallingford, Connecticut.

---

is the same composite measure that was computed for cost in Table 32–5. The weighted percentage difference in $R^2$ for APR-DRGs is much higher than for the other DRG systems. For APR-DRGs the weighted percentage difference in $R^2$ is 922.67, 3945.48, and 1974.03 for medical patients, surgical patients, and all patients combined, respectively. The weighted percentage difference in $R^2$ is very large, in part, because some high-volume MDCs (e.g., MDC 15) have a very low $R^2$ for Medicare DRGs, which results in a very large percentage difference. The weighted percentage difference in c-statistic for APR-DRGs is nearly twice as large as for the other DRG systems. For APR-DRGs, the weighted percentage difference in c-statistic is 10.30, 18.03, and 11.07 for medical patients, surgical patients, and all patients combined, respectively.

## MORTALITY BY AGE AND SEX

The mortality rate can vary by the age and sex of the patient. The mortality rate predicted by a DRG system for patients with a specific age and sex can be computed by summing across all patients with the specified age and sex the mortality rate (i.e., fraction died) in the DRG assigned to each patient and dividing the resulting sum by the number of patients with the specified age and sex. The predicted mortality rate can then be compared to the actual mortality rate. The predicted and actual mortality rate should be similar within each age and sex group. A large difference between predicted and actual mortality within an age and sex group would imply that the DRG system does not adequately account for the risk of mortality for patients with the age and sex characteristics. Table 32–26 shows the percentage difference between the predicted and actual mortality rate for each of the DRG systems. The percentage difference is computed by subtracting the actual mortality rate from the predicted mortality rate and dividing by the actual mortality rate. The value of –15.7 for the Medicare DRGs for males aged 0–28 days means that the predicted mortality rate is 15.7 percent lower than the actual mortality rate. The actual mortality displayed in Table 32–26 is for the Medicare DRGs. There were slight differences in the actual mortality across the different DRG systems due to differences in the number of patients in the excluded DRGs 469 and 470. The definition of chronic conditions for the pediatric patients is the same as the one used in the payment impact analysis. The predicted mortality rates for newborns and patients over age 79 were lower than the actual mortality rates, while the predicted mortality rates for pediatric patients and adults under age 65 were higher than the actual mortality rates for both sexes and all DRG systems. For patients between ages 65 and 79, the predicted mortality rates were lower than the actual mortality rates for males and tended to be higher for females. The predicted and actual mortality rates differed the most for pediatric patients without chronic illnesses. The actual and predicted mortality rates for APR-DRGs were much more consistent than for the other DRG systems. These results show that none of the DRG systems fully account for the impact of age on patient mortality.

## HOSPITAL-LEVEL ANALYSIS FOR MORTALITY

The mortality analysis has focused on the ability of the DRG systems to predict mortality at the individual patient level. The DRGs can also be used to predict mortality at the hospital level. A regression was performed with the hospital actual mortality rate as the dependent variable and the predicted hospital mortality rate as the only independent variable. In addition, a multiple regression was performed using the same hospital characteristics that were used in the hospital-level analysis for cost. The expectation is that the addition of hospital characteristics will not substantially increase the $R^2$ for mortality. Table 32–27 contains the $R^2$ results for mortality at the hospital level for each DRG system.

Relative to the Medicare DRGs, the hospital-level $R^2$ values are 4.84, 5.73, 4.87, and 9.92 percent higher for SDRGs, RDRGs, AP-DRGs, and APR-

**Table 32–26** Percentage Difference between Predicted Mortality Rate and Actual Mortality Rate

| Sex / Age | Actual mortality rate | Medicare DRGs | SDRGs | RDRGs | AP-DRGs | APR-DRGs |
|---|---|---|---|---|---|---|
| **Male** | | | | | | |
| 0–28 days | 0.83 | –15.7 | –11.0 | –18.5 | 2.6 | –1.2 |
| 29 days – 17 yrs w/o chronic DX | 0.31 | 145.2 | 131.3 | 138.7 | 193.3 | 48.4 |
| 29 days – 17 yrs w/ chronic DX | 0.98 | 77.6 | 72.6 | 87.2 | 117.9 | 10.7 |
| 18–64 yrs | 2.15 | 40.0 | 34.9 | 36.3 | 39.1 | 16.1 |
| 65–79 yrs | 5.39 | –10.9 | –7.8 | –10.2 | –13.2 | –2.0 |
| 80+ yrs | 9.22 | –37.0 | –30.8 | –33.8 | –35.0 | –21.1 |
| **Female** | | | | | | |
| 0–28 days | 0.69 | –17.4 | –9.1 | –13.0 | 10.6 | 7.7 |
| 29 days – 17 yrs w/o chronic DX | 0.20 | 175.0 | 131.8 | 170.0 | 210.0 | 65.0 |
| 29 days – 17 yrs w/ chronic DX | 1.21 | 79.1 | 61.7 | 79.1 | 94.9 | –3.4 |
| 18–64 yrs | 0.88 | 50.0 | 45.9 | 43.7 | 44.2 | 19.5 |
| 65–79 yrs | 4.22 | 0.9 | 1.2 | 1.4 | –2.9 | 6.2 |
| 80+ yrs | 7.14 | –26.9 | –24.7 | –26.5 | –27.7 | –14.6 |

Courtesy of 3M Health Information Systems, Wallingford, Connecticut.

**Table 32–27** $R^2$ for Mortality at Hospital Level across DRG Systems

|  | Medicare DRGs | SDRGs | RDRGs | AP-DRGs | APR-DRGs |
|---|---|---|---|---|---|
| $R^2$ expected mortality rate only | 0.6139 | 0.6436 | 0.6491 | 0.6438 | 0.6748 |
| $R^2$ expected mortality rate plus hospital characteristics | 0.6518 | 0.6778 | 0.6871 | 0.6778 | 0.6991 |
| Percentage increase in $R^2$ | 6.17 | 5.31 | 5.85 | 5.28 | 3.60 |

Courtesy of 3M Health Information Systems, Wallingford, Connecticut.

DRGs, respectively. The addition of the hospital characteristics increased the $R^2$ for all the DRG systems. The percentage increases in $R^2$ due to the addition of the hospital characteristics were 6.17, 5.31, 5.85, 5.28, and 3.60 for the Medicare DRGs, SDRGs, RDRGs, AP-DRGs, and APR-DRGs, respectively. The addition of the hospital characteristic did not substantially improve the hospital-level $R^2$ for mortality for any of the DRG systems. This is in contrast to the hospital-level $R^2$ for cost, for which the addition of the hospital characteristics resulted in substantial improvement in $R^2$ for the Medicare DRGs, SDRGs, and RDRGs.

## CONCLUSIONS

The ability of the five DRG systems to predict cost and mortality were evaluated across a broad range of patient and hospital characteristics. The major findings from the analysis are as follows:

- There are substantial differences in the ability of the different DRG systems to predict patient cost. Relative to Medicare DRGs, the untrimmed $R^2$ values for cost are 8.1, 13.5, 15.0 and 30.3 percent higher for SDRGs, RDRGs, AP-DRGs, and APR-DRGs, respectively. The percentage increase in $R^2$ is greater for medical patients than for surgical patients.
- The primary source of the difference in $R^2$ for cost is the secondary diagnosis subgroups within each DRG system. The increases in untrimmed $R^2$ due to the secondary diagnosis subgroups range from 2.69 percent for

the Medicare DRGs to 21.18 percent for APR-DRGs. The large contribution to $R^2$ due to the secondary diagnosis subclasses for APR-DRGs is likely the result of the APR-DRGs' being the only DRG system that explicitly recognizes the impact of multiple complications and comorbidities.

- The untrimmed $R^2$ for cost varies considerably across the individual MDCs, ranging from 0.0417 for the mental health MDC for Medicare DRGs to 0.6274 for the newborn MDC for APR-DRGs.
- Within individual MDCs, the untrimmed $R^2$ for cost differs substantially across the different DRG systems. For some MDCs the untrimmed $R^2$ for cost across the DRG systems differs by a factor of 3 or 4.
- The weighted percentage difference in untrimmed $R^2$ values for cost across MDCs relative to the Medicare DRGs are 18.78, 34.26, 30.45 and 70.62 percent for SDRGs, RDRGs, AP-DRGs, and APR-DRGs, respectively. Thus, at the MDC level the APR-DRGs have an untrimmed $R^2$ for cost that is 70 percent higher than the Medicare DRGs.
- Data trimming excludes more of the unexplained variability for DRG systems with a low untrimmed $R^2$. As a result of data trimming, the $R^2$ for the different DRG systems is artificially compressed.
- There are substantial differences in which patients are trimmed in each of the different DRG systems. A disproportionate number of severity-of-illness level 3 and 4 patients in APR-DRGs are high outliers in the other DRG systems, and a disproportionate number of severity-of-illness level 1 patients in APR-DRGs are low outliers in the other DRG systems.
- Relative to Medicare DRGs, the trimmed $R^2$ values for cost are 3.5, 8.3, 8.7 and 16.7 percent higher for SDRGs, RDRGs, AP-DRGs, and APR-DRGs, respectively.
- The weighted percentage differences in trimmed $R^2$ for cost across MDCs relative to the Medicare DRGs are 11.19, 20.62, 18.54, and 41.15 percent for SDRGs, RDRGs, AP-DRGs, and APR-DRGs, respectively.
- In general, the trimmed $R^2$ results for cost parallel the untrimmed results, except that the magnitude of the differences are compressed.
- The $R^2$ values for cost at the hospital level are 20–30 percent higher than at the patient level. Relative to the Medicare DRGs, the hospital-level $R^2$ values for cost are 1.27, 6.71, 14.63, and 21.15 percent higher for SDRGs, RDRGs, AP-DRGs, and APR-DRGs, respectively. The addition of hospital characteristics increases the hospital-level $R^2$ by 19.54, 20.67, 15.33, 7.98, and 4.83 percent for Medicare DRGs, SDRGs,

RDRGs, AP-DRGs, and APR-DRGs, respectively. With AP-DRGs and APR-DRGs, the need for payment adjustments based on hospital characteristics is greatly reduced.

- In general, the more refined DRG systems, especially the APR-DRGs, result in payment levels closer to hospital cost.

- The more refined DRG systems, especially APR-DRGs, tend to increase payments to nonnormal neonates; pediatric patients with chronic conditions; patients 65 years and older; patients transferred in from acute care hospitals or SNFs; patients discharged to nonacute institutions; patients who died; Medicare, Medicaid, and Title V patients; and patients treated in children's hospitals and major teaching hospitals.

- Conversely, the more refined DRG systems, especially APR-DRGs, tend to decrease payments for normal newborns; pediatric patients without chronic conditions; adult patients aged 18–64 years; patients discharged home; patients who left against medical advice; commercial, self-pay, workers' compensation, and "no charge" patients; and patients treated in rural hospitals.

- There are substantial differences in the ability of the different DRG systems to predict patient mortality. Relative to the Medicare DRGs, the percentage increases in $R^2$ for mortality are 54.5, 42.4, 40.1, and 145.2 percent for SDRGs, RDRGs, AP-DRGs, and APR-DRGs, respectively. Relative to the Medicare DRGs, the percentage increases in the c-statistic are 3.4, 2.9, 3.7, and 6.2 percent for SDRGs, RDRGs, AP-DRGs, and APR-DRGs, respectively.

- Within individual MDCs, the $R^2$ and c-statistic for mortality differs substantially across the DRG systems. The weighted percentage differences in $R^2$ for mortality across MDCs relative to the Medicare DRGs are 98.30, 391.14, 94.95, and 1974.03 for SDRGs, RDRGs, AP-DRGs, and APR-DRGs, respectively. The weighted percentage differences in the c-statistic for mortality across MDCs relative to the Medicare DRGs are 4.48, 5.61, 5.87, and 11.07, respectively.

- Across age and sex groups, the actual and predicted mortality are substantially closer for the APR-DRGs than for the other DRG systems.

- Relative to Medicare DRGs, the hospital level $R^2$ for mortality is 4.83, 5.73, 4.86, and 9.92 percent higher for SDRGs, RDRGs, AP-DRGs, and APR-DRGs, respectively. The addition of hospital characteristics increases the hospital level $R^2$ for mortality by 6.17, 5.31, 5.85, 5.28, and

3.60 percent for the Medicare DRGs, SDRGs, RDRGs, AP-DRGs, and APR-DRGs, respectively.

With the expansion of managed care, health plans are directing patients to selected hospitals that may appear more price competitive. States are increasingly disseminating information on hospital price and outcomes to consumers. A patient classification system is a critical component of these efforts, and the various DRG systems are being widely used. Based on the results of the analysis, there are several conclusions:

- If the DRGs are being applied to non-Medicare patients, then the Medicare DRGs, SDRGs, and RDRGs are not appropriate. This is particularly true for newborn and pediatric patients with chronic diseases.
- If the DRGs are being used for payment purposes, the use of the more refined DRG systems, especially the APR-DRGs, greatly reduces the need for payment adjustments based on hospital characteristics.
- Children's hospitals and major teaching hospitals will be financially disadvantaged in price negotiations or in a DRG-based payment system unless there is the kind of recognition of patient severity-of-illness provided for in the more refined DRG systems.
- The only DRG system that is applicable to mortality is the APR-DRGs. In the other DRG systems, death is one of the variables used to define the DRGs. Even if death is removed as part of the definition of the DRGs, the ability of these DRG systems to predict patient mortality is substantially lower than the APR-DRGs, especially for certain age and sex groups.
- If the DRGs are being used for internal management, the severity-of-illness levels in the more refined DRG systems provide a more clinically meaningful basis for communication of results to medical staffs.

The availability of severity-of-illness-adjusted pricing data and risk-adjusted data on the quality of the services being purchased is a fundamental requirement for managed care programs to be effective. There are more than 20 states that publicly disseminate information on provider performance. For example, the state of Florida annually publishes comparative information on charges, length of stay, and mortality for all hospitals in the state.[10] The Florida reports use APR-DRGs to adjust for severity of illness and risk of mortality.

The publicly disseminated information on provider performance will ultimately expand to include complication rates, readmission rates, and other measures of efficiency and quality. In 1996, California implemented a requirement that hospitals report for each secondary diagnosis an indication of whether the secondary diagnosis was present at admission.[11] This requirement will allow meaningful complication rates to be computed, admission severity of illness and risk of mortality to be determined, and patient deterioration or improvement during the hospitalization to be measured. For such data to be useful, they must be risk adjusted. If a multitude of risk adjustment methodologies are necessary to use such data, then this will be a burden for providers and will make communication of results difficult. The APR-DRGs added risk-of-mortality subclasses to the basic DRG structure. Similarly, the DRG approach can be expanded to encompass other measures of resource use and quality.

The limiting factor for expanding the applications of DRGs is not in the DRG methodology, but the International Classification of Diseases, Ninth Revision, Clinical Modification (ICD-9-CM), which is used to report diagnoses and procedures. With ICD-9-CM and the upcoming tenth revision of ICD, many important patient characteristics cannot be coded. In recent years, there have been some improvements to ICD-9-CM. For example, a specification of birth weight was added as a fifth digit for the newborn codes, and the number of days on mechanical ventilation was added to the mechanical ventilation codes. While these additions provide important information, there are still many clinical areas in which additional information is needed.

For the evaluation of certain diseases, specific vital signs, laboratory results, or health status information is essential. For example, the hematocrit would be useful in assessing patients with anemia or gastrointestinal bleeding. In a manner similar to the birth weight ranges for newborn codes, a fifth digit could be added to the codes for these diseases that specifies the range of the hematocrit. In addition, functional health status measures, such as activities of daily living, provide important information. Patient frailty and limitations in mobility impact both mortality and the ability to recover.

The additional information would only be collected on patients with specific diseases, which minimizes the data collection burden on providers. The collection of a large number of patient characteristics across all patients is neither practical nor necessary. Using ICD-9-CM to obtain selective additional information when necessary is a practical and cost-effective means of expanding the patient characteristics available to the DRGs. There are existing proposals on how ICD-9-CM could be expanded.[12]

With the appropriate additional information, the DRG methodology can be adapted to apply to a wide spectrum of resource use and quality measures. The DRGs are the most widely used and well-understood method of measuring case mix. As evidenced by the five DRG systems evaluated in this chapter, the DRG methodology has evolved and is continuing to evolve.

## NOTES

1. R. Fetter et al., "Case Mix Definition by Diagnosis-related Groups," *Medical Care* 18, no. 2 (1980): 1–53.
2. R. Averill et al., *Diagnosis Related Groups Definitions Manual, Version 12.0* (Wallingford, CT: 3M Health Information Systems, 1994).
3. J. Freeman et al., "Diagnosis Related Group Refinement with Diagnosis- and Procedure-Specific Comorbidities and Complications," *Medical Care* 33, no. 8 (1995): 806–827.
4. R. Berry et al., Final Report of Children's Hospitals Case Mix Classification Project. Alexandria, VA: NACRI, 1986.
5. R. Averill et al., All Patient Diagnosis Related Groups Definitions Manual, Version 12.0 (Wallingford, CT: 3M Health Information Systems, 1995).
6. *Federal Register* 16, no. 106 (2 June, 1995): 29209.
7. R. Averill et al., *All Patient Refined Diagnosis Related Groups* (Wallingford, CT: 3M Health Information Systems, 1995).
8. HCIA, Inc., Baltimore, Maryland, provided the data for the study, 1995.
9. R. Feldman, "Are We Splitting Hairs over Splitting DRGs?" *Health Services Research* 27, no. 5 (1992): 613–617.
10. *1996 Guide to Hospitals in Florida* (Tallahassee, FL: State of Florida Agency for Health Care Administration, 1996).
11. *California Assembly Bill 3639*, Chapter 1063, *Statutes of State of California*, 1994; effective January 1, 1996.
12. N. Goldfield et al., *Improving the Prediction of Outpatient Services Using Patient Characteristics: Results of a Six-Month Prospective Study*, final report (Wallingford, CT: 3M Health Information Systems, 30 June, 1996).

CHAPTER 33

# Using Severity-adjusted Data to Impact Clinical Pathways

*Carol Fridlin*

As managed care's impact on the health care industry continues to grow, St. Vincent Hospital and Health Services, Indianapolis, Indiana, has chosen to take a proactive approach. The hospital and its physicians have joined forces to reduce costs and average length of stay (LOS) in a key practice area—orthopedics. St. Vincent has achieved a 40-percent decrease in average length of stay over a three-year period, aided by exceptional cooperation on the part of its physicians and through the use of severity adjustment software to help measure outcomes.

St. Vincent is an 800-bed tertiary-care hospital. Approximately 50 percent of the hospital population are Medicare patients, with the remaining 50 percent representing a solid payer base fortunate for a large urban hospital.

The trend toward managed care, however, is making its presence felt in Indiana as in the rest of the country. Managed care has moved into certain areas of the Midwest at a slightly slower pace than it has on the East and West Coasts. This has given St. Vincent the opportunity to look to and learn from hospitals confronting more aggressive managed care programs elsewhere in the country.

*Source*: Reprinted with permission from C. Fridlin, Using Severity-Adjusted Data to Impact Clinical Pathways, *Healthcare Information Management*, Vol. 10, No. 1, pp. 23–30, © 1996, Healthcare Information and Management Systems Society and Jossey-Bass Inc.

As part of the Daughters of Charity national chain of hospitals, the largest Catholic hospital system in the United States, St. Vincent has access to useful outcomes data from its sister hospitals across the country. Today, measuring outcomes is a way for us to evaluate our effectiveness internally. Tomorrow, outcomes management will help us meet the challenge of managed care. It is critical that hospitals begin preparing now, for managed care is the future of health care. Those who are not prepared will be left behind.

At St. Vincent, outcomes measurement and management programs are under the direction of the Quality Review Department. The department is responsible for the hospital's utilization management program and quality improvement (QI) program for the medical staff. The rationale for combining these objectives in one department is the critical need to demonstrate continuous quality outcomes while reducing length of stay.

A major outcomes initiative over the past two years has been in the hospital's orthopedic department. Orthopedics is one of the fastest growing specialties at St. Vincent; the number of total joint orthopedic surgery patients increased 30 percent over the past three years, going from 572 patients in 1992 to a projected 800 in 1995. This growth mirrors the national trend. As the population ages, the number of potential candidates for orthopedic surgery increases. New, advanced technology also adds to the prevalence of such procedures. Orthopedic surgery is safer than it has ever been, and as a result, more people are willing to undergo these elective procedures.

The Quality Review Department began by gathering LOS data. Next, a multidisciplinary quality improvement team was assembled, made up of nurses, physical therapists, pharmacists, experts from medical records and finance, and physicians—in fact, half the members were physicians. Involving doctors at the very beginning turned out to be a wise strategy. They have come to trust the process because of their early involvement. They recognize that the process is not always perfect, but they also understand the importance of physician participation if the project is to succeed.

Our initial focus was on major joint surgery (DRG 209) because it is the highest-volume orthopedic procedure performed at St. Vincent. After an initial analysis of cost data for DRG 209, it became clear that the two areas needing most improvement from a utilization perspective were surgery (owing in part to the expense of prosthetic devices) and length of stay/bed changes. This chapter discusses improvements to length of stay.

For St. Vincent, as for most hospitals, about 75 percent of major joint surgery patients are Medicare patients. A very small percentage of the hospital's

Medicare patients are included in the externally managed commercial payer population, which makes an internal program for managing these cases and reducing the cost and length of stay even more critical.

In March 1993, the first clinical pathway for major joint surgery was initiated by the multidisciplinary team. The first pathway was an eight-day pathway. At that time, our average length of stay was just over eight days—80 percent of our patients were going home in eight days—and the Medicare geometric mean was 7.7 days. An eight-day pathway was a comfortable starting point, and physicians were in support.

It was obvious, however, that an average eight-day LOS for major joint surgery would not be winning St. Vincent many managed care contracts. It was critical that the average LOS for major joint surgery be reduced. We knew from third-party payers that daily bed charges make up a large portion of cost and that reducing length of stay very quickly reduces cost as well.

The industry benchmark is four days; a number that comes from Milliman and Robertson, an actuarial firm in California that contracts with the "Blues" of Indiana. The firm has a national reputation for setting aggressive industry standards, and the four-day benchmark is used extensively by third-party payers.

Making the transition from an eight day pathway to a four-day pathway represented a significant challenge. So, as an interim step, the multidisciplinary team established a pathway of six days. It soon became apparent that some additional data were needed in order to make this benchmark a feasible goal.

St. Vincent's Orthopedic Medical Staff Department had been receiving information from the Quality Review staff on average length of stay, both in department aggregate form and in separate reports for each individual physician. This type of information sharing is standard for most hospitals. There are some problems, however, in communicating average length-of-stay data. What cases should be included? Should an average LOS be calculated based on all cases or should outliers and mortality be deleted? This same question arises when calculating average cost per case. Another important issue is severity adjustment. Most physicians with a higher average LOS assume they have more complex cases. And, finally, what should be used as a benchmark for average LOS?

To address these issues, Quality Review first decided to change the way in which data was displayed by graphing the percentage of orthopedic patients that met a designated LOS. Using both the pathway LOS of six days and the four-day benchmark, the physician could graphically see the percentage of orthopedic patients discharged within these time periods (see Figure 33–1). This solved some of the problems associated with calculating average LOS. All patients could be included in the percentage, and the problem of outliers and mortality was eliminated.

Analyzing the data against the benchmark did not address the issue of severity, however. As discussed earlier, physicians with a higher average LOS maintain they are treating more complex cases. The orthopedic quality improvement team members soon realized that the only way to accurately measure length of stay and pinpoint specific areas needing improvement was to adjust the data by severity.

The Indiana Hospital Association had purchased 3M APR (all patient refined) DRG software in the summer of 1994 for the purposes of evaluating and comparing outcomes data from all Indiana hospitals. This, obviously, was a major incentive for St. Vincent in making a purchase decision. In addition, APR-DRG software integrated easily with the hospital's medical records systems. In October 1994 the hospital installed APR-DRG software on its CAD-CARS medical record system and backloaded it for the previous year in order to have a solid base of severity-adjusted data.

APR-DRG severity adjustment software uses computer logic to automatically read patients' Uniform Billing '95 discharge forms and to group patients into four severity classifications—from minor to extreme—based on diagnosis and treatment codes.

The software can be used to compare patients in each of four severity groups by hospital, department, and individual physician, in terms of length of stay, resource consumption, and mortality. Patients with similar severity can be compared both physician to physician within an institution and hospital to hospital, through data provided by the Indiana Hospital Association.

Once we severity-adjusted the data using APR-DRG software, we were able to demonstrate that most of the major joint patients were actually quite healthy. In fact, 91 percent of orthopedic patients who had received major joint surgery during the previous year were classified as severity levels 1 and 2, or minor and moderate severity (see Figure 33–1).

We reviewed with physicians how many of their patients were within the six-day guideline or the four-day best-practice LOS. We found that 82 percent of the patients met the six-day pathway and, of that, 52 percent met the four-day best practice rule.

It was clear that more patients should be meeting the four-day best practice. The question was, how many? For major joint procedures, 74 percent of St.

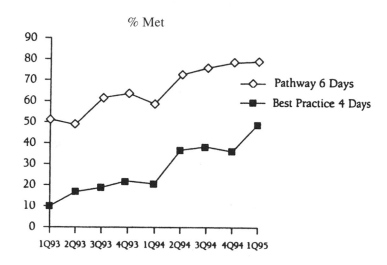

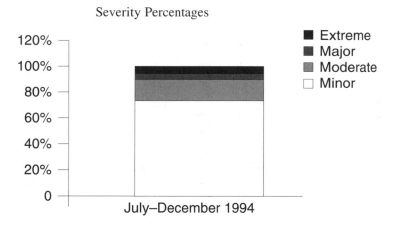

**Figure 33–1** APR-DRG 209—Major Joint (Percentage Met and Severity Percentages). *Note:* Best practice and clinical path goals have been established using minor severity level to equal best practice goal and severity level 1 and 2 to equal clinical path goal. Goals for July–December 1994: best practice = 74 percent, clinical path = 91 percent. *Source*: Reprinted with permission from C. Fridlin, Using Severity-Adjusted Data to Impact Clinical Pathways, *Healthcare Information Management*, Vol. 10, No. 1, pp. 23–30, © 1996, Healthcare Information and Management Systems Society and Jossey-Bass Inc.

Vincent patients are classified as severity level 1, or minor. This makes sense, since it is an elective surgery generally done on healthy people. There is no reason many of these patients cannot be sent home in accordance with the best-practice guideline of four days. St. Vincent does not operate an extended care facility, so a four-day length of stay seemed to be a reasonable benchmark for severity level 1 patients.

The next step was to provide orthopedic physicians with their own data, as compared with the department's. Figure 33–2 indicates the severity breakdown of patients for each physician (identified by alphabet letters). Most of each physician's cases fall into severity level 1. Taking this information one step further, we examined the cases in each severity level by physician and

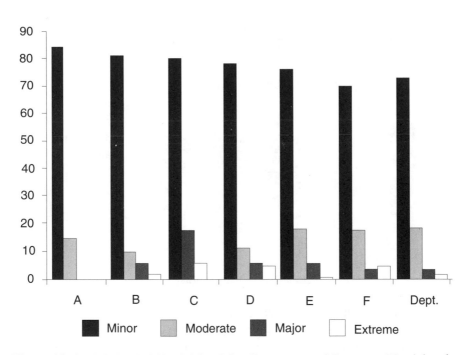

**Figure 33–2** APR-DRG 209—Major Joint (Percentage of Cases per Physician, by Severity Index). *Source*: Reprinted with permission from C. Fridlin, Using Severity-Adjusted Data to Impact Clinical Pathways, *Healthcare Information Management*, Vol. 10, No. 1, pp. 23–30, © 1996, Healthcare Information and Management Systems Society and Jossey-Bass Inc.

compared cost to LOS for each severity level. Figure 33–3 shows the individual data for each physician compared with their peers and the department for severity level 2, or moderate. From this data we were able to identify Doctors E and F as those physicians whose cases most closely met the benchmark goal. This information was a starting point for examining differences in practice methods that most influence cost and length of stay.

Physicians immediately question the integrity of the data. Presenting data such as this is challenging, especially the first time. Perfect data collection is

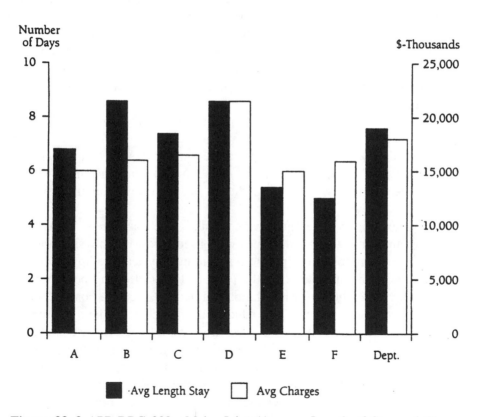

**Figure 33–3** APR-DRG 209—Major Joint (Average Length of Stay and Charge Comparison for Severity Level 2 [Moderate]) *Source*: Reprinted with permission from C. Fridlin, Using Severity-Adjusted Data to Impact Clinical Pathways, *Healthcare Information Management*, Vol. 10, No. 1, pp. 23–30, © 1996, Healthcare Information and Management Systems Society and Jossey-Bass Inc.

impossible when human beings are keying in the information. There is an error rate, which is monitored continuously. But because we have shared so much data with the physicians, they have become more comfortable with the validity of the severity-adjusted data. They understand that the goal is perfection, and they have assisted by reviewing and monitoring the data. The physicians also have the opportunity to thoroughly evaluate the severity adjustment software in advance and review its underlying logic.

Using outcomes information provided by the state of Indiana, we also were able to see how St. Vincent compared to other hospitals. We soon discovered that our severity did not warrant our costs. Were we underestimating our severity? The orthopedic physicians identified a twofold process problem: (1) physicians were not adequately documenting patients' problems, especially preexisting conditions, and (2) they felt they needed proactive education from the Health Information Management Department. Physicians did not know what they were supposed to be documenting. And they wanted that type of education. They wanted to know what made a difference.

We then examined those factors that have an impact on length of stay. What are the different protocols used? Did the patient get an epidural? What kind of pain medication was used? The faster these patients are up and mobile and going to physical therapy, the quicker they can go home. Pain management became a major initiative for orthopedics as one means of reducing length of stay.

We also examined different practice issues, such as when drains were pulled, whether or not CPM machines were used, and when physical therapy was initiated. A simple step involved providing physical therapy on weekends. Data analysis indicated that the primary factor affecting postoperative length of stay was whether or not the patient had attended the hospital's total joint program prior to surgery. This educational and physical therapy program prepares the patient for a successful recovery period. It includes pre- and post-surgery conditioning exercises and written diaries kept by the patient to aid in consultations with the physician. Formerly offered on a voluntary basis, this program is now mandatory for patients undergoing any major joint procedure.

Throughout the process of revising pathways, adjusting practice methods, and reducing length of stay, Quality Review carefully monitored complication rates and readmission rates. The result has been significant progress in reducing length of stay without compromise to the quality of patient care. At the end of second quarter of 1995, 86 percent of our major joint patients were discharged within six days, and 63 percent within four days. That is a big improvement over where we started. It also represents an approximate cost savings of $205,000.

Severity levels continue to be an issue. Approximately 70 percent of orthopedic patients continue to fall into a minor severity classification and could be discharged within the national best-practice guideline of four days. Given the progress made to date, however, the orthopedic QI team adopted a five-day pathway for major joint procedures on July 1, 1995.

Outcomes improvement initiatives at St. Vincent, such as the effort described in this chapter, move forward and find success in large part because of the longstanding partnership between the hospital and the medical staff. The hospital has been willing to share both cost and charge data with physicians in the spirit that the team cannot function without their total cooperation. St. Vincent also has allocated resources to the Quality Review Department to give each medical staff department an assigned quality review nurse. The nurse's role is to work with the department in an educational format. Physicians practice independently, and, unless the hospital is willing to share data on length of stay, complications, cost, charges, and so on, the physician is only guessing at his or her individual performance. The quality review nurse brings to the medical staff this internal comparative data, as well as external data from all available sources, such as Medpar (the national data bank for Medicare patients), managed-care companies, and state data.

The changing world of health care means a tremendous learning curve for physicians. They know that managed care companies will compare them to their peers and that outcomes data will often be the major factor in awarding managed care contracts Those of us managing outcomes measurement programs can help our doctors by giving them these data now so that they can learn from each other innovative ways in which to practice to the best standard. Tools like APR-DRG software help us help them prepare for the future.

# Concluding Comments

*Patrick Romano, Richard F. Averill, and Norbert Goldfield*

## POINT: IT IS IMPORTANT TO JUDICIOUSLY USE IN PROVIDER PROFILES SECONDARY DIAGNOSES THAT REPRESENT COMORBIDITIES OR, POSSIBLY, COMPLICATIONS

*Richard F. Averill and Norbert Goldfield*

With the advent of managed care the need for comparative information concerning the performance of health care providers has greatly increased. As a result many states have begun to publicly disseminate comparative data on provider performance to consumers. The assumption underlying the publication of such information is that consumers will use the performance information to select providers, which in turn will require providers to improve performance in order to avoid losing patient volume. The publication of comparative provider profiles will identify "winners" as well as "losers." Since the comparisons will be publicly available, the consequences of being a "loser" can be significant. Reputations, careers, and even financial viability can be at stake. The dissemination of provider profiles is by no means an academic exercise. The results have real consequences. Underlying our judicial system is the belief that it is more acceptable to allow some people who are guilty to go free than to allow one person who is innocent to be wrongly convicted. Thus, we maintain a high standard of reasonable doubt in favor of the accused party. Being labeled a "loser" in a provider profile is no different than being the accused in a legal proceeding. This is not an idle philosophical analogy. The philosophical premise from which one begins directly determines the choices that will be made on methodological issues. Hospitals should be given every reasonable doubt in the methodology used in the provider profiles. It is far more acceptable to fail to identify a hospital as a "winner" than it is to falsely identify a hospital as a "loser."

Provider profiles will often contain comparative information on provider resource use such as length of stay and charges and on outcomes such as mortality. In terms of outcome measures inpatient mortality and complication rates are the two outcome measures commonly considered for inclusion in provider profiles. The purpose of this paper is to evaluate the issues associated with the use of these two outcome measures in provider profiles.

## Complication Rates

The development of any outcome measure must reflect the strengths and limitations of the coding system that is used to record the data. For diagnoses, *International Classification of Diseases, Ninth Edition* (ICD-9-CM) is the coding system that is currently used. The first part of this discussion on complications will assume that only standard Universal Bill 92 (UB-92) data is available and that it is not known whether or not each secondary diagnosis was present at admission.

There are three basic issues associated with the use of ICD-9-CM for identifying complications.

1. Whether a diagnosis constitutes a complication is dependent on the patient's underlying disease and procedure.
2. A single ICD-9-CM code can specify both the underlying disease and a complication.
3. The section of ICD-9-CM that explicitly deals with complications lacks any clear definition or consistency of usage.

Each of these issues is discussed more fully below.

### Complications Are Related to the Underlying Disease and Procedure

Certain diseases represent complications for some underlying diseases or procedures but are in the normal course of other underlying diseases or procedures. For example, urinary retention is expected for a transurethral resection of the prostate, but can be an unexpected and avoidable complication for other surgical procedures. If urinary retention is considered as a complication and no adjustment is made for the surgical procedure, then hospitals who perform a large number of transurethral resections of the prostate would appear to have a high complication rate.

### ICD-9-CM Codes Can Specify Both The Underlying Disease and a Complication

Some ICD-9-CM codes contain both an underlying disease and a complication. For example, diabetes with ketoacidosis, appendicitis with peritonitis, and ulcer with perforation are all single ICD-9-CM codes. Clearly, peritonitis can be a complication for appendicitis patients. But an appendicitis patient with peritonitis may have no secondary diagnoses, but only the principle diagnosis (appendicitis with peritonitis). Thus, unless the principal diagnosis is evaluated to determine if it contains implicit complications, many complications may be missed. In addition, the interpretation of these codes for determining a complication rate is very difficult since it can not be determined whether the patient was admitted with a ruptured appendix with peritonitis or whether the patient developed peritonitis post admission due to delays in establishing the diagnosis and performing surgery.

### The Usage of the ICD-9-CM Codes Constituting a Complication Is Inconsistent

There is one section of ICD-9-CM (996-999) in which codes are explicitly designated as representing a complication. However, ICD-9-CM provides no good definition of when these codes should be used versus codes from the other sections of ICD-9-CM. There are a few codes which are both explicit and obvious in terms of their meaning and usage (e.g., code 9984 Foreign Body Accidentally Left During a Procedure). But the use of the vast majority of these codes is ambiguous. For example, ICD-9-CM instructs the coder to use the codes 9973 Respiratory Complications when the respiratory problem is resulting from the procedure. The determination of whether the problem "results" from the procedure or is a problem that can reasonably be expected to occur in some patients in the course of their disease is highly subjective. Is a post op pneumonia coded with 9973 or 480-486? For aspiration pneumonia in which the aspiration occurred during surgery, the use of code 9973 may be clear, but for any other pneumonia it is not. Since the need for surgery may indicate that the patient was in a compromised state prior to surgery, then he or she may have been more susceptible to pneumonia. Therefore, the pneumonia was not the result of the procedure, but something that simply occurs in the course of treating the patient. The use of the majority of codes in the 996-999 range is highly dependent on the coder and physician. Indeed, the

National Centers for Health Statistics recommends that postoperative compli-cation codes be used only when there is a clear statement by the physician that it is a complication, not just related to the surgery. Many physicians are very reluctant to record codes in the 996-999 range for their patients given the obvious malpractice implications of coding a complication.

Any reliance on codes in the 996-999 range to determine the presence of complication assumes that these codes reflect treatment during the current hospitalization. However, codes such as 9981 Hemorrhage Complicating a Procedure can be used to indicate the patient has a hemorrhage associated with a procedure performed during a previous hospitalization. (See *Coding Clinic For ICD-9-CM*, First Quarter 1993, pg. 26.) Indeed, the procedure may have even been performed at a different hospital. If code 9981 is considered a complication, then the hospital readmitting the patient will inaccurately be considered to have had a complication.

Unless all of the above issues are addressed, complication rates could be potentially misleading and may unjustly damage the reputation of some hos-pitals. The problems associated with using ICD-9-CM codes and UB-92 data to determine complication rates are inherent and in many cases unresolvable.

Some states, such as New York and California, now expand the standard UB-92 to include an indication of whether each secondary diagnosis is present at admission. With the availability of a present at admission indicator it is possible to develop meaningful complication rates. However, the avail-ability of such information is relatively new and there is little data available on the reliability of the recording of the present at admission indicator. While there is potential for the use of this indicator, more research is needed, and we are examining this issue with California data.

## Risk Adjusting Inpatient Mortality

In order to include inpatient mortality in provider profiles it is necessary to risk adjust the data. The issue of complications is also important in the risk adjustment methodology.

The issue is whether or not complications should be included in the data used to determine the risk adjustment. For the purposes of this discussion it will be assumed that the present at admission indicator is available for each secondary diagnosis. Given the availability of this indicator, the assumption could be made that all conditions that occur after admission represent a complication and, therefore, should not be used in the risk adjustment. The following discussion will examine the validity of this assumption. It is important to provide several definitions of terms which will be used throughout this discussion.

- *Comorbidity.* A disease or condition that was present prior to admission.
- *Complication.* A disease or condition that occurred after admission and was preventable if care was optimal.
- *Sequela.* A disease or condition that occurred after admission, represents a natural progression of the underlying disease and was not preventable even with optimal care.

As the above definitions emphasize, not all diseases or conditions that occur after admission are preventable complications. There are some diseases or conditions that develop after admission that simply represent a natural progression of a disease (referred to as sequela in this discussion). A post admission nosocomial infection due to poor hand washing practices is clearly a preventable complication. However, with respect to myocardial infarctions (MIs), it is clear that many secondary diagnoses that occur after admission most likely represent sequelae of the MI. Thus, if a patient develops a complete atrioventricular (AV)-block on the second day after admission, it is likely that the AV-block represents a sequela of the MI and not a complication and, therefore, should be included in the risk of mortality adjustment. It is important to note that it is not just the sequelae of the MI that should be included in the risk of mortality adjustment, but also the sequelae of all comorbidities. Thus, if the MI patient also had diabetes then both the sequelae of the MI and the sequelae of the diabetes should be included in the risk of mortality adjustment.

Many of the diseases and conditions that develop after birth for low birth weight neonates are not avoidable and are part of the natural progression associated with a low birth weight. It is difficult to make the argument that all conditions that develop after the birth of a low birth weight neonate should be treated as preventable complications. For example, intraventricular hemorrhage or necrotizing enterocolitis can develop several days or weeks after birth. In general, intraventricular hemorrhage and necrotizing enterocolitis are not preventable and it would be inappropriate to exclude them from the risk of mortality adjustment. Exclusion of post admission diagnoses such as intraventricular hemorrhage or necrotizing enterocolitis would inappropriately underestimate the risk of mortality for hospitals treating low birth weight neonates.

While the intent of excluding preventable complications from the risk of mortality adjustment is certainly laudable, it must be balanced by the reality of the ability to accurately identify the preventable complications. The above examples demonstrate that it is not correct to assume that all secondary diagnoses that occur after admission are preventable complications.

One must always be careful not to expect a single measure to accomplish multiple objectives simultaneously. The result of a measure that attempts to achieve multiple objectives is that usually none of the objectives are satisfactorily accomplished. Attempting to have the risk of mortality adjustment not only adjust for the risk of mortality, but also simultaneously identify preventable complications, is extremely difficult. The challenge is to give hospitals credit for diseases and conditions that represent a natural progression of the patient's underlying problem, but not to give credit for preventable complications.

There are two possible approaches to addressing the issue of sequelae (non-preventable) versus preventable complications. The first approach would be to identify for each underlying problem those diseases or conditions that are likely to represent non-preventable sequelae and those that are likely to represent preventable complications. In this approach, those secondary diagnoses which were sequelae of one of the patient's underlying diseases would be included in the risk adjustment even if they occurred after admission. Such an approach is only possible with the reliable implementation of the indicator which specifies which secondary diagnoses were present at admission.

A second approach would be to use most secondary diagnoses to assign the risk of mortality adjustment and to compute separately a complication index. The availability of the indicators which specify whether or not a secondary diagnosis was present at admission makes it possible to compute a meaningful complication index. A complication index would measure the rate at which a specific list of secondary diagnoses occurred after admission. The diagnoses in the complication index would be limited to those diagnoses for which there was a reasonable degree of confidence that they represented preventable complications. This approach would give hospitals the benefit of the doubt in determining the risk of mortality, and would identify separately any problems related to preventable complications through a complication index *which was clinically valid.*

The second approach is preferable since it provides payers, providers, and patients with valuable additional information about the care being provided. Lisa Iezzoni has done some initial work in this area. However, her work did not have available an indication of whether a secondary diagnosis occurred after admission, which is critical for developing a meaningful complication index.

## Approach to Complications in Version 15 of APR-DRGs

In Version 15 of the APR-DRGs released in April of 1998, some measured steps were taken to address the preventable complication issue. As previously discussed, in ICD-9-CM there is a section of diagnosis codes that identify complications of surgical and medical care (996–999). These codes are used when the diagnosis or condition is due to a specific surgical or medical intervention. For example, code 9971 relates to cardiac complications such as cardiac arrest or heart failure "during or resulting from a procedure". One can be relatively confident that these codes represent complications that may have been preventable. In APR-DRGs Version 15, codes in the 996–999 range are excluded from the risk of mortality and severity of illness adjustment. The only exception is the codes for complications of a transplanted organ will often relate to rejection of the transplanted organ. It was felt that the rejection of the transplanted organ was often not preventable and therefore, these codes should be used in the risk of mortality adjustment.

In order to address potential complications beyond those excluded in APR-DRGs Version 15, a separate complication index should be developed that would be used in conjunction with the risk adjusted mortality. Now that an indication of whether secondary diagnoses are present at admission is becoming available, the secondary diagnoses excluded from the risk of mortality adjustment in APR-DRGs are being reevaluated. In addition, there are a number of new base APR-DRGs which are based on the 996–999 codes (when they occur as a Pdx) such as an APR-DRG for cardiac bypass performed as a consequence of a malfunctioning bypass graft. These DRGs can assist in the tracking of patients readmitted for complications of previous care.

## COUNTERPOINT: ALL CONDITIONS THAT OCCUR AFTER HOSPITAL ADMISSION ARE POTENTIALLY PREVENTABLE COMPLICATIONS

### *Patrick Romano, MD*

Averill and Goldfield define a complication as "a disease or condition that occurred after admission and was preventable if care was optimal." From my perspective, this sounds more like a definition of a "preventable complication." There is nothing in the word "complication" that implies preventability.

Indeed, the Health Care Financing Administration's DRGs divide the world of secondary diagnoses into comorbidities and complications—with no mention of "sequelae."

This is a key point because I find Dr Goldfield's and Mr Averill's distinction between "complications" and "sequelae" to be artificial. For every diagnosis that develops after admission, a certain percentage of cases are potentially preventable with optimal medical care, while a complementary percentage are not. Third degree AV block after an AMI (acute myocardial infarction) might be 10% preventable and 90% nonpreventable. Fluid overload after minor elective surgery might be 90% preventable and 10% nonpreventable. Any effort to separate "complications" from "sequelae" is problematic because one would have to draw an arbitrary cutoff (e.g., 50% preventable) on the basis of very limited data. It may still be appropriate to draw such a cutoff for an individual project, but dichotomizing an inherently continuous variable (e.g., the percentage preventable with optimal medical care) still throws away useful data and oversimplifies a complex phenomenon.

Hence, I prefer not to use the term "sequelae." I reject the notion that there are diseases or conditions developing after admission which are completely (100%) beyond the control of health care providers. As health care providers, our goal for hospitalized patients is to intervene and thereby alter the natural history of the underlying disease. Using antibiotics, we alter the natural progression of pneumonia and pyelonephritis. Using thrombolytics, we alter the natural progression of myocardial infarction. We even alter the natural progression of metastatic cancer by palliative therapies such as radiation, laser ablation, etc. There is little reason to admit a patient to an acute care hospital in 1998 if we are powerless to alter the natural progression of his or her disease. Skilled nursing care, hospice care, and home visits would represent more cost-effective options for such patients.

I do not claim that all secondary diagnoses that occur after admission are preventable complications. Rather, I conclude that all such diagnoses could represent preventable complications. To the extent that one adjusts for such diagnoses in evaluating patients' risk of mortality, one potentially obscures true differences in the quality of care. After all, patients typically do not die "out of the blue." Instead, they experience a cascade of complications which become progressively more difficult to treat and eventually lead to death. So we could theoretically "explain away" every death by adjusting for the complications that precede it. But what would we then learn about quality of care?

By way of example, Dr Goldfield and Mr Averill state that "in general, intraventricular hemorrhage and necrotizing enterocolitis (NEC) are not preventable and it would be inappropriate to exclude them from the risk of mortality adjustment." In fact there is ample evidence that feeding hypertonic formula, advancing feedings too quickly, and other stresses such as hypoxia increase the risk of NEC. In fact, many cases of NEC appear to be preventable. So what does "in general" mean? Ten percent preventability? Forty percent preventability? Two factors overwhelmingly drive neonatal mortality: birth weight and congenital anomalies. Mortality rises exponentially with declining birth weight. Birth weight is also the most important predictor of neonatal complications such as intraventricular hemorrhage, necrotizing enteroclotis, respiratory distress syndrome, and bronchopulmonary dysplasia. To the extent that these complications are attributable to low birth weight, we can adjust for them simply by adjusting for birth weight. Remember that complications are not confounders (by definition) if they are in the causal pathway from low birth weight to mortality. To the extent that these same complications are attributable to factors other than birth weight (e.g., feeding schedules, nosocomial infection rates, endotracheal tube management), it is inappropriate to adjust for them.

Dr Goldfield and Mr Averill suggest that it would be necessary to identify when additional iatrogenic factors are present . . . by detailed record review before concluding that specific complications should be omitted in estimating the risk of mortality. That depends on the purpose of a risk-adjustment tool. If the purpose of a tool is, as Dr Goldfield and Mr Averill have argued, simply to screen for quality of care problems and identify promising areas for further investigation, then it is sufficient to say that "such additional factors were likely to have been present." In other words, sensitivity becomes more important than specificity if screening is the primary purpose of a tool. Adjusting for complications that may have been resulted from poor quality care will decrease the sensitivity of any screening instrument.

There are some purposes for which it might be appropriate to adjust for all complications, whether or not they appear to be preventable. Comparative regional or statewide reports on risk-adjusted mortality ("report cards") are not such a purpose for reasons described above. A hospital that rates poorly in the California Hospital Outcomes Project report (or similar efforts in Pennsylvania, New York, Cleveland, etc.) might use APR-DRGs Version 12 to clarify whether its poor performance is "explained by" post-admission diagnoses (e.g., complications). If so, that hospital would want to focus attention on its complications and clinically assess how many were preventable.

HCFA's Diagnosis Related Groups (DRGs) appropriately adjust for all significant complications because the system is designed to predict resource utilization rather than risk of mortality. Hospitals should not be denied some compensation for the complications their patients' experience, regardless of whether or not they are preventable. Otherwise, financial incentives (which are much stronger than any forces related to quality reporting) would drive hospitals to avoid high-risk patients who might experience complications.

I agree wholeheartedly that "one must always be careful not to expect a single measure to accomplish multiple objectives simultaneously." I think we are just defining our objectives differently. To me and others in this field, the objective of a "risk of mortality" score should be to estimate each patient's risk of dying given how sick the patient was when he or she was admitted to the hospital. This approach does not treat "all diseases and conditions that occur after admission as preventable complications"; rather, it treats them as "potentially preventable complications"—which I would argue they are. So I question the need for a second measure such as the "complication index" you suggest, because I doubt whether it is possible to define a set of diagnoses "for which there is a reasonable degree of confidence that they represent preventable complications."

California's Office of Statewide Health Planning and Development (OSHPD) and most other state/regional agencies are in the business of identifying not just hospitals with higher-than-expected mortality, but also hospitals with lower-than-expected mortality. This latter set of hospitals appear to be "star performers." Our recent AMI validation study actually suggests that OSHPD'S risk-adjustment system does a somewhat better job identifying star performers than identifying problem hospitals. And the information OSHPD publishes about star performers is just as, if not more prominent, in the news media than the information about problem hospitals. Here arises the fatal flaw in the "innocent until proven guilty" or "benefit of the doubt" approach that Dr Goldfield and Mr Averill advocate.

If one is comparing all of the hospitals in a region (e.g., California) with each other to develop regional benchmarks, and identify the best and worst performers in that region, one cannot "give credit" (in the form of expected deaths) to certain hospitals without taking it away from other hospitals. Overall, the analysis is constrained by the fact that the total number of expected deaths must equal the total number of observed deaths; a risk-adjustment tool cannot increase the total number of expected deaths in the region. If this constraint is dropped, then one is implicitly using national or historical rather than regional benchmarks, which is generally not politically acceptable. So if one boosts the expected mortality rate at certain high-mortality, high-complication hospitals, one simultaneously decreases the expected mortality rate at low-complication hospitals. This means that high-complication hospitals will emerge as winners but low-complication hospitals will emerge as losers. Some of these low-complication hospitals with low observed mortality might qualify as star performers, but would lose that designation under APR-DRGs. That's why giving hospitals "the benefit of the doubt" doesn't work—if some hospitals gain that benefit, others (which are likely to provide better-quality care, based on their lower complication rates) lose it. This is not an acceptable tradeoff. Dr Goldfield's and Mr Averill's comment that "being labeled a 'loser' in a risk adjusted mortality comparison (is) no different than being the accused in a legal proceeding" is a thought-provoking analogy. However, it does not completely fit. Being labeled as "neither better nor worse than expected" is similar to having a hung jury: one may be set free, but there is still a cloud over one's head. For example, hospitals that think they are outstanding performers, because they have developed a particular "center of excellence," truly feel the impact of this cloud. So mislabeling "winners" as being "neither better nor worse than expected" is not completely benign.

Finally, it is not clear to me how "the availability of the timing of the diagnosis greatly increases our ability to make 'reasoned judgments'." A diagnosis could be listed as "not present at admission" 100% of the time, but you would still include it in risk adjustment because it might (>25% probability) not be preventable. A diagnosis that is always present at admission is clearly a "safe" risk-adjuster because it is never preventable. But what if a diagnosis is present at admission 25% of the time? 50% of the time? 75% of the time? How does this information help you assess preventability?

Dr Goldfield and Mr Averill advocate separating the "preventable complication issue" from the "risk of mortality issue" by forming two outcome measures (complication index and risk adjusted mortality, respectively). This approach is conceptually attractive, but seriously flawed in practice. These two issues cannot be separated; any attempt to do so is doomed to failure. The reason is simply that preventable (or excess deaths) generally follow preventable complications, even though preventable complications are rarely fatal. In the real world, preventable complications and mortality are inextricably linked. If one adjusts for potentially preventable complications, then one's ability to find preventable (or excess) deaths is seriously compromised. Contrary to Dr Goldfield's and Mr Averill's assertion, adjusting for the risk of mortality and identifying preventable complications are not different objectives, but two sides of the same objective. Why are we interested in estimating the risk of mortality, if not to help us identify patients who had preventable life threatening complications (or providers who experienced clusters of such patients)?

# Episodes of Illness

CHAPTER 34

# Episodes of Illness: Introduction

*Norbert Goldfield*

Measuring episodes of illness represents the new frontier of case mix. It finally will allow researchers and providers alike to examine care provided across a continuum of care. We will not be able to argue anymore, for example, that we cannot measure the risk-adjusted mortality and resource consumption for

- diabetics for a year's period of time
- patients who have suffered a myocardial infarction and undergo not only hospitalization but 90 days of posthospitalization treatment
- specific pneumonias whether the care was provided on an inpatient or outpatient basis

As always, the first question the reader needs to ask is the purpose of using an episode-of-illness profiling system. In general, there are two purposes:

- Prospectively predicting costs for the coming year. This information is useful to adjust capitation rates for either an individual or specific disease category.
- Retrospectively profiling for purposes of comparing actual versus expected costs or actual versus expected performance on a variety of quality-of-care indicators.

Part V provides information on a number of approaches that look at episodes of illness. Most health care institutions are examining episodes of illness for the purpose of adjusting financial payments—either prospectively or retrospectively.

Exhibit 34–1 provides a list of currently available episode-of-illness systems, along with references to informative articles on the systems. Exhibit 34–2 provides the questions that a customer should consider when examining an episode of illness system.

**Exhibit 34–1** Episode-of-Illness Profiling Systems

---

**PAYMENT PURPOSES**

- Ambulatory Care Groups (ACGs)[1]
- Diagnostic Cost Groups (DCGs)[2]
- Hierarchical Cost Groups (HCGs)[3]
- Episode Grouper[4]
- The Disability Payment System (DPS)[5]

**PROFILING PURPOSES**

- Episode Treatment Groups (ETGs)
- Episode Grouper
- Diagnosis Episode Clusters (DECs)[6]

1. J. Wiener, et al., "Ambulatory Care Groups: A Categorization of Diagnoses for Research and Management," *Health Services Research* 26, no. 1 (1991): 53–74.
2. A. Ash, et al., "Adjusting Medicare Capitation Payments Using Prior Hospitalization Data," *Health Care Financing Review* 10, no. 4 (1989): 17–29.
3. R.P. Ellis et al., Diagnostic Cost Group (DCG) and Hierarchical Cost Conditions (HCC) Models for Medicare Risk Adjustment. (Prepared for the Health Care Financing Administration, Contract No. 500-92-0020), Washington, DC; April, 1996.
4. R. Averill, et al., "The Episode Classification System Project," *Journal of Ambulatory Care Management*, forthcoming.
5. R. Kronick, et al., "Diagnostic Risk Adjustment for Medicaid: The Disability Payment System," *Health Care Financing Review* 17, no. 3 (1996): 7–33.
6. D. Cave and E. Geehr, "Analyzing Patterns of Treatment Data To Provide Feedback to Physicians," *Medical Interface*, July 1994, 125.

---

**Exhibit 34–2** Questions To Consider When Choosing an Ambulatory Case Mix System

---

## CLINICAL

- Are the base units expressed in clinical terms easily understood and supported by health care professionals?
- Are the base units driven by *International Classification of Diseases*, Ninth Edition, Clinical Modification (ICD-9-CM) or *Current Procedural Terminology*, Fourth Edition (CPT-4) or both?
- Does a mapper exist to trace codes utilizing the code system currently in use in your system?
- If you are looking at episodes, is the unit of analysis the total episode of care (inpatient and outpatient), or are outpatient services only considered?
- Can case examples of the use of the system be provided?
- Does the episode-of-illness system distinguish complications from comorbidities, and if so, how does it do this?
- Is the episode-of-illness system best used for primary care physicians or specialists or both?

## STATISTICAL

- What is the predictive capability of the case mix adjustment?
- How are outliers treated?
- It should be pointed out that the more outliers removed, the more the statistics will improve at the expense of explaining the entire ambulatory care contact.
- Is it an ICD-9 code-driven system?
- Is the unit of analysis the total episode of care (i.e., links all ambulatory, outpatient, inpatient, and prescription drugs)?
- Does it have a large number of diagnostic groupings (i.e., medical conditions)?
- Is a valid method for assigning an ICD-9 code to encounters with missing and nonspecific ICD-9 codes available?
- Does it place all available encounter and claims data for each patient into at least one episode of care?
- Is an episode duration defined by the maximum number of days between contact with a physician (i.e., window period)?

*continues*

**Exhibit 34–2** Continued

- For multiple concurrent episodes, is an encounter placed into only one episode (e.g., one lab is placed into one and only one episode)?
- Do episodes have an adjustment for comorbidities, severity of illness, and patient age?
- Is the predictive ability of the episode adjustments very high?
- Can outlier episodes be excluded from analysis?
- To reduce fragmentation of episodes, are two years of encounter data required?
- Can pattern-of-treatment results for treating specific medical conditions easily be compared across networks and physicians?
- Is the system flexible enough to be used for the following software products?
  - Global patterns-of-treatment profiling
  - Prescription drug performance/risk
  - Clinical guideline development
  - Outcomes research
  - Physician compensation
  - Physician group composition
  - High-cost patient risk management
  - Medical capitation performance/risk
  - Workers' compensation performance/risk
  - Chronic disease management
  - Health Plan Employer Data and Information Set (HEDIS) 2.0/3.0 reporting

CHAPTER 35

# The Current State of Risk Adjustment Technology for Capitation

*Melvin J. Ingber*

Risk assessment and risk adjustment are terms whose meanings depend on context. Within the area of health care, one might be referring to the use of specific clinical measurements to indicate severity of disease and probabilities of outcomes. One also might be referring to the relationship of disease incidence and prevalence to measures of behavioral risk factors (smoking, bungee jumping) or environmental risk factors (exposure to heavy metals, radon). For purposes of this discussion, *risk adjustment* is a method of determining the expected value of medical care utilization of individuals or groups of people and the use of the assessed value in a payment system or analysis.

The risk adjuster score, in absolute or relative terms, has many potential uses. It can be a measure of general health status, serving as a control variable in studies of effects of changing financing and delivery systems, effectiveness of treatments, quality of care, access, and so on. It can be used as a tool for profiling health care providers, serving as a benchmark measure when making comparisons. The principal focus here, however, is risk adjustment as part of a system of rate setting for capitated managed care organizations (MCOs). (Because the organizational structure of capitated health care providers is changing, MCO is used rather than health maintenance organization.) In focusing on predictable utilization, the risk adjuster is actually an expected utilization adjuster; risk, the unpredictable, remains.

The need for risk adjustment, beyond simple experience rating of enrolled groups or setting rates based on assigning enrollees to rate cells according to age and sex, depends on the way the insurance and health care delivery system is organized. Especially important is the way MCOs and enrollees select each other. At one extreme is the situation in which neither the population nor the MCO has a choice—enrollees are assigned randomly and are locked in. At the other end of the spectrum is the situation faced by the Medicare program. Its beneficiaries may opt for a fee-for-service program or any participating MCO in their area. Until the Balanced Budget Act of 1997 (BBA), beneficiaries could change their enrollment status each month. (BBA created an annual open enrollment period in November for the subsequent year, with a lock-in after 6 months in 2002 and after 3 months in 2003. One change is allowed in the months before lock-in.) Employers offering multiple plans to employees, but with annual lock-ins, represent a middle case.

When MCOs can change how they are perceived in the market and potential enrollees can choose among health care plans and fee-for-service, systematic selection biases can occur. When enrollment is unstable, experience rating is not reliable and simple risk rating on demographics does not capture the biases. Among plans, and among capitated physician groups within plans, a non-average mix of enrollees may be attracted to a particular organization because of benefits offered, perceived expertise in a specialty, or access to a particular hospital or physician. Studies of selection bias in the Medicare system have shown that MCOs have favorable selection, on the average, compared with fee-for-service programs[1-6] The payment method, using county-specific rates, adjusted for characteristics such as age, sex, Medicaid eligibility and disability status, does not capture the relatively good health status of MCO enrollees within each rate cell. (The Medicare county rate book was part of the adjusted average per capita cost [AAPCC] method of payment. The rates were based on projected fee-for-service costs in each county. Among many other changes, BBA also mandated a rate floor, a blend of the local with a national rate, and a minimum annual percentage increase.) BBA mandated that a Medicare risk-adjustment system be instituted for the year 2000. Employer-based groups and state Medicaid programs are also implementing forms of risk adjustment.

Risk adjustment must be distinguished from risk elimination. In a cost-based payment system all the risk is on the payer. The providers or MCOs pass costs through to the payer. An MCO contracting in this way is, in essence, a fee-for-service provider. As capitation is introduced, the MCO becomes the risk taker—an insurer. Actual expenditures on behalf of a person or group will vary from the premiums paid. The plan could incur unexpectedly low or high expenditures for any individual. Limiting this form of risk—random events—is the function of reinsurance or a risk-sharing arrangement. On the other hand, pure risk adjustment is expected-cost adjustment; it adjusts for systematic expenditure differences that should be reflected in premiums, not random events. As will be seen, some risk adjustment systems combine features of risk sharing with pure expected-cost adjustment.

## STRUCTURES OF RISK ADJUSTER SYSTEMS

The standard rate cell classification of insured persons is not the form that the risk adjuster methodology usually adopts. Rate cells classify individuals into mutually exclusive categories. Each cell has a mean expenditure or relative expenditure associated with it. Risk adjusters incorporate more types of information than rate cell systems usually do, and generally they classify people along more dimensions. They are implemented using an equation that predicts the expected value of utilization for each person, rather than a rate table. Risk adjuster equations may be interpreted as determining rate cells, but some systems would be equivalent to many thousands of cells.

Typically, a risk adjuster is a formula with variables that characterize age, sex, and the presence of any of a number of conditions. Illustrative conditions include diseases, functional status measures, or responses to a survey. Each variable is associated with an incremental expenditure, which appears as its coefficient in the formula; $a_i$, in the simple example below. Continuous variables such as age could take on their actual values or they could be split into categories, as is done in the example. Variables indicating the presence of a condition or other categorical characteristic take on the value of 1 when present, and 0 otherwise. The sum of the terms is the risk adjuster (RA) score.

$$\text{RA score} = a_1 \cdot \text{age}(0–1) + a_2 \cdot \text{age}(1–17) + \ldots$$
$$+ a_3 \cdot \text{male} + a_4 \cdot \text{cond1} + a_5 \cdot \text{cond2} + \ldots$$

The coefficients are estimated using multiple regression techniques, with sets of data that should be large enough to get good estimates for all the conditions included in the model. Evaluating the models relies, in part, on statistics associated with the estimation.

## CLASSIFYING AND EVALUATING RISK ADJUSTERS

There are six ways in which risk adjusters may be characterized:

1. the type of data required to make the risk assessment and payment, the feasibility of collection, and the inherent limitations of the data;
2. the incentives in the system for MCO behaviors in provision of care and data reporting;
3. the relationship between the time of data collection and period of payment;
4. the degree to which randomly occurring events drive the adjustment;
5. the method for conversion of risk assessment into payment; and
6. the values of statistical validation criteria that may be used to grade the system.

The risk adjusters discussed here are those described in health research literature and government reports. No single dimension can be used to rank the systems. Any one consideration may predominate under particular circumstances.

The statistical evaluations reported in the literature must be used with caution. Few systems have been tested on a common benchmark data set. Defined subsets of people may have been removed from the data. In particular, high-cost people may have been removed or their costs set at a capped level. Data from different sources and of varying quality and pricing structures may have been used. Pricing may or may not have been standardized. Development and evaluation data sets may or may not have been the same. Some systems may have been developed on rather small data sets, others on large ones.

Two of the most easily interpreted, and potentially misinterpreted, statistics are the $R^2$ and the predictive ratio. The $R^2$ measures the proportion of person-to-person variation in expenditures predicted by the system. $R^2$ values for risk adjusters that predict for future periods are relatively low, reflecting the fact that many medical events are highly unpredictable, particularly with respect to timing. Newhouse, Manning, Keeler, and Sloss[7] estimate that the maximum $R^2$ that may be achieved using year 1 data to predict year 2 expenditures is about 20% in the general population. Risk adjusters that achieve the highest $R^2$ may use types of data that are not currently feasible to collect, or use types of data that would result in undesirable incentives.

Besides the caveats about comparing $R^2$ values reported for systems developed on data of different characteristics, there are other general warnings. The nature of the variable being predicted must be taken into account. Whereas predicting future expenditures results in a relatively low $R^2$, predicting expenditures for the period concurrent with the data collected can produce a relatively high $R^2$ in some systems. Predicting the costs of a known event is easier than predicting the event's occurrence as well as its cost. The variable "concurrent expenditures" is different from "future expenditures."

One also must be careful not to compare the $R^2$ for models predicting expenditures with those predicting mathematical transformations of expenditures. An example is the logarithm of expenditures. Only when the variables are expressed in the same units, preferably simple expenditures, is a comparison valid. Log models, for example, typically exhibit a relatively high $R^2$; it may not be compared directly to the $R^2$ for a simple expenditure model.

The value of $R^2$ reported may have been derived during the estimating of the model or it may have been computed by applying the estimated model to an independent validation data set. The $R^2$ computed from the estimation data reflects a best fit to the particular data used. To the extent that the estimation data are somewhat atypical, using the estimated model on a separate validation data set (preferably typical) will produce a smaller computed $R^2$.

One other difference may be found in the literature. Some researchers report the $R^2$, while others report the adjusted $R^2$. The adjusted $R^2$ is smaller because an adjustment has been made to the number of variables in the model relative to the number of observations. The adjusted $R^2$ is valuable when comparing the relative efficiency of different size models. The difference between the two measures is immaterial when the data sets are large.

The predictive ratio is the ratio of predicted expenditures to actual expenditures for a defined group. Its value should be close to 1. This number tests whether the model predicts well on an aggregate level. Even if the $R^2$ is not large at the individual level, predicting correctly for groups is an important characteristic. Groups might be defined by demographic characteristics, the presence of conditions, or by characteristics completely external to the model. Knowing whether the test is being made on the estimation sample or a validation sample is important for interpretation. One also should know whether the test group is characterized completely by a variable in the model. For example, for the previous model, using as a test group "persons aged 1 to 17," the predictive ratio for the group in the whole estimation sample would be 1 because the estimated coefficient for that group is in the model. If a separate validation sample were used for testing, the difference of the predictive ratio from 1 would indicate differences between the samples. If the difference is substantial, there may be overfitting of the data in the estimation, usually because the estimation sample is too small.

A more severe test is for groups defined by conditions or characteristics not identical to those in the model. Test groups, such as all teenagers, enrollees who were hospitalized, or enrollees who fell into a range of expenditure percentiles, are more of a challenge. They will often have predictive ratios different from 1. One can learn where models might benefit from tuning from such tests.

Another use of the predictive ratio is in evaluating how well the model works for groups defined by levels of predicted (rather than actual) cost. This test shows how well the actual group means track the predictions across the range predicted by the model. It usually reveals weaknesses at the extremes. Most models will do better on this test than on groupings by actual expenditures because the groupings are not driven by random events.

## PROSPECTIVE RISK ADJUSTERS BASED ON CLAIM OR ENCOUNTER DATA

One rich source of information on insured populations is administrative data. In the fee-for-service sector, billing records normally contain diagnosis and procedure information. Standardized forms and coding guidelines have made this source quite usable in recent years. Though coding practices vary, hospital and physician bills can be used as sources of diagnoses. Diagnoses are coded using *International Classification of Diseases, 9th Revision, Clinical Modification* (ICD-9-CM), and procedures are usually coded with ICD-9-CM on inpatient bills and *Current Procedural Terminology, Fourth Edition* (CPT-4) on ambulatory bills.

Risk adjusters can be built around any set of standard codes. MCOs, depending on their structure, may have full administrative data or electronic medical records retrievable; they may extract very little of the potential information from the data they receive, or they may have elected to collect very little from provider groups whom they pay through capitation. The realization that encounter/medical record data have multiple uses, however, has stimulated the development of better electronic record systems at many managed care plans in recent years. Other information needed for the risk adjusters, such as age and sex, is best taken from enrollment and eligibility files.

Medical records contain other data that could be used, particularly concerning severity of disease. Information is lost in coding with the current ICD-9-CM system. For example, ICD-9-CM does not capture degrees of hypertension with specific quantitative guidelines. However, the information in medical records is not currently available in machine-readable form at most sources of care. Because it is inaccessible for routine collection, as a matter of practicality, little use has been made of such data.

Although risk adjusters have been developed to be run on limited types of data (e.g., hospital and/or physician bills) development and calibration of the systems require data that can provide an estimate of the full costs that the system is to predict. Usually it means full encounter data. For example, the inpatient-based systems described later were developed with the full set of each individual's bills for the diagnostic cost groups (DCGs) and a preexisting summary file of such bills for the Payment Amount for Capitated Systems (PACS). The bills or encounter records must have costs associated with them for the development stage and any customization for a particular organization.

Recalibration on full data is also needed to compensate for behavioral effects of any risk-adjuster system. As with "coding creep" that occurred as hospitals adapted to the diagnosis-related group (DRG) payment system, risk adjusters provide an incentive to alter coding patterns and even treatment patterns. Periodic recalibration of the system using data from risk adjusted organizations will probably be needed. The data are also needed to adapt the systems to changes in the coding system as they accumulate. Recalibration will also capture changes in technology.

## SYSTEMS USING INPATIENT HOSPITAL DATA

One of the sources of clinical information considered most reliable and accessible is hospital billing data. Since the implementation of the Medicare DRG inpatient payment system in 1982, diagnoses on hospital bills have been a key part of the administrative billing system. Risk adjustment systems have been built on this base. Hospital encounter records are likely to play a part in risk-adjusting payments to MCOs participating in the Medicare program, because BBA requires capitated plans to submit hospital data first. Many of the considerations described in the case of hospital-based models also apply in general.

Medicare data have been used for much risk adjuster development. There are three eligibility subpopulations in Medicare. Those eligible because they have reached age 65 are designated "aged." A second population is eligible owing to classification by the Social Security Administration as "disabled." The third population consists of people having end-stage renal disease, ESRD.

## Inpatient DCG Model

One hospital-based model, which has gone through several developmental stages, is the PIPDCG (Principal Inpatient DCG) approach. Known simply as DCGs in the early stages,[8] DCG models are now a family of risk adjusters. The PIPDCG model uses only principal inpatient diagnoses for clinical input. Development of the model has concentrated on the Medicare population. The Health Care Financing Administration (HCFA) has supported much of the work on risk adjusters. The most recent published reports[9,10] describe development on 1991–1992 data, excluding persons eligible due to end-stage renal disease (ESRD). More recent refinements in progress are using 1995 to 1996 data. The costs being explained by the model are Medicare fee-for-service costs. They do not include most preventive visits, drugs, or extensive long-term care.

In the first stage of forming cost groups, ICD-9-CM codes are grouped with clinical and future cost characteristics as criteria. In the early work, a dimension of degree of discretion in admissions was included as a criterion.[11] Ranking of discretion proved to be highly variable across clinicians and was associated with the individual patient as much as the diagnosis. The criterion is being re-evaluated in current work. These diagnosis groups (DXGROUPS) are the building blocks of the cost groups. As with many of the other models to be described, a choice was made between degrees of additivity and hierarchy. All 144 PIP DXGROUPS could have been used in a regression model. Such estimates are frequently unstable because many of the groups are thinly populated, particularly in an inpatient model. Unlike DRGs, which model the cost of a hospital stay, risk adjusters model total costs, which have more variability. Even a database as large as the nearly 700,000 used for the 1996 published version of the DCGs is subject to overfitting of the data when some diagnosis groups have few persons. (Databases on younger populations generally have an even smaller proportion of persons hospitalized than the 20% in the Medicare population.) The DXGROUPS are themselves grouped into DCGs, which are defined by expenditure levels. The DCGs are put into a hierarchy so that a person's inpatient diagnosis having the most serious cost implications determines the DCG to which the patient belongs.

A person may have 0, 1, 2, or more hospitalizations in a given year. Each person is assigned to only one DCG, the highest applicable cost group, even though admissions may fall into more than one diagnosis group. With unique assignment to one of only 12 DCGs, the groups have adequate sample sizes.

For those persons with no inpatient stays, other variables are added to provide explanatory power. In this case, age/sex groupings (female < 65, female 65–69 . . . , male 85+) and a variable indicating a degree of Medicaid participation have been added. Medicare eligibility related to disability is indicated by the age less than 65.

The resulting model is relatively simple to apply. The equation adds expenditures related to age/sex, being associated with Medicaid, and expenditures related to one of 12 types of hospital stay. Data for every person to be risk adjusted must be run through the software whether hospitalized or not. Basic demographic information must be supplied even if no diagnoses exist. The program assigns to each person an age/sex group, the Medicaid group if applicable, diagnosis groups, and the highest DCG. Then, the prospective risk score is computed. Coefficients for the DCG groups range from about $2,000 to $23,000 per year in the 1992 data.

This model is the simplest of a number reported in Ellis et al.[12] and Ellis et al.[13] It does not have as high an explanatory power as other models using more data, but it requires only basic eligibility information and inpatient bills or encounter records. Explanatory power predicting future year expenditures, as measured by $R^2$, was 6%, compared with 1% using demographics only in the Medicare population. The $R^2$ was 5.5% when separate validation data were used. Diagnosis-based prospective models used on full Medicare data have rarely exceeded a $R^2$ of 10%. Such a model gets its power by distinguishing many of the most expensive persons, those hospitalized in the recent past. A limitation is that the many people who are not hospitalized are predicted only using demographic information.

Predictive ratios for nonrandom groups are as expected between the demographic models and models using more types of data. Many nonrandom groups were defined that did not correspond to variables in the model. For groups defined by actual expenditures in the base year, improvement over demographics can be seen (Table 35–1). Persons were ranked by expenditures and grouped into quintiles.

Relative to a demographic model, overpayment of the lowest prior use group is reduced by 38% (149% to 92%); underpayment of the highest is reduced by 71% (52% to 15%). The modest improvement in the lowest groups is related to the lack of ambulatory data that would distinguish the chronically ill from other nonhospitalized persons. Another nonrandom grouping of persons is by number of hospitalizations. The group having zero hospitalizations accounts for most of the people, and it is well predicted on the

**Table 35–1** Predictive ratios—Persons grouped by base-year expenditures

| Quintile | Demographics | PIPDCG |
|---|---|---|
| 1 | 2.49 | 1.92 |
| 2 | 1.78 | 1.37 |
| 3 | 1.30 | 1.01 |
| 4 | 0.92 | 0.78 |
| 5 | 0.48 | 0.85 |

Source: Copyright © 1998, Melvin J. Ingber.

average. However, with this type of model it is impossible to distinguish the nonhospitalized chronically ill from the well. For the hospitalized, even without counting admissions there is clear improvement in the average predictions (Table 35–2). For nonrandom groups based on particular chronic diagnoses found in ambulatory data, both the demographic and PIPDCG models predicted low, as one would expect. The underprediction was about 30% less for the inpatient model, however.

## Inpatient Models and Incentives

Models based on inpatient data are relatives of models incorporating "prior use" information. Such models use information on expenditures in the base year to predict future utilization. Past expenditures can be a fairly good indicator of future expenditures but this approach carries with it the taint of cost-based reimbursement when used in a payment system. Future payment depends on services rendered, not just patient condition. Many of the services

**Table 35–2** Predictive ratios—Persons grouped by number of inpatient stays

| Stays | Demographics | PIPDCG |
|---|---|---|
| 0 | 1.30 | 1.00 |
| 1 | 0.64 | 1.16 |
| 2 | 0.46 | 0.97 |
| 3+ | 0.29 | 0.73 |

Source: Copyright © 1998, Melvin J. Ingber.

may be related to time-limited conditions of little consequence for the future. Prior use measures bring practice style into the formula for payment, and incentives for efficiency are diminished. Hospital-based systems incorporate utilization by noting an inpatient stay as well as the existence of a diagnosis. The PIPDCG model limits the utilization effect by recording only the admission with the greatest future expenditure implication. However, there remains some incentive to hospitalize if a DCG incremental payment exceeds the difference between the cost of an admission and an outpatient procedure. It can occur depending on how an MCO contracts with hospitals.

Using the inpatient-based model prospectively mitigates some of the problems because the cost of the reported acute inpatient episode is not being predicted. Predicting the following year's expenditure results in a less extreme payment increment for most diseases.

Another characteristic of the inpatient-based risk adjuster is relatively low susceptibility to gaming. Demographic characteristics are least likely to be subjective or easily manipulated. Hospital data require an admission, are coded by the hospital, and are relatively easy to audit. Any diagnosis-based system is subject to upcoding. But admission rates are low enough to allow a substantial check of enrollment groups that appear unusual. High overall admission rates would be suspicious. In the case of the PIPDCG model, multiple admissions for individuals do not result in additional payment.

These considerations, and the relative ease of data gathering, make the system a candidate for a first risk adjuster for Medicare capitated organizations. It is adaptable for other age groups as well. Studies have been done in the Netherlands using sickness fund data for all ages.[14,15] DCG developers have also been working with data for the under-65 population. In younger populations the rate of hospitalization is lower than in the Medicare population. Thus, though the $R^2$ in the Dutch models are comparable to those for Medicare, there is a larger proportion of the population (the nonhospitalized) adjusted only by the demographic terms in the model.

### Inpatient PACS Model

Another risk adjuster using principally hospital inpatient data is the Payment Amount for Capitated Systems (PACS) model.[16,17] This model was developed using Medicare data from 1983 through 1984. Separate estimation and validation samples were used, including only the aged Medicare population. The estimation sample had more than 200,000 persons; the validation data had multiple groups of 5,000 persons chosen from a separate sample of about 200,000. The final report to HCFA contains variant models and estimates for the Medicare disabled population with disabilities; ESRD Medicare beneficiaries were not included.

The PACS model used the following demographic variables: years over 65, female, ever disabled. The principal inpatient diagnoses were classified according to their major diagnostic category (MDC). MDCs are the body system groupings developed for the DRG prospective payment system used by Medicare for hospital stays. MDCs are not defined by the costs of a hospital stay or total person costs, particularly for the future. The value assigned to each MDC variable is the number of admissions for a diagnosis in that group.

In addition there are variables indicating number of admissions for diseases deemed chronic and number of admissions for diseases expected to have sequelae. Two more variables indicate if the person had one admission or more than one. (They are set to zero for no admissions.) The last variable draws on ambulatory data for its definition—an indicator for the person having exceeded the Medicare Part B deductible. Part B includes physician services. The variable distinguishes nonhospitalized people who have had essentially no contact with the medical system from those who have. This variable goes beyond the hospital data and would probably not be collected if an inpatient-based system were adopted.

Application of the system is relatively simple. Demographic and encounter data are run through the program, categorical and count variables are set by the program logic, and the formula is computed predicting future utilization. For a count variable, the coefficient of the variable is multiplied by the number of times the event occurred. It is not immediately obvious what the maximum increment is for a hospitalization because a number of variables change. For a person meeting the Part B deductible and having one chronic admission in the highest coefficient category, the increment would be about $4,200 (in 1984 dollars). If the person had two admissions, the increment for the two hospitalizations would be somewhat more than double this amount. It is considerably less than the highest increment in the DCG model because there is no cost component used in defining the MDC groupings. The increment for this high group is an average over a wide mix of ear, nose, mouth, and throat and respiratory diseases. There is not enough information in the PACS report to compare the mappings of diseases in the two systems specifically. The PACS groups are sorted by body system, whereas the DCG groups are sorted by cost.

Evaluating the PACS system and comparing it with the DCG hospital-based model can be done only in a limited way. The DCG model used for comparison in the PACS report is an older version than the one in the more recent work cited above. The published article on PACS reports some limited validation statistics for models including demographics and the early DCGs. On a set of random samples of 5,000 Florida and Pennsylvania beneficiaries, the $R^2$ values were reported as 6% and 10% for DCGs and PACS, respectively. This gain in $R^2$ is not small or unexpected. The PACS model is much more utilization driven than the DCG model. The admissions are indicated not only by type of diagnosis, but also by number. The model is additive; a person may be assigned to many categories, not necessarily a unique one. Interpreted as cells, the PACS model has many more than the hierarchical and categorical DCG model. All the added information is for the hospitalized, however.

The predictive ratios for nonrandom groups show better results for the PACS model when multiple admissions have occurred. However, the reported groups are not comparable to most of those used in the DCG work and are few. The full definitions of the groups have not been given (Table 35–3).

A validation group comparable to one in the DCG report is the multiple admission category; the value reported there is higher. Examining the values for the two-stay and three-or-more-stay categories (see Table 35–2) the comparable DCG predictive ratio would likely be more than 0.8. Perhaps the difference is related to the somewhat different versions of the DCG models used or the relatively small sample in this validation. The disease-specific groups in the DCG report are not comparable because they were defined including ambulatory as well as inpatient diagnoses.

There are a few caveats for interpreting the findings. The data were trimmed by removing the top 1% ranked by second-year costs. This approach improves the $R^2$ value somewhat. It also appears that the prediction period

---

**Table 35–3** Predictive ratios—Persons grouped by type of inpatient stay

| Stays | Demographics | PIPDCG | PACS |
|---|---|---|---|
| Cancer | 0.34 | 0.78 | 0.79 |
| Heart disease | 0.44 | 0.93 | 0.98 |
| Multiple stays | 0.38 | 0.67 | 1.01 |

*Note:* PACS, Payment Amount for Capitated Systems.
*Source*: Copyright © 1998, Melvin J. Ingber.

was the 12 months after discharge, not the calendar year after discharge. This approach also improves the predictions.

In terms of explanatory power, this model clearly improves predictions at the high end. There are not enough validation tests reported to compare the model across the cost spectrum or by other grouping criteria. There are two factors at work in driving the model. Not separating out admission types by future cost implications would tend to lower explanatory power. However, counting the number of admissions in each MDC, as well as having variables that distinguish time-limited disease admissions from more chronic ones, adds significantly to the explanatory power. The indicator of nonhospital utilization, exceeding the deductible for Part B services, adds burden to running the system along with some power. The authors state that omitting it reduces $R^2$ by about 0.5 percentage points. What omitting it does to predictive ratios for nonhospitalized people is not stated.

This type of model is better used as a profiling tool than a payment model if one is concerned about incentive problems. Multiple admissions for the same or different diagnoses result in higher payments. Readmissions are rewarded. The results are more sensitive to practice patterns than the non-counting version of an inpatient-based model.

## FULL ENCOUNTER DATA MODELS

A goal in building risk adjustment models is to be relatively neutral in terms of incentives to treatment site. Clearly, models using inpatient data recognize people as being more expensive only after an inpatient stay. The nonhospitalized, high and low users of medical services, are averaged together. To distinguish among the nonhospitalized one must obtain encounter records, or at least diagnoses, from other providers. Incorporating hospital outpatient data would lessen incentives to admit a patient who could otherwise be treated in the outpatient department. Bringing in physician and other practitioner data essentially completes the diagnosis profile for the population covering encounters at even more sites of service. There are other bill or encounter types that may have diagnoses, but these are not brought into the systems because of concerns about the quality of diagnosis coding on the records. Physician and hospital bills and encounter records are not considered perfect, but they are viewed as more reliable.

In an encounter-based system adding the outpatient, and particularly the physician, encounters magnifies the data collection but greatly enriches the information on the 80% to 95% of the population that is not hospitalized. The benefit-cost ratio of collecting such information has been improving rapidly as the costs of storing and transmitting data have continued to fall and the benefits have become clearer. The ability of a managed care organization to manage both care and money is enhanced when there is a flow of data to identify patients who would benefit from monitoring, to compute utilization and expenditures by patient groups and providers, and to compute predicted expenditures (risk scores).

The risk adjuster systems described here use inpatient, outpatient, and physician data in varying ways to predict expenditures. They are all regression models estimated with utilization (usually total expenditures) as the dependent variable and demographic and condition groups as the independent variables. Unlike the PIPDCG model described previously, most do not assign people to only one of a set of mutually exclusive condition groups. The models are generally additive, with each type of condition adding its predicted incremental cost to the total prediction. The models are also linear. Though other functional forms, such as logarithms, may have been experimented with during the research, the final preferred models are the simple linear forms.

There are two aspects of the additive models using inpatient and ambulatory data that illustrate the two-edged sword of added information. It becomes possible to differentiate the healthy from those predicted to receive costly care using information from the ambulatory environment and then to pay differentially. On the other hand, the models are more subject to variant coding patterns, upcoding, and improper coding of diagnoses not firmly established. Researchers must consider not only the explanatory power of models, but also the integrity of the models when implemented in a payment system. Additive models employ various means to restrict the sensitivity to coding variations. Among these methods are aggregating codes into larger and fewer groups; excluding groups of easily coded, minor conditions, thereby capturing their costs in the demographic characteristics; and introducing hierarchies among conditions.

The models are not dramatically different from one another in principle. Differences reside in numbers of groups used, choices made in clustering codes into groups, and degree of hierarchy imposed. The ultimate limiting factor in models that depend on recorded diagnoses is the ability of diagnoses, as embodied in the coding system, to be predictive. The limits using this type of information in predicting total utilization, expressed as $R^2$, depend on the nature of the population being assessed. For the Medicare population the limit seems to be about 10%; for the general population, it is a bit higher. For populations with great numbers of children and pregnancies, such as Medicaid, $R^2$ is about 20%, and for people with disabilities it is about 20%. Models using more detailed information, such as time since first appearance of diagnosis, and multiple years of diagnoses can improve $R^2$ on the margin, but increase the burden. Continuous data on most populations are not available.

A step toward a full utilization risk adjuster is the ambulatory care group (ACG) model.[18] ACGs were developed predicting ambulatory care utilization using ambulatory diagnoses. The original developmental work was done using commercial plan and Medicaid data. The building blocks of the ACG system are the ICD-9-CM codes, aggregated into ambulatory diagnosis groups (ADGs), which are defined by a number of criteria such as disease persistence and likelihood of recurrence, likelihood of specialty care, expected treatment costs, and likelihood of hospitalization. Combinations of the ADGs and age-sex splits of the combinations resulted in the set of ACGs. The latter were such that a person would be assigned to 1 of 51 mutually exclusive groups.

The nomenclature of the system is helpful in understanding the concept behind the system without going into the exact codes. In a grouping of ADGs called chronic medical unstable, the ADGs have descriptors such as likely to recur: progressive; chronic medical: unstable; malignancy. Another grouping of ADGs is chronic specialty: unstable, consisting of four ADGs: orthopedic; ear, nose, throat; eye; and other. The ACGs are refinements of either these collapsed ADGs (CADGs) or refinements of combinations of the CADGs.

Examples of five ACGs are: acute: minor (split into 3 age groups); acute: major; acute: minor and major. Note that a person with both minor and major acute diseases does not have a prediction of the sum of incremental costs of these two categories. The combination has its own coefficient. Having variables representing some combinations of conditions allows the model to predict disproportionately higher or lower utilization due to exacerbations or efficiencies.

The main application of ACGs uses the concurrent form of the model, which was the principal focus of the development. The ACG system has gone through changes since the 1991 report, and it is being used by many health maintenance organizations (HMOs) as a case mix assessor or profiling tool.[19] An order of magnitude estimate of its explanatory power can be found in the early study. The estimation was done on five groups covering 160,000, mainly non-aged persons. There is no indication that separate validation groups were used to compute the $R^2$ values presented. The individual groups were not large; fewer than 8,000 were in the group used to estimate the prospective model. A variety of dependent variables was used: ambulatory visits, ambulatory charges, and total charges, though only the first two were estimated for the prospective model. The $R^2$ for number of visits is 20%; for ambulatory charges it is 18%. Visits are apparently less volatile than charges and consistently have higher $R^2$ values in the concurrent model as well. The only indication of how well the 1991 model would do for total charges has to be based on the concurrent estimate of total charges made for one of the plans. The concurrent model $R^2$ for total charges was less than half that for ambulatory charges. No other types of estimation or validation statistics were reported.

One of the other models reported is built on demographics and the 34 ADGs. This model is purely additive; there are no separate terms for particular combinations of ADGs. The $R^2$ for the prospective and concurrent versions is higher than the $R^2$ values for the ACG model. The ADG formulation was used in more recent work done for the Medicare population.

## MODELS FOR MEDICARE

HCFA contracted for further work to develop prospective risk adjusters based on the ACG system and the PIPDCG system, using a common set of data and validation criteria. Data for about 1.4 million Medicare fee-for-service enrollees in 1991 and 1992 were used (the standard Medicare 5% sample). Persons eligible because of ESRD were removed, as were those enrolled in HMOs and those with incomplete data (other than 1992 decedents). The main difference between the data sets used by the two groups was the choice by the DCG group to include beneficiaries with disabilities. The sample was split randomly into estimation and validation samples. Diagnoses from 1991 inpatient, hospital outpatient, and physician data were used to predict total expenditures in 1992.

### Medicare Models—ADG

The new models deviated from the rate-cell-like, mutually exclusive disease categories that were used in the earlier work. The preferred ACG-related models were denoted ADG MDC and ADG Hosdom.[20,21] The ADG MDC model has components of the PACS model and the ADGs. A person is assigned ADGs based on ambulatory data only. The MDC variables from PACS record the number of inpatient admissions in each diagnostic category. There are 13 ADG groups and 15 MDCs, as well as variables for age, sex, Medicaid, and whether an aged person was formerly classified as disabled. Age in both models was expressed as "years over 65" rather than by age interval categories.

The ADG groupings of ICD-9-CM codes were revised from the earlier ACG work. More codes than the original 5,000 were included, and some were reassigned. Only 13 ADGs were found to be significantly predictive in this study. Some MDCs were revised, some were dropped, and some MDC combinations were altered.

The ADG Hosdom model reduces the degree to which the model incorporates prior utilization; ADG assignments are made using inpatient and ambulatory diagnoses without distinction. The same demographic variables are included. The hospitalization count variables are replaced by the Hosdom (hospital dominant) variable. Hosdom is set to 1 if a person has a diagnosis that is associated with an admission at least half the time in the Medicare data. Interestingly, the absence of the counter variables does not result in a clearly inferior prospective model.

## Medicare Models—DCG

The DCG group also produced a number of models using the 1991–1992 Medicare data. In addition to the revised PIPDCG inpatient-based model, there is the ADDCG (all diagnosis DCG) model, similar to the PIP model, but incorporating diagnoses from ambulatory sources. Another set of models, DCG hierarchical coexisting conditions (DCG HCC), is of the additive type; a person is characterized by multiple condition groups and is not placed in a single, highest-cost group. Besides the diagnosis-driven HCC model is the (HCCP) model, which introduces variables indicating the presence of relatively nondiscretionary procedures with high cost implications, and the (HCCPH) model, which includes variables indicating the presence of principal inpatient diagnoses with high cost implications. Concurrent models and an HCC model that is updated monthly were also presented. Age-sex categories were included in all the models; age less than 65 indicates a beneficiary eligible for Medicare through disability.[22,23]

In early 1998, a report on revised Medicare HCC models was submitted to HCFA.[24] This work built on a separate project that extended the HCC system to cover non-aged individuals. The new model included revised diagnosis groupings, a Medicaid variable, additional age-sex categories for individuals with disabilities, a few condition-specific coefficient changes for those with disabilities, and a variable indicating that an aged beneficiary was formerly eligible because of disability. It was estimated on the full sample, rather than on the previous half sample.

The hierarchical part of the HCC refers to the method used to classify a person who has multiple related diagnoses that fall into groups distinguished by the level of predicted costs. Within this set of related conditions, only the condition with the greatest coefficient contributes to the prediction. For example, a person may be coded with a localized cancer and with metastatic cancer in the same year. When the program detects both diseases, the variable for high-cost cancers is set to 1 and the variable for lower cost cancer is set to 0.

The number of conditions in each HCC model is greater than the maximum number that could be recorded for an individual. Although three or four condition levels might exist for a given type of disease, the hierarchy will allow only the single highest to be recorded. The early HCC model used 34 condition groups, of which at most 21 can be flagged. The later model, which included pregnancy-related groups, used 62, of which 38 can be flagged. There are also six disease-specific increments for those with disabilities.

**Medicare Model—Comparison**

It is appropriate to look at the ADG Hosdom and the HCC models together, as they were developed with the same data and validation criteria. The validation criteria, particularly for disease groups, were specified by HCFA. The implementation of the validation was done by the model developers at Health Economics Research (Waltham, Massachuesetts) and Boston University (Boston, Massachusetts) in the case of the DCG models. For the ADGs the models were developed at Johns Hopkins University (Baltimore, Maryland) under subcontract to the Lewin Group (Fairfax, Virginia); the latter ran the validations. One limitation of the evaluations of these models is that the Medicare disabled were included in the HCC data and not in the ADG data.

The models presented here are relatively insensitive to prior utilization and site of service, although, as in any diagnosis-driven model, there must be some utilization to have a diagnosis recorded. The two models developed at the same time are denoted ADG and HCC; the later HCC model developed on the same data is denoted revised HCC. Two versions of the explanatory power are reported, the first for the data including very high-cost cases, the second for the data with individual costs capped at $50,000. The excess for these individuals is assumed to be compensated by a reinsurance mechanism (Table 35–4). The rationale for predicting capped expenditures is that the outlier cases are considered essentially unpredictable. Including the very high expenditures skews the coefficient estimates away from the more typical values.

It is evident that the HCC models, with more disease groupings, have a greater explanatory power than the smaller ADG model. The gain in explanatory power through more finely divided groupings appears to exhibit diminishing returns. The revised HCC model is a modest improvement over its predecessor, measured by $R^2$. It is an empirical question as to whether the hierarchies in the HCC models and the smaller number of conditions in the ADG models provide the same level of protection against discretionary coding. It has not been tested.

The predictive ratios for the models provide information on biases in predicting for nonrandom groupings of people. The ratios for selected groups are reproduced here. Some of the groupings are mutually exclusive (e.g., prior expenditures) and some are not (e.g., disease groups). A person may be in more than one of the latter and fall into both an underpredicted and overpredicted group. Successful selection could be made more easily on the former criteria than the latter (Table 35–5).

There are expected and unexpected patterns in these numbers. Generally models overpredict for people who are low users in the base year and underpredict for high users in the base year. All are better than simple demographic models in this respect, however. The value reported for the first quintile using the ADG model is remarkably good, and it breaks the pattern that characterizes all the other models. The authors state that they have no explanation for

**Table 35–4** Explanatory power of Medicare models including ambulatory diagnoses

|  | ADG | HCC | Revised HCC |
| --- | --- | --- | --- |
| $R^2$ | 5.5% | 8.1% | 8.8% |
| $R^2$ ($50,000 cap) | 8.0% | 13.9% | N/A |

Note: ADG, ambulatory diagnosis group; HCC, hierarchical coexisting condition; N/A, not available.
Source: Copyright © 1998, Melvin J. Ingber.

**Table 35–5** Predictive ratios—Persons grouped by base-year total expenditures

| Quintile | ADG | HCC | Revised HCC |
|---|---|---|---|
| 1 | 1.08 | 1.30 | 1.22 |
| 2 | 1.17 | 1.24 | 1.21 |
| 3 | 1.13 | 1.14 | 1.11 |
| 4 | 1.00 | 0.99 | 0.98 |
| 5 | 0.88 | 0.85 | 0.88 |

*Note*: ADG, ambulatory diagnosis group; HCC, hierarchical coexisting condition.
*Source*: Copyright © 1998, Melvin J. Ingber.

this finding. It remains to be seen whether the finding is robust in future tests. Also, models with better $R^2$ are not consistently better in this test.

Knowledge of prior year utilization will give a plan an advantage if it enrolls low users. The advantage is considerably less than if payment were based on demographic models, however. The advantage also is mitigated by plan size. These ratios hold, on the average, for very large groups. Actual enrollee groups may not live up to expectations.

Number of inpatient admissions in the base year offers another method of grouping (Table 35–6). This grouping was also used for the inpatient-based models above. It is easier to assemble data on hospitalizations than on total utilization. Selection on this basis would be potentially less profitable than on the total expenditure basis. Eighty percent of the Medicare population is in the 0 stay group, less than 3% in the 3+ group.

In this test one can see that the ratios are close to one for the nonhospitalized because they are the preponderance of the population modeled. There are slight overpredictions for this group that are balanced by the underpredictions

**Table 35–6** Predictive ratios—Persons grouped by number of inpatient stays

| Stays | ADG | HCC | Revised HCC |
|---|---|---|---|
| 0 | 1.03 | 1.05 | 1.03 |
| 1 | 1.06 | 0.99 | 1.02 |
| 2 | 0.91 | 0.91 | 0.96 |
| 3+ | 0.66 | 0.77 | 0.83 |

*Note:* ADG, ambulatory diagnosis group; HCC, hierarchical coexisting condition.
*Source:* Copyright © 1998, Melvin J. Ingber.

for the rarer multiple admission groups. The greater number of condition groupings in the revised HCC model predicts the multiple admission groups better than the smaller models. The Hosdom variable in the ADG model does not seem to capture the hospitalization effect as well as the more finely split condition groups in the other models.

Evaluating test groups formed by ICD-9-CM code clusters defined by HCFA was another validation task. Predictive ratios for these condition groups are more under the control of the system developers who base their models on condition groups. If the test groups overlap the model groups closely, the predictive ratios should be close to 1. Using validation data separate from the estimation data, and independently defining the groups of interest, can indicate where predictions for high prevalence or high-cost conditions could be refined. Selection of enrollees according to these base-year condition groups is possible. The predictive ratios for clinical groups are important in order to understand the consequences of risk adjustment for plans that attract enrollees with particular conditions. Plans might choose to develop expertise in treating certain patient groups rather than seek to avoid them if payment is correct (Table 35–7).

For disease groupings, models with finer splits track better than the smaller models. The revised HCC could have been optimized with respect to the known HCFA criteria, but the generally better predictive ratios are reflected in the higher $R^2$ generated by the more numerous condition groups. The more

**Table 35–7** Predictive ratios—Disease groups as identified in encounter data in the base year

| Condition | ADG | HCC | Revised HCC |
|---|---|---|---|
| Hypertensive heart/renal disease | 1.21 | 0.93 | 0.99 |
| Benign/unspecified hypertension | 1.06 | 0.97 | 1.00 |
| Diabetes with complications | 1.06 | 0.93 | 0.95 |
| Diabetes without complications | 0.86 | 1.02 | 1.01 |
| Heart failure/cardiomyopathy | 0.88 | 0.98 | 0.99 |
| Acute myocardial infarction | 1.00 | 0.87 | 1.01 |
| Chronic obstructive pulmonary disease | 0.92 | 0.98 | 0.98 |
| Breast cancer | 1.42 | 1.08 | 1.07 |
| Hip fracture | 1.05 | 0.99 | 1.00 |

Note: ADG, ambulatory diagnosis group; HCC, hierarchical coexisting condition.
Source: Copyright © 1998, Melvin J. Ingber.

parsimonious ADGs are more aggregate groups. Newer versions of this model have yet to be reported on.

Predictive ratios for other nonrandom groupings are in the ADG and HCC published reports and the government project reports. One other group that is of interest is the disabled Medicare population. This under-65 population was included in the HCC studies. The $R^2$ for Medicare expenditures for this subgroup is 9.37% with the early HCC model and 11.5% with the revised HCC. The predictive ratios for the subgroup are of little interest, because there are variables in the models indicating membership in this group; such ratios are very near 1 when large estimation and validation data sets are used. The disabled group has relatively few zero-expenditure members and an average expenditure almost as high as aged persons. Because the models cannot predict zero use, the $R^2$ is better when such persons are less frequent. The $R^2$ for the aged persons with disabilities receiving Medicaid is even higher, 14.5% in the revised HCC. This subgroup has average expenditures exceeding the non-Medicaid population with disabilities. One reason for special attention to this population is that there is interest in HMOs coordinating Medicare- and Medicaid-covered services for the dually eligible.

## A MODEL FOR MEDICAID EXPENDITURES FOR THE DISABLED

Risk adjustment models, specifically for the under-65 population with disabilities, have been developed and calibrated with Medicaid expenditure data. The Disability Payment System (DPS) model[25] differs in structure from the previous models by incorporating indicator variables in hierarchies for some conditions, but count variables for others. For the latter groups (e.g., central nervous system [CNS] diseases), there are splits into higher and lower cost groups with multiple diagnosis codes in each group. However, the value of the variable indicating the presence of a condition is set to the number of distinct diagnoses detected in the group. The value of the medium-cost CNS variable could be 0, 1, 2, 3 . . . , while the high-cost disease variable could also be 0, 1, 2 . . . . These counters are different from those used in the inpatient models. Here, a diagnosis is counted without the implied utilization of an admission. Protection against discretionary coding for this type of model depends on not having closely related or hard-to-distinguish diagnoses treated as distinct.

The published model has 25 condition groups that are clustered into 10 hierarchies, so that a person can be in a maximum of 10 of these condition groups. There are 17 non-hierarchical condition groups with counter variables. Demographic variables (age/sex) are also included. The target population for the model is the noninstitutionalized disabled in Medicaid who are not covered by Medicare. The model was estimated on multiple years of data from five states. Almost 400,000 distinct persons were present, some in more than 2 years; there were about 536,000 observations in the data.

Both prospective and concurrent models are reported. As found in the revised HCC model, the explanatory power of prospective diagnosis-based models for the disabled is better than that for the general population or older individuals. Although there was no distinct validation data set used, the order of magnitude of the explanatory power can be gathered from the $R^2$ reported for the regression run on the merged data sets—17.3%. The demographic model explains less than 1%.

It is not possible to compare the $R^2$ for DPS directly with the $R^2$ for the HCC computed for the subpopulation with disabilities in Medicare. The institutionalized are in the Medicare data, covered services differ, and the Medicare pricing structure is different. It is likely that the counter variables, however, are important for the relatively high DPS $R^2$. Although there are more groups in the revised HCC, groups such as the central nervous system (CNS) conditions are in a single hierarchy. In the DPS there are three non-mutually exclusive CNS groups, each of which uses a counter variable. A specialty model such as DPS may indeed be preferred by managed care organizations specializing in distinct populations.

The predictive ratios reported are also based on the estimation sample, not a validation sample. Because seven demographic variables are in the model, the predictive ratio for the demographically defined groups is 1. The same is true for the test condition groups that match the condition groups in the model. The most powerful test reported is the one that divides the population into quintiles by base-year expenditures (Table 35–8).

It is interesting that although the $R^2$ values for this model and population are higher than those for the overall Medicare models and population, the predictive ratios for these groups are not quite as close to 1. One might have expected the predictive ratio to be better because the $R^2$ is better. The disabled population, grouped by prior year costs, is overpredicted for all but the highest quintile. It may be because there are economies in treating multiple conditions that are not being captured by the constant increments of the counter variables. The groupings in this version of the model may also be sensitive to discretionary or inconsistent coding. The predictive ratio for

**Table 35–8** Predictive ratios—Persons grouped by base-year total expenditures

| Quintile | Demographic | DPS |
|----------|-------------|------|
| 1 | 4.82 | 1.95 |
| 2 | 2.76 | 1.71 |
| 3 | 1.66 | 1.41 |
| 4 | 0.96 | 1.10 |
| 5 | 0.37 | 0.71 |

*Note:* DPG, Disability Payment System.
*Source:* Copyright © 1998, Melvin J. Ingber.

those with no diagnoses in the base year is 1.02, indicating that the omitted diseases captured in the demographic variables are not responsible for the overprediction.

The state of Colorado is implementing a version of the DPS model. It is also being investigated for possible use risk-adjusting dual eligibles for a Medicare-Medicaid coordinated care demonstration. The model can be calibrated and tested on Medicare data for the disabled.

## MODELS DEVELOPED FOR THE GENERAL POPULATION AND MEDICAID

Already described in the discussion of full encounter data models is the ACG model. This model is being used in general population HMOs for profiling, but the model's behavior with total expenditures is not well documented. A retrospective version of the model (version 4.0) is being used as part of the risk adjustment system of the Minneapolis Buyers Health Care Action Group. An adaptation of the model has been made for use in a Maryland Medicaid managed care program.[26] The number of groups has been reduced by combining ACGs. There are 9 mutually exclusive groups for Aid to Families with Dependent Children (AFDC)-like recipients and eight for disabled. Maternity-related costs were carved out and separately paid. The nature of the report makes it difficult to compare the system with others.

### Models for the General Population and Medicaid—ADG

HCFA contracted for additional work that used the ACG family of models addressing data for the under-65 population.[27] The early analysis suggested that most of the work be done using the ADG-type models that were developed for Medicare rather than the mutually exclusive ACGs. There were two data sets used for most of the analysis, federal employees in Blue Cross Blue Shield (BCBS) and Washington State Medicaid. The differences are marked. The former covers working people and dependents spread over the United States. (The geographic distribution of federal workers is not the same as the general population.) The latter covers one state's Medicaid population with a disproportionate number of females and children. The people in the study had at least 6 months enrollment in the base year and at least 1 month in the second year. There were almost 900,000 people in the BCBS data and about 320,000 in the Medicaid data. The report states that the institutionalized were excluded from the sample.

An interesting finding was that the variables in the optimal models for both data sets differed. The distribution of people across the diagnostic categories differed between the data sets. The utilization patterns and ICD-9-CM coding patterns differed. The Medicaid data had a high proportion of inpatient data and coding at the 5-digit level. In the end the variables used in the models were optimized based on the BCBS data.

The reported $R^2$ for the ADG Hosdom formulation is 5.7%; the demographic model was 1%. The ADG MDC model had an $R^2$ of 6.2%. When the same models were estimated on the Medicaid data the $R^2$s were about 3.6%, a small improvement over the demographic model, which explained 1.6%. Because the Medicaid version of the private data models has a number of flaws (e.g., negative coefficients), it will not be discussed further. Versions of the ADG models were estimated with the costs of deliveries of newborns removed from the estimation. The mean delivery cost was then added to the estimated costs for each of the women who gave birth in the prediction year. The carveout of these expenses is reported to have had a slight improvement on the overall $R^2$. One would expect some improvement in predictive power for female subgroups.

Because the Washington Medicaid data were significantly different from the BCBS data, experiments were undertaken to produce an optimized model for these data. A four-part model was used that separated the population first into those with an ADG condition and those without a condition, then a split by ADFC or Supplemental Security Income (SSI) eligibility. Those without conditions were predicted on demographics. About 60% of the recipients were in this group. Those with conditions were predicted with full models. The Hosdom estimated $R^2$s for those with conditions were AFDC, 3.8%, SSI,

12.1%. The corresponding MDC model $R^2$s are 6.2% and 14.3%. These models are not mature, in part because the estimation data get thin when split into so many segments.

A number of predictive ratios for the BCBS-based models are presented. A validation half sample was used for these ratios. No one model was found to be consistently better for all groupings (Table 35–9).

Overall, the ADG models for the general population behaved much like the models for the Medicare population. Only 15 condition groups are in the models. They are additive, with no hierarchies. The MDC version has 13 additional groups for hospital admission types. These are count variables, as in the Medicare model. Allowing the utilization-based measures shows some advantage in $R^2$ and in the predictive ratio for the few people with multiple admissions. The report contains additional models—for expenditures limited to $50,000 and for retrospective models.

## Models for the General Population and Medicaid—DCG-HCC

HCFA also funded development of risk adjusters for the under-65 based on the DCG-HCC paradigm.[28] The method of hierarchical sets of conditions

**Table 35–9** Predictive ratios—Groups defined by base-year characteristic

|  | Demographics | ADG Hosdom* | ADG MDC* |
|---|---|---|---|
| Admissions |  |  |  |
| 0 | 1.13 | 1.06/1.08 | 0.99/0.99 |
| 1 | 0.39 | 0.88/1.42 | 1.04/1.05 |
| 2+ | 0.13 | 0.44/0.63 | 0.80/0.80 |
| Base-year costs |  |  |  |
| Quintile 1 | 2.94 | 1.48/1.45 | 1.57/1.52 |
| Quintile 2 | 1.85 | 1.12/1.12 | 1.15/1.12 |
| Quintile 3 | 1.42 | 1.17/1.17 | 1.12/1.13 |
| Quintile 4 | 1.02 | 1.16/1.17 | 1.07/1.08 |
| Next 10% | 0.67 | 1.01/1.05 | 0.93/0.95 |
| Next 5% | 0.51 | 0.92/1.09 | 0.87/0.88 |
| Next 5% | 0.27 | 0.66/0.89 | 0.68/0.68 |

*Without birth carveout/with birth carveout.
*Note:* ADG, ambulatory diagnosis group; MDC, major diagnostic category.
*Source:* Copyright © 1998, Melvin J. Ingber.

used in the Medicare modeling was applied. The underlying DXGROUPS, condition groupings, and hierarchies were revised to accommodate the younger population and fed back to the Medicare modeling in the revised HCC model. The groups and hierarchies are more clearly defined by chronic and acute clusters in addition to cost rankings.

The data used for the development included records for about 1.4 million persons insured through employer groups, 190,000 Massachusetts state employees covered by indemnity and HMO plans, and about 1.1 million Michigan Medicaid recipients. A reserved validation data set of 25% of the private data was not used in estimation. Similarly, 25% of the Medicaid data were set aside. The state data set was considered too small to split. Coding quality varied across the data sets. The private data were the basis for most of the modeling.

The condition groups in the model described here include some for children. They are used to produce an incremental payment for the condition that differs from that for adults with the same condition. There are pregnancy groups that differentiate completed from uncompleted pregnancies. The models are purely prospective.

The $R^2$s reported for the validation data were based on the model developed with the private data. The coefficients from that model were used. Results for the other data were derived by using a second regression that estimated a simple transformation of the base prediction. The coefficients were not reestimated for the state and Medicaid data (Table 35–10).

The explanatory power of the basic model was fairly uniform across all the data sets. Some of the experiments indicated that much greater improvements could be made on the Medicaid data with a model optimized on Medicaid. This model included five variables for Medicaid eligibility type and, for each eligibility type, the number of missing months in the base year data. The $R^2$ for this model, using the estimation data, is 21.5%.

---

**Table 35–10** Validation $R^2$s, optimized on private estimation sample

|  | Private | State | Medicaid |
|---|---|---|---|
| Demographic | 1.4% | 1.6% | 3.4% |
| DCG HCC | 8.2% | 9.2% | 11.7% |

Note: DCG HCC, diagnostic cost group hierarchical coexisting condition.
Source: Copyright © 1998, Melvin J. Ingber.

Predictive ratios were computed for the private data, some of which may be compared with the ADG model. The ratios for the Medicaid optimized model are also reported (Table 35–11).

The Medicaid optimized model is comparable to the private optimized model. The slightly better predictive ratios for cost groups probably reflect the high $R^2$. But some of the power for the Medicaid population is found in the demographics alone. The full DCG HCC report contains estimates of the models on the state data, comparisons across different plans in the state data, estimations on full databases, and estimates of concurrent models.

## Models for the General Population and Medicaid—CD-RISC

The Clinically Detailed Risk Information System for Cost (CD-RISC) was developed on data from two HMOs, an indemnity plan, and Michigan Medicaid.[29] There were about 360,000 persons in the data, almost half were Medicaid. The model is built on condition groups composed of groups of related ICD-9-CM codes. The conditions are split by severity and, in some cases, by age. A first-stage hierarchy is imposed within conditions so that only the

**Table 35–11** Predictive ratios—Groups defined by base-year characteristics, validation samples

| | Private data | | Medicaid data | |
|---|---|---|---|---|
| | Demographics | DCG HCC | Demographics | DCG HCC |
| Admissions | | | | |
| 0 | 1.20 | 1.03 | 1.17 | 1.03 |
| 1 | 0.44 | 1.01 | 0.68 | 0.99 |
| 2+ | 0.21 | 0.84 | 0.40 | 0.86 |
| 3+ | 0.09 | 0.61 | 0.19 | 0.55 |
| Base-year costs | | | | |
| Quintile 1 | 3.00 | 1.78 | 2.51 | 1.33 |
| Quintile 2 | 3.00 | 1.78 | 2.56 | 1.36 |
| Quintile 3 | 1.80 | 1.19 | 2.00 | 1.26 |
| Quintile 4 | 1.11 | 0.99 | 1.16 | 1.11 |
| Quintile 5 | 0.47 | 0.82 | 0.53 | 0.84 |

*Note:* DCG HCC, diagnostic cost group hierarchical coexisting condition.
*Source:* Copyright © 1998, Melvin J. Ingber.

highest severity is assigned. The conditions are organized by body system (circulatory system, nervous system, and so on), largely reflecting the ICD-9-CM coding structure. In a second stage, the assigned condition-severity groups within each body system have a hierarchy imposed according to predicted expenditures in the base year. At most, 16 groups could be assigned to a person, although about 140 coefficients for condition severity groups are estimated in a typical CD-RISC model. There are also 24 age/sex group variables in the models.

The condition grouping is based on, and a variation of, the Practice Review System (PRS) of Value Health Sciences (Santa Monica, California). The PRS is an extension of work done at RAND (Santa Monica, California) for the Health Insurance Experiment. The severity hierarchies are more elaborate than those of other models in this report. Although strictly diagnosis based, the system uses diagnoses that are comorbidities or complications not in the condition group being ranked. Severity of diabetes, for example, depends on the presence of diabetes ICD-9-CM codes and codes for other conditions—ischemic heart disease, renal failure, and so on. Indications of hospitalization or procedures are not used.

A variety of prospective models was developed. A major issue in models for the non-Medicare population is the method of predicting costs of future childbirth and the newborn. Pregnancy and birth are handled in different ways in variant models. In a purely prospective model the costs of a future newborn are accumulated in the pregnancy condition. There are also models that carve out these costs from the expenditures to be predicted. Incremental payments are estimated and are made for the birth episode or the birth and diseases of newborns when detected in the payment year. Episodes are defined and paid according to the fraction of the episode occurring in the payment year. The latter will be referred to as the New Baby model. This model differs from the ADG birth carveout model because the ADG carveout includes birth costs only. Other quasi-prospective models pay separately for episodes in the payment year for high-cost conditions and procedures such as ventilator dependence and transplants. A retrospective (concurrent) model with its own set of conditions and hierarchies is also described in the report as are models that build in expenditure-based, person-specific outlier payments.

The developmental data set used was complex. The HMO data were from two organizations with plans in the Northeast, Rocky Mountain states, and Southwest. The indemnity plan had members more geographically dispersed. The Medicaid data were all from Michigan. Only Medicaid recipients without

Medicare were included. Claims from covered services including drugs were collected, and the models predict total expenditures including drugs. The disparate data were combined, and algorithms were applied to standardize the pricing of services on hospital and physician bills. Charges were used for other bill types. An inflation adjustment was made to the Medicaid data to compensate for a difference in data years from the private data. The model does not reflect the pricing structure of any particular plan but the utilization patterns remain. Because the sample is about half Medicaid, the utilization pattern is more strongly influenced by that group than any other group. Because a person must have been continuously eligible to be in the sample, except for newborns and deaths, there is a disproportionate number of newborns in the Medicaid sample; their mothers become eligible only after having a child and are not eligible at the start of the data period to be in the sample.

The complex model was estimated on half the sample, about 180,000 people, and validated on the other half to test for overfitting. There is little indication of overfitting, but no tests for clinical subgroups are reported. The final models were fitted on the entire sample. For selected models the $R^2$ computed for the validation data and the regression $R^2$ for the final models estimated on the full sample are summarized here (Table 35–12).

While there are many other interesting statistics presented in the full report, it can be seen here that the fully prospective model explains roughly the same proportion of future expenditures as have been observed in the Medicare population. The New Baby model, which is not fully prospective, has its greatest impact on the groups with the most newborns. Clearly utilization patterns across groups vary. Secondary regressions were run to adjust the predicted scores for each group. The adjustment models shift and scale the scores

**Table 35–12** $R^2$ for selected models and data

|  | Demographic | Fully prospective | New Baby |
|---|---|---|---|
| Computed for validation data |  | 8.3% | 17.5% |
| From regression on full data | 3.1% | 7.8% | 17.5% |
| Computed for Medicaid | 3% | 8% | 21% |
| Computed for HMO 1 | 1% | 7% | 11% |
| Computed for HMO 2 | <1% | 4% | 9% |
| Computed for indemnity | 1% | 12% | 13% |

*Note:* HMO, health maintenance organization.
*Source:* Copyright © 1998, Melvin J. Ingber.

**Table 35–13** Predictive ratios—Persons grouped by base-year total expenditures

| Quintile | Demographic | Fully prospective | New Baby |
|---|---|---|---|
| 1 | 3.63 | 2.21 | 2.09 |
| 2 | 1.92 | 1.21 | 1.20 |
| 3 | 1.37 | 1.01 | 1.03 |
| 4 | 0.89 | 0.91 | 0.94 |
| 5 | 0.50 | 0.87 | 0.86 |

Source: Copyright © 1998, Melvin J. Ingber.

somewhat, but have a small effect on the $R^2$. Full customized fitting for each payer can only be done with large data sets.

The report provides information on under- and overpredictions the models make for people grouped by base-year expenditures. The newborns who are not in the base-year data are not in this computation, though the mothers are. The mothers carry birth costs in the fully prospective model, but not in the New Baby model, accounting for some of the observed differences. The ratios are in the range of the prospective Medicare and Medicaid models for those with disabilities though the models are not for the same populations (Table 35–13).

The CD-RISC models are interesting, and the full report provides insight into differences among payer groups and the effectiveness of some relatively simple methods to adjust for the differences. There is also much information about the effect of moving sets of conditions out of the prospective model in partially prospective models. CD-RISC has a more sophisticated severity calculation than most models, but it is not more effective than other hierarchies, as reflected in the $R^2$. Perhaps the model is robust with respect to coding idiosyncracies because of the body system hierarchy, while retaining a respectable $R^2$.

There are other encounter-based risk assessment systems in use at present. Few of them have been well documented in the literature. Other systems are being developed for particular situations and not for general adoption. Among the latter is the Health Insurance Plan for California (Sacramento, California) system for small employer groups. This system uses selected marker diagnoses from hospital stays to derive plan-level measures of selection in order to shift payments among plans.[30] The Washington State Health Care Authority (Olympia, Washington) is starting to risk adjust plans that serve state employees incorporating a version of the DCG grouper into its complex system. The expanded DCG (EDCG) model incorporates inpatient and ambulatory diagnoses, distinguished by source, and sorts them into mutually exclusive expenditure groups.

Commercially available profiling and risk assessment tools include the Clinical Complexity Index (CCI) distributed by Equifax and Symmetry, by Symmetry Health Data Systems. The CCI uses some procedures in addition to diagnoses. Symmetry builds episodes from the data and also uses procedures as part of distinguishing severity. They were both developed more as case mix adjusters than prospective risk adjusters.

## SURVEY-BASED MODELS

There have been attempts at using surveys, such as the SF-36, to predict expenditures prospectively and concurrently. These models are smaller than most encounter-based models but can capture dimensions of health status not usually available from encounters. Their basic explanatory power is not very great, but they may be useful for special populations. The surveys usually capture functional status information that can be useful to delineate frail populations. Surveys are most feasible when the assessed population is relatively small, or a sample of a group is sufficient to assess and make payment. Recent studies using the under-65 population include Hornbrook and Goodman[31] and Fowles et al.[32] The first uses the RAND-36 and the latter uses the identically worded SF-36, supplemented by a list of self-reported chronic conditions. (Though the RAND-36 and the SF-36 use the same questions, the scoring differs for some of the elements. Either the responses or the scores can be used in modeling.)

Two recent studies have used the Medicare Current Beneficiary Survey (MCBS) to develop a survey-based risk adjuster for the Medicare population.[33,34] Questions on the MCBS survey vary from those on the SF-36 and include chronic diseases. Both projects used data from the 1991 survey and utilization from 1992. The work by Pope and colleagues added 2 more years of data to check the stability of the model coefficients and to add to the size of the estimation sample. About 12,000 people were surveyed. Those who were in HMOs (insufficient data), those eligible because of ESRD (different population), first-year decedents, and those without part A and B coverage were eliminated from both studies. Gruenberg, Kaganova, and Hornbrook eliminated individuals with disabilities and those who were institutionalized. Pope and coworkers had about 10,600 in their sample; Gruenberg and associates had 8,600. Although the survey is identical for the two studies, each entered the information into the model differently. Both report a number of models; each has a comprehensive model using information from all dimensions of the survey—age, sex, overall health evaluation, activities of daily living (ADLs), instrumental activities of daily living (IADLs), and chronic diseases. Which variables were used and how they were used differ. Gruenberg, Kaganova, and Hornbrook[35] use individual measures triggered by whether the respondent needs help (e.g., bathing, dressing, lifting, meal preparation). Pope et al.[36] use counts of ADLs triggered by difficulty or inability to perform and whether only IADL difficulties are reported. Both models use self-stated health and a slightly different list of chronic diseases.

Given the difference in the modeled populations one cannot firmly compare the $R^2$. Gruenberg et al.[37] report a regression-adjusted $R^2$ of 6%. Pope et al.[38] report 3.2% for the regression $R^2$ and 4.2% on a separate validation year of data. The $R^2$ on the validation subsample of older persons is 4.3%, and the validation subsample of individuals with disabilities is 2.6%. The validation $R^2$ for the 750 institutionalized persons is very low.

The difference between the regression and validation $R^2$ in Pope et al.[39] is likely explained by the use of relatively small samples with year-to-year variation. The instability of coefficients from small samples is also demonstrated by Pope et al.[40] Some of the difference between the two models is also related to the people in the two samples. There is not much overlap in the test groups for which there are predictive ratios in the two reports. Even the expenditure quintiles are defined differently (actual cost versus predicted cost). A few similar test group ratios are reported here (Table 35–14).

The survey models constructed thus far have been on relatively small samples. More work is needed to get stable coefficients. Many of the measures are not very independent from one another in predicting expenditures, so variations in data sets create variations in what seem to be the best predictor variables. The values of the variables usually are matters of judgment and self-report by patients themselves. However, they are subject to manipulation by advice. It is parallel to some ICD-9-CM codes being subject to judgment calls. Survey data without utilization measures do not provide a basis for recalibration of models. Encounter data provide material for recalibration. Surveys do not require a massive data collection and transmission system. But surveys are expensive to field and only practical for small populations and samples.

**Table 35–14** Predictive ratios—Groups defined by base-year characteristic

| Group | Gruenberg et al. | Pope et al. |
|---|---|---|
| Hospitalized | 0.70* | |
| One stay | | 0.78* |
| Two or more stays | | 0.49* |
| Diabetes, self-report | 0.68 | 0.96 |
| Stroke, self-report | 0.62* | 1.06* |
| Any heart condition | 0.74 | |
|   Acute myocardial infarction | | 0.97 |
|   Angina | | 0.90 |
|   Other heart condition | | 0.96 |

*Group is not contained in the model.
*Note:* The predictive ratios in Gruenberg et al. are expressed as actual/predicted; they are inverted here for consistency with the other reported values.
*Source:* Copyright © 1998, Melvin J. Ingber.

## CONCLUSION

Many encounter-based prospective models have been outlined here. There are concurrent or retrospective counterparts to all these systems. The explanatory power of such models is in the range of 40% to 60%. These models capture diagnoses known to have occurred in the prediction year and frequently build on procedures or other utilization information. For reasons given earlier, they are not considered desirable in payment systems.

The prospective models fall along a continuum from totally hierarchical (e.g., PIPDCG, ACG) to completely additive (e.g., ADG). Many are partly additive and partly hierarchical. That is, the hierarchies are within conditions or body systems, and additivity occurs across the hierarchies. Typically, more additivity and more groups increase $R^2$. Unanswered is whether having more comprehensive hierarchies or fewer groups yields better resistance to discretionary and inconsistent coding. All the models will be subject to changes in coding patterns that result from use in payment—coding creep. Periodic recalibration on the data being received for risk adjustment is necessary due to coding creep and the need to accommodate new technologies and codes. For recalibration to take place, more data than the minimal amount for running the adjusters are required. All utilization is needed to derive the expenditures used to estimate the regression models. It is not an enormous leap from the inpatient, outpatient, and physician data to full data. Requirements for standard data formats will soon be effective, and they will reduce some of the nonuniformity problems now found.

The survey models seem better suited to niche applications. The particular questions asked add more information in describing a frail population than the general population. Problems with survey models include bias in responses or no responses from particularly ill or well populations. The use of proxy respondents also adds uncertainty. Gaming by interested parties is also possible, as mentioned above. Survey models still require periodic collection of encounter data in order to recalibrate the models, adding to the cost of fielding the surveys.

The uses of the encounter data for purposes other than profiling and payment are enormous. Most of the quality and access measures being used and proposed can be derived uniformly from encounter data. Instead of adding a new data collection system for each component of health care employer data information set, for example, one could simply use the diagnoses and procedures in the encounters to compute the measures. For MCOs attempting to understand and guide practice patterns across their providers and populations, the encounter data would be invaluable.

Risk adjustment is now sufficiently mature to be used in practice. Most systems use the same types of data. They can be used off-the-shelf as estimated on populations similar to the one to be assessed, or, for a large data set, recalibrations can be done. Simple transformations of the pre-estimated models often do quite well. Choice of model depends on ease of use, cost, and suitability for the insured group.

A final caveat on the use of risk adjusters. One must be wary about the use of these models in evaluating small groups. The models predict average utilization. The bigger the group, the more likely that the actual utilization of a group will deviate by only a small percentage from the the prediction. A capitated physician practice with substantially fewer than 1,000 patients could have relatively large deviations in incurred utilization from the prediction (lower as well as higher). Though risk-adjusted capitation rates for groups will be better than rates based on demographics only, risk remains. There will continue to be a place for risk mitigation through reinsurance and risk-sharing arrangements as long as a substantial unpredictable component to utilization remains.

## NOTES

1. Beebe, J., Lubitz, J., & Eggers, P. (1985). Using prior utilization to determine payments for Medicare enrollees in health maintenance organizations. *Health Care Financing Review, 6*(2), 27–38.

2. Brown, R.S., Clement, D.G., Hill, J.W., Retchin, M.S., & Bergeron, J.W. (1993). Do health maintenance organizations work for Medicare? *Health Care Financing Review, 15*(1), 7–24.

3. Eggers, P. (1980). Risk differential between Medicare beneficiaries enrolled and not enrolled in an HMO. *Health Care Financing Review, 1*(3), 91–99.

4. Eggers, P., & Prihoda, R. (1982). Pre-enrollment reimbursement patterns of Medicare beneficiaries enrolled in "at-risk" HMOs. *Health Care Financing Review, 4*(1), 55–74.

5. Hill, J.W., & Brown, R.S. (1990, September). *Biased selection in the TEFRA HMO/CMP program* (Prepared for the Health Care Financing Administration under Contract No. 500-88-0006). Mathematic Policy Research, Inc.

6. Riley, G., Tudor, C., Chiang, Y.P., & Ingber, M.J. (1996). Health status of Medicare enrollees in HMOs and fee-for-service in 1994. *Health Care Financing Review, 17*(4), 65–76.

7. Newhouse, J.P., Manning, W.G., Keeler, E.B, & Sloss, E.M. (1989). Adjusting capitation rates using objective health measures and prior utilization. *Health Care Financing Review, 10*(3), 41–54.

8. Ash, A., Ellis, R., Yu, W., McKay, E., Iezzoni, I., Ayanian, J., Bates, D., Burstin, H., Byrne-Logan, S., & Pope, G. (1998). *Risk adjustment for the non-elderly* (Prepared for the Health Care Financing Administration under Cooperative Agreement 18-C-90462). Boston: Boston University.

9. Ellis, R.P., Pope, G.C., Iezzoni, L.I., Ayanian, J.Z., et al. (1996). Diagnosis-based risk adjustment for Medicare capitation payments. *Health Care Financing Review, 17*(3), 101–128.

10. Ellis, R.P., Pope, G.C., Iezzoni, L.I., Ayanian, J.Z., Bates, D.W., Burstin, H., Dayhoff, D.A., Rensko, A., Dawes, T., & Ash, S. (1996, April). *Diagnostic cost group (DCG) and hierarchical coexisting conditions (HCC) models for Medicare risk adjustment* (Prepared for the Health Care Financing Administration under Contract No. 500-92-0020).

11. Ash, A., Porell, F., Gruenberg, L., Sawitz, E., & Beiser, A. (1989). Adjusting Medicare capitation payments using prior hospitalization. *Health Care Financing Review, 10*(4), 17–29.

12. Ellis et al., Diagnosis-based risk adjustment for Medicare capitation payments.

13. Ellis et al., *Diagnostic cost group and hierarchical coexisting conditions.*

14. van Vliet, R.C., & van de Ven, W.P. (1993). Capitation payments based on prior hospitalizations. *Economics and Health Economics, 2*(2), 177–188.

15. Lamers, L.M., & van Vliet, R.C. (1996). Multiyear diagnostic information from prior hospitalization as a risk adjuster for capitation payment. *Medical Care, 34*(6), 549–561.

16. Anderson, G.F., Lupu, D., Powe, N., Horn, S., Antebi, S., Whittle, J., & Steinberg, E. (1989, December). *Payment amounts for capitated systems* (Prepared for the Health Care

Financing Administration under Cooperative agreement number 17-C-98990). Baltimore: Johns Hopkins University.

17. Anderson, G.F., Steinberg, E.P., Powe, N.R., Antebi, S., Whittle, J., Horn, S., & Hervert, R. (1990). Setting payment rates for capitated systems: A comparison of various alternatives. *Inquiry, 27*, 225–233.

18. Weiner, J.P., Starfield, B.H., Steinwachs, D.M., & Mumford, L.M. (1991). Development and application of a population-oriented measure of ambulatory case mix. *Medical Care, 19*(5), 452–472.

19. Weiner et al., Development and application of a population-oriented measure.

20. Dobson, A., Coleman, K., Weiner, J.P., Starfield, B., Anderson, G., Abrams, C., & Hu, Y. (1996, August). *The development and testing of risk adjusters using Medicare inpatient and ambulatory data* (Prepared for the Health Care Financing Administration under Contract No. 500-92-0021). Baltimore: The Lewin Group and Johns Hopkins University.

21. Weiner, J.P., Dobson, A., Maxwell, S.L., Coleman, K., Starfield, B.H., & Anderson, G.F. (1996). Risk-adjusted capitation rates using ambulatory and inpatient diagnoses. *Health Care Financing Review, 17*(3), 77–100.

22. Ellis et al., Diagnosis-based risk adjustment for Medicare.

23. Ellis et al., *Diagnostic cost group and hierarchical coexisting conditions.*

24. Pope, G.C., Adamache, K.W., Walsh, E.G., & Khandker, R.K. (1998). Evaluating Alternative Risk Adjusters for Medicare. (Prepared for the Health Care Financing Administration under cooperative agreement number 17-C-903161). Center for Health Economics Research, Waltham, MA.

25. Kronick, R., Dreyfus, T., Lee, L., & Zhou, Z. (1996). Diagnostic risk adjustment for Medicaid: The disability payment system. *Health Care Financing Review, 17*(3), 7–33.

26. Johns Hopkins University, Health Services Research and Development Center. (1997, January). *The development and testing of an ACG-based risk-adjustment capitation methodology for the Maryland Medicaid 115-waiver managed care program* (Contract final report. Prepared for the Center for Health Program Development and Management of the University of Maryland, Baltimore County).

27. Dobson, A., Coleman, K., Weiner, J.P., Starfield, B., Anderson, G., Abrams, C., & Hu, Y. (1997, October). *The development of a diagnosis-based risk adjustment system for setting capitation rates for under-65 populations* (Prepared for the Health Care Financing Administration under Contract No. 500-92-0021). Baltimore: The Lewin Group and Johns Hopkins University.

28. Ash et al., *Risk adjustment for the non-elderly.*

29. Carter, G.M., Bell, R.M., Dubois, R.W., Goldberg, G.A., Keeler, E.B., McAlearny, J.S., Post, E.P., & Rumpel, J.D. (1997, September). "A Clinically Detailed Risk Information System for Cost," Contract number 500-92-0023. Prepared for the Health Care Financing Administration. RAND.

30. Shewry, S., Hunt, S., Ramey, J., & Bertko, J. (1996). Risk adjustment: The missing piece of market competition. *Health Affairs, 15*(1), 171–181.

31. Hornbrook, M., & Goodman, M. (1995). Assessing relative health plan risk with the RAND-36 health survey. *Inquiry, 32*(1), 56–74.

32. Fowles, J.B., Weiner, J.P., Knutson, D., Fowler, E., Tucker, A.M., & Ireland, M. (1996). Taking health status into account when setting capitation rates: A comparison of risk-adjustment methods. *Journal of the American Medical Association, 276*(16), 1316–1321.

33. Gruenberg, L., Kaganova, E., & Hornbrook, M. (1996). Improving the AAPCC with health status measures from the MCBS. *Health Care Financing Review, 17*(3), 59–75.

34. Pope, G.C., Adamache, K.W., et al. (1997, November). *Evaluating alternative risk adjusters for Medicare* (Interim report. Prepared for the Health Care Financing Administration, Center for Health Economics Research, under Grant 17-C-90316).

35. Gruenberg et al., Improving the AAPCC.

36. Pope, G.C., Ellis, R.P., Liu, C.F., Ash, A.S., Iezzoni, L.I., Ayanian, J.Z., Bates, D.W., & Burstin, H. (1998, February). Revised diagnostic cost group (DCG)/Hierarchical coexisting condition (HCC) models for Medicare risk adjustment. (Prepared for the Health Care Financing Administration under Contract No. 500-95-048.) Health Economics Research, Waltham, MA.

37. Gruenberg et al., Improving the AAPCC.

38. Pope et al., *Evaluating alternative risk adjusters for Medicare.*

39. Pope et al., *Evaluating alternative risk adjusters for Medicare.*

40. Pope et al., *Evaluating alternative risk adjusters for Medicare.*

CHAPTER 36

# Prospective Risk Adjustment Classes

*Norbert Goldfield, Richard Averill, Jon Eisenhandler,*
*John S. Hughes, John Muldoon, Barbara Steinbeck,*
*and Farah Bagadia*

The prevailing trend in American health care finance for the last two decades, and likely for the future, is the movement from a system based on fee-for-service payments to one dominated by capitation arrangements. At the core of this change is a shifting of risk from payers to providers.

Such a fundamental transition is not without difficulties. This is exemplified by some of the problems experienced by the Health Care Financing Administration (HCFA) as it has begun to encourage beneficiaries to move from traditional fee-for-service Medicare to capitated health maintenance organizations (HMOs). As a recent General Accounting Office (GAO) report stated:

> Our review of studies on risk selection shows that, because most HMOs benefit from favorable selection (the healthier individuals typically enroll in HMOs), Medicare has paid HMOs more than it would have paid for the same patient's care by fee for service providers.[1]

Adverse selection, of course, can easily work against providers if they accept rates that fail to cover the cost of care. The importance of risk selection cannot be overstated. For example, in 1992 less than 10 percent of Medicare beneficiaries with traditional Medicare fee-for-service benefits incurred almost 70 percent of the costs. In an environment where a disproportionate share of resources is consumed by a small number of individuals, both payers and providers place themselves in considerable financial jeopardy if they fail to adequately adjust their payment levels for their population. In the absence of adequate risk adjusters, competition is based on risk selection and the avoidance of costs rather than the quality and efficiency of health services.

Coupled with the problem of risk selection is the need to assure that the quality of care is not sacrificed in a cost conscious environment. For this need to be met, it is essential for payers and health care providers to have an in-depth understanding of the burden of risk presented by their enrolled population. By understanding the details of health care, as it is rendered for individual illnesses and for combinations of illnesses, payers and providers will be able to make informed decisions on cost control and quality assurance.

The solution to these problems is a reimbursement methodology that is sensitive to the different levels of risk posed by individuals based on the analysis of their medical history and treatment patterns. Such methodology would provide the basis for rates that are equitable for both payers and providers and encourage competition based on the quality and efficiency of care rather than risk selection. It would also provide the basis for a comparative understanding of treatment patterns, which is necessary if providers are to control costs while maintaining quality.

In response to these problems, 3M Health Information Systems (3M HIS), with the support of the National Institute for Standards and Technology, is developing a capitated risk adjustment system, the Prospective Risk Adjustment Classes (PRACs). 3M has also been joined by Actuarial Sciences Associates (ASA) and the National Association of Children's Hospitals and Related Institutions (NACHRI) in this effort. In addition, the project has received assistance from HCFA in the form of access to four years of the 5 percent sample of Medicare beneficiaries.

PRACs is a prospective capitation risk adjuster that provides an estimate of future health care costs. It will do this by assigning each individual a single capitation risk adjustment category based on an analysis of medical history and health care services rendered during a specific period of time. This assignment will be sensitive to the relative severity of illness and to the presence of multiple conditions.

There are many challenges facing the development of PRACs. Current prospective risk adjustment models tend to have limited explanatory power as measured by $R^2$. This is not surprising. Even discounting the inherently unpredictable effects of random events, new or previously unreported illnesses, uncertainty in disease progression, etc., the environment in which episode technology must function is a complex one. Prospective risk classification systems must be able to sort through massive amounts of data and accurately estimate a person's future health care expenditures without being overly sensitive to variations in data that stem from factors other than individual health status. This has led Newhouse[2] to suggest that the maximum explanatory power of prospective risk adjustment models is an $R^2$ of about 20%.

If risk adjustment technologies are to succeed they must focus on the diagnostic, procedure, and other information recorded in the medical records or claims of the population which they are trying to predict. They must be able to differentiate between the factors associated with high and low future costs. To do this they should be able to:

- Identify what is important and what is not. For example, minor trauma usually will have minimal impact upon future resource requirements and generally should be ignored.
- Distinguish between diagnoses or groups of diagnoses associated with high and low costs in immediate future. For example, an individual with emphysema will usually require more resources than an individual with asthma.
- Differentiate between less and more severe cases of the same illness. Within a given diagnosis or set of similar diagnoses, there are likely to be significant differences in resource requirements between an individual in the early stages of an illness and an individual in a more advanced stage. For example, a non–insulin-dependent diabetic will probably require fewer resources in the immediate future than a diabetic in the advanced stages of disease who has significant circulatory problems.
- Define the relationship between multiple diagnoses. Individuals may have more than a single recorded diagnosis. Many of these diagnoses will have no effect upon future health care costs, some will indicate differing levels of severity of some underlying condition, and others will indicate the presence of additional diseases. The technology should be able to distinguish at the individual level the importance of each diagnosis relative to an individual's health status. It should be sensitive to the whole constellation of an individual's diagnoses as well as the time frame in which they occurred. For example, angina occurring prior to a coronary bypass is unimportant as the bypass will have presumably resolved the angina for at least the immediate future. If, on the other hand, angina occurs after a bypass, it is very important as it means the problem either has not been resolved or it has recurred.

Current efforts, primarily ambulatory care groups (ACGs), diagnostic cost groups (DCGs), and their various implementations, have had some success addressing these issues. They have grown increasingly sophisticated and have experienced improvements in predictive power as they have developed solutions to the problems posed by prospective risk adjustment. While there are many important differences between ACGs and DCGs, both use one of two classification strategies. The first and simpler approach is to assign an individual a single group membership. The second and more complex approach is to assign each individual a unique weight based on membership in multiple groups. The latest commercial version of ACGs uses the first methodology and assigns each individual to one of 83 ACGs.[3] The 83 ACGs represent the combination of underlying diagnostic and demographic categories. The simpler form of DCGs is similar in that an individual is assigned a single weight based on the most costly DCG in which the individual has membership. DCGs with Hierarchical Coexisting Conditions (HCC) adopt the second, more complex approach.[4] It allows membership in multiple groups with individual weights equaling the sum of the group weights (albeit subject to some limitations as to which combinations of groups will be allowed) to which the individual belongs. Ambulatory Diagnosis Groups (ADGs), an interim step in ACG assignment, have also been used to experiment with multiple group membership and the prediction of health care utilization in a comparative study commissioned by the American Society of Actuaries.[5] The multiple group methodologies create a large number of distinct groups by allowing membership in multiple groups. The number of groups is equal to the number of allowed group combinations.

PRACs is a single category methodology. It assigns only a single clinically based risk class. It offers a more detailed clinically based classification system than other single category models. It also addresses the problems of differences in severity and multiple group membership by creating specific groups to reflect those differences where and whenever feasible. PRACs adopts a multiple group methodology by explicitly identifying groups it chooses to create rather than allowing the groups to interact freely with other groups.

PRACs has its strengths and weaknesses. The strengths of this approach are threefold. First, its detailed classification system is sensitive to differences between a greater number of illnesses. Second, it distinguishes between the relative severity of illnesses. Third, by only assigning an individual to a single risk class, it does not make assumptions about the mathematical nature of the interaction between the identifiable clinical factors that may influence an individual's future health care needs. The weakness of this approach is that a detailed classification system can produce cells that are overly sensitive to their underlying data, and it can become overspecified especially if many cells will be populated by relatively few cases.

## DATA PREPARATION

PRACs, a categorical model, predicts future health care utilization using clinical information derived from individual health claim histories. In its simplest form, PRACs works by reviewing an individual's history of medical claims, identifying pertinent clinical information, and assigning a single clinically based Prospective Risk Adjustment Class (PRAC). Each PRAC reflects the presence or absence of a chronic illness or illnesses, the relative severity of those illnesses, and where appropriate the individual's age and sex. An individual's predicted utilization is based solely on PRAC assignment with each PRAC being assigned a single weight.

PRAC assignment is a reasonably simple process that occurs in two stages. The first stage is data preparation, and the second stage is PRAC assignment.

PRACs requires individually linkable data for all contacts that an individual has with a health care provider. For the data analysis, which was used in developing the system, exposure issues also played a significant role. For every contact Prospective Risk Adjustment System needs diagnoses, procedures, dates of service, site of service, and type of provider. The data are then split into procedure and diagnostic categories.

### Procedure Data

Episode Procedure Categories (EPCs) collapse *International Classification of Diseases, Ninth Edition, Clinincal Modification* (ICD-9-CM), *Current Procedural Terminology, Fourth Edition* (CPT-4), and HCPCS procedure codes into comprehensive categories. Most EPCs, such as diagnostic tests and procedures, evaluation and management codes, etc., are inherently ambiguous and are not used. Others, such as chemotherapy, dialysis, etc, provide considerable insight into health status and future utilization and are retained.

### Diagnostic Data

ICD-9-CM diagnosis codes are collapsed into Episode Diagnostic Categories (EDCs), which are grouped by body system or Major Diagnostic Category

(MDC). If some of the EDCs are significantly different from clinical perspective from other EDCs in the same MDC or to facilitate manipulation of the data, some body systems are split into multiple MDCs. The grouping of EDCs within MDC is hierarchical in order of clinical significance.

EDCs are further classified as acute or chronic. Acute EDCs are categorized as minor or moderate acute. Minor acute is an acute EDC that has no sequelae and is not indicative of any underlying debility or health status (e.g., a minor fracture or upper respiratory infection). Moderate acute EDC is an acute EDC that either has sequelae or is indicative of an underlying health problem (e.g., an intercranial hemorrhage), which is not identified on any claims. Chronic EDCs are classified as dominant chronic, moderate chronic, minor chronic, or chronic manifestations. Chronic EDCs are defined as follows:

- Dominant chronic diseases (EDCs) are serious chronic illnesses that dominate an individual's consumption of health care resources over time and usually result in the progressive deterioration of an individual's health and often times lead or significantly contribute to an individual's debility and/or death. Congestive heart failure and emphysema are examples of dominant chronic EDCs.
- Moderate chronic diseases (EDCs) are illnesses that, though less severe than dominant chronic illnesses, tend to dominate an individual's consumption of health care resources and may also lead or contribute to an individual's debility and/or death. Prostate malignancies and peripheral vascular disease are examples of moderate chronic EDCs.
- Minor chronic diseases (EDCs) are illnesses that have an extended, frequently lifelong, duration. These are minor illnesses that occur in otherwise healthy individuals. While they tend to be serious in their advanced stages, they can usually be managed effectively and at relatively low cost throughout an individual's life with minimal effect upon the utilization of health services. Hypertension and osteoarthritis are examples of minor chronic EDCs.
- Chronic manifestations (EDCs) are diagnoses that include an underlying chronic diagnosis in their definition. For example, a diagnosis of diabetic neuropathy indicates the presence of diabetes at an advanced level. Chronic manifestations will be used to create that chronic diagnosis. In addition, they will be used to severely adjust (level) those diagnoses if they are present.

Chronic EDCs can also be created indirectly.

- Some acute EDCs (e.g., acute myocardial infarction [AMI]) can create chronic EDCs (history of AMI). The acute EDC is retained and available for severity adjustments later in the process of PRAC assignment (e.g., the impact of a second AMI). Some acute EDCs will conditionally create a chronic EDC based on recurrence over a defined period.
- Some chronic diagnoses can create other chronic diagnoses as discussed earlier.
- Some procedures, EPCs, (e.g., organ transplants) can create chronic EDCs (e.g., history of a transplant).

Diagnostic data are also refined and subjected to some basic edits.

- Diagnoses from nonprofessional providers (e.g., free-standing laboratories, ambulance services, durable medical equipment vendors) are not retained as presumably they should replicate diagnoses from the physicians and institutions ordering the services.
- Physician diagnoses associated with inpatient services are discarded. These diagnoses should duplicate institutional data for the same admission, and the data from institutional sources are more reliable than data from physician offices.
- All diagnoses associated with an inpatient admission are retained. Only those outpatient EDCs that are reported on two separate occasions are kept. If an EDC is associated with a hospital admission, is produced by a procedure, or is an important indicator of health status which may not receive active treatment (e.g., blindness), it will be retained based on only a single occurrence.

## ASSIGNING PROSPECTIVE RISK ADJUSTMENT CLASSES

The first task of PRACs is to sort through hundreds of diagnoses and procedures that may make up an individual's claim history and develop a description which best characterizes the individual's health status. The collapsing of data into EDCs and EPCs is the first step in data reduction. The next step is to identify chronic EDCs and select only the clinically relevant ones.

**Dominant Active Treatment Chronic Episode Diagnosis Category**

All chronic EDCs have been placed into a hierarchy within their respective MDCs based on their severity and likely impact upon the future consumption of resources. Only one chronic EDC will be selected for each MDC. That EDC will be called the Dominant Active Treatment Chronic Episode Diagnosis Category (DATCEDC). If an individual has more than a single chronic EDC from an MDC the following hierarchy will be used:

- Dominant chronic EDC is an inpatient primary diagnosis that has occurred in the last year.
- Dominant chronic EDC was treated on an outpatient basis within the last year with the first and last treatment dates being at least ninety days apart.
- Any dominant chronic EDC.
- Moderate chronic EDC is an inpatient primary diagnosis that has occurred in the last year.
- Moderate chronic EDC was treated on an outpatient basis within the last year with the first and last treatment dates being at least ninety days apart.
- Any moderate chronic EDC.
- The most significant minor chronic EDCs as determined by a hierarchy of EDCs within each MDC.

If more than one EDC meets the criteria and could be selected the EDCs are arranged hierarchically, and the most senior one is selected.

After DATCEDCs are identified, they are adjusted for severity. For each chronic EDC there is a leveling structure with up to four levels based on severity, and likely impact upon future resources will be defined. The leveling structure of chronic EDCs within the same MDC tend to be similar, but not identical, for all chronic EDCs in any given MDC. Variations in leveling structure address the specific clinical characteristics of different EDCs. The four levels will generally adhere to the following structure:

- DATCEDC with few if any symptoms.
- DATCEDC with minor symptoms.
- DATCEDC with moderate symptoms.
- DATCEDC with major or extreme symptoms.

The severity adjustment is based on the presence or absence of other EDCs from the same or other MDCs and selected EPCs. In order to avoid the possibility of double counting, if an EDC from another MDC is used to level a DATCEDC, that EDC (the one being used to level) cannot be used as the DATCEDC for its own MDC. The EDCs and EPCs used in the leveling matrix will themselves be subject to modification or inclusion based on specified rules. For example, an EDC with the first and last treatment dates being at least ninety or one hundred and eighty days apart will often produce a higher level than the same EDC which does not meet these criteria. The theory behind this is that all things being equal an EDC which persists or recurs over an extended period is more clinically significant than one which does not. Similarly, an EDC or EPC that has been noted within the last six months of data may receive a higher level than if it has not been recorded within that time period.

## PRACs

Every individual is assigned a PRAC. Unique PRACs are assigned for all chronic illnesses, combinations of chronic illnesses, and specified conditions. In addition, there are specific PRACs for people without chronic conditions. PRACs reflect severity adjustments and may also reflect an individual's demographic characteristics.

The PRAC number has seven digits. The first digit indicates the individual's health status. There are seven statuses:

1. Healthy
2. Moderate Acute
3. Single Chronic
4. Multiple Chronic
5. Three or more Dominant Chronics
6. Metastatic Malignancies
7. Catastrophic Illnesses and Conditions

The second through fourth digits indicate the EDC for status 3 and the group number for the other statuses. Each chronic disease has a unique set of status three PRACs. An individual with multiple independent chronic illnesses will be assigned a PRAC in status 4 or 5, except those with metastatic malignancies, human immunodeficiency virus (HIV), or one of a specified set of illnesses.

The fifth digit is the severity level. Healthy and moderate acute statuses are not leveled. Cases that fall into status 3 have four levels as discussed previously. Statuses 4 and 5, the multiple chronic illnesses statuses, are assigned 6 levels. These levels are based on the four severity levels of the component EDCs in the status 3 PRACS subject to modification by clinical factors associated with the EDC combinations (i.e. their interactions), which compose the groups. The metastatic malignancy and catastrophic statuses are assigned four levels. These levels reflect the presence of other serious conditions.

The sixth and seventh digits are the demographic categories, sex and age. These distinctions are available but are not always used.

## PRAC Assignment

Once an individual has his or her DATCEDCs assigned, PRAC assignment takes place. PRAC assignment is done hierarchically with PRACs assigned in reverse order of status.

Catastrophic PRACs are assigned first. These PRACs can be either procedure or diagnosis based. They include dialysis, HIV disease, total parenteral nutrition (TPN), mechanical ventilation, history of allogenic bone marrow transplant, history of major organ transplant (heart, lung, liver, or pancreas), outpatient gastrostomy, quadriplegia, and persistent vegetative state. Assignment is done hierarchically. Therefore, a person on dialysis who has also had a major organ transplant would be assigned to the dialysis group. Each of the catastrophic groups is further refined by severity structure unique to itself.

Status 6, metastatic malignancies, is assigned next. Individuals in status 6 include all those with evidence of metastases, multiple malignancies, or recurring malignancies. They are assigned to groups based on a primary malignancy and severity adjusted based on malignancy related EDCs and the presence of other EDCs.

Individuals with three or more dominant chronic DATCEDCs or an explicitly named combination of three DATCEDCs are assigned to status 5. Group assignment is hierarchical with combinations selected in a specific order. For example, if a person has congestive heart failure, emphysema, chronic renal failure, and some other dominant chronic DATCEDC, the first three DATCEDCs will always be used to form the PRAC as that combination comes first in the hierarchy. Cases are then assigned to one of six severity levels based on the underlying severity levels of the DATCEDCs which caused them to be assigned to the group. These assigned severity levels are subject to modification based on the presence of specified EDCs or EPCs.

If an individual meets the criteria for more than one DATCEDC and does not meet the criteria for status 5, he or she will be assigned to status 4. For the purposes of assignment to this status, minor chronic DATCEDCs with a severity level of 1 are ignored unless all of the other DATCEDCs are also minor chronic EDCs with a level of 1. As is the case with status, pairs are filled in a hierarchical order with cases assigned to the first pair combination whose criteria they satisfy. Cases are then assigned to one of six severity levels based on the underlying severity levels of the DATCEDCs that caused them to be assigned to the group and the relative significance or weight of the individual pair member. For example, in a pair consisting of a dominant chronic DATCEDC and a moderate chronic DATCEDC, the level of the dominant chronic DATCEDC receives more weight in assigning severity than the level of the moderate chronic DATCEDC. These assigned severity levels are subject to modification based on the presence of specified EDCs or EPCs. Status 4 also includes groups consisting of two and more than two minor chronic DATCEDCs with severity level 1. These groups are further refined by the sex and age.

Individuals with only a single DATCEDC (regardless of type or severity level) or a single DATCEDC that is not a minor chronic DATCEDC with severity level 1 and one or more minor chronic DATCEDCs with severity level 1 are assigned to status 3, single chronic illnesses. Status three severity level is that of the DATCEDC.

Individuals without any chronic illnesses but with a recent history of moderate acute illnesses are assigned to status 2. Status 2 groups may be optionally refined by sex and age. The latest version of the PRACs assigns three groups:

1. Two or more moderate acute illnesses from different MDCs.
2. One moderate acute illness with multiple occurrences of that EDC with the first and last occurrences of that EDC being at least ninety days apart.
3. One moderate acute illness or one of a specified set of EPCs.

Finally, healthy individuals, those without any chronic illnesses or moderate acute illnesses, are assigned to status 1. Status 1 could be further refined by sex and age.

For illustrative purposes, consider the following example of how PRAC assignment changes as diagnoses change.

A sixty-eight year old female with a few office visits for minor acute illnesses (e.g., EDC 658, Nonbacterial Infections–Minor) would be assigned to PRAC 1000028, Healthy Female, Aged 65–79. If she had a single outpatient diagnosis from EDC 652, Nonbacterial Infections—Major, a moderate acute EDC, she would still be assigned to the healthy PRAC because single outpatient occurrences of an EDC are ignored.

If she had more than one outpatient diagnosis from EDC 652 or if the diagnosis was a primary diagnosis on a hospital admission as well as if the last reported instance of that diagnosis was no more than six months prior to the end of the analysis period, she would be assigned to PRAC 2001028, Single Moderate Acute Diagnoses, Female Aged 65–79. If there were repeated claims for EDC 652 and more than ninety days separated the first and last claims that would indicate either a persistent or recurrent problem, she would be assigned to PRAC 2002028, Single Moderate Acute Diagnoses–Span 90, Female Aged 65–79. If on the other hand the last reported instance of the diagnosis was more than six months old, it would be ignored and she would be assigned to the healthy PRAC.

If she had a mild case of hypertension (EDC 121, a minor chronic illness) and had seen her physician several times about it, she would be assigned to PRAC 3121118, Hypertension–Level 1, Female Aged 65–79.

If she had also received care for diabetcs (EDC 315, a dominant chronic illness) but had no other symptoms, she would be assigned to PRAC 3315200 Diabetes–Level 2 as her moderate acute infection (EDC 652), which resulted in hospitalization is interpreted as indicative of a more severe case of diabetes. The hypertension, which is a minor chronic illness EDC, and the other acute illnesses would be ignored. If her diabetes worsened and the infection recurred or had to be treated over a prolonged period such that the interval between the initial and latest treatment was at least ninety days apart, she would be assigned to PRAC 3315300, Diabetes Level 3.

If her hypertension became worse and she was treated on several occasions for chest pains (EDC 95), the severity level of DATCEDC 121 (hypertension) would be assigned Level 2. Hypertension would no longer be ignored. She would now be assigned to PRAC 4146300, Diabetes and Hypertension–Level 3. The Level 3 is determined by the severity levels of the two DATCEDCs with greater weight being given to the clinically more important (i.e. the diabetes).

If her cardiovascular problems worsened and she had several diagnoses of angina (EDC 125), the cardiovascular DATCEDC would be angina. The chest pains and hypertension do not indicate a more severe case of angina relative to future expenditures and the level of the angina DATCEDC would be 1. Her PRAC assignment would become 4141200, Diabetes and Unstable Coronary Artery Disease–Level 2 (Unstable Coronary Artery Disease is a cluster of EDCs, one of which is angina). The assigned level of 2 would give equal weight to the diabetes and the angina.

If she later developed congestive heart failure, CHF, her cardiovascular DATCEDC would be CHF (EDC 129). The angina would raise the level of CHF DATCEDC from one to two. Her PRAC would 4111300, CHF and Diabetes–Level 3. Once again, the level reflects the underlying levels of the CHF and diabetes. If she also was treated for ulcers (EDC 175), her case would be likely to require more resources than if she had not developed ulcers and her PRAC would change to 4111400, CHF and Diabetes–Level 4, to reflect this. The ulcers act to increment the combination of CHF and Diabetes. The earlier diagnoses of hypertension and infections would not affect the PRAC assignment. If she was treated for an upper respiratory infection (EDC 90), there would be no effect on her PRAC assignment.

If the patient has developed kidney problems and was diagnosed with Chronic Renal Failure (EDC 345) in addition to the diabetes and CHF, her PRAC assignment would become 5001300, Renal Failure–Diabetes–Any Other Dominant Chronic Illness DATCEDC, Level 3. The CHF falls into the other dominant chronic illness group because CHF seldomly occurs in combination with diabetes and chronic renal failure to make reasonable estimates of future costs. The level assignment reflects the underlying levels of the three DATCEDCs. If there were additional diagnoses, such as asthma (EDC 78) or some psychiatric problems (e.g., Depression, EDC 929), these would either be ignored or, if clinically appropriate, raise the patient to a more severe level.

If the patient's renal failure worsened and she required dialysis on at least two separate occasions at least thirty days apart, she would be considered a catastrophic case or more correctly a person at high risk for high costs. She would be assigned to PRAC 7010300, Dialysis with Diabetes–Level 3. The assignment of level 3 would reflect the presence of CHF.

## DATA

PRACs has been under development for several years. Initial development is based on the Medicare Standard Analytical File, SAF, a 5 percent sample of Medicare patients with linkable data and encrypted individual identifiers to protect the privacy of beneficiaries. Two years of clinical data derived from fee-for-service Medicare claims (1991 and 1992) are being used to project total charges in the third year (1993). To be included in the analysis an individual had to have two full years of Medicare fee-for-service coverage and a third full year of coverage unless the reason for a shortened third year was death. Individuals with HMO coverage or whose claims indicated the possible presence of another primary payer were excluded from the analysis.

The project is ongoing. While the following results are preliminary, they illustrate the model, how it addresses issues like severity and disease interaction and, why these items should be addressed by risk adjustment technologies. It should be noted that these data will change as the model is further refined. For the purposes of the analysis, the data have been adjusted. First, total annual charges have been capped (cases kept but not allowed to exceed a predetermined level) at $100,000 for single chronic illness, $150,000 for multiple chronic illnesses, $250,000 for three or more dominant chronic illness, $250,000 for metastatic malignancies, and $500,000 for catastrophic cases. Second, the charges of individuals who died in 1993 have been annualized. Third, no demographic adjustments have been used.

The model, albeit with the aforementioned capping of catastrophic costs and annualization of the charges of people who died but without demographic adjustment, has an $R^2$ of 18.80%. When results are viewed by status, the differences are readily apparent and scarcely unexpected with healthier groups having lower charges (see Table 36–1). The only exception is between status 5, three or more chronic illnesses and status 6, metastatic malignancies.

For illustrative purposes, the examples of diabetes (DM), emphysema (COPD), and congestive heart failure (CHF) are displayed (see Table 36–2). All are relatively common illnesses. All have sufficient number of cases to assure consistent and stable results. Mortality also tends to track severity level reasonably closely, albeit imperfectly, as the model is not optimized for mortality. Of the three illnesses, CHF tends to be the most expensive. COPD, however, is more expensive at level 4. DM is the least expensive of the three.

When multiple DATCEDCs are present the same trends prevail, average charges increase as severity levels increase (see Table 36–3). Mortality also has a fairly unambiguous positive relationship with severity level. The differences between the combinations are particularly interesting. The six levels of the combination reflect the collapsing of sixteen possible cells. The lower levels of the combination roughly correspond to the lower levels of the single groups and the higher levels to the higher levels of the single groups. With this

**Table 36–1** Classification Results by Status

| Status | Frequency | Average Next Year Total Charges |
|---|---|---|
| Healthy | 210,538 | $2,750 |
| Moderate acute | 20,524 | $4,012 |
| Single chronic | 416,738 | $5,304 |
| Multiple chronic | 562,159 | $10,379 |
| Three or more Chronic illnesses | 67,841 | $25,683 |
| Metastatic Malignancies | 44,926 | $22,709 |
| Catastrophic | 7,732 | $64,730 |
| Total | 1,330,458 | $8,996 |

**Table 36–2** Selected Single Chronic PRACs by Level

*Emphysema (COPD)*

| Level | 1 | 2 | 3 | 4 |
|---|---|---|---|---|
| Cases | 6,352 | 4,248 | 2,477 | 974 |
| % Died In Year 3 | 4.71 | 4.76 | 5.53 | 14.89 |
| Avg Charge | $6,288 | $7,455 | $8,883 | $16,828 |

*Congestive Heart Failure (CHF)*

| Level | 1 | 2 | 3 | 4 |
|---|---|---|---|---|
| Cases | 3,697 | 2,180 | 4,551 | 1,949 |
| % Died In Year 3 | 8.74 | 9.36 | 10.46 | 12.67 |
| Avg Charge | $5,169 | $6,247 | $8,008 | $13,814 |

*Diabetes (DM)*

| Level | 1 | 2 | 3 | 4 |
|---|---|---|---|---|
| Cases | 18,838 | 8,957 | 2,903 | 3,158 |
| % Died In Year 3 | 2.81 | 2.33 | 3.69 | 4.59 |
| Avg Charge | $5,079 | $6,162 | $7,406 | $8,808 |

in mind, one can see that COPD and CHF have a largely additive relationship with average total charges of the pair being fairly close to the sum of the single chronic illness groups. CHF and DM are not additive. At the lower levels, average total charges tend to be less than the sum of the single chronic illness groups. At higher levels, the average total charges tend to be higher than the sum of the single chronic illness groups. COPD and DM behave in a totally different fashion with average charges of the combination tending to be lower than the sum of single groups at all levels except the highest.

When all three diagnoses are present as DATCEDCs the results are difficult to interpret because the six levels reflect the collapsing of sixty-four possible cells ($4^3$). Nonetheless, the following observations can be made (see Table 36–4). First, both charges and mortality consistently increase with severity. The difference between level 1 and level 6 is almost a factor of 4. Second, the addition of DM to the most expensive pair combination, CHF and COPD, has a limited impact on the lower levels (1 and 2) with average costs only being slightly higher that the pair combination. However, at level 3 and above, the

**Table 36–3** Selected Multiple Chronic PRACs by Level

### COPD and CHF

| Level | 1 | 2 | 3 | 4 | 5 | 6 |
|---|---|---|---|---|---|---|
| Cases | 85 | 1,487 | 1,547 | 2,143 | 2,232 | 3,145 |
| % Died In Year 3 | 7.06 | 11.90 | 13.38 | 14.37 | 17.34 | 22.58 |
| Avg Charge | $6,041 | $10,885 | $14,132 | $16,397 | $21,135 | $30,984 |

### CHF and DM

| Level | 1 | 2 | 3 | 4 | 5 | 6 |
|---|---|---|---|---|---|---|
| Cases | 607 | 1,324 | 2,716 | 2,399 | 2,397 | 2,102 |
| % Died In Year 3 | 7.41 | 8.84 | 9.83 | 10.30 | 14.31 | 17.89 |
| Avg Charge | $7,839 | $10,400 | $12,914 | $15,854 | $20,669 | $28,729 |

### COPD and DM

| Level | 1 | 2 | 3 | 4 | 5 | 6 |
|---|---|---|---|---|---|---|
| Cases | 562 | 883 | 640 | 573 | 510 | 585 |
| % Died In Year 3 | 4.27 | 5.44 | 6.56 | 5.58 | 9.80 | 12.14 |
| Avg Charge | $7,796 | $8,634 | $11,388 | $14,398 | $16,055 | $24,277 |

**Table 36–4** CHF and COPD and DM

| Level | 1 | 2 | 3 | 4 | 5 | 6 |
|---|---|---|---|---|---|---|
| Cases | 282 | 753 | 980 | 972 | 1,016 | 1,832 |
| % Died In Year 3 | 12.77 | 11.29 | 15.41 | 18.83 | 21.65 | 29.31 |
| Avg Charge | $11,911 | $15,843 | $19,864 | $27,931 | $33,068 | $50,549 |

effect is substantial with an almost $20,000 or 80 percent increase at level 6 of the three DATCEDC group.

## CONCLUSION

This preliminary analysis shows that charges vary considerably by the severity of an illness and that disease interaction is disease or disease combination specific. While further analysis is in order, it is reasonable to state that if prospective rate adjustment methodologies are to improve their predictive power they need to be sensitive to disease severity and disease specific relationships. Methodologies like PRACs are probably better than alternative methodologies, which fail to address these factors.

**NOTES**

1. General Accounting Office. November 8 1995. *Medical Managed Care: Growing Enrollment Adds Urgency to Fixing HMO Payment Problem.* GAO/HEHS-96-21.
2. J.P. Newhouse et al. Spring 1989. Adjusting Capitation Rates Using Objective Health Measures and Prior Utilization. *Health Care Financing Review* 10(3): 41–54.
3. Johns Hopkins University. 1998. *The Johns Hopkins University ACG Case-Mix Adjustment System, Version 4.1.* Baltimore: Johns Hopkins University.
4. R.P. Ellis et al. April 21 1996. *Diagnostic Cost Group (DCG) and Hierarchical Coexisting Conditions (HCC) Models for Medicare Risk Adjustment.* Waltham, MA: Health Economic Research, Inc.
5. D.L. Dunn et al. December 21, 1995. *A Comparative Analysis of Methods of Health Risk Assessment: Final Report.* Chicago: American Society of Actuaries.

CHAPTER 37

# The Development of a Risk-Adjusted Capitation Payment System: The Maryland Medicaid Model

*Jonathan P. Weiner, Anthony M. Tucker, A. Michael Collins, Hamid Fakhraei, Richard Lieberman, Chad Abrams, Gordon R. Trapnell, and John G. Folkemer*[*]

[*]The methodology described in this chapter was designed jointly by University of Maryland Baltimore County (UMBC), State of Maryland Department of Health and Mental Hygiene, Johns Hopkins University School of Public Health, and Actuarial Research Corporation. In addition to the chapter authors, other staff members of these organizations participated in various phases of this development process. Their contributions are gratefully acknowledged. This chapter provides a policy-relevant overview and empirical evaluation of the system and does not necessarily describe all current details of the system as implemented and updated. Readers are encouraged to obtain updates from the UMBC web site—www.umbc.edu/chpdm. This chapter reflects the opinions of the authors and does not necessarily represent the positions of their respective organizations.

*Source:* Adapted from Weiner, J.P., Tucker, A.M., Collins, A.M., Fakhraei, H., Lieberman, R., Adams, C., Trapnell, G.R., Folkemer, J.G., The Development of a Risk-Adjusted Capitation Payment System: The Maryland Medicaid Model, *Journal of Ambulatory Care Management*, Vol. 21, No. 4, pp. 29–52, © 1998, Aspen Publishers, Inc.

Nowhere in the U.S. health care system are changes more dramatic than within state Medicaid programs. In the past, federal guidelines have tended to limit a state's flexibility in implementing managed care options. Thus, as recently as 1994, less than 15% of the nation's 35 million Medicaid recipients were enrolled in capitated managed care plans.[1] As a vehicle for reform, the Clinton administration has used Title XIX, Section 1115, of the federal Social Security Act to grant most states waivers for research and development purposes under the Medicaid program. These waivers, known as 1115 waivers, are intended to encourage innovative delivery and financing arrangements. Most innovations are based on pre-paid managed care models. As a result of this waiver initiative, it is estimated that of all non-nursing home Medicaid eligibles, enrollment in managed care organizations (MCOs) has tripled to between 40%–50%.[2] Enrollment is expected to rise as states respond to the even greater Medicaid program flexibility afforded by recent congressional budget legislation.

Over the last decade, few Medicaid recipients were voluntarily enrolled in a limited number of traditional health maintenance organizations (HMOs), some of which specialized in Medicaid contracts. Most recipients were young mothers and children eligible under the Aid to Families with Dependent Children (AFDC) program. The 1115 waivers have increased not only the number of Medicaid recipients enrolled in managed care plans, but also the diversity of enrolled persons and plans. It is not uncommon for states to enroll people with disabilities and other "medically needy" persons in managed care. In some locales, the MCOs serving Medicaid recipients consist not only of traditional HMOs, but also innovative provider-based integrated delivery systems, such as physician hospital organizations (PHOs). Continued expansion in the needs of the population, welfare and child health insurance reform, and growing constraints on state and federal budgets suggest that reliance on capitated health plans can be expected to continue for the foreseeable future.

In the past, payments to Medicaid providers were typically made after the fact, on an open-ended, fee-for-service (FFS) basis. Pre-paid, capitation payment requires that HMOs and other organizations go "at-risk" and agree to provide a defined set of services for a fixed payment rate per enrollee. As the states move toward pre-paid alternatives, there is attendant concern that such flat-rate per-capita payment mechanisms may not fairly compensate all participating MCOs. In today's environment, many health policy experts are concerned that fixed payments based on overall average "community rates," or simple age and gender adjustment, are no longer adequate. They believe that an approach is necessary to help ensure that capitation rates fairly account for the expected medical need, or "health risk," of the Medicaid enrollees. Such an approach would protect against the adverse effects of patient groups that are sicker than average, or providers that specialize in treating them, under a fixed-budget reimbursement system.

Adverse or biased selection in pre-paid settings has also been considered a major policy issue, particularly as it relates to Medicare's "risk contract" HMOs, as well as state and national health care reform. In these contexts, health policy experts have identified the need for approaches to adjust capitation rates to account for the health status of MCO enrollees.[3–5] Accordingly, the risk-adjustment literature is replete with sophisticated approaches and methods for use in capitation rate adjustment. Although the market has yet to adopt these methods on a wide scale for payment purposes, the Medicare program has supported the development and evaluation of work in this area,[6,7] and a number of leading employer coalitions and large private health plans are beginning to apply mechanisms to risk adjust the capitation payments. Furthermore, private-sector MCOs are applying some risk-adjustment methods to serve other managed care objectives, such as utilization review and provider panel profiling.[8]

Maryland is viewed by many as a leader among states in applying innovative methods to the management of its Medicaid program. In 1991 Maryland introduced the then-largest mandated primary care case management program, the Maryland Access to Care program. Starting in June 1997, Maryland Medicaid continued on a path toward more comprehensive managed care controls by directing almost 90% of all noninstitutionalized and non-dually eligible (i.e., both Medicare and Medicaid) recipients (accounting for approximately half of annual program costs) to enroll in one of eight capitated MCOs on a mandatory basis. Maryland's 1115 waiver initiative, known as Health-Choice, possesses many innovative aspects, one of which is its approach to establishing risk-adjusted capitation payment rates for contracting providers.

Maryland's comprehensive risk-adjusted capitation system pays all contracting MCOs for enrollees on the basis of their health status. This chapter describes various facets of the Maryland capitation model. It also presents an empirical simulation analysis using data from 230,000 FFS Medicaid recipients that suggests the degree to which the new payment model is likely to help control for health status differences within the contracting MCOs when compared to more conventional, demographically adjusted capitation payments. The chapter is intended for a wide audience, including those involved in the design of systems of care for Medicaid patients, state and national policy makers concerned with managed Medicaid programs, and actuaries, analysts, and researchers involved in the development and implementation of risk-adjusted capitation payment systems.

## THE COMPONENTS OF THE PAYMENT SYSTEM

The Maryland Medicaid capitation payment model was designed to foster fairness and equity by balancing a system of fixed monthly risk-adjusted per-capita MCO payments with other financing mechanisms. These other mechanisms include global one-time payments for newborn deliveries, separate ongoing retrospective FFS payments for certain persons and for select services, and stop-loss protection. Exhibit 37–1 presents an overview of the key components incorporated into the Maryland risk-adjusted MCO payment model.

### Assigning ACGs

For those who were enrolled in the Medicaid program for at least 6 months, the Johns Hopkins University ambulatory care group (ACG) case mix methodology (version 3.00) was used to assign each recipient to one of approximately 50 case mix/risk adjustment categories. (Recently, the ACG system was renamed the adjusted clinical group system to better reflect the fact that it is applied to diagnoses treated in both the institutional and ambulatory settings.) This is done using both inpatient and ambulatory *International Classification of Diseases, 9th Revision, Clinical Modification* (ICD-9-CM) diagnosis codes assigned by the recipient's providers over a designated period of time (e.g., 6 to 12 months). A person's ACG category is determined by the particular mix of conditions for which he or she was treated over the designated risk assessment period. For example, a person with only one or more minor acute conditions (such as minor infections) is assigned to a specific ACG category, while a person with multiple serious chronic conditions (such as diabetes or asthma) is assigned to another. Each person is assigned to only one (mutually exclusive) category on the basis of the morbidities that were diagnosed during the designated time period (as well as his or her age and gender) regardless of the type or number of services actually provided to that person during the period. Because each ACG is designed to represent individuals with similar morbidity burdens and resource use expectations, ACGs can be viewed as a type of proxy health status designation. Readers are referred elsewhere (including on-line) for a description of this case mix system and its applications.[9–11] The ACG system is

**Exhibit 37–1** Summary of Maryland Medicaid Risk Adjustment Capitation Methodology

---

- Uses Johns Hopkins Universiy ambulatory care groups (ACGs) to develop 17 prospective risk-adjusted category (RAC) cells for all non-mental health services.
  - Applies ACGs for any person with 6 months or more ICD-9-CM diagnosis information derived from computerized claims or encounter data.
  - Uses separate rating cells based on two broad eligibiliy categories: Aid to Families with Dependent Children (and others without disability) and Supplemental Security Income (and others with disability).
  - Allows cells to vary by a factor of 24. Payments range from a low of about $45 a month to a high of $1,100 a month.
- Uses age/gender cells for new enrollees and others without claims/encounter data (always used for newborns).
- Carves out all services furnished by mental health providers to a special behavioral fee-for-service (FFS) managed care program; they are not included in capitation.
- Makes a separate retrospective global payment (about $4,000) for all deliveries.
- Gives persons with acquired immunodeficiency syndrome (as defined by the Centers for Disease Control and Prevention) their own capitation rates (about $2,000 a month).
- Pays for protease inhibitors and viral load testing for persons with human immunodeficiency virus on an FFS basis.
- Treats less than 1% of the population with one of approximately 30 "rare and expensive" conditions on an FFS case-managed basis.
- Provides a $61,000 hospital care stop-loss limit with a 10% risk share above that threshold for all capitated enrollees.

*Source*: Reprinted from Weiner, J.P., Tucker, A.M., Collins, A.M., Fakhraei, H., Lieberman, R., Abrams, C., Trapnell, G.R., Folkemer, J.G., The Development of a Risk-Adjusted Capitation Payment System: The Maryland Medicaid Model, *Journal of Ambulatory Care Management*, Vol. 21, No. 4, pp. 29–52, © 1998, Aspen Publishers, Inc.

---

used by more than 150 organizations around the world, making it the most widely adopted population-based diagnostic risk-adjustment methodology now in use.

## Collapsing ACGs into RACs

For ease of application within Maryland's Medicaid program, and to help ensure actuarial stability across time periods, the standard ACG cells were combined to form a more limited number of payment categories. They were termed "risk-adjusted categories" (RACs). The methods used to develop nine distinct RACs for AFDC and other recipients without a disability, and eight distinct RACs for Supplemental Security Income (SSI) program recipients and other persons with a disability are described in detail.

To determine the appropriate risk rating category for each person enrolled in Maryland's HealthChoice program, the ACG system (and all diagnosis-based risk measurement systems for that matter) requires access to ICD-9-CM codes from some designated time period—ideally the year immediately preceding a given contracting period. For practical reasons, even if a person is enrolled continuously for the entire period, the time lag between that risk assessment period and the contracting period is often greater. During the start-up phase of Maryland's HealthChoice program the lag was 3 months. That is, data describing Medicaid recipients' diagnoses for the period ending March 31, 1997 were used to determine each person's ACG risk rating for the period commencing June 1, 1997. (*Note*: During the second year of the program the rating will be updated annually with a lag between the rating period and enrollment period of no greater than 4 months. In future years, once encounter data systems become more established, monthly risk-adjusted payments may be calculated more frequently, that is, semiannually or quarterly.)

## Persons with No Diagnoses

Because diagnosis-based adjusters cannot be determined for persons who are new to any insurance program, or for whom computerized claim or encounter data are not otherwise available, alternative approaches must be used to set capitation payments. In Maryland, capitation payments for persons who are new to the Medicaid program, or for whom no claim or encounter data are available, are set (within each eligibility class) using age/gender and geographic cells. The geographic stratification distinguishes payments made on behalf of persons who reside within Baltimore City from those living elsewhere in the state. This geographic adjustment is intended to compensate for what are believed to be unmeasured health status differences between enrollees residing in Baltimore's inner-city area and suburban and rural locales.

During the start-up phase of the program, only those recipients who received services under FFS were paid on the basis of ACG/RAC adjustment. Prior to the implementation of the HealthChoice program, the submission of diagnosis data was not required from HMOs that enrolled Medicaid recipients in the state. (About 30% of HealthChoice participants were previously in a voluntary HMO program.) In the past, HMOs received demographically adjusted capitation rates. Starting in June 1997, all HMOs participating in HealthChoice (including those not previously submitting data) were required to provide encounter or claims data with ICD-9-CM codes adequate to facilitate ACG assignment. Through the program's second year, demographically adjusted capitation rates will be used to reimburse MCOs for all persons previously enrolled in the (pre-1115 waiver) HMO program. This blending of capitation methods will help phase in ACG-adjusted payments.

Payment to MCOs for new Medicaid recipients, defined as those with less than 6 months of eligibility in the program, is made using the demographic-based payment cells. HealthChoice coverage for infants less than 12 months of age is paid using a separate "under-age-1" demographic cell because of the limited diagnostic history available for newborns.

## Other Adjustment Mechanisms

In order to address the difficulty of setting a prospective capitation payment rate for pregnant women who deliver within a given time period, the Maryland payment model includes a separate retrospective global payment that covers costs related to delivery for any woman enrolled in an MCO when she delivers. All non-delivery–related services are included in the standard risk-adjusted monthly capitation payments. Also, pregnant women who enter the Medicaid program under the Pregnant Woman and Children (PWC) program (a program for those not otherwise eligible for Medicaid) are paid for based on a separate monthly capitation category.

Due to special concerns about the vulnerability of persons with mental illness and the fact that in the private sector it is common to carve out mental health care, all specialty mental health services are excluded from the base-capitation payment. These services are managed and paid (on an FFS basis) separately through the state's public mental health system. All services for substance abuse and non-specialty mental health services are, however, included in the capitation rate. It also should be noted that because persons with psychiatric diagnoses are known to experience higher-than-average use of general medical care, all mental health diagnoses are taken into consideration when calculating the ACG-based payment to be paid to the MCOs that have contracted to provide medical care to these individuals.

Persons with full-blown acquired immunodeficiency syndrome (AIDS; as defined by the Centers for Disease Control and Prevention) have a separate capitation category based on historical patterns of care. Persons with human immunodeficiency virus (HIV) are incorporated into the ACG-based capitation system and are included in the same categories as other persons with serious morbidities. For persons with HIV, a predetermined list of pharmaceuticals and services (notably protease inhibitors and associated monitoring tests) is paid for on an FFS basis separate from the monthly capitation payments to the MCOs.

In addition to adjusting fixed capitation payments to better reflect health status, most risk adjustment policy experts recommend application of two other approaches: stop-loss provisions and special criteria for excluding rare, very high cost conditions, often termed "high cost set-aside conditions."[12,13] Both of these methodologies were adopted as part of the Maryland Medicaid payment model.

Each MCO contracting with Maryland is at risk for the first $61,000 of inpatient expenses per enrolled individual within a 12-month period. The state reimburses MCOs for 90% of their hospital costs above that stop-loss threshold.

The HealthChoice program is intended to be inclusive. Other than the nursing home-bound and dual eligibles, virtually all Medicaid recipients (with and without disability) are included in the program on a mandatory basis. Because such a diverse group of recipients no doubt encompasses some very ill persons with extremely high expected resource use—use likely to be well above even the highest standard payment category—and given that these very ill persons are likely to require more intensive case management than most MCOs can provide, special payment and care delivery arrangements have been made for specific high-cost groups of individuals. While others have developed similar high-cost medical set-aside groupings[14–16] a relatively short list of 32 rare and expensive case management (REM) conditions were identified for the Maryland program. For HealthChoice, REM conditions were defined as conditions that accounted for less than 1% of the total recipient population, consisted of no more than 300 Medicaid recipients per condition, required over $10,000 of resources per year, and required specialized providers. Under the Maryland payment model, if a person has a REM condition, or develops one of these conditions during the contract period, he or she is excluded or released from the MCO pre-paid contract and special case management is arranged for his or her care (which is reimbursed on an FFS basis). A summary of the rare and expensive conditions incorporated into the payment model is presented in Exhibit 37–2. Note that many of the REM conditions focus on anomalies among neonates or represent serious genetically linked diseases in children. In the first year of the program, approximately 90% of all REM conditions involved children. It is estimated that approximately 2,400 persons and $68.5 million that would be otherwise eligible for the 1115 waiver capitation payments will be excluded based on the high-cost REM condition provision.

## THE ACG-BASED HEALTH STATUS ADJUSTER

A key component of the Maryland capitation payment system is the ACG case mix measure, which was developed over 15 years ago by faculty at the Johns Hopkins University School of Public Health.[17–19] For several years, the Maryland Department of Health and Mental Hygiene (DHMH) had been using ACGs for purposes of profiling within its mandated gatekeeper program.[20] The state had not used the ACG system for payment purposes prior to the implementation of its 1115 waiver. As noted earlier, the ACG system was incorporated into the overall capitation model in Maryland as a simplified grouping of multiple ACG categories, known as RACs. These risk-adjusted categories were designed by a team of staff from Johns Hopkins University (JHU), the Center for Health Program Development and Management (CHPDM) at the University of Maryland at Baltimore County, the Medical Care Policy Administration of the DHMH, and a consulting actuarial firm. It is these 17 rating cells, or RACs, that are used as the basis for payment to MCOs for all recipients for whom appropriate ICD-9-CM diagnostic data are available. The following sections describe the method used to construct the ACG-based risk adjusted category system.

## DATABASE CONSTRUCTION

To develop the ACG-based risk-adjusted categories, FFS claims data for all Maryland Medicaid recipients enrolled during state fiscal years 1993, 1994,

**Exhibit 37–2** REM Conditions

---

Congenital/neonate[*]
    Pediatric acquired immune deficiency syndrome (congenital)[†]
    Central nervous system anomaly, including hydrocephalus
    Respiratory system anomalies
    Cleft palate
    Tracheoesophageal fistula
    Severe digestive anomalies
    Biliary atresia, cystic disease of liver
    Serious urinary system anomalies
    Serious musculoskeletal anomalies
    Multiple congenital anomalies
    Neonatal necrotizing enterocolitis
Childhood degenerative/metabolic
    Extrapyramidal degenerative disease—myoclonus
    Other serious cerebral degenerative diseases
    Spinocerebellar degenerative disease
    Anterior horn cell disease
    Phenylketonuria, maple syrup urine disease, other amino acid metabolic
        disorders
    Urea cycle, other amino acid disorders
Other serious conditions/all ages
    Spina bifida
    Histiocytosis
    Cystic fibrosis
    Mucopolysaccharidosis, purine disease
    Hemophilia
    Ventilator dependent (non-neonate)
    Traumatic brain injury (blunt) after 30-day stay in state psychiatric hospital

*Note*: Persons with rare and expensive case management (REM) conditions are set aside from the capitation/payment system and included in a special case management program with FFS reimbursement. (A full list with specific diagnosis and age breaks is available at www.umbc.edu/chpdm.)

[*]Age cutoffs may apply for inclusion in REM program.
[†]Adults with this syndrome have a separate capitated payment category.

*Source*: Reprinted from Weiner, J.P., Tucker, A.M., Collins, A.M., Fakhraei, H., Lieberman, R., Abrams, C., Trapnell, G.R., Folkemer, J.G., The Development of a Risk-Adjusted Capitation Payment System: The Maryland Medicaid Model, *Journal of Ambulatory Care Management*, Vol. 21, No. 4, pp. 29–52, © 1998, Aspen Publishers, Inc.

and 1995 were used. Specific data elements relevant to this analysis included program eligibility status, months of eligible enrollment, ACG assignment based on all provider-designated ambulatory and inpatient diagnoses, a flag indicating the presence of maternity payments, and total incurred FFS expenditures for each fiscal year (FY). Because they are not included in the prospective capitation payment, costs related to deliveries, specialty mental health services, and 90% of claims above the hospital care stop-loss threshold were excluded from analyses, as were persons with specific rare and expensive conditions. AIDS patient costs, which for reasons of confidentiality could not be identified at the time the data files were created, were not excluded from these analyses. The effects of these limitations on both the development process and the simulation described later are believed to be modest. During the final actuarial review, costs for the approximately 2,100 persons with full-blown AIDS were removed from the published capitation rates, as was an adjustment for the estimated MCO cost sharing above the stop-loss threshold.

Although expenses related to delivery are reimbursed on a separate basis by the state, the standard JHU ACG grouper software uses pregnancy-related diagnoses to group pregnant women into a specific ACG subcategory. (*Note*: The latest version of the ACG system—version 4.0—uses pregnancy and delivery status as key grouping variables.) A method was therefore needed to account for the removal of delivery expenses from the monthly capitation rate calculation without removing information regarding comorbidities that might otherwise affect the ACG-based RAC payment for pregnant women for their other types of care. This was accomplished by assigning ACGs to each woman without using the specific subcategorization of the ACG system (known as ambulatory diagnostic groups [ADGs]) that reflects pregnancy. There were 11,276 waiver-eligible individual Medicaid recipients with maternity-related expenses in fiscal year 1993, the base year used to identify ACG assignment for the development of RACs. By eliminating all pregnancy-related diagnoses for those recipients, 9,313 individuals had their ACG assignment revised to another category that represented their illness burden without reference to pregnancy-specific diagnoses.

## CONSTRUCTION OF RACs BASED ON ACGs

Given the state's goal of an administratively simple, yet actuarially predictive risk-adjustment method, Medicaid program managers asked the developers to consider whether the 52 mutually exclusive ACG groupings could be reduced to a smaller set of payment cells. Moreover, regression-based models—using either ACGs or their component ADGs—were deemed too complex for wide scale use and understanding within the community. Consulting actuaries for the program suggested that fewer rating groups would increase cell stability and reduce the impact of any regression-to-the-mean. That is, persons in case mix groups who exhibit relatively high or low costs in a given year, tend to "regress" closer to the average in later years, all other things being equal. Greater time lags between the rating period and the payment period can be expected to exacerbate this problem even further.

While the full articulation of the original 52 ACG categories may be needed to support administrative applications that require clinical homogeneity within case mix categories (such as provider profiling), the decision to develop a simplified model was supported by previous research at JHU that indicated that a smaller number of groups may be adequate when the system is used for purposes of prospective payment.[21]

In order to collapse the full set of ACGs into a lesser number of RACs for the Maryland program, a "recursive partitioning classification" analysis of Medicaid data covering fiscal years 1993 through 1995 was performed using the PC-Group software that was originally used to develop diagnosis-related groups.[22] This computer software facilitates classification analysis such that a known set of independent (grouping) variables—in this case, ACGs—can be used to construct sets of categories based on the degree to which the groupings best "explain" a key dependent (outcome) measure. The dependent measure in this case was prospective costs associated with a person's health care utilization over a 1-year period of time.

Data for two broad categories of recipients, AFDC (and other nondisabled) and SSI (and other disabled) were analyzed separately, and distinct RAC assignment schemes were established for each population. Fiscal year (FY) 1993 ACG assignment and corresponding FY 1994 program costs for each eligible recipient were analyzed using the PC-Group software. That analysis was repeated using FY 1994 ACG assignment and FY 1995 program costs. Each of these multiyear analyses suggested a very similar assignment pattern of ACGs to RAC groupings. The final RAC assignments submitted to the state were derived from the analysis based on FY 1993 ACGs and FY 1994 payments.

The results of the ACG to RAC assignment process are presented in Appendixes 37–A and 37–B. They list the specific ACGs included in each RAC for AFDC (Appendix 37–A) and SSI (Appendix 37–B) populations. The appendixes also present the expected prospective resource use for persons falling into each ACG and RAC, as well as the relative weight for each cell, as compared with overall average payments. It is estimated that RAC payments under HealthChoice will cover approximately 65% of all service costs for the AFDC population and 86% for the SSI population.[23] That is, the numbers presented exclude special noncapitation costs such as those related to delivery, mental health provider services, and those costs above the inpatient stop-loss threshold.

While historical FFS payments for each risk category, such as those reflected in the appendixes, were a major factor used to determine the program's final RAC payment rates, other considerations were also taken into account. These other factors included expected trends of costs into the future, regression due to time lag between the risk assessment and payment periods, expected savings due to more intensive care management, estimates of biased selection in the existing voluntary HMO program, and the state's requirements for programmatic savings. The final RAC capitation rate table published for the HealthChoice program at the end of 1996 is summarized in Table 37–1. It presents the per member per month (PMPM) capitation rates for HealthChoice recipients eligible for ACG-based payment as well as rates for other key non-ACG–based payment categories. As discussed previously, persons for whom diagnostic data are not available are paid using demographic adjustment criteria. Those rates are available elsewhere.[24]

## SIMULATING THE IMPACT OF THE RISK-ADJUSTED MODEL

To help assess the degree to which an ACG/RAC–based risk-adjustment capitation model could be expected to improve the fairness and accuracy of MCO payments, a simulation analysis was performed using historical claims records. Alternative, prospectively determined capitation rates were calculated using RACs, ACGs, and age and gender categories based on Medicaid data from FYs 1993 and 1994. The various predetermined capitation rates were then compared to actual (in-scope) payment experience of large simulated groups of Medicaid recipients. Random sampling was used to establish 15 "pseudo" MCO groups, each consisting of 50,000 recipients. Five of those groups were skewed to reflect lower-than-average FY 1993 resource use, and five groups were skewed to reflect higher-than-average resource use. This skewing process simulated potential risk selection under the program. The

**Table 37–1** The Maryland Medicaid RAC Capitation Rate System

| RAC Categories | $ per month | Relative weight |
|---|---|---|
| AFDC and other families | | |
| RAC 1 | 45 | .26 |
| RAC 2 | 66 | .38 |
| RAC 3 | 75 | .42 |
| RAC 4 | 90 | .51 |
| RAC 5 | 136 | .77 |
| RAC 6 | 159 | .90 |
| RAC 7 | 245 | 1.40 |
| RAC 8 | 296 | 1.70 |
| RAC 9 | 372 | 2.11 |
| SSI and others with disability | | |
| RAC 10 | 95 | .54 |
| RAC 11 | 238 | 1.35 |
| RAC 12 | 277 | 1.57 |
| RAC 13 | 363 | 2.06 |
| RAC 14 | 441 | 2.51 |
| RAC 15 | 682 | 3.87 |
| RAC 16 | 556 | 3.15 |
| RAC 17 | 1,102 | 6.26 |
| Other categories* | | |
| Neonates (<1) | 247 | 1.69 |
| Persons with AIDS | 2,062 | 11.72 |
| PWC mothers | 310 | 1.76 |

*Average of Baltimore City and noncity rate.

*Note*: The text contains a full discussion of the services included and excluded from these rates. These rates reflect approximately 65% of all expected charges for the AFDC group and 86% of expected charges for the SSI group. A PMPM base rate of $176 was ued to calculate the relative weights. Appendixes 37–A and 37–B list the ACG case mix categories that fall into each RAC cell. Also, demographic cells are used for persons with less than 6 months of ICD-9-CM data. Last, the final rates put in place on June 1, 1997 were modified slightly based on a series of actuarial trend factors.

ACG, ambulatory care group; AFDC, Aid to Families with Dependent Children; AIDS, acquired immunodeficiency syndrome; PMPM, per member per month; PWC, Pregnant Women and Children; RAC, risk-adjusted category; SSI, Supplemental Security Income.

*Source*: Reprinted from Weiner, J.P., Tucker, A.M., Collins, A.M., Fakhraei, H., Lieberman, R., Abrams, C., Trapnell, G.R., Folkemer, J.G., The Development of a Risk-Adjusted Capitation Payment System: The Maryland Medicaid Model, *Journal of Ambulatory Care Management*, Vol. 21, No. 4, pp. 29–52, © 1998, Aspen Publishers, Inc.

percent deviation of the prospectively set capitation rates from actual (FY 1994) payments was calculated for each pseudo group to help assess the relative performance of the three alternative risk-adjustment methods.

## Simulation Methods

For this simulation, the underlying population was selected using the same criteria as those defined for the HealthChoice program. First, only those persons in the eligibility categories included in the 1115 waiver initiative were selected. The study population was limited to recipients with at least 6 months of FFS enrollment in FY 1993 and at least 1 month of FFS enrollment in FY 1994. Approximately 230,000 individuals met these criteria for inclusion. Using the actual claim experience for year 2 (FY 1994), PMPM capitation rates were derived for the entire study population using risk factors compiled with year 1 (FY 1993) diagnostic and demographic data. For all three adjusters, capitation rates were set separately for the AFDC and SSI populations. Stop-loss provisions modeled in this analysis removed approximately 1% of in-scope total charges for the AFDC population, and slightly more than 5% of total charges for the SSI population. Total charges included in the simulation were approximately $127 million for the AFDC and $165 million for the SSI populations.

As part of the overall analyses, regression analysis was used to establish predictive (1993 to 1994) $R^2$ values for each of the subpopulations independently. For the AFDC population, the $R^2$ values were age and gender, .025; ACGs, .082; and RACs, .081. For the SSI population, the $R^2$ values were age and gender, .005; ACGs, .123; and RACs, .122. It should be noted that the percentage of total variation in projected 1994 costs explained by the RAC model was nearly the same as that of the ACG model.

As noted previously, 15 pseudo MCO enrollment groups of 50,000 recipients were formed by selecting individuals at random (with replacement) from the overall study population. Five of those groups were then skewed to represent lower-than-average resource use, defined in terms of historical FY 1993 payments. Another five groups were constructed to represent higher-than-average resource use. Payments for each individual were ranked low, medium, or high within each of the designated resource use groups. Then randomly selected individuals who generated high FY 1993 program costs were moved from the low to the high use groups, and an equal number of individuals associated with low program costs were moved from the high to the low use groups. Approximately 5,400 individuals were moved from each designated low use group to a corresponding high use group, and vice versa. Five average use groups remained as originally selected, at random.

Year 1 (FY 1993) payments were chosen as the skewing factor because they are comparable to information MCOs would have available as they assess the ongoing resource use of their enrolled populations. Theoretically, MCOs could use such information to differentially influence their enrollment, somehow encouraging disenrollment among high-cost enrollees. As a result of the skewing process, low use groups had 29% lower resource use in FY 1993, on average, than the strictly random (average use) groups. High use groups had 23% higher resource use in FY 1993 than the average use groups. Because of regression-to-the-mean, the percentage differences were smaller across the resource use categories in terms of FY 1994 costs—low use groups were 21% below average, and high use groups generated 17% higher payments than the average use groups. (*Note*: This skewing methodology has been applied previously and is described in further detail in Fowles, Weiner, & Knutson,[25] and Fowles et al.)[26]

## Simulation Findings

The predictive accuracy of the three risk-adjustment methods is summarized and compared using the percent deviation of the "expected" costs (i.e., the prospectively set capitation payment rates) from the actual costs incurred for each large group (Table 37–2). If payments were actually made based on the alternative payment approaches, this measure (the percent deviation) would reflect the percentage that the overall MCO payments would be above—or below—actual costs (at least for the services covered by the risk-adjusted rates). A positive percentage in Table 37–2 indicates that the total capitation was greater than actual costs (i.e., an "overpayment"). A negative percentage indicates that payments were less than actual costs (i.e., an "underpayment"). To put this percentage in perspective, for groups of 50,000 recipients in the average use set of pseudo MCOs with average annual at-risk capitated expenditures of approximately $2,360 per person per year for the market basket of covered services, each percentage point of deviation coincides with a gain or loss to the MCO of about $1.2 million. (The value of each percentage point is about 20% lower for the low use MCO groups and 20% higher for the high use groups.)

In Table 37–2, columns headed "All" reflect the groups of 50,000 treated as a whole, including both eligibility categories. Columns headed "AFDC" and "SSI" show isolated results for persons in each of the two eligibility categories. The AFDC column includes an aggregation of all recipients without a disability that constituted approximately 80% of each pseudo enrollee group.

As can be anticipated when capitation rates are calculated from an underlying population and then assessed across large random subgroups drawn from the same population, the percent deviation of expected from actual costs for the five average use groups was low (nearly 0%) regardless of risk-adjustment method. This finding suggests that if assignment into MCOs under the Health-Choice program is strictly random, the particular risk-adjustment method applied would not be critical to the payment model's predictive performance. However, among the two sets of pseudo MCO groups selected on a biased basis (the low and high use groups), the results differ markedly when comparisons are made between the demographically adjusted payments and either the ACG or RAC methodologies. On average, age and gender adjustment

**Table 37–2** Predictive accuracy of alternative risk-adjusted capitation rates: Simulation for Maryland Medicaid 1993–1994*

| Use category | Age and gender | | | ACGs | | | RACs | | |
|---|---|---|---|---|---|---|---|---|---|
| | All | AFDC | SSI | All | AFDC | SSI | All | AFDC | SSI |
| Low | 19.2 | 15.9 | 22.0 | 3.8 | 6.5 | 1.6 | 4.9 | 7.4 | 2.7 |
| Average | −0.2 | 0.2 | −0.5 | −0.5 | 0.1 | −1.0 | −0.5 | 0.1 | −0.9 |
| High | −11.7 | −10.2 | −12.8 | −1.8 | −3.5 | −0.6 | −2.5 | −4.2 | −1.2 |

*Numbers reflect percent deviation of capitation rate from actual costs.

*Note*: Each use category row reflects five randomly selected groups of 50,000 members, drawn (with replacement) from a population of approximately 230,000 Maryland Medicaid recipients enrolled at least 6 months in 1993 and at least 1 month in 1994. Low use groups had an average of 29% lower 1993 costs than average. High use groups had an average of 23% higher 1993 costs than average. Only expenses covered in the 1997 Maryland 1115 waiver MCO capitation rate are included in this analysis. Eligibility status (AFDC versus SSI) was taken into account under all three rating approaches.

ACG, ambulatory care group; AFDC, Aid to Families with Dependent Children; MCO, managed care organization; RAC, risk-adjusted category; SSI, Supplemental Security Income.

*Source*: Reprinted from Weiner, J.P., Tucker, A.M., Collins, A.M., Fakhraei, H., Lieberman, R., Abrams, C., Trapnell, G.R., Folkemer, J.G., The Development of a Risk-Adjusted Capitation Payment System: The Maryland Medicaid Model, *Journal of Ambulatory Care Management*, Vol. 21, No. 4, pp. 29–52, © 1998, Aspen Publishers, Inc.

appeared to overpay across (the five) low use groups by 19% and underpay high use groups by more than 11%. In this simulation, both ACG-based methods somewhat overpaid low use groups—between 3.8% and 4.9%—and underpaid high use groups a more moderate 1.8% to 2.5%.

Results across eligibility categories also differed by rating method. Among the skewed groups for age and gender alone, average payment appeared to be less accurate for the SSI than for AFDC recipients. The reverse was true for the ACG-based methods, particularly for low use groups. On the whole, given the likely morbidity burden present among the SSI group, these results are consistent with the suggestion that diagnosis-based rating methods do a better job of accounting for costs associated with health status differences.

Another key conclusion to be drawn from these results is that the simpler RAC methodology has only slightly lower predictive accuracy than the full articulation of ACGs. Thus, it appears that Maryland's HealthChoice program can be expected to achieve a level of risk adjustment consistent with the existing ACG case mix system while maintaining a degree of administrative simplicity associated with fewer rating cells.

## Limitations

A series of limitations related to the simulation analysis should be noted. The simulation attempted to replicate the Maryland payment model as closely as possible. It should not, however, be viewed as an after-the-fact evaluation of actual capitated payment exchanges. Rather, it should be viewed as a benchmark for how well such a system potentially could operate once fully implemented.

When reviewing the results of the analysis, another limitation of a more technical nature should be noted. When predictive accuracy estimates for the simulated 50,000 member MCOs were developed, the persons included in these groups were randomly selected (with replacement) from the full 230,000-person FFS population meeting the 1115 waiver inclusion criteria. This full sample was used to develop "future" capitation weights for persons in each year 1 risk category (e.g., RAC or demographic cell) based on actual year 2 costs. Thus, the persons selected for inclusion in each of the 15 pseudo groups represented a subset of the persons whose data were used to calculate capitation weights. From a statistical perspective, results based on this approach reflect some degree of "overfitting" of expected to actual costs. In real practice, prospective capitation rates would also be derived from the same underlying population; the rates would probably be determined based on year 1 to year 2 forecasts and then risk ratings derived from charges in year 2 would be inflated to set capitation payments in year 3. Unlike the simulation, rates projected into the year 3 time period would be subject to actual (or mandated) inflation trends and other less predictable factors.

In any case, even if statistical overfitting led to a more optimistic picture of the accuracy of prospective risk-adjusted capitation than would be the case if applied in actual practice, this limitation should not affect the relative ranking of the alternative risk measures assessed. More specifically, the rating approach was applied uniformly across all three risk-adjustment methods, and the relative ranking of these rating methods, in terms of predictive accuracy, would not be expected to change.

## POLICY IMPLICATIONS

It should be reiterated that the goal of this chapter is not to review or compare the various capitation adjustment methodologies reported in the literature, nor is it meant to provide a comprehensive discussion of the general strengths and weaknesses of risk-adjusted capitation versus current approaches. Readers are referred elsewhere for such detailed reviews.[27–32] Readers new to the risk-adjusted capitation area should know that, although this literature is large and growing, the current chapter is one of few published works dealing with capitation adjustment within the Medicaid context. Rather, risk adjustment has been discussed and evaluated primarily within other environments, including regional or statewide purchasing cooperatives, internal applications within private MCOs, and risk-contract Medicare HMOs. Given the recent dramatic movement of Medicaid enrollees into prepaid managed care, the time is right for the development and evaluation of risk adjustment within the context of state medical assistance programs.

It also is worth noting that while many researchers and analysts (including the authors) have published describing the development and simulation of risk-adjusted capitation methods before, this chapter represents one of the few to describe and evaluate a payment system that has been implemented. Therefore, of necessity, the approach had to deal with the multitude of technical, administrative, and political factors always present when hundreds of real providers, hundreds of thousands of real patients, and hundreds of millions of real dollars are involved.

While the Maryland model is probably the most comprehensive risk-adjusted Medicaid payment system currently in place, a number of other states are also designing, or in the early stages of implementing, similar models.[33] As of winter 1998, several other states were in the midst of planning, or putting in place, risk-adjusted payment methods based on the JHU ACG system and other diagnostic risk measures including the Disability Payment System (DPS) and Diagnostic Cost Groups (DCGs).[34-36]

To help these and other states assess some policy implications of risk-adjusted capitation for Medicaid, the remainder of this article discusses a number of advantages and disadvantages of diagnosis-based capitation adjustment. It also offers some suggestions regarding the implementation and future assessment of such a system once put in place.

## SOME BENEFITS

Risk-adjusted payment methodologies such as the one used in Maryland have several positive attributes. First and foremost, such systems result in more fair and accurate payments to managed care organizations for the Medicaid recipients they enroll. As cost containment pressures continue to impinge on public programs, and as sicker and sicker persons become enrolled in capitated MCOs, risk-adjusted reimbursement mechanisms will increasingly become necessary to protect sick patients and the providers that serve them. Conversely, risk adjustment will also help Medicaid managers develop fairer and more cost-effective systems that do not overpay providers that disproportionately care for low-risk patients, at the expense of others in the program.

A second advantage of risk-adjusted systems for MCO payment within a Medicaid 1115 waiver program—or any other managed care context for that matter—is that risk measures such as those adopted in Maryland also have other practical applications beyond that of paying health plans' global fees. For example, versions of the risk-adjustment system described here can be used by Medicaid MCOs to reimburse their contracting clinicians, though as the numbers of persons covered get smaller, various "risk-absorbing" approaches, such as lower stop-loss provisions or more limited "risk corridors," should probably be adopted.

Risk-adjustment methods can also help facilitate resource use profiling. With such systems in place to assess patient mix, programs that must inevitably seek to eliminate waste and inefficiency need not unfairly target efficient providers who may look inefficient because they serve a sicker-than-average cohort of patients.[37–39] In addition to payment and resource management, risk adjustment can also be used for quality improvement or case management. For both of these clinically focused activities, risk measures that describe the number and scope of a person's comorbidities provide a useful means for case finding or report stratification.

Another beneficial aspect of diagnosis-based capitation adjustment is its likely impact on data collection. Compared with FFS, fixed capitation reimbursement has historically eliminated the MCO's most powerful incentive to provide timely and accurate claim and encounter data. Although other health care trends—such as performance monitoring and increasingly complex intra-MCO payment mechanisms—are adding pressures for improved transactional data, diagnosis-based capitation adjusters such as ACGs provide one more important incentive to document the diagnoses treated during the clinician–patient interaction. It is even possible that diagnosis-based capitation adjusters may one day help lead to calibration of ambulatory data in a manner similar to that which has already occurred within hospital databases since the wide-scale introduction of diagnosis-related groups and other inpatient case mix and severity adjusters.

## SOME PITFALLS AND CHALLENGES

The introduction of risk adjustment to setting capitation rates within Medicaid programs is not without its potential costs, concerns, and pitfalls. The first area of concern is one of administrative complexity and data requirements.

Paying contracting MCOs a flat community capitation rate, or one based on age/gender cells, is certainly less complex than basing a capitation rate on an annual (or even more frequent) diagnosis-based risk rating derived from each enrollee's claim or encounter histories. Payment systems not requiring diagnoses are obviously simpler for the payer and the participating plans, particularly if an MCO would otherwise not be required to submit claim and encounter data to the state. It should be noted, however, that few Medicaid agencies are likely to mandate claim and encounter reporting solely for the purpose of risk adjustment. There are many other important uses for these data, mainly for plan performance monitoring and general program management. Furthermore, only for a small minority of MCOs would the provision of diagnosis data require the de novo development of data systems. Today, virtually all organized providers reimbursed even partially by public or private FFS insurance are required to collect such administrative data. It also has been estimated that somewhere over 85% of providers that serve patients on a capitated or salaried basis have reasonably well-developed internal data systems as well.[40] Nonetheless, for those plans not currently collecting or retaining diagnostic data, development costs for these reporting systems will not be insignificant. Moreover, the reporting of encounter data to government agencies by some established (mainly staff/group model) HMOs has been a source of contention in the past; for the immediate future, a timely and accurate provision of these data may represent a challenge to program administrators.

Another weakness of risk-adjusted capitation is the potential incentive it provides for what can be termed "strategic manipulation," or more pejoratively, "gaming." As any public or private insurance administrator can attest, all health care provider payment systems are prone, to at least some degree, to attempted revenue maximization.

One advantage of age/gender capitation is that the rating process is virtually impossible to game. On the other hand, diagnostic-based, risk-adjusted capitation systems are likely to be prone to coding changes intended to place enrollees in the highest possible payment category. Some of these changes should be considered desirable, others not so. As identified earlier, one underlying incentive associated with the Maryland payment model is that in order to obtain higher payments for themselves and their plans, clinicians will have incentives to do a more complete job of documenting diagnosis codes. While this type of "upcoding" should not be considered gaming per se, it is likely to occur in the ambulatory setting, with its currently abridged coding practices.

The question of whether attempts to upcode will offer perverse incentives to consume more resources has been identified as an area of some concern by risk-adjustment policy analysts. For example, some risk measurement systems explicitly use type of service delivery (e.g., admission, surgery, drug prescription) as a classification variable. With regard to ACGs, upcoding should not result in greater utilization of resources, as service delivery is not directly linked to the risk measure itself. A person need only be diagnosed during one ambulatory contact to be placed into a given ACG or RAC category; no admission need take place, and no specific procedure need be performed to be assigned an ACG. However, with ACGs and all other morbidity-based risk measurement systems, it is possible that some potentially unnecessary diagnostic tests or return visits may result in instances where the provider wants to make sure that "expensive" diagnoses assigned to the patient are well documented in case of a chart audit.

While upcoding based on increased code completeness need not be a negative phenomenon, it could lead to cost overruns if the Medicaid agency is not prepared. It is important that any upward risk-category "creep" result in a "zero sum game," where MCOs play off against one another, rather than against the Medicaid program. That is, the size of the overall (per capita) Medicaid "pie" must be determined using other actuarial mechanisms. The risk-adjustment process should only be used to determine whether a given MCO will get a larger or smaller than average per capita slice of the pie based on the mix of its enrollees. Therefore, while any coding maximization that takes place within a single plan might give it a competitive advantage relative to the other MCOs in the system, if the capitation payment system is calibrated (and recalibrated) correctly, this upcoding should not translate into higher overall outlays for the state.

Regardless of these potentially mitigating factors, some sort of auditing and verification mechanism is a necessary part of any diagnostic-based, risk-adjustment capitation process to help ensure a level playing field for all and to root out the few providers that may unethically list nonexistent conditions. This auditing and verification protocol would likely include both computerized and manual components. For example, automated screens could help identify providers that experience unusual increases in the incidence rate of very expensive diagnoses compared to their peers or show where the "sickest" patients are receiving unusually low levels of services. Either of these situations could potentially suggest questionable upcoding or quality-of-care problems. In addition to medical record audits targeted on the basis of automated screens, some random chart audits, particularly of persons in high-cost risk categories, would be appropriate. Chart audits would help to deter diagnosis notation not meeting clinical standards.

Beyond the encounter data availability issue discussed previously, the data processing and analytic capabilities required of a state to develop and apply risk-adjusted capitation rates should not be too onerous. The requirements are similar to those needed to calculate age/gender capitation rates based on historical FFS claims data. One data/analytic challenge of particular note within the Medicaid context is that of new enrollees or enrollees with limited diagnostic claims history. That is, how does one set a diagnosis-based capitation rate for persons when no historical morbidity data are available? In Maryland this issue was handled by applying age/gender/eligibility capitation payments, as well as retrospective carve-out payments (e.g., for deliveries, mental health services, and rare conditions), but other approaches can be used as well. For example, data from enrollment surveys could be used. In any case, the issue of new and partial-year enrollees is not a trivial one when developing risk-adjustment systems.

Although a sound risk-adjusted capitation methodology can help ensure a more equitable and efficient managed Medicaid program, the payment methodology alone is not enough to attain this goal. A full discussion of the program components that are necessary to avoid unfair risk segmentation goes well beyond the scope of this chapter, but it must be acknowledged that many different design and regulatory factors are necessary.[41,42] For example, in Maryland and other states it is mandated that MCOs offer a required level of services for their special need patients and that no overt selection bias be practiced. Other innovative program controls in Maryland include an active ombudsman oversight and performance monitoring program (coordinated by county health officers) and an MCO enrollment process controlled by independent brokers (direct marketing by MCOs is prohibited). These and other related policy initiatives should potentially be part of any implementation strategy to help protect sick patients and their providers in a capitated Medicaid environment.

## CONCLUSIONS

The transition from an open fee-for-service Medicaid program to capitated (risk adjusted or otherwise) managed care will not be easy. It is critical that like other major program innovations, the capitation risk-adjustment process be subject to scrutiny, the goal of which is continuous quality improvement. After implementation, the state should seek input from all key parties in an open forum. To help inform the interchange, it will also be important to support adequate quantitative and qualitative evaluation including assessments of the actual accuracy of the payment system and its impact on patients and providers. With regard to the development of future generations of capitation adjustment methods, it will be important that states learn from not only internal evaluation, but also other states. Now that the national locus of innovative health care reform has shifted in large part to state houses and Medicaid agencies, states can learn much from one another in the quest for a more equitable and efficient health care system.

*Risk-Adjusted Medicaid Capitation*   565

## NOTES

1. U.S. Department of Health and Human Services, Health Care Financing Administration. (1996). Medicare and Medicaid Statistical Supplement, 1996. *Health Care Financing Review.*

2. Kaiser Commission on the Future of Medicaid. (1997, March). *Restructuring Medicaid: Key elements and issues in section 1115 demonstration waivers* (Policy Brief). Washington, DC: Author.

3. Alpha Center. (1997). *Risk adjustment: A key to changing incentives in the health insurance market.* Washington, DC: Alpha Center.

4. Luft, H. (1995). Potential methods to reduce risk selection and its effects. *Inquiry, 32,* 23–32.

5. Newhouse, J. (1994). Patients at risk: Health reform and risk adjustment. *Health Affairs, 13*(1), 132–146.

6. Ellis, R., Pope, G., Iezzoni, L., Ayanian, J., Bates, D., Burstin, H., & Ash, A. (1996). Diagnosis-based risk adjustment for Medicare capitation payments. *Health Care Financing Review, 17*(3), 101–128.

7. Weiner, J., Dobson, A., Maxwell, S., Coleman, K., Starfield, B., & Anderson, G. (1996). Risk-adjusted Medicare capitation rates using ambulatory and inpatient diagnoses. *Health Care Financing Administration, 17*(3), 77–99.

8. Goldfield, N., & Boland, P. (Ed.). (1996). Physician profiling and risk adjustment. Gaithersburg, MD: Aspen Publishers, Inc.

9. Johns Hopkins University. (1997, December). *The Johns Hopkins ACG case-mix system clinician's guide.* Baltimore: Health Services Research and Development Center, Johns Hopkins University School of Public Health. (Available on-line—www.hsr.jhsph.edu/acg/acg.htm.)

10. Starfield, B., Weiner, J., Mumford, B.L., & Steinwachs, D. (1991). Ambulatory care groups: A categorization for research and management. *Health Services Research, 26*(1), 53–74.

11. Weiner, J., Starfield, B., Steinwachs, D., & Mumford, L. (1991). Development and application of a population-oriented measure of ambulatory care case-mix. *Medical Care, 29*(5), 452–472.

12. Alpha Center, *Risk Adjustment.*

13. Newhouse, Patients at Risk.

14. Alpha Center, *Risk Adjustment.*

15. Andrews, J., Anderson, G., Han, C., & Neff, J. (1997). Pediatric carve-outs: The use of disease-specific conditions as risk adjusters in capitated payment systems. *Archives Pediatric Adolescent Medicine, 151,* 236–242.

16. Dobson, A., Weiner, J., Coleman, K., Abrams, C., Starfield, B., & Anderson, G. (1997). *The development and testing of risk adjustment methods for the under 65 population* (HCFA ORD Contract #560-92-0021). Fairfax, VA: The Lewin Group.

17. Johns Hopkins University, ACG-Case Mix.

18. Starfield et al., Ambulatory Care Groups.

19. Weiner et al., Development and Application of a Population-oriented Measure.
20. Stuart, M., & Steinwachs, D. (1993). Patient mix differences among ambulatory providers and their effect on utilization and payment for Maryland Medicaid users. *Medical Care, 31*, 1119–1137.
21. John Hopkins University, *The Johns Hopkins ACG Case-mix System Clinician Guide.*
22. Austin Data Management Associates. (1992). *PC-Group user's guide: Version 3.01.* Austin, TX: ADMA.
23. Actuarial Research Corporation. (1996). *Maryland Medicaid managed care program (1115 waiver).* Annandale, VA: Author. (Available on-line from: Center for Health Program Development and Management, University of Maryland Baltimore County—www.umbc.edu/chpdm.)
24. Actuarial Research Corporation, *Maryland Medicaid Managed Care Program.*
25. Fowles, J., Weiner, J., Knutson, D., (1994). *A comparison of alternative approaches to risk adjustment.* Selected External Research Series, Number 1. Washington, DC: Physician Payment Review Commission.
26. Fowles, J., Weiner, J., Knutson, D., Fowler, E., Tucker, A., & Ireland, M. (1996, October). Taking health status into account when setting capitation rates. *Journal of American Medical Association, 276*(16), 1316–1321.
27. Alpha Center, *Risk Adjustment.*
28. Ellis et al., Diagnosis-based Risk Adjustment.
29. Fowles et al., Taking Health Status into Account.
30. Kronick, R., Dreyfus, T., Lee, L., & Zhou, Z. (1996). Diagnostic risk adjustment for Medicaid: The disability payment system. *Health Care Financing Review, 17*(3), 7–33.
31. Luft, Potential Methods to Reduce Risk.
32. Newhouse, Patients at Risk.
33. St. Anthony's. (1997). Risk-adjusted physician compensation: A new frontier in managed care reimbursement. *St. Anthony's Physician Capitation Report, 3*(6), 1–2.
34. Dobson et al., *The Development and Testing of Risk Adjustment.*
35. Ellis et al., Diagnosis-based Risk Adjustment for Medicare.
36. Kronick et al., Diagnostic Risk Adjustment for Medicaid.
37. Powe, N., Weiner, J., Starfield, B., Stuart, M., Baker, A., & Steinwachs, D. (1996). System-wide provider performance in a Medicaid program: Profiling the care of patients with chronic illnesses. *Medical Care, 34*(8), 798–810.
38. Tucker, A., Weiner, J., Honigfeld, S., & Parton, R. (1996). Profiling primary care physician resource use: Examining the application of case-mix adjustment. *Journal of Ambulatory Care Management, 19*(1), 60–80.
39. Weiner, J., Starfield, B., Powe, N., Stuart, M., & Steinwachs, D. (1996). Ambulatory care practice variation within a Medicaid program. *Health Services Research, 30*(6), 751–770.
40. American Association of Health Plans. (1995). *1995, Annual industry survey.* Washington, DC: Author.
41. Luft, Potential Methods to Reduce Risk.
42. Newhouse, Patients at Risk.

# Distribution of Prospective Resource Use in Each ACG for RAC Capitation Payment Cells: AFDC and Other Nondisabled

| Category (RAC/ACG) | No. of enrollees | PMPM charges ($) | Relative weights* |
|---|---|---|---|
| RAC 1 | 83,061 | $31.30 | 0.40 |
| 1 Acute Minor, Age < 2 | 2,482 | 32.96 | 0.43 |
| 2 Acute Minor, Age 2–5 | 5,524 | 27.96 | 0.36 |
| 3 Acute Minor, Age 6+ | 11,759 | 37.81 | 0.49 |
| 5 Likely To Recur, without Allergies | 7,732 | 40.27 | 0.52 |
| 6 Likely To Recur, with Allergies | 507 | 32.83 | 0.42 |
| 11 Ophthalmological/Dental | 850 | 26.15 | 0.34 |
| 16 Preventive/Administrative | 14,347 | 29.29 | 0.38 |
| 19 Acute Minor and Likely To Recur, Age < 2 | 4,431 | 48.12 | 0.62 |
| 20 Acute Minor and Likely To Recur, Age 2–5 | 6,129 | 37.86 | 0.49 |
| 22 Acute Minor and Likely To Recur, Age > 5, with Allergy | 704 | 47.34 | 0.61 |
| 24 Acute Minor and Eye/Dental | 665 | 40.44 | 0.52 |
| 34 Acute Minor/Likely to Recur/Eye & Dental | 618 | 48.13 | 0.62 |
| 51 No Diagnosis or Other Unclassified Diagnosis | 1,093 | 77.05 | 0.99 |
| 52 Non-Users | 26,220 | 19.71 | 0.25 |
| RAC 2 | 13,835 | $58.25 | 0.75 |
| 9 Chronic Medical, Stable | 1,216 | 55.15 | 0.71 |
| 21 Acute Minor and Likely To Recur, Age > 5, without Allergy | 6,234 | 54.67 | 0.71 |
| 30 Acute Minor/Acute Major/Likely To Recur, Age 2–5 | 4,694 | 64.40 | 0.83 |
| 31 Acute Minor/Acute Major/Likely To Recur, Age 6–11 | 1,691 | 56.10 | 0.72 |
| RAC 3 | 31,846 | $69.80 | 0.90 |
| 7 Asthma | 571 | 61.49 | 0.79 |

*continues*

| Category (RAC/ACG) | No. of enrollees | PMPM charges ($) | Relative weights* |
|---|---|---|---|
| 8 Chronic Medical, Unstable | 334 | 85.28 | 1.10 |
| 10 Chronic Specialty | 123 | 53.03 | 0.68 |
| 12 Chronic Specialty, Unstable | 381 | 58.77 | 0.76 |
| 13 Psychosocial, without Psychosocial Unstable | 2,722 | 55.85 | 0.72 |
| 18 Acute Minor and Acute Major | 10,742 | 66.75 | 0.86 |
| 23 Acute Minor and Chronic Medical, Stable | 1,265 | 71.64 | 0.92 |
| 25 Acute Minor and Psychosocial, without Psychosocial Unstable | 1,834 | 65.26 | 0.84 |
| 29 Acute Minor/Acute Major/Likely To Recur, Age < 2 | 5,139 | 75.79 | 0.98 |
| 38 2–3 Other ADG Combinations, Age < 17 | 8,735 | 75.92 | 0.98 |
| RAC 4 | 21,591 | $87.67 | 1.13 |
| 4 Acute: Major | 6,902 | 71.94 | 0.93 |
| 28 Acute Major and Likely To Recur | 3,849 | 82.96 | 1.07 |
| 33 Acute Minor/Acute Major/Likely To Recur, Age > 5, with Allergy | 337 | 108.90 | 1.40 |
| 35 Acute Minor/Likely To Recur/Psychosocial | 1,869 | 92.72 | 1.20 |
| 39 2–3 Other ADG Combinations, Males Age 17–34 | 351 | 137.53 | 1.77 |
| 42 4–5 Other ADG Combinations, Age < 17 | 8,283 | 97.76 | 1.26 |
| RAC 5 | 9,768 | $138.55 | 1.79 |
| 32 Acute Minor/Acute Major/Likely To Recur, Age > 5, without Allergy | 4,343 | 131.72 | 1.70 |
| 36 Acute Minor/Acute Major/Likely To Recur/ Eye & Dental | 2,787 | 143.37 | 1.85 |
| 37 Acute Minor/Acute Major/Likely To Recur/ Psychosocial | 2,638 | 144.18 | 1.86 |
| RAC 6 | 16,580 | $163.71 | 2.11 |
| 14 Psychosocial, with Psychosocial Unstable, without Psychosocial Stable | 801 | 140.89 | 1.82 |
| 40 2–3 Other ADG Combinations, Females Age 17–34 | 3,678 | 143.72 | 1.85 |
| 41 2–3 Other ADG Combinations, Age > 34 | 1,562 | 142.89 | 1.84 |
| 43 4–5 Other ADG Combinations, Age 17–44 | 5,062 | 180.29 | 2.33 |
| 45 6–9 Other ADG Combinations, Age < 6 | 3,417 | 162.99 | 2.10 |

*continues*

| Category (RAC/ACG) | No. of enrollees | PMPM charges ($) | Relative weights* |
|---|---|---|---|
| 46 6–9 Other ADG Combinations, Ages 6–16 | 2,060 | 180.92 | 2.33 |
| RAC 7 | 4,341 | $258.01 | 3.33 |
| 15 Psychosocial, with Psychosocial Unstable, with Psychosocial Stable | 122 | 249.37 | 3.22 |
| 26 Acute Minor and Psychosocial, with Psychosocial Unstable, without Psychosocial Stable | 326 | 201.85 | 2.60 |
| 27 Acute Minor and Psychosocial, with Psychosocial Unstable and Stable | 162 | 166.27 | 2.14 |
| 44 4–5 Other ADG Combinations, Age > 44 | 453 | 274.30 | 3.54 |
| 47 6–9 Other ADG Combinations, Males Age 17–34 | 155 | 276.56 | 3.57 |
| 48 6–9 Other ADG Combinations, Females Age 17–34 | 3,123 | 265.62 | 3.43 |
| RAC 8 | 1,686 | $340.40 | 4.39 |
| 49 6–9 Other ADG Combinations, Age > 34 | 1,686 | 340.40 | 4.39 |
| RAC 9 | 1,657 | $435.55 | 5.62 |
| 50 10+ Other ADG Combinations | 1,657 | 435.55 | 5.62 |
| Total | 184,365 | $77.54 | 1.00 |

*Relative weights reflect per member per month payment for group divided by average AFDC payment ($77.54).

*Note:* ACG categories listed under each RAC are based on diagnosis codes identified from fiscal year (FY) 1993 Maryland Medicaid FFS claims data. Resource use reflects actual FFS charges for FY 1994. Only services included in capitation rate are included. The dollar values are not exactly comparable to final capitation rates (see Table 37–1) due to actuarial adjustments (Actuarial Research Corporation, 1996). ACGs reflect version 3.01 catgories. Pregnancy ICD-9-CM codes are excluded; thus ACG 17 "pregnancy only" is not used in the Maryland system.

Source of data: 184,365 AFDC and other non-disabled ("family") FFS Maryland Medicaid enrollees meeting criteria for inclusion in 1115 Waiver Program and enrolled at least 6 months in FY 1993 and at least 1 month in FY 1994.

ACG, ambulatory care group; ADG, ambulatory diagnostic group; FFS, fee for service; PMPM, per member per month; RAC, risk-adjusted category.

*Source:* Reprinted from Weiner, J.P., Tucker, A.M., Collins, A.M., Fakhraei, H., Lieberman, R., Abram, C., Trapnell, G.R., Folkemer, J.G., The Development of a Risk-Adjusted Capitation Payment System: The Maryland Medicaid Model, *Journal of Ambulatory Care Management*, Vol. 21, No. 4, pp. 29–52, © 1998, Aspen Publishers, Inc.

# Appendix 37–B

# Distribution of Prospective Resource Use in Each ACG for RAC Capitation Payment Cells: SSI and Other Disabled

| Category (RAC/ACG) | No. of enrollees | PMPM charges | Relative weights* |
|---|---|---|---|
| RAC 10 | 12,889 | $44.91 | 0.14 |
| 1 Acute Minor, Age < 2 | 6 | 63.10 | 0.19 |
| 2 Acute Minor, Age 2–5 | 37 | 165.49 | 0.50 |
| 3 Acute Minor, Age 6+ | 809 | 81.93 | 0.25 |
| 5 Likely To Recur, without Allergies | 384 | 101.75 | 0.31 |
| 6 Likely To Recur, with Allergies | 24 | 61.27 | 0.19 |
| 7 Asthma | 45 | 115.82 | 0.35 |
| 11 Ophthalmological/Dental | 66 | 47.01 | 0.14 |
| 13 Psychosocial, without Psychosocial Unstable | 686 | 70.56 | 0.21 |
| 16 Preventive/Administrative | 610 | 97.79 | 0.30 |
| 19 Acute Minor and Likely To Recur, Age < 2 | 4 | 149.82 | 0.45 |
| 20 Acute Minor and Likely To Recur, Age 2–5 | 27 | 104.32 | 0.32 |
| 21 Acute Minor and Likely To Recur, Age > 5, without Allergy | 369 | 93.07 | 0.28 |
| 22 Acute Minor and Likely To Recur, Age > 5, with Allergy | 40 | 84.02 | 0.25 |
| 24 Acute Minor and Eye/Dental | 32 | 62.16 | 0.19 |
| 25 Acute Minor and Psychosocial, without Psychosocial Unstable | 286 | 89.50 | 0.27 |
| 30 Acute Minor/Acute Major/Likely To Recur, Age 2–5 | 26 | 340.33 | 1.03 |
| 31 Acute Minor/Acute Major/Likely To Recur, Age 6–11 | 46 | 188.68 | 0.57 |
| 34 Acute Minor/Likely To Recur/Eye & Dental | 25 | 73.36 | 0.22 |
| 52 Non-Users | 9,367 | 28.53 | 0.09 |

*continues*

| Category (RAC/ACG) | No. of enrollees | PMPM charges | Relative weights[*] |
|---|---|---|---|
| RAC 11 | 5,669 | $162.76 | 0.49 |
| 9 Chronic Medical, Stable | 835 | 127.48 | 0.39 |
| 10 Chronic Specialty | 44 | 73.96 | 0.22 |
| 12 Chronic Specialty, Unstable | 100 | 121.69 | 0.37 |
| 14 Psychosocial, with Psychosocial Unstable, without Psychosocial Stable | 1,235 | 68.70 | 0.21 |
| 15 Psychosocial, with Psychosocial Unstable, with Psychosocial Stable | 180 | 76.16 | 0.23 |
| 18 Acute Minor and Acute Major | 632 | 190.70 | 0.58 |
| 23 Acute Minor and Chronic Medical, Stable | 446 | 123.27 | 0.37 |
| 26 Acute Minor and Psychosocial, with Psychosocial Unstable, without Psychosocial Stable | 221 | 112.71 | 0.34 |
| 27 Acute Minor and Psychosocial, with Psychosocial Unstable and Stable | 159 | 104.69 | 0.32 |
| 29 Acute Minor/Acute Major/Likely To Recur, Age < 2 | 17 | 104.21 | 0.32 |
| 35 Acute Minor/Likely To Recur/Psychosocial | 397 | 121.55 | 0.37 |
| 38 2–3 Other ADG Combinations, Age < 17 | 711 | 249.06 | 0.75 |
| 42 4–5 Other ADG Combinations, Age < 17 | 692 | 366.41 | 1.11 |
| RAC 12 | 4,810 | $263.75 | 0.80 |
| 4 Acute: Major | 928 | 256.35 | 0.78 |
| 28 Acute Major and Likely To Recur | 309 | 336.70 | 1.02 |
| 32 Acute Minor/Acute Major/Likely To Recur, Age > 5, without Allergy | 422 | 264.47 | 0.80 |
| 33 Acute Minor/Acute Major/Likely To Recur, Age > 5 with Allergy | 30 | 317.24 | 0.96 |
| 36 Acute Minor/Acute Major/Likely To Recur/ Eye & Dental | 685 | 312.82 | 0.95 |
| 37 Acute Minor/Acute Major/Likely To Recur/ Psychosocial | 672 | 250.14 | 0.76 |
| 39 2–3 Other ADG Combinations, Males Age 17–34 | 924 | 214.36 | 0.65 |
| 40 2–3 Other ADG Combinations, Females Age 17–34 | 645 | 192.70 | 0.58 |
| 45 6–9 Other ADG Combinations, Age < 6 | 195 | 507.28 | 1.54 |

*continues*

| Category (RAC/ACG) | No. of enrollees | PMPM charges | Relative weights[*] |
|---|---|---|---|
| RAC 13 | 5.855 | $291.95 | 0.88 |
|   8 Chronic Medical, Unstable | 379 | 271.38 | 0.82 |
|   41 2–3 Other ADG Combinations, Age > 34 | 4,754 | 250.25 | 0.76 |
|   48 6–9 Other ADG Combinations, Females Age 17–34 | 632 | 624.00 | 1.89 |
|   51 No Diagnosis or Only Unclassified Diagnosis | 90 | 318.11 | 0.96 |
| RAC 14 | 6,953 | $441.52 | 1.34 |
|   43 4–5 Other ADG Combinations, Age 17–44 | 2,876 | 437.31 | 1.32 |
|   44 4–5 Other ADG Combinations, Age > 44 | 3,664 | 437.28 | 1.32 |
|   46 6–9 Other ADG Combinations, Age 6–16 | 413 | 506.01 | 1.53 |
| RAC 15 | 5,812 | $712.65 | 2.16 |
|   49 6–9 Other ADG Combinations, Age > 34 | 5,812 | 712.65 | 2.16 |
| RAC 16 | 647 | $816.55 | 2.47 |
|   47 6–9 Other ADG Combinations, Males Age 17–34 | 647 | 816.55 | 2.47 |
| RAC 17 | 2,269 | $1,180.03 | 3.57 |
|   50 10+ Other ADG Combinations | 2,269 | 1180.03 | 3.57 |
| Total | 44,904 | $330.23 | 1.00 |

[*]Relative weights reflect PMPM payment for group divided by average SSI payment (330.23).

*Note:* ACG categories listed under each RAC are based on diagnosis codes identified from FY 1993 Maryland Medicaid FFS claims data. Resource use reflects actual FFS charges for FY 1994. Only those services included in capitation rate are included. The dollar values are not exactly comparable to final capitation rates (see Table 37–1) due to actuarial adjustments (Actuarial Research Corporation, 1996). ACGs reflect version 3.01 categories. Pregnancy ICD-9-CM codes are excluded.

ACG, ambulatory care group; ADG, ambulatory diagnostic group; FFS, fee for service; PMPM, per member per month; RAC, risk-adjusted category.

*Source:* Reprinted from Weiner, J.P., Tucker, A.M., Collins, A.M., Fakhraei, H., Lieberman, R., Abrams, C., Trapnell, G.R., Folkemer, J.G., The Development of a Risk-Adjusted Capitation Payment System: The Maryland Medicaid Model, *Journal of Ambulatory Care Management*, Vol. 21, No. 4, pp. 29–52, © 1998, Aspen Publishers, Inc.

CHAPTER 38

# Physician Profiling Using Outpatient Pharmacy Data as a Source for Case Mix Measurement and Risk Adjustment

*Douglas W. Roblin*

Patient case mix is a method of accounting for situations in which groups of patients are not necessarily comparable to one another regarding their need or potential demand for medical services. When allocating resources to providers or when comparing providers' performances, equitable allocation or comparison requires some accounting of patient case mix. Providers caring for a group of patients with relatively high prevalences of chronic diseases can be expected to have greater resource requirements and to have higher rates of use of selected medical services (e.g., emergency department visits, hospital admissions) than providers caring for a group of patients with relatively low prevalences of chronic diseases.

A goal of, and a challenge to, outpatient case mix measurement in a managed care organization (MCO) is to capture some information on the medical conditions for as large a proportion of the health plan population as possible. Realizing this goal has recently focused on two data collection and classification strategies.

*Source:* Reprinted from D.W. Roblin, "Physician Profiling Using Outpatient Pharmacy Data as a Source for Case Mix Measurement and Risk Adjustment," *Journal of Ambulatory Care Management*, Vol. 21, No. 4, pp. 68–84, Aspen Publishers, Inc., © 1998.

Physician visits are the most frequent point of medical service delivery to health plan members, with many patients having two or more physician visits per year.[1] Diagnoses, signs, and symptoms associated with medical conditions treated or recorded on clinic visits provide sources of data for outpatient case mix measurement. Ambulatory care groups (ACGs) and diagnostic cost groups (DCGs) are two of the more widely known diagnosis-based case mix systems with various risk adjustment applications, including profiles of physician practice.[2,3]

A large proportion of health plan members also are dispensed at least one prescribed medicine each year for outpatient treatment of a medical condition. Nearly two thirds of physician visits result in ordering of a prescription medication.[4] Properly classified into therapeutic groups and subgroups, the types of prescribed medicines dispensed to MCO members can identify the type of disease or disorder under treatment and, in some situations, can indicate the level of severity of illness under treatment. The Chronic Disease Score (CDS), developed initially at Group Health of Puget Sound, and the Kaiser Permanente Ambulatory Rx (KPARx) system are two recently developed pharmacy-based case mix systems with application to profiling of physician practices.[5-9]

The article describes characteristics of outpatient pharmacy data that make that data amenable to population case mix measurement. Then a discussion of issues surrounding the integrity of outpatient pharmacy data as a source of case mix measurement for the purpose of physician profiling is presented. The article concludes with several examples of the application of case mix measurement based on outpatient pharmacy data to risk adjustment of physician profiles.

## OUTPATIENT PHARMACY DATA

Computerized databases of prescribed medicines dispensed for outpatient therapy are widely available among MCOs. Data captured include records of dispensings from pharmacies directly managed by an MCO, from retail pharmacies contracting with an MCO, and from mail-order pharmacy arrangements with an MCO.

Common elements of each record of a prescribed medicine dispensed are a unique identifier for the MCO member, the date of dispensing, identifier(s) of the drug dispensed, number of units of th1e drug dispensed, and estimated supply of the drug dispensed in days. For the purpose of case mix measurement, the first three elements are particularly important. The last two elements may have potential application in monitoring physician compliance with guidelines for appropriate dosing and patient compliance with therapeutic regimens requiring sustained pharmacotherapy.

The unique identifier for the individual member (such as a medical record number) allows each member's drug dispensing history to be aggregated in a single record. The dispensing dates, in turn, determine which dispensings are relevant to a study timeframe. They may vary from one physician profiling application to another. In more advanced applications, for the sequencing of one dispensing in relation to another (e.g., for the purpose of staging development of disease states), dispensing dates will be necessary.

Drug identifiers come in a variety of forms. The National Drug Code (NDC) is a universal identifier; however, some outpatient pharmacy dispensing systems maintain proprietary product codes. Each NDC consists of three parts: the labeler, packager, or manufacturer of the drug; the therapeutic agent(s); and the package size (i.e., number of units). The combination of these three parts uniquely identifies a prescribed medicine.

Case mix measurement using outpatient pharmacy data will rarely rely directly on specific drugs as classes for measurement. Instead it will depend on the classification of drugs into therapeutic groups and subgroups. A therapeutic group or subgroup is a class of drugs having similar pharmacologic effect (e.g., vasodilation, diuresis), affecting the same body system (e.g., respiratory system), and/or achieving similar therapeutic results (e.g., control of serum glucose). A drug is classified into one and only one therapeutic group and subgroup.

The initial development of the CDS case mix system considered for inclusion the therapeutic groups and subgroups of prescribed medicines principally used for treatment of chronic medical conditions (Table 38–1) such as hypertension and diabetes.[10] Scoring rules were developed by consensus among various health care professionals to reflect the number of medical conditions under treatment, complexity of the drug regimen, and acuity of the medical condition. A recent revision to the CDS expanded the range of drugs and classes included, relying principally on American Hospital Formulary Service (AHFS) therapeutic groups for assignment of drugs to classes.[11]

The initial development of the KPARx case mix system also emphasized inclusion of prescribed medicines for treatment of chronic medical conditions

(Table 38–1). Recent revisions, however, have expanded the therapeutic groups and subgroups to include anti-infective agents (e.g., antibiotics and antifungals) because these drugs are among the most commonly prescribed in outpatient care.

The logic by which drug therapeutic groups and subgroups are defined in a case mix system requires substantial attention. Conflicting tendencies to aggregate and to disaggregate groups and subgroups must constantly be reconciled. Excessive aggregation may place drugs in the same therapeutic group or subgroup, which may represent different diseases or levels of severity within a disease. For example, in the acute version of KPARx case mix system, the therapeutic group of antidiabetic drugs is split into the subgroups of insulin and oral hypoglycemics because the former subgroup represents a more morbid disease state (and need for acute level care) than the latter subgroup represents.

Excessive disaggregation could make a case mix system based on pharmacy data sensitive to variation in physician prescribing patterns or to subtle variation in patient condition and comorbidity. For example, calcium channel blockers have application in the treatment of a range of cardiac, cardiovascular, and hypertensive conditions. Without contextual information, however, it is not possible to ascertain either which specific circulatory disorder is the target of therapy or what circumstances caused one type of calcium channel blocker to be chosen over another (e.g., diltiazem versus verapamil). Thus, in the present state of development of pharmacy-based case mix systems, these drugs remain in one class.

## DATA INTEGRITY

The integrity of pharmacy data for the purpose of case mix measurement can be affected by choices made by physicians and patients over the course of ordering, dispensing, and using prescribed medicines.[12,13] These issues include clinical relevance of the drug, disease specificity, and completeness of the database.

### Clinical Relevance

Because prescribed medicines legally require a physician order and, in generating that order, a physician makes a number of decisions related to patient

**Table 38–1** Therapeutic groups and subgroups for assignment of risk weights in selected pharmacy-based case mix measurement systems

| CDS-1 | CDS-2 | KPARx-O | KPARx-A |
|---|---|---|---|
| Cardiac/Cardiovascular/Hypertensive Rx Groups (2) | Cardiac/Cardiovascular/Hypertensive Rx Groups (3) | Cardiac/Cardiovascular/Hypertensive Rx Groups (7) | Cardiac/Cardiovascular/Hypertensive Rx Groups (7) |
| Obstructive Pulmonary Disorders Rx Groups (2) | Obstructive Pulmonary Disorders Rx Groups (3) | Obstructive Pulmonary Disorders Rx Groups (2) | Obstructive Pulmonary Disorders Rx Groups (2) |
| | | Antihistamines (1) | |
| | | Mucolytic Agents (1) | |
| Diabetes Rx Groups (1) | Diabetes Rx Groups (1) | Diabetes Rx Groups (1) | Diabetes Rx Groups (2) |
| | Anxiety/Depression/Psychoses Rx Groups (4) | Anxiety/Depression/Psychoses Rx Groups (4) | Anxiety/Depression/Psychoses Rx Groups (4) |
| Anticonvulsant Rx Groups (1) | Anticonvulsant Rx Groups (1) | | |
| Antiparkinson Rx Groups (1) | Antiparkinson Rx Groups (1) | | |
| Anti-infective Rx Groups (1) | Anti-infective Rx Groups (1) | Anti-infective Rx Groups (4) | Anti-infective Rx Groups (4) |
| | AIDS Rx Groups (1) | AIDS Rx Groups (1) | AIDS Rx Groups (1) |
| Antineoplastic Rx Groups (1) | Antineoplastic Rx Groups (1) | | |
| GI Hypersecretory Rx Groups (1) | GI Hypersecretory Rx Groups (1) | GI Hypersecretory Rx Groups (1) | GI Hypersecretory Rx Groups (2) |
| | Thyroid Rx Groups (1) | Thyroid Rx Groups (1) | Thyroid Rx Groups (1) |
| | Pain Control Rx Groups: NSAIDs, Opiates (2) | Pain Control Rx Groups: NSAIDs, Opiates (2) | Pain Control Rx Groups: NSAIDs, Opiates (2) |
| Systemic Corticosteroids (1) | Systemic Corticosteroids/Aurothiocyanates (1) | Systemic Corticosteroids (1) | Systemic Corticosteroids (1) |
| Aurothiocyanates (1) | | | |
| Ergot Derivatives (1) | | | |

*continues*

**Table 38–1** continued

| CDS-1 | CDS-2 | KPARx-O | KPARx-A |
|---|---|---|---|
| Ophthalmic Miotics (1) | Ophthalmic Miotics (1) | | |
| Uric Acid Agents (1) | Uric Acid Agents (1) | | |
| Antiacne Rx Groups (1) | Liver Disease Rx Groups (1) | | |
| | Renal Disease/ESRD Rx Groups (2) | | |
| | Transplant Rx Groups (1) | | |
| | Cystic Fibrosis Rx Groups (1) | | |
| | Crohn's/Ulcerative Colitis Rx Groups (1) | | |
| | | Replacement Preparations (1) | |
| | | Prenatal Multivitamin Supplements (1) | |

*Note:* Numbers in parentheses refer to the number of positions in the weight record for which a score might be computed. Many different medications or therapeutic groups and subgroups of medications might have to be identified to assign a score. For example, in CDS-1, the following therapeutic groups and subgroups must be identified: anticoagulants, cardiac agents (calcium channel blockers, ACE inhibitors, nitrates), loop diuretics, antihypertensive agents (other than calcium channel blockers, ACE inhibitors), beta blockers, and diuretics. Ultimately, two scores in the weight record are assigned: one for heart disease and another for hypertension.

*Note:* AIDS, acquired immunodeficiency syndrome; CDS-1, first version of Chronic Disease Score; CDS-2, second version of Chronic Disease Score; ESRD, end-stage renal disease; GI gastrointestinal, KPARx-O, outpatient version of KPARx case mix system; KPARx-A, acute version of KPARx case mix system; NSAIDs, nonsteroidal anti-inflammatory drugs; Rx, prescription.

*Source:* Reprinted from *Journal of Ambulatory Care Management*, Vol. 21, No. 4, pp. 71–72, Aspen Publishers, Inc., © 1998.

treatment, case mix systems based on pharmacy data convey substantial clinical significance. A physician evaluates a patient's presenting signs, symptoms, and history; makes a diagnosis; and determines that a selected form of pharmacotherapy is a necessary adjunct to the patient's treatment regimen. These aspects of clinical significance in prescribing medicines help to ensure both that the type of drug dispensed denotes a type of medical condition and that not ordering the drug denotes the absence of this type of medical condition (or the absence of a state of this type of medical condition requiring pharmacotherapy). Prescribing of a medicine, in the absence of appropriate indications for pharmacotherapy, may lead to adverse patient outcomes. A close correspondence between disease state and type of drugs dispensed ensures that a pharmacy-based case mix system meaningfully represents morbidity of a physician's panel population; and, the potential for adverse outcomes from inappropriate prescribing limits the likelihood that medicines will be prescribed to misrepresent the actual disease burden of a population.

By choosing drugs likely to be prescribed with such discretion, a case mix system based on outpatient pharmacy data can achieve a high level of acceptance by physicians as a reliable measure of morbidity of a patient population. Both the CDS and KPARx case mix systems aim to maximize clinical acceptance by including therapeutic groups and subgroups of drugs for which there is minimal variation in therapeutic choice among physicians and by excluding drugs for which there is substantial variation in therapeutic choice.[14] Drugs in the former group, "vital" drugs, are those whose use is vital to maintain the health status of a patient; that is, not prescribing the drug would potentially result in clinically significant deterioration in the patient's quality of life.[15] Drugs in the latter group are most often prescribed for self-limiting conditions, particularly for symptomatic relief. Examples include expectorants, analgesics, and antacids.

Both the CDS and KPARx case mix systems moderate variation in physician selection of specific drugs—given a diagnosis of a condition and decision to prescribe—by placing drugs of similar application into the same therapeutic group and subgroup. For example, while many types of insulin exist (e.g., fast acting and slow acting), all insulins are placed into one therapeutic subgroup. Insulin use denotes diabetes, specifically insulin-requiring diabetes. Prescribing of fast- or slow-acting insulin represents attempts by physicians to tailor a treatment regimen for insulin-requiring diabetes to unique patient circumstances.

## Disease Specificity

Reliability of a pharmacy-based case mix system is enhanced by selection and classification of drugs by their level of disease specificity. Some drugs have high specificity with respect to disease and severity of illness. Antidiabetic drugs (e.g., insulins and oral hypoglycemics) denote diabetes almost exclusively.[16] Diabetes requiring insulin represents a more acute state of diabetes than diabetes requiring oral hypoglycemics due to the generally higher rates of end-organ disease associated with the former disease state. Beta-agonist bronchodilators and orally inhaled steroids denote obstructive pulmonary disorders.[17] Nitrates are relatively specific to identification of angina.[18]

Other drugs have less specificity with respect to disease. Nevertheless they have value for inclusion in a pharmacy-based case mix system. Calcium channel blockers, for example, can treat a range of cardiac, cardiovascular, and hypertensive conditions. Although distinguishing among these medical conditions is highly desirable, knowing only that the dispensing of a calcium channel blocker has occurred, in the absence of other information, does not allow such a distinction to be made. Thus, definitions of some therapeutic groups and subgroups in a pharmacy-based case mix system must balance the ideal of clinical specificity with the reality of some clinical generality in use of relevant drugs.

## Completeness of the Database

Various factors can affect the completeness of a pharmacy database in capturing prescribed medicines. An incomplete accounting of drug dispensing history of an MCO member may be due to enrollment changes, patient noncompliance with physician orders to adhere to a treatment regimen, and effects of cost-sharing on drug purchases.

Enrollment in a managed care system is open. Members join, continue, and terminate their enrollment for a variety of reasons—birth and death, employment changes, changes in employer group health plan options, and so on. All else being equal, members do not have equal periods of enrollment. Therefore, they have unequal likelihoods of being dispensed prescribed medicines. This fact will ultimately affect whether individual MCO members are assigned to a class in a pharmacy-based case mix system. The effects of varying periods of enrollment on likelihood of assignment to a class in a case mix system can be handled by several techniques: either stratifying the population by duration of enrollment in the profiling period or by including in the risk adjustment method variables that define durations of enrollment.

Patients who have been ordered a drug as part of their therapeutic regimen may or may not adhere to that regimen over time. Noncompliant members will not be assigned to a class in a pharmacy-based case mix system during the time period that they are noncompliant. This loss of information about the member's disease state can best be reconciled if a database on drugs dispensed can be supplemented with a database on drugs ordered. It also may be possible to build a history of patient compliance into the risk-adjustment method to differentiate the impact on the measured outcome of compliant versus noncompliant patients in a case mix system class.

Compliance of a patient with a physician's order, as well as location of dispensing of a prescribed medicine, is affected by whether or not an outpatient pharmacy benefit is included in the member's total benefit package and, if included, the level of cost-sharing required of the member at the point of dispensing.[19–22] In an MCO, most non-Medicare members who receive benefits through an employer-sponsored health benefits offering have an outpatient pharmacy benefit; many Medicare members do not. Among members with an outpatient pharmacy benefit, the level of cost-sharing (i.e., the amount of copayment required of the patient at the point of dispensing) is usually nominal (typically in the range of a $1 to $5 copayment per dispensing).

In the absence of a benefit or with increased copayments among those with a benefit, the likelihood decreases that a drug ordered will be dispensed. The effect of a copayment on likelihood of dispensing is greatest for "nonvital" drugs and least for vital drugs.[23] Thus, the coverage of many MCO members with an outpatient pharmacy benefit and the emphasis of pharmacy-based case mix systems on vital drugs for health risk measurement minimizes the loss of data relevant to assignment to a case mix class. The effects of varying outpatient pharmacy benefits on likelihood of assignment to a class in a case mix system can be handled by several techniques: either stratifying the population by benefit type in the profiling period or by including variables that define benefit type in the risk-adjustment method.

Last, a drug may not be ordered or dispensed for clinically sound reasons. A physician may not prescribe a drug as part of a treatment regimen for a patient because it is not necessary, given alternatives to pharmacologic treatment. Chronic medical conditions, such as diabetes and hypertension, can, in some proportion of a patient population, be treated with modifications to existing patient behaviors (e.g., diet, nutrition, or exercise). Thus, some patients with a chronic medical condition, in legitimate absence of drugs prescribed for their condition, will not be assigned to a therapeutic group or subgroup in a pharmacy-based case mix system.

## CASE MIX MEASUREMENT

### Unit Records and Weight Records

Case mix measurement based on outpatient pharmacy data consists of two records: a unit record and a weight record (Table 38–2). A unit record summarizes the classification of drugs for a patient into therapeutic groups and subgroups for a defined study period, usually 1 year. Therapeutic group and subgroup are treated as binary variables: *yes*, the patient was dispensed at least one drug in the therapeutic group or subgroup; or, *no*, the patient was not

**Table 38–2** Example of assignment of risk weights in selected pharmacy-based case mix measurement systems

*Example:* Patient dispensed calcium channel blocker and loop diuretic in a year

|  | PMPY primary care visits | | PMPY overall morbidity | |
|---|---|---|---|---|
|  | Unit | Weight | Unit | Weight |
| CDS-1 |  |  |  |  |
| Heart disease | 1 | 4 | 1 | 4 |
| Hypertension | 1 | 1 | 1 | 1 |
| Total |  | 5 |  | 5 |
|  | PMPY primary care visits | | PMPY total cost | |
|  | Unit | Weight | Unit | Weight |
| CDS-2 |  |  |  |  |
| Coronary disease | 0 | 0.61 | 0 | $1,932 |
| Cardiac disease | 1 | 0.40 | 1 | $789 |
| Hypertension | 1 | 0.34 | 1 | $64 |
| Age: 45–54 | 1 | −0.24 | 1 | −$1,616 |
| Intercept | 1 | 1.44 | 1 | $2,011 |
| Total |  | 1.94 |  | $1,248 |

*continues*

**Table 38–2** continued

| | PMPY primary care visits | | PMPY admission probability | |
|---|---|---|---|---|
| | Unit | Weight | Unit | Weight |
| KPARx | | | | |
| CCH-1 | 0 | 0.87 | 0 | |
| CCH-2 | 0 | 1.27 | 0 | |
| CCH-3 | 0 | 0.62 | 0 | |
| CCH-4 | 1 | 1.22 | 1 | |
| CCH-5 | 0 | 1.94 | 0 | |
| CCH-6 | 0 | 0.74 | 0 | |
| Age: 40–54 (Intercept) | 1 | 1.03 | 1 | |
| Total | | 2.25 | | |

*Note*: PMPY indicates "per member per year." CDS- I refers to the first version of the Chronic Disease Score. CDS-2 refers to second version of the Chronic Disease Score. The "Total" for each of the CDS examples is computed by taking the sum of the products of the unit value and the weight value. KPARx refers to the KPARx case mix system. For primary care visits, the outpatient version of KPARx (KPARx-0) is applied; for admission probability, the inpatient version of KPARx (KPARx-A) is applied. With KPARx-O, the "Total" is computed by taking the sum of the products of the unit value and the weight value. For admission probability, the "Total" is computed by taking the sum of the products of the unit value and the weight value and then calculating a probability using the cumulative logistic probability function.

*Source*: Reprinted from *Journal of Ambulatory Care Management*, Vol. 21, No. 4, p. 75, Aspen Publishers, Inc., © 1998.

dispensed any drug in the therapeutic group or subgroup. By coding assignments as a binary variable, case mix measurement is insensitive to other attributes of a patient's dispensing history—strength, dose, days' supply, or number of dispensings over the course of the study period. The goal of this measurement approach is to place more emphasis on the likely presence or absence of a medical condition than on other factors that might affect these other attributes, such as pharmacy dispensing policies, physician prescribing preferences, or patient characteristics not otherwise readily available in electronic format (e.g., the effect of body mass on dosing).

A weight record is a set of numeric estimates, one estimate for each therapeutic group or subgroup, of the relationship between an outcome and whether or not dispensings of drugs in a particular therapeutic group or subgroup have occurred. An outcome can be a quality measure such as the proportion of patients dispensed a drug in the therapeutic group or subgroup who die or a quality-of-life score for patients dispensed a drug in the therapeutic group or subgroup. An outcome can also be a utilization or cost measure such as the proportion of patients dispensed a drug in the therapeutic group or subgroup who are admitted to the hospital or the average total cost of medical services for patients dispensed a drug in the therapeutic group or subgroup.

## Estimation of Weights

Weights for the association between an outcome and each of the classes in a pharmacy-based case mix system have been estimated several ways. In the initial version of CDS, weights were assigned to a therapeutic group or subgroup according to physician judgments about the relative morbidity implied by use of drugs in the case mix system classes.[24] This subjective system of weights establishes an ordinal system between use of a drug and implied morbidity. Diabetes is a more morbid state than hypertension; therefore, use of an antidiabetic drug assigns a weight of 2 to a patient's potential overall score while use of an antihypertensive drug assigns a weight of 1 to a patient's potential score.

The more recent versions of the CDS and KPARx case mix systems rely on weights derived from statistical estimation of the association between an outcome and the therapeutic groups and subgroups of drugs dispensed.[25] Statistical methods of estimation are principally multiple linear regression for outcomes with continuous normally distributed values (e.g., log-transformed total medical expense) and multiple logistic regression for outcomes that have categorical values (e.g., whether or not a hospital admission occurs).

Whether subjective weights or empirically derived weights are chosen for application in physician profiling becomes a matter of preference and convenience. CDS subjective weights cannot be used to compute quantitative estimates of the occurrence of an outcome in a population. Patient populations can be stratified and compared, however, on the basis of the distributions of scores computed from subjective weights.[26-28] Subjective weights are fixed and do not vary from one outcome to another. Thus, the ordinal relationship implied by subjective weights may be more or less accurate from one outcome to another. A noteworthy advantage of subjective weights is that they are readily available and no further statistical analysis is required before application in physician profiling.

Empirically derived weights for a therapeutic group or subgroup will vary from one outcome to another and may vary from one setting to another.[29,30] For example, the weight for the proportion of members dispensed insulin in one year who die in the next year is not likely to be the same as the proportion of members dispensed insulin in one year who are admitted to the hospital in the next year. Similarly, a health plan that is quite efficient in managing chronically ill patients so that hospital admissions are avoided and more appropriate medical services are provided will have quite different empirically derived estimates of probabilities of hospital admission for therapeutic groups and subgroups of drugs dispensed for treatment of chronic medical conditions than a health plan that is inefficient in managing comparable patients.

## CASE MIX MEASUREMENT AND PRACTICE PROFILING FOR IMPROVED PANEL SYSTEM DESIGN AND MANAGEMENT

Primary care practice serves several important functions in the overall care for an enrollee in a managed care organization.[31] First, the primary care physician is often an enrollee's first point of contact with an MCO. Second, the primary care physician ensures continuity of care for an enrollee within the MCO across multiple (different or recurrent) episodes of illness. Third, the primary care physician coordinates care within or across episodes of illness with physician specialists whose knowledge and skills are relevant to treatment of the enrollee's illnesses.

A recent trend in primary care management MCOs is implementation of primary care panels. A *panel* is the conceptual and institutional unit that associates a primary care physician, or physician team, with a defined population of enrollees. A primary care panel system holds primary care physicians, or teams of primary care physicians, "accountable" for their performance of these functions in providing medical care to populations of enrollees.

The apparently solo primary care physician in an MCO must practice medical care both as a patient advocate and as a corporate advocate.[32,33] A primary care panel system tightens accountability of the primary care physician in these roles. The physician must act as gatekeeper, mediator, and negotiator in balancing demand for medical care (particularly physician time) generated by a panel's enrollees with the MCO's constraints on available resources (including physician time) and corporate goals (such as lowered costs and improved quality). A critical concern in the design of primary care panel systems is how to ensure that accountability of primary care physicians can be reasonably fair and equitable with regard to these roles.

One principle of fairness and equity in management of a primary care panel system is that similar commitments of time to primary care practice by physicians should be aligned with similar patient workloads. Workloads mean the demand for primary care time that is generated by the burden of illness of patients on a panel. Demand is partly a function of the number of enrollees on a panel (i.e., the panel population) and partly a function of the case mix of the panel population. If two primary care physicians have similar time commitments to primary care practice and are accountable for panels with similar populations, but one panel's cases are, on average, 25% more complex than the other panel's cases, then the workload of the one panel will be approximately 25% greater than the workload of the other panel. Unless there is some adjustment to primary care physician staffing, primary care panel population, or physician compensation, the panel system is inherently inequitable. This inequity affects the physicians directly and may affect the panels' patients and the MCO indirectly by influencing patient access and by inefficient use of resources.

In managing primary care panels, an MCO is in a position to design a panel system so that demand for and supply of physician time are reasonably well aligned. Alignment may be achieved by various adjustment strategies. One adjustment strategy might be to adjust demand for physician time by opening or closing enrollment to selected panels. Another adjustment strategy might be to adjust supply of physician time by adjusting physician staffing time or to compensate physicians in proportion to the workload that they manage and in relation to their efficiency in the management of that workload.

Primary care panel workload is a concept to represent the demand for primary care physician time from a panel. Several factors enter into determining a panel's workload. One factor is the number of enrollees in the panel's population. Another factor is the burden of illness, or case mix, of enrollees comprising that panel's population. Case mix is a concept that encompasses several dimensions of measurement. One dimension is the relative incidence or prevalence of disease among enrollees on a panel. Another dimension is the relative severity of specific diseases, independent of the incidence of disease. Above average workload, therefore, can be expected as a function of higher incidence of disease (chronic or acute) or as a function of disease (independent of its incidence) that requires above-average rates of primary care visits for each episode of that disease. Conversely, below-average workload can be expected as a function of lower incidence of disease or as a function of disease with low average rates of primary care visits for each episode of that disease.

Inequities in demand for physician time are created when panel workloads are not aligned with physician time allocated to the panels. A critical question in panel management in an MCO, therefore, is how to align demand for primary care physician time with supply of primary care physician time in the interest of equity, fairness, and efficiency. Design and management of a primary care panel system in an MCO require measurement of the factors that generate demand for primary care physician time and the efficiency of physician practice style in the management of that demand. Case mix systems and physician practice profiling are several techniques that can be adopted in design and management of a primary care panel system to improve on simple but problematic strategies for aligning supply and demand relative to primary care physician time.

## CASE MIX MEASUREMENT AND STATISTICAL MODELS OF HEALTH RISK

Measurement of the case mix of each primary care panel is central to estimating demand for primary care physician time. Age and gender are acceptable, but limited, measures of case mix.[34,35] Neither age nor gender explicitly measure the incidence of disease in a population or the relative effects of specific diseases on generating demand for primary care physician visits, and hence time. Panels with similar age and gender distributions may differ substantially and significantly in disease case mix because diseases may be non-randomly distributed across primary care panels—whether due to differences in disease distributions in the communities from which panel populations are selected, processes by which patients choose physicians, or processes by which physicians orient their practice to patients of certain types.

Demand for primary care physician time within the MCO population is estimated by regression models. Because demand for primary care time is not measured directly, volume of visits per enrollee per month (PEPM) is the proxy measure for time demand and, hence, for workload. A regression model yields a weight record, which measures, for each health risk class in the case mix system, the effect of that class on increasing (or decreasing) average numbers of PEPM primary care visits. Case mix is measured in the 12-month time period *prior* to the month in which utilization is measured. Age and gender effects are also factored into the regression model.

An enrollee's estimated PEPM primary care visits are an estimate of the demand for primary care physician time from that enrollee. To compute this estimate, the weight record from the primary care visit regression is multiplied by an enrollee's unit record of health risks. For each month over the course of eligibility of an enrollee, the enrollee's primary care panel assignment is known (which may be a specific primary care panel or the pool of unimpanelled enrollees). The estimated PEPM primary care visits of an enrollee accrue to the assigned panel. The average of all estimated PEPM primary care visits for a primary care physician panel represents the average expected workload for that panel. We also refer to this latter measure as the case complexity factor (CCF):

$$CCF_p = (\Sigma \; w \cdot u_i)/\Sigma \; EM_{ip}$$

where p indexes the panel, i indexes the enrollee, w is the weight record from the regression, u is the unit record of the ith enrollee; and EM is enrollee months of eligibility of the ith enrollee on the pth panel. The sum of all PEPM primary care visits represents the total expected workload (total number of primary care visits) for a panel.

The case mix measurement and physician profiling methods just described are being applied in the design and management of primary care panels at Kaiser Permanente. The overall goal of these applications is to support resource allocation strategies—where to allocate primary care physician time, which panels to open to new enrollees and which to close, and whether physician compensation should be adjusted to pay for varying workloads.

## Where to Allocate Primary Care Physician Time

If burden of illness is neither randomly nor equally distributed from one primary care clinic service area to another, then primary care physician time will be optimally allocated when distributed in proportion to the estimated volume of demand for primary care in each service area—not necessarily in proportion to the number of enrollees in each service area. Table 38–3 illustrates

**Table 38–3** A model for allocation of primary care physician time among clinics in proportion to standardized primary care workloads

| Clinic | Observed enrollee months | Case complexity factor | Primary care visits | | Primary care physician time allocation† | | | Primary care visits per session | |
|---|---|---|---|---|---|---|---|---|---|
| | | | Observed | Adjusted* | Observed | Adjusted‡ | Change | Observed | Adjusted |
| 001 | 102,018 | 0.217 | 24,479 | 22,138 | 2,514 | 2,213 | –301 | 9.79 | 10.00 |
| 002 | 57,623 | 0.207 | 10,285 | 11,928 | 1,080 | 1,192 | +112 | 9.52 | 10.00 |
| 003 | 132,400 | 0.200 | 25,142 | 26,480 | 2,341 | 2,647 | +306 | 10.74 | 10.00 |
| 004 | 82,714 | 0.210 | 17,436 | 17,370 | 1,826 | 1,737 | –89 | 9.55 | 10.00 |
| 005 | 56,636 | 0.202 | 11,197 | 11,422 | 1,157 | 1,142 | –15 | 9.68 | 10.00 |
| 006 | 72,549 | 0.226 | 17,791 | 16,396 | 1,713 | 1,639 | –74 | 10.39 | 10.00 |
| Overall | 503,940 | 0.211 | 106,330 | 106,330 | 10,630 | 10,630 | 0 | 10.00 | 10.00 |

*Note:* Overall observed and predicted measures may differ slightly due to rounding error.

*Adjusted primary care visits = $CCF_c \cdot \Sigma\,EM$, where $CCF_c$ represents the case complexity factor of the clinic and EM is the enrollee months of the panel population.

†Physician time allocation is measured in sessions, with one session equal to four clinic hours.

‡Adjusted sessions = Total budgeted sessions $\cdot \rho_c$, where $\rho_c$ = Adjusted visits$_c$/$\Sigma$ Adjusted visits$_c$; $\Sigma\alpha_c = 1$ $[\Sigma]$ $[r][_c] = 1$, where $_c$ is the index for the clinic.

*Source:* Reprinted from Douglas W. Roblin, Applications of physician profiling in the management of primary care panels, *Journal of Ambulatory Care Management,* Vol. 19, No. 2, p. 68, © 1996 Aspen Publishers, Inc.

how primary care physician time might be allocated across six primary care clinic service areas in proportion to burden of illness. The number of enrollee months is the number of months of eligibility in 1992 for all enrollees impanelled to each primary care clinic. All enrollees are impanelled to one clinic as their primary care clinic. The case complexity factor is the average number of PEPM primary care visits predicted on the basis of (1) the age, gender, and health risk distributions (measured by the KPARx case mix system) and (2) the PEPM primary care visit rates for the risk classes as estimated by regression models for this MCO's entire population. The adjusted number of primary care visits is the product of the observed enrollee months and the CCF.

Physician time is measured in sessions—one session represents 4 hours in the clinic. The observed allocation of primary care physician time is the amount of time actually recorded on physician time records. Assuming a fixed global budget for primary care physician time (i.e., 10,630 sessions), the adjusted allocation of primary care physician time is the number of sessions that would be optimal for each clinic if the total time were distributed in proportion to the adjusted primary care visits predicted from the burden of illness at each clinic. By this allocation strategy, Clinic 001 appears to have had 300 more observed sessions than required by the burden of illness of that clinic's primary care panel. Clinic 003 appears to have had 300 less clinic sessions than required by the burden of illness of that clinic's primary care panel.

When primary care physician time is allocated in proportion to the number of actual enrollee months at each clinic, primary care physicians at Clinic 001 provide approximately 9.8 visits per session; however, primary care physicians at Clinic 006 provide approximately 10.4 visits per session. At Clinic 006, primary care physicians are either working harder or working more productively than primary care physicians at Clinic 001 given the allocation of time to provide primary care services to the enrollee populations for which they are accountable.

## Which Primary Care Panels to Open and Which to Close

A primary care physician who is working full time in an MCO will typically be accountable for the care of a fixed number of enrollees. The number of enrollees might, for example, be determined simply by dividing the enrollee population by the number of primary care physician full-time equivalents (FTEs) so that, on average, the workload—or volume of visits per primary care physician panel—would be expected to be the same. The decision to open or to close a panel to new enrollees would depend simply on whether or not the actual number of enrollees impanelled to a particular primary care physician is less than this computed number per primary care physician FTE.

If primary care panels' burdens of illness are equal, then this allocation rule will, on average, be optimal. On the other hand, if primary care panels' burdens of illness vary substantially, then this allocation rule will create substantial discrepancies in primary care physician panel workload.

Table 38–4 illustrates how CCFs might be considered in management decisions as to which primary care panels to open and which primary panels to close to new enrollees. In this example, four pediatricians (P01 through P04) comprise a pediatric module (M01)—or accountable team of pediatricians— at a primary care clinic. By a simple allocation rule, each pediatric primary care physician is assumed to be responsible for a workload of 3,600 visits per year or 1,200 enrollees (assuming a system average of 0.300 pediatric visits per enrollee per month and an average of 10 months of eligibility per pediatric enrollee per year).

The case complexity of pediatric enrollees on each of the four primary care panels, however, is substantially different. Panel P04 has a CCF (0.352 primary care visits PEPM) that is 34% higher than the CCF of panel P01 (0.263 primary care visits PEPM).

After adjusting these four panels for differences in both case complexity and number of enrollee months, the workload of P01 is much less than the target workload; and, the workloads of the other three pediatricians in this module are greater than the target workload. For example, given the case complexity and patient population of panel P01, the patient population of that panel is expected to generate a workload of 447 primary care visits less than the target necessary for equitable workloads—3,600 primary care visits. Thus, panel P01 should remain open to new enrollees while panels P02, P03, and P04 should remain closed to new enrollees.

The same assumptions that were used to compute the targeted allocation can, in turn, be used to compute estimates of the changes to panel composition that will achieve equity in workload. For panels P02, P03, and P04—closed to new enrollees—adjustment to workload will be achieved through attrition of existing enrollees comprising their primary care panels. On the other hand, for panel P01, adjustment to workload will be achieved through addition of new enrollees beyond the current panel composition.

**Table 38–4** A model for determination of which primary care panels to open and which primary care panels to close to new enrollment

| | Case com-plexity factor | Enrollee months | Primary care visits | | | Enrollment changes | |
|---|---|---|---|---|---|---|---|
| | | | Adjusted | Targeted* | Difference | Enrollee months† | Enrollees‡ |
| Panel | | | | | | | |
| P01 | 0.263 | 11,988 | 3,153 | 3,600 | –447 | +1,480 | +148 |
| P02 | 0.303 | 13,103 | 3,970 | 3,600 | +370 | –1,233 | –123 |
| P03 | 0.325 | 12,274 | 3,989 | 3,600 | +389 | –1,297 | –130 |
| P04 | 0.352 | 12,265 | 4,317 | 3,600 | +717 | –2,390 | –239 |
| Module | | | | | | | |
| M01 | 0.311 | 49,630 | 15,429 | 14,400 | +1,029 | –3,440 | –344 |

*Assumes a system average per enrollee per month primary care visit rate of 0.300 and a fully populated panel of 12,000 enrollee months.

†The difference in primary care visits adjusted to the system average.

‡Enrollees adjusted to the system average number of months of eligibility in a year—10 months/enrollee less than 19 years of age.

*Source:* Reprinted from Douglas W. Roblin, Applications of physician profiling in the management of primary care panels, *Journal of Ambulatory Care Management*, Vol. 19, No. 2, p. 70, © 1996 Aspen Publishers, Inc.

In application, however, a decision to open or close primary care panels that accounts for case complexity of panels will require ongoing measurements of case complexity and updates of estimates of enrollment changes necessary to achieve targeted, equitable workloads. The enrollees who join or leave a particular panel may be healthier or sicker than the panel average; and, each month, this factor would alter the CCF for each panel. For example, enrollees who leave panel P04 may be healthier on average than enrollees who remain on panel P04. If so, more enrollees than the expected number (239) would need to be lost through attrition in order for this panel population to achieve the targeted workload.

## CONCLUSIONS

A case mix system based on outpatient pharmacy data is particularly easy to implement. Computerized records of drugs dispensed are widely available and can be retrieved quickly and inexpensively. Data can be collected in a consistent format, and continuous data collection can ensure that unit records of patients are updated continuously. Several validated pharmacy-based case mix systems, CDS and KPARx, can be applied to records of drugs dispensed to classify drugs, and subsequently patients, into meaningful therapeutic groups and subgroups.

Case mix measurement using outpatient pharmacy data can be applied in those areas of administration of medical care where a population's burden of illness must be considered. For a managed care organization, improving primary care panel system design and management presents opportunities for improved access, appropriate continuity and coordination of care for a disease episode, and efficient use of resources. Patients, physicians, and payers all stand to benefit from strategies that improve the alignment of demand for primary care physician time with supply of primary care physician time in an MCO.

Many other applications in MCOs can be found. Per capita budgets for units providing medical services can be adjusted to reflect variation in disease burdens across those units. Utilization and case management programs can be targeted to the subset of patients whose drug dispensing profiles indicate that they are at significantly elevated risk of incurring potentially unnecessary, high-cost services in the near future.

## NOTES

1. Woodwell, D.A. (1997). *National ambulatory medical care survey: 1996 summary, advance data from vital and health statistics, no. 295.* Hyattsville, MD: National Center for Health Statistics.

2. Ellis, R.P., Pope, G.C., Iezzoni, L.I., Ayanian, J.Z., Bates, D.W., Burstin, H., et al. (1996). *Diagnostic cost group (DCG) and hierarchical coexisting condition (HCC) models for Medicare risk adjustment.* Boston: Health Economics Research, Inc.

3. Weiner, J.P., Starfield, B.H., Steinwachs, D.M., & Mumford, L.M. (1991). Development and application of a population-oriented measure of ambulatory care case mix. *Medical Care, 29*(5), 452–472.

4. Woodwell, *National ambulatory medical care survey.*

5. Clark, D.O., von Korff, M., Saunders, K., Baluch, W.M., & Simon, G.E. (1996). A chronic disease score with empirically derived weights. *Medical* Care, *33*(8), 783–795.

6. Johnson, R.E., Hornbrook, M.C., & Nichols, G.A. (1994). Replicating the chronic disease score (CDS) from automated pharmacy data. *Journal of Clinical Epidemiology, 47*(10), 1191–1199.

7. Roblin, D.W. (1996). Applications of physician profiling in the management of primary care panels. *Journal of Ambulatory Care Management, 19*(2), 59–74.

8. von Korff, M., & Marshall, J. (1996). High cost HMO enrollees: Analysis of one physician's panel. *HMO Practice, 6*(1), 20–25.

9. von Korff, M., Wagner, E.H., & Saunders, K. (1992). A chronic disease score from automated pharmacy data. *Journal of Clinical Epidemiology, 45*(2), 197–203.

10. von Korff, Wagner, and Saunders, A chronic disease score from automated pharmacy data.

11. Clark, von Korff, et al. A chronic disease score with empirically derived weights.

12. Hornbrook, M.C., & Goodman, M.J. (1992a). Health plan case mix: Definition, measurement, and use. *Advances in Health Economics and Health Services Research, 12*, 111–148.

13. Hornbrook, M.C., Goodman, M.J., & Bennett, M.D. (1992). Assessing health plan case mix in employed populations: Ambulatory morbidity and prescribed drug models. *Advances in Health Economics and Health Services Research, 12*, 197–232.

14. von Korff, Wagner, & Saunders, A chronic disease score from automated pharmacy data.

15. Harris, B.L., Stergachis, A., & Ried, L.D. (1990). The effect of drug co-payments on utilization and cost of pharmaceuticals in a health maintenance organization. *Medical Care, 28*(10), 907–917.

16. O'Connor, P.J. et al. (in press). Identifying managed care plan members with diabetes or heart disease: Sensitivity, specificity, predictive value and cost of survey and database methods. *American Journal of Managed Care.*

17. Osborne, M.L., Vollmer, W.M., Johnson, R.E., & Buist, S. (1995). Use of an automated prescription database to identify individuals with asthma. *Journal of Clinical Epidemiology, 48*(11), 1393–1397.

18. Cannon, P.J., Connell, P.A., Stockley, I.H., Garner, S.T., & Hampton, J.R. (1988). Prevalence of angina as assessed by a survey of prescriptions for nitrates. *Lancet, 1*(8592), 979–981.

19. Harris, Stergachis, & Ried, The effect of drug co-payments on utilization and cost of pharmaceuticals in an HMO.

20. Johnson, R.E., Goodman, M.J., Hornbrook, M.C., & Eldredge, M.B. (1997). The effect of increased prescription drug cost-sharing on medical care utilization and expenses of elderly health maintenance organization members. *Medical Care, 35*(11), 1119–1131.

21. Leibowitz, A., Manning, W.G., & Newhouse, J.P. (1985). The demand for prescription drugs as a function of cost sharing. *Social Science and Medicine, 21*(10), 1063–1069.

22. Soumerai, S.B., Avom, J., Ross-Degnan, D., & Gortmaker, S. (1987). Payment restrictions for prescription drugs under Medicaid: Effects on therapy, cost, and equity. *New England Journal of Medicine, 317*(9), 550–556.

23. Harris, Stergachis, & Ried, The effect of drug co-payments on utilization and cost of pharmaceuticals in an HMO.

24. von Korff, Wagner, & Saunders, A chronic disease score from automated pharmacy data.

25. Clark, von Korff, et al. A chronic disease score with empirically derived weights.

26. Johnson, Hornbrook, & Nichols, Replicating the chronic disease score.

27. von Korff & Marshall, High cost HMO enrollees.

28. von Korff, Wagner, & Saunders, A chronic disease score from automated pharmacy data.

29. Clark, von Korff, et al. A chronic disease score with empirically derived weights.

30. Roblin, Applications of physician profiling in the management of primary care panels.

31. Starfield, B. (1992). Primary care: Concept, evaluation, and policy. New York: Oxford University Press.

32. Reagan, M.D. (1987). Physicians as gatekeepers: A complex challenge. *New England Journal of Medicine, 317*(27), 1731–1734.

33. Relman, A.S. (1988). Salaried physicians and economic incentives (Editorial). *New England Journal of Medicine, 319*(12), 784.

34. Blumberg, M.S. (1986). Risk-adjusting health care outcomes: A methodologic review. *Medical Care Review, 43*(2), 352–393.

35. Hornbrook, M.C., & Goodman, M.J. (1992b). Adjusting health benefit contributions to reflect risk. *Advances in Health Economics and Health Services Research, 12*, 41–76.

CHAPTER 39

# Profiling the Health Service Needs of Populations Using Diagnosis-based Classification Systems

*John H. Muldoon, John M. Neff, and James C. Gay*

Managed care presents the challenge to deliver health care services to enrolled populations from a fixed pool of dollars and the imperative to be accountable for doing so. This challenge begs the question of how to describe the population groups to be served. The population group is the basis for five key functions: (1) identifying health services needs, (2) organizing the delivery of health services, (3) tracking quality indicators and patient satisfaction, (4) profiling the practice patterns of individual providers and provider groups, and (5) risk adjusting the capitation payment rates. It, therefore, becomes critical to have classification systems that adequately describe the health service needs of the population.

There are a number of different types of classification systems with the population group as the unit of analysis. Each has its own strengths and limitations. This article briefly reviews these systems to illustrate their uses (not to critique them) and then describes and illustrates the uses of the National Association of Children's Hospitals and Related Institutions (NACHRI) Classification of Congenital and Chronic Health Conditions. This is a system recently developed by NACHRI and intended to describe the entire population with one or more ongoing chronic health conditions.

*Source:* Reprinted from J.H. Muldoon, J.M. Neff, and J.C. Gay, Profiling the Health Service Needs of Populations Using Diagnosis-based Classification Systems, *Journal of Ambulatory Care Management* Vol. 20, No. 3, pp. 1–18, © 1997 Aspen Publishers, Inc.

## BRIEF REVIEW OF EXISTING POPULATION-BASED CLASSIFICATION METHODS

This section will briefly describe some of the more common population-based classification systems focusing on their major uses and limitations and how they might be used in conjunction with one another. This includes demographic models, prior health service utilization, health status questionnaires, and diagnosis-based classification systems. These systems have the population as the unit of analysis and must be distinguished from other systems in which the unit of analysis is an encounter or an episode of care.

Age and gender are *demographic* variables commonly used to classify populations. They are commonly available, easy to collect, and not subject to manipulation. Age and gender provide some information about the number and types of health services that individuals might need (e.g., well-child and immunization services to young children, obstetrical and gynecological services to women of child-bearing age). However, they provide only very general information and do not differentiate for sickness and wellness within age and gender categories. Numerous studies have shown age and gender to have limited predictive power for identifying current- or future-year health service utilization and cost.[1-3]

*Prior health service utilization models* attempt to predict health service utilization and cost in a future time period based on utilization in a prior time period. Prior utilization models have greater predictive power than age and gender and are administratively feasible if a claims- or encounter-level database is available, but they have drawbacks. They do not provide an understanding of the population group, do not provide the most appropriate incentives for cost management, and do not necessarily relate to the future course of an illness.[4-6]

*Health status questionnaires* vary in their specific focus but generally seek to ascertain the individual's self-perceived health status. They can provide useful information, especially about a person's functional status, but they, too, have limitations. Health status questionnaires require administration and regular updating; are subjective and, therefore, subject to manipulation; and have not been shown to be very powerful as a predictor of health service utilization and costs.[7,8]

*Diagnosis-based classification models* can identify specific diseases and disease combinations that are predictive of health service utilization and costs and are administratively feasible if a claims- or encounter-level database is available. They, too, have their limitations. The existing diagnosis codes do not always contain the level of specificity needed to describe fully a patient's condition, and certain diseases have a very variable course.[9–12]

There are also models that combine different classification methods. Age and gender can be used with any of the other models. Diagnostic classification systems and health status questionnaires can be combined broadly or in selective areas. Prior utilization can be used in conjunction with either of these models. The Supplementary Security Income (SSI) disability program is perhaps the best known system that combines diagnostic and functional status information as part of a detailed assessment of the individual's status. It is a time-consuming and expensive process, necessary for the eligibility determinations for cash benefits and medical assistance that it makes, but it is probably not practical for many other programs. Its focus is also limited to certain types of health conditions.[13]

One of the most recently developed diagnosis-based classification systems is the NACHRI Classification of Congenital and Chronic Health Conditions. The NACHRI system provides a conceptual and operational means through *International Classification of Diseases, Ninth Edition, Clinical Modification* (ICD-9-CM) codes to identify individuals who have a congenital or chronic health condition expected to last 12 months or longer. The system classifies chronic disease by body system, condition category, severity level, and disease progression. The condition categories within a body system are organized into hierarchies to facilitate classification of individuals with multiple chronic conditions. The system also classifies certain at-risk categories to the extent possible with existing diagnostic code information.

The NACHRI classification system is intended to identify the many different populations with ongoing chronic health conditions. It is intended to be used in conjunction with age and gender to provide a more complete description of expected health service needs for different populations. It does not include acute illnesses except in selective circumstances to describe further the status of a chronic health condition. Acute illness and wellness care represents a large component of the population's health service needs but is generally not very predictive of future health service needs. Age and gender are used by the NACHRI classification system to anticipate these needs. One limitation to this approach is in the area of provider profiling. Certain physicians by virtue of their specialization treat a large number of serious acute conditions in not chronically ill persons; this is not reflected in the case mix measurement of the NACHRI classification system.

The NACHRI classification system is intended to be a useful tool for managed care systems in understanding and serving their many populations. Specifically with regard to the five functions identified at the beginning of this article, the NACHRI system is intended to serve the following functions:

- identifying health service needs through establishment of disease prevalence rates for the full spectrum of chronic physical and mental health conditions and certain at-risk categories to the extent possible with existing diagnostic information
- organizing the delivery of health care services based on frequency and types of chronic health conditions as well as the age and gender of the population served
- tracking quality indicators and patient and family satisfaction for distinctive subgroups of the population, the chronically ill population as a whole, and subgroups thereof
- profiling the practice patterns of individual physicians, physician groups, and entire health plans, case mix adjusted for the prevalence and types of chronic health conditions
- risk adjusting capitation payment rates based on the prevalence and types of chronic health conditions

This chapter describes the design and structure of the NACHRI Classification of Congenital and Chronic Health Conditions, illustrates its management applications from its first testing on a full-service claims database, and discusses issues regarding its successful implementation and use. In order to understand the capabilities and limitations of this system or any similar classification system, it is necessary to understand the concepts, definitions, and informational building blocks (ICD-9-CM diagnosis codes) used to create the system. Therefore, a fairly in-depth presentation of the design and structure of the NACHRI classification system precedes the illustrations of its uses.

## DESIGN AND STRUCTURE OF NACHRI CLASSIFICATION OF CONGENITAL AND CHRONIC HEALTH CONDITIONS

The NACHRI classification system is a clinical model built with extensive involvement of physicians from many disciplines. The key strategy behind the system is to develop as complete a clinical profile of the population as is practical from readily available information on the patient's diagnostic conditions. It has been built through an interactive, three-stage process:

1. Identify clinically meaningful and recognizable groupings of patients. This is done with the guidance and assistance of a 14-member medical advisory committee, the pediatric medical and surgical division chiefs at two children's hospitals, a part-time pediatric physician consultant, and continuous reference to pediatric medicine and general medicine textbooks.
2. Identify the ICD-9-CM diagnosis codes that represent chronic health conditions. This is done by first reviewing the titles of all 15,000 ICD-9-CM diagnosis codes (valid codes plus "header record" codes); then reviewing the illustrated examples of conditions included in each diagnosis code in the tabular section of the ICD-9-CM manual; then, if necessary, conducting a complete computer index search of all terms and conditions that ICD-9-CM assigns to the code. In the case of mental health conditions, all of the diagnoses, terms, and definitions in the *Diagnostic and Statistical Manual of Mental Disorders, Fourth Edition* (DSM-IV) were first reviewed and then crosswalked to the corresponding ICD-9-CM codes.
3. Identify the case volume of the chronic disease diagnoses and statistics on health service utilization and costs. Several databases were used for this. The primary data set was a full-service, paid-claims database for the state of Washington Medicaid recipients, ages 0 to 64 years. A second full-service, claims-paid database was a state of Washington private health insurance plan data set for enrollees ages 0 to 17 years. In addition, to examine conditions associated with frequent inpatient hospitalization, a large national database of inpatient discharges from 40 children's hospitals and 840 general hospitals was used.

There are a number of key concepts and definitions necessary for understanding the structure, capabilities, and limitations of the NACHRI classification system, including chronic health condition, major diagnostic category, individual chronic condition category, supplemental status indicator, severity level assignment, disease progression, hierarchy of chronic condition category, at-risk category, valid ICD-9-CM code, and fourth- and fifth-digit specificity in ICD-9-CM codes.

## Chronic Health Condition

*Chronic health condition* refers to physical, mental, emotional, behavioral, or developmental disorders expected to last 12 months or longer or having sequelae that last 12 months or longer. The condition is one that requires treatment and/or monitoring. Approximately 4,000 of the 15,000 ICD-9-CM diagnosis codes meet these criteria.

In instances where there is variability in the severity or progression of a disease, there must be an expectation that at least 75% of patients will have the condition or sequelae for 12 months or longer. This criterion means that most individuals identified as having a chronic disease will in fact have a chronic condition, but there will also be some individuals who really do have a chronic condition and are not identified as such.

## Major Diagnostic Category

*Major diagnostic categories* (MDCs) are major body systems, such as cardiovascular and musculoskeletal systems, and major disease processes, such as blood disorders and malignant neoplasms. The organization of MDCs generally follows the chapters in the ICD-9-CM manual except where the disease clearly overlaps chapters of ICD-9-CM or the chief manifestation of a disease is clearly in a different chapter than its etiology. In the instance of mental health conditions, the organization of MDCs generally follows the chapters of DSM-IV.

## Individual Chronic Condition Category

*Individual chronic condition categories* are clinically distinct and recognizable categories at a broad population level, defined based on one or more of the following factors plus case volume: anatomy/physiology of condition, disease progression of condition, congenital/inherited versus acquired condition, interaction between conditions. There are approximately 250 chronic condition categories, of which 40 are mental health categories.

## Supplemental Status Indicators

*Supplemental status indicators* are supplemental status V codes and related ICD-9-CM diagnostic codes that identify major medical assistive devices and ongoing treatment modalities. These codes provide additional information about the status of persons with chronic health conditions. For example, chemotherapy status indicates that a malignant neoplasm is active, and renal dialysis status indicates that chronic renal failure has progressed to an end stage.

## Severity Level Of Individual Diagnosis

Each *diagnosis* is given an initial *severity-level* assignment based on expected complexity and costliness of all health care services over a 12-month period. There are four chronic disease severity levels: mild, moderate, major, and extreme. The severity-level assignment for each diagnosis takes into account the expected number of different services, intensity of each service, and frequency of each service.

## Severity Level of Person

The *severity-level assignment for each person* takes into account the severity level of individual diagnoses, disease progression, interactive effects of multiple conditions, and supplemental status indicators. For example, a congenital anomaly that can be cured or substantially improved may receive a high severity-level assignment in the first year or first several years of life followed by a lower severity level thereafter.

## Disease Progression

Each diagnosis is assigned to one of the following *disease progression* types based on the expected course of the disease and treatment goal: cure/substantially improve, substantially improve/continuous treatment, static/improve function, progressive, supportive care, or mixed course.

## Hierarchy of Chronic Health Condition Categories Within Body System

For most body systems, the chronic condition categories are organized and listed in hierarchical order. The purpose of the *hierarchy* is to help determine the patient's primary chronic condition within a body system when the patient has multiple chronic diseases from that body system. For example, a patient with the diagnoses of cystic fibrosis and asthma would be viewed as having cystic fibrosis as his or her primary respiratory chronic disease condition. The following factors were considered in developing the hierarchies:

- *primary versus secondary*: Conditions that are usually primary diseases are placed higher in the hierarchy, whereas conditions that may be either primary or secondary diseases are placed lower in the hierarchy.
- *disease progression*: Conditions that are permanent and especially conditions that are progressive are placed higher in the hierarchy.
- *severity level*: Conditions that are considered high severity level chronic diseases are placed higher in the hierarchy.

### "At-Risk" Categories

*"At-risk" categories* are conditions that do not meet the criteria used to define chronic conditions (i.e., expected to last or have sequelae that last 12 months or longer at least 75% of cases) but usually require services of an amount and type greater than that for not chronically ill persons and place the individual at risk for ongoing chronic conditions. Examples include premature infant, light-for-date infant, failure to thrive, child abuse/neglect, and adult abuse/neglect.

### Valid, Out-of-Date, and Header Record ICD-9-CM Diagnosis Codes

Approximately 4,000 of the currently valid ICD-9-CM diagnosis codes meet the criteria for inclusion in the classification system as a congenital/chronic health condition. Approximately 125 ICD-9-CM diagnosis codes that were valid for earlier time periods are included so that the classification system can be applied to multiple years of data. These codes are included along with the year in which they became out of date.

"Header diagnosis" codes are 3- or 4-digit codes that describe a family of diseases. They are not valid ICD-9-CM codes but are included in the NACHRI classification system and identified as such when three criteria are met: (1) the chronic disease is discrete, (2) all of the specific ICD-9-CM codes for the disease entity represent chronic illnesses, and (3) the header diagnosis provides as much information as the not otherwise specified (NOS) version of the diagnosis codes. For example, the header diagnosis of cerebral palsy (343) provides the same information content as cerebral palsy NOS (343.9). Approximately 250 header diagnosis codes are included in the NACHRI classification system.

### Fourth- and Fifth-Digit Specificity in ICD-9-CM Diagnosis Codes

The precision of the severity-level assignments depends on the specificity of the ICD-9-CM diagnosis codes together with the logic of the NACHRI classification system that examines the interactive effect of multiple chronic conditions. Here are two examples:

1. For epilepsy, the fourth digit of the ICD-9-CM code distinguishes the general form of epilepsy (e.g., generalized convulsive, generalized nonconvulsive, partial epilepsy), and the fifth digit distinguishes whether or not the epilepsy is intractable. Thus, a good deal of information is available from which to make the initial severity assignment for epilepsy.
2. For cerebral palsy, the fourth digit of the ICD-9-CM code distinguishes between congenital quadriplegia, congenital diplegia, congenital hemiplegia, and cerebral palsy NOS. This provides helpful information for a first sorting into severity levels, but there is still a spectrum of severity (or functional impairment) within these categories. The ICD-9-CM codes do not have a fifth digit providing further information on cerebral palsy, but the NACHRI classification system is able to make a final severity-level assignment based on the existence of multiple chronic conditions (e.g., epilepsy, mental retardation, cortical blindness, esophageal reflux, gastrostomy status).

## ILLUSTRATION OF USES OF NACHRI CLASSIFICATION OF CONGENITAL AND CHRONIC HEALTH CONDITIONS

The uses of the NACHRI classification system are illustrated here from its first testing on a full-service, paid-claims database from the state of Washington Medicaid program. Some more general information is also presented from a state of Washington private health insurance database.

The Washington Medicaid database includes noninstitutionalized recipients, ages 0 to 64 years, with eligibility for service for at least 9 months of fiscal year (FY) 1993. There were 312,544 recipients meeting this eligibility criteria and passing edit tests, the most important of which was removing mothers whose paid claims records included the diagnoses and bills for their newborn children. Of the 312,544 recipients, 201,330 were children including 7,461 SSI disabled recipients; 111,214 were adults including 39,253 SSI disabled recipients. Of the 312,544 recipients, 291,924 or 93.4% had one or more paid claims for health services in this time period. The average total of billed charges for all recipients in the study database was $2,700.

The state of Washington private health insurance database had paid claims information on 404,923 children from 11 of the 17 largest health plans in the state in 1993. It was built as part of an effort by the state of Washington Health Care Advisory Board to identify the population of children with special health care needs and make recommendations to the governor and legislature on "a system for managing health care services to children with special health care needs."[14]

It is important to be aware that the Medicaid and non–Medicaid populations are different from each other in a number of ways. One difference is that Medicaid recipients are from lower income families than the population as a whole and low income is often associated with additional health status risk factors. A second difference is that the Medicaid program includes health coverage for the SSI disabled, a population group served by the Medicaid and Medicare programs, but not by private-sector health insurance. This group by definition has certain chronic disabling conditions, at least at the time of enrollment. A third difference is that the Medicaid program income eligibility levels are higher for mothers, newborns, and young children, so there will be a larger population of young children and mothers in the Medicaid program than in the population as a whole. The result is that there are certain to be differences in the age distribution of the Medicaid population and likely to be differences in health status factors and the prevalence of chronic health conditions. The Medicaid adult population is particularly different from non–Medicaid adults as it consists primarily of mothers and SSI disabled recipients.

For this analysis, chronic disease prevalence and cost profiling were performed for the Medicaid population as a whole and separately for children and adults. The profiling was also generated separately for the SSI disabled and non–SSI disabled but, for brevity's sake, only selective highlights of these profiles are presented here.

The chronic disease prevalence and cost profiling was performed at the following levels of aggregation:

presence or absence of chronic condition
* presence of chronic condition and severity level
* chronic physical versus chronic mental condition versus mental retardation
* major diagnostic category (body system)
* individual chronic condition category
* multiple chronic conditions

Table 39–1 presents overall chronic disease prevalence rates. The overall chronic disease prevalence rate for children was 18.3% with rates slightly higher for infants and adolescents (20%) and slightly lower for preschool- and grade-school–age children (16.5%). The overall rate for adults was 46% with very different rates for 18- to 34-year-olds (37.2%) and 35- to 64-year-olds (60.7%). Part of this is attributable to the increased prevalence of chronic conditions generally for older adults, but much is also attributable to the fact that a larger proportion of the 35- to 64-year-old Medicaid recipients were SSI disabled.

The overall chronic disease prevalence rate for children in the Washington private health insurance plan database was a little lower than that for Medicaid children. Exact comparisons cannot be made because the databases were

**Table 39–1** Overal chronic illness prevalence rates, state of Washington Medicaid, FY 1993, noninstitutionalized recipients, ages 0 to 64 years

|  | Recipients ages 0–17 yrs | Recipients ages 18–34 yrs | Recipients ages 35–64 yrs | All recipients |
|---|---|---|---|---|
| With chronic condition | 36,894 (18.3%) | 25,967 (37.2%) | 25,189 (60.7%) | 88,050 (28.2%) |
| Without chronic condition | 164,436 (81.7%) | 43,776 (62.8%) | 16,282 (39.3%) | 224,494 (71.8%) |
| Total | 201,330 (100%) | 69,743 (100%) | 41,471 (100%) | 312,544 (100%) |

*Source:* Data from National Association of Children's Hospitals and Related Institutions, Inc., 1996.

not exactly comparable, but the overall rate appeared to be 2% to 3% below the 18.3% for Medicaid. Though the overall prevalence rate was only a little lower, there were some large differences in the frequency of individual chronic diseases.

In the private health insurance plan database, there were fewer children with neuromuscular conditions, such as cerebral palsy, spina bifida, muscular dystrophy, and acquired paralytic syndromes; fewer children with mental retardation; fewer children with conduct disorders and other behavioral disorders; fewer children with certain other mental health conditions, such as depression and anxiety disorders; somewhat fewer children with asthma; and fewer children with some of the rarer conditions, such as blood disorders, malignancies, and human immunodeficiency virus. There were also fewer children with congenital anomalies and developmental delays, but this is probably mostly a reflection of the fact that there was an older distribution of children in the private health insurance plan database. In contrast, there were many more children with musculoskeletal disorders in the private health insurance database, though some of the difference appears to be a result of coding issues.

Table 39–2 presents chronic disease prevalence rates and billed charges by severity level. The higher severity level persons represent a very small percentage of the population but a dramatically large percentage of billed charges for health care services. This relationship is less dramatic but still substantial for individuals with moderate and mild chronic conditions. Of the entire Medicaid population, 28.2% have chronic illnesses and account for 73% of all billed charges for health services.

Table 39–3 presents chronic disease prevalence rates for mental and/or physical conditions. For this analysis, the 250 chronic condition categories were aggregated to six very broad categories that relate to distinctive health delivery services. Each person is assigned to one and only one of these categories. Transplant patients represent less than 0.1% of the population. Individuals with mental retardation or encephalopathy and physical chronic conditions represent 0.5% of the population. Those with mental retardation or encephalopathy but without chronic physical condition represent 0.3% of the population. There is a greater proportion of adults with these conditions than children, but it must be remembered that Medicaid adults do not represent a cross-section of the adult population, with one-third being SSI disabled. Those with both chronic physical and mental health conditions represent 3.7% of the population. For adults, this percentage is much greater

**Table 39–2** Chronic disease prevalence rates and charges by severity level, state of Washington Medicaid, FY 1993, noninstitutionalized recipients, ages 0 to 64 years

|  | Recipients ages 0–17 years | | Recipients ages 18–64 years | |
|---|---|---|---|---|
|  | *% Persons* | *% Charges* | *% Persons* | *% Charges* |
| With chronic conditions |  |  |  |  |
| Severity 3+4 | 1.3 | 20.8 | 8.6 | 36.5 |
| Severity 2 | 5.9 | 18.7 | 20.9 | 31.7 |
| Severity 1 | 11.1 | 19.2 | 16.5 | 18.3 |
| Subtotal | 18.3 | 58.7 | 46.0 | 86.5 |
| Without chronic DX | 81.7 | 41.3 | 54.0 | 13.5 |
| All persons | 100.0 | 100.0 | 100.0 | 100.0 |

*Note:* DX = diagnosis. *Source:* Data from National Association of Children's Hospitals and Related Institutions, Inc., 1996.

than for children. Part of the explanation may be that many adults with a substance dependence condition also have chronic physical illnesses. Another 18% of the Medicaid population have a physical chronic condition only, and 5.7% have a chronic mental health condition only. The proportion of adults with a chronic condition is higher than for children, partly due to the increased incidence of chronic illness with age and partly due to the larger proportion of Medicaid adults who are SSI disabled. This six-way breakout of the population, while very broad, helps to provide an initial understanding of who the chronically ill are and what health delivery services they might need.

Table 39–4 presents chronic disease prevalence rates by body system, and Table 39–5 presents chronic disease prevalence rates by individual chronic condition category. These are counts of conditions, so individuals with multiple chronic conditions will be counted as many times as they have chronic conditions. At the body system level, mental health conditions are by far the most prevalent chronic condition at 9.7%, followed by respiratory at 6.6%, brain/cerebrovascular at 4.2%, musculoskeletal at 3.7%, and endocrine at 3.2%.

**Table 39–3** Chronic illness prevalence rates by mental and/or physical conditions, state of Washington Medicaid, FY 1993, noninstitutionalized recipients, ages 0 to 64 years

|  | Recipients ages 0–17 yrs | Recipients ages 18–64 yrs | All recipients |
|---|---|---|---|
| Transplant status | 31 | 69 | 100 |
|  | (0.0%) | (0.1%) | (0.0%) |
| Mental retardation/encephalopa-thy with physical chronic DX | 619 | 845 | 1,464 |
|  | (0.3%) | (0.8%) | (0.5%) |
| Mental retardation/encephalopa-thy without physical chronic DX | 495 | 444 | 939 |
|  | (0.2%) | (0.4%) | (0.3%) |
| Physical chronic DX and mental health DX | 2,417 | 9,052 | 11,469 |
|  | (1.2%) | (8.1%) | (3.7%) |
| Physical chronic DX only | 25,655 | 30,546 | 56,201 |
|  | (12.7%) | (27.5%) | (18.0%) |
| Mental health DX only | 7,677 | 10,200 | 17,877 |
|  | (3.8%) | (9.2%) | (5.7%) |
| Subtotal, with chronic DX | 36,894 | 51,156 | 88,050 |
|  | (18.2%) | (46.1%) | (28.2%) |
| Subtotal, without chronic DX | 164,436 | 60,058 | 224,494 |
|  | (81.8%) | (53.9%) | (71.8%) |
| Total, all persons | 201,330 | 111,214 | 312,544 |
|  | (100%) | (100%) | (100%) |

*Note:* DX = diagnosis. Individuals with multiple chronic conditions are only coutned once in these prevalence rates, based on the heirarchy as listed above. *Source:* Data from National Association of Children's Hospitals and Related Institutions, Inc., 1996.

For adults, chronic mental health conditions are especially common, with a prevalence of 17.9%, 5.5% of which is substance dependence, 6.2% is depressive disorders, and 3.5% is anxiety disorders. Chronic mental health conditions are also common for children with a prevalence of 5.2%, 1.8% of which is attention deficit hyperactivity disorder; 0.8% is developmental delays; and 0.8% is depressive disorders. Actually, the chronic mental health prevalence rates are even higher than what these figures show. Close inspection of the

**Table 39–4** Chronic illness prevalence by body system, state of Washington Medicaid, FY 1993, noninstitutionalized recipients, ages 0 to 64 years

| Body system | Recipients ages 0–17 yrs (%) | Recipients ages 18–64 yrs (%) | All recipients (%) |
|---|---|---|---|
| Mental/developmental/substance dependence | 5.2 | 17.9 | 9.7 |
| Respiratory | 5.7 | 8.3 | 6.6 |
| Brain/cerebrovascular | 2.1 | 7.8 | 4.2 |
| Musculoskeletal | 2.1 | 6.7 | 3.7 |
| Endocrine | 0.8 | 7.5 | 3.2 |
| Neuromuscular | 0.9 | 5.0 | 2.4 |
| Cardiovascular | 0.7 | 4.6 | 2.1 |
| Gastroenterology | 0.9 | 5.3 | 2.1 |
| Renal | 1.0 | 3.2 | 1.8 |
| Peripheral vascular | 0.2 | 3.2 | 1.3 |

*Note*: Individuals with multiple chronic conditions are counted multiple times in these prevalence rates. *Source*: Data from National Association of Children's Hospitals and Related Institutions, Inc., 1996.

ICD-9-CM codes in the Washington Medicaid claims files has identified additional "header record" diagnosis codes that meet the criteria for inclusion in the NACHRI classification system. These have since been added.

The most common respiratory condition for both adults and children is asthma. Chronic bronchitis/chronic obstructive lung disease is also very common among adults. The most common brain/cerebrovascular condition among adults is migraine; the most common among children is epilepsy. In the musculoskeletal system, back disorders are by far the most common problem among adults, whereas children's musculoskeletal disorders are more diverse. In the endocrine system, diabetes mellitus is by far the most common condition with thyroid gland disorders as the other very common disorder among both adults and children. Of the low-prevalence endocrine conditions, pituitary growth hormone deficiency is more common among children and adrenal gland disorders are more common among adults.

In most areas, the mix of chronic health conditions is different for adults and children, as might be expected. This is especially evident in body systems, such as the neuromuscular system where cerebral palsy is the most common

**Table 39–5** Chronic illness prevalence by condition category, state of Washington Medicaid, FY 1993, noninstitutionalized recipients, ages 0 to 64 years

| Chronic condition category | Recipients ages 0–17 yrs (%) | Recipients ages 18–64 yrs (%) | All recipients (%) |
|---|---|---|---|
| Asthma | 4.9 | 5.6 | 5.2 |
| Depressive disorder | 0.8 | 6.2 | 2.7 |
| Diabetes mellitus | 0.4 | 4.9 | 2.3 |
| Substance dependence | 0.2 | 5.5 | 2.2 |
| Spinal disorder except curvature of the back | 0.2 | 4.2 | 1.6 |
| Anxiety disorder | 0.4 | 3.5 | 1.5 |
| Migraine | 0.3 | 3.5 | 1.4 |
| Chronic bronchitis/chronic obstructive pulmonary disease | 0.3 | 2.9 | 1.2 |
| Attention deficit hyperactivity disorder | 1.8 | 0.1 | 1.2 |
| Peripheral nervous system disorder | 0.1 | 2.8 | 1.1 |

*Note*: Individuals with multiple chronic conditions are counted multiple times in these prevalence rates. *Source*: Data from National Association of Children's Hospitals and Related Institutions, Inc., 1996.

---

childhood condition and peripheral nervous system disorders are the most common adult condition. In the cardiovascular system, congenital heart disease is by far the most common childhood condition, whereas coronary heart disease is the most common adult condition.

There are also, as might be expected, dramatic differences in the prevalence of specific conditions among the SSI-disabled and non–SSI-disabled populations. In the childhood population, to illustrate, there is among the SSI disabled a much higher percentage of children with mental retardation, mental illnesses, and certain neurological conditions, such as cerebral palsy, spina bifida, and muscular dystrophy.

These many illustrations of chronic illness prevalence rates are important for understanding health service needs and, in turn, for organizing appropriate delivery systems and tracking quality indicators and patient satisfaction. The number and types of chronic conditions vary greatly from the child to the adult population and from the Medicaid to non–Medicaid population. Accordingly, the number and types of physicians and other health professionals needed to serve them will also vary. Quality tracking mechanisms need to be tailored to the population—in particular, individuals with complex chronic conditions will often need very individualized care plans and a tracking mechanism that spans multiple years and continues intact if the individual changes health plans. What is important from a classification system perspective is the capability to identify and track these individuals. The next series of illustrations focuses on the costs of treating the different subgroups of the population.

Figure 39–1 presents average per annum charges by chronic disease severity level for children and adults. It shows a very similar pattern for adults and children with average charges increasing two- to threefold from the not chronically ill to those with mild chronic conditions and likewise from one chronic condition severity level to the next. Average charge levels for adults and children with major (S3) and extreme (S4) chronic conditions are nearly identical. Average charge levels are a little higher for adults than for children with moderate (S2) and mild (S1) chronic conditions. This relates primarily to the presence of multiple chronic conditions, which is not shown. The adults who are not chronically ill are also a little more expensive than children. Much of this is probably attributable to childbirth expenses for women. Nonetheless, the overall pattern for this first-cut viewing of charge levels is one of great similarity between adults and children. It is not shown in Figure 39–1, but the average charge levels among different adult age groups are especially consistent. The average charge levels are more variable among pediatric patients, with newborns and infants/toddlers being more expensive than other children.

Figure 39–2 presents average per annum charges by severity level and presence of multiple chronic conditions. This adds greatly to the predictive power of the system. To illustrate, all individuals with one or more moderate chronic conditions had average annual charges of $6,146. Those with multiple moderate chronic conditions from different body systems had average charges of $12,072; those with multiple chronic conditions from the same body system had average charges of $8,868; those with a single chronic condition had average charges of $4,807. Thus, within the range of moderate chronic conditions, there is a two and one-half–fold difference in charges based on the presence of multiple chronic conditions and their involvement of different body systems.

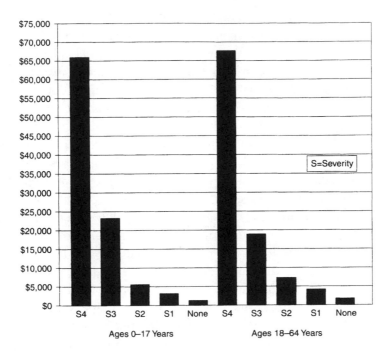

**Figure 39–1** Per annum charges by severity level for children and adults, state of Washington Medicaid, fiscal year 1993, noninstitutionalized recipients ages 0 to 64 years. Courtesy of National Association of Children's Hospitals and Related Institutions, Alexandria, Virginia.

The final version of the software for the NACHRI classification system places all persons into mutually exclusive categories based on the system's logic for disease combinations and hierarchies. This provides greater differentiation in average cost levels, less variability within each category, and greater clinical meaningfulness. This, in turn, will enable more effective provider profiling and capitation risk adjustment.

Figure 39–3 presents average per annum charges by presence or absence of chronic health condition for SSI-disabled and non–SSI-disabled Medicaid recipients. The presence of a chronic health condition is a consistent and very powerful predictor. Those who do not have chronic health conditions have relatively low charge levels. Those with chronic conditions have much higher

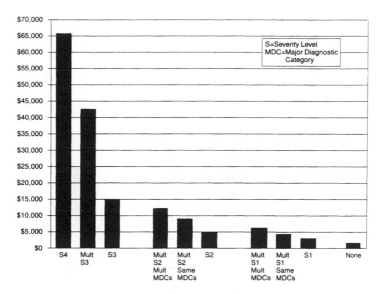

**Figure 39–2** Per annum charges by severity level and combinations for all Medicaid patients, state of Washington Medicaid, fiscal year 1993, noninstitutionalized recipients ages 0 to 64 years. Courtesy of National Association of Children's Hospitals and Related Institutions, Alexandria, Virginia.

charges. The charge levels are particularly high for those who are SSI disabled with chronic health conditions. Though not shown in Figure 39–3, this reflects a greater proportion of high severity chronic diseases and a greater proportion of multiple chronic conditions.

It is particularly noteworthy that the SSI-disabled recipients identified by the classification system as not having any chronic disease diagnoses have billed charges for health care services that are essentially the same as those for the non–SSI-disabled recipients who do not have a chronic disease diagnosis. It is possible that these are individuals whose chronic disabling condition has resolved but who have not yet come up for recertification. Another possibility is that they still have a chronic disabling condition but are not seeking or receiving health care services. This is not well understood, but what is important from a classification perspective is the ability to identify

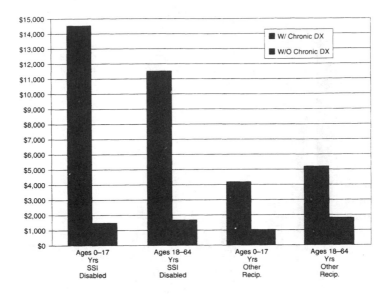

**Figure 39–3** Per annum charges by presence of chronic condition, state of Washington Medicaid, fiscal year 1993, noninstitutionalized recipients, ages 0 to 64 years. *Note*: SSI, Supplemental Security Income. *Source*: Data from National Association of Children's Hospitals and Related Institutions, Inc., 1996.

such persons and situations. Once the circumstance is identified, then focused management review can take place to gain a greater understanding of the population's health needs and whether they are being met.

## CODING AND CLASSIFICATION ISSUES

The key to the usefulness of any classification system is its clinical credibility. This depends on the concepts, definitions, and information building blocks of the system. The NACHRI classification system has attempted to develop these components very rigorously in its design and testing.

The *concepts and definitions* for the NACHRI classification system are based on how clinicians view and describe the patient population. Over 50 pediatric physicians and psychologists representing nearly 25 medical and surgical disciplines have been involved in its design and testing. The same group of pediatric division chiefs at two children's hospitals have worked with the system at different stages of development, and a medical advisory committee has overseen its development, focusing on the overall design and consistency of its many components. This has provided essential guidance as well as insight into the limitations of the system.

The system has been developed to comprehensively cover chronic conditions for patients of all ages. The first testing suggests its statistical performance may be as strong for adults as for children. The system has not, however, had the benefit of extensive review by adult physicians. Such review would certainly be beneficial, especially for the more subtle aspects of disease interactions, and it is intended for the next version of the system.

The *informational building blocks* for the NACHRI classification system and any other diagnosis-based classification system are the ICD-9-CM diagnosis codes and supplemental status codes. While often criticized for lacking sufficient specificity—and this is true to a certain extent—there is a wealth of information in the 15,000 ICD-9-CM diagnosis codes. There are also established coding principles and guidelines, and there is an established process through the ICD-9-CM Coordination and Maintenance Committee to update the codes annually. Many important changes are introduced each year.

Three important starting-point strategies, therefore, are (1) to understand and make maximum use of the existing information in the ICD-9-CM codes, (2) to encourage and support the full and accurate reporting of ICD-9-CM diagnosis and supplemental status codes by health plans for all patient care encounters, and (3) to continue to formulate proposals to the ICD-9-CM Coordination and Maintenance Committee for new and revised codes. It is especially important in the area of outpatient services that greater attention be given to a complete recording of all pertinent diagnoses, with full fourth- or fifth-digit specificity, and in accordance with established coding principles and guidelines.

It is important to recognize that even with complete and accurate recording of ICD-9-CM diagnosis codes, there is not always all the information that might be desired for a full description of a person's medical condition and needed interventions. If resources were not a constraint, full history and physical, response to treatment to date, stage of illness, and prognosis might be sought. Actually, even with all this information, it is not always possible to predict the course of an illness and needed interventions. The strategy has to be to identify the most essential information items that are readily available to describe a person's health conditions and likely needed interventions.

There are some diagnostic conditions that might be further illuminated by supplemental information on stage of illness or functional status. Stage or status can sometimes be inferred from viewing all the person's diagnoses. For example, a person with diabetes mellitus who also has peripheral neuropathy or nephropathy has a more advanced form of diabetes mellitus. Supplemental status V codes can also be very helpful. To illustrate, the ICD-9-CM committee recently considered adoption of a new code for wheelchair-dependent status. This will be very helpful for a number of patients, muscular dystrophy being just one example. Age can also be very helpful for conditions that generally follow an age-specific predictable course. For example, there are some congenital anomalies that require intensive treatment in the first several years of life but then are mostly or entirely cured.

Another approach is to combine selectively prior health service utilization with diagnostic information. This can be an effective approach when the diagnosis codes lack the desired specificity, and the utilization of certain services is associated with more severe or advanced forms of the disease and is not subject to any significant degree of practice pattern variation. This approach is one of the most practical for maximizing the clinical content and predictive power of a diagnosis-based classification system with available information. It will be given increased attention in future efforts to refine the NACHRI classification system.

## PUBLIC HEALTH AND POLICY APPLICATIONS

In addition to its many managed care uses, the NACHRI classification system has many public health and policy applications. The same applications that are possible at the health plan level are also possible at the community level. There are also specific applications for the Medicaid program and for identification and servicing of the population of children with special health needs.

At the community level, the classification system can be used to profile health needs and health delivery issues for the entire population. To do this, all health plans would need to maintain their own data sets and contribute to a central data repository on a regular basis. Once the central data repository is created, it would then be possible to set up systems for tracking the chronically ill over time as they enroll, disenroll, and reenroll in different health plans. Patient satisfaction and long-term outcomes could be tracked to the extent that appropriate quality indicators exist or could be developed.

Medicaid programs in many states are implementing managed care programs. The ability to risk adjust capitation rates and to track patient satisfaction and enrollment and disenrollment rates in health plans could be greatly facilitated through use of the NACHRI classification system. Many Medicaid programs have only risk adjusted for age and gender. Some have included SSI recipients in managed care, while others have excluded them. Neither approach is very effective. Some SSI recipients require very extensive health care services; others require very few. There are also many chronically ill persons who do not meet the SSI criteria but are very sick; in fact, among children, the vast majority of chronically ill are not SSI recipients.

In the state of Washington, only 12% of chronically ill children are SSI recipients. This is because SSI disability is based on ability to engage in substantive gainful employment or its functional equivalent for children—ability to function independently and effectively at an age-appropriate level. Accordingly, a large number of children with mental retardation or certain neurological and mental health conditions qualify for SSI, but many other children with complex health care needs do not. From a policy perspective, it is important that SSI disability not be mistakenly used as a proxy definition for children with special health care needs.

The NACHRI classification system provides a tool to identify the population of children with special health care needs. The term *children with special health care needs* is widely used but generally not well defined. At one extreme, it is sometimes used to describe all chronically ill children plus the at-risk population. At the other extreme, it is used to describe children with the most complex conditions. The differences in definition often reflect differences in context and purpose. An operational definition can only be developed if the purpose and intended scope are clear. Once they are established, an operational definition could be developed working with the categories and severity levels of the NACHRI classification system.

## CONCLUSIONS

Managed care has the challenge of delivering health care services to populations from a fixed pool of dollars and the imperative to be accountable for doing so. From a health plan and a community perspective, it is critical to have classification systems that adequately describe the health service needs of the population. For a classification system to be clinically credible, it must be developed from specific diagnostic information with clear definitions and medical logic that gives order and meaning to the many pieces of diagnostic information. For it to be practical on a broad scale, it must be developed from readily available information. The NACHRI Classification of Congenital and Chronic Health Conditions endeavors to operationalize such an approach, and its first testing on a full-service, paid-claims database gives encouraging support to this approach.

## NOTES

1. Ellis, R., Pope, G., Iezzonni, L.I., Ayanian, J., Bates, D., Burnstein, H., & Ash, A. (1996, Spring). Diagnosis-based risk adjustment for Medicare capitation payments. *Health Care Financing Review, 17*(3), 101–128.
2. Kronick, R., Dreyfus, T., Lee, L., & Zhou, Z. (1996, Spring). Diagnostic risk adjustment for Medicaid: The disability payment system. *Health Care Financing Review, 17*(3), 7–33.
3. Weiner, J., Dobson, A., Maxwell, S., Coleman, K., Starfield, B., & Anderson, G. (1996, Spring). Risk adjusted Medicare capitation rates using ambulatory and inpatient diagnoses. *Health Care Financing Review, 17*(3), 77–99.
4. Ellis et al., diagnosis-based risk adjustment for Medicare capitation payments.
5. Kronick et al., Diagnostic risk adjustment for Medicaid.
6. Weiner et al., Risk adjusted Medicare capitation rates.
7. Ellis et al., Diagnosis-based risk adjustment.
8. Division of Services for Children with Special Health Care Needs. (1996, December). *Children with special health care needs in managed care organizations: Definitions and identification, family participation, capitation and risk adjustment, quality of care—Summary of expert work group meetings.* Rockville, MD: Maternal and Child Health Bureau, U.S. Department of Health and Human Services.
9. Ellis et al.,
10. Division of Services for Children with Special Health Care Needs, *Children with special health care needs in managed care organizations.*
11. Kronick et al., Diagnostic risk adjustment for Medicaid.
12. Weiner et al., Risk adjusted Medicare capitation rates.
13. Division of Services for Children with Special Health Care Needs, *Children with special health care needs in managed care organizations.*
14. Washington State Health Care Advisory Board. (1997, January). *Children with special health care needs report.* Olympia, WA: Author.

# CHAPTER 40

# Predicting Mental Health Outpatient Services Using Non-claims-based Characteristics

*Norbert Goldfield, Richard Averill, Herbert Fillmore, and Dennis Graziano*

The study described in this chapter examined whether additional data elements not currently collected on the standard claim form would increase the ability of ambulatory patient groups (APGs) to predict resource consumption. This issue is important to pursue, as there are certain medical services that, on the basis of claim form data, have been historically difficult to understand from a resource consumption perspective.

APGs were developed, pursuant to a grant from the Health Care Financing Administration, as a classification system for ambulatory services. The APGs can be used as the basic unit of payment in a prospective payment system for outpatient services. The initial APG research was completed in December 1990 and resulted in a classification system (APG 1.0) consisting of 298 patient groups covering all outpatient services provided in hospital outpatient departments. The most recent APG research resulted in a second version of the APGs (APG 2.0), consisting of 290 groups—some changed from the first version. Both versions of the APGs use only information present on the existing claim form. For mental health services, there are APGs such as family therapy, extended individual therapy, and partial hospitalization. Their construction is, in turn, dependent on time and type of therapy. No patient characteristics are utilized.

Data not currently collected on the claim form may be useful for clinical areas that historically have not been well defined in either *International*

Courtesy of 3M Health Information Systems, Wallingford, Connecticut.

*Classification of Diseases, Ninth Edition, Clinical Modification* (ICD-9-CM) or *Current Procedural Terminology, Fourth Edition* (CPT-4). Current ICD-9-CM codes for mental health, for example, have been found to be relatively poor predictors of inpatient resource consumption.[1] In addition, current CPT codes for mental health are largely based on length of visit, not patient characteristics. As a consequence, it is important to consider the use of additional patient-level variables that might characterize patient conditions better than is possible using the existing ICD-9-CM or CPT-4 codes. In turn, consideration of these variables may have the effect of improving the APG classification system, as APGs are dependent on these two coding systems.

A thorough description of the data elements collected in this research project, together with instructions on how to collect the data elements, was developed into a document termed the H-Code chapter. The data elements were extensively reviewed by many researchers, as well as Health Care Financing Administration officials, before they were finalized.

In summary, the research discussed in this chapter had the following objectives:

- to identify a discrete set of clinical signs, symptoms, or findings that are not currently collected on the Universal Bill 92 (UB-92) claim form or used in ICD-9-CM or CPT-4 but that could improve the ability of specific APGs to predict resource consumption
- to collect a sample of outpatient data with the additional data elements and test the extent to which the additional data improve the ability of specific APGs to predict resource consumption

## STUDY DESIGN

The study involved the collection of information not included on the standard claim form from a variety of clinical settings over a six-month period. This additional information consists of patient characteristics thought to be useful in improving the ability of APGs to predict resource consumption.

The study was nonrandom and nonrepresentative and thus was not meant to be definitive. It was intended as a starting point for further research. The testing of the proposed diagnosis code modifications was performed in many sites in New York State in conjunction with the New York Department of Health (NYDOH). New York State was chosen because a considerable amount of work has been done by NYDOH to better understand outpatient services.

The four specific hypotheses tested in this study were as follows:

- Patient characteristics, such as mental health status, predict resource consumption of outpatient mental health services over a one-month period of time.
- Patient characteristics, such as functional health status, predict resource consumption of outpatient rehabilitation health services over a one-month period of time.
- Patient characteristics, such as blood pressure, identify different categories of chronic illness for patients seen in an outpatient setting.
- Patient characteristics, such as temperature, identify different categories within, for example, the upper respiratory infection (URI) or other infectious disease APGs for patients seen in the emergency room setting.

### Site Selection and Data Collection Process

Appropriate sites were identified by New York State Department of Health (NYDOH) personnel, and were varied in terms of ownership and types of patient served. For example, in the area of mental health, both private and public, managed care and non-managed-care sites were sought. NYDOH representatives contacted the institutions to determine their level of interest.

If a site expressed an interest in the project, representatives from NYDOH and 3M HIS presented to the site's clinical and administrative staff the purpose and the mechanics of the data collection process. If the staff still expressed interest in participating in the project, they were trained in the objectives and content of the study. NYDOH staff assisted in all the data collection and processing issues. Additionally, in an effort to maintain a high level of interest in the project, site personnel were provided inter- and post-project presentations of their data.

The following sites participated:

- Community Health Plan—not-for-profit staff model HMO
- Kingston Psychiatric Center—state-run and -funded community-based outpatient facility
- Creedmore Psychiatric Center—a state-run and -funded community-based outpatient facility

- Horizon Community Center—not-for-profit community-based health centers
- Mid-Hudson Family Practice Center—an interdis
- ciplinary medical group practice

Definition and resolution of all issues pertaining to data collection and processing constituted a key administrative project objective. Both claims data and clinic-based data had to be collected and merged. There were challenges associated with each data source. The vast majority of sites that agreed to participate submitted data that could be analyzed. However, the data collected from several sites (e.g., mental health services at Columbia Presbyterian Medical Center) had to be excluded because of data-processing problems.

There were two general data-processing issues applicable to all sites:

- working with clinical settings and information services at participating sites to determine the formats in which data collected on site would be sent to the NYDOH
- working with information services at participating sites to ensure that claims data extracts were sent by the institution to the NYDOH in a timely and accurate manner
- Once the data processing issues were resolved, on-site training and data collection began. On-site training utilized a detailed training manual developed to assist individual sites in collecting the data. The manual consists of
- project background information
- an H-Code chapter
- examples on how to code data elements
- most frequently asked questions pertaining to the research project
- background scientific articles providing further details

- A newsletter was sent to every participating site on a bimonthly basis to encourage commitment to the project.

After four to six weeks of data collection, initial data were processed, and a health professional from either NYDOH or 3M HIS (or both) visited each site to provide feedback to clinical and administrative professionals. This was done in an effort to maintain interest in the project and to ensure the highest possible accuracy and completeness in the data items collected. Once the project was completed, 3M/HIS personnel offered to return to the sites to provide a summary of data results.

When data collection was completed, claims and clinical data were sent to the NYDOH. Clinical data were first transferred, if necessary, from paper to electronic format. The two data streams were then merged, and dummy record numbers were assigned to replace the patient record numbers. A data tape containing both claims and clinical data was then sent to 3M HIS.

## Development of H-Codes

Each of the variables described below was included in the H-Code chapter for several reasons. Each was

- thought to have a high probability of representing an indication of severity, thus making the reason for a visit more difficult to treat and requiring more resources
- based on information either routinely collected by health care professionals or very familiar to them
- derived, whenever possible, from standardized items already tested in the literature (e.g., mental health status and functioning, which is derived from Axis V of DSM-IV)

Independent and dependent variables considered useful in refining rehabilitation and mental illness APGs were not collected for every visit. This was due to the difficulty of collecting additional information on every visit, together with a move toward managed care, which reimburses for services provided over a period of time. While the type of visit (e.g., family visit versus individual therapy) could be identified on a visit basis, additional patient information was collected monthly. A month was adopted as a "bridge" between an individual visit in traditional fee-for-service and a one-year period of time summarized under capitation.

Version 2.0 of the medical APGs uses ICD-9-CM diagnosis and CPT procedure codes. Due to frequent provider change from one visit to the next in the ambulatory medical setting, improvement in the medical APGs was sought at the individual visit level. As data would have to be collected for every visit, a very short additional data set for potential refinement of the medical APGs was developed. Similarly, refinement of the medical APGs with specific attention to the emergency room also needed to be done at the individual visit level. Again, a short additional data set was developed.

The additional information in the H-Codes completely yet briefly describes health services in the areas tested in the project.

Two types of H-Codes were collected: independent and dependent variables. Each category of codes is described, along with a reason the information was collected.

### Independent Variables

- *Medications.* Medications, legally used as part of the doctor-patient relationship, can be associated with provider time differences. Medications can require monitoring or may be indicative of the seriousness of the underlying condition. Only medications of this type were included in the list of medications. For example, Clozapine is a medication used for the treatment of chronic schizophrenia. Extensive monitoring from both a laboratory and a practitioner time point of view is needed whenever a physician prescribes Clozapine.
- *Living arrangements.* Living arrangements can result in provider time differences. A homeless individual may require more case management time to coordinate intervention strategies than an individual who is not homeless.
- *Work/school status.* Changes in work/school status may be associated with provider time differences. An individual who misses several days of work or school may utilize more services than an individual who does not miss any work or school. Time lost from work or school may be an indication of a severely ill individual requiring increased provider time. For the purposes of this study, unpaid work activity, such as participation in a work program, was defined to constitute work.
- *Suicide assessment.* A patient with a suicide gesture may require more provider time than a patient with no suicide ideation or gesture.
- *Substance abuse effect.* A person who abuses drugs (legal or illegal) may require more provider time, making substance abuse a marker for increased severity of illness. This variable examined the degree of substance abuse, a characteristic not collected in ICD-9-CM. More time may be necessary to manage the interaction between the drug problem and the mental health problem.
- *Family/support system available (if applicable).* This variable was derived from the Patient Evaluation and Conference System (a health status measure utilized particularly for patients undergoing physical rehabilitation). A person without a family or social support system may

require more provider time than one with a family or social support system. This domain does not indicate whether the patient is or is not living with the available family or social support system.

- *Family/support system communication.* This variable was derived from the Patient Evaluation and Conference System. This measure defines discrete levels of family or support system communication. It is hypothesized that a patient with poor social support communication may require more provider time than one with good family or social support communication.
- *Previous psychiatric hospitalization.* This variable provides the common periods of last hospital discharge. An individual who was recently discharged from the hospital may consume more provider time than an individual not recently hospitalized.
- *Chronic medical conditions.* The most frequently occurring medical conditions that might represent a marker for increased severity of illness and result in provider time differences were identified. The list was obtained through discussion with participating sites. Examples include obesity and AIDS.
- *Number of ER visits.* A demographic variable thought to be relevant in predicting provider time. An individual with one or more emergency room visits may consume more non-ER outpatient provider time than an individual who has no emergency room visits. Use of the emergency room may represent a marker for increased severity of illness.
- *Symptoms and functioning.* The symptoms and functioning scales are based on the Global Assessment Scale. This scale is present in Axis V in DSM-IV, the principal coding and nomenclature system for mental health disorders. Modifications were made to reflect current thinking among some researchers that symptoms and functioning should, if at all possible, be separated.[2] The current version of the Global Assessment Scale integrates both symptoms and functioning within the same scale.

### Dependent Variables

The dependent variables were

- primary provider time
- case management time

Resource consumption is considered to be the sum of these two variables. (Under fee-for-service, resource consumption consists only of primary provider time.) Increased primary provider time and case management time result in higher charges.

Primary provider time was obtained from claims data utilizing already existing CPT codes (e.g., code 90843 was used to refer to visits of 20 to 30 minutes). Case management time was collected on a monthly basis from supplemental forms. This information was collected by either the primary care provider or an individual specifically assigned the task of providing case management.

For the purposes of this study, case management time is defined as time spent in any professional activity, including family meetings and/or meetings with significant others and/or agencies; phone contacts with patient or family member or significant other and/or other agencies; court business; case conferences (e.g., meetings between therapist and psychiatrist, formal case presentations, peer supervision meetings) with patient present or absent; escorting patient for appointment; and letters or completion of forms for other agencies.

## DATA ANALYSIS

### Editing Data Process and Analysis Framework

Supplemental encounter forms were merged with patient claim data. The merge algorithm used to ensure that patient months of data for mental health services are valid is shown below:

- Dummy record numbers replaced patient record numbers to preserve patient confidentiality.
- A month of patient data was allowed only if a supplemental form was completed during the month. This was done to eliminate any instances in which the supplemental form was misplaced or not completed.
- The supplemental form completion date and dummy record number were used as the keys to join the patient visit(s) that occurred during the month. This was done to ensure patient services were assigned in a consistent manner to the appropriate supplemental form.
- Patient visits were limited to 20 visits a month. This was done to deal with a situation in one institution in which services from a day rehabilitation program were classified as direct patient care services.

- Patients must have had case management time. This eliminates any instances in which the supplemental form was misplaced or not completed.
- Primary provider time spent on each visit was limited to 3 hours. This was done to deal with a situation in one institution in which services from a day rehabilitation program were classified as direct patient care services.

The merge algorithm resulted in patient records being eliminated, as shown in Table 40–1.

Approximately, 60 percent of all monthly patient encounters were included in the analysis. Over 11,000 months of data were maintained and almost 8,000 months of data were eliminated (for a total of approximately 19,000 months). As described in Table 40–1, records were discarded for the following reasons:

**Table 40–1** Mental Health Edits Count and Logic

| Step | Description | Total | Percent-age |
|------|-------------|-------|---------|
| 1 | Identify patients with supplemental form(s) for one month. | 19,014 | 100.00 |
| 2 | Eliminate patient months without any visit. | 16,690 | 87.78 |
| 3 | Eliminate patient months in which total monthly visits exceeded 20. | 16,557 | 87.08 |
| 4 | Eliminate patients who did not have case management time. | 14,049 | 73.89 |
| 5 | Eliminate patients with primary provider visits that exceeded 3 hours. | 13,811 | 72.64 |
| 6 | Eliminate patients with primary provider visits that did not exceed 0 minutes. | 13,792 | 72.54 |
| 7 | Eliminate patients who did not have functioning/behavior and symptomology scores. | 13,196 | 69.40 |
| 8 | Eliminate patients who do not have either family communication status code or use medicine code. | 11,624 | 61.13 |

*Note: Total* refers to patient months of mental health services.

Courtesy of 3M Health Information Systems, Wallingford, Connecticut.

- No visits in a month.
- Number of visits exceeded twenty. (One site included participation in a day program for the chronically mentally ill as a visit and the data for these patients was eliminated.)
- Case management time was not recorded.
- Symptoms or functioning fields were not completed.

After the data were edited, reports were created for further analysis. The analysis was conducted to examine possible clinical and statistical relationships that could assist in the development of a tree-based classification structure. This report was produced for each relevant H-Code. Table 40–2 provides a sample report that was analyzed in detail as part of the process of creating the classification of mental health disorders.

## Results

Table 40–3 contains final statistical results for the groups that were created after detailed examination of the data in conjunction with clinical input. Both averages and coefficients of variation statistics are presented. The verbal headings of the vertical columns are virtually the same as in Table 40–2. Figure 40–1 graphically depicts the relationship between the different groups.

## Classification Tree

The process for formulating the mental health classification tree was highly iterative, involving statistical results from collected data combined with clinical judgment. A preliminary classification was developed based solely on clinical judgment. Thus, for example, from a clinical perspective it is important to incorporate in the tree structure as early as possible significant symptoms or function deficits, as these patient characteristics are easily obtained and represent important aspects of the patient.

Sixteen categories were created using a decision tree type of process. That is, the initial groups were created using those H-Codes deemed to be most important clinically: the Assessment of Symptoms and the Assessment of Functioning codes. Additional groups were then created based on clinical judgment. Untrimmed $R^2$ for this grouping structure of 16 categories was 0.08; trimmed $R^2$ was 0.10 (136 records were discarded). From a statistical perspective, 1 percent of the data at either end were trimmed.

**Table 40-2** Hospital: All Sites—Model 5: Group 20—Service Area: Mental Health Aggregated Report across Months for Assessment of Functioning/Behavior

| H Code | Pat cnt | Avg vst cnt | Avg PPTM/ vst | Avg PPTM/ pat | Pri phys T/M | Avg cstm/pat | Case mgmt tm (cstm) | Tot time p/pat | Total time | H-Code description |
|--------|---------|-------------|---------------|---------------|--------------|--------------|---------------------|----------------|------------|---------------------|
| H902 | | | | | | | | | | Extremely severe impair |
| H903 | | | | | | | | | | Severe impairment |
| H904 | | | | | | | | | | Extremely serious impair |
| H905 | | | | | | | | | | Serious impair |
| H906 | | | | | | | | | | Moderate impair |
| H907 | | | | | | | | | | Some impairment |
| H908 | | | | | | | | | | Mild impairment |
| H909 | | | | | | | | | | Good functioning |

*Patient count (Pat cnt)* refers to the number of months of treatment for individual patients.
*Average visit count (Avg vst cnt)* refers to the average number of face-to-face provider visits that occurred per month.
*Average primary provider time per visit (Avg PPTM/vst)* refers to the average provider time per visit.
*Average primary provider time per patient (AVG PPTM/pat)* represents a multiplication of the second and third column and is the total average provider time per patient per month.
*Total primary provider time per month (Pri phys T/M)* refers to the total amount of provider time spent with a patient during a month.
*Average case management time per patient (Avg cstm/pat)* represents the average case management time per patient per month.
*Case management time (cstm)* is a multiplication of the patient count by average case management time per patient.
*Total time per patient (Tot time p/pat)* is the sum of the average provider time per patient added to the case management time per patient.
*Total time* represents the total time per patient multiplied by the number of monthly patient encounters.

Courtesy of 3M Health Information Systems, Wallingford, Connecticut.

**Table 40-3** Statistics for Mental Health Grouping Structure

| Mental Health Group | Pat cnt | Vst cnt | | PPTM Per Vst | | PPTM Per Pat | | CSTN Per Pat | | Total Tm Per Pat | | Group 2 |
|---|---|---|---|---|---|---|---|---|---|---|---|---|
| | | Avg | CV | Avg | CV | Avg | CV | Avg | CV | Avg | CV | |
| Grp1 | 36 | 8.58 | 0.51 | 32.54 | 0.77 | 279.31 | 0.80 | 175.00 | 0.55 | 454.31 | 0.49 | With Clozapine, recent (past 6 months) hospital discharge |
| Grp2 | 165 | 7.71 | 0.53 | 31.21 | 0.71 | 240.59 | 0.77 | 119.27 | 0.65 | 359.87 | 0.55 | With Clozapine |
| Grp3 | 124 | 4.77 | 0.59 | 43.71 | 0.54 | 208.69 | 0.70 | 168.39 | 0.74 | 377.07 | 0.58 | Significant symptoms & behavior disturbances (Sig symp & behav disturb), poor family support (FS), suicide attempt, with substance abuse/recent hosp discharge or AIDS |
| Grp4 | 272 | 3.83 | 0.63 | 41.42 | 0.53 | 158.82 | 0.72 | 148.46 | 0.75 | 307.27 | 0.56 | Sig symp & behav dist, poor FS, suicide attempt |
| Grp5 | 612 | 4.20 | 0.63 | 38.15 | 0.59 | 160.14 | 0.77 | 126.32 | 0.81 | 386.46 | 0.61 | Sig symp, poor FS, with substance abuse/recent hospital discharge or AIDS |
| Grp6 | 80 | 3.15 | 0.66 | 39.49 | 0.46 | 124.39 | 0.81 | 67.88 | 0.86 | 192.26 | 0.68 | Sig symp & behav disturb, poor FS |
| Grp7 | 2230 | 3.89 | 0.63 | 38.31 | 0.53 | 148.99 | 0.77 | 114.50 | 0.85 | 263.49 | 0.66 | Sig symp & behav disturb, poor FS, not full time work status (WS) |
| Grp8 | 689 | 4.18 | 0.61 | 39.89 | 0.54 | 166.84 | 0.67 | 116.17 | 0.86 | 283.01 | 0.58 | Sig symp & behav disturb, good family support (FS), not full-time WS, w substance abuse/attempt suicide/ recent hospital discharge or AIDS |

*continues*

**Table 40–3** continued

| Mental Health Group | Pat cnt | Vst cnt | | PPTM Per Vst | | PPTM Per Pat | | CSTN Per Pat | | Total Tm Per Pat | | Group 2 |
|---|---|---|---|---|---|---|---|---|---|---|---|---|
| | | Avg | CV | Avg | CV | Avg | CV | Avg | CV | Avg | CV | |
| Grp9 | 3135 | 3.71 | 0.65 | 39.08 | 0.63 | 141.40 | 0.87 | 86.55 | 0.93 | 227.95 | 0.71 | Sig symp & behav disturb, not full-time WS |
| Grp10 | 230 | 3.24 | 0.75 | 35.42 | 0.52 | 114.73 | 0.83 | 53.35 | 1.20 | 168.07 | 0.72 | Sig symp & behav disturb |
| Grp11 | 948 | 3.44 | 0.65 | 40.59 | 0.51 | 139.48 | 0.69 | 95.16 | 0.82 | 234.64 | 0.59 | Mild symp & behav disturb, poor FS, not full-time WS, w substance abuse/suicide attempt/recent hospital discharge or AIDS |
| Grp12 | 181 | 3.67 | 0.58 | 40.56 | 0.59 | 149.03 | 0.69 | 108.90 | 0.76 | 257.92 | 0.56 | Mild symptoms & behavior disturbances (Mild symp & behav disturb), poor FS, not full-time WS |
| Grp13 | 147 | 2.78 | 0.58 | 36.88 | 0.50 | 102.61 | 0.75 | 64.29 | 0.95 | 166.89 | 0.65 | Mild symp & behav disturb, poor FS |
| Grp14 | 279 | 3.74 | 0.66 | 40.74 | 0.60 | 152.31 | 0.84 | 86.67 | 0.89 | 238.97 | 0.66 | Mild symp & behav disturb, not full-time WS, w substance abuse/attempt suicide/recent hospital discharge or AIDS |
| Grp15 | 2046 | 3.21 | 0.64 | 39.14 | 0.58 | 125.79 | 0.84 | 69.38 | 0.91 | 195.17 | 0.68 | Mild symp & behav disturb, not full-time WS |
| Grp16 | 450 | 2.48 | 0.56 | 33.69 | 0.50 | 83.48 | 0.68 | 55.33 | 0.86 | 138.81 | 0.55 | Mild symp & behav disturb |

CV, coefficient of variation.
Courtesy of 3M Health Information Systems, Wallingford, Connecticut.

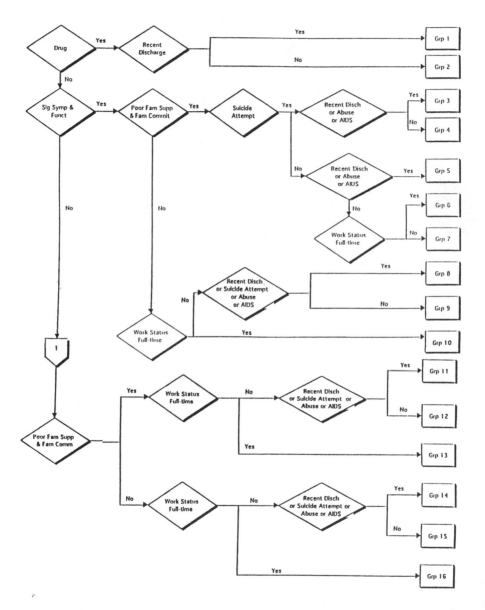

**Figure 40–1** Mental Health Classification Tree. Courtesy of 3M Health Information Systems, Wallingford, Connecticut.

Figure 40-1 provides a "branching tree" of the different groups created from the data and a separate summary of the statistics pertinent to each group. While decisions were made iteratively looking at the data, decisions always had a clinical basis. A description of the tree follows.

From an overarching perspective, it was important to include in the tree structure differences in resource consumption based on the significance of either symptoms or function deficits or both.

The first two groups used the medication Clozapine and the date of hospital discharge, if any, as the axes of classification. It is known that the use of Clozapine for the treatment of schizophrenics results in the consumption of numerous resources, both primary provider time (e.g., reviewing results of blood tests with the patient) and case management time (making sure the medication is being taken). While only a relatively small number of patients take Clozapine, the cost of the medication, in combination with the amount of both primary provider and case management time spent per patient, necessitated the creation of a separate group for these patients. Recent discharge from a hospital was found, as expected, to significantly predict differences in resource consumption between patients. The amount of resources utilized for Group 1 was 454 minutes per month for those patients on Clozapine who had a recent discharge from the hospital and 359 minutes per month for those patients on Clozapine who did not have a recent discharge (Group 2). The coefficients of variation (CVs) for these two groups were 0.47 and 0.55, respectively.

An examination of the importance of mental health symptoms and functioning represented the next important axis of classification. Two groups were created with respect to symptoms and functioning: significant and mild. A patient was considered to have significant symptoms or function deficits if he or she had H-Codes 901–907 or H-Codes 911–916. Eight separate groups, described in more detail below, were created based on the presence of, at a minimum, significant symptoms and function deficits. The average amount of time spent per patient per month in each group ranged from 377 to 168 minutes, with CVs ranging from 0.56 to 0.72.

If significant symptoms and function deficits were present, the presence of poor family social support communication (defined as H692–H692) was perceived to be the next most important factor. Five of the eight groups with significant symptoms and function deficits also had poor family or social support communication. Several other factors, including suicide attempt, recent discharge from a psychiatric hospital, substance abuse, the presence of AIDS, and the work or school status, were all utilized for further distinctions among these eight groups.

- Group 3 included patients who had significant symptoms and behavior disturbances; poor family support; a suicide attempt; and a recent hospital discharge, substance abuse problems, or AIDS. This group had an average provider time of 377 minutes and a CV of 0.58.
- Group 4 contained patients who had significant symptoms and functioning deficits, poor family support, and a suicide attempt. This group of patients had an average provider time of 307 minutes per month and a CV of 0.56.
- Group 5 consisted of patients who had significant symptoms and functioning deficits; poor family support; and a recent hospital discharge, substance abuse problems, or AIDs (there were no suicide attempts in this group). There were 612 patients in this category, and they had an average provider time of 286 minutes per month. The CV for this group was 0.61.
- Group 6 had significant symptoms and functioning deficits, had poor family communication, and were not working or going to school full time. There were 2,230 patients in this group, and they had an average provider time of 263 minutes per month. The CV for this group was 0.66.
- Group 7 had significant symptoms and function deficits, had poor family communication, but were going to work or school full time. There were only a small number of patients in this group. They had an average provider time of 192 minutes per month and had a CV of 0.68.

Three groups were created whose axis of classification began with significant symptoms and function deficits but did not have poor family support or communication.

- Group 8 did not work full time or go to school and had a recent psychiatric hospital discharge, a suicide attempt, substance abuse problems, or AIDS. These patients consumed an average of 283 minutes of provider time per month and had a CV of 0.58.
- The patients in Group 9, a much larger group (3,135), also did not work full time and had significant symptoms and function deficits. This group of patients consumed an average of 227 minutes of provider time per month and had a CV of 0.71.

- Group 10 consisted of patients who only had significant symptoms and function deficits. These patients consumed an average of 168 minutes of provider time per month and had a CV of 0.72.

Six separate groups were created for patients with mild symptoms and function deficits. The same variables utilized for patients with significant symptoms and function deficits were also utilized for those patients with mild symptoms and function deficits. The time spent per patient per month for those with mild symptoms and function deficits ranged from 257 to 138, with CVs ranging from 0.55 to 0.66.

- Group 11 consisted of patients with poor family communication and a recent discharge from a psychiatric facility, a suicide attempt, substance abuse problems, or AIDS. This group of patients had an average provider time of 257 minutes per month and a CV of 0.56.
- In Group 12, a much larger group of patients, patients had poor family communication and were not working or going to school full time. This group of patients had an average provider time of 234 minutes per month and a CV of 0.59.
- Group 13 consists of patients with poor family communication.

The last three groups consisted of patients who had neither significant symptoms or function deficits nor poor family communication.

- Group 14 consisted of patients who did not work full time and had a recent psychiatric discharge, a suicide attempt, substance abuse problems, or AIDS. This group of patients consumed an average of 238 minutes of provider time per month and had a CV of 0.66.
- Group 15 also consisted of patients who did not work or go to school full time. This group of patients consumed an average of 195 minutes of provider time per month and had a CV of 0.68.
- Group 16, the last group, did not have significant symptoms or function deficits, did not have difficulties with family communication, and worked or went to school full time. These patients consumed an average of 138 minutes of provider time per month and had a CV of 0.55.

It should be pointed out that the data were also analyzed on a visit-specific basis (as opposed to a monthly basis) and that patient characteristics never explained more than 1 percent of the variation in per visit costs of the mental health services provided.

## Clinical Characterization of Study Sample

This patient sample had a wide variety of symptoms and function deficits. Interestingly, the symptoms and function deficits often did not coincide, a finding that supports the recent suggestion by Goldman to separate Axis V into separate scales for symptoms and functioning.[3] Table 40–4 provides a simplified version of the relationship between equivalent levels of symptoms and functioning/behavior. The differences are statistically different at a 0.001 level.

Clinical aspects of the database were also examined from a variety of perspectives. Thus, the relationship between symptoms or function deficits and family or social support or communication and work status were examined. While statistically significant, it needs to be emphasized that this study, because of study design, was not able to examine issues pertaining to causality. All that can be concluded is that good family communication is strongly related to fewer mental health symptoms.

This study also came up with results regarding changes in symptoms and functioning over a period of time. Twenty-five percent of patients had data available for analysis for at least three consecutive months. Using regression analysis, the statistical relationship between change in symptoms and other variables, such as family communication, family support, or work status was shown to be relatively weak (4 percent), with the work status explaining the most.

## DISCUSSION

This study attempted to identify a discrete set of variables that might improve the ability of several types of APGs to predict resource consumption: mental health, rehabilitation, chronic medical conditions, and emergency room services.

In particular, the study examined the following hypothesis: selected patient characteristics, such as mental health status and family communication, correlate with resource consumption of mental health services over a one-month period of time. (Resource consumption was defined here as a combination of face-to-face primary provider time and case management time.)

While this study is the first study of its kind for outpatient mental health services, several practical implications are evident from the results demonstrating, with resource consumption, as the dependent variable an $R^2$ of 0.10. One can consider a month of services as either a portion of an episode of illness or the potential basis for a capitated rate for this type of patient. A small number of easily collected variables do improve prediction of resource consumption. These variables are both well known to providers and intuitively reasonable from a clinical point of view.

This prospective study represents the first time selected patient characteristics were utilized to predict resource consumption for health services over a mini-episode period of time. This work is particularly important at a time of significantly increased interest in managed care. In addition, this study represents the first effort to quantify the relationship between selected patient characteristics and case management time.

The results highlight the importance of better understanding the relationship between patient characteristics and resource consumption of health services. This is important, for example, for those patients with chronic mental illness. The Rand HIS study clearly documented how financial barriers decrease access to needed mental health services.[4] The current push toward managed care mandates more research to increase our understanding of the determinants of resource consumption in health services.

This study begins the process of understanding the relationship between resource consumption and patient characteristics for those patients whose consumption of resources have been historically difficult to understand utilizing data available from a claim form.

## RECOMMENDATIONS

The work summarized in this chapter suggests several recommendations:

- For certain services, such as mental health services, the Health Care Financing Administration could consider a demonstration project that would evaluate payment for outpatient mental health services or rehabilitation services using a quasi-capitated (e.g., monthly) methodology based on the variables collected in the study. The research summarized herein could provide a methodological approach and create a bridge between fee-for-service and managed care. There are carve-outs for managed care mental health services in the private sector, and thus a similar project would have relevance to today's health care market.

- An important follow-up research project could examine the patient characteristics that would predict resource consumption of inpatient and outpatient rehabilitation and/or mental health services. This project would complete the bridge between fee-for-service and managed care. Such a research project would examine the costs of services for stroke patients, for example, not only in the outpatient setting but also in the hospital and nursing home setting.

- Further research is necessary to better understand consumption of general medical services over differing periods of time, not just during a single visit. This is especially important in light of the capitation payments made for general medical services provided by primary care physicians. It is possible that additional patient variables, such as those collected in this study, are relevant for predicting resource consumption of episodes of illness for chronic medical illnesses.

**NOTES**

1. S.F. Jencks et al., "Bringing Excluded Psychiatric Facilities under the Medicare Prospective Payment System: A Review of Research Evidence and Policy Options," *Medical Care* 25 (1987): S1–S51.
2. H.H. Goldman et al., "Revising Axis V for DSM-IV: A Review of Measures of Social Functioning," *American Journal of Psychiatry* 149 (1992): 1148–1156.
3. Goldman et al., "Revising Axis V for DSM-IV."
4. J.P. Newhouse, "A Summary of the Rand Health Insurance Study," *Annals of the New York Academy of Sciences* 387 (1982): 111–114.

CHAPTER 41

# Predicting the Cost of General Medical Outpatient and Emergency Services Using Non-claims-based Characteristics

*Norbert Goldfield, Richard Averill, Jon Eisenhandler,*
*Herbert Fillmore, and Dennis Graziano*

**ABSTRACT**

**Background:** This study examines whether additional data elements not currently collected on the standard claim form would increase the ability of Ambulatory Patient Groups (APGs) to predict resource consumption. APGs are a patient classification tool which in part can be used for the prospective payment of outpatient services.

**Objective:** The specific hypotheses tested in this study were:

- Patient characteristics, such as blood pressure level, identify different categories of chronic illness for patients seen in an outpatient setting.
- Patient characteristics, such as temperature, identify different categories within, for example, the upper respiratory infection (URI) or other infectious disease APGs for patients seen in the emergency room setting.

This report was performed with the support of the Health Care Financing Administration, Office of Research and Demonstrations under cooperative agreement No. 17-C-90057/5-01 to 3M Health Information Systems. The opinions are solely of the authors and do not necessarily represent those of the Health Care Financing Administration.

Courtesy of 3M Health Information Systems, Wallingford, Connecticut.

**Design:** Non-random testing of additional data elements in many sites in New York State.

**Setting:** Physician offices in private practice, academic and non-academic hospital outpatient department.

**Measurements:** Claims- and non-claims-based clinical and cost information

**Results:** Selected patient characteristics, such as blood pressure level and aspects of functional status, do not correlate with resource consumption of general medical services or emergency room services for a visit or mini-episode.

**Conclusion:** Independent variables such as health status and blood pressure level did not correlate with facility and physician resource consumption. This study begins the process of understanding the relationship between resource consumption and patient characteristics for those patients whose consumption of resources has been historically difficult to understand utilizing data available from a claims form.

Data not currently collected on the claim form may be useful for clinical areas that historically have not been well defined in either *International Classification of Diseases, Ninth Revision, Clinical Modification* (ICD-9-CM) or *Current Procedural Terminology, Fourth Edition* (CPT-4). Additional data might also be useful in distinguishing between visits to the emergency room and visits to the outpatient department. For emergency room visits, certain patient variables, such as the patient's temperature and the patient's living situation, may be important predictors of resources consumed during the visit. This information is not currently collected in either ICD-9-CM or CPT-4.

The hypotheses tested in the study described in this chapter were these:

- Patient characteristics, such as blood pressure, identify different categories of chronic illness for patients seen in an outpatient setting. This occurs both at an individual visit and mini-episode level.
- Patient characteristics, such as temperature, identify different categories within, for example, the URI or other infectious disease APGs for patients seen in the emergency room setting.

The patient characteristics collected during the six-month collection period were

- thought to have a high probability of indicating severity (associated with the consumption of more resources)

- based on information either routinely collected by health care professionals or very familiar to them
- derived, whenever possible, from standardized items already tested in the literature

## METHODS

### Study Design

This study, which lasted from 1991 to 1994, involved the collection of information not included on the standard claim form from a variety of clinical settings over a six-month period. The study is nonrandom and nonrepresentative and is not meant to be definitive. The testing of the proposed diagnosis code modifications was performed in New York State in conjunction with the New York Department of Health. New York State was chosen, as a considerable amount of work has been done by the department of health to better understand outpatient services.

### Data Collection

Due to the change in provider that often occurs from one visit to the next in the ambulatory medical setting, improvement in the medical APGs was sought at the individual visit level. As data would have to be collected for every visit, a very short additional data set for potential refinement of the medical APGs was developed. Similarly, refinements in the medical APGs, with specific attention to the emergency room, also needed to be performed at the individual visit level. Again, a short additional data set was developed. The specific variables selected for collection included the following:

- *General health status.* A person who has poorer health status may consume more provider time than a person with good health status. Increased provider time could result in either longer or more frequent visits. This study analyzes the possibility that, for example, visit times are longer for patients with poor health status than patients with good health status. The symptoms and functioning scales are based on the Dartmouth Coop chart, a well-validated health status measure.[1] The measure is typically completed by the patient and contains only six items. No changes were made in the questionnaire for this study. All domains collected in the traditional Dartmouth Coop chart were included in this study (General Health, Social Health, Mental Health, Activities of Daily Living, and Physical Health). Both English and Spanish versions were used.

- *Blood pressure level.* Both systolic and diastolic blood pressure levels were collected. Higher blood pressure may be associated with expenditure of more provider time than normal blood pressure. Blood pressure level is routinely collected at every visit for virtually every patient.
- *Blood glucose level or its equivalent (e.g., HgbA1C).* Higher blood glucose may be associated with expenditure of more provider time than normal glucose. Glucose level, either tested at the time of the visit or at home by the patient, is routinely collected at every visit for virtually every patient. Furthermore, diabetes is a common chronic illness.
- *Primary care provider costs.* Estimation of these costs was based on time reported for each visit on the supplementary form by the primary care provider. Time was converted to cost using Medicare primary provider rates for CPT Evaluation and Treatment codes for primary care services.
- *Ancillary test costs.* Estimation of these costs was based on the frequency and type of tests performed. Charges from the most frequently occurring tests were obtained from a participating site.

With respect to episodes of illness, three visits per individual patient was defined as the minimum for an episode of illness. More could not be included, as this was only a six-month study. Averaging of the health status independent variable was done after patients were divided into three groups.

## Statistical Methods

Data were analyzed using SAS. Statistical tests performed included T tests and multiple regression.

## DATA ANALYSIS

### General Medicine Data Editing Processing and Analysis Framework

Data from supplemental encounter forms were merged with data from patient claims. Tables 41–1 through 41–4 provide sample reports with actual data included. A description of each vertical column heading follows:

**Table 41–1** Sample Report Description  (Academic Health Sites Only)

| Health status level | Count | Avg pri | Avg sup | Phy chg | Anc chg | Tot chg |
|---|---|---|---|---|---|---|
| Excellent | 440 | 32.97 | 11.25 | 40.64 | 18.13 | 58.77 |
| Very good | 920 | 32.77 | 10.61 | 40.69 | 20.62 | 61.31 |
| Good | 1693 | 34.69 | 11.32 | 42.50 | 23.29 | 65.78 |
| Fair | 1669 | 34.46 | 9.02 | 42.27 | 21.76 | 64.03 |
| Poor | 458 | 34.05 | 5.94 | 40.26 | 19.85 | 60.11 |

Courtesy of 3M Health Information Systems, Wallingford, Connecticut.

**Table 41–2** Sample Report Description (Nonacademic Health Sites Only)

| Health status level | Count | Avg pri | Avg sup | Phy chg | Anc chg | Tot chg |
|---|---|---|---|---|---|---|
| Excellent | 218 | 20.02 | 6.74 | 36.82 | 22.50 | 62.33 |
| Very good | 601 | 19.82 | 6.43 | 36.40 | 27.63 | 64.04 |
| Good | 1069 | 19.73 | 7.49 | 36.19 | 22.06 | 58.25 |
| Fair | 926 | 20.15 | 6.37 | 37.18 | 25.85 | 63.04 |
| Poor | 312 | 21.88 | 6.56 | 40.91 | 34.81 | 75.71 |

Courtesy of 3M Health Information Systems, Wallingford, Connecticut.

**Table 41–3** Sample Report Description (Academic Health Sites Only)

| Diastolic BP | Patient count | Average visit time |
|---|---|---|
| ≥100 | 181 | 4.08 |
| 95–100 | 34 | 3.41 |
| 90–95 | 186 | 3.26 |
| <90 | 899 | 2.95 |

Courtesy of 3M Health Information Systems, Wallingford, Connecticut.

**Table 41–4** Sample Report Description (Nonacademic Health Sites Only)

| Diastolic BP | Patient count | Average visit time |
|---|---|---|
| ≥100 | 62 | 3.50 |
| 95–100 | 29 | 3.17 |
| 90–95 | 89 | 2.75 |
| <90 | 224 | 2.20 |

Courtesy of 3M Health Information Systems, Wallingford, Connecticut.

- *Health status level* refers to one of the health status domains measured at every visit. This domain is the general health status assessment.
- *Count* refers to the number of visits for that health status category. This information was obtained from both the supplemental and claim forms. These two forms needed to match by date and patient dummy identifier for the information to be included in the data analysis.
- *Avg pri* refers to the average primary provider time during the visit This information was obtained from the supplemental form.
- *Avg sup* refers to the average number of supplies (radiology, ancillary tests) ordered per patient. This was obtained from the claim form.
- *Phy chg* refers to the translation, using salary information obtained from Medicare RBRVS, of time to charges.
- *Anc chg* refers to the translation, using HCFA payment rates, of specific ancillary categories, such as cardiograms, into dollars.
- *Tot chg* refers to the sum of the physician and ancillary charges.

| Change | Median health status | Cases | Provider time |
|---|---|---|---|
| Stable | 1 | 13 | 31.9 |
| | 2 | 36 | 30.4 |
| | 3 | 104 | 31.7 |
| | 4 | 177 | 32.3 |
| | 5 | 61 | 38.1 |

Courtesy of 3M Health Information Systems, Wallingford, Connecticut.

## Results

The independent variables tested in this study did not have a strong or meaningful relationship with resource consumption at the visit level. Thus, while the data are virtually always in the expected direction (as demonstrated in the sample tables), the $R^2$ is always quite low, whether the independent variable is a functional status measure or a physiologic measure, such as glucose level. The highest $R^2$ for any variable is approximately 0.03.

## Emergency Room Services Data Analysis

Data from supplemental encounter forms were merged with data from patient claims. Once the data were determined to be valid, they were formatted into several reports. Table 41–5 is a sample report with actual data included. A description of each vertical column heading follows:

- All categories beginning with the letter *a* refer to an APG.
- *Tmp* refers to temperature.
- *Pul* refers to arterial blood gas.
- *Glu* refers to glucose.
- *Sys* refers to systolic blood pressure.
- *Dias* refers to diastolic blood pressure.
- *Hct* refers to hematocrit.
- *N* refers to the number of records that had the independent variable in question.

The remaining columns refer to statistical measures.

The independent variables tested in this study do not have a strong or meaningful relationship with emergency room contact time:

- *Physician time.* The correlation between physician time and these clinical indicators is virtually nonexistent. None of the variables had an $R^2$ higher than 0.015. Only two, $ARTO_2$ (arterial oxygen) and alcho (alcohol) had an $R^2$ greater than 0.01, with alcohol having a negative relationship. The other variables have an $R^2$ of less than 0.01.
- *Nonphysician time.* The relationship between nonphysician time and the clinical indicators tends to be stronger, albeit marginally so. ARTPH (arterial PH) and O2 (oxygen saturation) have an $R^2$ of 0.06. The rest of the variables had an $R^2$ of less than 0.01.

**Table 41–5** Sample Report Description

| Variable | N | Missing | Mean | Median | TrMean | StDev | SEMean |
|---|---|---|---|---|---|---|---|
| timeoth | 25448 | 9883 | 35.203 | 23.000 | 28.605 | 46.933 | 0.294 |
| timemd | 25448 | 9883 | 42.39 | 30.00 | 37.02 | 42.58 | 0.27 |
| timetot | 25448 | 9883 | 77.59 | 56.00 | 68.41 | 72.13 | 0.45 |
| a501tmp | 209 | 35122 | 2.6459 | 3.0000 | 2.6085 | 0.6927 | 0.0479 |
| a501pul | 209 | 35122 | 3.9665 | 4.0000 | 3.9471 | 0.7492 | 0.0518 |
| a502tmp | 554 | 34777 | 2.2978 | 2.0000 | 2.2189 | 0.5859 | 0.0249 |
| a502pul | 571 | 34760 | 3.5797 | 3.0000 | 3.5322 | 0.6638 | 0.0278 |
| a503tmp | 221 | 35110 | 2.0271 | 2.0000 | 2.0000 | 0.1629 | 0.0110 |
| a503pul | 238 | 35093 | 3.0462 | 3.0000 | 3.0140 | 0.2793 | 0.0181 |
| a542tmp | 2800 | 32531 | 2.2557 | 2.0000 | 2.1794 | 0.5282 | 0.0100 |
| a542pul | 2857 | 32474 | 3.6241 | 4.0000 | 3.5986 | 0.7072 | 0.0132 |
| a562tmp | 195 | 35136 | 2.3436 | 2.0000 | 2.2686 | 0.6091 | 0.0436 |
| a562pul | 195 | 35136 | 3.7128 | 4.0000 | 3.6743 | 0.7862 | 0.0563 |
| a661tmp | 352 | 34979 | 3.1222 | 3.0000 | 3.0823 | 0.3840 | 0.0205 |
| a661pul | 352 | 34979 | 3.1222 | 3.0000 | 3.0823 | 0.3840 | 0.0205 |
| a651glu | 31 | 35300 | 318.8 | 318.0 | 309.6 | 157.8 | 28.3 |
| a572sys | 147 | 35184 | 3.2381 | 3.0000 | 3.1955 | 0.5654 | 0.0466 |
| a572dias | 146 | 35185 | 2.5342 | 2.0000 | 2.4848 | 0.6763 | 0.0560 |
| a692hct | 32 | 35299 | 25.531 | 25.000 | 25.214 | 5.483 | 0.969 |
| a692pul | 102 | 35229 | 3.0686 | 3.0000 | 3.0326 | 0.3521 | 0.0349 |

Courtesy of 3M Health Information Systems, Wallingford, Connecticut.

---

It is conceivable that controlling for diagnosis would enhance the predictive power of at least some of these variables. Accordingly, controls by APG were introduced and selected indicators (those relevant to the diagnosis associated with the APG) were analyzed.

- *Physician time.* Controlling for diagnosis by using APG does improve the correlations between physician time and clinical indicators. However, the $R^2$ never exceeded 0.04 (a692hct, hematocrit in APG 692, Anemia). Even these results are somewhat questionable, as there were only 32 cases. Other correlations were somewhat less; most had an $R^2$ of slightly more than 0.01.

- *Nonphysician time.* Controlling for diagnosis does not strengthen the relationship between nonphysician time and clinical indicators. Correlations remain about the same.
- *Total time.* As above, the correlation between total time and clinical indicator is a function of both physician and nonphysician time.

## DISCUSSION

This study attempted to identify a discrete set of variables that might improve the ability of several types of APGs to predict resource consumption: chronic medical conditions and emergency room services. In particular, this study examined the following hypotheses.

*Selected patient characteristics, such as level of blood pressure and aspects of functional status, correlate with resource consumption of general medical services during a visit.* Resource consumption was defined here as a combination of primary care provider time and the cost of ancillary services. Of note, this study did document a significant difference in visit time between academic and nonacademic health sites. However, health status and selected clinical findings, such as blood pressure level, did not improve the $R^2$ of the medical APGS. Thus, for example, knowing the blood pressure level did not enhance the ability of the hypertension APG to better predict resource consumption during an ambulatory visit or mini-episode. In addition, knowing aspects of functional status, such as the level of mobility, did not enhance the ability of the back APG to better predict resource consumption during an ambulatory visit.

There are two likely explanations for these findings. The most likely explanation is that, while variables, such as blood pressure level, are relevant in explaining resource consumption over a period of time, they may not be important for explaining resource consumption during a single visit. Thus, for example, a hypertensive patient with consistently high blood pressure may have more visits over a period of time than a hypertensive patient who typically has normal blood pressure and thus has only occasional check-ups.

The second possible explanation for the negative findings is that variations in practice patterns exist between facilities and between providers within a single facility. Wennberg and colleagues have amply documented the phenomenon of variations in practice patterns of different procedures between hospitals in geographic proximity with each other.[2]

*Selected patient characteristics, such as blood pressure level and temperature, correlate with resource consumption during an emergency room visit.* Resource consumption was defined here as a combination of provider time and the cost of ancillary services. The lack of confirmation for the hypothesis pertaining to emergency room services may relate to the quality (reliability) of the data collected. While all emergency room directors were supportive of the study and understood its potential financial implications for the payment of emergency room services in New York State, many data elements were not collected for all appropriate visits.

A number of limitations in this study must be highlighted. First, it is possible that variations in resource consumption might occur over longer episodes of time. Variations in resource consumptions may not be apparent during a visit or mini-episode. This study was also conducted in one geographic area (New York State), not at sites throughout the United States. The issue of episodes of illness does not identify possible limitations in the data collected from emergency rooms. Issues pertaining to data quality at the collection site were identified. For example, providers often did not record the time they spent with patients. Over 30 percent of patients did not have any visit time coded for any physician personnel—a clearly impossible option. Further study of resource consumption in emergency rooms is important, as significant resources are consumed in this setting and managed care organizations have different rules regarding emergency room access.

NOTES

1. J.H. Wasson et al., "Adolescent Health and Social Problems: A Method for Detection and Early Management," *Archives of Family Medicine* 4 (1995): 51–56.
2. J. Wennberg et al., "Variations in Medical Care Among Small Areas," *Scientific American* 246 (1982): 120–134.

# APPENDIX 41–A

# New York State (New York Department of Health Project Participants)

## Mental Health Services

- Community Health Plan: Not-for-profit staff model HMO
- Kingston Psychiatric Center: State run and funded community-based outpatient facilities
- Creedmore Psychiatric Center: State run and funded community-based outpatient facilities
- Horizon Community Center: Not-for-profit community-based health centers
- Mid-Hudson Family Practice Center: Interdisciplinary medical group practice

## Rehabilitation Services

Private, not-for-profit institutions:

- Rusk Rehabilitation Institute
- SUNY Upstate Medical Center
- Strong Memorial Hospital
- Lutheran Medical Center

Publicly funded, state-administered:

- Helen Hayes Rehabilitation Institute

## General Medical Services

- Mid-Hudson Family Health Center: Private, not-for-profit family practice

- Strong Memorial Hospital: Private, not-for-profit academic, medical center
- Lutheran Medical Center: Private, not-for-profit, hospital outpatient department
- Hudson Headwaters Health Center: Private, not-for-profit, rural health center
- Montefiore General Medical Clinic: Private, not-for-profit academic center

CHAPTER 42

# Improving the Prediction of Rehabilitation Outpatient Services Using Patient Characteristics

*Norbert Goldfield, Richard Averill, Thelma Grant, Yvette Wang, Dennis Graziano, Herbert Fillmore, and William Fisher*

The study described in this chapter examined whether additional data elements not currently collected on the standard claim form would increase the ability of ambulatory patient groups (APGs) to predict resource consumption of rehabilitation services. For six months, various clinical settings were used to collect additional information not included on the standard patient claim form. The testing of the proposed additional data elements was performed in many sites in New York State in conjunction with the New York Department of Health.

The specific hypothesis tested in this study was that patient characteristics, such as functional health status, predict resource consumption of outpatient rehabilitation health services over a one-month period of time. The results of the study were as follows: selected patient characteristics, such as diagnosis and aspects of functional status, correlate with resource consumption of rehabilitation health services over a one-month period of time. Diagnosis alone, a patient characteristic already collected on the claim form, has an $R^2$ of 0.092. Inclusion of additional elements, such as time since hospital discharge, if any, and aspects of functional status, increased the $R^2$ to 0.195.

This prospective study represents the first time selected patient characteristics were utilized to predict resource consumption for rehabilitation health

Courtesy 3M Health Information Systems, Wallingford, Connecticut.

services over a mini-episode period of time. The results highlight the importance of better understanding the relationship between patient characteristics and resource consumption of health services. This study begins the process of understanding the relationship between resource consumption and patient characteristics for those patients whose consumption of resources has been historically difficult to understand utilizing data available from a claim form.

## BACKGROUND

APGs were developed, pursuant to a grant from the Health Care Financing Administration, as a classification system for ambulatory services. The APGs can be used as the basic unit of payment in a prospective payment system for outpatient services. The initial APG research was completed in December 1990 and resulted in a classification system (APG 1.0) consisting of 298 patient groups covering all outpatient services provided in hospital outpatient departments. The most recent APG research resulted in a second version of the APGs (APG 2.0), consisting of 290 groups—some changed from the first version. Both versions of the APGs use only information present on the existing claim form.

Data not currently collected on the claim form may be useful for clinical areas that historically have not been well defined in either *International Classification of Diseases, Ninth Edition, Clinical Modification* (ICD-9-CM) or *Current Procedural Terminology, Fourth Edition* (CPT-4).[1] For rehabilitation, patient descriptors, such as health status aspects or when (and if) the patient was discharged from a hospital for the condition under outpatient treatment, may also be important predictors of resource consumption. As a consequence, it is important to consider the use of additional patient level variables that might characterize patient conditions better than is possible using the existing ICD-9-CM or CPT-4 codes. Any improvement may have the effect of improving the APG classification system, as APGs are dependent on these two coding systems.

Additional data might also be useful in distinguishing between visits to the emergency room and visits to the outpatient department. The latter are classified into a medical APG. For emergency room visits, certain patient variables, such as the patient's temperature and the patient's living situation, may be important predictors of resources consumed. This information is not currently collected in either ICD-9-CM or CPT-4.

In summary, the research discussed in this chapter had the following objectives:

- Identify a discrete set of clinical signs, symptoms, or findings that are not currently collected on the Universal Bill 92 (UB-92) claim form or used in ICD-9-CM or CPT-4 but that could improve the ability of specific APGs to predict resource consumption.
- Collect a sample of outpatient data with the additional data elements and test the extent to which the additional data improve the ability of specific APGs to predict resource consumption.

## STUDY DESIGN

This study involved the collection of information not included on the standard claim form from a variety of clinical settings over a six-month period. The additional information consists of patient characteristics thought to be useful in improving the ability of APGs to predict resource consumption.

This study is nonrandom and nonrepresentative and is not meant to be definitive. It is a starting point for further research. The testing of the proposed diagnosis code modifications was performed in many sites in New York State in conjunction with the New York Department of Health (NYDOH). New York State was chosen because a considerable amount of work had been done by the department of health to better understand outpatient services.

### Site Selection and Data Collection Process

Appropriate sites were identified by New York State Department of Health personnel. These sites varied in terms of ownership and types of patients served. For example, in the area of mental health, both private and public, managed care and non-managed-care sites were sought. NYDOH representatives contacted the institutions to determine their level of interest.

If a site expressed an interest in the project, representatives from NYDOH and 3M HIS presented to the site's clinical and administrative staff the purpose and the mechanics of the data collection process. If the staff still expressed interest in participating in the project, they were trained in the objectives and content of the study. NYDOH staff assisted in all the data collection and processing issues. Additionally, in an effort to maintain a high level of interest in the project, site personnel were provided interim and post-project presentations of their data.

The following rehabilitation sites participated (all are private, not-for-profit institutions except the last, which is publicly funded and state administered):

- Rusk Rehabilitation Institute
- SUNY Upstate Medical Center
- Strong Memorial Hospital
- Lutheran Medical Center
- Helen Hayes Rehabilitation Institute

Definition and resolution of all issues pertaining to data collection and processing constituted a key administrative project objective. Both claims data and clinic-based data had to be collected and merged. There were challenges associated with each data source. The vast majority of sites that agreed to participate submitted data that could be analyzed.

There were two general data-processing tasks that required attention:

- working with clinical settings and information services at participating sites to determine the formats in which data collected on site would be sent to NYDOH
- working with information services at participating sites to ensure that claims data extracts were sent by the institution to NYDOH in a timely and accurate manner

Once these data-processing tasks were accomplished, on-site training and data collection began. On-site training utilized a detailed training manual developed to assist individual sites in collecting the data. The manual contained

- project background information
- an H-Code chapter
- examples on how to code data elements
- most frequently asked questions pertaining to the research project
- background scientific articles providing further details

A bimonthly newsletter was sent to every participating site to encourage commitment to the project. After four to six weeks of data collection, initial data were processed, and a health professional from either NYDOH or 3M HIS (or both) visited each site to provide feedback to clinical and administrative professionals. This was done in an effort to maintain interest in the project and to ensure the highest possible accuracy and completeness in the data items collected. Once the project was completed, 3M HIS personnel offered to return to sites to provide a summary of data results.

When data collection was completed, claims and clinical data were sent to NYDOH. Clinical data were first transferred, if necessary, from paper to electronic format. The two data streams were then merged, and dummy record numbers were assigned to replace the patient record numbers. A data tape containing both claims and clinical data was then sent to 3M HIS.

## Development of H-Codes

Each of the variables described below was included in the H-Code chapter because it was

- thought to have a high probability of indicating severity (associated with the consumption of more resources)
- based on information either routinely collected by health care professionals or very familiar to them
- derived, whenever possible, from standardized items already tested in the literature (e.g., mental health status and functioning derived from Axis V of DSM-IV)

Independent and dependent variables considered useful in refining rehabilitation and mental illness APGs were not collected for every visit. This was due to the difficulty of collecting additional information on every visit together with a move toward managed care that reimburses for services provided over a period of time. While the type of visit (e.g., family visit versus individual therapy visit) could be identified on a visit basis, additional patient information was collected monthly. A month was adopted as a "bridge" between an individual visit in traditional fee-for-service and a one-year period of time summarized under capitation.

Version 2.0 of the medical APGs uses ICD-9-CM diagnoses and CPT procedure codes. Due to frequent change of provider in the ambulatory medical setting, improvement in the medical APGs was sought at the individual visit level. As data would have to be collected for every visit, a very short additional data set for potential refinement of the medical APGs was developed. Similarly, refinements in the medical APGs with specific attention to the emergency room also needed to be performed at the individual visit level. Again, a short additional data set was developed.

The additional information in the H-Codes completely yet briefly describes health services in the areas tested in the project.

Two types of H-Codes were collected: independent and dependent variables. Each category of code is described below, together with an explanation why the information was collected.

## Independent Variables

- *Functional health status.* Determination of which domains of functional health status to monitor was challenging. Two functional health status measures were studied for possible use: the Patient Evaluation and Conference System (PECS) and the Functional Independence Measure (FIM). A significant amount of research has been performed on both measures.[2] The PECS was chosen because it was intended to cover both inpatient and outpatient settings, whereas the FIM covers inpatient settings only. Many different domains (specific functional status areas, such as eating or walking) were considered for possible use as independent variables.

  There are two reasons for including a large number of domains in the final data set collected in this part of the project. First, no literature was available on which domains were likely to be most useful in predicting resource consumption. Second, the panel of experts consulted for this phase of the project felt that a large number of variables was necessary to be certain that all the appropriate domains were chosen.

- *Time of discharge from a hospital.* Time of discharge from a hospital may be relevant. For example, an individual recently discharged from the hospital for a stroke may consume more resources than a stroke patient at the same functional status level discharged more than one year ago.

## Dependent Variables

- *Provider cost.* Provider cost was based on the time per patient per month spent by each of the treating therapies (physical, occupational, and speech therapy). Time spent with the patient was converted to dollars based on salaries of therapists in the New York City area. Salary structure was obtained from two of the participating sites, both in the New York City area.

- *Equipment cost.* Equipment cost was based on equipment used by or given to the patient. Equipment used was identified on a monthly basis on the supplemental form by the treating therapist.

## DATA ANALYSIS

### Data Editing Process and Analysis Framework

Data from supplemental encounter forms were merged with data from patient claims. The merge algorithm for rehabilitation services is shown below.

- Dummy record numbers replaced patient record numbers to preserve patient confidentiality.
- A month of patient data was allowed only if a supplemental form was completed during the month. This was done to eliminate any instances in which the supplemental form was misplaced or not completed.
- Patient months without any visits were discarded. This was done to eliminate any instances in which the patient visits were misplaced or not completed.
- The supplemental form completion date and dummy record number were used as the keys to join the patient visits that occurred during the month. This was done to ensure patient services were assigned in a consistent manner to the appropriate supplemental form.
- Patient months with no diagnoses coded were discarded, as these data could not be used in any analysis.
- Patients for whom disequilibrium or mental illness diagnostic categories were identified as the reason for visit were discarded. This was done for two reasons: disequilibrium was treated at only one institution, and mental illness treatment in a rehabilitation setting was not considered to be part of the rehabilitation portion of this study.

The merge algorithm resulted in patient records being eliminated in the manner shown in Table 42–1. Once the data were edited to be certain that only valid data were analyzed, they were formatted into a variety of reports. Table 42–2 provides a sample report with actual data included. A description of each vertical column heading follows:

- *H-Code* refers to the H-Code specified in the supplementary code. *H56-* refers to the supplementary forms for which no code in this domain was checked off.

**Table 42–1** Rehabilitation Edits Count and Logic

| Step | Description | Total | Percentage |
|------|-------------|-------|------------|
| 1 | Identify patients with supplemental form(s) for one month. | 2,365 | 100.00 |
| 2 | Eliminate patient months without any visit. | 1,991 | 84.19 |
| 3 | Eliminate patient months with no rehabilitation diagnostic category defined. | 1,946 | 82.28 |
| 4 | Eliminate patient months for whom disequilibrium or mental illness diagnostic categories were identified as the reason for visit. | 1,872 | 79.15 |

Note: Total refers to patient months of rehabilitation services.

Courtesy of 3M Health Information Systems, Wallingford, Connecticut.

- *Patient count (pat cnt)* refers to the number of months of patient visits for which a supplementary form was coded. This is derived from the claim form.
- *Average visit count per patient per month (avg vst cnt/pat/month)* refers to the average number of visits per patient for a month of services for physical therapy (PT), occupational therapy (OT), or speech therapy (SP). This is derived from the claim form.
- *Total average (tot avg)* refers to the number arrived at by averaging all three therapy averages. This is derived from the claim form.
- *Average equipment count per patient per month (Avg equip cnt/pat/month)* refers to the number of pieces of equipment used during a month of services for either PT, OT, or SP services. The specific items were checked off by treating therapists at the time of completion of the supplementary form.
- *Total average equipment per patient per month (tot avg)* refers to the average equipment count per month used in all three therapies.
- *Per visit (per vst)* refers to the average equipment count used in a patient visit.
- *Cost per patient per month (cost/pat/month)* is divided into staff, equipment (equip), and total.
- *Group description* refers to the level of functional status for that particular domain (acceptance/understanding of disability). The level ranges from extremely poor to good.

**Table 42–2** Aggregated Report across Months for Acceptance or Understanding of Disability

| H-Code | Pat cnt | Avg vst cnt/pat month | | | | Avg equip cnt/pat month | | | | | Cost/pat/month | | | Group description |
|---|---|---|---|---|---|---|---|---|---|---|---|---|---|---|
| | | PT | OT | SP | Total avg | PT | OT | SP | Tot avg | Per vst | Staff | Equip | Total | |
| H56- | 0 | 0.00 | 0.00 | 0.00 | 0.00 | 0.00 | 0.00 | 0.00 | 0.00 | 0.00 | 0.00 | 0.00 | 0.00 | No code |
| H561 | 6 | 5.50 | 0.00 | 6.00 | 5.67 | 0.25 | 0.00 | 0.00 | 0.17 | 0.03 | 170.10 | 0.00 | 170.10 | Extremely poor |
| H562 | 20 | 6.00 | 0.00 | 6.88 | 6.70 | 1.50 | 0.00 | 0.62 | 0.80 | 0.12 | 201.00 | 12.65 | 213.65 | Moderately to mildly satisfactory |
| H563 | 65 | 5.43 | 0.00 | 6.41 | 6.31 | 0.14 | 0.00 | 0.55 | 0.51 | 0.08 | 189.30 | 8.00 | 197.30 | Mostly satisfactory |
| H564 | 31 | 3.83 | 0.00 | 5.80 | 5.42 | 0.00 | 0.00 | 0.96 | 0.77 | 0.14 | 162.60 | 3.19 | 165.79 | Good |

Courtesy of 3M Health Information Systems, Wallingford, Connecticut.

## Results of Data Analysis

Tables 42–3 and 42–4 contain final statistical results for the groups that were created after detailed examination of the data in conjunction with clinical input. The average cost of personnel services and average amount of equipment are provided in the first table. The verbal headings of the vertical columns are virtually the same as in Table 42–2. In Table 42–4 coefficient of variation, standard deviation, and mean are provided for each of the groups created after data analysis and clinical input.

## Classification Tree

This portion of the analysis describes the classification of rehabilitation services and details the explanatory power of this classification.

The final model has an $R^2$ of 0.133 for total visits during one month and an $R^2$ of 0.195 for total cost during one month. The description of the final model follows. Quadriplegia represents an illness that typically consumes sigiiificant treatment resources. Two groups of quadriplegics were created, with the axis of classification being the presence or absence of a feeding problem. The quadriplegia group that did have a feeding problem (Group 1) consumed on average $293 of services per month, while the quadriplegia group that did not have a feeding problem (Group 2) consumed on average $192 per month.

The next set of groups (Groups 3–6) used diagnostic information as the initial axis of classification. The second axis of classification was whether or not a recent discharge, if any, occurred from a hospital. Recent discharge from the hospital might indicate reception of more services than in the case of a patient who had not been recently discharged. Two other variables were utilized in the formation of these groups: ability to prepare a light meal and acceptance or understanding of disability.

Group 6 consisted of patients who had hemiplegia, above-knee amputation, or complicated fractures; were recently discharged from a hospital; and had difficulty preparing light meals. These patients consumed $342 per month. Patients who had the same diagnoses and were recently discharged from a hospital but could prepare a light meal consumed $170 per month (Group 5). Patients with the same diagnoses but who were not recently discharged and who did have acceptance or understanding of the disability under treatment consumed $165 (Group 4), while those with the same diagnoses, also not

**Table 42–3** Rehabilitation Statistics for Grouping Structure

| Grp | Pat cnt | Avg vst cnt/pat/month | | | | Avg equip cnt/pat/month | | | | | Cost/pat/month | | | Group description |
|---|---|---|---|---|---|---|---|---|---|---|---|---|---|---|
| | | PT | OT | SP | Total avg | PT | OT | SP | Tot avg | Per vst | Staff | Equip | Total | |
| 1 | 74 | 5.56 | 7.80 | 7.11 | 6.45 | 6.00 | 8.40 | 3.54 | 5.39 | 0.84 | 193.50 | 99.84 | 293.34 | Quadriplegia & with feeding prob |
| 2 | 188 | 4.97 | 5.25 | 6.13 | 5.66 | 2.45 | 1.25 | 0.60 | 1.31 | 0.23 | 169.80 | 24.74 | 194.54 | Quadriplegia & without (wo) feeding prob |
| 3 | 198 | 3.51 | 4.72 | 4.34 | 4.03 | 1.76 | 2.44 | 0.48 | 1.19 | 0.29 | 120.90 | 13.34 | 134.24 | Hemiplegia, above-knee (AK) amput, complicated (comp) fracture with acceptance of disability |
| 4 | 211 | 4.01 | 5.10 | 5.35 | 4.89 | 2.00 | 1.20 | 0.88 | 1.27 | 0.26 | 146.70 | 17.90 | 164.60 | Hemiplegia, AK amput, comp fracture & wo acceptance of disability (accept) |
| 5 | 158 | 3.82 | 5.69 | 5.33 | 4.78 | 2.03 | 4.85 | 1.01 | 1.72 | 0.36 | 143.40 | 27.10 | 170.50 | Hemiplegia, AK amput, comp fracture & with ability to pre-pare light meal & recent hosp discharge |
| 6 | 64 | 6.00 | 9.33 | 8.42 | 8.22 | 3.73 | 3.73 | 5.37 | 4.70 | 0.57 | 246.60 | 95.44 | 342.04 | Hemiplegia, AK amput, comp fracture & wo recent hosp discharge & with ability to prepare light meal |

*continues*

**Table 42–3** continued

| Grp | Pat cnt | Avg vst cnt/pat/month | | | | Avg equip cnt/pat/month | | | | | Cost/pat/month | | | Group description |
|---|---|---|---|---|---|---|---|---|---|---|---|---|---|---|
| | | PT | OT | SP | Total avg | PT | OT | SP | Tot avg | Per vst | Staff | Equip | Total | |
| 7 | 514 | 2.58 | 2.15 | 3.40 | 2.67 | 1.98 | 2.14 | 0.85 | 1.71 | 0.64 | 80.10 | 20.51 | 100.61 | Paraplegia, burns, pain, simp fracture & with accept |
| 8 | 305 | 2.97 | 3.42 | 3.91 | 3.25 | 2.85 | 3.36 | 0.97 | 2.43 | 0.75 | 97.50 | 40.40 | 138.00 | Paraplegia, burns, pain, simp fracture & wo accept |
| 9 | 98 | 2.76 | 1.86 | 4.66 | 3.32 | 1.53 | 1.71 | 0.78 | 1.30 | 0.39 | 99.60 | 21.07 | 120.67 | Paraplegia, burns, pain, simp fracture with recent hosp discharge with ability to prepare light meal |
| 10 | 62 | 4.47 | 6.73 | 8.89 | 5.66 | 5.11 | 2.00 | 6.22 | 4.52 | 0.80 | 169.80 | 92.73 | 262.53 | Paraplegia, burns, pain, simp fracture & with recent hosp discharge & wo ability to prepare light meal |

Courtesy of 3M Health Information Systems, Wallingford, Connecticut.

recently discharged, but who did not have understanding of the disability under treatment consumed $134 per month (Group 3).

The last set of groups (Groups 7–10) used the following diagnoses as the axis of classification: paraplegia, burns, pain, and simple fracture. Those patients who had a recent hospital stay and who could not prepare a light meal consumed $262 per month of rehabilitative services (Group 10). Similar patients who could prepare a light meal consumed $120 per month (Group 9). Similar patients who did not have a recent hospitalization but did have an acceptance or understanding of the disability consumed $138 per month (Group 8), while those who did not have an acceptance or understanding of the disability consumed $100 per month (Group 7).

The coefficients of variation for the different rehabilitation groups are provided in Table 42–4. The relatively low CVs (ranging from 0.53 to 0.96) emanate from the relatively tight (0.65 to 1.31) distribution of staff costs. The group (Group 10) with a relatively high CV (1.31) had only 62 patients. There is considerable variation in equipment costs (CVs from 0.8 to 2.5), and several categories have patient months with minimal to no equipment costs. The question of reliable coding of equipment use arises in those categories having patient months with no equipment costs.

## DISCUSSION

This study attempted to identify a discrete set of variables that might improve the ability of several types of APGs to predict resource consumption for rehabilitation services. In particular, it examined the following hypothesis: Selected patient characteristics, such as diagnosis and aspects of functional status, correlate with resource consumption of rehabilitation health services over a one-month period of time. (Resource consumption was defined as a combination of rehabilitation treatment therapies and equipment cost.)

Diagnosis alone, a patient characteristic already collected on the claim form, has an $R^2$ of 0.092. This is not surprising, as many diagnoses, such as quadriplegia, include aspects of functional status within the diagnosis itself. However, the inclusion of additional elements, such as time since hospital discharge, if any, and aspects of functional status, improve the $R^2$ to 0.14 for total visits and 0.195 for total cost for one month. At the same time, functional health status measurement is familiar to the vast majority of providers of rehabilitation services. Many institutions already collect this type of information

**Table 42–4** Coefficients of Variation, Means, and Standard Deviations for Rehabilitation Grouping Structure

| Group | N | Staff Cost | | | Equipment Cost | | | Total Cost | | |
|---|---|---|---|---|---|---|---|---|---|---|
| | | Mean | SD | CV | Mean | SD | CV | Mean | SD | CV |
| 1 | 188 | 169.95 | 116.29 | 0.6843 | 24.74 | 51.94 | 2.0991 | 194.69 | 133.39 | 0.6851 |
| 2 | 74 | 193.38 | 127.29 | 0.6563 | 99.84 | 93.53 | 0.9368 | 293.22 | 156.43 | 0.5335 |
| 3 | 198 | 120.91 | 106.14 | 0.8778 | 13.34 | 33.53 | 2.5135 | 134.25 | 114.47 | 0.8527 |
| 4 | 211 | 146.59 | 95.84 | 0.6538 | 17.90 | 39.01 | 2.1787 | 164.49 | 102.53 | 0.6233 |
| 5 | 158 | 143.35 | 115.80 | 0.8078 | 27.10 | 48.91 | 1.8049 | 170.46 | 134.54 | 0.7893 |
| 6 | 64 | 246.56 | 172.83 | 0.7010 | 95.44 | 82.64 | 0.8659 | 342.00 | 192.01 | 0.5614 |
| 7 | 514 | 80.20 | 77.88 | 0.9711 | 20.51 | 44.21 | 2.1551 | 100.71 | 88.88 | 0.8825 |
| 8 | 305 | 97.77 | 87.68 | 0.8968 | 40.50 | 61.00 | 1.5063 | 138.27 | 100.72 | 0.7284 |
| 9 | 98 | 99.49 | 104.42 | 11.0496 | 21.07 | 40.59 | 1.9260 | 120.56 | 116.10 | 0.9630 |
| 10 | 62 | 169.84 | 222.52 | 1.3102 | 92.73 | 81.36 | 0.8773 | 262.57 | 237.66 | 0.9051 |

Courtesy of 3M Health Information Systems, Wallingford, Connecticut.

on a regular basis. Further research on larger groups of patients is necessary to evaluate the impact of specific aspects of functional status (e.g., functional deficits in hearing) that could not be assessed for lack of a large enough data set.

## CONCLUSIONS

This prospective study represents the first time selected patient characteristics were utilized to predict resource consumption for rehabilitation health services over a mini-episode period of time. This work is particularly important at a time of significantly increased interest in managed care. In addition, this study represents the first effort to quantify the relationship between selected patient characteristics and case management time.

The results of this study highlight the importance of better understanding the relationship between patient characteristics and resource consumption of health services. The current push toward managed care demands more research be done to increase our understanding of the determinants of resource consumption in health services.

This study begins the process of understanding the relationship between resource consumption and patient characteristics for those patients whose consumption of resources have been historically difficult to understand utilizing data available from a claim form.

## RECOMMENDATIONS

The work summarized in this chapter suggests several recommendations:

- For certain services, such as rehabilitation services, the Health Care Financing Administration could consider a demonstration project that would evaluate payment for outpatient mental health services or rehabilitation services using a quasi-capitated (e.g., monthly) methodology based on the variables collected in the study. The research summarized in this chapter could provide a methodological approach and represent a bridge between fee-for-service and managed care. There are carve-outs for managed care rehabilitation services, and thus a similar project would have relevance to today's health care market.

- An important follow-up research project could examine the patient characteristics that would predict resource consumption of inpatient and outpatient rehabilitation and/or mental health services. This project would complete the bridge between fee-for-service and managed care. Such a research project would examine the costs of services for stroke patients, for example, not only in the outpatient setting but also in the hospital and nursing home setting.

---

**NOTES**

1. S.F. Jencks et al., "Bringing Excluded Psychiatric Facilities under the Medicare Prospective Payment System. A Review of Research Evidence and Policy Options," *Medical Care* 25 (1987): S1–S51.
2. R.F. Harvey and H.M Jellinek, "Functional Performance Assessment: A Program Approach," *Archives of Physical Medical and Rehabilitation* 62 (1981): 456–461.

# Index

## A

Abrams, Chad, 541
Accountability, 96–97
  and benchmarking, 98
  meaning of, 96
  multiple approaches for, 96–97
Accutrex, Inc., 113
Acuity adjustment, 102–105
  adjustment methods, 104–105
  audiences for, 102–104
  dangers to validity of, 104
  data sources for, 105
  rates, information from, 103
  as research information, 103–104
Acute illness, episodes-of-illness systems, 528
Adjustment of data. *See* Case mix adjusted data; Risk adjustment
Admission source, payments by, 425–427
Aetna Health Plan, 113, 113–114
A. Foster Higgins, Inc., 113
Age
  mortality analysis, 446–447
  payments by patient age, 423–425, 434–437
Agency for Health Care Administration (Florida), 122–127

Agency for Health Care Policy and Research, 23, 78
Age per se, 166
Aid to Families with Dependent Children, 542, 552
AIDS, Maryland Medicaid model, 548, 551
All-inclusive packaging, 306–306
All-patient DRGs (AP-DRGs), 395–397
  development of, 395–397
  updates, 397
  use of, 164
All-patient-refined DRGs (APR-DRGs), 160, 162–168, 397–399
  applied to managed care, 162
  basis of, 166
  class assignments, development criteria, 166–167
  information systems configuration, 355–363
  managed care example, 364–368
  patient descriptors, 398
  and quality improvement, 162
  recent developments, 168
  risk adjustment software, 138
  scope of use, 165
  scores in, 166
  secondary diagnosis, impact of, 167
  severity logic, 356–364
  subclasses of, 166, 397–399

All-payer DRGs (AP-DRGs), 166
Ambulatory care
    administrative complexity of, 158–159
    classification problems, 159–160
    profiling of services, 225–228
Ambulatory care groups (ACGs), 158
    Maryland Medicaid model, 544, 546–547
    risk adjustment, 49
Ambulatory case mix systems (ACMS),
    157–160
    bundling of classes, 157, 158
    clinical questions in, 226
    components of, 157–158
    obstacles in development of, 158–160
    statistical questions in, 226–227
Ambulatory patient categories (APCs), 160
Ambulatory patient groups (APGs), 153,
    160–163, 284–286, 289–299
    ancillary service APGs, 161, 296–299
    classification of procedures, 287–288
    compared to DRGs, 160–161, 282, 321
    and continuous quality improvement
        (CQI), 161–162
    databases used for development of, 302–
        303
    data elements, sources of, 286
    historical development of, 155
    initial classification variable, 286–289
    Iowa hospitals system, 215–220
    major diagnostic categories, 286
    medical APGs, 160, 291–296
    for misuse of services, 162
    packaged APGs, 161
    patient characteristics, 285
    payment under, 161
    recent development trends, 168
    risk adjustment, 49
    setting utilized by, 285–286
    significant procedure APGs, 160, 287,
        289–291
    Version 2.0, list of APGs, 337–350
    Versions 1 and 2, 281–282, 301–303
Ambulatory patient groups (APGs) payment
    system, 305–321

alternative systems, 317–321
ancillary discounting, 320
ancillary packaging, 305–308, 310, 333
applicability, 334
charge to cost conversion, 314–315
compared to inpatient payments, 334
components of system, 209, 308
discounting, 308–309, 310
evaluation of alternative formulations,
    313–314
fragmentation of costs, 332
historical charges, 334
hospital characteristics, 322–330
hospital-specific payment adjustments,
    334
identification of visits, 333
outliers, 310, 312–313, 319
outside-hospital ancillaries, 333
payment simulation, 309–313
relative weights computation, 315–317
upcoding, 332
volume of visits, 332
window of time, 310–313, 320–321
American Association of Health Plans
    (AAHP), 7–8
American Medical Accreditation Program
    (AMAP), xix, 30, 229–241
    flowchart of accreditation process, 237
    functions of, 229–230
    physician accreditation approach, 232–
        233
    and professional accountability, 233
    public information provided by, 234–235
    standards in, 235–236, 239–240, 247–
        250
American Medical Association (AMA)
    on collection/release/use of physician-
        specific data, 245–246
    origins of, 229
    physician profiling principles, 243
Ancillary packaging, 161
    alternative lists, 317–319
    APG payments, 305–308, 310
    nonhospital settings, 333

payment outside of hospital, 333
Ancillary service APGs, 161, 296–299
    ancillary tests/procedures, 298
    anesthesia, 298
    chemotherapy, 298–299
    laboratory tests, 297
    pathology, 298
    radiological tests, 297–298
Ancillary service capitation, 202–203
    laboratory services example, 202–203
    pharmacy example, 202
Anesthesia, as APG, 298
Army Ambulatory Care data, 299
Atlas MQ, 115
At-risk conditions, meaning of, 606
Attributes
    control charts for, 182–184
    critical values for, 185
Averill, Richard F., 281, 391, 465, 523, 623, 643, 655

**B**

Bagadia, Farah, 523
Bailey, R. Clifton, 251
Balanced Budget Act of 1997, 282, 484
Barbanel, Josh, 85
Benchmarking, 98–99
    and accountability, 98
    in health care, 98–99
    meaning of, 95, 98
    and outcomes research, 98
    output rates, 98–99
    regional, 377
Bennett, Gregg, 373
Berman, Harris A., 39, 191
Bernstein, Geoffrey, 251
Berwick Hospital Center, 114
Best clinical practice, 268–269, 271
Best demonstrated practice, 369–370
Blue Shield of California. *See* Outpatient
    payment program
Bonus payment, 198
Bradford Regional Medical Center, 114
Breakthrough Initiatives, 133

**C**

California Hospital Outcomes Project, 51
Capitation, 193–198, 201–203
    ancillary service capitation, 202–203
    basis of, 193
    fee-for-service with group capitation, 195
    financial risk, 194
    forms of, 195–196
    group capitation, 196–197
    impact on physician behavior, 196
    physician-hospital organization capitation, 195
    pre-paid, 542–543
    risks involved in, 194
    specialist capitation, 201–202
    withholding, 197–198
Cardiac Surgery Reporting System (New York), 136
Case complexity factor (CCF), computation of, 590
Case mix adjusted data, 72–74
    universal standards for, 131
    value measures in, 133
Case mix systems
    all-patient-refined DRGs (APR-DRGs), 160, 162–168
    ambulatory case mix systems (ACMS), 157–160
    ambulatory patient groups (APGs), 153, 160–163
    complex, meaning of, 392
    diagnosis-related groups (DRGs), 155–156
    historical view, 155–156
    pharmacy data for measurement, 576–595
    purposes of, 575
Central limit theorem, and statistical process control (SPC), 177
Chemotherapy, as APG, 298–299
Chronic illness
    episodes-of-illness systems, 528
    hierarchy of, 606

individual chronic conditions, 604
meaning of, 604
National Association of Children's Hospitals
and Related Institutions (NACHRI) classification, 599–622
Claims data, for physician profiling, 27–29
Classification tree
mental health services study, 632, 636–640
rehabilitation outpatient services study, 664–667
Clinical Complexity Index (CCI), 515
Clinical pathways, severity-adjusted data in computation of, 455–463
Code creep, 58–59
manifestations of, 58
Code fragmentation, minimizing, 284
Codman, Ernest Amory, 64, 155
Collins, Arlene, 191
Collins, Michael, 541
Common Working File (CWF), 300
Comorbidity, meaning of, 469
Completeness of data, 136
Complication, meaning of, 469, 471
Complications of care
APR-DRGs Version 15 of, 471
categories of, 466–468
and ICD-9-CM, 77, 138–139, 156, 466–468
preventable complication issue, 472–475
risk adjustment for mortality, 468–469, 473–475
Computerized severity index (CSI), 162
Confidentiality, and physician profiling, 32
Congenital conditions, National Association of Children's Hospitals and Related Institutions (NACHRI) classification, 599–622
Consultative pools, 199
Consumer Guides to Coronary Artery Bypass Surgery, 112, 114
Continuous quality improvement (CQI)
and ambulatory patient groups (APGs), 161

basis of, 129–132
benefits of, 68, 69
and case-mix adjusted information, 72–74
educational component, 71–72
and feedback to physicians, 34
and low-income/uninsured patients, 76
process of care versus outcomes, 76–77
versus public's right to know, 69–71
Control charts, 174, 178, 181
for attributes, 182–184
critical attributes, 185
cumulative sum chart (CUSUM), 185
out-of-control indications, 179, 180, 182
SDEV chart, 177, 180, 183
XBAR chart, 177, 182
Cooperative Cardiovascular Project, 50
Cooperative Health Care Reporting Initiative (California), 6
Cooper, Richard, 191
Cost containment council, public disclosure of data, 111–116
Cost-to-charge ratios, 314–315
Crawford, Raymond S., III, 251
Cumulative sum chart (CUSUM), 185
Current Procedures and Terminology, Fourth Edition (CPT-4), 159
ambulatory patient groups, 286
procedure data, 527
purpose of, 159

D

Databases
in ambulatory patient groups (APGs) design, 299–300
in case mix measurement study, 401–402
and Maryland Medicaid model, 549, 551
New York State, 229
for pharmacy data for case mix, 582–584
Decision support tools
Greater Southeast Community Hospital, 353–355
Military Health Services System, 259

Decision tree
  application in decision rules, 274
  example of use, 271–272
Deming, W. Edwards, 34, 65, 86, 87, 88
Diagnosis-based classification, National
    Association of Children's Hospitals and
    Related Institutions (NACHRI) system,
    599–622
Diagnosis-related groups (DRGs)
  all patient DRGs, 395–397
  all-patient DRGs (AP-DRGs), 164
  all-patient-refined DRGs (APR-DRGs),
    160, 162–168, 164, 397–399
  compared to APGs, 160–161, 282, 321
  comparison of major features of, 399–
    454
  goals of, 156
  HCFA DRGs, 164
  historical development of, 155–156, 391–
    392
  Medicare DRGs, 393
  mortality analysis, 438–449
  payment redistribution and alternative
    DRG systems, 420–427
  Principal Inpatient DRG approach, 490
  recent development trends, 168
  refined DRGs, 393–395
  and resource utilization, 92
  severity DRGs, 397
  severity of illness refinements, 163–165
  structure of, 156
  types of, 164
  Yale refined DRGs, 164
Disability, Supplementary Security Income
    (SSI), 552–553, 571–573, 601
Disability Payment System (DPS) model,
    505–507
  Maryland Medicaid model, 571–573
  risk adjusters, 505–507
Discharge destination, payments by, 427–
    429
Discounting
  ancillary discounting, 320
  APG payments, 308–309, 310

Dragalin, Daniel, 191
Duke Case-Mix System, 49
DXGROUPS, 490

**E**

Eisnehandler, Jon, 523, 643
Emergency room
  resource consumption study, 643–652
  risk pools, 199
Empowerment of patient, increasing by
    MCOs, 7–8
Encounter data
  for physician profiling, 29–31
  for risk adjusters, 496–499
Episodes-of-illness systems
  acute illness, 528
  chronic illness, 528–529
  for clinical purposes, 481
  for payment purposes, 480
  for profiling purposes, 480
  for statistical purposes, 481–482
  uses of data, 479–480

**F**

Fakhraei, Hamid, 541
*Federal Register*, 160
Feedback, from physician profiling, 383–385
Fee-for-service, 192
  basis of, 192
  global fees, 192–193
  target expenditures, 193
Fetter, Robert, 155–156, 171
Fillmore, Herbert, 623, 643, 655
Financial risk, 194
Fineran, Elizabeth C., 391
Fisher, William, 655
Folkemer, John G., 541
Foundation for Accountability (FACCT), 29
Fridlin, Carol, 455

**G**

Global fees, 192–193
  basis of, 192
  examples of, 193

Goldfield, Norbert, 3, 21, 67, 145, 153, 191, 223, 281, 391, 465, 479, 523, 623, 643, 655

Goodspeed, Ronald, 91

Grant, Thelma M., 281, 391, 655

Graziano, Dennis, 623, 643, 655

Greater Southeast Community Hospital system
  APR-DRG logic, 355–363
  decision support function, 353–355
  information systems configuration, 355
  managed care contracting example, 364–368
  physician profiling for PHO, 368–371

Greenwald, Jeffrey, 251

Gregg, Laurence W., 281

Group capitation, 195, 196–197

**H**

Hammons, Terry, 229

Hannan, Edward L., 135

H-Codes
  mental health services study, 627–630, 633
  rehabilitation outpatient services study, 659–660

Health Care and Insurance Reform Act of 1993 (Florida), 123

Health Care Cost Containment Council (Pennsylvania), 80–81, 111–116

Health Care Financing Administration (HCFA), 78, 109
  ambulatory patient groups, Versions 1 and 2, 281–282
  DRG implementation, 155–156
  DRG update, 393
  HCRA DRGs, 164
  hospital mortality data, 89, 109–110

Health care market, priority issues for purchasers, 93

Health Chex, 149

HealthChoice, 543, 547, 548–549, 555

Health Plan Employer Data and Information Set (HEDIS), 30, 54, 70

Hershey Foods Corp., 113

*Hospital Effectiveness Reports*, 112

Hospital Outcomes Project (California), 51

Hospital type, RPAC payments by, 434–437

Hughes, John S., 523

Hughes, Richard, 229

**I**

Iezzoni, Lisa I., 79

Impartiality, of physician, 14

Individualism, of physician, 14

Influence, versus power, 10

Ingber, Melvin J., 483

Inpatient models, diagnostic cost groups (DCGs), 490–496

Inspection, meaning of, 172

Institutional review boards (IRB), 79

Institutional risk pools, 199

*International Classification of Diseases, Ninth Edition, Clinical Modification* (ICD-9-CM), 26, 28, 49, 54
  ambulatory patient groups (APGs), 286
  complications of care, 77, 138–139, 156, 466–468
  diagnostic data, 527–528
  fourth/fifth-digit specificity, 607
  header diagnosis codes, 606–607
  procedure data, 527
  purpose of, 159
  for SSF codes, 291–293

Iowa, ambulatory patient groups (APGs), system development, 215–220

**J**

Jessee, William F., 229

Jia-Yeong, Monica, 251

Joint Commission on Accreditation of Healthcare Organizations, 29, 231
  function of, 172

Jones, Patricia, 353

**K**

Kazandjian, Vahé, 95
Kilberg, Laura, 373
Kingsdale, Jon, 39
Kongstvedt, Peter, 191
Krakauer, Henry, 251

**L**

Laboratory services
  as APG, 297
  capitation, 202–203
Leverton, Ian H., 57
Lieberman, Richard, 541
Lilienfeld, David E., 251
Lynch, Tim, 121

**M**

Major diagnostic categories (MDCs), uses
  of, 494, 604
Managed care organizations (MCOs)
  MCO/physician/patient trust, 14–16
  patient choice, elements of, 14–15
  patient empowerment methods, 8
Management, involvement in physician profiling, 381–383
Maryland Access to Care, 543
Maryland Medicaid model, 543–564
  ambulatory care group (ACG) assign-
    ment, 544, 546–547
  aspects of model, 545
  database construction, 549, 551
  disabled/SSI, 552, 571–573
  HealthChoice, 543, 547, 548–549, 555
  as innovative program, 543
  positive/negative aspects of, 560–564
  rare and expensive case management
    conditions (REM), 549, 550
  risk-adjusted categories (RACs), 549,
    551–560
  risk adjustment factors, 547–549
  simulation methods, 555–556
Massachusetts Medical Society, 6
Mayo digit, 73, 85–86, 110

McKee, William, 373
Media, 85–90
Medicaid
  Disability Payment System (DPS) model,
    505–507
  Maryland Medicaid model, 543–564
  outcome of care, 132
  past payment-bases, 542
  quality of care, 117–118
  risk adjusting data for, 118–119, 507–515
  severity of illness on admission, 76
Medical APGs, 160, 291–296
  classification variables, 293–295
  new/old patient factors, 295–296
  signs/symptoms/findings (SSF) codes,
    291–293
Medical Assessment Project (Maine), 27
Medical Outcomes Study SF-36, 49
Medical Practice Study, 117
Medical staff, involvement in physician profiling, 381–383
Medicare
  Medicare DRGs, 393
  Prospective Payment System (PPS), 156
  risk adjuster data, 498, 499–507
Medicare Current Beneficiary Survey, 515
Medicare Standard Analytical File, 535–536
MediQual Systems, 115, 162
MedisGroups, 115, 162
MEDPAR database, 140
Mental health services study, 623–642
  characteristics of sample, 640
  classification tree, 632, 636–640
  data analysis, 630–632
  data collection, 626–627
  data processing issues, 626
  dependent variables, 629–630
  grouping structure statistics, 634–635
  H-Codes, 627–630, 633
  hypotheses tested in, 625
  independent variables, 628–629
  recommendations from, 641–642
  sites participating in, 625–626
Mercy Hospital, 114

Military Health Services System
    analytic activity of, 251–252
    case sampling, 253–254
    data acquisition, 254
    decision support tools, 259
    outcomes-based practice guidelines, 262–263
    outcome scoring, 254–257
    overview of operation, 252–254
    practice guidelines, 257–258, 271–274
    predictive models, 259–262
    report cards, 257–258, 263–271
    statistical analysis, 257–259
Miller, Richard C., 251
Monte Carlo simulation, physician profiling, 48
Morbidity, assessment of, 255
Mortality analysis, 438–449
    age/sex and mortality rate, 446–447
    hospital-level analysis, 447–449
    purpose of, 438
    risk adjustment for, 468–469, 473–475
    statistical analysis, 438–446
Mortality rate, and birth rate, 473
Muldoon, John H., 391, 523
Mullin, Robert L., 281, 391
Mutter, Randy, 121

header diagnosis codes, 606–607
hierarchy of conditions, 606
individual chronic condition category, 604
informational building blocks, 619
major diagnostic categories, 604
Medicaid populations, 608
public health/policy applications, 620–621
severity level of diagnosis, 605, 607
severity level of person, 605
supplemental status indicators, 605
National Committee for Quality Assurance (NCQA), 29, 54, 231
National Drug Code (NDC), 577
National Institutes of Health (NIH), 79
Need for intervention, meaning of, 154
Nelson, Eugene C., 129
New York State
    database, 299
    Department of Health Project participants, 653–654
    non-claims based study, 643–652
Non-claims-based data, resource consumption study, 643–652
Northeast Pennsylvania Regional Health Care Coalition, 113

N

National Ambulatory Care Survey, 299
National Association of Children's Hospitals and Related Institutions (NACHRI), Classification of Congenital and Chronic Health Conditions, 164, 599–622
    age/gender in, 600, 601
    at-risk categories, 606
    chronic health conditions, 604
    coding/classification issues, 618–620
    concepts/definitions, basis of, 618–619
    design/structure of, 602–603
    disease progression, 605
    examples of use, 607–618
    functions of, 602

O

Obligations
    challenges for physicians, 13
    in physician/patient relationship, 12–14
Omnibus Budget Reconciliation Act (OBRA), 281
On-site review, and health plan accreditation, 231
Outcome of care, 97–98
    meaning of, 97
Outcomes-based practice guidelines, development of, 262–263
Outcomes research, 97–98
    and benchmarking, 98
    meaning of, 95

Outliers
    APG payments, 310, 312–313, 319
    physician profiling, 376–377
Outpatient Code Editor, 332
Outpatient patient classification system,
    282–284
Outpatient payment program
    development of, 208–211
    effects of program, 212
    objectives of, 207–208, 212
    program requirements, 210–211
    work flow requirements, 210–211
    work plan, 209–211
Output rates, benchmarking, 98–99

## P

PacifiCare, 15
Pacific Business Group on Health, 30
Packaging APG payments, 305–308
    all-inclusive packaging, 306
    partial packaging, 306–307
    relative weights, 316–317
Panels. *See* Primary care panels
Park, Dae, 251
Partial packaging, 306–307
Pathology, as APG, 298
Patient classification system, 282–284
    administrative aspects, 283
    clinical meaningfulness of, 283–284
    code fragmentation, minimizing, 284
    comprehensiveness of, 283
    flexibility of, 284
    homogeneous resource use, 283
    necessity of, 392
    reduction of variance ($R2$) measure, 402–
        420
    upcoding, minimizing, 284
Patient compliance, and trust in physician,
    6–7
Patient education
    from continuous quality improvement
        (CQI), 71–72
    elements of, 130

Patient types, and secondary diagnosis, 139
Payment redistribution
    and admission source, 425–427
    and age range, 423–425
    and discharge destination, 427–429
    hospital service line/age, 431–434
    hospital type and age, 434–437
    payment redistribution impact, calcula-
        tion of, 421–422
    and primary payer, 429
    and types of DRGs, 420–427
Payment simulation, APG payments, 309–
    310
Payson, Norman, 191
Peer group, specialty comparisons, 378
Pennsylvania Power and Light, 113
Per enrollee per month (PEPM) measure,
    589–590, 592
Performance data
    adjustment of. *See* Case mix adjusted
        data; Risk adjustment
    completeness of data, 136
    data quality, 135–136
    difficulties of data distinctions, 84
    as power to consumers, 122–123
    process-outcome links, 141
    and providers of care, 100
    requirements of, 24
    and researchers, 101
    validity of, 137–140
Pharmacy data for case mix, 576–595
    basis of measurement, 577–578
    and database completeness, 582–584
    data integrity, requirements for, 578,
        581–584
    disease specificity, 582
    pharmaceutical groups/subgroups, 577–
        580
    pharmacy record, components of, 576–
        577
    unique identifier of record, 577
    unit records, use of, 584–585
    weight records, 585–586
    weights, estimation of, 586–587

Physician/patient relationship
  and managed care organizations, 4–18
  obligations in, 12–14
  patient/physician/managed care organiza-
    tion relationship, 14–18
  power in, 9–12
  strengthening of, 16–18
  trust in, 5–8
Physician profiling
  AMA program. *See* American Medical
    Accreditation Program (AMAP)
  bad information problem, 47–53
  basic limitation of, 50
  better patient care, requirements for, 45
  claims data for, 27–29
  and code creep, 59–60
  consumer profiling, 40–41
  encounter data for, 29–31
  feedback, use of, 383–385
  future requirements for, 31–34, 53–54
  Greater Southeast Community Hospital
    system, 368–371
  importance to patient, 61
  internal/external use of, 24, 33–34, 60–61
  Monte Carlo simulation, 48
  patient-derived data for, 29
  physician defenselessness for faulty
    information, 51–53
  physician involvement in process, 40
  principles of, 243
  Provident Medical Center example, 373–
    389
  and quality improvement, 223–228
  risk-adjustment for, 48–53
  scoring, example of, 378–379
  severity of illness element, 25–26, 54,
    376
  and statistical errors, 48
  statistical requirements, 53
  uses of profiling data, 24–25, 57, 60–61,
    62
Physician reimbursement
  bonus payment, 198
  capitation, 193–198, 201–203

  fee-for-service, 192
  global fees, 192–193
  research issues related to, 204
  risk-based payment, 198–200
  stop-loss, 200–201
Pocono Medical Center, 114
Poisson distribution, 184
Political aspects, public disclosure, 91–92
Population-based classification, 600–602
  units of analysis in, 600–601
Population group, uses as measure, 599
Poverty level patients. *See* Medicaid patients
Power
  aspects of, 9
  versus influence, 10
  and physician/patient/MCO relationship,
    9–14
  in physician/patient relationship, 9–12
Practice guidelines, Military Health Services System, 271–274
Practice Review System (PRS), 512
Predictive models
  application of, 261
  development process, 259
  Military Health Services System, 259–
    262
  statistical processes, 261
Predictive ratio
  groups by base-year characteristic, 517
  groups by base-year expenditures, 491–
    492
  groups by base-year total expenditures,
    507
  groups by type of inpatient stay, 495
  interpretation issue, 486–487
  from published reports, 505
  purpose of, 487
  uses of, 487–488
Pre-paid capitation, 542–543
  bias issue, 543
Primary care, functions of, 587
Primary care panels, 587–589, 587–595
  case mix measure of panels, 589–595
  closing panels, 592–595

physician time allocation decisions, 590–592
purpose of, 587, 588–589
workload of, 588–589
Primary payer, and RPAC payments, 429
Prior use information, 492
Process, components of, 174
Process control, 174–175
meaning of, 174–175
*See also* Statistical process control (SPC)
Pro/File, 368
Prospective payment system design ambulatory patient groups (APGs), 284–286, 289–299
ambulatory patient groups (APGs) payment system, 305–321
databases used, 299–300
initial classification variable, 286–289
patient classification system, 282–284
Version 2.0 modifications, 302–305
Prospective Payment System (PPS), impact on Medicare expenditures, 156
Prospective risk adjustment classes (PRAC)
assignment of classes, 529–535
data preparation, 527–529
diagnostic data for, 527–529
illness hierarchy, 532–535
initial data sources, 535–536
issues in development of, 524–525, 535–539
PRAC number, components of, 531–532
procedure data for, 527
pros/cons of, 526–527
prospective payment system design, dominant active treatment chronic episode diagnosis category, 530–531
purpose of, 524
as single category method, 526
Provident Medical Center physician profiling, 373–389
feedback/counseling, 383–385
information distribution, 380
management/medical staff support, 381–383

outcome, 385–387
outlier removal, 376–377
physician scoring, 378–380
regional benchmarks, 377
resource improvement, 374–376
service line identification, 377
severity adjustments, 376
specialty peer-group comparisons, 378
variance calculations, 377
variance roll-ups by physicians, 378
Public data, versus research information, 79–80
Public data initiatives, 80
Public disclosure
acuity adjustment in QI project, 95–106
case mix adjusted data, 67–78
cost containment council case, 111–116
employer response to, 107–110
health care for all concept, 117–119
impact, evidence for, 112–114
and media, 85–90
political aspects, 91–92
and proprietary information, 92–93
research information, cautions in presentation of, 79–84
usefulness of, 99–100
Putting Patients First, 7–8, 10

**Q**

Quality assurance
definitions in, 171–172
meaning of, 172
Quality circles, 186, 187
Quality conformance, meaning of, 172
Quality control, meaning of, 172
Quality improvement
and physician profiling, 60–61, 223–228
*See also* Continuous quality improvement (CQI)
Quality management
basis of, 173–174
process control, 174–175
required conditions for, 173–174

**R**

Radiology, as APG, 297–298
Rare and expensive case management conditions (REM)
  Maryland Medicaid model, 549
  types of conditions, 550
Reduction of variance (R2) measure, 402–420
  for cost by major diagnostic category (MDC), 406–409
  data trimming, 409–413
  interpretation issues, 486–487
  for mortality analysis, 440–446
  trimmed results, 413–417
  untrimmed results, 402–406, 418–420
Refined DRGs, 393–395
  secondary diagnosis, 394
  sources of, 395
  versions of, 395
Rehabilitation outpatient services study, 655–670
  classification tree, 664–667
  data analysis, 661–664
  data collection, 658–659
  dependent variables, 660
  H-Codes, 659–660
  independent variables, 660
  sites participating in, 657–658
Reinsurance, 200–201
  risk adjustment, 150
Relative value scales, 299, 300–301
Relative weights
  APGs, computation of, 315–317
  charge-based, 317
  cost-based, 317
Reliability, case mix adjusted data, 131
Report cards, 6, 52
  of military Health Services System, 263–271
  risk-adjusted mortality, 473
Research
  acuity adjustment information, 102–104
  researchers use of performance data, 101

Research information
  cautions in presentation of, 79–84
  versus public data, 79–80
Resource Based Relative Value Scale (RBRVS), 299
Resource intensity, meaning of, 154
Resource utilization
  and diagnosis-related groups (DRGs), 92
  Military Health Services System, 255–257
  resource use reduction, 374–376
  and risk-adjustment methods, 560–561
Restuccia, Robert, 117
Risk-adjusted categories (RACs)
  Aid to Families with Dependent Children, 567–569
  disabled persons/SSI, 571–573
  Maryland Medicaid model, 549, 551–560
Risk adjusters
  ambulatory care group model, 498–499
  classification of, 485–488
  component of RA score, 485
  data sources for, 488–489
  encounter-based information for, 496–499
  inpatient hospital data for, 489–496
  Medicaid models, 507–515
  Medicare models, 489, 499–507
  nature/purpose of, 485
  score, uses of information, 483
  survey-based models, 515–517
Risk adjustment
  Ambulatory Care Groups, 49
  Ambulatory Diagnostic Groups, 49
  case mix adjusted data, 72–74
  compared to risk elimination, 484–485
  Duck Case-Mix System, 49
  information for, 49–50, 145–150
  Maryland Medicaid model, 545–564
  Medical Outcomes Study SF-36, 49
  for mortality, 468–469
  for physician profiling, 48–53
  problems related to, 146–150
  process-outcomes link, 141

purpose of, 483–484
reinsurance approach, 150
and resource use profiling, 560–561
risk corridors and capitation rates, 150–151
software for, 138
variables in models, 149
Risk Adjustment Work Group, 149
Risk-based payment, 198–200
high-cost services impact, 200
and risk-pools, 198–200
Risk corridors, and capitation payments, 150
Risk fund, elements of, 198
Risk pools, 198–200
consultative pools, 199
for cost containment, 198
emergency room risk pools, 199
institutional risk pools, 199
limitations of, 200
quality of care-based payment, 199–200
Roblin, Douglas W., 575
Rogers, Barbara, 251
Romano, Patrick S., 47, 465
Roughan, John F., 207

**S**

St. Joseph's Hospital, 114
St. Vincent's Health Center, 114
Schone, Eric M., 251
Schutt, David C., 251
SDEV chart, 177, 180, 183
Secondary diagnosis, 139–140
and APR-DRGs, 167
Sequela, meaning of, 469, 472
Service line identification, 377
and RPAC payments, 431–434
Service lines, categories of, 431–434
Service risk, and capitation, 194
Sessa, Ernest J., 111
Severity
level assignment for persons, 605
levels of, 605
meanings of, 154
Medicaid patients, 76

and physician profiling, 25–25, 54, 376
refinements for DRGs, 163–165
severity adjustment tool, 167–168
severity-adjusted data and clinical pathways, 455–464
Severity DRGs, 397
development of, 397
Severity of service, meaning of, 154
Shafir, Boris V., 281
Shewhart, Walter, 172
Siegel, David, 191
Significant procedure APGs, 160, 287, 289–291
body systems classification, 289–290
complexity of procedure, 290–291
procedure classification, 290
Signs/symptoms/findings (SSF) codes, 291–293
*Small Area Analysis Reports*, 112
Social Security Act, Title XIX, Section 1115, 542
Software
for physician screening, 368
for risk adjustment, 138
Southham, Arthur, 191
Specialists
peer-group comparisons, 378
specialist capitation, 201–202
Stable system of chance causes, 175
Stahl, Sidney M., 251
Stark, Marcia J., 215
Statewide Planning and Research Cooperative System (SPARCS), 139
Statistical analysis
physician profiling, 53
quality improvement, 130
reduction of variance ($R2$), 402–420
validity for specific outcome, 137
Statistical errors
and physician profiling, 48
Type I/Type II errors, 48
Statistical process control (SPC), 175–187
application of health care processes, examples of, 176–182

and central limit theorem, 177
charts. *See* Control charts
Poisson distribution, 184
principles of, 175–176, 177
and total quality management (TQM), 186–187
variables, types of, 186
Statistics, mortality analysis, 438–446
Steinbeck, Barbara, 391, 523
Stoeckle, John D., 43
Stop-loss, 200–201
   buying decisions, 201
   level of loss decisions, 201
   levels of, 200–201
Strudgeon, George, 353
Study sections, 79
Supplemental status indicators, meaning of, 605
Supplementary Security Income (SSI), ambulatory care groups, 552–553, 571–573
Survey-based models, risk adjusters, 515–517

T

Target expenditures, basis of payment, 193
Technical Advisory Group, 115
3M/Health Information Systems, 164, 216, 355, 365, 458, 524
Time allocation
   primary care physician, 590–592
   sessions as measure, 592
Total quality management (TQM)
   meaning of, 172
   and statistical process control (SPC), 186–187
Trapnell, Gordon R., 541
Treatment difficulty, meaning of, 154
TRENDSTAR, 354, 355
Trust
   aspects of, 5–8, 14
   and compliance of patient, 6–7
   ideal type of, 12

in physician/patient relationship, 5–8
Tucker, Anthony M., 541
Type I/Type II errors, 48

U

UB-92-based data
   limitations of, 126–127
   use of data, 124–127
Unbundling, 58
Unit records, pharmacy data for case mix, 584–585
Upcoding
   APGs, 332
   and cost overruns, 563
   minimizing, 284, 332

V

Validity, 137–140
   assessment for specific outcome, 137
   case mix adjusted data, 131
   meaning of, 137
   threats to, 138–140
Variances
   calculation, 377
   reduction of variance ($R2$) measure, 402–420
   roll-up by physicians, 378
Vertrees, James C., 215, 391
Vital Solutions, Inc., 6$n$
Volume of visits, APG payments, 332
Vulnerability, of patient, 5–6

W

Wang, Yvette, 655
Wasson, John, 45
Weight records, pharmacy data for case mix, 585–587
Weiner, Jonathan P., 541
Weis, Ernest, 191
Window of time, APG payments, 310–313, 320–321

Withholding, capitated payment, 197–198

**X**

XBAR chart, 177, 182

**Y**

Yale-refined DRGs, use of, 164

**Z**

Zhang, Mona Z., 391